Communications
in Computer and Information Science   434

T0215682

Constantine Stephanidis (Ed.)

HCI International 2014 – Posters' Extended Abstracts

International Conference, HCI International 2014
Heraklion, Crete, Greece, June 22-27, 2014
Proceedings, Part I

 Springer

Volume Editor

Constantine Stephanidis
Foundation for Research and Technology - Hellas (FORTH)
Institute of Computer Science
N. Plastira 100, Vassilika Vouton
70013 Heraklion, Crete, Greece
and
University of Crete
Department of Computer Science
Heraklion, Crete, Greece
E-mail: cs@ics.forth.gr

ISSN 1865-0929   e-ISSN 1865-0937
ISBN 978-3-319-07856-4   e-ISBN 978-3-319-07857-1
DOI 10.1007/978-3-319-07857-1
Springer Cham Heidelberg New York Dordrecht London

Library of Congress Control Number: 2014940387

Typesetting: Camera-ready by author, data conversion by Scientific Publishing Services, Chennai, India

Printed on acid-free paper

Springer is part of Springer Science+Business Media (www.springer.com)

Foreword

The 16th International Conference on Human–Computer Interaction, HCI International 2014, was held in Heraklion, Crete, Greece, during June 22–27, 2014, incorporating 14 conferences/thematic areas:

Thematic areas:

- Human–Computer Interaction
- Human Interface and the Management of Information

Affiliated conferences:

- 11th International Conference on Engineering Psychology and Cognitive Ergonomics
- 8th International Conference on Universal Access in Human–Computer Interaction
- 6th International Conference on Virtual, Augmented and Mixed Reality
- 6th International Conference on Cross-Cultural Design
- 6th International Conference on Social Computing and Social Media
- 8th International Conference on Augmented Cognition
- 5th International Conference on Digital Human Modeling and Applications in Health, Safety, Ergonomics and Risk Management
- Third International Conference on Design, User Experience and Usability
- Second International Conference on Distributed, Ambient and Pervasive Interactions
- Second International Conference on Human Aspects of Information Security, Privacy and Trust
- First International Conference on HCI in Business
- First International Conference on Learning and Collaboration Technologies

A total of 4,766 individuals from academia, research institutes, industry, and governmental agencies from 78 countries submitted contributions, and 1,476 papers and 225 posters were included in the proceedings. These papers address the latest research and development efforts and highlight the human aspects of design and use of computing systems. The papers thoroughly cover the entire field of human–computer interaction, addressing major advances in knowledge and effective use of computers in a variety of application areas.

This volume, edited by Constantine Stephanidis, contains extended abstracts of posters addressing the following major topics:

- Design Methods, Techniques and Knowledge
- The design of everyday things
- Interacting with information and knowledge

- Cognitive, perceptual and emotional issues in HCI
- Multimodal and Natural Interaction
- Algorithms and Machine Learning methods in HCI
- Virtual and augmented environments

The remaining volumes of the HCI International 2014 proceedings are:

- Volume 1, LNCS 8510, Human–Computer Interaction: HCI Theories, Methods and Tools (Part I), edited by Masaaki Kurosu
- Volume 2, LNCS 8511, Human–Computer Interaction: Advanced Interaction Modalities and Techniques (Part II), edited by Masaaki Kurosu
- Volume 3, LNCS 8512, Human–Computer Interaction: Applications and Services (Part III), edited by Masaaki Kurosu
- Volume 4, LNCS 8513, Universal Access in Human–Computer Interaction: Design and Development Methods for Universal Access (Part I), edited by Constantine Stephanidis and Margherita Antona
- Volume 5, LNCS 8514, Universal Access in Human–Computer Interaction: Universal Access to Information and Knowledge (Part II), edited by Constantine Stephanidis and Margherita Antona
- Volume 6, LNCS 8515, Universal Access in Human–Computer Interaction: Aging and Assistive Environments (Part III), edited by Constantine Stephanidis and Margherita Antona
- Volume 7, LNCS 8516, Universal Access in Human–Computer Interaction: Design for All and Accessibility Practice (Part IV), edited by Constantine Stephanidis and Margherita Antona
- Volume 8, LNCS 8517, Design, User Experience, and Usability: Theories, Methods and Tools for Designing the User Experience (Part I), edited by Aaron Marcus
- Volume 9, LNCS 8518, Design, User Experience, and Usability: User Experience Design for Diverse Interaction Platforms and Environments (Part II), edited by Aaron Marcus
- Volume 10, LNCS 8519, Design, User Experience, and Usability: User Experience Design for Everyday Life Applications and Services (Part III), edited by Aaron Marcus
- Volume 11, LNCS 8520, Design, User Experience, and Usability: User Experience Design Practice (Part IV), edited by Aaron Marcus
- Volume 12, LNCS 8521, Human Interface and the Management of Information: Information and Knowledge Design and Evaluation (Part I), edited by Sakae Yamamoto
- Volume 13, LNCS 8522, Human Interface and the Management of Information: Information and Knowledge in Applications and Services (Part II), edited by Sakae Yamamoto
- Volume 14, LNCS 8523, Learning and Collaboration Technologies: Designing and Developing Novel Learning Experiences (Part I), edited by Panayiotis Zaphiris and Andri Ioannou

- Volume 15, LNCS 8524, Learning and Collaboration Technologies: Technology-rich Environments for Learning and Collaboration (Part II), edited by Panayiotis Zaphiris and Andri Ioannou
- Volume 16, LNCS 8525, Virtual, Augmented and Mixed Reality: Designing and Developing Virtual and Augmented Environments (Part I), edited by Randall Shumaker and Stephanie Lackey
- Volume 17, LNCS 8526, Virtual, Augmented and Mixed Reality: Applications of Virtual and Augmented Reality (Part II), edited by Randall Shumaker and Stephanie Lackey
- Volume 18, LNCS 8527, HCI in Business, edited by Fiona Fui-Hoon Nah
- Volume 19, LNCS 8528, Cross-Cultural Design, edited by P.L. Patrick Rau
- Volume 20, LNCS 8529, Digital Human Modeling and Applications in Health, Safety, Ergonomics and Risk Management, edited by Vincent G. Duffy
- Volume 21, LNCS 8530, Distributed, Ambient, and Pervasive Interactions, edited by Norbert Streitz and Panos Markopoulos
- Volume 22, LNCS 8531, Social Computing and Social Media, edited by Gabriele Meiselwitz
- Volume 23, LNAI 8532, Engineering Psychology and Cognitive Ergonomics, edited by Don Harris
- Volume 24, LNCS 8533, Human Aspects of Information Security, Privacy and Trust, edited by Theo Tryfonas and Ioannis Askoxylakis
- Volume 25, LNAI 8534, Foundations of Augmented Cognition, edited by Dylan D. Schmorrow and Cali M. Fidopiastis
- Volume 27, CCIS 435, HCI International 2014 Posters Proceedings (Part II), edited by Constantine Stephanidis

I would like to thank the Program Chairs and the members of the Program Boards of all affiliated conferences and thematic areas, listed below, for their contribution to the highest scientific quality and the overall success of the HCI International 2014 Conference.

This conference could not have been possible without the continuous support and advice of the founding chair and conference scientific advisor, Prof. Gavriel Salvendy, as well as the dedicated work and outstanding efforts of the communications chair and editor of *HCI International News*, Dr. Abbas Moallem.

I would also like to thank for their contribution towards the smooth organization of the HCI International 2014 Conference the members of the Human–Computer Interaction Laboratory of ICS-FORTH, and in particular George Paparoulis, Maria Pitsoulaki, Maria Bouhli, and George Kapnas.

April 2014   Constantine Stephanidis
                                          General Chair, HCI International 2014

Organization

Human–Computer Interaction

Program Chair: Masaaki Kurosu, Japan

Jose Abdelnour-Nocera, UK
Sebastiano Bagnara, Italy
Simone Barbosa, Brazil
Adriana Betiol, Brazil
Simone Borsci, UK
Henry Duh, Australia
Xiaowen Fang, USA
Vicki Hanson, UK
Wonil Hwang, Korea
Minna Isomursu, Finland
Yong Gu Ji, Korea
Anirudha Joshi, India
Esther Jun, USA
Kyungdoh Kim, Korea

Heidi Krömker, Germany
Chen Ling, USA
Chang S. Nam, USA
Naoko Okuizumi, Japan
Philippe Palanque, France
Ling Rothrock, USA
Naoki Sakakibara, Japan
Dominique Scapin, France
Guangfeng Song, USA
Sanjay Tripathi, India
Chui Yin Wong, Malaysia
Toshiki Yamaoka, Japan
Kazuhiko Yamazaki, Japan
Ryoji Yoshitake, Japan

Human Interface and the Management of Information

Program Chair: Sakae Yamamoto, Japan

Alan Chan, Hong Kong
Denis A. Coelho, Portugal
Linda Elliott, USA
Shin'ichi Fukuzumi, Japan
Michitaka Hirose, Japan
Makoto Itoh, Japan
Yen-Yu Kang, Taiwan
Koji Kimita, Japan
Daiji Kobayashi, Japan

Hiroyuki Miki, Japan
Hirohiko Mori, Japan
Shogo Nishida, Japan
Robert Proctor, USA
Youngho Rhee, Korea
Ryosuke Saga, Japan
Katsunori Shimohara, Japan
Kim-Phuong Vu, USA
Tomio Watanabe, Japan

Engineering Psychology and Cognitive Ergonomics

Program Chair: Don Harris, UK

Guy Andre Boy, USA
Shan Fu, P.R. China
Hung-Sying Jing, Taiwan
Wen-Chin Li, Taiwan
Mark Neerincx, The Netherlands
Jan Noyes, UK
Paul Salmon, Australia

Axel Schulte, Germany
Siraj Shaikh, UK
Sarah Sharples, UK
Anthony Smoker, UK
Neville Stanton, UK
Alex Stedmon, UK
Andrew Thatcher, South Africa

Universal Access in Human–Computer Interaction

Program Chairs: Constantine Stephanidis, Greece, and Margherita Antona, Greece

Julio Abascal, Spain
Gisela Susanne Bahr, USA
João Barroso, Portugal
Margrit Betke, USA
Anthony Brooks, Denmark
Christian Bühler, Germany
Stefan Carmien, Spain
Hua Dong, P.R. China
Carlos Duarte, Portugal
Pier Luigi Emiliani, Italy
Qin Gao, P.R. China
Andrina Granić, Croatia
Andreas Holzinger, Austria
Josette Jones, USA
Simeon Keates, UK

Georgios Kouroupetroglou, Greece
Patrick Langdon, UK
Barbara Leporini, Italy
Eugene Loos, The Netherlands
Ana Isabel Paraguay, Brazil
Helen Petrie, UK
Michael Pieper, Germany
Enrico Pontelli, USA
Jaime Sanchez, Chile
Alberto Sanna, Italy
Anthony Savidis, Greece
Christian Stary, Austria
Hirotada Ueda, Japan
Gerhard Weber, Germany
Harald Weber, Germany

Virtual, Augmented and Mixed Reality

Program Chairs: Randall Shumaker, USA, and Stephanie Lackey, USA

Roland Blach, Germany
Sheryl Brahnam, USA
Juan Cendan, USA
Jessie Chen, USA
Panagiotis D. Kaklis, UK

Hirokazu Kato, Japan
Denis Laurendeau, Canada
Fotis Liarokapis, UK
Michael Macedonia, USA
Gordon Mair, UK

Jose San Martin, Spain
Tabitha Peck, USA
Christian Sandor, Australia

Christopher Stapleton, USA
Gregory Welch, USA

Cross-Cultural Design

Program Chair: P.L. Patrick Rau, P.R. China

Yee-Yin Choong, USA
Paul Fu, USA
Zhiyong Fu, P.R. China
Pin-Chao Liao, P.R. China
Dyi-Yih Michael Lin, Taiwan
Rungtai Lin, Taiwan
Ta-Ping (Robert) Lu, Taiwan
Liang Ma, P.R. China
Alexander Mädche, Germany

Sheau-Farn Max Liang, Taiwan
Katsuhiko Ogawa, Japan
Tom Plocher, USA
Huatong Sun, USA
Emil Tso, P.R. China
Hsiu-Ping Yueh, Taiwan
Liang (Leon) Zeng, USA
Jia Zhou, P.R. China

Online Communities and Social Media

Program Chair: Gabriele Meiselwitz, USA

Leonelo Almeida, Brazil
Chee Siang Ang, UK
Aneesha Bakharia, Australia
Ania Bobrowicz, UK
James Braman, USA
Farzin Deravi, UK
Carsten Kleiner, Germany
Niki Lambropoulos, Greece
Soo Ling Lim, UK

Anthony Norcio, USA
Portia Pusey, USA
Panote Siriaraya, UK
Stefan Stieglitz, Germany
Giovanni Vincenti, USA
Yuanqiong (Kathy) Wang, USA
June Wei, USA
Brian Wentz, USA

Augmented Cognition

**Program Chairs: Dylan D. Schmorrow, USA,
and Cali M. Fidopiastis, USA**

Ahmed Abdelkhalek, USA
Robert Atkinson, USA
Monique Beaudoin, USA
John Blitch, USA
Alenka Brown, USA

Rosario Cannavò, Italy
Joseph Cohn, USA
Andrew J. Cowell, USA
Martha Crosby, USA
Wai-Tat Fu, USA

Rodolphe Gentili, USA
Frederick Gregory, USA
Michael W. Hail, USA
Monte Hancock, USA
Fei Hu, USA
Ion Juvina, USA
Joe Keebler, USA
Philip Mangos, USA
Rao Mannepalli, USA
David Martinez, USA
Yvonne R. Masakowski, USA
Santosh Mathan, USA
Ranjeev Mittu, USA

Keith Niall, USA
Tatana Olson, USA
Debra Patton, USA
June Pilcher, USA
Robinson Pino, USA
Tiffany Poeppelman, USA
Victoria Romero, USA
Amela Sadagic, USA
Anna Skinner, USA
Ann Speed, USA
Robert Sottilare, USA
Peter Walker, USA

Digital Human Modeling and Applications in Health, Safety, Ergonomics and Risk Management

Program Chair: Vincent G. Duffy, USA

Giuseppe Andreoni, Italy
Daniel Carruth, USA
Elsbeth De Korte, The Netherlands
Afzal A. Godil, USA
Ravindra Goonetilleke, Hong Kong
Noriaki Kuwahara, Japan
Kang Li, USA
Zhizhong Li, P.R. China

Tim Marler, USA
Jianwei Niu, P.R. China
Michelle Robertson, USA
Matthias Rötting, Germany
Mao-Jiun Wang, Taiwan
Xuguang Wang, France
James Yang, USA

Design, User Experience, and Usability

Program Chair: Aaron Marcus, USA

Sisira Adikari, Australia
Claire Ancient, USA
Arne Berger, Germany
Jamie Blustein, Canada
Ana Boa-Ventura, USA
Jan Brejcha, Czech Republic
Lorenzo Cantoni, Switzerland
Marc Fabri, UK
Luciane Maria Fadel, Brazil
Tricia Flanagan, Hong Kong
Jorge Frascara, Mexico

Federico Gobbo, Italy
Emilie Gould, USA
Rüdiger Heimgärtner, Germany
Brigitte Herrmann, Germany
Steffen Hess, Germany
Nouf Khashman, Canada
Fabiola Guillermina Noël, Mexico
Francisco Rebelo, Portugal
Kerem Rızvanoğlu, Turkey
Marcelo Soares, Brazil
Carla Spinillo, Brazil

Distributed, Ambient and Pervasive Interactions

**Program Chairs: Norbert Streitz, Germany,
and Panos Markopoulos, The Netherlands**

Juan Carlos Augusto, UK
Jose Bravo, Spain
Adrian Cheok, UK
Boris de Ruyter, The Netherlands
Anind Dey, USA
Dimitris Grammenos, Greece
Nuno Guimaraes, Portugal
Achilles Kameas, Greece
Javed Vassilis Khan, The Netherlands
Shin'ichi Konomi, Japan
Carsten Magerkurth, Switzerland

Ingrid Mulder, The Netherlands
Anton Nijholt, The Netherlands
Fabio Paternó, Italy
Carsten Röcker, Germany
Teresa Romao, Portugal
Albert Ali Salah, Turkey
Manfred Tscheligi, Austria
Reiner Wichert, Germany
Woontack Woo, Korea
Xenophon Zabulis, Greece

Human Aspects of Information Security, Privacy and Trust

**Program Chairs: Theo Tryfonas, UK,
and Ioannis Askoxylakis, Greece**

Claudio Agostino Ardagna, Italy
Zinaida Benenson, Germany
Daniele Catteddu, Italy
Raoul Chiesa, Italy
Bryan Cline, USA
Sadie Creese, UK
Jorge Cuellar, Germany
Marc Dacier, USA
Dieter Gollmann, Germany
Kirstie Hawkey, Canada
Jaap-Henk Hoepman, The Netherlands
Cagatay Karabat, Turkey
Angelos Keromytis, USA
Ayako Komatsu, Japan
Ronald Leenes, The Netherlands
Javier Lopez, Spain
Steve Marsh, Canada

Gregorio Martinez, Spain
Emilio Mordini, Italy
Yuko Murayama, Japan
Masakatsu Nishigaki, Japan
Aljosa Pasic, Spain
Milan Petković, The Netherlands
Joachim Posegga, Germany
Jean-Jacques Quisquater, Belgium
Damien Sauveron, France
George Spanoudakis, UK
Kerry-Lynn Thomson, South Africa
Julien Touzeau, France
Theo Tryfonas, UK
João Vilela, Portugal
Claire Vishik, UK
Melanie Volkamer, Germany

HCI in Business

Program Chair: Fiona Fui-Hoon Nah, USA

Andreas Auinger, Austria
Michel Avital, Denmark
Traci Carte, USA
Hock Chuan Chan, Singapore
Constantinos Coursaris, USA
Soussan Djamasbi, USA
Brenda Eschenbrenner, USA
Nobuyuki Fukawa, USA
Khaled Hassanein, Canada
Milena Head, Canada
Susanna (Shuk Ying) Ho, Australia
Jack Zhenhui Jiang, Singapore
Jinwoo Kim, Korea
Zoonky Lee, Korea
Honglei Li, UK
Nicholas Lockwood, USA
Eleanor T. Loiacono, USA
Mei Lu, USA

Scott McCoy, USA
Brian Mennecke, USA
Robin Poston, USA
Lingyun Qiu, P.R. China
Rene Riedl, Austria
Matti Rossi, Finland
April Savoy, USA
Shu Schiller, USA
Hong Sheng, USA
Choon Ling Sia, Hong Kong
Chee-Wee Tan, Denmark
Chuan Hoo Tan, Hong Kong
Noam Tractinsky, Israel
Horst Treiblmaier, Austria
Virpi Tuunainen, Finland
Dezhi Wu, USA
I-Chin Wu, Taiwan

Learning and Collaboration Technologies

**Program Chairs: Panayiotis Zaphiris, Cyprus,
and Andri Ioannou, Cyprus**

Ruthi Aladjem, Israel
Abdulaziz Aldaej, UK
John M. Carroll, USA
Maka Eradze, Estonia
Mikhail Fominykh, Norway
Denis Gillet, Switzerland
Mustafa Murat Inceoglu, Turkey
Pernilla Josefsson, Sweden
Marie Joubert, UK
Sauli Kiviranta, Finland
Tomaž Klobučar, Slovenia
Elena Kyza, Cyprus
Maarten de Laat, The Netherlands
David Lamas, Estonia

Edmund Laugasson, Estonia
Ana Loureiro, Portugal
Katherine Maillet, France
Nadia Pantidi, UK
Antigoni Parmaxi, Cyprus
Borzoo Pourabdollahian, Italy
Janet C. Read, UK
Christophe Reffay, France
Nicos Souleles, Cyprus
Ana Luísa Torres, Portugal
Stefan Trausan-Matu, Romania
Aimilia Tzanavari, Cyprus
Johnny Yuen, Hong Kong
Carmen Zahn, Switzerland

External Reviewers

Ilia Adami, Greece
Iosif Klironomos, Greece
Maria Korozi, Greece
Vassilis Kouroumalis, Greece

Asterios Leonidis, Greece
George Margetis, Greece
Stavroula Ntoa, Greece
Nikolaos Partarakis, Greece

HCI International 2015

The 15th International Conference on Human–Computer Interaction, HCI International 2015, will be held jointly with the affiliated conferences in Los Angeles, CA, USA, in the Westin Bonaventure Hotel, August 2–7, 2015. It will cover a broad spectrum of themes related to HCI, including theoretical issues, methods, tools, processes, and case studies in HCI design, as well as novel interaction techniques, interfaces, and applications. The proceedings will be published by Springer. More information will be available on the conference website: http://www.hcii2015.org/

General Chair
Professor Constantine Stephanidis
University of Crete and ICS-FORTH
Heraklion, Crete, Greece
E-mail: cs@ics.forth.gr

Table of Contents – Part I

Design Methods, Techniques and Knowledge

The Design of Everyday Things

Interacting with Information and Knowledge

Cognitive, Perceptual and Emotional Issues in HCI

Multimodal and Natural Interaction

Algorithms and Machine Learning Methods in HCI

Virtual and Augmented Environments

Table of Contents – Part II

Social Media and Social Networks

Learning and Education

Design for All, Accessibility and Assistive Environments

Design for Aging

Games and Exergames

Health and Well-Being

Ergonomics and Safety

HCI in Business, Tourism and Trasport

Human-human and Human-Agent Communication

User Experience Case Studies

Design Methods, Techniques and Knowledge

Using Color Guidance to Improve on Usability in Interactive Environments

Michael Brandse[1] and Kiyoshi Tomimatsu[2]

[1] Graduate School of Design, Kyushu University
michaelbrandse@kyudai.jp
[2] Faculty of Design, Kyushu University,
4-9-1 Shiobaru Minami-ku Fukuoka 815-0032, Japan
tomimatu@design.kyushu-u.ac.jp

Abstract. In this paper, we examine the need for usability methods for game design and argue that within the level design discipline in game design there is a distinct lack of usability methods for users with low game literacy. Therefore, we propose that there is a need for guidance methods to properly accommodate players of all levels of game literacy in the game world. With the player having to spend the majority of its time in digital game environments and color being a basic component of any environment, we have decided to use color contrasts to determine whether color is suitable for player guidance. The goal of this paper is to determine whether player behavior, both in decision making and in viewing behavior, can be influenced through color contrasts.

Keywords: Color Design, Design Patters and DUXU, Navigation Design, Usability Methods and Tools, Video Game Design.

1 Introduction

Within the game design discipline, level design is a fairly new practice. Whereas at first it was just a task delegated to the programmers, when video games started to become more technically advanced, specialized level designers became a necessity. It could be argued that for modern game design, level design is of utmost importance to the design process [1, 2]. However, as of yet there is no real formal understanding of what makes for good level design, apart from rules of thumb and design lore[3]. Furthermore, we feel that the current design lore within level design mostly requires a medium to high game literacy, alienating less experienced players. Therefore we postulate that it is necessary to create a body of formal knowledge in regards to level design. The aim of this study is to create new methods to make the progression through levels more intuitive for players of games. Our research focus is on how the user perceives the environment visually and how the user deals with this information. Past studies in interior design have proven the effectiveness of colour on visitors [4, 5]. However, a weakness of these studies is that they mostly relied on the psychological effects of colour, which can be argued to have different effects depending on culture. Therefore, we seek to find whether colour at its most basic can influence user

C. Stephanidis (Ed.): HCII 2014 Posters, Part I, CCIS 434, pp. 3–8, 2014.
© Springer International Publishing Switzerland 2014

behaviour. We therefore researched how users would perceive contrasting colours (based on the definitions by Itten, J.[6]) and whether these contrasts had any effect on their viewing behaviour and decision making.

2   Method

2.1   Participants and Equipment

Two experiments were conducted, with 12 participants each. For the first experiment, the average age of the participants was 28.6 with a standard deviation of 7.3. There were a total of 6 females and 6 males. For the second experiment, the average age of the participants was 26.2 with a standard deviation of 3.9. There were a total of 5 females and 7 males. For both experiments the participants were of varying nationalities. To get the RGB values used in the experimental prototype, we used the color values of the color circle on which the contrasts were based. For the paints used to construct the color values, we have used the standard print colors. The paints that were used are Holbein Artists' Gouache G651 Primary Magenta, Holbein Artists' Gouache G652 Primary Yellow and Holbein Artists' Gouache G654 Primary Cyan. We used 218GSM paper for the color samples. To convert the colors to waveform values, the Konica Minolta CM_2600d spectrometer was used. To convert the colors from waveform to digital, the Konika Minolta Spectroradiometer CS-1000 was used. To get colors mixed with black or white, we overlaid an additional layer of black or white over the colors of the color circle and adjusted the transparency as needed. A BENQ G2400WDLCD monitor was used for the experiment. The computer used for the experiment was an Intel Core i5-2400 3.10GHz, with 4.0 GB RAM and a AMB RADEON HD 6450 1.00GB. The operating system used was Windows 7 Enterprise (64 bits). Additional hardware to control the experimental prototype was used in the form of a Microsoft Wireless XBOX360 Controller for Windows. For the eye tracker hardware, we used a Mirametrix S2 eye-tracker, model MRS2.

2.2   Preparation

An experimental prototype to contain the stimuli was designed using the Unreal Development Kit July 2012 Beta. A side scrolling action type game was prepared, where the game camera is always fixated to the side of the environment. The prototype features only the most basic controls to allow for interaction with the environment. Two sequences of stimuli, a tutorial room and a finish room were prepared. One sequence of grey rooms and one sequence of coloured rooms were created. The contrasts used in the colored stimuli rooms are the hot and cold contrast, complementary contrast, saturation contrast, light and dark contrast and the contrast of hue. 3 to 4 stimuli were prepared for each of the contrasts.

The Areas of Interest (AOI) were determined as the colored areas around the entrances and went from left to right.

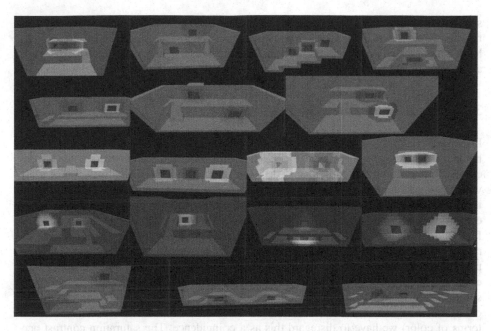

Fig. 1. Stimulis used for the experiment. 1st row contains hot and cold, 2nd row contains complementary, 3rd row contains saturation, 4th row contains light and dark and the 5th row contains hue contrasts.

2.3   Protocol Design

Experiments were conducted in a well lit room, whose settings could be adjusted if there was a need for it. Participants were requested to not wear glasses or make-up, due to interference with the eye-tracking hardware. Participants were first explained the contents of the experiment, after which the examiner would proceed to calibrate the eye-tracking hardware. In order to get accustomed to the controls, participants would first play a tutorial room in which the examiner explained how to operate the XBOX360 controller. After the tutorial room was finished, the participants would be assigned either the monochrome or the colour stimuli. The stimuli would appear in randomized order, until the participant had finished all the stimuli after which the participant would be taken to the finish room. Once the participant had reached the finish room, they were required to fill in a questionnaire to make up for lacking data.

2.4   Data Analysis

For the contrasts, there was not a clear definition on which color was more dominant, so we will conclude their effects by the frequency of entrances being chosen. According Holmqvist, K., & Nystrom, M.[7], a typical fixation is anywhere between 200-300ms. Therefore, everything below 200ms was not considered a fixation and therefore ignored. Furthermore, eye tracking data after the player had made a choice was not recorded either. We consider a decision to be made the moment the player has pressed the button to proceed to the next room, as this action cannot be undone since the act of entering entrances is automated. Once the transition between two rooms is finished, if the player's gaze happened to be inside of an area of interest, but hadn't moved since before the transition was finished, the gaze is not considered to be a hit, but a coincidence. ANOVA was used to analyze the significance of the data.

3   Results and Discussion

Looking at figure 2, we can conclude that a few contrasts have distinct effects on player behavior, whereas the majority doesn't. The complementary contrast does not have a distinct influence on the participants' decision making, nor on their dwell times. Only with the third stimulus did participants choose exit with the complementary color, leading to believe that this may have had to do with preference rather than the contrast being effective. Furthermore, the contrast of hue also performed rather poorly, with only the first stimulus having the intended effect, even if slightly. Even so, the dwell times do not reflect this, making this contrast ineffective for player guidance. The hot and cold contrast performs rather poorly, with no distinct preference given for either the hot or cold color, both in terms of dwell times as well as decision making. The second stimulus is somewhat of interest however, in how the dwell times are completely contrary to the decision making. However, since the second stimulus is not unlike the third stimulus (in terms of color) we have to disregard this as a coincidence. The saturation contrast performs rather well. There is a preference towards the more saturated colors as opposed to the unsaturated colors. While the first stimulus only have a 50% chance of choosing the more saturated color, both the average and total dwell times on the more saturated color of the first stimulus was higher than that of the unsaturated color. The light and dark contrast also performs okay, though to lesser extent than the saturation contrast. While decision making is only influenced in two of the four stimuli, the reported average and total dwell times on the stimuli are in favor of the lighter colors as opposed to the darker colors, for all stimuli apart from the fourth stimulus.

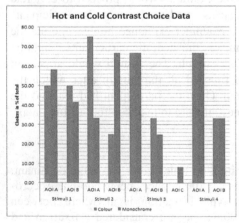 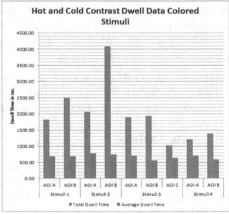

Fig. 2. Contrasts choice and dwell data cont.

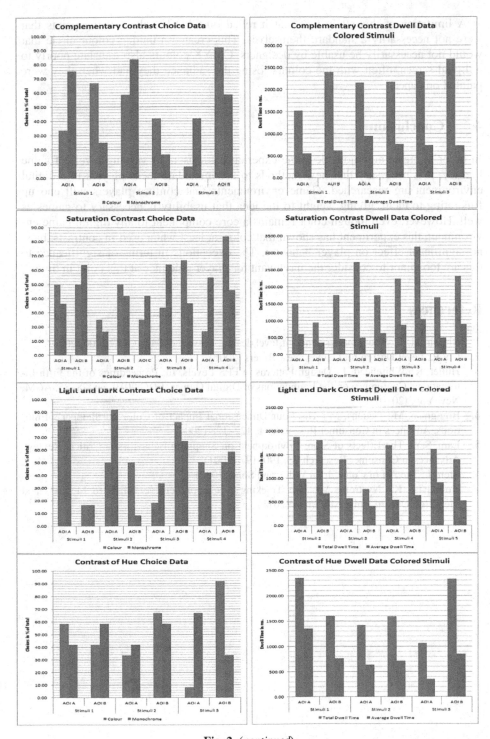

Fig. 2. (*continued*)

A limitation of this study was that it relied on CMYK values, using paints that were not necessarily a standard themselves. This created a unique colour circle that would not necessarily be usable by designers. CMYK colours also translate poorly to a digital screen, often with the colours losing the radiance they had when they were painted on paper.

4   Conclusion

In order to create an enjoyable game experience for users of varying levels of game literacy, it is necessary that new methods to accommodate these players in a digital environment are researched. Game environments that confuse players will end up frustrating to them, giving weight to the idea that usability is necessary to games as well. However, even though color remains a core component to any digital game environment, this experiment has shown that color, at least when used in contrasts, have no significant effect on player behavior. The exceptions in terms of significance to this are too minor to consider them relevant for player guidance at this point in time.

References

1. Blezsinski, C.: The art and science of level design, Session 4404 at GDC 2000 (2000)
2. Co, P.: Level Design for Games. New Riders (2006)
3. Hullet, K., Whitehead, J.: Design Patterns in FPS Levels. In: Proceedings of the Fifth International Conference on the Foundations of Digital Games, FDG 2010, pp. 78–85. ACM, New York (2010)
4. Brengman, M., Geuens, M.: The Four Dimensional Impact of Color on Shopper's Emotions. Advances in Consumer Research 31, 122–128 (2004)
5. Lam, S.Y.: The Effects of Store Environment on Shopping Behaviors: a Critical Review. Advances in Consumer Research 28, 190–197 (2001)
6. Itten, J.: The Art of Color. John Wiley and Sons (1997)
7. Holmqvist, K., Nystrom, M.: Eye Tracking A Comprehensive Guide to Methods and Measures. Oxford University Press (2011)

Medium – Media – Post-media

Jiří Bystřický, Jan Brejcha, and Katrin Vodrážková

FI, Post-Media-Theory Research Prague, Czech Republic
jiribystricky@seznam.cz,
{jbrejcha,vodrazkova.katrin}@gmail.com

Abstract. The poster shows the fundamental difference between the concept of *medium* and *media*. Does the difference exist in each imaging and information system? The topic is focusing on the model of post-media thinking in our post-information society. We would like to analyze *how* the basic difference of *medium – media* influences the human cognition, thinking about the future imaging and information systems, computing processes and future trends of imaging techniques. The concept of science within the post-media theory of thinking focuses on constitution proceeding through critical reflexive medium. It is using still more and more deeply methods for further researches. Critical reflexive form is the methodology used for analysing of the term *medium* which is understand as mediate factor. Here we are investigating the autonomous medium related to itself – this is called, as Luhmann said in his theory of the social systems, Self-reference. On the other hand the medium is able to develop a relation to open universal entity (Other-reference) that just enables self-emancipation of the objects. There is a difference between the individual and general relation. Each medium evinces a possiblity of contradiction in relation to another *media*, that are based on different and authentic conditions.

Keywords: difference, dispositive, double-reality model, imaging, media, medium, Other-reference, post-media, system, the social system theory.

In this poster we put a basic question: on what basis could the fundamental difference of the double-reality model of medium – media be analyzed? On what philosophical background could the post-media thinking be examined? We are using the theory of reflexive media, conception of dispositive (Giorgio Agamben) and the theory of the social systems (Niklas Luhmann) and coding of: Self-reference – Other-reference, system and its environment, information and non-information. The social systems are very complex, and the system complexity is not only based on the binary coding of yes – no, but it especially rises from complex system relations and system communication.

We can explain the main difference of post-media thinking following way: one entity is delimited in relation to another entity within the original quality that is enhanced only by the specific medium at the specific time. This is the difference that makes the difference. The concept of the new model of post-media thinking would like to expound the medium as an exclusively unity with its own separate essential wholeness and its own negativity, not only defined as one of the „also". The medium has ability

C. Stephanidis (Ed.): HCII 2014 Posters, Part I, CCIS 434, pp. 9–12, 2014.
© Springer International Publishing Switzerland 2014

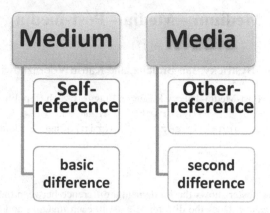

Fig. 1. Difference of medium and media

to produce „other" (related to the system Other-reference), that differentiates one factor from another factors. The secondary difference involves the media that exist in the form of double-reality model, it means for example the system of masmedia. The system Other-reference is a mode and clue to explain the complex bindings in each system and the way of how the system communication is working and how it influences the cognition and thinking. The system Other-reference is also able to clarify the process of how the system is performing an operation and how the system is observing because of the two levels of observation: firstly we are talking about the facts (the observer is observing) whereas second reality, the double-reality model is related to the observation of another observers (how the other observers are observing).

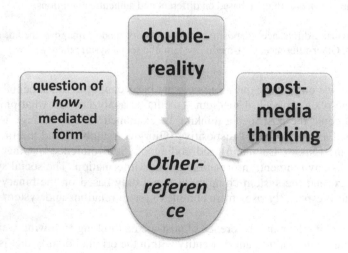

Fig. 2. The system Other-reference

The system of media, especially the mass-media system is a world in itself (Self-reference), environment with information that are circulating in the system environment, the electronic, digital and imaging processing and transport, but also the major limitation: within the system of media are information and system communication spreading in all directions, but their content ends not only by the recipients, but again with emitents. It is therefore a more or less autonomous, self-reference system that lacks the basic form: the relationship to the conception of general. Therefore should the mass-media system prepare the basic information and always update them. Medium is preparing huge, but limited realm of possibilities, from which the system communication could choose new forms for further communication process. Technologically produced objects of seeing are acting with new rule: not only that it does not allow sufficient difference between thinking and knowing, but mainly because some redirecting perspectives lead to "overlap" of the difference between the current view and its subsequent simulations.

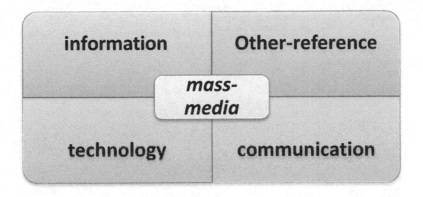

Fig. 3. The system of massmedia

The reflexive medium and system Other-reference is closely related to the concept of dispositive. Dispositive is a form, mode and heterogeneous whole (rules, architecture, institution, script, computer) that can explain the complex structure of each social, imaging and information system. The dispositive rises as a plan in the society. For example as the first dispositive is considered the language. The dispositive is being based on usability, control and power. It is a system and net of complex operational processes and functions that produces the knowledge and control and could form the identity and autonomy. Because there are more possibilities in the current post-information society that we could use at the same time, the system should select the information and reduce the social complexity, of course the system has to choose the right dispositive for further operating.

References

1. Agamben, G.: What is a dispositive? Minnesota Press, Minneapolis (1993)
2. Brejcha, J., Marcus, A.: Semiotics of Interaction: Towards a UI Alphabet. In: Kurosu, M. (ed.) HCII/HCI 2013, Part I. LNCS, vol. 8004, pp. 13–21. Springer, Heidelberg (2013)
3. Bystřický, J.: Techno-imagination and implicit knowledge. In: Marcus, A. (ed.) DUXU 2013, Part I. LNCS, vol. 8012, pp. 22–28. Springer, Heidelberg (2013)
4. Bystřický, J.: Denkbare Hintergründe. In: International Flusser Studies 5/2007 (2007b)
5. Luhmann, N.: The Reality of the Massmedia. Polity Press, Maldon (2000)
6. Lyotard, J.-F.: The Differend: Phrases in Dispute. Minnesota Press, Minneapolis (1988)

Research on the Cultural Product Design
Based on Consumer Cognition

Jianxin Cheng, Junnan Ye, Le Xi, and Wangqun Xiao

School of Art, Design and Media, East China University of Science and Technology
M. BOX 286, NO. 130, Meilong Road, Xuhui District, Shanghai 200237, China
cjx.master@gmail.com, yejunnan971108@qq.com, xilutar@sina.com,
xiaoyao-1916@163.com

Abstract. With the development of cultural creative industry, cultural product design has shifted from "production-oriented" of batch design to "consumer-oriented" of personalized design, on the basis of function, shape, material, color, brand, economic, cultural and other factors of product design. The consumer's emotional appeal should also be investigated fully and comprehensively. How to master the general rule of consumers' psychology, follow the law of consumer behavior, design marketable products and finally promote the customers' satisfaction will be significant subjects of current cultural product design.

This paper studies on the current cultural product from targeted consumers' cognition point of view based on theories such as Demand Psychology, Consumption Psychology, Cognitive Psychology, Kansei Engineering, Ergonomics, Semantics of Design and Semiotics and etc, and proposes three hierarchy theory of consumer cognition on cultural product by analyzing cultural products' connotation, characteristic and category and combining human cognitive system in Cognitive Psychology, which are interpretation, experience and cognition. Also present the cultural product design procedure based on consumer cognition on the basis of this theory, including research and analysis of consumers' cognition, image space establishment of cultural product cognition, cultural product concept design and implementation and cultural product test and evaluation.

Keywords: Consumer Cognition, Cultural Product Design, Design Method, Design Procedure.

1　Introduction

With the development of social economy, people are not satisfied with the material enjoyment of modern products, and try to pursue the intrinsic cultural connotation and artistic value, which change people's material life, improve their life quality and bring people with higher spiritual enjoyment, making the world much more wonderful. Therefore, cultural influence on product design should be strengthened; unique cultural quality should be added to the products so as to show products' unique style and charm, which could make product design in a dominant position in international market competition. Liu,2009).

C. Stephanidis (Ed.): HCII 2014 Posters, Part I, CCIS 434, pp. 13–18, 2014.
© Springer International Publishing Switzerland 2014

Designers must learn to cater to the desire of consumers from user's point of view, make the shape of product meet their emotional demand. They should realize the emotional communication between people and product in the designation and make the product not only satisfy people's living needs, but also an emotion-bearing companion (P. M. A. Desmet. C. J. Overbeeke. S. J. E. T. Tax,1993).

Thus how to master the general rule of consumers' psychology, follow the law of consumer behavior, design marketable products and finally promote the customers' satisfaction will be significant subjects of current cultural product design.

2   Research Background

2.1   Cultural Products' Ponnotation, Characteristic and Category

In the latest document "1994-2003, the International Flow of Cultural Products and Services" released by UNESCO, it said that cultural products are the products provided by culture industry activities, which are divided into two categories of cultural products and cultural service (li,2013).

Professor Bai Ying in Central South University thinks cultural products have the following characteristics: first, it reflects in the creativity of symbols in pragmatic sense used by communicators; second, it reflects in the value deferring by added value of symbolic values; third, the cultural resources regeneration or proliferation regurgitation-feeding that formed by value deferring; fourth, the ideology of significant social and cultural responsibility by symbolic interaction (Bai,He,2006).

Sun Anmin divides cultural products into three categories: art, handicrafts, and industrial products. Art is personalized, created by a single person , such as drama, calligraphy, and painting; handicrafts is done manually by some person or persons , such as tourism dance, sculpture; industrial products are standardized and can carry out mass production, such as television, DVDs, books and magazines (Sun Anmin, 2005).

2.2   Consumer Cognitive Model

Cognitive system in the psychology is made up of four parts: the information transmission and processing system of limited capacity, cognitive system, knowledge system and self -monitoring system.

Modern cognitive psychology thinks that the human brain is an information processing system. When people are awake, they will continue to carry out processing activities from the stimulation of external environment information. This system mainly includes the following components: sensors, registration, pattern recognition, short-term memory and long-term memory (Zhang, 2007).

3   Research Methods

3.1   Three Levels of Consumers' Cognition on Cultural Product

Consumers' cognition for cultural products is based on their cognitive model, and in this process, we can include the consumers' cognition process into three levels, namely, interpretation, experience, and cognition, as shown in Figure 1.

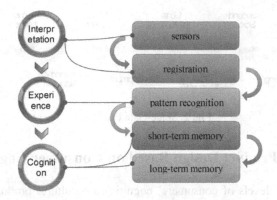

Fig. 1. Three Levels of Consumers' Cognition for Cultural Products

Interpretation

Interpretation is the receptor and sensory register part in cognitive models of consumers where consumers can do cognitive experience of initial level on properties such as cultural products' color, texture, shape, surface ornamentation, detail processing, and component through the visual, tactile, auditory, olfactory, and gustatory sense .

Experience

Experience is a part of recognition pattern in consumers' cognitive model, and in the process consumers, according to their social, cultural, economic, political environment, and their own cultural cognition, have the deep experience in   cultural products ,which means the deeply-cognized experience in attributes such as the process, function, operation, safety, and relationship .

Cognition

Cognition is a short-term memory and long-term memory part in consumers' cognitive model .In the process of interpretation and experience of cultural products, consumers understand properties of products such as a special meaning intrinsically expressed, narrative, emotionality, and cultural characteristics, and stored internal information of these products in short-term memory. After repeating product experience cognition, consumers formed a cultural stereotype in their thinking set, so as to achieve the long-term memory.

3.2   Access Management Product Design Program

For the product design procedure, Canada's new product development expert Robert G.Copper proposed the "gateway management procedures" in 1993. Now the design management process has been adopted by many international well-known large companies, including familiar Carlsberg public limited company, Kodak company, Lego company, Microsoft Corp, Hewlett-Packard Co, DuPont Co and many other well-known enterprises, which is proved to be very effective. The main individual stages of the "Stage gate process" are   shown in figure 2:

Fig. 2. Stage-Gate Process

4   Cultural Product Design Based on Consumer Cognition

According to three levels of consumers' cognition on cultural products and product design procedures, cultural product design based on consumers' cognition can be divided into research and analysis of consumers' cognition, image space establishment of cultural product cognition, cultural product concept design and implementation and cultural product test and evaluation .These four phases are   shown in figure 3.

4.1   Research and Analysis of Consumers' Cognition

With certain designed object, designers, first of all, do research and analysis of the designed target consumers and carry out a comprehensive test and research on their countries,   city, occupation, age, gender, educational level, marital status, income, family income and other aspects. Second, they carry out in-depth investigations and studies in cognitive experience of culture products from the perspective of the three levels : interpretation, experience and cognition.

4.2   Image Space Establishment of Cultural Product Cognition

According to the analysis of cognitive three level contents of target consumers, the designer pursue product cultural design elements from the three aspects of culture, people, and goods environment.

Designers collate these collected cultural design elements, on which target consumer groups design cognitive tests so as to establish image space of product culture.

4.3   Cultural Product Concept Design and Implementation

The main work of this stage is conversion, application, and integration of cultural elements, which makes the design process more clear, and systematic. Designers can achieve implantation of cultural concept and draw concept sketches through design semantics, and pictograph, self-explanatory, ideographic, and phonetic in semiotics.

Then the designers test and evaluate concept sketches early through people, color, material, process, function, structure, environment and other aspect, finally choose the best design sketch and form concept model scheme through CAD or the traditional design performance. At the same time, the best design concept model selection scheme of a certain amount of cognitive test by the target consumer groups, to determine whether the design of the products meet three hierarchy needs of consumers' cognition. Qualified products will next be put into three dimensional model making, and those not accord with the demand will be tested again after the selection or improved design.

They select a certain amount of best design concept model scheme, which is to be under cognitive test by target consumer groups to make sure whether the design of products meets three hierarchy needs of consumers' cognition.

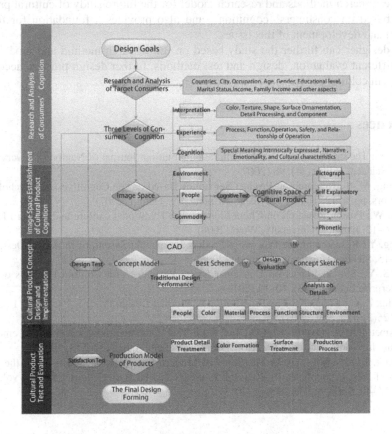

Fig. 3. Cultural Product Design Based on Consumer Cognition

4.4   Cultural Product Test and Evaluation

Designers produce models through 3D software and they research product detail treatment, color formation, surface treatment, and production process through produced model ones. Production model of products to meet consumers' cognition is made after repeated scrutiny and verification. The final production model passes customer satisfaction testing, thus the final design forming.

5   Conclusion and Suggestion

This paper makes a deep intensive study of design method and model of cultural product design based on consumers' cognition according to Psychology, Consumer

Psychology, Cognitive Psychology, Mental Engineering, Ergonomics, Design Semantics , Semiotics and other theories. According to human cognitive system in the cognitive psychology, it proposes consumers' interpretation ,experience, and cognition ,these three hierarchy theory on cultural products, and raises cultural product design process based on consumers' cognition on the basis of the theory, which provides effective research methods and research model for the future study of cultural product design based on consumers' cognition , and also provides a foundation for further research and development of this issue.

The designer can further the study based on the research method and model, proposes different evaluation, design and test methods, further design practice according to different cultural products.

References

1. Xu, Y.: The modern design of the cultural connotation. Journal of Nantong University Social Sciences Edition (4), 98 (2007)
2. Zhang, M.-S.: Research on Product Semantics Based on the Cognitive and Psychological Factors, pp. 8–12. Tianjin Polytechnic University, Tianjin (2007)
3. Lin, W.: Fusion Research on China Elements of Traditional Culture and Modern Design, pp. 6–12. Jiangnan University, Wuxi (2008)
4. Peng, Y.: Research on the Process of Product Innovation System of Industrial Design, pp. 13–15. Sichuan University, Chengdu (2006)
5. Li, S.-Y., Shi, J.: Impact on Consumer Brand Preference for Cultural Products demand. Enterprise Economy (3), 10–12 (2013)
6. Wang, Z.-G.: Comparison and Innovation of Product Design Process. Packaging Engineering 25(2), 154–159 (2004)
7. Desmet, P.M.A., Overbeeke, C.J., Tax, S.J.E.T.: Designing products with added emotional value. In: Conference on Very Large Data Bases, Dublin, pp. 134–145 (1993)
8. Cheng, J., Zhou, M., Ye, J.: The Study of Modern Emergency Products under the Direction of New Ergonomics. In: Rau, P.L.P. (ed.) CCD/HCII 2013, Part I. LNCS, vol. 8023, pp. 31–40. Springer, Heidelberg (2013)

Towards an Interactive and Iterative Process to Design Natural Interaction Techniques

Lucio Cossio, Felipe Eduardo Lammel, and Milene Selbach Silveira

Faculdade de Informática – PUCRS, Avenida Ipiranga 6681, Prédio 32 – 90619-900,
Porto Alegre - RS, Brazil
{lucio.cossio,felipelammel}@gmail.com,
milene.silveira@pucrs.br

Abstract. With the rise of different interaction modalities, several different devices are available to users that need to learn how to interact with them. To avoid problems in the future, developers need to create intuitive interaction techniques, which is not a trivial task. To support the design of these techniques, we present a process where users interactively and iteratively participate in the design, through a series of individual interviews and focus groups. We also present two case studies, for a multimodal and a multi-touch application.

Keywords: Natural Interaction, Multimodal and Multi-touch applications.

1 Introduction

As envisioned in the 90's [12][15], today computers are present all around our daily environment and a person can own and interact with several of them during the day. This increased use and the different contexts in which computers can be found, requires more natural types of interaction [1][12][13], like touch, gestures and speech.

The interaction with these natural modalities needs to be studied to generate the best interface design principles. There are several characteristics that must be addressed to provide the best design or these natural interfaces may suffer from bad decisions [9]. It is important to generate gestures, like body or motion device gestures, that are socially acceptable [10]. It is also important to define gestures that are intuitive to use, or users may forget how to execute them [6].

A solution to overcome possible design problems is to execute user studies before implementing the system. As stated by [8], this approach can lead to gestures that are easy to perform, easy to remember, intuitive, iconically logical towards functionality and more ergonomic. Morris et al [7] compared surface gestures created by users and researchers, and concluded that participants preferred gestures created by large groups of people, such as those created by end-users or proposed by more than one researcher.

Moreover, there are other works that propose user studies to generate natural gestures for different systems [4][8][11][14][16]. This work presents an enhanced approach to extract the interaction with the system using user studies before implementation.

C. Stephanidis (Ed.): HCII 2014 Posters, Part I, CCIS 434, pp. 19–23, 2014.
© Springer International Publishing Switzerland 2014

This work present a process focused on the final implementation, introducing a focus group phase to improve the interaction of the initial interviews. The process description and examples of its application are presented in the next sections.

2   Proposed Process

The process definition focuses on the generation of the input interaction with the system, although it also exposes ideas for output. Therefore we use the term interaction1 from this point on in the paper to focus on the input, unless explicitly stated. Next sections present the five phases of the process.

2.1   Definition of the System

For the first phase of the process we start with an initial set of commands based on the defined purpose of the intended system, or we could execute a user study to explore and understand the use of the system and generate its initial commands, as used by Henze et al [4].

2.2   Individual Interviews

We recommend a semi-structured interview process, using a qualitative approach [2] with a restricted number of users (5 to 10), in order to deepen the discussion. The interview allows us to extract possible interaction techniques and capture participants' opinions and ideas. Here we are concerned about presenting the user a general vision of the system, and immersing them in its context of use.

We propose the following steps to conduct the interview: (I) Introduction: Introduce and present the research goal and sign the consent form; (II) Participant profile: question the user about his/her experience with technologies that share common characteristics to those that will be used by the system; (III) Interaction Proposals: present the idea of the reference system to the user and for each command that the system will provide ask them to propose the best way to perform it using some modality (according to the system being studied).

2.3   Interview Analysis

Based on the results of step III, the researcher should generate an initial set of interaction techniques. For each command, the users' proposals can be categorized by similarity. Since the focus of the process is on the implementation of a specific system, we recommend that the categorization also be done based on the limitations of the referenced system technology. For instance, a free-hand gesture recognizer may not be able to perceive individual fingers, but only the whole hand. If a gesture proposal was made with the movement of the finger in the air, and another participant made a similar movement using the whole hand, these two proposals could be categorized into only one category. However, we should validate in the next phase, the Focus Group, the system's known limitations that may affect the proposed gestures' implementation.

---

[1] In this work we use the terms interaction and interaction techniques in the same sense: the way users interact with a system.

The frequency of proposals for each category can be filtered and only a subset of all gestures proposed in the interviews may be used for the next phase.

2.4   Focus Group

The next phase is to use a focus group to validate, reduce, expand or enhance (or a combination of these) the set of interaction techniques proposed in the interviews. This study method was used in other HCI research [3][5], and can reveal feelings and beliefs that benefit from discussion in a social setting. We recommend the number of 3 to 10 users in the group, as suggested in the literature [3][5].

We suggest the following steps for the group meeting: (I) Research introduction: Introduce and present the research goal to the participants and sign the consent forms; (II) Participant profiles: Questions about the participants' profile and their experience with similar technologies; (III) Present the system: Introduce to the participants to the system's concept; (IV) Interaction Discussion: For each command the system has, we should (a) Explain the command to the participants, (b) Present the participants with the selected interaction ideas generated from the individual interviews. (c) Validate them and ask for better alternatives if they are not accepted by most of the participants, (d) Ask participants about further details of the interaction for possible implementation, taking into consideration the known limitation aspects of the technology.

The researcher should encourage the discussion about the participants' opinions in order to build a general understanding of what they want the system to be. In this phase, as generally executed for focus groups [3][5], more than one group could be used to have different possible groups opinions and user profiles. As additional part of the focus group, a prototype or a similar system could be shown to the users, so they can better understand possible uses, ideas and provide feedback.

2.5   Converging Interaction Definition

The interpretation of the focus group results should be related to the improvement of the initial set of interactions proposed by the individual interviews. If participants from the focus group do not approve a gesture that was previously chosen as one of the most suggested (from the interview phase), the gesture should not be promptly discarded and replaced by a new and not similar suggestion from the participants. It's interesting to question the participants about the reasons they do not like it. New suggestions that are more consistent with the scenario may be used in place of others, but this evaluation needs to be based on the designer's interpretation.

3   Case Studies

We executed two case studies, following the proposed process. The first, focusing on interaction techniques for a multimodal presentation system (including interaction through smartphone, body and hand gestures, and speech), and the second one a visualization information tool, with data manipulation by selection and zoom commands through multi-touch devices (exploiting the use of multiple fingers).

In the first study – multimodal system - nine participants were recruited using a convenience sampling for the interview process. Five of them were female. All nine participants were students in computer science programs. The age of the participants ranged from 19 to 32. In the second study – visualization information tool - we conducted seven interviews with undergraduate and graduate students from different areas, such as law, economics and computer science. All of them were also recruited by convenience sampling and they were between 20 and 33 years old.

In both cases, the Interviews phases allowed us to gather several interaction possibilities for each system, which were consolidated in the Focus Group phases. The most preferred interaction actions for each command were chosen and then presented to the groups, with the purpose of validating and reducing the initial set of interaction. In the multimodal system case study, two focus groups were conducted. The first group was composed of a convenience sample of eight undergraduate students in computer science programs, ages ranging from 17 to 20. The second group was composed of six undergraduate students in computer science programs, ranging in age from 19 to 26. In the visualization information tool case study, only one focus group was conducted with six participants and they were between 18 and 32 years old. The group was made up of undergraduate and postgraduate students from economics and computer science areas, also recruited by convenience sampling.

The main difference of the proposed process - the use of focus groups - made it possible to discuss the ideas suggested by the participants and to find the best ways to interact with the focused systems based on the opinions of several users. The focus group was a good source of ideas and reflection on interaction for real use. In the first case study, for instance, a big concern was how the use of the system could be affected by the context (for example if the presenter is moving or speaking a lot, a non-desired command cannot be recognized and activate the system); in this case the use of two groups gave an interesting diversity to the research, some commands were generally accepted as they were, or only slightly modified, whereas others had different outcomes for each group. Without the focus group, could be a hard task to decide the gestures/movements to implement. In the second case study, for example, the designer could opt for more elaborate gestures but users chose simple gestures with a few fingers.

4   Final Considerations

We proposed a new process that aims to involve users in the elaboration of interaction techniques through the use of individual interviews and focus groups. The process provides us with a quick and simple way of obtaining the users' interaction preferences. The main difference between our process and related work is that it relies on the addition of an additional phase where, after initial interaction derivation from individual interviews, we use a focus group research for further evaluation, interaction detailing, and to resolve possible conflicts that may arise. As a method carried out before the final development, it reduces the possibility of having rework in implementation and also allows for adjustments or further evaluation.

The results of the case studies carried out show us that the process could help the designers to understand users' preferences and difficulties in the use of some techniques. This can help them to generate the interaction techniques needed for the applications they are developing. Future steps in this proposed process should be applied research in other case studies, especially dealing with distinct modalities, to help us to refine and improve it.

References

1. Abawajy, J.H.: Human-computer interaction in ubiquitous computing environments. International Journal of Pervasive Computing and Communications 5(1), 61–77 (2009)
2. Denzin, N.K., Lincoln, Y.S.: Collecting and Interpreting Qualitative Materials. Sage Publications, London (2007)
3. Heikkinen, J., Olsson, T., Väänänen-Vainio-Mattila, K.: Expectations for user experience in haptic communication with mobile devices. In: Proceedings of the 11th International Conference on Human-Computer Interaction with Mobile Devices and Services (MobileHCI 2009), Article 28, 10 pages. ACM, New York (2009)
4. Henze, N., Löcken, A., Boll, S., Hesselmann, T., Pielot, M.: Free-hand gestures for music playback: deriving gestures with a user-centred process. In: Proceedings of the 9th International Conference on Mobile and Ubiquitous Multimedia (MUM 2010), Article 16, 10 pages. ACM, New York (2010)
5. Mazza, R.: Evaluating information visualization applications with focus groups: the CourseVis experience. In: Proceedings of the 2006 AVI Workshop on Beyond Time and Errors: Novel Evaluation Methods for Information Visualization (BELIV 2006), pp. 1–6. ACM, New York (2006)
6. McGlaun, G., Althoff, F., Lang, M., Rigoll, G.: Towards multi-modal error management: experimental evaluation of user strategies in event of faulty application behavior in automotive environments. In: Proceedings of the Seventh World Multiconference on Systemics, Cybernetics, and Informatics, pp. 462–466 (2003)
7. Morris, M.R., Wobbrock, J.O., Wilson, A.D.: Understanding users' preferences for surface gestures. In: Proceedings of Graphics Interface 2010 (GI 2010), pp. 261–268. Canadian Information Processing Society, Toronto (2010)
8. Nielsen, M., Störring, M., Moeslund, T.B., Granum, E.: A procedure for developing intuitive and ergonomic gesture interfaces for HCI. In: International Gesture Workshop 2003, pp. 409–420 (2003)
9. Norman, D.A.: Natural user interfaces are not natural. Interactions 17(3), 6–10 (2010)
10. Rico, J., Brewster, S.: Usable gestures for mobile interfaces: evaluating social acceptability. In: Proceedings of the SIGCHI Conference on Human Factors in Computing Systems (CHI 2010), pp. 887–896. ACM, New York (2010)
11. Ruiz, J., Li, Y., Lank, E.: User-defined motion gestures for mobile interaction. In: Proceedings of the SIGCHI Conference on Human Factors in Computing Systems (CHI 2011), pp. 197–206. ACM, New York (2011)
12. Salber, D., Dey, A., Abowd, G.: Ubiquitous computing: Defining an HCI research agenda for an emerging interaction paradigm, GVU Technical Report, Georgia Institute of Technology (1998)
13. Schmidt, A., Kranz, M., Holleis, P.: Interacting with the ubiquitous computer: towards embedding interaction. In: Proceedings of the 2005 Joint Conference on Smart Objects and Ambient Intelligence: Innovative Context-aware Services: Usages and Technologies, pp. 147–152 (2005)
14. Vatavu, R.-D.: User-defined gestures for free-hand TV control. In: Proceedings of the 10th European Conference on Interactive Tv and Video (EuroiTV 2012), pp. 45–48. ACM, New York (2012)
15. Weiser, M.: The Computer for the 21st Century. Scientific American 265(3), 94–104 (1991)
16. Wobbrock, J.O., Morris, M.R., Wilson, A.D.: User-defined gestures for surface computing. In: Proceedings of the SIGCHI Conference on Human Factors in Computing Systems (CHI 2009), pp. 1083–1092. ACM (2009)

Agile Software Teams Can Use Conflict to Create a Better Products

Broderick Crawford[1,2], Ricardo Soto[1,3], Claudio León de la Barra[1], Kathleen Crawford[1], and Eduardo Olguín[4]

[1] Pontificia Universidad Católica de Valparaíso, Chile
[2] Universidad Finis Terrae, Chile
[3] Universidad Autónoma de Chile, Chile
[4] Universidad San Sebastián, Chile

{broderick.crawford,ricardo.soto,claudio.leondelabarra}@ucv.cl,
kathleen.crawford.a@mail.pucv.cl,
eduardo.olguin@uss.cl

Abstract. Agile Software processes emphasize collaboration more than traditional methods. Collaborations and interactions are cited directly in two of the four values listed in the agile manifesto. Because of everything that involves communication contains the potential for conflict, we are interested in knowing how to manage conflicts to enhance agile projects.

Keywords: Software Engineering, Agile Development, Conflict Management.

1 Introduction

Some amount of conflict is required in a team to motivate change and encourage creativity. The relation between conflict and team effectiveness approximates an invert U-curve, where too much or too little conflict impacts negatively. Therefore, management to maintain an appropiate level of conflict is crucial for optimizing team effectiveness.

Conflict is defined as an interactive process manifested in incompatibility, disagreement or dissonance within or between social entities (individual, group, organization, ...) [26]. In recent years the concept has taken an unexpected turn around its qualities, being discovered that the appearance of conflict in small amounts could bring great benefits to organizations in terms of creativity and innovation [21,23,13,18]. Seeing that the conflict is necessary to a creative process like software development.

2 The Conflict within Organizations

We can find many ways to classify the conflict within organizations: interpersonal, intrapersonal, intergroup and intragroup [26]. Interpersonal conflict refers to the most basic type of conflict that is developed between two people or colleagues either by differences in personality or work style also a personal history.

C. Stephanidis (Ed.): HCII 2014 Posters, Part I, CCIS 434, pp. 24–29, 2014.

Meanwhile the conflict intra staff is one where the purpose and vision of an individual differs from the overall vision of the organization. When an individual is faced with a group and is unwilling or unable to conform to the dynamic, he left the team due to an intragroup conflict. In intergroup conflict meanwhile, two teams are involved in the problem, threatening the successful completion of a project due to differences in group dynamics.

2.1 Dysfunctional and Functional Conflict

Conflict must be managed, not only as a way to optimize project success, but also to increase the satisfaction of project team members.

Persistent conflict complicates the management of the projects, causes participants to constantly disagree with each other about requirements, methods, techniques and solutions. The continued conflict damages the communication, coordination and control, reducing the team performance level affecting the final quality of the product, the project deadline accomplishment and costing. In this way we are talking about dysfunctional conflict [21].

On the other hand and with the new discoveries, we see that constructive or functional conflict is considered to have beneficial effects. Where functional conflict is present, people feel free to express their opinions, beliefs, assumptions and to challenge ideas of others [21,23,13,26]. Functional conflict works like an antidote to groupthink [6], a psychological phenomenon that occurs within a team, in which the desire for harmony or conformity in the group results in correct decisions. Group members try to minimize conflict and reach a consensus decision without critical evaluation of alternative ideas or viewpoints.

In [26] Rahim describes the main characteristics of each type of conflict.

Dysfunctional Outcomes:

- Conflict may cause job stress, burnout, and dissatisfaction.
- Communication between individuals and groups may be reduced.
- A climate of distrust and suspicion can be developed.
- Relationships may be damaged.
- Job performance may be reduced.
- Resistance to change can increase.
- Organizational commitment and loyalty may be affected.

Functional Outcomes:

- Conflict may stimulate innovation, creativity, and growth.
- Organizational decision making may be improved.
- Alternative solutions to a problem may be found.
- Conflict may lead to synergistic solutions to common problems.
- Individual and group performance may be enhanced.
- Individuals and groups may be forced to search for new approaches.
- Individuals and groups may be required to articulate and clarify their positions.

3   Developing Software

Software development projects depends mostly on team performance: "Software is developed for people and by people" [19]. But surprisingly, most of software engineering research is technical and deemphasizes the human and social aspects. It is interesting to consider the new proposals of agile methodologies for software development in order to study them considering the teamwork practices. The agile principles and values have emphasized the importance of collaboration and interaction in software development. Scrum Agile Development Process [29], the most notorious competitor of eXtreme Programming XP [4] between agilists, has attained worldwide fame for its ability to increase the productivity of software teams by several magnitudes through empowering individuals, fostering a team-oriented environment, and focusing on project transparency and results.

There are recent studies reporting efforts to improve agile process. Agile software development addresses software process improvement within teams. The work in [27][24] argue for the use of diagnosis and action planning to improve teamwork in agile software development. The action planning focused on improving shared leadership, team orientation and learning. We believe that the innovation and development of new products is an interdisciplinary issue influenced by different aspects [30][25][14], we are interested in the study of the potential of new concepts and techniques to foster knowledge management, creative problem solving and conflict management in software engineering [17][12][11].

Software engineering is a knowledge intensive process that includes some aspects of knowledge management and creative problem solving in all its phases: eliciting requirements, design, construction, testing, implementation, maintenance, and project management [19]. No worker of a development project has all the knowledge required to fulfill all activities. This underlies the need for communication, collaboration and knowledge sharing support to share domain expertise between the customer and the development team [9].

The traditional approaches (often referred to as plan-driven, task-based or Tayloristic), like the waterfall model and its variances, facilitate knowledge sharing primarily through documentation. They also promote usage of role based teams and detailed plans of the entire software development life-cycle. It shifts the focus from individuals and their creative abilities to the processes themselves. In contrary, agile methods emphasise and value individuals and interactions over processes. Tayloristic methods heavily and rigorously use documentation for capturing knowledge gained in the activities of a software project life-cycle [8]. In contrast, agile methods suggest that most of the written documentation can be replaced by enhanced informal communications among team members internally and between the team and the customers with a stronger emphasis on tacit knowledge rather than explicit knowledge [5].

One possibility to improve the software development process is to design a process which can manage conflicts. In management and business, researchers have done much work about conflict management and obtained evidence that conflict must be managed to optimize projects and boosting the satisfaction of team members. The employees who had appropriate skills - negotation and conflict resolution, problem modeling and creative problem solving, critical thinking, written and verbal communication - worked on complex, challenging jobs, and were supervised in a supportive, noncontrolling fashion, produced more creative work. Then, according to the previous ideas the use of conflict and creativity in software development is undeniable. In a few publications the importance of creativity has been investigated in all the phases of software development process [17][16][10][20] and mostly focused in the requirements engineering [28][22]. Nevertheless, the use of techniques to foster conflict management is still shortly investigated.

4   Conflict in Software Development

Conflict management in software development must certainly take into account many factors [15,31,7,2]. We can even observe the importance of individual and interpersonal conflict mentioned above, related to levels of participation, influence and personal traits such as personality and emotions. We can also see the importance of the organization and the context in which software is developed, linked to the different views in which workers are trained. This is the *organizational culture* that has a number of rules and patterns in which the work is performed daily in an organization [3,1].

One of the most important points in the development of software is communication, it is identified as one of the critical factors [32]. This is because much of the work can be developed virtually, work teams fall into problems of misunderstanding or lack of communication which demonstrates the importance of collaborative work for the creation of better products.

5   Conclusion

We believe that the latest research shows that the use of conflict within organizations brings fruitful results around creativity and innovation projects. It is important to consider new theories of conflict management within organizations, and not to forget that we are working with human emotions and relationships.

References

1. Managing conflict in software development teams: A multi-level analysis. Journal of Product Innovation Management 15, 423–435 (1998)
2. Altay, A., Kayakutlu, G., Topcu, Y.I.: Win-win match using a genetic algorithm. Applied Mathematical Modelling 34(10), 2749–2762 (2010)
3. Barki, H., Hartwick, J.: Interpersonal conflict and its management in information system development. MIS Q. 25(2), 195–228 (2001)
4. Beck, K.: Extreme programming explained: embrace change. Addison-Wesley Longman Publishing Co., USA (2000)

5. Beck, K., Beedle, M., Bennekum, A.V., Cockburn, A., Cunningham, W., Fowler, M., Grenning, J., Highsmith, J., Hunt, A., Jeffries, R., Kern, J., Marick, B., Martin, R.C., Mellor, S., Schwaber, K., Sutherland, J., Thomas, D.: Manifesto for agile software development (2001), http://agilemanifesto.org

6. BÉnabou, R.: Groupthink: Collective delusions in organizations and markets. Working Paper 14764, National Bureau of Economic Research (March 2009)

7. Carneiro, D., Novais, P., Neves, J.: Using genetic algorithms to create solutions for conflict resolution. Neurocomputing 109, 16–26 (2013); New trends on Soft Computing Models in Industrial and Environmental Applications A selection of extended and updated papers from the SOCO 2011 International Conference

8. Chau, T., Maurer, F.: Knowledge sharing in agile software teams. In: Lenski, W. (ed.) Logic versus Approximation. LNCS, vol. 3075, pp. 173–183. Springer, Heidelberg (2004)

9. Chau, T., Maurer, F., Melnik, G.: Knowledge sharing: Agile methods versus tayloristic methods. In: Twelfth International Workshop on Enabling Technologies: Infrastructure for Collaborative Enterprises, WETICE, pp. 302–307 (2003)

10. Crawford, B., Leon de la Barra, C.: Enhancing creativity in agile software teams. In: Concas, G., Damiani, E., Scotto, M., Succi, G. (eds.) XP 2007. LNCS, vol. 4536, pp. 161–162. Springer, Heidelberg (2007)

11. Crawford, B., Leon de la Barra, C., Soto, R., Misra, S., Monfroy, E.: Knowledge management and creativity practices in software engineering. In: Liu, K., Filipe, J. (eds.) KMIS, pp. 277–280. SciTePress (2012)

12. Crawford, B., Leon de la Barra, C., Soto, R., Monfroy, E.: Agile software engineering as creative work. In: CHASE, pp. 20–26. IEEE (2012)

13. Deutsch, M.: A Theory of Co-operation and Competition. Human Relations 2(2), 129–152 (1949)

14. Fernandez-Sanz, L., Misra, S.: Analysis of cultural and gender influences on teamwork performance for software requirements analysis in multinational environments. IET Software 6(3), 167–175 (2012)

15. Gallivan, M.J.: The influence of software developers' creative style on their attitudes to and assimilation of a software process innovation. Information & Management 40(5), 443–465 (2003)

16. Glass, R.: Software creativity. Prentice-Hall, USA (1995)

17. Gu, M., Tong, X.: Towards hypotheses on creativity in software development. In: Bomarius, F., Iida, H. (eds.) PROFES 2004. LNCS, vol. 3009, pp. 47–61. Springer, Heidelberg (2004)

18. Jehn, K.: Impact of Intragroup Conflict on Effectiveness: A Multimethod Examination of the Benefits and Detriments of Conflict. UMI Dissertation Services (1992)

19. John, M., Maurer, F., Tessem, B.: Human and social factors of software engineering: workshop summary. ACM SIGSOFT Softw. Eng., Notes 30, 1–6 (2005)

20. León de la Barra, C., Crawford, B.: Fostering creativity thinking in agile software development. In: Holzinger, A. (ed.) USAB 2007. LNCS, vol. 4799, pp. 415–426. Springer, Heidelberg (2007)

21. Massey, G., Dawes, P.: Functional and Dysfunctional Conflict in the Context of Marketing and Sales. University of Wolverhampton Business School Working Papers WP009/04. Management Research Centre, Wolverhampton University Business School (2004)

22. Mich, L., Anesi, C., Berry, D.: Applying a pragmatics-based creativity-fostering technique to requirements elicitation. Requir. Eng. 10, 262–275 (2005)

23. Miron-Spektor, E., Gino, F., Argote, L.: Paradoxical frames and creative sparks: Enhancing individual creativity through conflict and integration. Organizational Behavior and Human Decision Processes 116(2), 229–240 (2011)
24. Moe, N., Dingsoyr, T., Dyba, T.: A teamwork model for understanding an agile team: A case study of a scrum project. Information and Software Technology 52, 480–491 (2010)
25. Nonaka, I., Takeuchi, H.: The Knowledge Creating Company. Oxford University Press, USA (1995)
26. Rahim, A.: Managing Conflict in Organizations. Praeger (1992)
27. Ringstad, M.A., Dingsøyr, T., Brede Moe, N.: Agile process improvement: Diagnosis and planning to improve teamwork. In: O'Connor, R.V., Pries-Heje, J., Messnarz, R. (eds.) EuroSPI 2011. CCIS, vol. 172, pp. 167–178. Springer, Heidelberg (2011)
28. Robertson, J.: Requirements analysts must also be inventors. IEEE Software 22, 48–50 (2005)
29. Sutherland, J.: Agile can scale: Inventing and reinventing scrum in five companies. Cutter IT Journal 14, 5–11 (2001)
30. Takeuchi, H., Nonaka, I.: The new new product development game. Harvard Business Review (1986)
31. van Lamsweerde, A., Letier, E., Darimont, R.: Managing conflicts in goal-driven requirements engineering. IEEE Trans. Softw. Eng. 24(11), 908–926 (1998)
32. Zhang, X., Stafford, T.F., Dhaliwal, J.S., Gillenson, M.L., Moeller, G.: Sources of conflict between developers and testers in software development. Information & Management 51(1), 13–26 (2014)

Sketches in Embodied Interaction:
Balancing Movement and Technological Perspectives

Cumhur Erkut, Sofia Dahl, and Georgios Triantafyllidis

Aalborg University Copenhagen, Department of Architecture, Design and Media Technology
A.C. Meyers Vænge 15, 2450 Copenhagen SV, Denmark
{cer,sof,gt}@create.aau.dk

Abstract. We present an approach for teaching and designing embodied interaction based on interactive sketches. We have combined the *mover perspective* and *felt experiences* of movement with advanced technologies (multi-agents, physical simulations) in a generative design session. We report our activities and provide a simple example as a design outcome. The variety and the qualities of the initial ideas indicate that this approach might provide a better foundation for our participants, compared to the approaches that focus only on technologies. The interactive sketches will be demonstrated at the conference.

Keywords: Embodied Human-Computer Interaction, Design Pedagogy.

1   Introduction

Embodied interaction embraces possibilities of gestural or whole-body interaction. Yet, the affordances and the design space of these new media need to be carefully studied, experienced and thought to the future-generation interaction designers. Practitioners of interaction design consider sketching a core generative and evaluative activity [1], and great examples of incorporating bodily knowledge into the design exploration and teaching are reported, e.g., in [2] and [3]. While [2] de-emphasizes the movement philosophy in embodied interaction for pragmatic exploration, [3] calls for a balance between its movement and technological perspectives.

In this paper, we present an approach for teaching and designing embodied interaction based on the felt qualities of the movement, informing interactive sketches created in popular, open-source, audio-visual creative coding environments, such as openFrameworks[1] and Processing[2]. These sketches are considered as main design artifacts in our approach, which is based on the methodology "Moving and Making Strange" (MMS) by Lian Loke [3]. MMS centers on the lived body in interaction design practice, and emphasizes the moving body both as a creative material and embodied knowledge for design. Our interpretation and facilitation of these foundations in the context of a graduate Embodied Interaction course are the main themes of our paper.

---

[1] http://www.openframeworks.cc
[2] http://processsing.org

C. Stephanidis (Ed.): HCII 2014 Posters, Part I, CCIS 434, pp. 30–35, 2014.
© Springer International Publishing Switzerland 2014

Loke points out two possible limitations of MMS: 1) an underdeveloped machine perspective, and 2) a focus only on video-based motion sensors. While there are emerging approaches that focus on how to explore embodied interaction from the machine perspective [4, 5], in this paper, we explore this domain with developing sketches based on our exploration with the felt qualities of movement. Our sketches combine the textbook examples of simple computer vision [6] with other modalities (e.g., sonic interaction [7]).

The rest of this section summarizes the MMS framework and its technology perspective by computer. Then, in Section 3, we summarize our activities in exploring the felt qualities of movement, within a pedagogical context and in collaboration with a contemporary dance choreographer. Section 4 presents our sketching process to explore embodied interaction with a design funnel [1]. Examples developed by the participants will be demonstrated during the HCI International 2014. Finally, Section 5 draws our conclusions.

1.1   MMS: An Embodied Approach for Movement-Based Interaction Design

Studies of embodied cognition show how body movements may shape our perception in ways that may not always be apparent to us. For instance, recent research has shown a close relationship between body movement and perceived rhythmic accents [8]. In their paper, Loke and Robertson [3] state the need for designers of movement-based interactions to acquire movement expertise. Not only from observing, recording, and analyzing movement, but also bodily mastery based on first-person, lived experiences of movement.

Loke and Robertson [3] propose the use of defamiliarization ("making strange") as a means of breaking up our automatic percept of movement and highlighting the felt aspect. As a methodology, they combine activities for each of the three perspectives:

1. Mover: (a) Investigating movement, (b) inventing and choreographing movement, and (c) re-enacting movement
2. Observer: (a) Describing and documenting movement and (b) Visual analysis and representation of movement
3. Machine: (a) Exploring and mapping human-machine interaction, (b) representing machine input and interpretation of moving bodies.

As part of the activities for getting first-person perspective of movement, Loke and Robertson propose movements from imagery, playing with everyday movements, and variations on traditional movements. Activities for the observer perspective involve scripts and movement-oriented scenarios, as well as describing movement qualities using Laban Movement Analysis.

1.2   Computer Vision

Computer vision technologies are employed in motion sensor devices to facilitate motion sensing and capturing. These technologies allow experiences that bridge the physical and virtual worlds. Such long or short range motion sensing devices have been available for decades and are designed to be able to detect differences in the levels of infrared energy of moving objects. Recently they became mainstream due to some innovative low-cost implementations. These include, e.g., Kinect for Xbox/Windows, Leap Motion, DepthSense Cameras, and Wii controller.

The methods are referring to different software implementations, which are based in the corresponding computer vision techniques, e.g., detection of moving objects by *background subtraction, frame differencing,* or *movement direction tracking,* [6], *speed of movement estimation, depth calculation of objects in a scene,* object position in the 3d space, gesture recognition, and skeleton or joint movement tracking.

2   Exploring the Felt Qualities of Movement

2.1   Context and Activities

The activities were performed with the master students on the education in Medialogy, Aalborg University Copenhagen. In an elective course, students learn the theory of embodied interaction together with basic computer vision (see Sec. 2.2), creative coding [9, 10], embodied agents, multi-agent systems and AI engines [11]. Working with students of media technology and not with designers, our approach and objective differ some from that of Loke and Robertson [3]. For guiding our students in their project work, we have organized a session with five students and a contemporary dance choreographer on the felt experiences of movement. The choreographer was provided both the theory and practical exercises presented in [3], and our focus and interest in embodied interaction. She prepared four exercises based on this formation, and discussed her action plan before the session, out of which three activities were tried out in a single session, following an action-reflection pattern.

Generating Movement from Imagery: A Drop of Oil. As a start, the participants have engaged in a meditative whole body warm-up exercise with their eyes closed. Directed by the choreographer, participants imagined each of their joints being made more movable by a drop of oil, traveling through the body. This imagery puts focus and awareness on different parts of the body.

Participants reported to like the calm feeling of this activity. Some felt heat sensation in hands and other parts of the body. One participant stated that he felt as if the imagined oil was "lubricating a robot". Some participants did not know whether or not to move, but a general effect on movement qualities were that the movement patterns of hands and body sway became more circular as focus went through the body.

Playing with Everyday Movements: Act of Walking. Directed by the choreographer, participants walked around and experimented with changing direction (forward, backwards, sideways all with maintained walking speed), as well as changes in walking speed (normal, fast, slow), half and double tempo. Participants were asked to pay attention to the effect on movement kinematics and felt qualities. Then different walking rhythms (double, triple and counting to five) were introduced and participants were instructed to alternate between the dominant and non-dominant foot leading, again noting the difference in sensation.

In discussion, changes in movement kinematics were noted. In particular, the slow walking speed led to different use of arms and some difficulties in maintaining balance. Backwards movement also changed focus: the facilitator noted a tendency for participants to lean forward, mainly for protection.

In discussing the felt qualities of tempo and speed, the participants pointed out the difficulty of maintaining the balance in slow tempo, and that of varying kinematics and expressive qualities in fast tempo walking. Again related to kinematics, they identified differences on how we use our feet in different directions: in walking backwards, for instance, the regular rolling of the foot from heel to ball is reversed. Participants also brought about the tendency to relate spatial perception and tempo (e.g., while climbing up and down the stairs). While moving sideways, they reported to switch between the actual and double tempo.

The introduced walking rhythms made participants aware of the difference in movement quality between their dominant and non-dominant sides. Movers were unsure if the effect was only felt (mental in their description), or if it could be observed from outside. Again, the relationship between our body movements and perception becomes apparent as humans have a clear tendency to perceive isochronous and identical sounds as divided into groups (e.g. tic-tock of clocks, see e.g., [12]) The choreograph facilitator commented that some changes in movement quality were observable. For instance, there was a tendency for more circular movements by the using the pelvis in imagined triple pattern.

The discussion has continued on describing the felt qualities of movement in Laban dimensions, and relation between the movement and cognitive processes (e.g., solving a math problem while walking, or tests will elderly people).

The Body in Space: Focus. This activity was conducted in four stages: 1) eyes closed, ii) gaze and focus within 1 meter, ii) within the room, and iv) beyond the room. The movement material and instructions were the same as in the drop exercise; the emphasis here was on feeling how the focus changes the movement qualities. Participants noticed bigger movements when their focus was expanding. The inward focus when the eyes were closed had a different quality compared to outward focus. They reported that when their eyes were open, they have hard time to pull in their focus. The choreographer commented that this task could be too ambitious for novices, as these difficulties do not occur when working with dance and movement professionals. She also pointed out that this activity is usually performed in a longer period compared to what we had.

The session as finalized with a visit to multisensory experience laboratory so that the facilitator and the participants were introduced to the technologies related to activities. Fig. 1 illustrates a snapshot of walking in virtual reality (a farm scene) with optical motion tracking and realistic auditory feedback (walking and cloth sounds) [13].

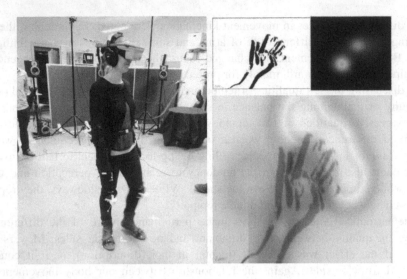

Fig. 1. Left: Repeating the walking activity in VR: optical motion tracking and audio-visual feedback [13]. Right: Detecting motion with *frame differencing* [6, 9] and superposing heat-map[3]. If desired, liquid sounds may be added [7, 14].

3   Sketches: Design Funnel and an Example

Two weeks after the movement session, a brain/body-storming session was conducted with four participants. After a lively 10+10 Design Funnel session [1] and subsequent discussion, participants have generated concepts and sketches to form mini-projects to be completed in Spring 2014. For the first ten concepts of the Funnel, a design brief guiding the design funnel was as follows (*edited*):

Brief: "We have generated movement from imagery with the image of an oil drop. This puts focus and awareness on different parts of the body. Now, please send the digital "oil" to the focus area. *Constraints*: None (Input / Output): Any modality."

From the analysis of the ten initial concepts, central themes such as figure/ground merging (fitting to shapes or movement bitmaps), auditory feedback, and particle movement have emerged. Then the brief has been constrained to include agents [11] or physical simulations (related to learning objectives of the curriculum). Again, interesting concepts related to augmented reality, games, education, and music and movement interfaces have emerged. The final projects will be demonstrated at the conference. Here we present the instructor's solution (see Fig. 1, left). It was conceived while preparing the briefs, and realized by in short time by combining two examples in Processing. First, the example code of frame differencing was modified to convert the detected movement to a mouse click at a single coordinate by center of mass extraction, and then applied to a heat map[3]. The coordinates and the movement intensity were then used to excite liquid sounds models in Sound Design Toolbox [7].

---

[3] "Heat Distribution" by Justin Dailey, licensed under Creative Commons Attribution-Share Alike 3.0 and GNU GPL license. Work:
`http://openprocessing.org/visuals/?visualID=46554`

4   Conclusions

In this paper, we have presented an approach for teaching and designing embodied interaction. We have combined the *mover perspective* and *felt experiences* of MMS [3] with advanced technologies (multi-agents, physical simulations) in a generative design session [1]. We have reported our activities and provided a simple example as a design outcome.

We expect this approach to provide a better foundation for our participants compared to the approaches that focus only on technologies. Subsequently, it would be interesting to compare the outcomes of different foundations, in terms of creativity.

References

1. Buxton, B.: Sketching user experience. Morgan Kaufmann, San Francisco (2007)
2. Klemmer, S., Verplank, B., Ju, W.: Teaching embodied interaction design practice. Presented at the DUX 2005: Proceedings of the 2005 Conference on Designing for User Experience, San Francisco, CA, USA, November 1 (2005)
3. Loke, L., Robertson, T.: Moving and making strange: An embodied approach to movement-based interaction design. ACM Transactions on Computer-Human Interaction (TOCHI) 20, 7–25 (2013)
4. Sundström, P., Taylor, A., Grufberg, K., Wirström, N., Belenguer, J.S., Lundén, M.: Inspirational bits: towards a shared understanding of the digital material. In: Proc. CHI Conference on Human Factors in Computing Systems (May 2011)
5. Hansen, L.A.: Making do and making new: Performative moves into interaction design. International Journal of Performance Arts & Digital Media 9, 135–151 (2013)
6. Levin, G.: Computer vision for artists and designers: pedagogic tools and techniques for novice programmers. AI and Society 20, 462–482 (2006)
7. Delle Monache, S., Polotti, P., Rocchesso, D.: A toolkit for explorations in sonic interaction design. In: Proc. Audio Mostly, Piteå, Sweden (September 2010)
8. Phillips-Silver, J., Trainor, L.J.: Hearing what the body feels: Auditory encoding of rhythmic movement. Cognition 105, 533–546 (2007)
9. Shiffman, D.: Learning Processing. Elsevier (2008)
10. Perevalov, D.: Mastering openFrameworks. Packt Pub., UK (2013)
11. Wooldridge, M.: An introduction to multiagent systems. John Wiley & Sons, Chichester (2009)
12. Brochard, R., Abecasis, D., Potter, D., Ragot, R., Drake, C.: The "Ticktock" of Our Internal Clock: Direct Brain Evidence of Subjective Accents in Isochronous Sequences. Psychological Science 14, 362–366 (2003)
13. Sikstrom, E., Nilsson, N.C., Nordahl, R., Serafin, S.: Preliminary Investigation of Self Reported Emotional Responses to Approaching And Receding Footstep Sounds in A Virtual Reality Context. Presented at the Audio for Games, London, UK (February 2013)
14. Farnell, A.: Designing Sound. MIT Press, Cambridge (2010)

Participant Observation and Experiences in the Design for Affectibility

Elaine C.S. Hayashi and M. Cecília C. Baranauskas

UNICAMP – Universidade Estadual de Campinas
Institute of Computing, Brazil

Abstract. This paper reports on our experience as Participant Observers in a Project introducing the XO laptop at an elementary school in Brazil. Working together with all members of the school community, we experienced their daily activities with and without technology. Our objective was to build a better understanding of the affective and emotional relationships developed among the community. Moreover, we wanted to understand how users made use and sense of technology. In this article we investigate the presence of affect in our study scenario using the method of Participant Observation. This study was one of the initial steps towards the design of an educational system to be used at elementary schools.

1   Introduction

Understanding final users of a given technology within their social and cultural context, has recognized importance in the process of designing such technology [3,6]. Besides the technical comprehension needed, designers need to understand other informal aspects of use. In order to consider requirements from levels that go beyond the technical one, it is important that social-cultural strategies are adopted. Such strategies should amplify the vision of the general context of the problem and of the stakeholders involved in the solution.

In order to construct this social-technical view of the school context and of the educational technologies, we have adopted, among others, Participant Observation (PO) [1] as research method. In this method, the researcher becomes part of a group and he observes behavior as it happens in the real daily settings – and not only the behavior that is described in formal documents. The researcher interacts with the members of the group as if s/he was one of them. At the same time that s/he is interacting with the group, the researcher also observes their actions. This allows him/her to construct a view from his/her perspective as the human being that belongs to that group, sharing ideas, sensations and mainly living and understanding the affective relationships.

Affect in the educational context has been studied since long. Piaget, for example, argues that for the intellectual development to take place it is necessary to consider also the affective issues and not only the cognitive ones [9, 15]. However, designers of systems for the support of learning usually converge their efforts only to the aspects that facilitate the development of cognition. The aspects that support or facilitate

C. Stephanidis (Ed.): HCII 2014 Posters, Part I, CCIS 434, pp. 36–41, 2014.

communication and expression of affect are frequently left aside. We argue that technology in education has the potential to benefit students' development to even higher levels if it considers the affective aspects of interaction, together with the didactic content and other requirements like usability and accessibility. One of the means to bring affect into the design process, especially in the earlier phases, is by adopting the PO as research method.

The work we present here is part of a research that investigates how affect (including emotions, feelings, opinions [12]) can be incorporated in the process of designing technology. We base our studies in the concept of Affectibility (related to the characteristics that help triggering affective responses during user's interaction [7]) to guide our system design, explicitly considering affect and the creation of affective responses. In this work we discuss the results of our experience as participant observer at a public elementary school in Brazil, in a context of introduction of the XO laptop. Our practices as observers had the main goal of understanding the diverse possibilities of manifestation of affect in the school practices, to inform a design process.

First we present, on Section 2, the school community and we describe our research plan. Then, on Section 3, we present the data collected during the PO of the students from the 2nd and 8th grades. In Section 4 we discuss the results and in Section 5 we conclude.

2   Participants, Material and Method

This research took place at an elementary school located at the city of Campinas in the state of São Paulo, Brazil. The school community is composed of around 530 people, including teachers, students, and other employees. Even though the school had a computer lab (with circa 15 desktop computers) and educational laptops (a little less than 500 XO laptops from OLCP), not all teachers were familiar with technology. While few students were not used to the computer mouse, most of them had basic computer skills and were familiar with communication technologies like smart phone.

We were present in most of the school activities and we were in touch with students and teachers from the 1st until the 9th grades. The deeper immersion occurred within two groups: the 2nd graders and their two general teachers; and the 8th graders and their science teacher. Due to absences, school transfers and/or dropouts the sizes of each group varied. It ranged between 25 to 30 students per group. 2nd graders ages varied from 8 to 10 years old and 8th graders, from 14 to 16 years old. We were part of their classes, as participant observers, helping teachers and students in their daily tasks, which included activities with and without technology.

Results from PO are usually saved as notes from the researcher [13]. Such notes include contents that go beyond the central point of the research. Our notes were transcribed, coded (i.e., keywords were attributed to blocks of texts) and categorized. Using specific software [2] we grouped codes and tested different associations. This process is commonly used in qualitative analysis, especially in social studies. From the categories generated from coding we were able to observe some recurring themes and important concepts. This process was the basis for the development of principles for the design that considers affective aspects of the interaction (more on this in [8]).

The concept of Validity, associated to quantitative analysis, has its equivalent in the qualitative analysis in the concept of Confiability [5,11]. Some techniques are suggested for the results of a qualitative research to present Confiability. These techniques are related to the constructs of Credibility, Reliability, Transferability, and Confirmability. According to the authors, Credibility (i.e., one can trust the results) can be obtained by a prolonged relationship with the observed community. Our participation at the school could be considered as of a 'prolonged relationship'. We had direct interaction with teachers, students and other employees for three times a week during two consecutive semesters - and with less frequency during two years at the beginning of the project. This should count for the Credibility of our work.

The technique recommended for Reliability (i.e. verify that the results or conclusions reflect the data) is the Internal Audit. In his technique, a different researcher observes the activities from distance (he does not participate directly). He also guides the process and reviews results and conclusions. The Transferability refers to the capacity to apply the conclusions or results in different situations. This is different from the concept of Generalization from quantitative approaches, which seeks to make sure that it is possible to generalize results that were obtained in small groups to the population as a whole. The idea behind Transferability is to encourage readers to articulate elements from one study to the elements from their own experience. For this to be possible, it is important that researchers provide a detailed description of their research context and participants. Finally, Confirmability (i.e., how well findings are supported by the data collected) can be obtained by Audit trails. This technique consists in the description of the research process so that other researchers are able to understand the path followed [5,11].

Our participation at the school started in 2009 and was followed by a certain distance by an experienced researcher, who guided the process and reviewed the data collected. This provides for the reliability of our work. Due to space restrictions, we were not able to inform here all the details needed for Transferability and Confirmability. Such information, however, are provided in separate publications: [4] and [8]. Table 1, however, already provides for Audit trail.

3   Results and Discussion

The manifestations of affect are inherent to human beings. It is present in all social interactions, being influenced and influencing the behaviors of each person and of the group. Filtering this information to direct to the development of digital artifacts can be a challenge. In the design of educational technology, we used PO method to collect data. The data was then coded and categorized. Table 1 shows results of this process.

Fondness, care, kindness, eagerness, fear and all other forms of manifestation of affect cannot be substituted by technology. What technology can do is to present itself in a way to awaken affective responses from users during their interaction with such technology, according to their contexts and needs. It can also allow or support the expression of affect - at least, it should not prevent its manifestation. How to design and develop systems in line with this mindset is a challenge for the designers of educational technology. The qualitative method of PO was of vital importance for us to better identify affect in daily interactions. The final objective is to include similar affective interactions in the design of a system.

Table 1. Examples of extracts from field notes and their coding

Extracts from field notes	Coding	Subcategory	Key Category
The unexpected arrival of different children in the classroom caused great commotion among the students.	Presence of strangers in the group.	Self x Group	Awareness of others
(…) she [a student] constantly looked around to see if other students were looking at what she was doing.	Need of acceptance/approval from peers	Self x Group	
Students from grade 9 demanded to be recognized as such. They valued being in the 9th grade and they were very proud of it.	Sense of belonging; Age as status	Pride as a social value	Social values
Their [group of girlfriends] place of chatting was the girls' restroom, since they could talk without the presence of the boys.	Sense of belonging; Privacy	Privacy as a social value	
A student drew hearts on the blackboard, expressing her affection to another person.	Expression of affect; drawing	Expression of affect	Communication/ expression and interpretation of affective states
The students welcomed the researcher with hugs, kisses and compliments on her look.	Expression of affect	Expression of affect	
The "S2" meant "heart", which in turn, meant "loves".	Expression of affect; Interpretation	Communication and interpretation of affect	
Students felt a positive sense of accomplishment when they were able to help their peers in the use of the laptop.	Collaboration among peers	Collaboration	Collaborative construction and participation of adults
Students were experiencing technical difficulties. Frustration and deception might had arisen if a researcher had not helped them.	Adult participation in learning process	Collaboration	
A text read by the teacher about a Chinese tale seemed more interesting and made students more curious when the researcher, who has oriental looking and roots, entered and joined the classroom.	Content in context; Meaning and understanding	Context	Context-rich environments
Two kids started to sing. Soon the entire group was singing, building an informal and fun atmosphere in the classroom.	Rhythm; mood contamination; music	Atmosphere/ environment	Media contamination
One girl started to cry when she saw her friend in a convulsion seizure. The class was calm until then, but then they all became nervous and out of control.	Mood contamination	Atmosphere/ environment	

Observing and participating together with users in their activities allowed us to see clearly the presence of affect in the interactions. By including such affective interactions in the system we expect to design systems that are more meaningful to the users. PO resulted in a vast material of field notes that highlight affect. The process of coding the notes and its categorization resulted in key categories (Table 1). The concepts from these key categories should now be translated into requirements or guidelines that should direct the design of a system that we will develop for use at the school. For example, we noted the importance of social values (e.g., pride, privacy) for users. Therefore, we shall consider what are valuable for those users when designing for them. 'Awareness of others' is another concept or key category that emerged from PO. When designing for these users we shall think about means of letting people know about other users' (presence, intentions, moods, emotions, etc.).

PO also provided us with insights about the importance of considering users affective response during the design process. How they felt during the PO activities, their opinions on their participation in system design activities (e.g., participatory practices) as well as their willingness or not in participating must be considered. It is important to mention that all students were aware of our purposes and their parents signed official permissions for their involvement. They all were aware of the fact that they could interrupt their participation whenever they felt like. The principal and pedagogue of the school, as well as a few parents, followed some of the activities and agreed with them.

Considering the affective responses of students in this process seems to have bestowed on students with confidence, pride and self respect. They seemed to have enjoyed being considered and cared for. The researcher's affective responses were present during the interactions within the school but they were left aside when taking notes and analyzing results. Having one researcher following the process from distance helped keeping the analysis within a certain degree of objectivity.

4   Conclusion

The understanding of the context of use and the affective interests of a community of users demand an approach that allows close and deep investigation of that community. In this challenge, we found in the qualitative research method of Participant Observation a strategy to interpret and understand, under the perspective of the community of users, the interactions that take place at the school. This paper described the process and results of the application of the PO within a public school in Brazil. Our objective was to propose new ways of treating design of educational technology, aiming at the explicit inclusion of affect in the design process.

As a contribution to the community of HCI, this paper pointed towards the importance of affect in the process of designing of technology. We presented examples of the use of PO in this context. PO helped us to gather information, unveiling elements that are particular to the culture of that specific community and untangling the real practical implications of the introduction of a new computational system into the organization of the community. The mapping of main concepts resulting from the coding of notes from PO would then serve as basis for us to define requirements for the design and development of educational application (i.e., design principles [8]).

Our challenge and goal was to think about technological solutions in a way that the affective responses from the stakeholders were a priority. This way of approaching design, working within the school community may represent an important differential, especially to the most excluded parcels of the population.

References

1. Atkinson, P., Hammersley, M.: Ethnography and participant observation. In: Handbook of qualitative research. Sage, Thousand Oaks (1994)
2. ATLAS/ti, http://www.atlasti.com (last accessed: October 2012)
3. Baranauskas, M.C.C.: Socially aware computing. In: ICECE 2009 VI International Conference on Engineering and Computer Education, pp. 1–5 (2009)
4. Baranauskas, M.C.C., Martins, M.C., Assis, R.: XO na escola: construção compartilhada de conhecimento - lições aprendidas (2012)
5. Denzin, N.K., Lincoln, Y.S.: Introduction: Entering the field of qualitative research. In: Handbook of Qualitative Research, pp. 1–18. Sage Publications, Thousand Oaks (1994)
6. Friedman, B.: Value-Sensitive Design. Interactions 3(6), 16–23 (1996)
7. Hayashi, E.C.S., Baranauskas, M.C.C.: The affectibility concept in systems for learning contexts. International Journal for e-Learning Security 1(1/2) (2011)
8. Hayashi, E.C.S., Baranauskas, M.C.C.: Design Principles for Affectibility. Technical Report IC-13-17 (2013)
9. La Taille, Y., de Oliveira, M.K., Dantas, H.: Piaget, Vygotsky, Wallon: teorias psico-genéticas em discussão. Summus editorial (1992)
10. Macaulay, C., Benyon, D., Crerar, A.: Ethnography, theory and systems design: from intuition to insight. Intern. Journal of Human-Computer Studies, 35–60 (2000)
11. Miles, M.B., Huberman, A.M.: Qualitative data analysis: A source book of new methods. Sage, Beverly Hills (1984)
12. Ortony, A., Norman, D.A., Revelle, W.: Effective functioning: A three level model of affect, motivation, cognition, and behavior. Who Needs Emotions, 173–202 (2005)
13. Smith, L.M.: An Evolving Logic of Participant Observation, Educational Ethnography, and Other Case. Review of Research in Education 6, 316–377 (1978)
14. Tedlock, B.: From Participant Observation to the Observation of Participation: The Emergence of Narrative Ethnography. Journal of Anthropological Research 47(1), 69–94 (1991)
15. Wadsworth, B.J.: Piaget's theory of cognitive and affective development: Foundations of constructivism. Longman Publishing (1996)

mGQM: Evaluation Metric
for Mobile and Human Interaction

Azham Hussain, Nor Laily Hashim, and Nazib Nordin

School of Computing, Universiti Utara Malaysia, 06010 UUM Sintok, Kedah, Malaysia
{azham.h,laily,Nazib}@uum.edu.my

Abstract. The constant developments in technology of mobile devices are rapidly increasing the demand for applications on these devices. In June 2013, there were 900,000 applications for iPhone available on the iTunes store to be downloaded, and the application store had over 50 billion downloads. Demand for Android phones is also increasing and exceeds analysts' expectations. As a result of the rapid evolution of mobile device development, a new challenge has emerged for application developers; how to improve the usability of mobile applications. This research examines usability issues of mobile devices, and proposes a metric based model which may be used to evaluate applications on mobile devices.

Keywords: ISO and usability, Mobile, Evaluation, Goal Question Metric.

1 Introduction

A number of evaluation methods and tools are readily available to examine software usability. However, usability measures that are specifically intended for mobile devices are very limited indeed. Limitations on current measures to evaluate mobile applications include 1) Their ability to generalize to other domains, 2) The focus on mobile devices instead of the applications and 3) They are not designed to measure applications that use the new features on mobile devices. In addition to limited usability measures, evaluation becomes more challenging due to the unique features of mobile devices such as limited bandwidth, unreliability of wireless networks, changing mobile context (e.g., location), small screen size, and limited memory. Hence, this study will propose a conceptual model called mGQM to evaluate mobile applications.

The objective of this study is to propose a usability metric that can be used to evaluate mobile applications. The proposed evaluation model is based on a goal-driven method for developing and maintaining a meaningful metrics program, Goal Question Metric (GQM). The proposed metric, mGQM (Mobile Goal Question Metric) consists of usability metrics to assess both quantitative and qualitative measures of mobile phone applications, which other models do not offer.

2 Evaluation of Mobile Applications

Evaluation has grown into a well-established research area. The first rule to evaluate the application system is ISO 9241 – 11 standards which, in fact, is today"s mainstream.

C. Stephanidis (Ed.): HCII 2014 Posters, Part I, CCIS 434, pp. 42–47, 2014.
© Springer International Publishing Switzerland 2014

For several years, these guidelines focus on the generic usability metric that has been countered by others who argue in favor of using the specific usability metric. The discussions of this difference between generic and specific have mostly been a matter of opinion, and it has not been prominent in literature on the comparison of usability metric, e.g. [1] and [2].

Evaluations based on user perception are accomplished by developing procedures for capturing the problem that users have while trying the software system. The results of user perception are based on the actual views of valid users on interface problems. However, user evaluation is expensive and time consuming. Expert-based evaluation is similar to design reviews of software projects and model-based evaluation is based on predictions of performance from the model. As expert-based and model-based evaluations are less expensive, thus many interface designs can be tested. Whether the evaluation is user-based, expert-based or model-based, there is no agreement yet in the community about which evaluation method is the most practical [3].

The evaluation on mobiles is slightly different from desktops due to the unique features of mobile phones such as limited bandwidth, small screen, changing mobile context (e.g., location) and limited memory. However, many studies which proposed methods and guidelines for evaluations on desktop applications may not be directly applicable to mobile applications [4] and [5]. Examples of studies on mobile evaluation include [6] and [7] which suggest design guidelines and evaluations of mobile applications, Jun & Tarasewich [8] which creates user interface guidelines for mobile devices, Jin & Ji [9] which provides usability evaluations on the physical user interface for mobile phones but not for applications

3 Methodology

In order to derive a usability metric using the GQM approach, a literature search and review are conducted to obtain usability characteristics, which become the goals of the initial model. The questions are subsequently developed to assess each goal and finally the metrics are derived by refining all the questions into metrics.

A set of usability metrics specifically for mobile phone applications is proposed, in which the metrics are divided into two; objective metrics and subjective metrics. In order to validate the metric and ensure that the model is effective and reliable, usability tests were conducted. The metric has been employed in usability tests to evaluate two different applications on two different mobile phones.

3.1 Systematic Literature Review

The three main steps in SLR are Planning the review, Conducting the Review and Reporting the review. The main focus in planning is to collect relevant information related to this study, i.e. usability evaluation of mobile application and usability issues. Five (5) topmost human computer interaction (HCI) journals and three (3) conference proceedings have been selected from 2007 ahead and this method of selection has a basis from Seffah [10]. After conducting the review, the only related papers were selected as shown in table 1 below:-

Table 1. Selected Papers

Journals/Conference	Year							Total
	2007	2008	2009	2010	2011	2012	2013	
IJHCI	1	-	1	-	2	2	1	7
Software Quality Journal	-	1	-	1	2	-	-	4
Journal for usability studies	-	-	2	-	2	3	1	8
IJCSE	-	-	-	2	2	2	1	7
IJMHCI	-	-	1	1	2	2	1	7
ICHFCS	1	-	1	2	1	1	-	6
ICHCIMDS	-	-	2	-	2	1	2	7
Hawaii ICSS	2	1	-	-	-	-	-	3
Total	4	2	7	6	13	11	6	49

Once completing the analysis of selected papers, 6 dimensions have been selected as follows; simplicity, accuracy, time taken, features, safety and attractiveness. These 6 dimensions will be the input to the next steps to derive the usability metrics.

3.2 Goal Question Metric

GQM has been selected to derive usability metric for mobile phone applications. The dimensions created in the SLR will initiate the method of generating questions and finally deriving metrics. We are unable to discuss step by steps to derive the metrics due to limited pages. 37 different metrics for evaluation of mobile phone applications were derived. 18 can be assessed objectively and 19 were subjective measures.

Table 2 shows the usability metrics derived from GQM approach and named as mGQM. All metric will be tested by implementing usability study as explain in the next section.

Table 2. The mGQM usability metrics

	Objective Measure	Subjective Measures
1	Time taken to key-in the data	Satisfaction with physical/virtual keypad
2	Number of errors while keying in the data	Satisfaction with output
3	Time taken to install	Satisfaction with the installation process
4	The number of interactions while installing the application	Satisfaction with screen size optimization
5	Time taken to learn	Satisfaction with help
	The number of mistakes while learning	Satisfaction with Contents
7	Number of errors	Enjoyment
8	Time taken to complete the task	Satisfaction with interface
9	Number of tasks successful in the first attempt	Safety while driving
10	Number of tasks successful in given time	Easy to find help

Table 2. (*Continued*)

11	Time taken to start the application	Stress
12	Time taken to respond	Satisfaction with signal indicator
13	Time taken to connect to the network	Satisfaction with virtual joystick
14	Number of times voice assistance provided in a task	Satisfaction while learning
15	Number of system resources displayed	Satisfaction with text
16	Number of requests to update the application	Satisfaction with system navigation
17	Percentage of battery used during installation	Satisfaction with touch screen
18	Percentage of battery used	Satisfaction with menu button
19		Satisfaction with voice assistance

3.3 Usability Study

Usability study is a common method to evaluate and identify problems of an application. Users usually use the application, then provide feedback by completing questionnaires or participate in interviews. For objective measure, data such as 'time taken' or 'error rate' can be collected by analyzing recorded video. Usability studies (also called usability tests) are usually conducted in a lab, but may be carried out in the field depending on the objectives of the study. The purpose of the usability test in this study is to verify mGQM by using the proposed metrics to test several applications on mobile devices. The tests comprised three stages; experiment, questionnaire and interview. The experiment was conducted to collect objective data and the questionnaire and interview provided subjective data. Application used in this study are Facebook and CoPilot while two mobile platforms are iOS on iPhone and Android on Samsung Phone.

4   Result

The result is presented based on three instruments taken in this study to ensure all usability metrics can be used to evaluate mobile application. Data collected during usability study are mixed and can be triangulated to support each others. To investigate the difference between applications on iPhone and android device, a t-test was conducted to compare two separate independent and identically distributed samples. All 18 metrics from mGQM model have been tested individually using the t-test. Subjective data were obtained from the amended QUIS questionnaire and the interview sessions.

The result from questionnaire present how user satisfies with application on mobile device based on metric provide by mGQM. Figure 2 below shows comparison between 2 applications on both phones. Some metrics are unable to measure for instance satisfaction on joystic (metric no 13) and safety while driving (metric no 9). Metric no 13 are unable to measure due to no joystic are needed for both applications. Metric no 9 are unable to measure on Facebook only. Overall result shows that participants were happy with application on iPhone compare to Android phone. However, the purpose of this study is not to compare the application on different devices, but to test the validity of the metrics.

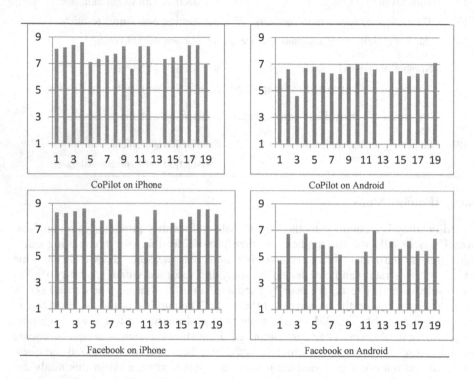

Fig. 1. Satisfaction on application based on questionnaire

Among the problem faced by participants during the test is the use of virtual keypad. Usability test on co-pilot application shows that the participants have to deal with difficulties to input data due to the tiny virtual keypad particularly on Android phone. Virtual keypad on iPhone is also small but some participants know how tilt to landscape view and the virtual keypad getting bigger. Only a few participants who are very familiar with Copilot took less time to key-in the address or save the address into a favorite address. Similar problem happens during a usability test on Facebook application. Only a few participants that familiar with iPhone know how to tilt the phone into landscape view making the virtual keypad look bigger. Participant six made many criticises about small virtual keypad and he also mentioned about his big fingers. However, the QWERTY keyboard layout for both phones helps participants to enter data more quickly. We also realized that the processor and the network connection are crucial to to users and it has influenced usability of mobile application.

5   Conclusion

The study presented in this paper has been concerned with usability metrics to evaluate applications on mobile devices. Evaluation of mobile applications is different from applications on immobile devices. The unique characteristics of mobile applications have become the main challenge in evaluation. The model presented in this paper contributes an option to the field of evaluation related to mobile devices.

Acknowledgements. This study, funded by Universiti Utara Malaysia under LEADS grant.

References

1. Bertoa, M.F., Troya, J., Vallecillo, A.: Measuring the usability of software components. Journal of Systems and Software 79(3), 427–439 (2006)
2. Ahmed, S., Mohammad, D., Rex, B.K., Harkirat, K.P.: Usability measurement and metrics: A consolidated model. Software Quality Control 14(2), 159–178 (2006)
3. Scholtz, J.: Usability Evaluation (2004), http://www.itl.nist.gov/iad/IADpapers/2004/Usability%20Evalution_rev1.pdf
4. Constantinos, K.C., Dan, K.: A research agenda for mobile usability. In: CHI 2007 Extended Abstracts on Human Factors in Computing Systems, pp. 2345–2350. ACM (2007)
5. Zhang, D., Adipat, B.: Challenges, Methodologies, and Issues in the Usability Testing of Mobile Applications. International Journal of Human-Computer Interaction 18(3), 293–308 (2005)
6. Marco, S., Carrico, L., Duarte, L., Tiago, R.: A framework for mobile evaluation. In: CHI 2008 Extended Abstracts on Human Factors in Computing Systems, pp. 2673–2678. ACM (2008)
7. Marco, S., Carrico, L.: Defining scenarios for mobile design and evaluation. In: CHI 2008 Extended Abstracts on Human Factors in Computing Systems, pp. 2847–2852. ACM (2008)
8. Jun, G., Tarasewich, P.: Guidelines for handheld mobile device interface design. In: Proceedings of DSI Annual Meeting, Northeastern University (2004)
9. Jin, B.S., Ji, Y.G.: Usability risk level evaluation for physical user interface of mobile phone. Computers in Industry 61(4), 350–363 (2010)
10. Ahmed, S., Mohammad, D., Rex, B.K., Harkirat, K.P.: Usability measurement and metrics: A consolidated model. Software Quality Control 14(2), 159–178 (2006)

Viewpoints to Introducing the Human-Centered Design (HCD) Process to the Development Process

A Survey of Japanese Companies

Toru Mizumoto[1], Atsuko Kuramochi[2], and Ryota Mori[3]

[1] Graduate School of Systems Engineering, Wakayama University, 930 Sakaedani,
Wakayama-shi, Wakayama, 640-8510, Japan
mizumoto.toru@sysmex.co.jp
[2] Design Center, SHARP Corporation, 22-22 Nagaike-Cho, Abeno-ku,
Osaka-shi, Osaka, 545-8522, Japan
kuramochi.atsuko@sharp.co.jp
[3] Department of Life Science, Nagano Prefectural College,
8-49-7 Miwa, Nagano-shi, Nagano, 380-8525, Japan
mori@nagano-kentan.ac.jp

Abstract. The objective of this research is to clarify the relationship between the practice of human-centered design (HCD) and the obstacles to applying this approach. Our study is based on research into several factors in the HCD process as applied to the development of hardware devices with embedded software, such as office equipment, home electronics, medical devices and information equipment. From the results of our investigation of 13 companies, we identified several obstacles to applying HCD methods to the development process. Also discussed are the nature of these obstacles, and methods to make better use of the HCD process to avoid such obstacles in future. Previous studies of the HCD process have presented new perspectives by performing various analyses of the benefits of using HCD methods. However, previous studies have not discussed proposals to avoid obstacles, or how to apply the HCD process to company workflows. Therefore, we collected 79 "good cases" and 53 "bad cases" through interviews and questionnaires. We then analyzed those cases, and summarized 4 viewpoints on introducing the HCD process to companies, and 12 approaches for solving these problems. Viewpoints: 1) Establish methods appropriate to each company. 2) Indicate the effects. 3) Share goals. 4) Participate in upstream processes.Approaches: 1) Use easy words. 2) Match HCD methods to the development process. 3) Create simple methods. 4) Compare with other companies. 5) Compare with in-house practices. 6) Share results with users. 7) Publish results as a reference. 8) Create industry standards. 9) Recognize a good point that already exists. 10) Share goals with the relevant departments. 11) Participate in requirement definition process. 12) Create valuable features through observation.

Keywords: human-centered design (HCD) process, survey, Japanese.

C. Stephanidis (Ed.): HCII 2014 Posters, Part I, CCIS 434, pp. 48–52, 2014.
© Springer International Publishing Switzerland 2014

1   Background

In order to survive, and to avoid price competition in commodity markets, companies should make an effort not only to improve the performance and functionality of their products, but also to improve the usability and the user experience. Japanese companies have begun the introduction of a Human-centred design (HCD) process to improve the usability and the user experience.

The HCD process was established as ISO13407 (Ergonomics - Human-centred design processes for interactive systems) [1] in 1999, after which Japanese companies began to use it. The HCD process is comprised of four key activities (Fig.1).

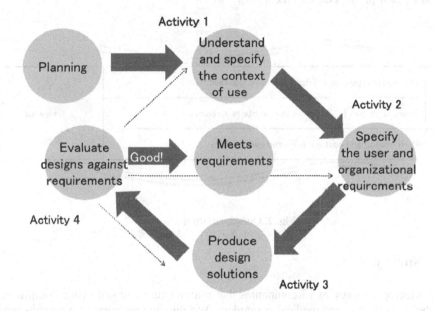

Fig. 1. Human-centered design (HCD) process

Knowing users well, understanding their problems and requirements, creating a prototype to solve these problems, and evaluating whether the prototype can really satisfy users: through these steps, companies can create products that result in high customer satisfaction.

ISO13407 was revised to ISO 9241-210:2010, "Ergonomics of human-system interaction – Part 210: Human-centred design for interactive systems" [2] in 2010. The most important point of this revision is that the "user experience" has been defined. It shows that thought has been shifting from providing convenience to users to bringing positive experiences to them.

2   Purpose

Previous studies of the HCD process have presented new perspectives by performing various analyses of the benefits of using HCD methods. However, these studies have not discussed proposals to avoid obstacles, or how to apply the HCD process to the development process. Also, the ISO only shows the process. It does not show a concrete implementation method. Accordingly, companies are using trial and error to increase the effectiveness of their HCD process.

Therefore, by carrying out interviews and questionnaires (Fig.2) about the situation of various companies, we could examine viewpoints for introducing the HCD method. We shared these viewpoints with companies who are struggling to introduce the HCD process to their product development flow.

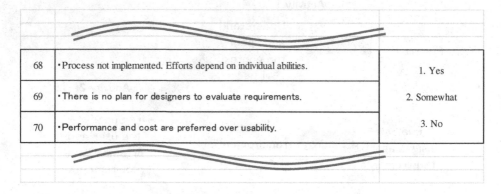

68	• Process not implemented. Efforts depend on individual abilities.	1. Yes
69	• There is no plan for designers to evaluate requirements.	2. Somewhat
70	• Performance and cost are preferred over usability.	3. No

Fig. 2. Questionnaire items

3   Survey

We conducted a survey of 13 companies that manufacture and sell office equipment, household appliances and medical equipment. We directed the survey to persons who have a high knowledge of the human-centered design within each company. We also carried out an interview survey to persons from 5 companies who responded to the survey with detailed comments. We investigated in detail the causes of problems revealed by the survey.   By analyzing the interviews, we were able to extract 53 failure cases and 79 success cases. Through the result of analyses using the KJ method for a total of 132 cases, we were able to extract 12 approaches to succeed in the introduction of HCD to Japanese companies.

4   Results

Approaches were extracted as follows.

Table 1. 12 approaches

Viewpoint 1:   Establish methods appropriate to each company
Approach 1: Use easy words   Using terms which are familiar to employees in their office will increase their understanding of the process.
Approach 2: Match HCD methods to the development process   Designers should be given processes that will reduce their tasks.
Approach 3: Create simple methods   Simple tools that provide effective methods for HCD should be prepared and implemented. These tools will provide designers with ease of use.
Viewpoint 2: Indicate the effects
Approach 4: Compare with other companies   The comparison should be shown as a comparative ranking of usability of products to evaluate the company's performance against others in the same field.
Approach 5: Compare with in-house practices   Products based on HCD and other products should be compared through an analysis of data.
Approach 6: Share results with users   Usability testing should be shown to users, especially in B-to-B consumer products.
Approach 7: Publish results as a reference   Procedures for HCD should be shown and taught to each section as in-house standards.
Viewpoint 3: Share goals
Approach 8: Create industry standards   Standardization within industry organizations should provide requirements for each section in a company's office.
Approach 9: Recognize good points that already exist   Effective design phase methods should be retained.
Approach 10: Share goals with relevant departments   Shared values should be discussed to strengthen links between sections.
Viewpoint 4: Participate in upstream processes
Approach 11: Participate in requirement definition process   Shared values should be discussed to strengthen links between sections.
Approach 12: Create valuable features through observation   A design idea based on observation should be adopted in the planning phase as a product feature.

5   Conclusion

The approaches that we have presented in this paper are very concrete. Our study serves as a window to understanding the process for introducing HCD. We believe these will help the introduction of the Human-centered Design process to Japanese companies.

References

1. ISO13407:1999, Human-centred design processes for interactive systems
2. ISO9241-210:2010, Ergonomics of human-system interaction – Part 210: Human-centred design for interactive systems

The Possibility of Human-Better Centered Design

Haiying Ni[1,2], Qi Luo[2], and Yan Chen[2]

[1] Center of Buddhist Studies, The University of Hong Kong*, Hong Kong
[2] Customer Research and User Experience Department,
Tencent Inc., Shenzhen, P.R. China
{amieeni,sybil,enya}@tencent.com

Abstract. The assumption of the "human" has not been agreed universally in Human-centered design. As the aim of design is to solve human's problem, the evaluation standard of a "good" design is ambiguous in this context. The marketing designs based on the usage of the weaknesses of human nature, which cause the impulse buying and the immersion of online games easier, made people depressed. The traditional "human" assumption is based on cognition and social requirements. The former should be respected but the latter need a reconsideration. Inspirations from Buddhism are proposed as a solution to the evaluation standard and the problem of "depression": the general "good" standard transcended culture and religions is happiness based on Dependent Arising, which means to be a "better" existence and realizing the responsibility of self, for both designers and users.

Keywords: Human-centered, human-better centered, Buddhism.

1 Introduction

1.1 The Problem of "Human-Centered" Design

With more than 20 years development, "Human-centered" design principles are well accepted, especially in the Internet application design on PC and Mobile Device. This principle is also expressed in product managers' handbook as "Don't make me think" or "Users are lazy, they are voting with ass".

The cognition psychology made a great help on the research of the limits of human's cognition, which could be called as a hardware of human. However, the social value, what kind of functions do users need, is not generally agreed. Based on survey, it seems that users always wants more than they really need. Some designers considered this character should be used as this will give a great chance to have large number of users. This ideology is very popular in Internet products, named as "insight the human nature".

This usage of the weaknesses of human nature, which cause the impulse buying and the immersion of online games easier, made people depressed. More and more users become unhappy and even lonelier after they "enjoy" a service or game "happily" online.

C. Stephanidis (Ed.): HCII 2014 Posters, Part I, CCIS 434, pp. 53–57, 2014.
© Springer International Publishing Switzerland 2014

1.2   Design Is Just a Tool in Neutrality?

Living on the greedy of new functions of users, designers working for international large companies do not want to take this responsibility: "I just design a game for their fun, what the users become after this game is none of my business."

Many online games made the most use of people's sense of "honor". Lots "losers" in the actual life refined their "self-esteem" in the game, then they became addict to it, which means they pay less attention and endeavor their real life.

Based on our research, the Social network do not decrease people's loneliness, and the online game, as the game player admit: "When I quit the game, back to the actual life, I feel vanity. I fear this sense of feeling. In order to avoid it, I return the game, without thinking those unhappy things."1

These "Fun" "Tool" give people space to kill time, avoid the real problems of life. Could this tool be innocent? Just as a money earning tool for designers and an unhappy feeling avoid tools for users?

2   The Inspiration from Buddhism

2.1   Dependent Arising

Dependent Arising is a root theory of early Buddhism, also the whole Buddhism. "Strictly speaking, 'dependent' means 'co-dependent' (dependence on many factors), and 'arising' means 'co-arising' (arising together with many other factors)."2

Big Data Analysis is a good example to explain this theory. In the past, when an online product manager would like to find a way to promote the user's vitality of his products, he would always design some questionnaires sending to some of their users (sampling). Meanwhile, the researcher, could be regarded as a condition, a factor, as he picked up some "factors" which might be not as that important as he thought in the reality. That's why a researcher's cognitive bias is easily to cause the results he needed. It's common and extension version is "we only collect the data we wanted". A practical example is the Customer Satisfactory Model. The answer to the general satisfactory question is always not match with the means of all the sub-factors, even after Structure Equation Modeling or Artificially weighted adjustment. The fundamental reasons for of this problem is that some factors of the satisfactory have not been put in on the data collection design stage.

In contrast, in the big data analysis context, researchers rely more on the natural user generating dates (such as the logs, duration of stay, feeds on the main page and com-ments in YouTube while watching etc.), and the whole one (all users data). This degrade the subjectivity of the researcher's past experience, and respect each factor equally, believe each factor could be a possible one depending which some special phenomenon arises, such as the dissatisfactory of customers. With the full natural data, data researchers have more chance to find valuable connections between factors and the arisings. These connections, do not become week or strong according to the researcher's expect. They follow their rules all along, while with the progress of data acquirement, researchers could aware the map clearer.

It reminds us the relationship between designers and users. The human-computer interaction is actually a time-lagged human-human interaction: the designers and users. And their attitudes and behaviors delivered by the products in the environments interacts, which will affect them consciously and unconsciously on the timeline.

2.2   General "Good" Standard

According to Dependent Arising, there is no distinction between your own good and the good of others in ethics. The moral order is universally applicable out of the reason that "Greed, hatred and delusion and their opposites are not confined to one geographical region, nor are they confine to one historical period."2 That's why "the Buddhist evaluation of what is morally good and what is morally bad is not relative in this sense that it does not change in relation to shifting social conventions, cultural norms, government-enforced laws, or political ideologies."3

In "Kalama Sutta: To the Kalamas", The Buddha tells the Kalamas that "when a person is overcome with hatred and delusion, he behaves in such a way that causes harm to himself as well as others. Then the Buddha tells Kalamas that when a person is free from greed, hatred and delusion, what he does is beneficial to himself as well as others."4

"There is no single effect from a single cause, there are always multiple causes and multiple effects."2"Buddhism recognizes that every intentional action bears its fruits, whether good or bad, wholesome or unwholesome and that there are causal relations between the very act and the consequences." 3"Therefore, the doer is entirely responsible for the consequences of his own actions no matter them are good or bad."3

In the "Sammaditthi Sutta: The Discourse on Right View"3, 5, a list of "unwholesome" specifies as:

- Onslaught and harm of living beings,
- Taking what is not given,
- Sensual misconduct
- Lying speech
- Back-biting speech
- Harsh speech
- Empty gossip
- Covetousness
- Ill-will
- Wrong view (particularly the view that one should not be held responsible for one's action, that actions matter)

All these above are easily enlarged online.

3   The Possibility of "Human-Better Centered" Design

3.1   The Responsibility of Designers

According to the definition of "the world" the Buddha gave, if a Designer do something evil, the first victim is himself : as he contaminate his own world firstly. If he consider others' good, he is learning de-egocentricity, although there is a long way to "Non-self", it is a valuable start.

In Mahayana Buddhism, practitioners learn how to extinguish "Greed, hatred and delusion" by helping others to release "Greed, hatred and delusion". In other words, a designer could start by an aim of extinguishing his own and others' unhappiness in a board view in time and space, although at the beginning, his works, the solution of some problems of the users, may be not complete the aim well. However, with the awareness of the standard of "good" and his own responsibility, he could make the works, actually the reflection of his mind, better and better.

3.2   The Responsibility of Users

When a product has been designed and sold out, the interaction of designers and users begin. What the designer consider mostly do not match with the users' situation. It just like apple are planted to eat and enjoy the shade of the tree, but some people chose to use the apple to hit others or use the tree to build their house.

Users also need to take responsibility of their life: A man's life online and offline is connected. Every person's life is just like a river, which means that the flow of one's world could not be completely separated between online life and offline life.

People may also hear some "terrible" things online, such as one person who is "good" in "actual/real" life, but acted as an erotomania nymphomania online. Or some game players are willing to spend thousands of dollars to by a virtual weapons in a particular game (WOW: World of Warcraft; DNF: Dungeon N' Fight, etc.) out of self-display. It seems that the online environment gives people an atmosphere to do something crazy. Without the "identity" in "actual/real" life, someone seemed experiencing a kind of "liberation".

As a matter of fact, the life online and offline combined one's whole life map. In actual life, because of the "identity", which are mostly could be recognized by "Name" "Appearance" "Sound" "Fingerprint" "Feeling" "Ideal" "Fame and social status", normal people have more consciousness of his own action. However, when online, these identity are obstacle, then someone need to condense his glory, by special deco-ration of his website or homepage of Facebook, while others feel it is so easy to do something which could not be allowed to do in his actual life out of law or his fearing of being blamed, such as browsing pornographic websites.

The awareness to face our life and control our desire, no matter when and where, is a requirement of real happiness in a board context. Leo Babauta uses Zen to treat his mind online and offline, it seems very useful and worth spreading6.

4   Conclusion

With the observation of this world's perceptions, Buddhism proposes the idea of "the ceasing of annoyance" for human. The purpose of Buddhist ethics is for the transformation of man's character to a higher level of perfection such an enlightened being. The Noble Eightfold Path is of threefold: (1) virtue or ethics, (2) concentration and (3) wisdom. Then ethics is an essential ingredient on the path to the final goal. One starts with morality and ends up with moral perfection.

This wisdom could be used in every business and professional, including design fields. By aware of the conditional identity as a designer or user, both personas could take their own responsibility for a better existence in the future.

References

1. Luo, C., Chen, S., et al.: Social Network Relationship in Mainland China. Internal Project Sources. The research was based on Tencent's great large number of users. As of (December 31, 2012), the active QQ users' accounts for QQ IM amounted to 798.2 million while its peak concurrent users reached 176.4 million. Tencent 2012, http://www.tencent.com/en-us/at/abouttencent.shtml
2. Karunadasa, Y.: Public lecture on The Relevance of Morality: How Buddhism Sees it (September 3, 2013)
3. Karunadasa, Y.: Early Buddhist Teaching: The Middle Position in Theory and Practice, Centre of Buddhist Studies, the University of Hong Kong (2013)
4. Kalama Sutta: To the Kalamas (AN 3.65), translated from the Pali by Bhikkhu, T. Access to Insight (Legacy Edition), http://www.accesstoinsight.org/tipitaka/an/an03/an03.065.than.html (November 30, 2013)
5. Sammaditthi Sutta: The Discourse on Right View (MN 9), translated from the Pali by Thera, N., Bodhi, B. Access to Insight (Legacy Edition) (November 30, 2013), http://www.accesstoinsight.org/tipitaka/mn/mn.009.ntbb.html
6. Babauta, L.: Zen Habits: http://zenhabits.net/

Flourishing Adaptive Systems (FAS)

Juan F. Suarez

Antioch University, USA
jsuarez1@antioch.edu

Abstract. Humans are not just complex adaptive systems; we are flourishing adaptive systems (FAS), because we have human aspirations and tend to flourish. Our wisdom system is multidimensional, and it develops over time. A flourishing adaptive system is guided by its wisdom system to achieve a higher purpose. It seems plausible to augment human practice by developing 8 particular dimensions of wisdom or "wisdom senses". Further exploration of these 8 wisdom senses could lead to designing "wise organizations", and even developing "synthetic flourishing adaptive systems", exploring the frontiers of "artificial wisdom".

Keywords: flourishing, adaptive, system, wisdom.

1 Introduction

The world is changing fast, and we live in turbulent times accelerated by the speed of technological change and massive amounts of information. It seems like society has decided to walk the Data-Information-Knowledge-Wisdom Hierarchy [1] in reverse mode, in search for answers in a sea of big data. Revolutions and recessions have caused some analysts and policymakers to believe we are facing what they call a big global reset, a new normal where many people suffer the consequences of increasingly more difficult conditions of living.

Bringing wisdom back to the center of our societal development could result in a better redefinition of our systems and structures of living. A wiser socio economic system, "by design" and not "by chance", may well benefit from a series of design principles drawn from the well of wisdom. Provided actors follow these "wise design" principles, one could assume that a wiser outcome might be achieved. Is there value in using principles inspired in the multi-dimensionality of wisdom to design "wise" innovations, including organizations themselves? Can we design organizations that are more adaptive and thrive in complex social ecosystems, aiming at individual and organizational flourishing?

2 Flourishing Adaptive Systems

My flourishing adaptive systems model stems from wisdom research by [11] and the work on flourishing by [16] and [17]. I posit that humans have a "wisdom system" whose mission/purpose is "flourishing of self and others." I concentrate on eight subsystems

C. Stephanidis (Ed.): HCII 2014 Posters, Part I, CCIS 434, pp. 58–63, 2014.

of the wisdom system (cognitive, intuitive, practical, humane/ethical, aesthetic, adaptive, balanced, and temporal perspective of past, present and future) and their sense and response (i.e., aesthetic sense and aesthetic response). I have chosen these eight because I could research them in the context of human organizations. My research explored this model with a panel of those "seen as wise" by stakeholders in a given social system to discuss these eight elements in the context of "flourishing of self and others," and how/if they have applied these dimensions in past successful change and innovation projects. I'm also exploring how/which ones they would apply in order to design future change (processes, products, organizations, or system change) that will potentially "flourish" in a complex environment. I call this "Wise by Design".

3   Research and Analysis of Findings

My study was based on two methods broadly used in futures research, forecasting and backcasting. The research took participants through an exploration of past, present, and future, aimed at better understanding if, how, and when they would invoke any of the eight dimensions under investigation in their construction of individual and shared perspectives of future organizations in their field of work.   There was no explicit mention of the eight dimensions until the end of the third step in a study designed in four steps. The panel recognized wisdom as a complex multidimensional concept that is context dependent [2], time-bound, related to values, knowledge, and experience below consciousness, and requires consistence and judgment to make informed decisions. Out of the more than 33 traits or characteristics that panelists found associated with wisdom, the following 10 where invoked more frequently in different forms during the course of this research: time sensitive, cognitive, higher purpose, ethical, experienced, adaptive, balanced, outcomes oriented, aesthetic, and intuitive. The eight principles under study were part of the ten wisdom senses more used.

Higher Purpose, Higher Outcomes. In a complex and uncertain world, wise leaders [20] prioritize common purpose before personal interests. The pursuit of virtuous outcomes [21] is seen as a sign of responsible leadership, a balancing act between the good, the true, and the beautiful. In this regard, I refer to "higher outcomes" as the result of pursuing a "higher purpose." Panelists also mentioned the concept of intentionally developing "wise processes" in the context of achieving "higher outcomes" and fulfilling the "higher purpose." There seems to be room for systematizing wisdom in practice, as a proactive reflective form of practice rather than just a sentimental reactive form of interpretation of current realities, starting with a clear articulation of a higher purpose and measurable higher outcomes.

ETHOS: Essential to Higher Outcomes Skills. Another important finding of this research is the need to develop intentional skills in order to achieve higher outcomes. Panelists pointed to traditions and rituals as important elements in the culture of institutions that could only be redesigned and aligned to higher outcomes with the presence of the necessary [13], management, and innovation skills. These three categories of distinct skills, leadership, management, and innovation and change, could be augmented by wisdom traits in what I call "Wisdom-Augmented Practices." This type of "augmentation" would require a systematic application of certain wisdom dimensions. This research found that certain leadership, management, and innovation and change skills could greatly benefit by a "wise" approach. I encourage the reader to think about it this way: If leadership leads organizations to achieve their outcomes, wisdom-augmented leadership is the type of "wise leadership" that leads organizations to obtain higher outcomes.

Wisdom Dimensions and Their Interplay. According to [19] wisdom integrates and balances several spheres of human functioning. This interplay of wisdom attributes was empirically tested in several studies. As authors [2] put it, the outcome is an orchestration of mind and virtue in a quest for excellence. The eight dimensions under study appeared several times during the course of this research, with clear overlaps across them. When a sense is not fully developed, experts tend to reach out to their trusted networks for advice.

Sense of Time. This was the most invoked dimension of all, even above knowledge and experience. The sensitivity toward the future was characterized by concepts of vision, longevity, long term-ness, sustainability, and planning. The present was characterized by the ability to stay tuned to internal and external variables and conditions, monitoring and scanning the environment to look for trends and signs that could help anticipate the future. The relevance of the past was mentioned several times. It is important not to forget history in order to understand the present and foresee the future. Being aware of organizational foundations, strengths, and weaknesses, and what has made the institution successful in the past.

Sense of Balance. There seemed to imply the need for a balanced approach between vision and action, being mindful that decisions need to be tested before implementation. This sense cuts across all others. Panelists were also confronted with reacting to dilemmas in their industry, and how they think the field will evolve in addressing those tensions. According to [8], wisdom develops in response to wrestling with important dilemmas in life, whether emotional, interpersonal, or existential. Using wisdom as a way to balance competing visions will be essential of complex social sectors.

Practical Sense. The intentional use of experience to avoid "pie in the sky" approaches was mentioned several times. "Learning what worked" for the organization, and seeking out "what works" in other places, being able to assess and evaluate progress versus outcomes, and always keeping the goal in mind, were suggestions on how to implement practical approaches. The study of "phronesis" as practical wisdom has dominated the discourse of organizational wisdom research and the professions. I posit that an intentional pursuit of a higher purpose and setting measurable higher outcomes creates a different dynamic, a dynamic of human flourishing, connecting more dimensions than practical, rational, and ethical in a balanced, forward-looking, beautiful, and adaptive enterprise beyond phronesis.

Ethical Sense. This constitutes the ability to articulate core values, live them, and reinforce them, remaining mindful of the higher purpose and doing what is right and fair. According to [10], being wiser will require more than technical rationality in organizations, but leaders will have to be capable to help others navigate through complex realities, identify the differences between fad and necessary change, and be consistent and prepared to interpret realities as humanely and sensibly as and when necessary. The panel also articulated the ethical dimension as "not being averse to difficult/uncomfortable conversations" and "always asking who benefits and how do they benefit." Part of the challenge of wisdom in practice is that some dimensions, like ethics, could be perceived as "falling outside" [11] the utilitarian values of organizations.

Intuitive Sense. Sometimes referred to as "unconventional wisdom" [11], the intuitive sense is probably the most difficult to explain, precisely because it is about acknowledging visceral and sensory dimensions of judgment, "seeing the unseen," following instincts. A way to develop this sense for panelists in this research was to have "good listening and observation" skills, and "being open to the unexpected and unknown." Some panelists mentioned creativity, while others pointed to monitoring the environment, as processes related to developing an intuitive sense. In the field of knowledge management, wisdom is commonly referred as "intuition based on experience" [18]. Intuition was also paired with forward looking skills and foresight, in association with time-sensitivity.

Aesthetic Sense. This research established a strong connection between "aesthetic" and "authenticity of discourse," as well as pursuing "beautiful outcomes." On the note of this, [10] made reference to the ability to "clearly articulate judgments in an aesthetically pleasing way" (p. 40).Other concepts associated with the aesthetic sense were "sustainability," "trust," "clarity," "simplicity," "long-term shared vision," and "engaging others. This dimension can easily be discussed from the negative side, addressing what "ugly outcomes" [4] would be. Interestingly, some of these comments referred back to the ethical dimension like "unfair" and "unequal." As [14] put it, aesthetics in relation to what he calls Social Practice Wisdom (SPW) is the ability to communicate ideas that are difficult to convey in an expressive, equanimous, pleasurable, and rewarding way.

Cognitive Sense. I captured mentions to rationality, knowledge, love of learning, use of data, effectiveness, and evidence-based decisions. This is the dimension that most often refers to measurement and facts. Another important reference was the ability to ask questions about progress, study itself, and systematically gathering data and analyzing it frequently. There were references to using "vision" as guidance, and "facts" as points of reference for course-correction. According to [3], "Knowledge is necessary but not sufficient for wisdom."

Adaptive Sense. This research showed this dimension related to the capacity of understanding the underlying principles, practices, and structures; also the ability to recognize differences in the beneficiaries of the work (students in this case); taking the ego of the decision making out of the equation in what has been called "ego-transcendence" [12] in developmental psychology; proactively scanning and seeking feedback from its environment, stakeholders, and someone's own gut (in a clear interplay with two other dimensions, time-sensitivity and intuition).

4 Conclusions

This research could lead to explore human wisdom as a multidimensional subsystem that can be nurtured and fed, and even accelerated if we embrace all the possibilities. Would we be opening the doors for a new generation of research in pursuit of artificial wisdom? Can humans and their creations be wiser by design?

Wisdom. Wisdom is both a journey and a destination with the "higher" purpose of human flourishing for self and others. For that journey, all humans have the capacity to develop their own Wisdom System (analogy: the "nervous system") with the 8 dimensions acting as "subsystems" or senses. Wisdom requires time and use. It's not about aging - it's about maximizing the exposure and use of all subsystems over time (aging in a cave doesn't maximize the exposure).

State of Flourishing. At any given time, all "subsystems" are fully operational and ready to engage in a "sense-and-respond" mode, generating outcomes seen as "wise" by others.

Trust. It is the connector between wisdom systems. When a wisdom system feels imbalanced - any of the 8 subsystems is not fully operational -, it reaches out via a "trust pipe" to other wisdom systems to fill the gap.

Flourishing Adaptive Systems. Human creations (products, organizations, systems) can achieve a State of Flourishing if a) the "creation" exhibits "wise markers" in its genetic code that could reveal it was created using "wise principles"; and, b) the "creation" is conceived in a way that has its own "wisdom system" to be able to sense-and-respond with the 8 subsystems.

References

1. Ackoff, R.L.: From data to wisdom. Journal of Applied Systems Analysis 15, 3–9 (1989)
2. Baltes, P.B., Staudinger, U.M.: Wisdom: A metaheuristic (pragmatic) to orchestrate mind and virtue toward excellence. American Psychologist 55, 122–136 (2000)
3. Bierly, P.E., Kessler, E.H., Christensen, E.W.: Organizational learning, knowledge and wisdom. Journal of Organizational Change Management 13, 595–618 (2000)
4. Burke, W.W.: Aesthetics and wisdom in the practice of Organization Development. In: Kessler, E.H., Bailey, J.R. (eds.) Handbook of Organizational and Managerial Wisdom, pp. 243–260. Sage, Thousand Oaks (2007)
5. Gilding, P.: The Great Disruption. In: Why the Climate Crisis Will Bring On the End of Shopping and the Birth of a New World. Bloomsbury Publishing, London (2011)
6. Iley, R.A., Lewis, M.K.: Has the global financial crisis produced a new world order? Accounting Forum 35(2), 90–103 (2011)

7. Kaletsky, A.: Capitalism 4.0: The Birth of a New Economy in the Aftermath of Crisis. Perseus/Public Affairs, New York (2011)
8. Kramer, D.A.: Wisdom as a classical source of human strength: Conceptualization and empirical inquiry. Journal of Social and Clinical Psychology 19(1), 83–101 (2000)
9. Lombardo, T.: The Psychology of the Future: Flourishing in the Flow of Evolution (2013), http://www.academia.edu/3509044/The_Psychology_of_the_Future_Flourishing_in_the_Flow_of_Evolution_-_Synopsis_of_Forthcoming_Book
10. McKenna, B.: Wisdom, Ethics and the Postmodern Organization. In: Rooney, D., Hearn, G., Ninan, A. (eds.) Handbook on the Knowledge Economy, pp. 37–53. Edward Elgar, Cheltenham (2005)
11. McKenna, B., Rooney, D.: Wisdom management: Tensions between theory and practice in practice. In: KMAP 2005 Knowledge Management in Asia Pacific Conference: Building a Knowledge Society. Victoria University, Wellington (2005)
12. Peck, R.: Psychological developments in the second half of life. In: Conference on Planning Research. American Psychological Association, Bethesda (1955, 1956)
13. Phillips, C., Hall, S.: Nurses and the wise organisation: techne and phronesis in Australian general practice. Nursing Inquiry 20(2), 121–132 (2013)
14. Rooney, D.: Empirical Wisdom Research: A Community Approach. Wise Management in Organisational Complexity 34 (2013)
15. Schultz, R.: Unconventional wisdom: Twelve remarkable innovators tell how intuition can revolutionize decision making. Harper Business, New York (1994)
16. Seligman, M.: Flourish. Simon & Schuster, New York (2011)
17. Sitrin, M.: Horizontalism and the Occupy Movements. Dissent 59(2), 74–75 (2012)
18. Smith, E.A.: The role of tacit and explicit knowledge in the workplace. Journal of Knowledge Management 5(4), 311–321 (2001)
19. Sternberg, R.J.: Wisdom: Its Nature, Origins, and Development. Cambridge University Press, Cambridge (1990)
20. Verhezen, P.: Managerial Wisdom in Corporate Governance: The (Ir) Relevance of Accountability and Responsibility at Corporate Boards. Wise Management in Organisational Complexity 198 (2013)
21. Waddock, S.: Wisdom and responsible leadership: Aesthetic sensibility, moral imagination, and systems thinking. In: Aesthetics and Business Ethics, pp. 129–147. Springer, Netherlands (2014)

Research on Design Approach
Based on Cultures Comparison

Tengku Idora Ilyanee[1] and Yamazaki Kazuhiko[2]

[1] Graduate School of Engineering, Chiba Institute of Technology, Japan
ilyanee@gmail.com
[2] Chiba Institute of Technology, Japan
designkaz@gmail.com

Abstract. This research aims to propose designs based on cultures comparison. Taking Malaysian and Japanese cultures as the target of this case study, their common and different points are studied before proposing a new design concept which will suit on both cultures. Using the new combination of design concepts, a prototype is built. For the first prototype, a rattan floor chair is designed. To verify the acceptance of the design on both of the cultures, design evaluation and user experience design evaluation is made.

1 Introduction

Differences in cultures usually resulted in the misunderstanding and get people separated in their own culture. In this research, Japanese and Malaysian are taken to be the sample of two different cultures. Japanese and Malaysian have their own culture which are unique and different from each other. Thus, designing based on comparison of cultures can create a new design and thus narrowing the gap of differences between cultures.

2 Research Objective

This research aims to find out the differences and common points between two different cultures which in this case, between Malaysian and Japanese cultures. By understanding the common and different points between Malaysian and Japanese cultures, the connection between their culture and their lifestyle can be found.

Another purpose of this research is to create a new design that suits both of the cultures. After understanding their lifestyles and cultures, a new design based on the new concepts derived from the first objective will be made.

3 Research Definition

In this research, the word "culture" is defined as the collective programming of the mind which distinguishes the members of one group or category of people from another based on the Cultures and Organizations : Software of the Mindbook written by Geert Hofstede.

C. Stephanidis (Ed.): HCII 2014 Posters, Part I, CCIS 434, pp. 64–69, 2014.

4   Research Approach

In order to perform this research, step by step approaches are to be taken accordingly to ensure the research originality. The research is started by doing observations to gain more information regarding the cultures.

The result of the observation is then analyzed to get a clearer image on the differences and common points between the cultures. Then only the concept visualization and prototyping will be done.

The concepts will be derived from the results of the observations. After the prototype is completed, an user evaluation test will be held to ensure the prototype fulfill the research objective.

Using the data and feedback collected from the evaluations, another prototype will be designed and evaluated. Based on both of the evaluations, the conclusion of this research will be done.

5   Research Observation Method

5.1   Fieldwork to the Respondent House/Room

Based on the ethnography method, a fieldwork to the respondent room is done to see how the respondents live their daily life. The influence of their culture in their lifestyle is also observed.

5.2   Interview the Respondents

An interview was held after the fieldwork to ask some question regarding what they think about their culture and lifestyle. The respondent are 2 Malaysian students and 2 Japanese students

6   Analyzing the Observation

In order to analyze the observation, four work models; Sequence Model, Physical Model, Artifacts Model and Cultural Model which are developed by Hugh Beyer and Karen Holtzblatt in Contextual Design book are used (Fig. 1).

These work models are used to observe how related some objects to one`s daily life. It is also used in order to understand the different aspects of the work that matter for design.

To make the common points and differences clearer, all the points taken from the observation are filled in a matrix sheet (Fig. 2). The first sheet is for the origin culture use which in this research is Malaysian.

It is filled in as the basic points that will be use as the base when comparing with the targeted culture which is Japanese culture. The second sheet is filled in based on the observations and interviews comparison with the targeted culture which is Japanese culture.

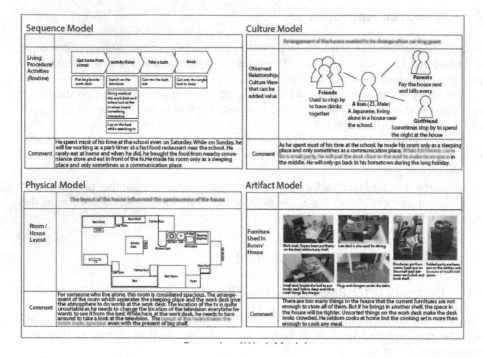

Fig. 1. Work models used to analyzed the observation

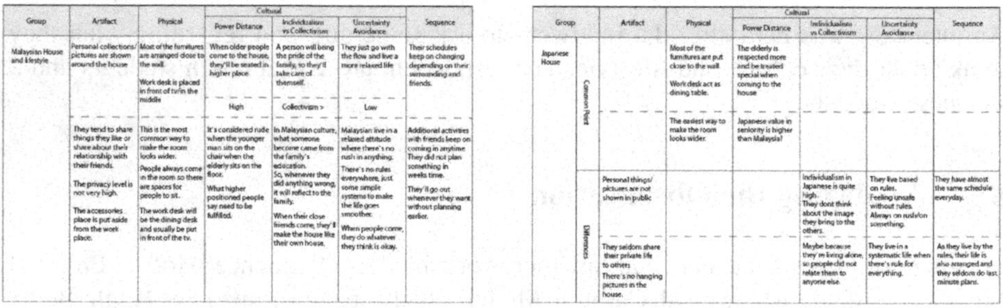

Fig. 2. Filled in matrix sheet

After analyzing the observation, it can be concluded that Japanese and Malaysian share some common points in the following matters :

  i. usually sit on the floor
  ii. furniture alignment in the house
  iii. prefer multifunctional furniture
  iv. prefer nature-based products
  v. traditional

Meanwhile, the differences between these two cultures are concluded as in Table 1 below.

Table 1. Differences between Malaysian and Japanese

Malaysian	Japanese
Heavy furniture	Light furniture
Low privacy level	High privacy level
House prepared for guest	House unprepared for guest
Mostly with religion	Mostly without religion
Usually having party at home	Usually having party outdoor
Spacious home	Cramped home

7   Concept Visualization

While considering those common and different points between Japanese and Malaysian, some important points from the observation are taken to be the concepts for the new design. For the first concept visualization, a new furniture is designed. The concepts for this furniture are as follow:

    i.   Practical
    ii.   Suit both country needs (sit on the floor)
   iii.   Combining Japan and Malaysia element
          (floor chair and rattan furniture)
   iv.   Using nature-based material

8   First Prototyping

For the first prototype, a rattan floor chair is designed (Fig. 3). It combines both of Japanese and Malaysia elements in the design. While taking the concept of Japanese floor chair, it uses the rattan material which is widely used in Malaysia. With the size of 600mmx800mmx600mm, it is more than comfortable for one to sit on it.

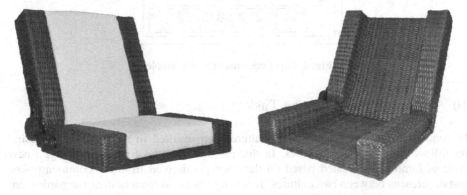

Fig. 3. First prototype; Rattan Floor Chair

Some other characteristics are as shown bellow:

    i.   Removable cushions
   ii.   Reclining function
  iii.   Washable cushions

9   User Evaluation

In order to evaluate the prototype, user evaluation   (Figure 4) was made on four users
which consist of two Malaysian students and two Japanese students.   This evaluation
objective is to find out on how far does the designed furniture suit both of the countries and how relevant the furniture is to their life. Based on the result, it can be concluded that the design of the furniture get a higher evaluation than the cultural aspect.
The lack of image of another country can be say as the cause of the result.

Another user evaluation on the experience map was also done to two of the users, a
Japanese and a Malaysian. The objective of this experience map evaluation is to find
out about what they are thinking and their opinions while experiencing using this
rattan floor chair. The result example of this test can be seen in Figure 3.

The conclusion that can be made from this experience map are as follows :

    i.   Users are satisfied with this chair
   ii.   The size of this chair is quite big and heavy
  iii.   The Japanese can accept the design even are not very
          familiar with rattan furniture
  iv.   It is not very suitable for a small room

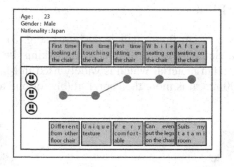

Fig. 4. Experience map result example

10   Summary and Future Task

In conclusion, comparison between cultures can resulted in a new style of design
regardless the gap of the cultures. In this research, for the first prototyping, a new
style of furniture is created based on the concepts derived from the common points
and differences between two cultures. It gets the approval from both of the parties that
the design suits with their cultures.

For the future task, another new design will be created using the same approach thus approving the way of designing new things based on cultures comparison.

References

1. Hofstede, G.: Cultures and Organizations: Software of the Mind
2. Holtzblatt, K.: Contextual Design

The Design of Everyday Things

Research on the Design of Cross-Age Interaction Toys

Chia-Ling Chang[1,*], Wang-Chin Tsai[2], and Chen-Chih Sun[1]

[1] Department of Creative Product Design and Management, Far East University
No.49, Zhonghua Rd., Xinshi Dist., Tainan City 74448, Taiwan (R.O.C.)
{idit007,jackxz8}@gmail.com
[2] Department of Product and Media Design, Fo Guang University
No.160, Linwei Rd., Jiaosi, Yilan County 26247, Taiwan (R.O.C.)
forwangwang@gmail.com

Abstract. In response to the aging society and change of family structure, intergenerational learning: getting help from the children, has become a new trend of elderly care. However, the elders and children differ a lot in body function, physical perception and mental cognition, and few studies take into account the physical and mental condition of both groups. Products designed for the elders and children to interact and play are even rarer. The study investigates the physical and mental capacity and prerequisite knowledge of the elders and children, analyze the overlapping characteristics of their physical and mental capacity, and provide cross-age body-mind interaction product design guidelines, including: (1)Reviving motor function, (2)Divergent creativity, (3)Intergenerational learning, and(4) Safety. With this product, both groups can strengthen their physical and mental capacity through the joyful game playing process, optimizing the development of synesthesia, and build friendship among them, as well as reducing the cost of social resources for long-term caring.

Keywords: Cross-Age, Elderly Toys, Interaction, Product Design.

1 Introduction

With the economy and society going through transformation and the trend of aging population, the family structure has changed rapidly. Besides, people nowadays are busy with their work and mostly form dual-earner families. The phenomenon of "grandparent family" is becoming increasingly common, and grandparents and grandchildren (elderly and children) are spending more and more time together, which makes it mostly the elderly and children keeping each other's company at home. In the leisure activities of the elderly in Taiwan, playing with their grandchildren accounts for 50% to 60% (Chen, 2001). Toys suitable for both the elderly and children become an important medium of physical and mental interaction between them, which can further serve as a platform for greater family intimacy, so cross-age toy design gradually shows its significance under the new social trend.

In general, "grandparents capable of child care" are aged 50-70, while the children cared for are about 3-12 years old, indicating that the average age gap between

---

* Corresponding author.

C. Stephanidis (Ed.): HCII 2014 Posters, Part I, CCIS 434, pp. 73–78, 2014.
© Springer International Publishing Switzerland 2014

grandparents and grandchildren are 40-60 years. The two groups differ a lot in physical and mental condition, as well as in their body function and respective need for mental cognitive development. As a result, this kind of toy design has to take into account both groups' physical and mental development in various stages, which needs more open thinking and room for discussion.

2   Literature Reviews

The WHO estimates that in 2050, the elderly aged over 60 will account for 22% of the world population. According to the Ministry of Education in Taiwan, the average age when Taiwanese nationals first become grandparents is 53, so if compared with Taiwanese people's average life expectancy of 79.15 years in 2010, the time of being a grandparent could be as long as 26 years. The get-along between the elderly and children has been an indispensible part of family relationship. When the grandparents and grandchildren spend time together and play games, the elderly often view the roles they play in a positive way (Lu & Chen, 2002). The grandparents place great importance on the interaction with their grandchildren, whereby they can get a sense of life continuity. Positive interaction can increase the intimacy between the grandparents and grandchildren, and on the other hand, the children can also learn life experience from their elders, which is the energy of "intergenerational learning" derived from good interaction between the elderly and children (Kazemek & Logas, 2000; Hannon, 2004).

2.1   Physical and Mental Functioning of the Elderly

Changes that come with aging are the degeneration of senses and slower movement (Wang,2009), among which the most obvious include: (1)Skeletal muscle: reduced bone density, (2)Muscular strength and muscular coordination (Kawakami, Inoue, and Kumashiro, 1999; Lin, 2008); (3)Action: change of reflex time and response speed; (3)acuity: lower visual and hearing acuity and hearing impairment; (4)Balance: one of the important indicators of the aging process, normally people aged over 60 would begin to show initial signs of impaired balance, especially the degeneration of bones, joints and muscular system would all affect gait biomechanics, lowering the stability of gait (Wu & Chan, 2009); (5)Body coordination: hand-brain and hand-leg coordination deteriorate. Therefore, the elderly doing activity should keep using their muscles and joints to prevent the loss of muscular strength and pliability, and they need a sense of safety when doing physical activity (Lu and Li, 2001). They can increase lower body muscle and strengthen muscular endurance by simply walking or knee bend. Besides, exercises can improve the balance of the elderly, especially those with instant vertical or horizontal movement can help with the sense of balance

Mentally, the elderly also go through some apparent changes with age, including poorer memory and judgment, and failure to achieve what they are originally familiar with (Hsieh, 2007). The mental characteristics of the elderly are as follows: (1) logic: logical reasoning is an important indicator of understanding cognitive development and intelligence (Bjorklund, 2000; Siegler, 1998); (2) memory: poorer memory, failure to achieve what they are originally familiar with; (3) creativity: when people get older, the ability to repress gets weaker, which unleashes their creativity and makes them stronger artistically.

2.2   Physical and Mental Condition of the Children

The study looks into the physical and mental condition of 3-12-year-old children raised by cross-generational parenting. This stage lays the foundation for children's growth physically, mentally or in character development. So if their physical and mental growth can be enhanced through the interactive toys for grandparents and grandchildren, it will be very beneficial to their future development (Marcus, Selby & Rossi, 1992). The movement skills developed by children aged 3-7 are basic locomotor and non-locomotor skills, such as running, sliding, bending, turning, hopping on one foot and hopping on both feet, jumping over, dodging, swaying, swinging, and stretching. When they turn 8-9 years old, they perform these fundamental skills more easily and efficiently, and start to develop complicated locomotor, non-locomotor, and manual skills. In the meantime, due to an increase in body strength during this period, accompanied by growth in perception and cognition, children are able to complete coordinated movement more quickly and accurately. 10- to 12-year-olds emphasize more special movement skills needed in competition, dancing or gymnastics (Lin, 2004).

In terms of psychological development theory, with regard to creativity: children aged over 3 years have endless inspiration, and 3- to 5-year-olds can find association between different concepts, expressing their imagination or ideas through analogy and comparison; 4- to 6-year-olds try to turn analogical concepts into actual concepts that apply to the outside world. In respect of spatial perception: 3- to 7-year-olds can use themselves as the center to feel the things in the surrounding, and gradually develop spatial concepts. A 3-year-old child can already distinguish the direction of up and down; a 4-year-old can distinguish front and back; a 5-year-old can start using himself/herself as the center to distinguish left and right; and a 6-year-old can correctly distinguish up and down, front and back. 6- to 12-year-olds have the abstract spatial and temporal concepts.

3   Product Design

Through references analysis, the study first proposes the design guidelines for toys targeted at grandparents and grandchildren, and then conducts product design accordingly. The guidelines are as follows:

3.1   Design Guidelines of Cross-Age Toy

1. Reviving motor function: the elderly are faced with the degeneration of senses, during which they gradually lose muscular strength, while the children are going through muscular and skeletal growth. Therefore, toys for grandparents and grandchildren should make both groups' bones and muscles feel refreshed in the game process, enhancing physiological movement functions such as hand-eye training, muscular strength, and body coordination.
2. Divergent creativity: In order to prevent the intellectual deterioration of the elderly and to train the children's creative thinking, toys for grandparents and grandchildren should have the quality of divergent creativity, enabling both groups to brainstorm and improvise to create toys that fit in their own scenarios.

3. Intergenerational learning: the elderly are experienced and skilled, while the children have good memory and flexibility, so the toys should use both groups' characteristics to help them complement each other, and increase the sense of participation, making the grandparents feel recognized in the game.
4. Safety: Since the target users are the elderly and children, the product should not have sharp corners, and should be made of soft material or have protection measures, in order to lower the risk of accident during the game.

3.2   Cross-Age Toy Design and Development

According to the above design guidelines and considering the revival of motor function and divergent creativity, the cross-age toy design in the study is set up as a large assembled toy for three reasons: (1) the process of assembly involves movement of the whole body; (2) the process of assembly can develop the users' creative thinking; (3) the scale of the game can be determined by the users' physical strength, which makes it suitable for both the elderly and children. The design of the cross-age toy components is shown below:

1. The unit pieces are hexagon-shaped like honeycomb cells for the maximum possibility of assembling.
2. There are three kinds of unit pieces with different-sized raised spots respectively, used to assemble a variety of obstacle courses.
3. The unit pieces are made of EVA soft material and the reverse is covered with slip-resistant material, which makes them quite safe and reduces injury from falls or bumps.
4. Each unit piece has hidden blocks at the edges, which can be taken out, turned 90 degrees and inserted back into the original groove, so they become curbs that prevent the ball from rolling out of range. The game can proceed without being interrupted and causing a waste of energy (Figure 2).

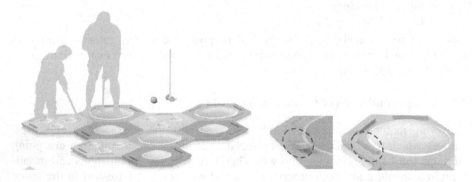

Fig. 1. The design of unit pieces   **Fig. 2.** The design of hidden blocks

Before the game, the grandparents and grandchildren can assemble three kinds of unit pieces together to form a variety of obstacle courses. The ways of assembly can be adjusted according to their creativity and surroundings, by means of which the elderly and children can develop creative thinking. During the game, both sides strike the ball with the mallet, making it move along the courses surrounded by raised spots, even choosing different colors to alter the difficulty level of the game, which leads the elderly and children to think and react. The game is simple but can be played in a variety of ways, making it quite flexible. For example: you can request the course of the ball to include the yellow area or exclude the yellow area (the latter is more difficult), and the person who reaches the goal is counted as successful.   The product features are as follows:

1. Developing motor function: the process of assembly can help the elderly and children develop motor function such as limb movement and improve concentration, increasing hand-eye coordination and balanced development of small muscles and extensor muscles.
2. Encouraging creative thinking: the number of unit pieces can increase freely, and there are a variety of ways to play the game. The product is expandable, and it can train the users' ability of spatial planning through the process of assembly, which is helpful to the grandparents and grandchildren's creative development.
3. Developing color vision: the product is colored in yellow, green and blue to help develop the elderly and children's ability of color discrimination, as well as left and right brain stimulation.
4. Building family ties: through playing the game together, the grandparents and grandchildren develop the relation of mutual support, which not only reduces the gap of physical functions, but also strengthens their interaction and care for each other, building family ties.
5. Suitable for grandparents and grandchildren to play together or on their own: considering that the grandparents do not always have time to play with their grandchildren, the product allows the grandparents or children to play individually, with the same effect of physical and mental development. The product's usage rate can also be increased.

4   Conclusion

From the preparation of physical and mental prerequisite knowledge of the elderly and children, the study finds the overlapping characteristics of their physical and mental capacity, and develops the interaction toy for both groups accordingly. Through working together in the game, the grandparents can train their physical and mental functions, reducing the speed of aging; for the children, they can develop physical strength and mental growth. Both groups can enhance their physical and mental capacity, optimizing the development of synesthesia and, most important of all, improving their interaction relationship to become closer to each other.

In terms of the production process, the product is made of EVA, which is bendable, non-toxic, low cost in material, easy to process, and recyclable, so the feasibility of production is very high.

In terms of commercial potential, products targeted at the elderly and children have a big market with a lot of consumers. The product spans the industries for the elderly and children, and covers the physical and mental development of both groups, making it possible for family members to play together, which leads to promising commercial potential.

Acknowledgements. This paper is partially sponsored by National Science Council, Taiwan (NSC 102-2221-E-431-004).

References

1. Chen, C.N.: Leisure Activities and Life Satisfaction Among Taiwanese Elderly. Journal of Population Studies 26, 96–136 (2001)
2. Lu, L., Chen, H.H.: An Exploratory Study on Role Adjustment and Intergenerational Relationships among the Elderly in the Changing Taiwan. Research in Applied Psychology 12, 221–249 (2002)
3. Kazemek, F., Logas, B.: Spiders, Kid Curlers, and White Shoes: Telling and Writing Stories across Generations. The Reading Teacher 53(6), 446–451 (2000)
4. Hannon, P.O.: An Investigation of the Impact of Short-Term Quality Intergenerational Contact on Children's Attitudes toward Older Adults. Unpublished doctoral dissertation. The university of Pennsylvania State (2004)
5. Wang, H.S.: Exercise and Physical Activity for Older Adults. American College of Sports Medicine MSSE 41(7), 1510–1530 (2009)
6. Kawakami, M., Inoue, F., Kumashiro, M.: Design of a Work System Considering the Needs of Aged Workers. Experimental Aging Research 25(4), 477–483 (1999)
7. Lin, G.U.: Aging effect on the elderly workers. Newsletters of Labor Safety and Health 91, 17 (2008)
8. Wu, M.T., Chan, Y.S.: The Effects of Aging and Exercise Intervention on Balance Control in the Elderly. Taiwanese Gerontological Forum 2, 1–12 (2009)
9. Lu, Y.J., Li, M.R.: Exploration of Socialization Development and Needs of Leisure Stage. National Taiwan University of Physical Education and Sport 8, 97–112 (2001)
10. Hsieh, K.J.: Feasible ways to slow communication fear of elderly learners. Quarterly Journal of Community Development 120, 283–295 (2007)
11. Bjorklund, D.F.: Children's Thinking: Developmental Function and Individual Difference, 3rd edn. Wadsworth/Thomson Learning, Belmont (2000)
12. Siegler, R.S.: Children's thinking. Prentice-Hall, Englewood Cliffs (1998)
13. Lin, F.G.: Physical and Mental Development of Children. Bimonthly Journal of School Sports 80, 18–24 (2004)

Using Smart Textiles in Customized Product Design Children's Drawings as Example

Aqua Chuan-Yu Chen

Department of Product Design, Ming Chuan University, Taiwan
aquachen@mail.mcu.edu.tw

Abstract. This is a project based analysis of interactive elements by using smart textiles as media. The effective design processes and methods of turning a concept into a real product in textiles industry are demonstrated. First children's' drawings were collected to analyzed the interaction performance expected on soft toys. Second, adapting suitable Smart Textile and the desirable electronic circuits which corresponding to the mode of the situational reaction as well as input and output context design. Finally, customized design process was established for the on-line smart textiles service.

Keywords: product design, work organization & agent modeling, e-fabric, customization.

1   Introduction

Characteristics of Smart Textiles are not only have the tactile of somatosensory, warm, soft, etc., but also provides the effects of light, temperature regulation, power storage, water, and other functions, and mean while preserving the fabric originally unique soft feature which can be braided, stitching, folding, extended class organic qualities, to replace chilled dangerous plastic products, more affinity exists in life. The research starts with children's drawings for soft toys. And base on the setting function of children's drawings to adapt customized modules and proper interactions modes that are suitable for Smart Textile corresponding to the situational reaction as well as input and output context design for the desirable electronic circuits. The establishment of an integrated modeling original design draft, electronic circuits, and smart textile design flow of customized products provide niche related industry to establish a smart fabric in the integrity of the program of customized products designed to integrate the use of technology model.

We also aimed at suggesting the systematized construction of the project management of Smart Textile applied in customized design process by practice cases to find how to improve the inconveniency that customers, material providers and designers confronted and help to integrate the electronic, information, fabric and consumer product.

The development of modes by smart textiles is according to the investigations of interaction concept from drawings, then design and develop the interaction IC boards. For the outlook we need to turn analog children's drawing into digital data by 2D computer drawing, 3D modeling, fabric material, making prototypes, and sewing.

C. Stephanidis (Ed.): HCII 2014 Posters, Part I, CCIS 434, pp. 79–84, 2014.

For the interaction, we need to decide the interactive scenarios corresponding to the behaviors, design electronic circuits and control program. Overall, a well-designed process integration management will be introduced. The use of digital printing and embroidery to accurately reproduce the original creative spirit. The establishment of this design research of customized textile goods providing benefit to establish a niche model in the relevant industry. Based on this, the purpose of the study is as follows:

(1) The establishment of the custom product design process of smart textile in order to understand their customers and designers coordination between each issues.

(2) Analysis of the interaction scenario from children's drawings to develop interaction modes of smart textiles.

(3) Apply textiles on soft toys developed from children's drawings, and dissemble performance of smart textiles.

2   Functional Application of Smart Textiles

2.1   Smart Textiles, E-Textiles

Multi-functional demands on textile fiber material instead of the end product, often reminiscent of smart textiles can be passed with light, sound, electricity, and other special functions with input and feedback fibers. Taiwan Textile Research Institute (hereinafter referred to as TTRI) is the legal entity belongs Ministry of Economic Affairs, has a strong R & D capabilities and resources, and is also a major source of functional fabrics scientific knowledge and education. The following table shows the smart textiles related nature and performance characteristics of their applications which Textile Research Institute published in 2011. (Table 1)

Table 1. Related Smart textiles technologies in TTRI (TTRI, 2011)

Energy	Sensor	Processing	Feedback
Development of Mobile Energy Textile Technology	Physiology Monitoring Textiles Development (health indicators: heart rate, respiratory rate and body temperature)	Application of Conductive Materials Processing Technology	Monitor(Mobile phone, Nursery Station)
		Development of Conductive Nano Silver Ink	LED Embedded and Photonic Textiles Technology
			Development of Electro-Thermal Textile

Smart fabrics with different definitions from functional fabrics generally defined as the detection of physiological signals or mood changes (Philips Design, SKIN probe project, 2006), and feedback information to enable the user to determine the response. Here are some examples of applications of smart textiles: "Bubelle Dress is composed of two layers. The inner layer features biometric sensors that analyze the wearer's emotions and show them in form of different colors projected onto the outer layer. The dress is the brainchild of researchers at Philips. It functions by analyzing physical alterations linked with different feelings. For example, stress, arousal, or fear are linked with body temperature and sweat that change the colors of the dress. Thus, when a person is stressed the color of the dress becomes green and when the wearer is calm the dress turns green."

We seek to conduct applied research from analyzing interaction results from children's drawing within the smart fabrics included items such as fabrics covering sensing and feedback technologies. Study will present the results from research and development of the textile. The preliminary plan were from the previous experiences of the smart textile as following:

Table 2. Artifacts empowered by Smart textiles technologies. (Source: research result of smart-textile Lab hosted by Aqua Chuan-Yu Chen in Ming Chuan University).

Static electricity,	Light transmission	Conductive	
Sensatex: smart shirt	LED Embedded Yarns	Electro-thermal isolation fiber	electro-thermal Fabric

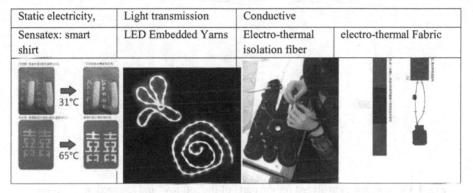

2.2 Customized On-line Service

Smart textiles' characteristics are different from ordinary fabric due to sensing and feedback function, but still with the softness and intimacy experience the plastic product can't achieve. Specific smart fabrics that can replace the hard circuit, plastic, or presented the light and temperature feedback.

Table 3. Related Smart textiles technologies in TTRI (TTRI, 2011)

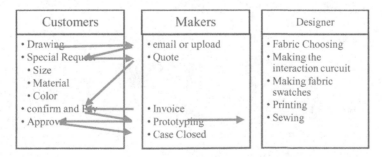

With appropriate design process management to complete design ideas which can communicated to idea provider, and get expected performance of user behavior are important topics of this study. According to the aforementioned study flowchart of table 2. The smart fabric design development process proposed in the preliminary design phase differences mode as Table 3 above.

3   The Design Process

3.1   Soft toys by E-textiles

The research started from questionnaires by asking children to draw their own soft toys and asking what are their expectations of these toys if they come alive. The expressions data were analyzed by four aspects: Physio, Socio, Psyco, and Ideo (Jordan, 2002). There are different forms in place for the different children's drawing. We found there are three types of interactions of intimacy: Touching, Hugging and Talking.

Fig. 1. Questionnaires analyzed for the parts of the soft toys and interaction scenarios

3.2   Development of Interaction Corresponding to the Scenario

With the interaction scenarios, three interactive scenarios corresponding to the behaviors are decided. 1) Touching and the soft toy will react by sound of heart beat and breathing frequency of lighting. 2) Hugging to activate the electro-thermo fiber to feel warm. 3) Talking to and the soft toys will reply back.

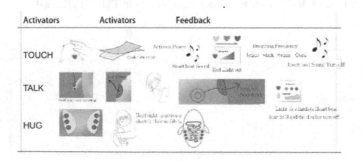

Fig. 2. Three patterns of intimacy

3.3   Applying Smart Textiles to Achieve the Interactions

We used conductive fabric with sensors, electro-thermo fiber, and LED Yarns to achieve the interaction modes. Two different electronic circuits and control program were made. The establishment of this design research of customized textile goods providing benefit to establish a niche model in the relevant industry.

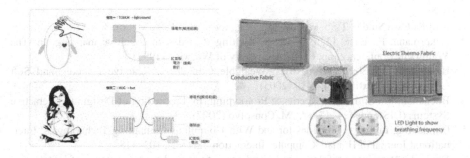

Fig. 3. Two modes of intimacy. The electronic circuits and the smart textiles used.

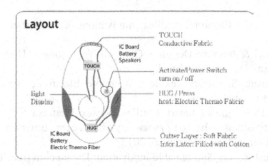

Fig. 4. The integration layout corresponding to the structure of soft toys from children's drawing

4   Summary and Discussion

From the child's drawing, we find the intimacy needs. And the application of smart textiles to presents the interactive results of children's expectation were studied. Currently we can show the interaction of temperature, heartbeat sound. For the next step, we will construct on-line site to collect more children's works and found innocent expectations that smart textiles could be used to develop intelligent interactive modules.

Acknowledgements. The researcher would like to thank National Science Council of Taiwan sponsored this research (NSC102-2221-E-130-023-) and Taiwan Textile Research Institute (TTRI) and Dr. Nian-Hao Wang and his team provided advanced functional textiles and the experts from TTRI to offer treasurable opinions and technical suggestions. I am grateful to the Prof. Wen-Chang Chen, Institute of Polymer Science and Engineering (IPSE) at the National Taiwan University (NTU) for providing invaluable support in making reliable working prototypes.

References

1. Child's Own Studio, Tsao, Wendy, http://www.childsown.com/
2. Ackermann, F., Eden, C., Cropper, S.: Getting started with cognitive mapping. In: The Young OR Conference, pp. 65–82. University of Warwick (1992)
3. Berzowska, J.: Electronic Textiles: Wearable Computers, Reactive Fashion, and Soft Computation. Textile 3(1), 2–19 (2005)
4. Buchenau, M., Suri, J.F.: Experience Prototyping. In: Proceeding of Designing Interactive Systems (DIS), pp. 424–433. ACM, Consolvo (2007)
5. Conducting In Situ Evaluations for and With Ubiquitous Computing Technologies. International Journal of Human–Computer Interaction 22(1&2), 103–118
6. Davis, F.: Perceived usefulness, perceived ease of use, and user acceptance of information technology. MIS Quarterly, Michigan (1989)
7. Dow, S.P., Glassco, A.: Paralled Prototyping Leads to Better Design Results, More Divergence, and Increased Self-Efficacy. ACM Transactions on Computer-Human Interaction 17(4) (2010)
8. Kholiya, R., Jahan, S.: Electronic textiles: Innovations & diversified. Colourage, 45–54 (December 2010)
9. Nielsen, J.: Parallel & Iterative Design + Competitive Testing = High Usability. (2011), http://www.useit.com (retrieved)
10. Park, S., Jayaraman, S.: Smart Textiles: Wearable Electronic Systems. MRS Bulletin 28(08), 585–591 (2003)
11. SYSTEX (n.d.). Definition of Smart Textiles, Systex_Platform for Smart Textiles and Wearable Microsystems, http://www.systex.org/content/definition-smart-textiles (retrieved March 16, 2013)
12. TTRI, 2011 Annual Report_Substainable innovation: Dream com true. Taiwan Textile Research Institute, Taipei (2011)
13. Visser, T., Vastenburg, M.H., Keyson, D.V.: Designing to support Social Connectedness: The Case of SnowGlobe. International Journal of Design 5(3), 129–142 (2011)

A Proposal for User's Intervention
in Interactive Evolutionary Computation
for Optimizing Fragrance Composition

Makoto Fukumoto and Shimpei Koga

Fukuoka Institute of Technology
fukumoto@fit.ac.jp

Abstract. Fragrance is one of important media types that effect on our psycho-physiological states. However, adjustment of fragrance composition is difficult for most of users. Interactive Evolutionary Computation (IEC) is known as an efficient method to optimize media contents, and we have already proposed IECs for optimizing fragrance composition. To enhance the optimization ability of IEC, some previous studies proposed that IEC accepts user's active intervention as operations on solution candidate. Referring to these previous studies, this study proposes a new IEC for optimizing fragrance composition with user's intervention. While the user just evaluates the presented fragrance with scoring or comparison in the conventional IECs, the user not only evaluates the fragrance but also operates the composition in the proposed IEC. The user's intervention is performed on solution candidate directly. In construction of the system, Aromageur, which blends six aroma sources, is used to create the fragrance based on the composition.

Keywords: Interactive Evolutionary Computation, Fragrance, Optimization, Intervention.

1   Introduction

Recently, we use various types of media contents in various situations. We enjoy these media contents, furthermore, some of them are effective to change mood. In the use of the media contents, it is ideal that each of the users use the media contents suited to each user's preference. However, it is still difficult to obtain the media contents, because preference of the users is very different and complex.

Interactive Evolutionary Computation (IEC) is known as an effective method to create contents suited to each user, and IEC was applied for creating various media contents [1]. Most of IEC applications were related to sense of sight such as image, movie, and graphics [1, 2]. Music and sound were next candidates of IEC applications. In recent years, with helps of development of information technology, the area of IEC applications were spread to various fields related to other human senses such as taste [3], touch [4], smell [5-8].

The present study focuses on IEC for optimizing fragrance composition. Fragrance is important for us. Some persons wear fragrance every day, and the fragrance is used

C. Stephanidis (Ed.): HCII 2014 Posters, Part I, CCIS 434, pp. 85–89, 2014.
© Springer International Publishing Switzerland 2014

for therapeutic purposes. However, these fragrances are ready-made: Most of the users do NOT use fragrance suited to each user's preference and objectives to use. Fragrance is composed of various source materials. If we could obtain the fragrance suited to each of us, the effect of the fragrance must be stronger than ever.

Objective this study is to propose a new IEC optimizing fragrance composition with user's intervention. We have already proposed IEC methods for optimizing the fragrance composition [5-8]. However, there have not been proposed any IEC optimizing fragrance pattern with the user's intervention, which is direct operation by the user on solution candidate in IEC.

2 Related Works of Optimization of Fragrance with IEC and Intervention in IEC

Evolutionary Computation (EC) is used for optimizing several variables suited to certain problem. In other words, EC searches best combination of several variables for solving the problem. IEC is an interactive type of EC by using human as a function of problem (Fig. 1). Therefore, IEC searches best combination of several variables suited to each user's subjective evaluation.

Before we describe the proposed IEC, this chapter shows previous related works of IECs optimizing fragrance composition. Most of them were works of us. Furthermore, the section 2.2 explains what IECs with user's intervention by introducing previous related studies.

2.1 IEC Optimizing Fragrance Composition

Obtaining fragrance suited to each user is difficult because preference of each user is very different and fragrance composition is complex. Optimizing fragrance composition is also difficult task, however, there is a possibility of the optimization by using information technology related to fragrance. A previous study has proposed a method to obtain fragrances by manually adjusting the fragrance composition. Zhang et al. have tried to obtain the fragrance suited to image of a university by manually adjusting the fragrance composition [9]. In the previous study, Aromajeur, blending six aroma sources was used. Although the user's task was adjusting just six variables related to each aroma's intensity, it seems difficult to obtain the fragrance composition suited to image. Furthermore, if the user was satisfied with the obtained fragrance, it must not be the best composition.

IEC is effective method to obtain good combination of variables related to media contents. In IEC, the user sees or smells presented media contents and evaluate them subjectively by scoring or selecting. The authors have proposed IEC method searching the fragrance composition suited to each user [5-8]. First try [5] of the IEC used Genetic Algorithm [10,11] as Evolutionary Algorithm (EA). In next study [6], we have adopted Differential Evolution [12] as EA. In recent approach [7, 8], Tabu Search (TS) [13] was employed.

2.2 IEC with User's Intervention

As described in Introduction, IEC is effective method to search media contents suited to each user. However, less number of evaluation times with small population size and short generations remains as problem in IEC [1]. The problem is come from fatigue of human users. Therefore, effective search method is demanded.

Some previous IEC studies have proposed IEC method with user's intervention. The user's interventions are done by several ways. Bleeding enables the user to select parent individual [14]. HIEC permits the user to select the parent and operations (crossover and mutation) [15]. Ono et al. enables the user to operate directly individuals. These previous studies with the intervention are applied for only problem related to computer graphics [16].

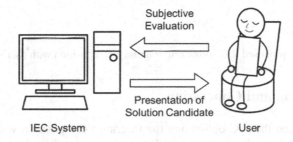

Fig. 1. A fundamental relationship between IEC system and a user

Table 1. Example of Setting Intensities of Fragrande Composition

	Aroma Source 1	Aroma Source 2	...	Aroma Source N
Intensity of Aroma Source	10	92		53

3   Proposed Method: IEC for Optimizing Fragrance with User's Intervention

By combining the IEC optimizing fragrance composition and intervention technique in IEC, this study proposes an IEC optimizing the fragrance composition with user's intervention. Fig. 2 shows outline of the proposed IEC. The user evaluates the presented fragrance by scoring and selecting, and the IEC system progress search of the fragrance composition. As the intervention, the user can manually adjust the intensity of each aroma in the composition of the presented fragrance when user wanted to. After the intervention, the user smells the fragrance and evaluates it.

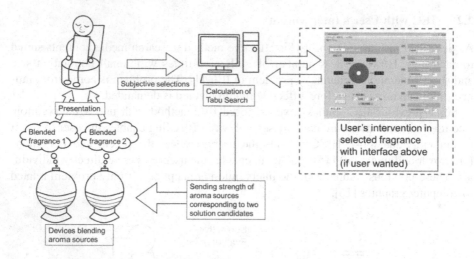

Fig. 2. Outline of proposed IEC optimizing fragrance composition with user's intervention

4   Discussion and Conclusion

This study proposed the IEC optimizing the fragrance composition with user's intervention. Different from the conventional IECs, the proposed method searches better fragrance composition with user's manipulation. A concrete system was constructed based on ITS.

As next step, we will investigate efficacies of the proposed IEC method through smelling experiment as same as the previous IEC studies: efficacy of EA for searching better and best solutions is guaranteed, however, the efficacy of IEC is not because human feelings are unstable.

Acknowledgements. This work was supported in part by Ministry of Education, Culture, Sports, Science and Technology, Grant-in-Aid for Young Scientists (B) and Grant from Computer Science Laboratory, Fukuoka Institute of Technology.

References

1. Takagi, H.: Interactive Evolutionary Computation: Fusion of the Capabilities of EC Optimization and Human Evaluation. Proc. the IEEE 89(9), 1275–1296 (2001)
2. Dawkins, R.: The Blind Watchmaker. Penguin Books (1986)
3. Herdy, M.: Evolutionary optimization based on subjective selection – evolving blends of coffee. In: Proc. 5th European Congress on Intelligent Techniques and Soft Computing, Aachen, pp. 640–644 (1997)
4. Nishino, H., Takekata, K., Sakamoto, M., Salzman, B.A., Kagawa, T., Utsumiya, K.: An IEC-Based Haptic Rendering Optimizer. In: Proc. the IEEE WSTST 2005, pp. 653–662. Springer (2005)

5. Fukumoto, M., Imai, J.: Design of Scents Suited with User's Kansei using Interactive Evolutionary Computation. In: Proc. KEER 2010, Paris, pp. 1016–1022 (2010)
6. Fukumoto, M., Inoue, M., Imai, J.: User's Favorite Scent Design Using Paired Comparison-based Interactive Differential Evolution. In: Proc. 2010 IEEE Congress on Evolutionary Computation, pp. 4519–4524 (2010)
7. Fukumoto, M., Kawai, K., Inoue, M., Imai, J.: Interactive Tabu Search for Creating Fragrance Suited to User's Preference. In: Proc. ISAE 2013, Kitakyusyu, pp. 237–240 (2013)
8. Fukumoto, M., Inoue, M., Kawai, K., Imai, J.-I.: Interactive Tabu Search with Paired Comparison for Optimizing Fragrance. In: IEEE SMC 2013, pp. 1690–1695 (2013)
9. Zhang, P., Mitani, A., Miyazaki, M.: Development of Control System for Blending and Generating of Scent. In: Proc. KEER 2007, Sapporo, L-18 (2007)
10. Holland, J.H.: Adaptation in Natural and Artificial Systems: An Introductory Analysis with Applications to Biology, Control and Artificial Intelligence, The University of Michigan Press, Ann Arbor. (1975)
11. Goldberg, D.: Genetic Algorithms in Search, Optimization and Machine Learning. Addison-Wesley Professional, Reading (1989)
12. Storn, R., Price, K.V.: Differential evolution–A simple and efficient adaptive scheme for global optimization over continuous spaces. Institute of Company Secretaries of India, Chennai, Tamil Nadu. Tech. Report TR-95-012 (1995)
13. Glover, F., McMillan, C.: The general employee scheduling problem: an integration of MS and AI. Computers & Operations Research 13(5), 563–573 (1986)
14. Unemi, T.: A Design of Multi-Field User Interface for Simulated Breeding. In: Proceedings of the Third Asian Fussy and Intelligent System Symposium, pp. 489–494 (1998)
15. Bush, B.J., Sayama, H.: Hyperinteractive Evolutionary Computation. IEEE Transactions on Evolutionary Computation 15(3) (June 2011)
16. Ono, S., Maeda, H., Sakimoto, K., Nakayama, S.: User-system cooperative evolutionary computation for both quantitative and qualitative objective optimization in image processing filter design. Applied Soft Computing 15, 203–218 (2014)

Development of the Estimate of Computer Assistance Program for Checkmark Position by Different Bend Radius of Curvature of Different Lanes in 4x100m Relay

Tai-Yen Hsu

Department of Physical Education, National Taichung University of Education,
Taichung City, Taiwan
hsu@mail.ntcu.edu.tw

Abstract. This study aims to discuss the effect of radius of curvature on the checkmark in different lanes of 4×100m relay and offer appropriate suggestion of checkmark according to the speed of different runners. The objects of research were sixteen outstanding players of senior high school and college who had accepted the long-term training in 4×100m relay. The research obtained the interval time of checkmark calculation of each runner in 130m to calculate the interval speed by SPM100. This study found that the forecast formula of bend speed developed by Greene in 1985 could be used in present PU track, thus we applied it to substitute the actual measurement. Experimental checkmark was calculated from the interval speed of incoming runner in last 30m and the starting speed of outgoing runner in 30m. Traditional checkmark was the original used distance. Both of them had the obvious differences ($P< .05$). Hence, the two checkmarks had different results. Comparing the individual grade, the grades of experimental checkmark were better than the grades of traditional checkmark. Therefore, the estimate of computer assistance program for checkmark position by the different bend radius of curvature of different lanes in 4×100 m relay could be applied to the real competitions which can provide the runners and coaches as prompt references, which expect to reduce the possibility of mistakes of baton exchange and let relay process more easily completed.

Keywords: checkmark, takeover zone, 4×100m relay, bend, computer assistance program.

1 Introduction

1.1 Research Background

The set of the checkmark position is affected by the speeds of the incoming and outgoing runners. The speed is divided into two parts, namely the linear speed and the bend speed. According to the scientific theory, the bend speed is affected by the bend radius of curvature and the linear speed, but all three takeover zones cover the bend part, and the different lane has the different bend radius of curvature(please refer to Fig. 1). Therefore, the bend radius of curvature is recognized as an important factor

C. Stephanidis (Ed.): HCII 2014 Posters, Part I, CCIS 434, pp. 90–94, 2014.
© Springer International Publishing Switzerland 2014

that may affect the set of the checkmark position, and will be also an important un-controllable condition that will affect the baton exchange.

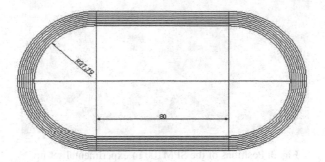

Fig. 1. Typical track and field stadium of double semicircle

1.2   Research Objectives and Problems

This study aims to discuss the effect of radius of curvature on the checkmark in different lanes of 4×100m relay and offer appropriate suggestion of checkmark according to the speed of different runners.

2   Research Methods

2.1   Test Subjects

The subjects of research were sixteen outstanding players of senior high school and college who had accepted the long-term training in 4×100m relay. Their age, height, mass were 19 ± 2.9yr, 170.6±6.9cm, 59.6 ± 8.8 kg, separately.

2.2   Research Process

• Measurement of the Interval Speed

The research obtained the interval time of checkmark calculation of each runner in 130m to calculate the interval speed including the first 30m and the last 30m linear speed and bend speed by SPM100(please refer to Fig.2 & Fig.3).

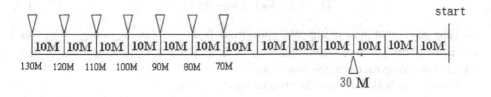

Fig. 2. Positions of the interval time of checkmark in experimental set-up

Fig. 3. Positions of the SPM100 in experimental set-up

- Estimate of Bend Speed

According to the results of Greene in 1985 :

$$\omega=\left[\frac{r^2}{2}+\sqrt{\frac{r^4}{4}+\frac{r^6}{27}}\right]^{\frac{1}{3}}+\left[\frac{r^2}{2}-\sqrt{\frac{r^4}{4}+\frac{r^6}{27}}\right]^{\frac{1}{3}} \tag{1}$$

$$r = Rg/V_0^2 \tag{2}$$

$$V = V_0\sqrt{\omega} \tag{3}$$

(g : 9.8m/s^2 ; R : bend radius of curvature ; V_0 : linear speed ; V : bend speed)

So, we could get the estimate of bend speed for the specific lane.

- Calculation of The Experimental Checkmark

In this experiment, the position of the baton exchange was set at 3m from the end of the takeover zone, and in this moment, the free space between outgoing and incoming runners was 1.5m. Experimental checkmark was calculated from the interval speed of incoming runner in the last 30m and the starting speed of outgoing runner in the first 30m. So, we get the formula for checkmark position:

$$D = (27/V_2) * V_1 - 25.5 \tag{4}$$

(D : the position of the experimental checkmark from the outgoing runner ; V_1 : the estimate of bend speed of incoming runner in the last 30m ; V_2 : the estimate of bend speed of outgoing runner in the first 30m)

Traditional checkmark was the original used distance.

2.3   Data Processing

The Relay team randomly selected two different lanes, and performed two 4X100 m relay using experimental Checkmark and traditional checkmark, respectively. The grades were analyzed and tested for significance via paired-sample t-test ($\alpha = .05$).

3   Results and Discussion

3.1   Comparison between Estimate and Actual Measurement of Bend Speed

In this study, we measured the linear speed and the bend speed in the 30m actually. We found bend radius of curvature are still major factors influencing the bend speed just like mentioned by Chang, Campbell, and Kram [1] [2]. Research results show that there were no significant differences between estimate and actual measurement of bend speed (p> .05). It meant that the forecast formula of bend speed developed by Greene in 1985 could be used in present PU track [3] (please refer to Fig. 4), thus we can apply it to substitute the actual measurement.

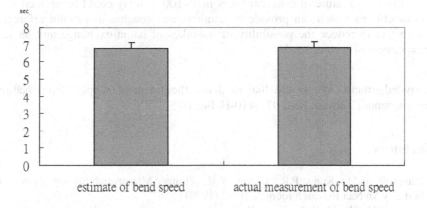

Fig. 4. Comparison between estimate and actual measurement of bend speed

3.2   Comparison between the Grades of Experimental Checkmark and Traditional Checkmark

The grades of experimental checkmark were better than the grades of traditional checkmark (p < .05) (please refer to Fig. 5). Therefore, the estimate of computer assistance program for checkmark position by the different bend radius of curvature of different lanes in 4×100 m relay could be applied to the real competitions which can provide the runners and coaches as prompt references, which expect to reduce the possibility of mistakes of baton exchange and let relay process more easily completed.

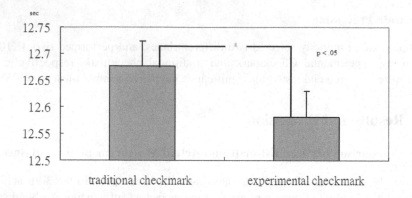

Fig. 5. Comparison between grades of traditional and experimental checkmark

4   Conclusion

The estimate of computer assistance program for checkmark position by the different bend radius of curvature of different lanes in 4×100 m relay could be applied to the real competitions which can provide the runners and coaches as prompt references, which expect to reduce the possibility of mistakes of baton exchange and let relay process more easily completed.

Acknowledgement. We would like to thank the financial support from National Science Council, Taiwan, NSC 97-2410-H-142-015-

References

1. Campbell, K.M., Kram, P.R., Chang, Y.H.: Human Maneuverability on Curves. The Berkeley McNair Research Journal, 21–32 (1999)
2. Chang, Y.H., Campbell, K., Kram, R.: Running speed on the curve is limited by the inside leg. In: Proceedings of the 25th Annual Meeting of the American Society of Biomechanics, pp. 435–436 (2001)
3. Green, P.R.: Running on flat turns: experiments, theory, and applications. Journal of Biomechanical Engineering 107, 96–102 (1985)

Dashboard Design Factors on Emotional Change: How Separation between Center-Fascia and Center-Console, Button Orientation and Button Arrangement Influence Emotion

Joongyeon Kim and Kwanghee Han

Cognitive Engineering Lab., Yonsei University, Seoul, Korea
yonttykkaro@naver.com, khan@yonsei.ac.kr

Abstract. This study aims to find out which kind of car interior design factors influence human emotion change. A special focus was given on emotional effects of dashboard design. The selected design factors of dashboard, which are commonly observed in luxury cars, were the separation between center-fascia and center-console, the orientation of each button and the arrangement of buttons. Perceived luxuriousness and preference were measured out of seven points via an online questionnaire. It was hypothesized that i) when center-fascia and center-console are divided than when they are integrated, ii) when button orientation is horizontal than when it is vertical, iii) when buttons are arranged horizontally than when they are arranged vertically, perceived luxuriousness and preference would be increased. 2 x 2 x 2 repeated-measures ANOVA was conducted on perceived luxuriousness and preference with division, orientation and arrangement as factors. Results showed that when button orientation is horizontal, perceived luxuriousness and preference were higher. Perceived luxuriousness and preference were also higher when buttons are arranged horizontally. An interaction effect between button orientation and arrangement on preference was found. This implies that higher preference can be triggered when at least one factor is horizontal. No other significant effects were found. This study was conducted to make a car interior design guideline which associates particular design factors that trigger particular emotional response. Future studies should investigate low-level psychological elements and conduct factor analysis of various emotional adjectives.

Keywords: Dashboard, Kansei-enginerring, Car Interior, button, center-fascia, luxuriousness.

1 Intro

The market for imported cars in Korea has grown in recent years. For that reason, manufacturers have to consider various factors of car design to satisfy a wide range of users. The number of consumers who consider Kansei-design is increasing and so is the competitiveness within the design industry. Car manufacturers focus more on

C. Stephanidis (Ed.): HCII 2014 Posters, Part I, CCIS 434, pp. 95–100, 2014.
© Springer International Publishing Switzerland 2014

Kansei-factors – luxury material, elaborate finishing touches, convenience system, etc. – than traditional specs – speed, horse-power, fuel efficiency, etc. (Bahn et al. 2006). This international market trend triggers the Kansei study on design and engineering factors of the car exterior and interior. There are many Kansei studies on car interiors: the Kansei-evaluation of car interior materials(Shin et al, 2002), developing luxuriousness-model of car crash pad(Bahn et al, 2006), research on car seat design factors(Han et al, 2000), evaluation of touch sense on car interior(Park et al, 2013), the Kansei-engineering on car interior image(Tanoue et al, 1997), and study on Kansei-study on car interior(Jindo et al, 1997).

Most of these studies focus on responses to visual or tactile characteristics of interior details. However, it is necessary to study interiors holistically because the same trend might not be observed uniformly across the individual components. Leder et al(2005) have studied the overall frontal interior by using holistic view image. In this study, they chose three design factors and combined these factors to make their stimuli, which looked like the general front interior of a car and could be perceived more holistically. They controlled the rest of the factors that can affect one's kansei – interior materials (Shin et al., 2002), seat design (Han et al., 2002), crash-pad material, color, surface (Bahn et al., 2006) – and by doing so just the form of the interior could be evaluated

In this study, we are interested in emotional change with respect to design factors of the car dashboard. We observed three flagship models of major Europian luxury car brands and a representative domestic luxury model. Because the focus was on luxuriousness, we selected the most high-end model of each brand and extracted the common design factors.

2   Experiment

We studied the effect of particular design factors on perceived luxuriousness and preference by using the methodology from Leder et al. (2005). The models chosen for stimuli creation   were Mercedes Benz S-Class (2014), BMW 7 Series (2013), Audi A8 (2014), and Hyundai Equus (2013). Each of these is the flagship models of their respective brand and represent the brand's pride, and therefore seemed appropriate in studying about perceptions on luxuriousness. We discovered three common design factors, as indicated in Figure 1.

Three extracted design factors are 1) separation between center-fascia and center-console, 2) the orientation of each button, 3) and the arrangement of buttons. These characteristics are commonly observed in many luxury cars.

From these findings, we set up our hypothesis as below. Perceived luxuriousness and preference would increase when:

1. the center-fascia and center-console are divided than when they are integrated,
2. the button orientation is horizontal than when it is vertical,
3. the buttons are arranged horizontally than when they are arranged vertically

Fig. 1. Design factors of each brand flagship(from left Audi A8, BMW 7 series, Benz S-Class, Hyundai Equus)

2.1   Participants

There were a total of 88 participants (39 male and 49 female). The average age was 26.16 and the range was 20 – 34 years.

2.2   Apparatus and Stimuli

Experimental stimuli were generated through Adobe Illustrator CS6 , similar to those used in Leder et al. (2005) and based on the interior of the BMW 7 Series. All other design factors except independent variables were controlled for experiment. The three independent variables were i) separation between center-fascia and center-console(integration/separation), ii) orientation of each button(horizontal/vertical), iii) arrangement of buttons(horizontal/vertical). The stimuli created for this study are shown in Figure 2.

The experiment was carried out as an online survey using Google Docs Form. The URL generated by this form was sent to participants via e-mail or mobile phone.

Orientation	Horizontal		Vertical	
Arrangement	Horizontal	Vertical	Horizontal	Vertical
Separation				
Integration				

Fig. 2. Experimental stimuli

2.3   Experiment Design and Procedure

The experiment used a within-participant design. Participants completed the survey by choosing answers about luxuriousness and preference on a 7-point Likerts scale, where 1 means "Not luxurious or preferred at all" and 7 is "Most luxurious or preferred". After finishing each stimulus evaluation, participants clicked the "next" button to continue. There were 8 combination stimuli based on three independent variables. To prevent any ordering effects and learning effects, the order of stimulus presentation was randomized by a balanced Latin square.

3   Result

Collected data were analyzed using the statistics package program PASW Statistics 18. A 2x2x2 repeated measures ANOVA was conducted.

3.1   Luxuriousness

Valid data on perceived luxuriousness from 86 participants were analyzed by repeated measures ANOVA. Data from two participants missing data was excluded. Value of descriptive statistics is indicated in Figure 3.

A main effect of button orientation on perceived luxuriousness was observed (F(1, 85) = 4.643, p = .034). They were perceived more luxurious when button orientation is horizontal (m = 4.009, s.e. = .097) than when vertical (m = 3.846, s.e. = .103). Moreover, a main effect of arrangement of buttons was found as well (F(1, 85) = 7.008, p = .010). When buttons were arranged horizontally (m = 4.029, s.e. = .099), they were perceived more luxurious than when arranged vertically (m = 3.826, s.e. = .102). There were no other main effects or interactions.

	m	sd	n
S11	4.06	1.056	85
S12	3.91	1.175	85
S21	4.00	1.256	85
S22	3.76	1.168	85
I11	4.13	1.282	85
I12	3.94	1.277	85
I21	3.93	1.225	85
I22	3.70	1.398	85

Fig. 3. Desciptive statistics value on luxuriousness

3.2   Preference

Value of descriptive statistics of preference is indicated in Figure 4. Data from six participants with incomplete values were excluded from analysis and repeated measures ANOVA on 82 values were conducted.

A main effect of button orientation on preference was observed ($F_{(1, 81)} = 7.433$, $p = .008$). This means people preferred the design when each button were laid out horizontally ($m = 4.006$, *s.e.* $= .108$) than when shown vertically ($m = 3.805$, *s.e.* $= .110$). Similarly, a main effect of arrangement of buttons was found ($F_{(1, 81)}= 6.709$, $p = .016$). Participants preferred having buttons arranged horizontally($m= 4.012$, *s.e.* $=.111$), than buttons arranged vertically ($m = 3.799$, *s.e.* $= .111$).

In addition, an interaction effect between button orientation and arrangement of buttons was found ($F_{(1, 81)}= 5.302$, $p= .016$). Figure 5 indicates that when each button was laid out horizontally, there was no effect of button arrangement on preference. However when laid out vertically, horizontal arrangement of buttons is more preferred than otherwise. Likewise, when buttons were arranged horizontally, people didn't show a clear preference for arrangement direction. Nevertheless, if buttons were arranged vertically, the horizontal buttons were preferred. No other significant effects were found.

	m	sd	n
S11	4.10	1.096	81
S12	3.98	1.227	81
S21	4.05	1.323	81
S22	3.63	1.262	81
I11	3.99	1.252	81
I12	3.96	1.271	81
I21	3.91	1.229	81
I22	3.62	1.254	81

Fig. 4. Descriptive statistics value on preference

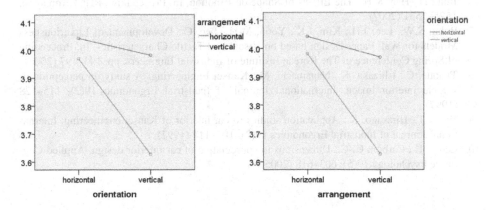

Fig. 5. Interaction effect between orientation and arrangement on preference

4   Discussion and Future Direction

This study examined the car interior design factors–button orientation, arrangement of buttons–which affect people's emotion. The effect of separation between center–fascia and center-console on both emotion–perceived luxuriousness and preference – were not found. Participants' inability to detect the differences of this factor could have influence this outcome. Nevertheless, the other two factors were identified as valuable for use in design guides. The observed effects were significant between these two factors on perceived luxuriousness and preference.

It is recommended that future research employ stimuli with different viewing perspectives. For example, the separation between the center-fascia and center-console can be more noticeable from a more diagonal angle. Moreover, low-level research dealing with luxuriousness is scarce. It would be valuable if Kansei-design factors can be explained by low-level perception research. Finding the perceptual mechanism involved in feelings of luxuriousness will be the next step in this line of research.

References

1. Korea Automotive Research Institute, 2013 Korea Automotive Industry (2013)
2. Han, G.J., Yoon, H.G.: A Study on the Design of Fabric of Automobile based on an Analysis of Constumer's Sensibility. Journal of Design Research 6(2), 469–483 (2000)
3. Bahn, S.W., Lee, C., Lee, J.H., Yoon, M.H.: Development Luxuriousness Models for Automobile Crash Pad based on Subjective and Objective Material Characteristics. Journal of the Ergonomics Society of Korea 25(2), 187–195 (2006)
4. Park, N.C., Jeong, S.W.: Extraction of Representative Emotions for Evaluations of Tactile Impressions in a Car Interior. Journal of Korean Society for Emotion and Sensibility 16(2), 157–166 (2013)
5. Shin, S.W., Ryu, T.B., Lim, I.K., Oh, K.H., Min, D.K., Seon, M.S., Yoo, H.C., Kim, K.J., Keum, W.Y., Yoon, M.H.: An Ergonomic Approach for Improvement of a Passenger Car Interior Design. In: Proceeding of Conference of The Ergonomics Society of Korea (2002)
6. Jung, D., Han, K.H.: The Effects of Shape on Emotion. In: Proceeding of HCI Korea, pp. 1525–1531 (2007)
7. Bahn, S.W., Lee, J.H., Kim, I.K., Yoon, M.H., Lee, C.: Development of Luxuriousness Models for Wall Paper Design based on Visual and Tactile Characteristics. In: Proceeding of Spring Conference of The Korean Institute of Industrial Engineers, pp. 193–197 (2006)
8. Tanoue, C., Ishizaka, K., Nagamachi, M.: Kansei Engineering: A study on perception of vehicle interior image. International Journal of Industrial Ergonomics 19(2), 115–128 (1997)
9. Jindo, T., Hirasago, K.: Application studies to car interior of Kansei engineering. International Journal of Industrial Ergonomics 19(2), 105–114 (1997)
10. Leder, H., Carbon, C.-C.: Dimensions in appreciation of car interior design. Applied Cognitive Psychology 19(5), 603–618 (2005)

Developing Intelligent Interior Design Decoration Components by BIM Technologies

Ju-Hung Lan and Ming-Shu Tsai

Department of Interior Design, National Taichung University of Science and Technology,
Taichung, 404, Taiwan, ROC
jhlan@nutc.edu.tw

Abstract. This study develops intelligent interior design components that enhance design communications, based on the concepts and technologies of the building information modeling (BIM) to resolve data inconsistencies in relevant graphics of an interior design project. The developed intelligent decorative wooden walls possess intelligent dynamic correlation functions, with parameters that can control the wooden wall material, size, and restrictions. This study identified that the graphical data inconsistency problem was resolved, and effective communication was promoted among the participants who were involved in the various stages of an interior design project.

Keywords: BIM, building information modeling, interior design.

1   Introduction

Traditional execution process of interior design project relies on two-dimensional drawings. However, when 2D view is used to express construction entity of interior decoration, often, it has pretty many simplification, omission and confliction. Especially, when design modification are taken during the project process, the negligence and errors of description update may highlight the problem severity of contradictions and inconsistencies on drawing related information even more.

In recent years, Building Information Modeling (BIM) takes the new concept of consistency of whole project engineering life cycle information exchange, multi-disciplinary integration and cross-phase collaboration communication method. It can provide effective communication and coordination mechanisms of whole project. Therefore, the study goal is to develop an intelligent interior design decoration element with design communication efficiency aiming at the inconsistent information problems related with general interior design project execution via BIM concepts, methods and techniques.

2   The Practices of Carpentry Decoration Wall

With the research schedule limitations, this paper uses carpentry decoration wall as discussion objects. Carpentry decoration wall plays roles of compartment, decorative

C. Stephanidis (Ed.): HCII 2014 Posters, Part I, CCIS 434, pp. 101–106, 2014.
© Springer International Publishing Switzerland 2014

decoration and accommodating utilities, information, communications wiring and other related functions. It is designed by designer, constructed by carpenter master and piping configuration is finished by related operation personnel.

2.1   Carpentry Decoration Wall Design Practice Interview

Carpentry decoration wall design practice interview in the study invites 4 professional interior designers. Main points of the design practice interview are design type and category, construction position, application range, typical decorative wall molding and drawing description of decoration carpentry wall in design stage. The design practice interview results are summarized as in Table 1.

Table 1. Summary of Design Practice Interview Results

Design Type	Perpendicular Wall	Two-sided Partition Wall
Design Category	Depending on the attached construction, wall width can be divided into two design categories: 1).equal to wall width, 2). Less than wall width.	
Construction Location Type	Constructing on original wall in the space, it can be divided into 4 construction location types: Left, center, right and full wall width, as in Figure 1.	Constructing on room width (depth), it can be divided into 4 construction location types: Left, center, right and full room width, as in Figure 2.
Typical Decoration Wall Molding	It takes even separation or partition for width or height of wall surface, and creates simple and refreshing shape and three-dimension effect after being separated by concave joint emphasized line of plywood or skinning plywood. See Figure 3. Typical Decoration Wall Molding.	

| Left | Center | Right | Full Wall Width |

Fig. 1. Construction Location Type of Perpendicular Wall (Plan Sketch)

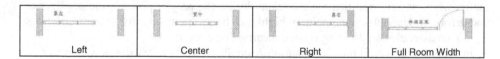

| Left | Center | Right | Full Room Width |

Fig. 2. Construction Location Type of Two-sided Partition Wall (Plan Sketch)

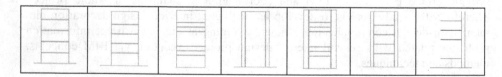

Fig. 3. Typical Decoration Wall Molding (Facade Schematic)

2.2   Carpentry Decoration Wall Construction Practice Interview

Construction practice interview in the study invites 4 professional carpenter masters, and all of them have more than 25 years of business experiences and interior decoration engineering contractors. Main points of the construction practice interview are commonly used materials and specifications, size limits, structure type, design drawing description and actual construction differences of decoration carpentry wall. The construction practice interview results are summarized as in Table 2.

Table 2. Summary of Construction Practice Interview Results

Design Type	Perpendicular Wall	Two-sided Partition Wall
Commonly used materials and specifications	Wood strips: generally adopted 1.2cun x1cun	Wood strips: generally adopted 2cun x1cun
	Plate: No matter for Perpendicular Wall or Two-sided Partition Wall, the generally used plate is 2fen plywood or 2fen Calcium silicate board (which shall be adopted when it has fire 0 proof regulations). 2fen Calcium silicate board: 3chi x 6chi (90cm x 180cm) 2fen plywood: 3 chi x 6 chi (90cm x 180cm), 4 chi x 8 chi (120cm x 240cm). See Figure 4 on detail.	
Design drawing description and actual construction differences	As all wood strips structures of decoration engineering are restricted by two kinds of commonly used plate specifications, i.e. 3 chi x 6 chi and 4 chi x 8 chi. Therefore, the construction method of wood strips structure has fix construction mode and formula rule for reference (Figure 5 and Figure 6). This is the necessary professional knowledge for interior design related employees. Unless the carpentry wall has complicated shape and structure, which requires sectional detail drawing for expression, the drawing description may simplify and omit sectional elevation drawing or detail drawing if it is general carpentry wall.	

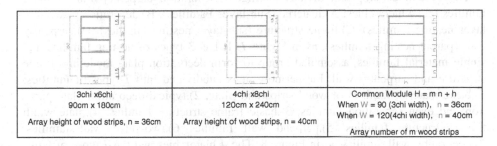

3chi x6chi 90cm x 180cm Array height of wood strips, n = 36cm	4chi x8chi 120cm x 240cm Array height of wood strips, n = 40cm	Common Module H = m n + h When W = 90 (3chi width), n = 36cm When W = 120(4chi width), n = 40cm Array number of m wood strips

Fig. 4. 3chi x6chi and 4chi x8chi Ply Wood Specifications

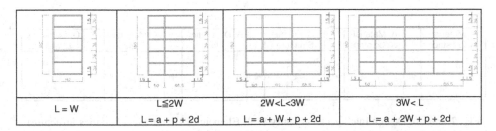

L = W	L≦2W L = a + p + 2d	2W<L<3W L = a + W + p + 2d	3W< L L = a + 2W + p + 2d

Fig. 5. Modular Analysis for 4 Types of Wood strips Structures(3chi x6chi Perpendicular Wall)

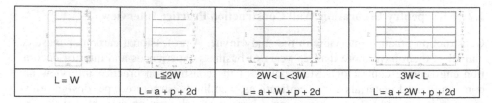

L = W	L≦2W	2W< L <3W	3W< L
	L = a + p + 2d	L = a + W + p + 2d	L = a + 2W + p + 2d

Fig. 6. Modular Analysis for 4 Types of Wood strips Structures(4chi x8chi Perpendicular Wall)

3 Developing Intelligent Interior Design Decoration Carpentry Wall Element

The study takes Autodesk Revit BIM development tool to develop intelligent interior design and decoration carpentry wall element. Revit takes Families as construction core of BIM and uses parametric modeling techniques and 3D visualization design. The development of intelligent interior design and decoration carpentry wall element in the study takes the families of Revit BIM as basis. With the above stated carpentry wall design and construction practices interview, the paper makes the following illustrations for the development of intelligent interior design and decoration carpentry wall element.

The system development divides intelligent decoration carpentry wall element families into 4 hierarchies: A).material (Sub-layer Families), B).decoration plate (sub-layer nesting families), C).frame structure (sub-layer nesting families), D).carpentry wall (parent nesting families), as in Figure 7. It has 3 types of nesting families, i.e. single material families, assembled group to form decoration plate modeling, frame structure and carpentry wall. Furthermore, it is subdivided into 7 types of families: 1).basic material families of wood strips and plate, 2).typical decoration plate partition and even separation families, 3).basic frame structure families, 4).plate width frame structure families, 5).perpend wall families 6).two-sided wall families, 7).decoration wall families, as in Figure 8. The 4 hierarchies and the 7 types of families are the results of system development in the study: interior design intelligent decoration carpentry wall element.

A. Material-Wood strips		A. Material-Wood strips		C. Frame Structure		B. Decoration Plate		A. Material-Plate		D. Carpentry wall
	+		→		+		+		→	

Fig. 7. Interior Design Intelligent Carpentry Wall Element (4 Hierarchical Families Structure)

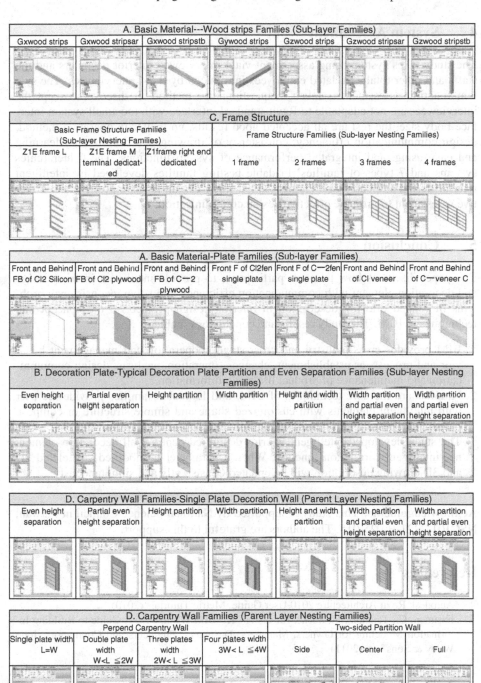

Fig. 8. Interior Design Intelligent Decoration Carpentry Element

4   System Assessment

The study takes system using assessment via 4 interviewed interior designers and the staffs and other total 32 related employees introduced by the 4 interviewees. The system function assessment is taken in questionnaire method. It discovers except the interviewees are not adaptable to Revit standard interface with too small system interface body size, the rest are all accepted good results, no matter in operation method, design communication efficiency, consistency of drawing description, easy-learning and easy using, and integrated performance of system functions. The 4 hierarchies systems and 7 types of families' loadable nesting families developed by intelligent interior design carpentry wall element in the study can all achieve positive and effective assessment to promote effective design communication.

5   Conclusion

The paper discusses how to assist participants to provide intelligent interior design and decoration element with communication efficiency and solve inconsistency problems of related drawing description in interior design project via the concept and techniques of BIM. The study results and conclusions include:

1. BIM provides cross-industry and cross-stage cooperation and management behavior and process, as establishment, changes, operation, analysis, design communication and maintenance of product life cycle information.
2. Families are the core techniques of BIM, and Loadable families provide the user with intelligent elements with customized shape and simple structure or compose parent layer nesting families by several modular sub-layer families.
3. The study developed intelligent interior design carpentry wall decoration element has intelligent correlation function. When a parameter is modified, all related 2D and 3D drawing description will be updated consistently and simultaneously.

Acknowledgements. This study is supported by National Science Council in Taiwan, NSC101-2221-E-025-015. The authors are grateful to this support.

References

1. Autodesk Revit Architecture 2010 User Guide, Metric Tutorials (2010)
2. Eastman, C., Teicholz, P., Sacks, R., Liston, K.: BIM Handbook: A Guide to Building Information Modeling for Owners, Managers, Designers, Engineers and Contractors. John Wiley & Sons Inc. (2011)

Application of the Multi-touch Tabletop to the Design Evaluation during the Initial Phase of Product Development

Hyun-Chul Lee

Division of I&C and Human Factors, Korea Atomic Energy Research Institute,
305-353, 989-111 Daedeok-daero, Yusong-gu, Daejeon, Republic of Korea
leehc@kaeri.re.kr

Abstract. To support human factors evaluators, a cooperation system using the multi-touch tabletop computer is developed. The cooperation system, so called COSY, can show static information from drawings and dynamic information from design documents on the multi-touch tabletop computer. Because multiple human factors evaluators can discuss their opinions and draw the final conclusion on the current product design around the COSY. The COSY was applied to evaluate digital indicators for nuclear power plants from the human factors perspective iteratively from the initial design phase before high fidelity prototyping. It is concluded from the application that (1) since human factors evaluators could easily figure out the dynamic behavior, work together for each design issue, and complete their design reviews in a short time, they preferred the COSY as the evaluation support system (2) product designers liked the COSY because they could get fast design feedbacks.

Keywords: Multi-touch, Tabletop, Human Factors Evaluation, Cooperation.

1 Introduction

Since nuclear facilities pay much attention to safe operation of themselves, every component of them should be inspected individually and independently from various engineering areas' points of view. After TMI-2 accident in 1970s, importance of human factors engineering was recognized and countermeasures, such as emergency response facilities and safety parameter display systems, were rapidly deployed in nuclear power plants.

Most valuable reaction to the accident is the introduction of the process of human factors engineering which is composed of main 4 phases including planning and analysis (P&A), design, evaluation (V&V), and implementation and operation (I&O) [1]. The process should be applied to the development of all nuclear systems, equipment, and even devices. Regulatory bodies require plan documents and result reports for all phases and activities.

The successful adopt of the process needs systematic process management from the beginning of the product development. Several practical reasons had prohibited the initial activation of the process: lack of understanding of human factors engineering,

C. Stephanidis (Ed.): HCII 2014 Posters, Part I, CCIS 434, pp. 107–111, 2014.
© Springer International Publishing Switzerland 2014

lack of development resources, lack of engineers, and misunderstanding of the necessity.

The process has assigned many points in which developer/designers can get feedbacks from human factors design evaluation. In general, the design discrepancies found in early points may be modified with a little resource and later discrepancies may consume much resource to fix them (refer to Fig.1.).

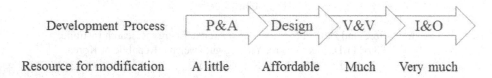

Fig. 1. Process vs. resource required to fix

Many nuclear industries in Korea have experienced temporal and economic losses caused by design changes resulted from human factors evaluation in the final phase of product development. For instance, one company had to destroy its high-fidelity prototype after human factors evaluation performed in the late V&V phase, and had to start new design development. Therefore, they like to iteratively perform the human factors evaluation from the beginning phase of product development.

Available information on the design may be different for each development process. In early phases such as P&A and design, design concept documents and drawings might be available. In the V&V phase, prototypes (or real products) should be available additionally.

As developers/designers issue their design concepts through many drawings and documents, human factors evaluators have to integrate information from drawings and documents and specify the product by themselves. In most cases, the shape or physical and static characteristics of the product can be easily imagined, however dynamic behavior of the product hardly simulated. As the results of insufficient understanding of dynamic behavior, confused design comments between evaluators are generated and much time are consumed to build correct behavior model within evaluators and to draw conclusive design comments agreed by all evaluators.

To support human factors evaluators and to avoid unnecessary conflicts between them, a cooperation system, so called COSY, is proposed in this presentation.

2   Development of COSY

To develop the COSY, information requirements and interface requirements were analyzed.

2.1   Information Requirements

In general, design documents and drawings are available for human factors evaluation in the early phase of development process. Contents in the documents and drawings can be classified into static information and dynamic information. Static information is much related to the size and shape, for example width, height, space, layout etc. Dynamic information means behavior of the product, such as shape changes for each mode, physical changes according to time. It was required that the COSY should display both information from design documents and drawings. Usually static information is derived from design drawings and dynamic information from design documents or style guides.

2.2   Interface Requirements

The evaluation in the early phase of development process is formative rather than summative [2]. To secure many valuable design comments, multiple human factors specialists have to participate in the evaluation. Discussion is necessary to reach design comments which every evaluator agrees to. It will be very desirable and efficient of all evaluators to get together at the same place at some time. Thus it was required that the COSY provides meeting place where many evaluators can present their opinions and discuss with others to draw design comments. The COSY selected a multi-touch tabletop as the meeting place. It is well-known that the multi-touch tabletop is efficient for cooperation.

From interviews with human factors evaluators, it was required that

- Evaluators can easily pick up drawings and documents.
- Evaluators can adjust the size of information to emphasize or skip their opinions.
- No scaled (1:1) products can be shown on the screen.
- Display of dynamic information can be controlled by evaluators
- All evaluators can join discussion at any time without any permission on the screen.

By using finger touches and drags on the COSY, human factors evaluators can do the followings;

- search drawings
- freely enlarge, reduce, shrink, rotate the static/dynamic information
- set the static/dynamic information to the real size (1:1)
- activate, freeze, or de-activate dynamic behavior of the product

Because multiple human factors evaluators can be positioned around the multi-touch tabletop, they can discuss their opinions and draw the final conclusion on the current product design with the COSY.

It was infrequently observed that a human factors evaluator issues a design discrepancy but, in fact, the discrepancy is identified from insufficient understand of design. The COSY is an effective system for screening wrong design comments because the COSY enables evaluators to show their design comments (or discrepancies) to other evaluators.

3   Application to the Digital Indicator

The COSY was applied to evaluate digital indicators for nuclear power plants from the human factors perspective iteratively from the initial design phase before high fidelity prototyping.

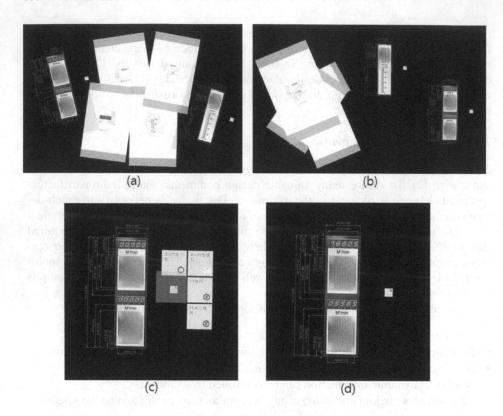

Fig. 2. Captures from the COSY

Fig.2 shows the capture from the COSY. Six drawings are displayed in the screen of the COSY (refer to Fig. 2.(a)). Four drawings in the middle (white background) show static information, that is, physical drawings. Two drawings (transparent background) in left-side and right-side include dynamic information. Fig. 2.(b) shows the screen resulted from re-arranging drawings by finger touches and dragging. Four drawings with static information moved to the left-side and one with dynamic information moved to the right side. Each drawing with dynamic information has a button on the right side away. When the button is touched, four control buttons appeared (refer to Fig. 2.(c)). Control buttons, (1) dynamic behavior activation (2) deactivation of dynamic behavior (3) set the drawing to the real size (1:1) (4) unset the real size fixation, are arranged in the clockwise direction.

A screen capture after the dynamic behavior activation is shown in Fig. 2.(d). One of the dynamic behaviors of an indicator was the indication of digital value on the top side of each device.

4   Conclusion

A multi-touch tabletop based cooperation system (COSY) was developed to support human factors evaluators in the early phase of development process. The COSY was applied to the digital indicator evaluation and human factors evaluators showed positive responses because

- They can easily understand the dynamic behaviors and their impact on other design attributes
- Opinions are correctly transferred to other evaluators so that design comments from individual evaluators were efficiently integrated.
- Time required to evaluate was reduced so that developer/designers can have fast design feedbacks.

References

1. Nuclear Regulatory Commission: Human Factors Engineering Program Review Model. NUREG-0711, US NRC, Washington DC (2002)
2. Lewis, J.R.: Usability Testing. In: Salvendy, G. (ed.) Handbook of Human Factors and Ergonomics, pp. 1267–1312. John Wiley & Sons, New Jersey (2012)

Color Imagery of Skin Tone and Eyeglass Frames

Kuen-Meau Chen, Ying-Sin Lin, and Hsueh-Cheng Chou

Department of Industrial Design, National United University,
1 Lien Da, Kung-Ching Li, Maioli 36003, Taiwan
1kmchen0721@gmail.com

Abstract. This study aimed to explore the colour imagery of skin tone and eyeglass frames, and whether this affects the preferences of consumers. Glasses are a focal point on the face and we wished to understand whether the frame colour along with skin tone affects the entire facial image. Many businesses provide suggestions on choosing frames that complement one's skin tone, but what is the basis of these recommendations? We conducted a questionnaire survey and analysed the results using two-way ANOVA and regression analysis. Results were as follows: (1) skin tone significantly influences preference; (2) the colour of eyeglass frames significantly influences preference; (3) the interaction of skin tone and frame colour does not significantly affect preference; (4) consumers with lighter skin tone tend to prefer black frames; (5) elegant, simple, fresh imagery significantly and positively influences preference. Our results showed that when consumers are choosing glasses, the colour relationship between skin tone and glasses frames does not significantly influence their decisions; however, when it comes to choosing the frames, consumers place more emphasis on their skin tone or colour preferences.

Keywords: Glasses design, colour imagery.

1 Introduction

1.1 Motivation and Objectives

In addition to correcting one's vision, eyeglasses have become an accessory capable of expressing one's individual style. Occasionally, the difference between skin tones and eyeglass frames is quite striking, such as when a black person wears white frames or a white person wears dark frames. Salespeople and websites dealing with eyeglasses often recommend that their customers select the correct color for their eyeglass frames as a marketing ploy, while consumers tend to maintain personal preferences. This paper explores the relationship between skin tone and the color of eyeglass frames with the following objectives:

1. To explore the emotional imagery evoked by the arbitrary combination of various skin tones and frames of different colors;
2. To understand the inclinations of consumers with regard to skin tones and the color of eyeglass frames.

C. Stephanidis (Ed.): HCII 2014 Posters, Part I, CCIS 434, pp. 112–117, 2014.

This research may provide a useful reference for eyeglass designers in the selection of colors.

1.2   Scope and Limitations

Hairstyle, facial characteristics, and the style of eyeglasses all play a role in the selection of eyeglasses. This study selected "skin tone" as the sole variable affecting one's decision in the selection eyeglass frames in the hope of eliminating factors that might otherwise confound the research results.

2   Literature Review

Stylish product design has become an important global trend. Style can be a unique characteristic, which is presented as an outward expression of oneself (Schmitt & Simonson, 1997). Trends in product design have been steered from functionalism toward product semantics Krippendorff, 1996）. Krippendorff and Butter（1984）defined product semantics as 1. "research that focuses on the meanings and symbols of objects in the psychological and social dimensions" and 2. "research on the forms and symbolic features of manmade objects in the users' environment and an application of such knowledge on industrial design" (Krippendorff & Butter，1991). Krampen （1996） claimed that every commodity (structures or products) has its own stylistic or connotative significance. A wide range of eyeglasses are available on the market and in addition to the function of holding optical lenses, the eyeglass frame also serves as an adornment that helps to express oneself and alter one's image. Eyeglass frames also indicate one's social status, professional appearance, and fashion acumen. Mature markets include a wide range of consumers with different preferences and needs. This study is based on the assumption that style can be analyzed using a recognition-coding system based on the emotional connotations shared by most people.

Designers provide strong and emotional design skills and uses provide their "experience skills". These two skills are the two factors which connects the design objects and the users. (Norman, 2004). According to Khaslavsky and Shedroff (1999), designers use enticement, relationship, and fulfillment to project sentimental expression. Designs are determined by the color, shape, and materials used in the product as well as the latest trends. From computer accessories and headphones to household appliances and vehicles, people consider the color of a product when making decisions related to purchasing behavior (Nagamachi, 1995).

Chen (2008) claimed that humans undergo physical and psychological changes when they see things and receive stimulation from the outside world. Skin tone and the color of the eyeglass frames are two important factors to be considered. When working on the design of spectacles, the matching of skin tones and the color of eyeglass frames can make a pronounced difference with regard to visual effect. This paper sought to identify the inclinations of the general public with regard to skin tones and the color of eyeglass frames.

3   Research Design

This study progressed through the following three phases: First, we assembled sampling pre-tests by making a glossary of skin tones, the colors of eyeglass frames, and the terminology used to describe style. This led to the drafting of a questionnaire for a public opinion survey. Two-way ANOVA was used to analyze the inclinations and preferences of consumers with regard to the matching of skin tones and the color of eyeglass frames. In the third phase, we employed regression analysis to investigate the impressions that could influence the decisions involved in the selection of eyeglass frames with the aim of identifying the crucial elements believed to embody good style.

3.1   Sampling of Skin Tones

Samples were obtained from the skin-tone chart proposed by Felix von Luschan, an Austrian anthropologist, who classified human skin colors into 36 degrees, ranging from nearly pure white to black. The chart was then compared with the skin color distribution map by Italian geographer Renato Biasutti. The resulting map indicated that the skin tones of Taiwanese people range from 12-14. We used Photoshop to adjust the skin tones and color intensity in the sample images to the near-average complexion found in Taiwan, resulting in 15 skin samples. The questionnaire was administered to 14 college students with a major in design. The questionnaire included two questions: (1) What skin tone do you think can best represent the Taiwanese people? (2) Please choose three samples of "light, average, and dark" skin tones that are most typical of Taiwanese people. We then collected the questionnaires and selected Sample 5 (for light complexion), Sample 9 (for average complexion), and Sample 13 (for darker complexion) as representative samples (see Figure1).

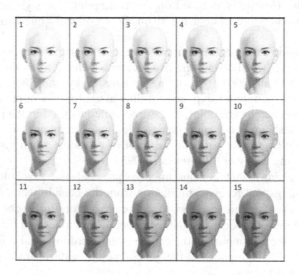

Fig. 1. Sampling of skin tones

3.2   Selection of Adjectives Related to Imagery

This study assembled several comparative adjectives from a study on color recognition and the color of plastic eyeglass frames (Liang et al. 2010) and organized a conference of experts to discuss the issue. Feedback from the experts was used for the selection of the following eight pairs of adjectives appropriate for the glossary: (1) cool vs. warm; (2) gloomy vs. refreshing; (3) immature vs. mature; (4) dusky vs. bright; (5) lowly vs. noble; (6) serious vs. sprightly; (7) nerdy vs. glamorous; and (8) delightful vs. unlikeable.

3.3   Colors Selection for Eyeglass Frames

For the selection of the colors of eyeglass frames, we adopted the Practical Color Coordinate System (P.C.C.S) and selected a color every 60 degrees, with additional neutral tones (grey, black, and white). We made the samplings for eyeglass frames in accordance with the P.C.C.S-RGB-CMYK, and obtained a total of nine colors: Y, G, gB, V, RP, rO, grey, black, and white.

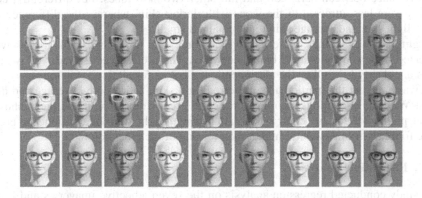

Fig. 2. Sampling of eyeglass-wearing icons

3.4   Questionnaire Design and Testing

Photoshop was used to apply the nine colors of eyeglass frames onto the three types of skin tone. The location where we put the eyeglass on the face was based on the standard adopted by most people who wear eyeglasses. This resulted in 27 samples (9*3) (see Figure 2). This study employed a questionnaire survey to collect information from students. The order of testing ran as follows: (1) Assemble adjectives to describe skin tones and the color of eyeglass frames by recruiting ten college students majoring in design; (2) Assemble a sample of skin tones by recruiting 14 college students with a major in design; (3) Conduct a survey with 30 students to identify "emotional imagery" produced by matching skin tones and the color of eyeglass frames as well as "levels of preferences".

We then listed a sample icon on each page (27 icons in total), with eight scoring items. The color of the eyeglass frames was matched with the three skin tones (light, average, dark). This study employed a Osgood Sematic Differential, scoring ranged from 1 through 7. SPSS 20.0 was used for two-way ANOVA in exploring the degree of preferences and impressions perceived by consumers in the matching of skin tones and the color of eyeglass frames.

4　Results and Analysis

4.1　Analysis of Two-Way ANOVA and Preference Levels

We discerned that (1) the significance of "skin tone" (P value = 0.000) suggests that skin tone has a noticeable impact on one's preferences; (2) the significance of the "color of the eyeglass frame" (P value = 0.000) shows that the color of the eyeglass frame has a noticeable impact on one's preferences; (3) the significance of the matching of "skin tone and color of eyeglass frames" (P value = 0.903, which is far above 0.05) does not reach significance, suggesting that "the matching of skin tone and the color of the eyeglass frames" does not have noticeable effects on one's preferences.

From the multiple comparisons of skin tone preferences, we discovered a noticeable difference between dark skin and the other two skin tones. Put differently, consumers were less attracted to the icons with darker skin, whereas the difference between light skin and average skin tone remained small.

Light skin was slightly preferred over average skin tones and black frames were preferred, followed by orange, blue, and white. The preferences for red, yellow, and green are clearly lower than the aforementioned colors for all three skin tones.

It was apparent that participants preferred light skin, followed by average and dark skins. With the exceptions of orange, red, and green colors, the participants show a higher preference for any color when matched with light skin. In addition, the preference for black frames was far higher than for any of the other colors.

4.2　Regression Analysis

This study conducted regression analysis on the seven adjective imageries and levels of preferences, producing three models to explain the phenomenon. Model 3 presents the highest explanatory power, which produced three adjective pairs, as follows: (1) gloomy vs. refreshing; (2) lowly vs. noble; (3) nerdy vs. glamorous. The predicted variable equation runs as follows:

$y = 0.999 + 0.866*(noble) + (-0.379)*(glamorous) + 0.262*(refreshing)$, illustrating the impact of the three adjective pairs on the participants in evoking an emotional response. "Noble" and "refreshing" exert positive effects on consumers whereas "glamorous" has a negative effect on perceptions of eyeglass frames.

5　Conclusions

It was discovered that skin tones and the color of eyeglass frames play a pivotal part in one's preferences, while the relationship between skin tone and the color of eyeglass frames has almost no influence. Darker skin had a less positive impression on the viewers, while fair skin was admired. The difference between light and average skin tones is smaller, because the preference level depended on the fairness of the skin.

The participants showed a higher preference for all frames exhibited on light skin, regardless of the color. This confirms that skin tone, rather than the color of the eyeglass frame, had a greater impact on the viewers. The most popular color for eyeglass frames was black. The adjectives indicating preference were noble, quiet, and refreshing. These results provide a useful reference for further research and designers in the eyeglass industry for the selection of colors used in future design.

References

1. Schmitt, B., Simonson, A.: Marketing Aesthetics: The Strategic Management of Brands, Identity, and Image. Simon & Schuster (1997)
2. Khaslavsky, J., Shedroff, N.: Understanding the seductive experience. Communications of the ACM 42(5), 45–49 (1999)
3. Krampen, M.: Semiotics in Architecture and Industrial/Product Design. In: Margolin, V., Buchanan, R. (eds.) The Idea of Design, 2nd Printing, pp. 89–103. The MIT Press, Massachusetts (1996)
4. Krippendorff, K.: On the Essential Contexts of Artifacts or on the proposition that Design is Making Sense (of Things). In: Margolin, V., Buchanan, R. (eds.) The Idea of Design, vol. 184, pp. 56–184. MIT Press, Massachusetts (1996)
5. Krippendorff, K., Butter, R.: Product Semantics: Exploring the Symbolic Qualities of Form. Innovation, The Journal of IDSA 3(2), 4–9 (1984)
6. Liang, C.C., Chen, K., Ho, C.H.: A Study on Color Emotion for Plastic Eyewear. In: New World Situation: New Directions in Concurrent Engineering, pp. 147–162 (2010)
7. Mitsuo, N.: Kansei Engineering: A new ergonomic consumer-oriented technology for product development. International Journal of Industrial Ergonomics 15, 3–11 (1995)
8. Norman, D.A.: Emotional design: Why we love (or hate) everyday things. Basic Books, New York (2004)
9. Chen, K.M., Wang, M.J.: The Influence of Single Colour Preference and Area Ratio on Dichromatic Colour Preference. Colour: Design & Creativity (2), 5, 1–9 (2008)

Evolution of a Laboratory for Design of Advanced Ship Bridges

Kjetil Nordby[1] and Sashidharan Komandur[2]

[1] Oslo School of Architecture and Design, Maridalsveien 29, 0175 Oslo, Norway
kjetilnordby@gmail.com
[2] Aalesund University College, Larsgardsvegen 2, 6009 Aalesund, Norway
sash.kom@gmail.com

Abstract. In this paper we describe the process of constructing a design laboratory oriented towards designers re-conceptualizing ship bridge interaction. We
offer a description of the laboratory itself and the rationale for its form and the
current experiences from using it.

Keywords: Design, design-lab, ship bridge interaction, H5.m, Information interfaces and presentation, documentation.

1   Introduction

Ship bridges, in particular offshore support vessels (e.g. platform supply vessels -
PSVs) are complex and include equipment from multiple vendors that often user
entirely different user interface methodologies. To quote an experienced captain
working within the Norwegian offshore industry "they are all prototypes, each one is
unique".

Recently, technological developments have made it possible to design integrated
ship bridges where the ship builder can make an overarching interface steering all
equipment on the bridge. Such development opens up for more holistic user oriented
design. However, it also means the new design tasks are very complex and needs to
take the entire ship bridge into account in the design process. To cope with such a task
in a multidisciplinary project there is a need for tools that support multiple design
professions to collaborate efficiently in designing a complex system.

In this poster we report one such design and research project from the Norwegian
maritime industry. In particular we describe how we created a space oriented towards
supporting holistic development of entire ships bridges. We describe why we created
the space, how it functions and what we learnt from using it. Key challenges in designing the work space is to bridge the gap between the lab environment and the very
different environment of a ship in practice (Lurås & Nordby, 2014). Also, we need to
connect and maintain relationship between multiple different research groups in
Norway in a seamless way.

C. Stephanidis (Ed.): HCII 2014 Posters, Part I, CCIS 434, pp. 118–122, 2014.
© Springer International Publishing Switzerland 2014

2   The Project

The lab is created in context of Ulstein Bridge Concept, a joint research and design project. The project is sponsored by the Norwegian research council and a large Norwegian ship yard developing advanced PSVs. Designing ship bridges for advanced offshore vessels is complex and demands collaboration between many participants. In the project practitioners and research from industrial, graphical, sound and interaction design collaborate with software and human factors engineers. The research and development project uses a mix of methodologies related to collaborative and participatory design disciplines. Important in this process is to have a place where we collaborate in creating new design proposals. Our project draws on experiences from design and HCI research related design collaboratoriums (Buur & Bødker, 2000; Bødker & Buur, 2002). We do so by creating a lab particularly oriented towards allowing multiple participants to work hands-on with the design problems. Also, we draw on experiences form CSCW (computer supported collaborative work) that outline how we might use video connected spaces as part of our toolbox.

3   The Collaboratoriums

The collaboratarium is distributed over two separate locations. The main lab is in Oslo where we continuously run design processes. The other lab is located in Ålesund where we will conduct usability testing. Ålesund is a city which can be considered the hub of shipbuilding in Norway.

3.1   The Collaboratorium Features

In essence the ship bridge is an enclosed space where we control much of the environmental aspects of the situation. This makes such a space ripe for experiments within the genre of ubiquitous computing. Because of this the collaboratarium is constructed so as to support live experiments with a range of technologies allowing by means of hardware and software infrastructure. Following is an overview of the various elements available for the participants in the lab space.

3.2   Physical Bridge Rig

Central in the lab is a wood rig representing the sloping glasses of a bridge from a Platform Supply Vessel. These are equipped with covers so as to be suitable to represent both front and rear bridge. The glass panes are only made for half the bridge to save space and out of the experiences that most bridges have a symmetrical structure.

3.3   Simulator

The operation of the ship in various environmental conditions are critical I ship bridge design. To introduce marine context to the design processes we have integrated a ship simulator inside the lab. This is done by placing a projection foil on the sloped windows and a projector connected to a computer housing the simulator. This enables a tighter integration with realistic maritime situations while maintaining the flexibility of the lab environment. Currently we have access to three simulator systems in the lab: A commercial naval simulator, one based on games engines and finally an in-house built custom simulator. In addition to offering visuals, the simulators provide data about the simulated environment and the virtual ship that we use in the interaction design demonstrators.

3.4   Video Communication and Capture System

There are installed three video cameras in the lab. Camera one is located in one corner above a large monitor (46 inch). The camera is used for documenting workshops and for video communication. It is also capable of taking 10mp images.

The second camera is mounted on the bridge rig in front so as to be able to take pictures of console concepts from a side/front position. This camera is also used for video communication. This camera is also mounted for image capture.

The third camera is mounted on a moving arm. This camera is used for capturing images of sketches and models as they are produced in the collaboratorium. It is made easily available to make is possible to scan images as they are created.

3.5   Field Related Data

The lab has access from extensive data captured from both in operations in the north seas. The data have been collected during 1700 hours of field studies and comprise of extensive image, audio and video archives as well as written reports. The use of images are particular important in the lab and work have been carried out to make images easily accessible for design processes. (Nordby et al. 2011)

3.6   Bridge Prints

All equipment from a real life bridge is printed (10x10cm to 60x60cms) and used. This is mainly used for Building low level mock-ups of early concept designs. This system were used in the early phases of our project. However, as the project have matured all preexisting interfaces have been replaced with new systems.

3.7   CAD Station

Three well equipped stationary computers are centrally placed in the lab. They are used to run simulator software, do 3D renderings, CAD work and control experimental screens and projectors.

3.8   Building Equipment

In addition to large workshops including wood, plastic, metal and rapid prototyping workshops close to the lab a number of low end prototyping tools for console mockup is made available in the lab. This include cardboard, plywood and a large number of XPS "bricks" which is used to rapidly build large mockups.

3.9   Software

A software middleware layer is made available for the collaboratorium. The software offers a communication layer between all the ship functions and the interfaces we design as well as offering connection to commercial ship simulators. The system allows for efficient prototyping of novel interface concepts and make them testable in a simulated environment. All new interface technologies introduced in the lab (like gesture sensors, haptic systems or novel display types) are integrated into the labs middleware with the purpose to make their functionality available across the lab network.

3.10   Board Walls

All walls are used for visual communication. The walls facing away from the cameras are used for visual reference material, including ergonomic overviews, ship control systems and inspirational mood boards covering competitors, style guides and current inspirational materials.

In the front facing wall we have mounted a whiteboard. This is positioned to enable the cameras to capture the 'writing on the wall'.

4   Experiences and Reflections

Together the facilities of the lab makes for an efficient environment for collaborate design processes where users, marine experts and designers can work together. The lab has functioned well so far in the project. It offers a great inspirational place as well as a good place for interacting with the emerging design artifacts. We have found that in particular the sharing of digital field data function well in the lab as well as the tools for developing interactive prototypes.

Despite the many tools available in the lab we have experienced that   the distance between real life ship bridges and the lab is a concern (Lurås &Nordby, 2014). Although the visual data, mockups and simulator equipment allow much of the marine context to be expressed in the lab, it does not relieve the need for extensive fieldstrips to understand marine settings. The extreme nature of the marine context involves both physical, cultural and psychological factors hard to understand outside the actual marine context. Consequently, our experiences using the lab for designing for marine use is that it ns necessary to   combine a rich lab with frequent trips to real life user context.

Acknowledgements. We would like to thank Ulstein business group and the Norwegian Research Council without whose support it would be difficult to set up such a laboratory. We are particularly thankful to the efforts of Sigbjorn Windingstad & Sigrun Lurås.

References

1. Buur, J., Bødker, S.: From usability lab to "design collaboratorium": reframing usability practice. Paper Presented at the 3rd Conference on Designing Interactive Systems: Processes, Practices, Methods, and Techniques (2000)
2. Bødker, S., Buur, J.: The design collaboratorium: a place for usability design. ACM Trans. Comput.-Hum. Interact. 9(2), 152–169 (2002)
3. Nordby, K., Komandur, S., Lange, C., Kittilsen, A.: Mapping of work areas on a platform supply vessel: A case study. In: Proceedings of Human Factors and Ship Design Conference. Royal Institution of Naval Architects, London (2011)
4. Lurås, S., Nordby, K.: Field studies informing ships' bridge design at the Ocean Industries Concept Lab. In: Proceedings of Human Factors in Ship Design and Operation. Royal Institution of Naval Architects, London (2014)

The Relationship between Active Heating Power and Temperature of the Fingers in EVA Glove

Yinsheng Tian, Ding Li, and Heqing Liu

School of Biological Science and Medical Engineering,
Beihang University, No.37 XueYuan Road,
HaiDian District, Beijing 100191, China
muser_tt@163.com, ding1971316@buaa.edu.cn

Abstract. The low temperature and low pressure in the space restrict astronauts' operation when they are wearing Extravehicular (EVA) gloves. Active heating is an effective method for maintaining temperature stability in the gloves; however, research findings in the field are scarce at present. In the study, we designed a structure of active heating in EVA glove, and explore a heating scheme for the structure. We designed a system including environment simulation device, hand simulation device as well as temperature measuring equipment to simulate the parameters of space surroundings and human hands. A electric heating structure was fixed in the limiting layer of the gloves. This structure could maintain the surface temperature of hands which was gauged by the sensors. We adjusted the heating power of heating structure, and confirmed 4 Watt was ideal. The other result is the thumb finger needs more power than middle finger.

Keywords: EVA glove, active heating, temperature of fingers.

1   Introduction

Heat loss is a very universal issue when the astronauts are in extravehicular activity (EVA). Heat loss seems to be related to the task and safety. There is an effective solution to compensate the heat loss of the human body, especially the hands, which is called active heating. In our previous studies, we focused on the effect of low temperature on work efficiency of EVA gloves. The result showed that the low temperature could significantly reduce the grip and fatigue of the hands, the number could be more than 50%. The lower the temperature was, the faster body heat lost. Therefore, design a feasible active heating scheme for EVA gloves is necessary. This technology has been applied and proved in US gloves [1], but China is still in initial stage. For different glove structure and pressure, hand heat loss rate of our gloves would be different with the United States. As a result, we should establish a new active heating scheme to study the relationship between the active heating power and the temperature of the fingers, our target is determining the reasonable choices of the power.

C. Stephanidis (Ed.): HCII 2014 Posters, Part I, CCIS 434, pp. 123–128, 2014.
© Springer International Publishing Switzerland 2014

2   Method

2.1   Heating Method

There were two kinds of heating: body produced heat and active heating. We used heating plates to attach on the inner wall of medical rubber hand in order to simulate human body heat production. Inside the hand was filled with heat insulation material so that the heat conduction could not to the internal. Through reference, the average heat dissipation power of human hand is about 4W [2]. We could consider the fingers and the palm skin area were roughly the same; besides heat dissipating capacity of each finger was the average. Therefore, the number is 0.4W.

Other heating plates were fixed in the back side of limiting layer of the fingers in EVA glove. There were two reasons for this design: one was the temperature of back side was lower than the inner, so the back needed more protection. The other reason was the experiment needed subjects to grip low temperature bar, this design could prevent the heating plate damage.

Heating plates had equal length as the fingers, and the rated heating capacity was 1W/cm2, the maximum operating temperature was 125 °C. Glove active heating on each finger was average so that the heating plates were easy to be controlled. Heating systems in the hand and the gloves independent of each other could be adjusted separately.

Target of active heating was to keep the surface temperature of the fingers exceeded 15.6 °C [3]. Previous studies showed that temperature on the tip of the middle finger held on 15.6 °C could be used as the minimum standard of spacesuit ergonomics design. Although human also could endure when the temperature on the tip of the middle finger lower than 10 °C, work efficiency had been a serious decline, as well as the helmet of the space suit would be fogged. Therefore, we would start active heating if the temperature of the fingers dropped to 15.6°C.

2.2   Environment Simulation

Generally, the heat transmission is realized from the following four ways: convection, conduction, radiation and sweat evaporation. In the space heat transmission is much simpler. The main heat exchange from EVA gloves to the space is radiation. We designed a vacuum tank to simulate the vacuum environment and temperature in the space. As shown in Figure 1, liquid nitrogen flowed into the tank from liquid nitrogen inlet, and vaporized into low temperature nitrogen in circulating pipeline. The low temperature nitrogen would change the environmental temperature in the tank. Residual low temperature gas flowed out from liquid nitrogen outlet. We used vacuum pump to empty the air in the tank in order to simulate the vacuum environment, the pump was connected to air outlet. There were two interfaces on the top of the tank: one connected to vacuum gauge to measure the pressure in the tank; the other one is data interface, the sensors used to test the temperature of the tank and glove transferred the data from this interface. The glove was in the tank and the pressure between inside and outside of the glove was the same; it is different from the EVA glove standard pressure (39.6KPa) because the pressure is not the target of the study, and this design was safer.

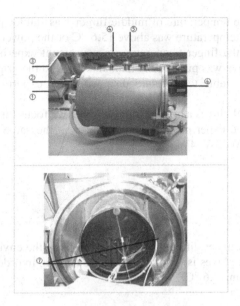

Fig. 1. Vacuum tank (Where, 1 Liquid nitrogen inlet; 2 Air outlet; 3 Liquid nitrogen outlet;4 Interface for vacuum gauge; 5 Data interface; 6 Door; 7 Circulating pipeline)

2.3   Measurement

Two kinds of data were needed to measure in the study. One class was used to adjust the experiment parameters, such as temperature and pressure in the tank, as well as the heating plate temperature. Another kind was used for data analysis, such as hand skin temperature. Pressure was measured by vacuum gauge, temperature data was acquainted by sensors of real-time monitoring. Based on data acquisition channels restriction, we only selected 15 representative temperature measuring points.

Although each finger had one heating plate, the heating power is basically the same because the resistances were connected in parallel. Therefore, we could estimate each heating plate temperature by measuring only one of the heating plates. According to the pre-experimental results, we selected middle finger. The measurement points should be hung in the test tank in order to ensure the data was the environmental temperature, not the temperature of tank surface.

2.4   Procedures

The experiment has three main goals:

1. Find a pressure suitable for the formal test;
2. Simulate a vacuum environment, and observed temperature of fingers dropping without active heating.
3. Ensure an active heating scheme, and gives its heating effect.

At the beginning of the experiment, giving the fingers active heating power was 2W in a specified pressure. If the temperature of the finger was more than 15.6 °C when the inner surface temperature of middle finger was stable, The experiment only stopped in two cases: temperature was above 15.6 °C or the power reached to 4.5W.

The part two was the finger temperature measurement experiment without active heating. The EVA glove was put into the tank and fitted to the grip bar before the test. We could record the stable temperature data when the experiment was performed 1-1.5 hours.

The third part tested gloves active heating scheme, we focus on two fingers: middle finger and thumb. The experimental conditions t was the same as part two, active heating power were 2W, 3W, 4W.

3   Results

3.1   Experiment 1

As shown in Figure 2, under different pressure conditions(the environmental temperature is -130 °C), EVA gloves is supplied the active heating in order to keep the finger temperature higher than 15.6 °C.

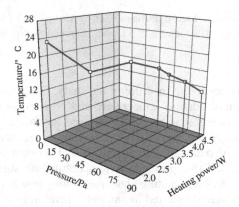

Fig. 2. Finger temperature under different pressure (active heating)

3.2   Experiment 2

As shown in Figure 3, environmental pressure drops to 0.1Pa, each layer temperature of middle finger has different temperature curve. It is shown that the environmental temperature drops to -120 degree 50 minutes later. Because of the heat insulation ability of EVA gloves, hand surface temperature is maintained at 20°C. With the extension of time, hand temperature is declining. After about 75 minutes, the temperature lower than 15.6 °C. The result is thermal protection of EVA gloves may not enough to sustain the normal manual operation (5-8 hours) in space, Active heating is necessary.

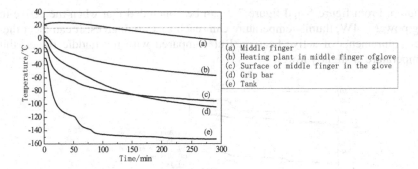

Fig. 3. Each layer temperature of middle finger under low environmental temperature (0.1 Pa)

3.3   Experiment 3

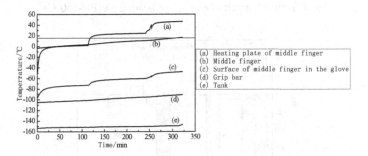

Fig. 4. Middle finger temperature in active heating (0.1Pa,-150°C)

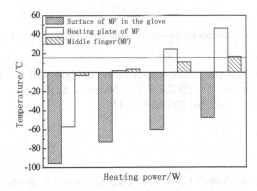

Fig. 5. Comparison of middle finger temperature in different heating power (0.1Pa, -150°C)

1. Figure 4 and 5 can be shown that the middle finger temperature reach to 15.6 degrees only when the heating power is 4W, although the temperature rise with the increase of heating power. The power of heat is higher than optimum value (2.5W) because the heating is average. This result is consistent with theoretical calculation [2].

2. Thumb: From figure 6 and figure 7 it can be concluded that when the active heating power is 4W, thumb temperature can reach to 15.6 degrees. It can meet the basic requirements of active heating. But compared with the middle finger, thumb temperature is slightly lower.

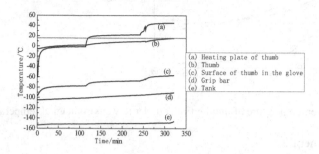

Fig. 6. Thumb temperature in active heating (0.1Pa,-150°C)

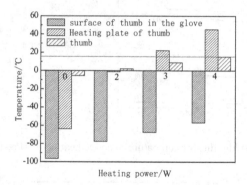

Fig. 7. Comparison of thumb temperature in different heating power (0.1Pa, -150°C)

Acknowledgements. This project is supported by the National Natural Science Foundation of China, Grant No. 51175021 & the National Science and Technology Support Program of China, Grant No.2014BAK01B05.

References

1. Graziosi, D., Stein, J.: Phase VI Advanced EVA Glove Development and Certification for the International Space Station. Johnson Space Center, NASA (2001)
2. Li, D.: Study on Thermal Protection of EVA Glove. Beihang University, Beijing (2000) (in Chinese)
3. Li, D., Longzhu, H., Chunxin, Y., et al.: Study on Effects of Active-heating-system for EVA Gloves on Working Performance. Space Medicine & Medical Eengineering 18(1), 47–51 (2005) (in Chinese)

Study on "Intuitive Semantics" of Orient Traditional Creation Wisdom Contained in the Design of Modern Mechanical Products

Wangqun Xiao, Jianxin Cheng, Junnan Ye, and Le Xi

School of Art, Design and Media, East China University of Science and Technology
M. BOX 286, NO. 130, Meilong Road, Xuhui District, Shanghai 200237, China
xiaoyao-1916@163.com, cjx.master@gmail.com,
yejunnan971108@qq.com, xilutar@sina.com

Abstract. The traditional mechanical products have been considered to be structured products all the time. The concept of "priority to function" dominates the design philosophy in the long term, but it unilaterally stresses "technique" and "performance" of the "product" but overlooks "emotion" and "care" of "human", thus making the relationship between "human" and "product" "disharmonious" and violating the original intention of human for creation. Then this requires us to think deeply. In the aspect of things perception in China, starting from characters invention by Cang Jie, there were cultural heritages being good at abstraction including "intuitive realization", "sudden enlightenment" and "empathizing and understanding" since ancient times. The six methods of character creation reflect the "intuitive semantics" or the information referred to as "intuitive semiology" formed very early in Chinese culture. The theoretical achievements of domestic and overseas mechanical product design are presented and analyzed firstly in this essay; and then starting with the study on Chinese traditional creation culture and practical activities, the orient traditional creation wisdom that contains substantial thinking and elements related to "intuitive semantics" will be researched; finally, the "intuitive semantics" will be infused into design of modern mechanical products to think and study and survey the relationship between human emotion and technical principles, thus perfecting the innovation theory of modern mechanical product design.

Keywords: product design, emotional experience, intuitive semantics.

1 Introduction

The traditional mechanical products have been considered to be structured products all the time. The concept of "priority to function" dominates the design philosophy in the long term, but it unilaterally stresses "technique" and "performance" of the "product" and overlooks "emotion" and "care" of "human", resulting in fatigue and boredom of laborers working for long time and "disharmony" of relationship of "human" and "product" as well as violation of initial intention of human for creation. Then this requires us to think deeply and the orient traditional creation wisdom will be a bright lamp to indicate the right directions.

C. Stephanidis (Ed.): HCII 2014 Posters, Part I, CCIS 434, pp. 129–133, 2014.
© Springer International Publishing Switzerland 2014

2   Analysis on Research Status of Modern Mechanical Product Design

With rapid development of research on "technical character of product" made by human, the natural science researches with subjects of engineering and science progress significantly and the researches achievements about modern mechanical product design throughout the world are too numerous to mention one by one. For example, Lu Yongxiang, the academician of CAS and CAE, pointed out in his essay-Guide of Development of Chinese Mechanical Engineering Technology and Industry Innovation that "Technology Roadmap of China Mechanical Engineering has been published and made prediction and outlook about development of mechanical engineering technology in the next 20 years" (Lu, 2011).

The researches on "product spirituality" are significantly less than those on "technical character of product" in the aspect of modern mechanical product design around the world. The reasons contain various aspects. Profess Cheng Jianxin, a Chinese scholar pointed out in his keynote speech-Oriental Culture and Modern Design Ethics that "the technical development of western developed countries is so rapid that human social ethics may not follow, thus causing serious 'negative control of technology'. Some other scholars also conducted the researches from different aspects, for instance, Aesthetics and Modern Mechanical Product Design (Yang, Jin, Wu,2000), Study on Industrial Design of Mechanical Product Based on Using Philosophy (Jiang, Xu, 2011), Mechanical Product Design Based on Ergonomics (He, Zhang, 2010), Study on Affective Component in Appearance Design of Mechanical Product (Wei, Zhong, 2011), the Application of Color Perception on the Humanization Design of Mechanical Products (Cao, Cheng, 2007) etc.

3   "Intuitive Semantics" of Orient Traditional Creation Wisdom

Five thousand-year Chinese culture runs a long history and is extensive and profound. No matter the Book of Changes, Book of Diverse Crafts, Exploitation of the Works of Nature, Ying-tsao fah-shih, Shan Hai Ching or armillary sphere, Houfeng Seismograph, southward pointing cart, mileage drum wagon and gold and silver sachet, they are all sparkling with orient traditional creation wisdom and show the great creation thinking in the early stage of China as well as deliver the information about "intuitive semantics" of Chinese creation.

In the aspect of things perception in China, starting from character creation by Cang Jie, there were cultural heritages being good at abstraction including "intuitive realization", "sudden enlightenment" and "empathizing and understanding" since ancient times. As for six methods of character creation that include self-explanatory characters, pictographic characters, echoism characters, associative characters, synonymous characters and loan characters, "self-explanatory character" stands in the breach. The other methods such as "pictographic characters", "echoism characters" and "associative characters" reflect the "intuitive semantics" which is also referred to as "intuitive semiology" formed early. For pictographic character formation, Xu Shen explicated as: "the pictographic character is created through drawing the outline or features of certain objects." (Xu, 1963)

Zhang Heng, a Chinese scientist in the Eastern Han Dynasty, created the Houfeng Seismograph in A.D.132——the first seismoscope in the world but failed to be handed down between A.D.132~418. Fan Ye used 196 characters to record in his Book of the Later Han • Zhang Heng to keep it handed down (Feng, Wu, 2003). Upon studies, we found out that the decorations on the seismograph applied by Zhang Heng are mainly pictorial symbols and symbol marks, both of which contain the implications about "intuitive realization" including: superficial functional significance, inner symbolic meaning and deep concept of natural law. These contents visually enrich the connotations of creation, strengthen the poetic imagery beauty of ware and show the understanding and application of "intuitive symbol" of our ancestors (Figure 1).

Fig. 1. Restoration model of new bronze seismograph

According to the archaeological materials open to public currently, 13 gold and silver sachets of Tang Dynasty have been excavated so far (Duan, 2011). The artistic modeling of gold and silver wares of Tang Dynasty are distinctive. The close attention are not only paid to the change of external contour but also paid to the delicacy and smooth(Zhu, 2010). After reading Six Code in Tang Dynasty and other classical documents, we found out that gold and silver sachets of Tang Dynasty not only are integrated with functionality, aesthetic character, decorative nature, interestingness and emotionality but also possess the "universality" or "general character" that enables the user to know the function and usage at a glance. It is solid evidence that the appreciation and understanding of "intuitive realization" are contained in Chinese traditional creation ideology.

4   Oriented and Western Division History

The first industrial revolution of UK starting in the 1860s brought human society into the industrial age, resulting in separation of technology and art and split between substance function and moral function which are shown in Modern Times of Chaplin or reflected in the current society where the technology are highly developed, but the human is more lonely, doleful and despondent.

Among Chinese traditional creation ideology, the sages in the ancient times advocated adaption to the law of natural development and to be kind to all things on earth, such as the ecological philosophical view put forward by Lao Tse and design idea of "making methods of human to meet natural law" proposed by Chuang Tse. However, the development of China was also limited. Firstly, mystique was excessive, "capability of comprehension" was highly praised and the feudal thoughts toward heritage of creation culture and technique, resulting in failure in handing some heritages down to next generation. Secondly, thousands of years development of civilization in China leaded to the emperors and officials unconsciously cultivating a kind of superiority feeling toward the historic culture, great power psychology and self-seclusion, giving rise to lag in modern science and technology, thus making Chinese excellent traditional creation thought to be deserted and forming division history of Chinese creation ideology.

5 Research on "Intuitive Semantics" of Modern Mechanical Product Design

Although almost 100 years has passed since appearance of Moder Times, the mechanical products in all plants around the world are still running in cycles and they are simply equipped with more advanced technology and higher level of automation and informatization. People had tried to change the "relationship between mechanical products and human" from the status of "human being enslaved by product" formed in the industrial age, but looking around, the mechanical products that "uphold technology" and "give priority to function" but ignore human "emotions" and "care" can be seen everywhere. Thousands of years of Chinese traditional creation activities have been taking family production system as the structure and self-sufficient cottage craft and workshops formed by specialized households for the purpose of making a living as the form for long time. The creators virtually stressed the emotionalization during product creation and a kind of imperceptible harmonious atmosphere that was naturally revealed was embodied in the works.

It is not hard to find out that infuse Chinese traditional creation ideology into design of modern mechanical products and apply "intuitive semantics" as the theoretical guidance for design and practice so as to inherit the inner thoughts including "experience design", "interactive design", "emotional design" and "general design" contained in Chinese traditional creation activities and effectively find out a solution to the inharmony of "mechanical products" and "human" caused by mechanized mass production dominated by high technology.

6 Conclusion

The unilateral development of modern design philosophy taking western design concepts as subject in today's world cannot properly solve the harmonious relationship between "human" and "product" as well as "human" and "nature", especially in the field of mechanical product design. Therefore we have reasons to search the advanced creation ideology made by our ancestors and gain the theory of "intuitive semantics" for guiding modern design practice through conducting scientific summary about information about "intuitive realization" or elements of "intuitive conformity" and learning western science ideology and technology so as to form unique orient design ideology, enabling China to catch up with or even lead the global design current.

References

1. Lu, Y.: Guide of Development of Chinese Mechanical Engineering Technology and Industry Innovation. Science & Technology Review 29(25), 8 (2011)
2. Yang, J., Jin, M., Wu, Y.: Aesthetics and Modern Mechanical Product Design. Shanxi Machinery 109(4), 41–42 (2000)
3. Jiang, M., Xu, T.: Study on Industrial Design of Mechanical Product Based on Using Philosophy. Machinery Design and Manufactur 5(5), 266–268 (2011)
4. He, C., Zhang, L.: Mechanical Product Design Based on Ergonomics. Mechanical Management and Developmen 25(2), 38–40 (2010)
5. Wei, Y., Zhong, L.: Study on Affective Component in Appearance Design of Mechanical Product. Mechinery Design 28(12), 6–8 (2011)
6. Cao, J., Cheng, J.: The Application of Color Perception on the Humanization Design of Mechanical Products. Machinery Design and Manufacture 4(4), 163–164 (2007)
7. Xu, S., Shuo, W.J.Z.: Zhonghua Book Company, Beijing (1963)
8. Feng, R., Wu, Y.: Rehabilitation Study on Principle of Houfeng Seismograph Made by Zhangheng. China Earthquake 19(4), 358–376 (2003)
9. Duan, B.: Research on Gold and Silver Sachet of Tang Dynasty. Journal of the Central University for Nationalities (Humane and Social Sciences Edition) 38(197), 58–63 (2011)
10. Zhu, H.: Chinese Arts and Crafts History. Hunan University Press, Changsha (2010)

Research on Behavioral Semanteme Form Based on Early Education Products

Ying Cao, Tian Lei, and Xun Wu

HuangZhong University of Science and Technology, P.R. China
{331393782,12739731}@qq.com, caoying@mail.hust.edu.cn

Abstract. Currently, there are a variety of the early education products in the market. A strict approach for classification of these products, however, is generally absent. But even so, any kind of the early education products are indeed built on the same principle that almost all devisers are making attempts to attract users for participation and experience from the three aspects--the visual sense, the auditory sense and the sense of touch. The way for experience is also limited to some certain operant behavior including "press", "twist" and "thump". Due to the fact that young children are the targeted users for the early education products and because of their unique characteristics—the so-called "realistic feature" embedded into their intelligence, their behavioral norms are conspicuously distinguishing from adults. It is therefore that the development of related products should not be conducted in the logical way of adults. It is proper to cultivate the cognitive ability, judgment and logics of infants in a simplistic and pleasant context and circumstances.

This research will delve into behavior from a perspective of Semantics by initiating a study on "Form", which is the carrier for products' semanteme. Experimental data of a series of early education products will be reviewed for reference and for making contributions to the quantitative research on the influence of forms on behavior. Three key concepts, which are the "form", the "semanteme" and the "behavior", will also be effectively integrated into and contributing to the two new concepts, the "Behavioral Semanteme Form" and the "Semanteme Form Model". The research aims at providing the entire and detailed explanations to the formation, structural characteristics and category of the semanteme by adopting the operable and controllable approaches.

Keywords: Product semantics States; Behavioral semantics States; user experience.

1 The Present Situation of Market for Devise of Early Education Products

Product Semantics refers to a discipline which focuses on the symbolic features of the forms of artificial products. The forms of products indeed reflect devisor's philosophy and ideas, as well as the functions and appearance of the products. The designing of the form is conducted through the entire process of devise.

C. Stephanidis (Ed.): HCII 2014 Posters, Part I, CCIS 434, pp. 134–138, 2014.
© Springer International Publishing Switzerland 2014

As the increasing attentions and investments being directed on the early childhood education, a variety of early education products spring up in the market, some of which are devised based on the adults' logics and from adults 'perspective rather than in compliance with the children's behavioral semantemes and therefore fail to draw the interests from them. Conversely, these kinds of products will have a counterproductive function in causing children's resentments and make them abandon the use of products, which makes the early education meaningless. This research is concerned about how to understand the features of behavioral forms which exactly results in children's basic operation by an accurate and controllable approach. This research is also, based on these features, pursuing the improvement of the user experience of the early education products and the avoidance of the misoperation and delay of the operation in order to guarantee the safety of children during their experience.

2   Consistency of Behavioral Semanteme Form and Semanteme Form Model, and Its Influence on Early Education Products

In an attempt to depict more clearly and accurately the forms of products which are appropriate for children's use, this article integrates three concepts, the Forms, the Semanteme and the Behavior, into two new ones, the "Behavioral Semanteme Form" and the "Semanteme Form Model", aiming at offering explanations to the formation, structural features and category of the semanteme by adopting a controllable and operable approach. The ultimate purpose is to contribute the feasible and operable devising guidance and thoughts the early education products.

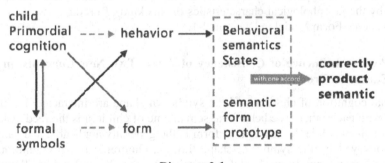

Diagram 2-1

2.1   Behavioral Semanteme Form

Behavioral Semanteme Form refers to the semanteme reflected by people's behavior to pursue their own goals. For instance, when a person is thumping the protuberance, he basically pursues the purpose to flatten that protuberance. Due to the fact that early education products are targeting at the children whose intelligence is under development and devised to direct children to have a positive and correct reactions towards subjects and events, the functions, structures and forms should be devised in a way that is mostly consistent with children's behavioral semanteme.

In order to explain Behavioral Semanteme Form in details, the processes regarding children's behavioral semanteme form have been decomposed. (See Diagram 2-1) The targeted users of the early education products are mostly children who have not yet received education. Characteristically, this group of children possesses the incomplete understandings on subjects surrounding them and has the under-constructing mental model. Their innate characters, instinctive reaction and innate conditioned reflex mainly constitute their cognition towards subjects, which can be highly summarized into the initial cognition demonstrated in the diagram. Children's initial cognition will generate feedbacks to the given symbolic forms, which includes behavior of "touching", "thumping", "twisting" and "pinching". In another word, the semanteme demonstrated by this behavior depicts the behavior's purpose, which is the Behavioral Semanteme Form generated during the cognition.

2.2   Semanteme Form Model

Single symbolic form does not have the effect to convey semanteme form due to the limitations that semanteme form is the general, applicable and subjective feeling obtained after cognition. Meanwhile, symbols of the shape will produce the morphological characteristics after the subjective cognition. The morphological characteristics of early education products are the symbols of shape for children's initial cognition. Human beings will define the morphological characteristics by the mental models which come from the past experience. For instance, if the symbol of the annulus perceived in the past is curved and rounded, then human beings tend to believe this kind of shapes to be rounded when they see the quasi-annulus next time. Regarding the forms of early education products which target at children with incomplete mental models, the initial cognition of children on the forms is exactly the semanteme expressed by the morphological characteristics of this kind of products, which refers to the Semanteme Form Model in Diagram 2-1.

2.3   Positive Influence of Consistency of These Two New Concepts on Early Education Products

The initial cognition of children and the symbol of shape are interacted and interdependent with each other. The behavioral semanteme of children is the feedback of the symbol of shape while the semanteme form is the generally applicable and subjective image conveyed by the symbol of shape through children's initial cognition. Only when the Semanteme Form Model is consistent with the Behavioral Semanteme Form, the morphological characteristics of the products can be appropriate to children's initial cognition and the products being devised can be most effective.

3   Morphological Experiment Based on Initial Cognition of Preschool Children

3.1   Planning and Methodology of the Experiment

In order to figure out what symbols of shape are consistent to forms of children's initial cognition, 12 basic symbols of shape have been abstracted from some early education products as shown in Diagram 3-1, 3-2 and 3-3. Four forms in Diagram 3-1 are marked as A1, A2, A3 and A4 and the same for the latter two models. Meanwhile, each behavior and conduct produced during children's interaction with the early education products will be recorded and classified into three major categories, the "Press", the "Thump" and the "Twist". The "Press" category was matched with four basic symbols of shape in Diagram 3-1. Children pressed the model in this diagram as they pleased without instructions from adults. Through these four typical symbols of shape, the ones to which children are most and least sensitive will be figured out. The remaining two models can be deducted by analogy. The "Thump" models in Diagram 3-2, and the "Twist" models in Diagram 3-3 are tested.

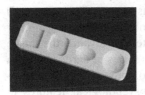

| Diagram 3-1 | Diagram 3-2 | Diagram 3-3 |

3.2 Experimental Results and Data

52 children at age between 2 and 5 have been randomly selected in a kindergarten in Wuhan, of whom 27 are girls and 25 are boys. They have conducted the above experiment respectively. In addition, 52 parents were also selected randomly. The following is the result.

The result demonstrates that in the "Press" category, A4 (Square Form) caused children's impulsive to press and touch while A2 was the one that least children touched or pressed. In the "Thump" category, B4 (Square Form) was thumped for the most times while least children thumped B1. In Experiment C, C2 and C3 (two middle buttons) attracted the almost equal twists while C4 was seldom twisted.

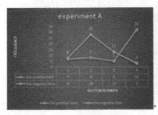

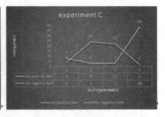

| Diagram 3-4 | Diagram 3-5 | Diagram 3-6 |

4 Conclusion

The experiment suggested that children's initial cognition under an incomplete mental model is different from the one of adults. The style of children's initial cognition is approaching a simplistic, linear, flat and original symbol of shape. The square form will offer a sense of security to children when they are interacting with the model. The quasi-ball square form changes at an uncontrollable and complicated way and is less stable than the morphological change of the square form, which is beyond children's understanding. Therefore, the devisors should consider designing the linear and simple form, as well as the adoption of stable morphological change during the devise. In Experiment C, children had the strongest impulsive to twist the obviously sunken form despite that adults would mostly choose buttons like C1. This suggested that the mental model of adults regarded some forms resembling the gas switch, air fan switch as the basis to obtain experience while children tended towards the innate cognition on complete forms. Therefore, when designing the forms of early education products, the designers may consider using another form to compensate the incomplete forms, maximally utilizing and guiding children's psychological features to compensate the incomplete forms.

Acknowledgements. The central university special funding for basic scientific research business expenses, project approval NO.2013QN013

Interacting with Information and Knowledge

MOSAIC: A Multi-modal Surveillance System
to Enhance Situation Awareness and Decision Making

Richard Adderley[1], Atta Badii[2], Rubén Heras Evangelio[3], Matteo Raffaelli[4],
Patrick Seidler[1], and Marco Tiemann[2]

[1] A E Solutions (BI) Ltd., Badsey, UK
{rickadderley,patrickseidler}@a-esolutions.com
[2] University of Reading, Reading, UK
{atta.badii,m.tiemann}@reading.ac.uk
[3] Technische Universität Berlin, Berlin, Germany
heras@mailbox.tu-berlin.de
[4] Synthema srl, Pisa, Italy
matteo.raffaelli@synthema.it

Abstract. With increasing complexity of systems under surveillance, demand grows for automated video-based surveillance systems which are able to support end users in making sense of situational context from the amount of available data and incoming data streams. Traditionally, those systems have been developed based on techniques derived from the fields of image processing and pattern recognition. This paper presents MOSAIC (Multi-Modal Situation Assessment and Analytics Platform), a system which aims at exploiting multi-modal data analysis comprising advanced tools for video analytics, text mining, social network analysis, and decision support in order to provide from a richer context an understanding of behaviour of the system under surveillance and to support police personnel in decision making processes.

Keywords: Multi-modal data mining, social and criminal network analysis; video analytics; semantic interoperability; decision support system.

1 Introduction

As we attempt to monitor increasingly complex behaviour in larger systems, understanding this behaviour from the amount of available data becomes less manageable for the human analyst, possibly leaving a knowledge gap that hinders effective decision-making. One of the key problems for end users of surveillance systems is to 'connect the dots' or to quickly find the few pieces of relevant information from disparate systems and data to establish a greater picture of current situational context. Available information may be structured or un-structured, quantitative and qualitative, of multiple formats, e.g. text, documents, images, videos, or streaming data such as social media or news feeds; be from multiple sources, be of varying quality and reliability, sparse, streaming, and represent rapidly changing situations. Having greater insight would enable officials such as law enforcers, policy makers, and decision

C. Stephanidis (Ed.): HCII 2014 Posters, Part I, CCIS 434, pp. 141–146, 2014.
© Springer International Publishing Switzerland 2014

makers, to deal more effectively with uncertainty, provide timely warning of threats, and to support operational activity by analysing crime.

MOSAIC, a Collaborative Project within the 7th Framework Programme's Research Theme, sets out to improve targeted surveillance by combining data intelligence and advanced video analytics to provide a decision support system for responsible authorities in complex situational contexts. The MOSAIC system enables end users such as police personnel including analysts, administrators, CCTV operators, and staff supervisors to localise and visualise real-time and recorded CCTV video and alerts generated by smart cameras and video analytics nodes to initiate and support police investigations. Providing data mining, text mining and social network analysis, the system also enables the processing, analysis and visualisation of criminal structures and behaviour under investigation. Video analytics and data intelligence tools are being integrated within a unified scalable and modular framework.

The MOSAIC system provides a high-level of usability and effective information display to improve situational awareness and enable faster decision making. Intelligent decision support functionalities support end users in assessing situations and in improving surveillance activities in order to better monitor and respond to identified threats.

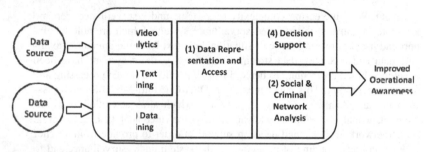

Fig. 1. Overview of the MOSAIC analytical framework with four subsystems: (1) Data representation subsystem; (2) Social & Criminal network analysis subsystem with (2a) Text- & (2b) Data Mining components; (3) Video analytics subsystem; (4) Decision support subsystem.

2   Semantic Interoperability and Data Representation

In order to identify previously unknown connections between disparate data from the enriched operational and analytical picture, the data to be integrated must be queryable using a single query language and return a unified data representation in response to queries. The available information must become semantically interoperable.

Semantic interoperability for MOSAIC involves three main aspects: first, the definition of a semantic domain model, a "world model" which can represent the available information in a way that preserves its meaning; second, the development of a system that organises the available information using the developed model and that also makes it accessible in a unified way; third, the connection to the individual data sources (and to any further "consumers" of the data). The world model for MOSAIC is being defined as an OWL-Lite ontology model [1]. This model represents actors, objects, actions and other relevant information types as subject-predicate-object triples that establish object types, their properties and their relations to other object types. Newly arriving data is analysed for consistency and converted into suitable OWL-Lite instances that are added to the MOSAIC data model stored in the data store. A semantic triple store based on Apache Jena manages the processes of creating, reading, updating and deleting instance data within the semantic representation model. Data in the MOSAIC data model can be queried and updated using the SPARQL query language [2]. The Apache Jena data store implementation has been extended with additional MOSAIC-specific features such as the ability to subscribe with queries in order to allow users to receive notifications when new relevant data has arrived.

The described data representation and data store system allows analysts and operators to query a single data representation for information across information provided by all of the data sources described. The ontology used in MOSAIC extends this by allowing users to make use of the knowledge encoded in the ontology while querying it – a trivial example for this is the ability to query for persons involved in violent crimes without having to enumerate the individual identifiers for violent crimes as might be necessary in a conventional SQL database.

3   Social and Criminal Network Analytics Subsystem

The MOSAIC system will offer data mining support that has been tailored to analysts' need for immediately actionable operational intelligence inside the intelligence cycle. At the lower level, the Entity Resolution Component based on the Apache Lucene framework resolves entities over specified personal attributes, thus alleviating problems regarding poor data quality and supporting identification of all relevant entity data that might not be easily identifiable through global unique identifiers.

Further, following [3], we have formalised analysis tasks using CRISP-DM [4] in conjunction with the intelligence cycle to structure the set of typical analyst tasks. A MOSAIC Data Mining Workbench has been created to assist analysts in manipulating data without the hassle of having to access data from disparate systems. Using the workbench, analysts can search, link, explore, model and visualise data through a process of interconnected nodes; previous knowledge on querying languages is not required. Specific support is provided for: (1) Offender mining and automatic assignment of domain based priorities; (2) Identification of crime series and mapping of known offenders to unsolved crimes; (3) Identification of criminal roles and profiles. Resulting processes are reusable, can be re-run any time taking into account new data, thus accommodate for various possible end user requirements.

In MOSAIC text mining is applied through a pipeline of linguistic and semantic processors (morpho-syntactic tagging, multiword detection and word-sense disambiguation) that share a common knowledge. A domain specific knowledge base with crime patterns, abbreviations and technical terms extracted mainly from anonymised police reports is created. To support analysis tasks specifically, extensive effort is being spent on the recognition of named-entities: dates, addresses, person names, locations, license plate numbers, brands, web entities, bank accounts and phone numbers. Entities are reduced to their semantic roles (agent, predicate, theme, recipient, time and location, i.e. who does what to whom, how, when and where), identified as a result of the dependency parsing. The linguistic processor is then able to extract all kinds of relationships between the entities mentioned above. Entity relationships are visualised in user-friendly network graphs (see Figure 2(b)).

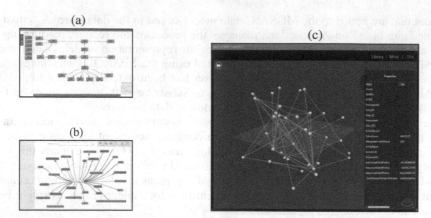

Fig. 2. (a) Data Mining Workbench; (b) Text Mining – Entity Network Visualisation (c) 3D Criminal Network Visualisation and Analysis Tool

Social network analysis specifically is believed to be key in leveraging the operational gap between intelligence analysis and the operational side of businesses [5]. A 3D criminal network visualisation and analysis tool (see Figure 2 (c)) enables the user to conduct Social Network Analysis modified for its application on criminal networks from data accumulated through the data and text mining components, facilitated by the semantically enabled data representation.

4   Video Analytics Subsystem

The video analytics subsystem consists of a number of Networked Video Analytics (NVA) components used to detect events of interest in CCTV footage. Functionalities include visual analytics at low-level such as the detection of change [6] or the computation of optical flow between consecutive video frames [7], at mid-level such as people tracking [8] (also across multiple cameras), and at high level such as crowd behaviour analysis [9], multi-movement identification, automatic detection of human activity [10], mugging detection, etc. The video analytics subsystem is defined as a set of modular NVAs that provide ONVIF [11] metadata in form of events and/or scene descriptions. In this way, mid- and high-level NVAs can use the information gathered by lower levels of analysis and provide higher level semantics (see Figure 3(a)). Combined information provided by the NVAs is collected by the decision support and control sub-system and displayed by means of 3D maps (see Figure 3(b)). This allows for the representation of the gathered information at different levels of abstraction. Furthermore, feedback information of the users can be sent to the NVAs over web services. Following [12], the video analytics sub-system consists of four classes of devices: (1) Network Video Transmitter (NVT) to provide video streams; (2) Network Video Analytics (NVA) for video, audio or metadata analysis; (3) Network Video Display (NVD) for representation of media stream and the gathered information to human operators; (4) Network Video Storage (NVS) for recording streamed video and associated metadata. This architecture provides the common base for a fully interoperable network comprised of products from different network vendors based on Web Services using open and independent standards.

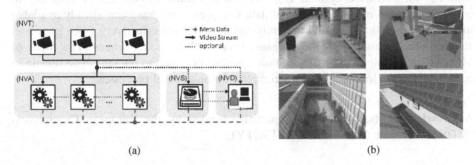

(a)   (b)

Fig. 3. (a) ONVIF Network (b) 3D representation of information provided by video analytics. Left: input video. Right: 3D representation

5   Decision Support Subsystem

Decision support in MOSAIC is concerned with the operational support of both intelligence analysts and monitoring systems operators given an environment that is characterised by increasing complexity. Rule-based decision support engines provide configurable support to operators using the MOSAIC system. MOSAIC includes both a high-speed near-real-time rule processing mechanism to provide timely rule processing, and a rule engine that performs complex analyses using the data store's semantic data representation and an advanced rule engine with complex event processing capabilities. Latter can monitor complex events that may be hard to spot by human operators, but that can be defined as sets or sequences of events that taken together either lead to new information or should trigger a specific (re-)action [13].

At the same time, MOSAIC focuses on representing data in context, be it through the presentation of video analytics and event data on a locations' 3D visualisation or the visualisation of relations between relevant actors in an investigation integrating domain priorities and thus producing directly actionable intelligence.

Finally, MOSAIC focuses on empowering users to make better informed decisions. A limited range of direct actions is available through the system, specifically to store information deduced from available data, communicate information to relevant actors and guide further information gathering in particular in the video analytics domain by reorienting cameras and selecting video analytics algorithms based information provided by decision support system components. Additionally, intelligence analysts can simulate intervention strategies based on social network topological measures and domain based priorities for input into operational decision making processes.

6   Conclusions

This paper shows the main building blocks and techniques used in order to realise the vision of the MOSAIC system. Together, the integrated system components aim to empower users to make better use of data that previously has been already available to them but could not be used efficiently and thus also not effectively given personnel and resource pressures affecting organisations such as police forces. The focus of MOSAIC is on improving the operational picture provided to humans, who remain in control and in the loop rather than a complete automation of processes.

Acknowledgments. This work is partially funded by the European Commission (MOSAIC Project, 261776 FP7-SECURITY).

References

1. Horrocks, I.: From SHIQ and RDF to OWL: the making of a web ontology language. Web Semantics: Science Services, and Agents on the World Wide Web 1 (2003)
2. Perez, J., Arenas, M., Gutierrez, C.: Semantics and complexity of SPARQL. ACM Transactions on Database Systems 34(3) (2009)
3. Adderley, R.: Exploring the Differences Between the Cross Industry Process for Data Mining and the National Intelligence Model Using a Self Organising Map Case study. In: Business Intelligence and Performance Management, pp. 91–105. Springer (2013)
4. Shearer, C.: The CRISP-DM model: the new blueprint for data mining. Journal of Data Warehousing 5, 13–22 (2000)
5. Seidler, P., Adderley, R.: Criminal network analysis inside law enforcement agencies – a data mining system approach under the National Intelligence Model. International Journal of Police Science & Management 15(4), 323–337 (2013)
6. Evangelio, R.H., Paetzold, M., Keller, I., Sikora, T.: Adaptively Splitted GMM with Feedback Improvement for the Task of Background Subtraction. Accepted for Publication in: IEEE Transactions on Information Forensics and Security (2014)
7. Senst, T., Geistert, J., Keller, I., Sikora, T.: Robust Local Optical Flow Estimation using Bilinear Equations for Sparse Motion Estimation. In: 20th IEEE International Conference on Image Processing (2013)
8. Eiselein, V., Arp, D., Paetzold, M., Sikora, T.: Real-time Multi-human Tracking using a Probability Hypothesis Density Filter and Multiple Detectors. In: IEEE AVSS (2012)
9. Kuhn, A., Senst, T., Keller, I., Sikora, T., Theisel, H.: A Lagrangian Framework for Video Analytics. In: IEEE Workshop on Multimedia Signal Processing (2012)
10. Acar, E., Senst, T., Kuhn, A., Keller, I., Theisel, H., Albayrak, S., Sikora, T.: Human Action Recognition using Lagrangian Descriptors. In: IEEE MMSP (2012)
11. Open Network Video Interface Forum, http://www.onvif.org
12. Senst, T., Paetzold, M., Evangelio, R.H., Eiselein, V., Keller, I., Sikora, T.: On building decentralized wide-area surveillance networks based on ONVIF. In: IEEE AVSS (2011)
13. Pan, J.: A flexible ontology reasoning architecture for the semantic web. IEEE Transactions on Knowledge and Data Engineering 19(2), 246–260 (2007)

CAPER: Collaborative Information, Acquisition, Processing, Exploitation and Reporting for the Prevention of Organised Crime

Carlo Aliprandi[1], Juan Arraiza Irujo[2], Montse Cuadros[2],
Sebastian Maier[3], Felipe Melero[4], and Matteo Raffaelli[1]

[1] Synthema srl, Pisa, Italy
{carlo.aliprandi,matteo.raffaelli}@synthema.it
[2] Vicomtech, San Sebastián, Spain
{jarraiza,mcuadros}@vicomtech.org
[3] Fraunhofer IGD, Darmstadt, Germany
sebastian.maier@igd.fraunhofer.de
[4] S21sec, Pamplona, Spain
fmelero@s21sec.com

Abstract. Law Enforcement Agencies (LEAs) are increasingly more reliant on information and communication technologies and affected by a society shaped by the Internet and Social Media. The richness and quantity of information available from open sources, if properly gathered and processed, can provide valuable intelligence and help drawing inference from existing closed source intelligence. This paper presents CAPER, a state-of-the-art platform for the prevention of organised crime, created in cooperation with European LEAs. CAPER supports information sharing and multi-modal analysis of open and closed information sources, mainly based on Natural Language Processing (NLP) and Visual Analytics (VA) technologies.

Keywords: Open Source Intelligence (OSINT), Focused Crawling, Social Web, Natural Language Processing (NLP), Named-Entity Recognition (NER), Semantics, Visual Analytics (VA).

1 Introduction

The revolution in information technology is making open sources more accessible, ubiquitous, and valuable. LEAs have seen open sources grow increasingly in recent years and most valuable intelligence information is often hidden in files which are neither structured nor classified. The process of accessing all these raw data, heterogeneous in terms of source, format and language, and transforming them into information is therefore strongly linked to multi-modal and multi-lingual data analysis and VA technologies with powerful Human Computer Interfaces.

CAPER is an open source intelligence (OSINT) platform that supports collaborative multilingual analysis of unstructured text and audiovisual contents (video, audio,

C. Stephanidis (Ed.): HCII 2014 Posters, Part I, CCIS 434, pp. 147–152, 2014.
© Springer International Publishing Switzerland 2014

speech and images). CAPER is not focused on the development of new technology, but on the fusion and real validation of existing state-of-the-art to solve current bottlenecks faced by LEAs.

Traditionally, text and data mining systems can be seen as specialised systems that convert raw data into a structured database, allowing people to find information. For some domains, text mining applications are well-advanced, for example in the domains of medicine, military and intelligence, and aeronautics [1]. In addition to domain-specific miners, general technology has been developed to detect named-entities [2], co-reference relations, geographical data [3], and time points [4].

Current baseline information systems are either large-scale, robust but shallow (standard information retrieval (IR) systems), or they are small-scale, deep, but ad hoc and maintained by experts in language technologies, not by people in the field (Semantic-Web and ontology-based systems). The table below gives a comparison across different state-of-the-art information systems (ad hoc Semantic Web solutions, WordNet based information systems and traditional information retrieval are compared with CAPER).

Table 1. Comparison of semantic information systems

Key features	Semantic Web	WordNet based	IR	CAPER
Large scale and multiple domains	NO	YES	YES	YES
Deep semantics	YES	NO	NO	YES
Automatic acquisition and indexing	NO	YES/NO	YES	YES
Multi-lingual	NO	YES	YES	YES
Cross-lingual	NO	YES	NO	YES

2   Interoperability and Central Management Application

CAPER is a broad platform that aims at providing LEAs with integrated, advanced modules for capturing, analysing, storing and intelligently displaying large data sets collected from open sources. Both semantic and operational interoperability received specific attention throughout the design and development phases, as CAPER comprises multiple modules, systems and applications, developed globally by numerous partners, varying in expertise and focus.

Semantic interoperability and standardisation of information processing are guaranteed through the adoption of KAF (Knowledge Annotation Format) [5]. There have been numerous attempts to standardise different aspects of natural language processing [6][7][8][9]. KAF is a multi-layered XML format for the semantic annotation of unstructured text documents that has been proven to be suitable as data representation standard and has been extended within CAPER in order to be able to represent also multimedia audiovisual contents.

Operational interoperability is guaranteed through a service-oriented architecture (SOA). All system modules are called by an orchestrator, which executes the data collection and analysis workflow that the end-user has configured on the CAPER

Central Management Application (CMA). The CMA is the end users' workbench, built on a web based collaborative platform, and is one of the two modules developed within CAPER with graphical user interface (the other being the VA application, described in §5). It allows LEA analysts to:

- Configure a Research Line (RL) by setting up a web crawling process.
- Configure the analysis modules. These may require parameterisation depending on the gathered content.
- Control the overall system by monitoring servers, services and processes and applying corrective actions.
- Manage system security (access control, authentication and authorisation).
- Obtain system reports: check the actions performed within the platform.
- Configure alerts among other features.

Fig. 1. CMA - Configuration of the analysis modules

3   Data Acquisition

The CAPER crawler is a multimedia content gathering and storing system, whose main goal is to manage huge collections of data coming from heterogeneous and distributed information sources. Text, audio and video content is retrieved via crawling of the worldwide web in three ways:

- Looking for documents in a given URL until a parametric depth of levels. A focused crawler has been developed. Users can specify key-words when setting up the crawling process. The crawler follows all the links of the web page and rejects the pages that don't contain the specified key-word.
- Looking for a parametric number of documents on the web with a key-words search. Users can specify queries that are redirected to the principal search engines in order to retrieve their results.
- Looking for a parametric number of pages on Facebook with a key-words search. The crawler is able to capture collaboratively created content and to retrieve specific information from Facebook, like users names and IDs, users networks based on "likes", friends networks.

4   Information Analysis

Whilst data are raw the interpretation of those data in a given context produces information. In OSINT solutions data are crawled from publicly available sources and then stored in normalised formats that are ready to be processed by the system. At this stage data are ready to be analysed. The analysis of the data can take many different forms depending on the purpose. The same data can be analysed with different approaches and therefore different information can be obtained out those same data. The results produced by a contextualised (focused) analysis of a set of data produces focused knowledge. In the CAPER project an OSINT platform has been built with the aim of producing valuable knowledge for the prevention of organised crime from publicly available data. For the multimedia data collected CAPER develops automated networks of entities and their relationships, one of the most (if not the most) important objectives of OSINT solutions when fighting crime [10].

When a RL is created on the CMA, end users can select the set of languages they want for the analysis of the text and audio files and they can upload a set of images and/or audio reference files as well. Then every time a new normalised text is sent for analysis the text analysis module will identify the language of that text and redirect it to the appropriate linguistic processor. Additionally, every time a new image and/or audio is crawled and normalised it will be compared against those reference files that the user might have configured when creating the RL by the corresponding analysis modules.

CAPER includes the following six analysis modules: (1) Image analysis, which compares crawled images and video frames with a set of reference images and/or classes of objects (images) and provides a similarity score; (2) Multilingual text analysis, which covers 13 different languages including Arabic, Basque, Catalan, Chinese, English, French, German, Italian, Japanese, Portuguese, Romanian, Russian, and Spanish; and which uses natural language processing techniques to identify entities and relationships among them; (3) Multilingual analysis of audio content so that it can be reduced to its base components for deeper analysis (i.e. text transcripts of voice, speaker recognition and tracking, gender and age identification); (4) Analysis of videos so that they can be reduced to their base components for deeper analysis (i.e. scenes, frames, audio); (5) Integration of semantic-Web technologies and data to improve and relate analysis results (e.g. in the Named Entity Recognition process) and analysis of data coming from Social Media; and (6) Biometric analysis, which includes face recognition and speaker identification.

5   Visual Analytics Application

Large information spaces like the one created by the CAPER Information Analysis module call for a suitable way to explore, drill-down and analyse this information [11]. The CAPER VA Application provides several ways to access the information, including an overview of the different cases currently assigned to the analyst. It also provides an overview of the documents which have been collected for a single case.

Here the analyst can access the contents of a single document, whether it is a text, audio, video or image document with recognised entities being highlighted.

Before the data are presented to the human analyst we create an integrated model of all entities and their relationships as they are in the analysed documents. Relations between entities are either provided by the Information Analysis Module or are created based on co-occurrence by the VA Application. Each relationship is given a certain degree of credibility. For text documents this degree of credibility is currently based on the distance of the entities in the text but could also be based on the actual syntactic or semantic relationship as expressed within the text.

The social graph can be explored using the VA Browser and Editor to manually select those parts of the graph which are of interest to the investigator. Here it is also possible to annotate the graph with custom relations and entities. This is used to enhance the automatic model with knowledge coming from other sources like an interrogation.

Another way to access the information space is the search for specific patterns in the data. For this use-case we provide a visual query interface to define graph patterns which can then be searched within our database. Search results are then visualised using a circular graph layout, showing all entities being part of the specified pattern.

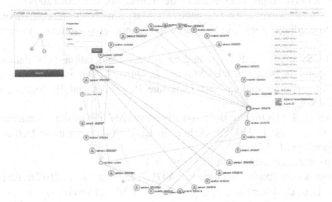

Fig. 2. VA Application – Visualisation of entity relationships

6   Conclusions

This paper has presented CAPER, a state-of-the-art OSINT platform for the prevention of organised crime, created in cooperation with European LEAs. LEAs have special intelligence analysis units to support extended investigations against organised crime. In these units analysts might work for months or even years on specific investigations. Today the intelligence cycle is characterised by manual collection and integration of data. CAPER supports the automatic collection and analysis of unstructured text and audiovisual contents (video, audio, speech and images) and develops automated networks of entities and their relationships. These networks are automatically integrated into LEAs' systems, thus drastically reducing data integration efforts for intelligence analysts.

Acknowledgments. This work is partially funded by the European Commission (CAPER Project, 261712 FP7-SECURITY SEC-2010.1.2-1).

References

1. Grishman, R., Sundheim, B.: Message Understanding Conference - 6: A Brief History. In: Proceedings of the 16th International Conference on Computational Linguistics, Kopenhagen, vol. I, pp. 466–471 (1996)
2. Hearst, M.A.: Untangling Text Data Mining. In: Proceedings of ACL 1999: The 37th Annual Meeting of the Association for Computational Linguistics, College Park, pp. 123–129 (1999)
3. Miller, H.J., Han, J. (eds.): Geographic Data Mining and Knowledge Discovery, 2nd edn., London (2009)
4. Wei, L., Keogh, E.: Semi-Supervised Time Series Classification. In: Proceedings of the 12th ACM SIGKDD International Conference on Knowledge Discovery and Data Mining, New York, pp. 748–753 (2006)
5. Bosma, W., Vossen, P., Soroa, A., Rigau, G., Tesconi, M., Marchetti, A., Aliprandi, C., Monachini, M.: KAF: a generic semantic annotation format. In: 5th International Conference on Generative Approaches to the Lexicon, Pisa, pp. 157–164 (2009)
6. Clément, L., Villemonte de La Clergerie, É.: Maf: a morphosyntactic annotation framework. In: Proceedings of the 2nd Language & Technology Conference, Poznań, pp. 90–94 (2005)
7. Declerck, T.: Synaf: Towards a standard for syntactic annotation. In: Calzolari, N., Choukri, K., Gangemi, A., Maegaard, B., Mariani, J., Odijk, J., Tapias, D. (eds.) Proceedings of the 5th Conference on International Language Resources and Evaluation, Genova, pp. 229–233 (2006)
8. Ide, N., Romary, L.: Outline of the international standard linguistic annotation framework. In: Proceedings of ACL 2003 Workshop on Linguistic Annotation: Getting the Model Right, Sapporo, pp. 1–5 (2003)
9. http://semantic-annotation.uvt.nl
10. U. S. Army: Open-Source Intelligence ATP 2-22.9 (p. 91). (2012), http://www.fas.org/irp/doddir/army/atp2-22-9.pdf (retrieved)
11. Keim, D., Mansmann, F., Schneidewind, J., Ziegler, H.: Challenges in Visual Data Analysis. In: 4th International Conference on Information Visualisation, Washington, DC, pp. 9–16 (2006)

Privacy Protection of Biometric Templates

Moazzam Butt, Olaf Henniger, Alexander Nouak, and Arjan Kuijper

Fraunhofer Institute for Computer Graphics Research IGD
Fraunhoferstr. 5, D-64283 Darmstadt, Germany
{moazzam.butt,olaf.henniger,
alexander.nouak,arjan.kuijper}@igd.fraunhofer.de

Abstract. Although many biometric characteristics are not secrets, biometric reference data (also known as biometric templates) need to be stored securely and to be protected against unauthorized use. For this purpose, biometric template protection techniques have been developed that do not only prevent privacy leakage and provide confidentiality of the stored biometric templates, but address also problems like identity theft and cross-matching of biometric templates stored in different systems. This paper describes the security and privacy risks associated with storing biometric data and highlights the necessity of using biometric template protection as a potential remedy to these risks. Privacy considerations are discussed with respect to using fingerprint verification for access control to a public outdoor swimming pool.

1 Introduction

Biometrics, i.e. the automated recognition of individuals based on their biological and behavioural characteristics, is a promising technology for automating user authentication at human-machine interfaces. Common biometric modalities used at human-machine interfaces nowadays are face, fingerprint, iris, vein pattern, voice, handwritten signature, or gait. Biometric authentication methods provide convenience to the users and enhance the binding of the authentication process to persons provided that their recognition accuracy and resistance against fraud are sufficiently high. An increase in the deployment of biometric systems is observed in the civil domain (such as UIDAI Aadhaar [1], US-VISIT programmes [2]) and in the forensic domain (such as AFIS). On the other side, security and privacy fears like personal data misuse or hacking, mass surveillance, personal data peering or sharing via centralised storage in the cloud and cloud-based services have become major concerns these days. Hence, use of biometrics in systems needs to preserve privacy by design and must not violate the human right to privacy and freedom from surveillance.

The remainder of this paper is organized as follows: Section 2 describes the general flow of information and vulnerabilities in biometric systems. Section 3 gives an overview of biometric template protection. Section 4 discusses the concerns raised by a recent practical deployment experience at a public outdoor swimming pool in Germany. Section 5 comprehends the conclusions.

C. Stephanidis (Ed.): HCII 2014 Posters, Part I, CCIS 434, pp. 153–158, 2014.

2 Privacy and Security in Biometrics

Fig. 1 illustrates the general flow of information within a biometric system: Biometric samples are acquired from a subject via a sensor. The sensor output is sent to a processor that extracts distinctive, repeatable biometric features. The resulting features can be stored in the biometric enrolment database as a biometric template. In some cases, the captured biometric data themselves (without prior feature extraction) are stored as reference. A probe biometric sample can be compared to a specific reference, to many references, or to all references in the enrolment database to determine if there is a match. A decision regarding acceptance or rejection is taken based upon the similarity between the features of the probe and those of the references compared. Fig. 1 also identifies potential points of attack within a biometric system.

A main threat to a biometric system is that of impersonation, i.e. of an impostor masquerading as another person who is enrolled and gaining access to the protected assets. The success rate of zero-effort impostor attacks (in which an impostor presents the own biometric characteristics in order to get falsely accepted as somebody else's biometric look-alike) is related to the system's false accept rate. If unwatched, an impostor may also attempt to impersonate an enrolled person by use of a dummy such as a silicone or gummy finger or a reproducing device such as a voice recorder.

Although many biometric characteristics are not secrets (e.g., anyone can rather easily take photographs of someone else's face), biometric data are considered personal data as defined in [3]. Personal data is required to be stored securely and to be used in a privacy preserved manner [4]. Unlike the ubiquitous passwords, biometric templates can only a limited number of times be replaced with different biometric traits of the same person due to limited availability (only one face, two eyes, ten fingers, etc.). Furthermore, they do not only contain information about biometric features of a person, but may also contain personal information beyond what is needed for authentication. For instance, information about gender, ethnic origin, body conditions and diseases, which one may like to keep private, can be inherently attached to a face template. Because biometric data are highly sensitive personal data, many people are troubled by the risks associated with storing biometric templates in computer systems [5,6,7,8].

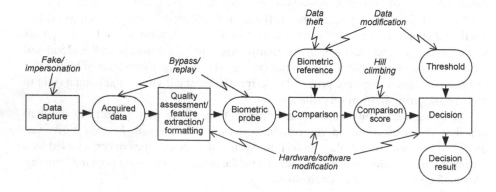

Fig. 1. Examples of attacks against a biometric system

Biometric template protection is not only needed for privacy preservation, but also for protecting against identity theft and other attacks. Cross-matching attacks could allow an impostor, who gets hold of the biometric reference of another person stored in one system, to intrude all other systems where the same biometric reference is used. A stolen biometric template must not be usable as a blueprint for biometric presentation attacks, e.g. for the generation of an artificial gummy fingerprint (spoofing).

Also other vulnerable points indicated in Fig. 1 may be attacked to gain access to protected assets. For instance, if bypass and replay attacks are possible, an impostor could send recorded or otherwise acquired biometric data to the comparison component, evading the regular data capture device. If comparison scores are revealed, an impostor could systematically modify biometric probes in a hill climbing attack to obtain comparison scores closer and closer to the decision threshold until the threshold is met. There are long-established standards and best practices for ensuring IT security that must be applied also to protect biometric systems.

3 Biometric Template Protection

The confidentiality of stored passwords is usually protected by cryptographic hash functions. The hash value of a presented password must match bit by bit the stored hash value. This approach cannot be applied directly to biometric data because the biometric data captured from the same person are never completely the same due to their natural variability. Using general-purpose cryptographic algorithms for encrypting the stored biometric references is also not a satisfying solution because encrypted biometric data must be decrypted for comparison with the claimer's data, which makes them vulnerable to attacks at the comparison stage.

One of the solutions to cope with the threats to biometric templates is to store and to compare biometric data in tamper-proof smart cards. However, smart-card based systems are not always applicable.

For the protection of biometric templates in an insecure environment, special biometric template protection techniques have been developed. Biometric template protection techniques generate binary templates that can be used for biometric authentication and at the same time preserve privacy. It is computationally hard to retrieve the original biometric characteristic or any personal or private information attached to it from these binary templates. For that reason, they are called protected biometric templates or pseudonymous identifiers (PI) [9].

Biometric template protection techniques do not only prevent privacy leakage, but also resolve the risk of cross-matching by allowing to generate multiple templates that are statistically independent from each other. The number of templates that can be generated depends on the entropy of the biometric modality. These templates can be stored in different biometric application servers for personalizing different services. Multiple templates, extracted from a single biometric sample, also offer revocability (or cancelability), i.e., a new biometric template can be assigned if a template is compromised.

Biometric template protection techniques must also not lead to a significant degradation of the recognition accuracy, i.e. of the false reject rate and false accept rate, of a biometric system.

Several biometric template protection techniques have been proposed under a unified architecture [9]. These techniques can be categorized into two types, biometric cryptosystems and feature transformation [10]:

- Biometric cryptosystems have been developed utilizing cryptographic primitives. In these schemes, either a consistent key is generated from the biometric sample (key generating biometric cryptosystems) or a bound cryptographic key is released (key binding biometric cryptosystems) provided the error correction coding [11] can overcome the difference between the biometric probe and the samples given at enrolment. In order to overcome the intra-class variance between the biometric samples at the enrolment and authentication stages, helper data (also called auxiliary data [9]) is stored in addition to the protected biometric template. At the authentication stage, this helper data is used for error correction. Key binding biometric cryptosystems lead to a binary match/non-match decision. Hence, there is no possibility that an adversary could exploit comparison scores to regenerate biometric templates in an iterative fashion in a hill-climbing attack [6].
- Feature transformation methods transform the biometric features extracted from the original biometric sample using a non-invertible transformation [12,13] or a user-specific invertible transformation (salting) [14]. These techniques inherently support template diversity and revocability as changes in transformation parameters may result very conveniently in many new templates from one single biometric sample. The challenge is to design a transformation that is irreversible and robust to intra-class variance [15]. The transformed data may or may not have the same domain as the original data [12]. The comparison takes place using distance measures resulting into a score. The score is compared with a pre-adjusted threshold resulting in a match/non-match decision. In salting-based approaches, the transformation parameters are derived from a user password. In this case, the security of the protected biometric template is tied to the security of the user password [16,17].

4   Use Case: Access Control to Public Outdoor Pool

In the following, we discuss a deployment scenario of using biometrics for access control to a public outdoor swimming pool in Germany. The pool entrance was originally operated by staff and the ticket to the pool was not personalized, i.e. no information about the holder was printed on the ticket. The motivation for using biometrics here was to bind the season tickets to their holders and to prevent sharing the same season ticket between several persons by providing a mechanism of identity verification. Season-ticket holders received RFID chip cards (Mifare) with stored encrypted fingerprints, and a RFID reader with integrated fingerprint sensor was installed at the pool entrance. To enter the pool, the user had to first touch the card on the RFID reader in order to upload the fingerprint template to the reader. As next step, the user gave his fingerprint and the access-control terminal compared the template with the live scan. In case the probe sample matched the template, the gate was opened; otherwise not. The advantage of storing the fingerprint template on a card is that the reference template is always in the custody of the user. The use of fingerprints for access-control to the pool was all voluntarily, i.e. the users signed declarations of consent.

However, after petitions from citizens who did not accept being fingerprinted for accessing a public swimming pool, the regional data protection authority complained about the above scenario [18]. The data protection authority considered the use of fingerprints objectionable because of

- lack of an equivalent alternative (holders of season tickets without fingerprint had to wait for the pool attendant to open the entrance door) and
- disproportionality of using fingerprints in local-government services for the public.

As a result, the use of biometrics for access-control was abandoned. This resulted in termination of the option of season tickets (allowing any number of entries during a season). The RFID chip cards are now used as rechargeable payment cards at an unstaffed access-control terminal instead.

This example suggests that the use of biometrics for local government services for the public is far from certain although methods of biometric template protection already exist. In private-sector recreation facilities (fitness clubs etc.), biometrics may still be used on a voluntarily basis, provided that biometric template protection schemes are deployed. A lesson learnt is that there must be an equivalent alternative for people who do not accept using biometrics. The use-case scenario also highlights the need to raise awareness of the potential of biometric template protection techniques.

5 Conclusions

The use of biometric data for public-domain applications is subject to EU data privacy regulations [3,4]. Often, the use of biometric data is perceived to bring less added value than added privacy and security risks even if being convenient for citizens.

Central storage of biometric references is susceptible to cyber-attacks and misuse of personal data. Smart cards can be used as an alternative to central storage. In this way, access to a biometric template and demographic data associated with it remains limited and, hence, also protected from many external attacks described in Section 2. Moreover, the personal data can always be used only on a voluntary basis, and the data remains at the disposal of the actual owner. Smart cards can also provide a tamper-proof platform for biometric comparison on card [19]. Nowadays, smartphones can replace smart cards and, therefore, a dedicated separate hardware token is not necessary. New technologies like near-field communication (NFC) can make the transmission of biometric data feasible and interoperable.

Irreversible biometric templates created by biometric template protection techniques can aid in overcoming the issue of proportionality. The development of certifiably secure and privacy-enhancing biometric systems will increase the level of trust in biometric systems. Methods for assessing the privacy and security properties of the biometric template protection techniques have already been investigated e.g. in [20].

Acknowledgement. This work has received funding from the European Community's Framework Programme (FP7/2007-2013) FIDELITY project under grant agreement no. 284862.

References

1. Unique Identification Authority of India. AADHAR, http://uidai.gov/in
2. US Department of Homeland Security, http://www.dhs.gov/us-visit-traveler-information
3. European Parliament, Directive 95/46/EC of the European Parliament and of the Council of 24 October 1995 on the protection of individuals with regard to the processing of personal data and on the free movement of such data (october 1995), http://eur-lex.europa.eu/LexUriServ/LexUriServ.do?uri=CELEX:31995L0046:en:HTML
4. European Convention on Human Rights (December 1950), http://www.echr.coe.int/Pages/home.aspx?p=press/factsheets&c=
5. Hill, C.: Risk of masquerade arising from the storage of biometrics, B.S. thesis, Australian National Univ., Canberra, Australia (2013), http://chris.fornax.net/biometrics.html
6. Adler, A.: Vulnerabilities in biometric encryption systems. In: Kanade, T., Jain, A., Ratha, N.K. (eds.) AVBPA 2005. LNCS, vol. 3546, pp. 1100–1109. Springer, Heidelberg (2005)
7. Mohanty, P., Sarkar, S., Kasturi, R.: Privacy and security issues related to match scores. In: Proc. Conf. Computer Vision and Pattern Recognition Workshop, pp. 162–165 (2006)
8. Jain, A.K., Bolle, R., Pankanti, S. (eds.): Biometrics: Personal Identification in Networked Society. Kluwer Academic Publishers (1999)
9. ISO/IEC, ISO/IEC 24745 Information technology - Security techniques - Biometric information protection, ISO/IEC JTC 1/SC 27 (2010)
10. Jain, A.K., Nandakumar, K., Nagar, A.: Biometric template security. EURASIP Journal on Advances in Signal Processing, Special Issue on Biometrics, 1–20 (January 2008)
11. Hall, J.I.: Generalized Reed-Solomon codes. Notes on Coding Theory, 63–76 (2003)
12. Ratha, N., Connell, J., Bolle, R.: Enhancing security and privacy in biometric-based authentication systems. IBM Syst. J. 40(3), 614–634 (2001)
13. Teoh, A., Goh, A., Ngo, D.: Random multispace quantization as an analytic mechanism for biohashing of biometric and random identity inputs. IEEE Trans. Pattern Anal. Mach. Intell. 28(12), 1892–1901 (2006)
14. Ngo, D., Teoh, A., Goh, A.: Biometric hash: High-confidence face recognition. IEEE Trans. Circuits Syst. Video Technol. 16(6), 771–775 (2006)
15. Sutcu, Y., Sencar, H., Memon, N.: A secure biometric authentication scheme based on robust hashing. In: Proc. Seventh Workshop Multimedia and Security, pp. 111–116 (2005)
16. Teoh, A.B.J., Connie, T., Ngo, D., Ling, C.: Remarks on biohash and its mathematical foundation. Inf. Process. Lett. 100(4), 145–150 (2006)
17. Lumini, A., Nanni, L.: An improved biohashing for human authentication. Pattern Recognition 40(3), 1057–1065 (2007)
18. Ronellenfitsch, M.: 40. Tätigkeitsbericht des Hessischen Datenschutzbeauftragten (2011)
19. Eurosmart, Smart biometrics for trust and convenience – Analysis of use cases and best practice recommendations, Eurosmart Reference Paper (April 2012)
20. Zhou, X.: Privacy and security assessment of biometric template protection, PhD thesis, TU Darmstadt (2011)

Understanding User Requirements for the Design of a Semantic Digital Library Interface

Cristina Emilia Costa[1] and Marco Ronchetti[2]

[1] CREATE-NET, Trento, Italy
cristina.costa@create-net.org
[2] DISI, University of Trento, Trento, Italy
marco.ronchetti@unitn.it

Abstract. This paper discusses the role of interaction and user experience in the design of an interface of search for digital libraries. We present our preliminary work in the design of an advanced interaction interface for "Publicamente", a web based semantic multimedia digital library that allows the archiving, management and access to a collection of heterogeneous documents types. In this paper we explore the user requirements, and present the design guidelines for the interface of the system. Users of "Publicamente" are be both expert users and casual users and the interface need to being able to accommodate different search styles, make semantic technologies transparent to casual users, and leverage on the semantic layer in the presentation of the retrieved information and its context.

Keywords: HCI, search user interface, digital libraries.

1 Introduction

A digital library is an information system designed to collect, organize, retrieve and access digital documents, integrating them with information coming from metadata from different sources. The search user interface plays an important role in it, since it supports the multiple functions needed during information search. First of all it has to support the user, or searcher, in formulating the more appropriate query for his needs or in browsing through the content available. Then, it should help him in the understanding and interpretation of the search results, subsequently aiding him in the selection of the content more appropriate to his information needs. Finally, it should keep track of the recent search activities, making them accessible during the search session in order to allow the user to improve and refine his research.

In modern digital libraries, text based documents are placed side by side to multimedia content, and the information is distributed over multiple and mixed formats. Besides, the role of multimedia has gradually shifted from being mostly entertaining to informative or documentary. These factors influence both the search and fruition of data, making the design of the user interface more challenging and complex.

Recently research has focused in making multimedia content fully searchable and easy to access as traditional text documents, using various techniques able to enrich

C. Stephanidis (Ed.): HCII 2014 Posters, Part I, CCIS 434, pp. 159–164, 2014.

the interpretation of the content, such as text to speech converters, speaker recognition, and automatic evaluation of the visual content.

In some types of digital libraries, such those containing content from conferences, lectures, formal meetings or public administration activity documentation, contents with different formats are often related to each other. These relationships are part of a context that plays an important role in the comprehension of the documents themselves, and therefore they should be preserved, and correctly presented in the visualization interface.

The introduction of semantic technologies empowers the search, making it more robust, improving results presentation that can be supported by significant contextual information. Indeed, being able to work with semantically enriched documents, especially if extended to multimedia, allows emerging significant relationships between documents and contextual information.

2   The "Publicamente" Platform

"Publicamente" is a web based semantic multimedia digital library that allows the archiving, management and access to a collection of heterogeneous documents types. "Publicamente" is able to manage a wide variety of content types: documents may be video, audio (podcasts), images and text based documents (such as PDF, HTML, PowerPoint, Word, OpenOffice, and Excel document formats).

The platform was created to support digital libraries where multimedia is predominant and where the content is connected to each other by temporal and location constraints, such as in documentation from conferences, lectures, meetings, etc.

"Publicamente" groups related documents, and their metadata information, into "event" entities, and uses additional metadata to markup documents with time, date and location. These entities may be assimilated to a collection of temporal related content, where various heterogeneous types of documents that are related to each other are grouped together forming a complex entity, where information is delivered as a whole over multiple heterogeneous channels. The semantic layer is able to link the groups (or collections) of documents with others in the library and assists the users in the retrieval of the content relevant with respect to their information needs. This structure is then used to search and access data and to display the content taking into account user preferences.

Presenting the entity as a whole gives the advantage to emphasize the context in which the content has been created.

Since video is predominant in this type of digital library, the platform fully supports features designed for dealing with video based content. Video can be searched through the transcripts of the audio (either already available in form of subtitles or automatically generated thanks to a speech to text engine), or through other types of synchronized content (e.g. slides). Therefore, besides text documents, also videos can be semantically enriched with automatic processes. Search result contains the exact time stamp in which the information was retrieved, allowing the user to quickly check the results.

3   Use Cases

"Publicamente" is a platform that gives access to the general public to documentation on specific topics. The search system interface is the main point of access for the user to the digital library, and it has an important influence in the user experience (UX) and on the accessibility of the content. We consider as potential users of the system both expert users and casual users: therefore the interface needs to be able to accommodate different search styles, make semantic technologies transparent to casual users, and leverage on the semantic layer in the presentation of the retrieved information and its context.

The interface should be intuitive and graphically appealing in order to satisfy the needs of first time or casual users, supporting both query search and explorative search. These users may expose a more exploratory form of search, for example for learning about a topic, discover events, and understand complex topics as a part of a course. At the same it should support also expert groups of users that need to search specific information or documents in the library. The objectives and motivations of these two user groups, as well as the type of information search, may therefore be quite different. Due to the specific type of content, there is need for an interaction interface that does not just return results but is also able to provide an effective user experience, letting users to see and explore the richer context connected to the documents.

Since we are working with a heterogeneous collection of information, depending on the nature of the content (audio, video, text) it requires to be read, seen or listen. The interface should not only give the user the control over his findings, but also provide easy and practical tools for interacting with the content and checking their interest on it.

For defining the principles of the design of the user interface we defined tree real world use cases that generalize tree implementations of the system.

3.1   Event Document Repository

Big recurrent events such as Festivals and Expos produce in time a large library that archives various types of connected documentation and represents a history memory of the event. "Publicamente" is used to create a portal that collects a great variety of contents over a single topic (e.g. Economy) provided in various formats such as video of keynotes, audio of interviews, slides, photographs, biographies of speakers. The portal allows retrieving documents related to a specific moment of the event, such as a keynote (and related documents) as well allow exploratory search, but the more interesting feature its capability in making connections between past and new information, thus allowing emerging the evolution of a specific topic in time, and its key players.

3.2   Academic Environment

In academic environment "Publicamente" can be used to create a portal that collects courses and related lecture materials. Lecture content is by its nature mixed media, containing videos, presentations and reading material. These can be enriched with information from the academic library and journals. The semantic organization of the information allow to make cross-links between materials of various courses (for example linking material from 101 courses to more advanced ones), helping students to connect information acquired in different moments of their academic path.

3.3   Public Administration

Transparency in the political life of public administration is becoming a more and more central issue for local communities. For increasing the access of citizen to the information discussed during debates, sometimes these are video recorded and made available to the public. Unfortunately being able to access to recorded information without other forms of support does not help the citizen in find in an efficient way the information he needs."Publicamente" allows creating an archive of the information indexing the video information and connecting it to textual documentation, such as minutes and resolutions, and to profiles of the politicians involved.

4   Advanced Interaction Interface Design

In "Publicamente" it is fundamental that the visualization and interaction strategy adopted in the interface is able to reflect the information needs that drive the users' search in each use case. The main common element that emerges is the importance of context in which the document is created and subsequent referred to. The user interface should present to the user the semantic enrichments and the connections with other documents in a form that he can use it.

Publicamente requires an advanced interaction interface, able to efficiently present to the user a collection of heterogeneous documents types and is able to manage a wide variety of content types: documents may be video, audio (podcasts), images and text based documents (such as PDF, HTML PowerPoint, Word, OpenOffice, and Excel document formats), supporting the range of use cases and finding an interface that best if fits into more than one category.

The use of interactive and graphical information has the goal of amplifying and reinforcing human cognition, thus enabling the viewer to gain knowledge about the internal relationships between documents and information, and making it emerge the structure of the library organization. The interface supports human interaction for exploration and understanding using graphical and layout elements for visualizing context elements (being it metadata such temporal, meaning, author information, relationships or semantic enrichment) and mapping them in the screen, taking advantage of psychological principles, such as selective proximity of the search results, alignment of the elements, and chosen shared visual properties such as color or size.

Diversity of users search styles is supported by exploiting the interaction properties of the interface: for example selective hiding of data contributes keeping the displayed information clean and simple, while additional details remains available to users that require deeper information; giving more space to the information related to key documents help to maintain the focus of the search. Interaction can be designed to enable users to make discoveries, getting understanding and take decisions and adapting the layout as the user refines the search.

In the design of the search user interface (SUI), we take into consideration the four types of features [3]:

-   Input Features: search box based (natural language query), facets, clusters categories, ontology, context
-   Control Features: Sorting, filters, grouping, suggestions
-   Informational Features: previews, usable information, social information
-   Personalisable Features: current search, persistent

Each of these features contributes to improve the user search experience: the ideal SUI should include elements that combine as more of these features as possible. For understanding from the usability point of view what makes search easy or difficult, we analyzed the interface so that it could support each phase of the four-phase search framework [2] mapped in the range of the envisioned use cases:

-   Formulation, represents what happens before the search. It is connected with the objectives of the user and with the motivation that brings him to the portal.
-   Action, which type o search he performs.
-   Review of results, presentation of the found data
-   Refinement, improving the search

The interface should be keep simple ("produce a search interface that is both highly functional, but not cluttered and distracting" [1]), but allow various levels of exploration.

5   Conclusions

During the design process of the user interface of the "Publicamente" for different use case, some key characteristics of the platform emerged. In particular two aspects needed n special attention. First the presentation of the search results that involved multimedia content: it is not sufficient to list audio or video titles, but it is necessary to give the user a quick access to them in relevant points, fully exploiting in the presentation the richer semantic information available. Secondly, the organization of documents in logical entities need to be supported and visualized side by side to other less structured connections between documents suggested by the semantic engine. These connections, enriched by metadata information, create the context around the documents during the search, and contribute to the correct interpretation of the found results.

Acknowledgements. This work was partially supported by the Publicamente project, co-funded by the Province of Trento (PAT) under the POR FESR 2007-2013 EU program, bando n.2/2010.

References

1. Wilson, M.L., Kules, B., Schraefel, M.C., Shneiderman, B.: From Keyword Search to Exploration: Designing Future Search Interfaces for the Web. Found. Trends Web Sci. 2(1), 1–97 (2010), http://dx.doi.org/10.1561/1800000003, doi:10.1561/1800000003
2. Shneiderman, B., Byrd, D., Bruce Croft, W.: Sorting out searching: a user-interface framework for text searches. Commun. ACM 41(4), 95–98 (1998), http://doi.acm.org/10.1145/273035.273069, doi:10.1145/273035.273069
3. Wilson, M.L.: Search User Interface Design. In: Marchionini, G. (ed.) Synthesis Lectures on Information Concepts, Retrieval, and Services. Morgan & Claypool (2011)

Autonomous Search: Towards the Easy Tuning of Constraint Programming Solvers

Broderick Crawford[1,2], Ricardo Soto[1,3], Rodrigo Olivares[1], Rodrigo Herrera[1]
Eric Monfroy[4], and Fernando Paredes[5]

[1] Pontificia Universidad Católica de Valparaíso, Chile
[2] Universidad Finis Terrae, Chile
[3] Universidad Autónoma de Chile, Chile
[4] CNRS, LINA, Université de Nantes, France
[5] Escuela de Ingeniería Industrial, Universidad Diego Portales, Chile
{ricardo.soto,broderick.crawford}@ucv.cl,
rodrigo.olivares@uv.cl,
rodrigo.herrera.1@mail.pucv.cl,
eric.monfroy@univ-nantes.fr,
fernando.paredes@udp.cl

Abstract. Constraint programming (CP) allows users to solve combinatorial problems by simply launching the corresponding model in a search engine. However, achieving good results may clearly depend on the correct search engine configuration, which demands advanced knowledge from the modeler. Recently, Autonomous Search (AS) appeared as a new technique that enables a given search engine to control and adapt its own configuration based on self-tuning. The goal is to be more efficient without the knowledge of an expert user. In this paper, we illustrate how the integration of AS into CP is carried out, reducing as a consequence the user involvement in solver tuning.

Keywords: Constraint Programming, Constraint Satisfaction, Autonomous Search.

1 Introduction

Constraint programming (CP) is a relatively modern software technology for solving constraint-based and optimization problems that has been successfully used in different application domains. Varied examples can be found, specially in rostering [13], manufacturing [14], games [9,10] and in engineering design [8,11]. Under the CP technology, a problem is modeled as a Constraint Satisfaction Problem (CSP), which roughly consists in a sequence of variables holding a domain of potential values and a set of constraints. A CSP is basically solved by using a search tree, where the potential solutions are distributed and explored by a backtracking-like algorithm. The exploration of potential solutions is performed by interleaving two main phases: propagation and enumeration. The propagation attempts to delete from domains the values that do not lead to

C. Stephanidis (Ed.): HCII 2014 Posters, Part I, CCIS 434, pp. 165–168, 2014.
© Springer International Publishing Switzerland 2014

any solution in order to accelerate the exploration. In the enumeration phase, a variable of the problem and then a value from its domain are selected in order to construct a potential solution to be verified. The order in which variables and values are selected is determined by the variable and value ordering heuristics. This pair is known as the enumeration strategy; and together with the propagation technique form the solving strategy. Selecting the right solving strategy is known to be dramatically important to achieve efficient solving processes, however predicting its behavior is quite hard. This decision is typically left to the modeler, which obviously requires a significant amount of expertise to success. Recently, Autonomous Search (AS) appeared as a new technique that enables the solver to control and adapt its own heuristics based on self-tuning. The goal is to be more efficient without the knowledge of an expert user. In this paper, we illustrate how the integration of AS into CP is carried out, reducing as a consequence the user involvement in solver tuning.

2   Discussion

The main idea of integrating AS in CP is to enable the self-adaptation of the solver when a poor performance of the search process is detected, this also implies that modelers are not forced to configure the solver by hand. This obviously simplify the experimentation task allowing users with a limited expertise in tuning to obtain good solving results. The current architecture of AS in CP performs its self-adaptation by dynamically replacing the strategies that show a lower performance than the desired one. The replacement is performed "on the fly" by measuring the quality of strategies through a choice function. The choice function determines the performance of a given strategy in a determined amount of time, and it is computed based upon a set of indicators and control parameters. Additionally, to guarantee the precision of the choice function, an optimizer tunes the control parameters. The architecture for integrating AS in CP, firstly presented in [2], is composed of four components: SOLVE, OBSERVATION, ANALYSIS and UPDATE.

- The SOLVE component solves the CSP by interleaving propagation and enumeration phases through a classic CP solving algorithm . The enumeration strategies used are selected from a quality rank, which is controlled by the UPDATE component.
- The OBSERVATION component regards and stores the information relevant about the resolution process.
- The ANALYSIS component inspect the information stored by OBSERVATION, and evaluates the strategies via a set of indicators (a common list of indicators employed can be seen in [1]).
- The UPDATE component computes a choice function, which is composed of indicators and then decides if the current strategy must be replaced by a more promising one.

The original architecture has smoothly been modified and improved over the five past years. Indeed, a hyperheuristic approach was included in [1,4]. The idea was to improve the UPDATE component in order to perform a better rank generation. The hyperheuristic is a heuristic that operates at a higher level of abstraction than the solver. It is the responsible for deciding which enumeration strategy to apply at each decision step during the search. The choice function computes the performance through the indicators and control parameters. In this approach, a genetic algorithm controls the relevance of indicators within the function. Experimental results on different benchmarcks validated this approach. The implementation details of this framework can be seen in [6], and a extended versions considering more elaborated statistical analysis of results were reported in [3].

The work done in [7] can be seen as an extension of previous works. The idea here is to dynamically manage some strategies and components of the solver. The framework can hence be used to reactively manage some solvers inside an hybridization of solving processes. This is achieved by some rules that trigger some solvers or functions of solvers reacting to some observations of the search. Let us note that in this work, a hybrid Branch and Bound-based algorithm allows to support also optimization problems, previous work only support constraint satisfaction problems. Finally, in a recent work the genetic algorithm that tunes the choice function has successfully been replaced by a particle swarm algorithm. The new optimizer exhibited competitive results, which are illustrated in [5]. A more detailed performance analysis of both optimizers has later been reported in [12].

3 Conclusion

In this paper, we have illustrated how AS can be integrated into CP, which leads to a reduction of user involvement in solver tuning. The idea is to enable the self-adaptation of the solver when a poor performance of the search process is detected, this implies that modelers are not forced to configure the solver by hand. This obviously simplify the experimentation task allowing users with a limited expertise in tuning to obtain good solving results. The AS-CP architecture has been largely improved over the past five years and it has been validated through several experimentation phases. We expect to continue improving this architecture by for instance designing new choice functions, strategy rankers, or more efficient AS-CP components.

Acknowledgements. Ricardo Soto is supported by Grant CONICYT/ FONDE-CYT/INICIACION/11130459, Broderick Crawford is supported by Grant CON-ICYT/FONDECYT/REGULAR/1140897, and Fernando Paredes is supported by Grant CONICYT/FONDECYT/REGULAR/1130455.

References

1. Crawford, B., Soto, R., Castro, C., Monfroy, E.: A Hyperheuristic Approach for Dynamic Enumeration Strategy Selection in Constraint Satisfaction. In: Ferrández, J.M., Álvarez Sánchez, J.R., de la Paz, F., Toledo, F.J. (eds.) IWINAC 2011, Part II. LNCS, vol. 6687, pp. 295–304. Springer, Heidelberg (2011)
2. Castro, C., Monfroy, E., Figueroa, C., Meneses, R.: An approach for dynamic split strategies in constraint solving. In: Gelbukh, A., de Albornoz, Á., Terashima-Marín, H. (eds.) MICAI 2005. LNCS (LNAI), vol. 3789, pp. 162–174. Springer, Heidelberg (2005)
3. Crawford, B., Castro, C., Monfroy, E., Soto, R., Palma, W., Paredes, F.: Dynamic Selection of Enumeration Strategies for Solving Constraint Satisfaction Problems. Rom. J. Inf. Sci. Tech. 15(2), 106–128 (2012)
4. Crawford, B., Soto, R., Castro, C., Monfroy, E.: Extensible CP-based autonomous search. In: Stephanidis, C. (ed.) Posters, Part I, HCII 2011. CCIS, vol. 173, pp. 561–565. Springer, Heidelberg (2011)
5. Crawford, B., Soto, R., Monfroy, E., Palma, W., Castro, C., Paredes, F.: Parameter tuning of a choice-function based hyperheuristic using particle swarm optimization. Expert Syst. Appl. 40(5), 1690–1695 (2013)
6. Crawford, B., Soto, R., Montecinos, M., Castro, C., Monfroy, E.: A framework for autonomous search in the $ecl^i ps^e$ solver. In: Mehrotra, K.G., Mohan, C.K., Oh, J.C., Varshney, P.K., Ali, M. (eds.) IEA/AIE 2011, Part I. LNCS, vol. 6703, pp. 79–84. Springer, Heidelberg (2011)
7. Monfroy, E., Castro, C., Crawford, B., Soto, R., Paredes, F., Figueroa, C.: A Reactive and Hybrid Constraint Solver. J. Exp. Theor. Artif. Intell. 25(1), 1–22 (2013)
8. Soto, R.: Controlling search in constrained-object models. In: Kuri-Morales, A., Simari, G.R. (eds.) IBERAMIA 2010. LNCS, vol. 6433, pp. 582–591. Springer, Heidelberg (2010)
9. Soto, R., Crawford, B., Galleguillos, C., Monfroy, E., Paredes, F.: A hybrid ac3-tabu search algorithm for solving sudoku puzzles. Expert Syst. Appl. 40(15), 5817–5821 (2013)
10. Soto, R., Crawford, B., Galleguillos, C., Monfroy, E., Paredes, F.: A Pre-filtered Cuckoo Search Algorithm with Geometric Operators for Solving Sudoku Problems. The Scientific World Journal, Article ID 465359 (2014)
11. Soto, R., Crawford, B., Misra, S., Monfroy, E., Palma, W., Castro, C., Paredes, F.: Constraint programming for optimal design of architectures for water distribution tanks and reservoirs: a case study. Tehnicki Vjesnik 21(1), 99–105 (2014)
12. Soto, R., Crawford, B., Misra, S., Palma, W., Castro, C., Paredes, F.: Choice functions for Autonomous Search in Constraint Programming: GA vs PSO. Tehnicki Vjesnik 20(4), 525–531 (2013)
13. Soto, R., Crawford, B., Monfroy, E., Palma, W., Paredes, F.: Nurse and Paramedic Rostering with Constraint Programming: A Case Study. Rom. J. Inf. Sci. Tech. 16(1), 52–64 (2013)
14. Soto, R., Kjellerstrand, H., Durán, O., Crawford, B., Monfroy, E., Paredes, F.: Cell formation in group technology using constraint programming and Boolean satisfiability. Expert Syst. Appl. 39(13), 11423–11427 (2012)

Mining Navigation Histories
for User Need Recognition

Fabio Gasparetti, Alessandro Micarelli, and Giuseppe Sansonetti

Roma Tre University, Via della Vasca Navale 79, Rome, 00146 Italy
{gaspare,micarel,gsansone}@dia.uniroma3.it

Abstract. The time spent using a web browser on a wide variety of tasks such as research activities, shopping or planning holidays is relevant. Web pages visited by users contain important hints about their interests, but empirical evaluations show that almost 40-50% of the elements of the web pages can be considered irrelevant w.r.t. the user interests driving the browsing activity. Moreover, pages might cover several different topics. For these reasons they are often ignored in personalized approaches. We propose a novel approach for selectively collecting text information based on any implicit signal that naturally exists through web browsing interactions. Our approach consists of three steps: (1) definition of a DOM-based representation of visited pages, (2) clustering of pages according with a tree edit distance measure and (3) exploiting the acquired evidence about the user behaviour to better filtering out irrelevant information and identify relevant text related to the current needs. A comparative evaluation shows the effectiveness of the proposed approach in retrieving additional web resources related to what the user is currently browsing

1 Introduction

Implicit Feedback techniques monitor the user behavior gathering usage data to build a profile of the user needs and, for this reason, users do not have to explicitly indicate which documents are relevant. Typical sources of usage data are: viewed or edited documents, query histories, emails, purchased items, etc.. Browsing and query histories in particular have been considered in some personalized search systems (e.g. [1]). Search engines' toolbars and desktop search tools can easily access that information, which has proven to be very useful to disambiguate query terms and personalize the search results, identifying the current user context [2,3].

Even though browsing activities are an important source of information to build profiles of the user interests, empirical evaluations show that browsing sessions contain around 40-50% of elements considered irrelevant w.r.t. the user interests driving the browsing activity [4]. HTML pages include noise data, such as ads and navigation menus. Moreover, pages might cover several different topics. For these reasons they are often ignored in personalized approaches.

We propose a novel approach for implicitly recognizing valuable text descriptions of current user needs based on the implicit feedback revealed through web

C. Stephanidis (Ed.): HCII 2014 Posters, Part I, CCIS 434, pp. 169–173, 2014.
© Springer International Publishing Switzerland 2014

browsing interactions. The remainder of this article describes the process of extraction of relevant cues from usage data collected from browsing sessions.

2   Related Works

Early attempts show that query histories and clicked results, namely, title and summary have the chance to recognise the current search context improving the retrieval of relevant information [5,6]. Further techniques take advantage of those aggregated click-through data extensively collected by popular search engines confirming that hypothesis [5,7,8]. But, on the other hand click-through data remain an exclusively advantage of large search engines and, therefore, out of reach of other entities.

In [9,10], the authors propose a preliminary attempt for extracting cues of user information needs based only on the user's most recent activity. In that model, the browsing activity is exploited in order to identify a set of words that characterize the current needs of the user.

3   Identifying User Needs from Browsing Sessions

A *browsing session* is defined as an ordered set of web pages $\langle p_1, p_2, \ldots p_N \rangle$ that one user visits following the links that bind them. Empirical evidence shows that the external content introduced by hyperlinks sometimes tends to be of high quality and useful. Links convey recommendations and users make judgments about which links to follow according with the potential value of the distal objects w.r.t. their needs. On the web, however, hyperlinks bind documents of varying quality and purposes. Anchors and surrounding text can sometimes introduce noise and degrade potential representations of user current interests. Anchor text is usually vague and imprecise especially if consisting only of a few words or, even worse, these words are just for surfing support. Moreover, if the link is used only to organize information, it conveys no recommendation to the user.

Users decide whether or not access the distal content, that is, the page at the other end of the link, analyzing the text snippets associated to links [11]. We assume that if the user decides to follow a link, she is expressing a particular interest that corresponds with her perception of the information source pointed by that link. Because this perception depends on the links anchor, that text can be considered strongly correlated to the current user needs governing the browsing activity. Collecting this information during a browsing session may be valuable for profiling users in personalized systems.

3.1   Web Page Representation

A DOM-based tree representation of each HTML page is defined. A pre-processing step involves a syntax checker[1] that cleans up malformed and faulty code. A simplified DOM-based tree is obtained filtering out unnecessary tags and considering the following most relevant ones.

A further step aims at generalizing groups of blocks forming a single *data region*. A group of data records that contains descriptions of a set of similar objects are typically rendered in a contiguous region of a page and formatted using similar tags. The identification of data regions on web pages relies on the approach proposed by Liu *et al.* [12].

The DOM-based representation is also useful to cluster pages with similar templates. A *template* corresponds to the set of common layout and format features that appear in a group of pages. A common tree edit distance [13] allows us to compare and cluster together pages presented by the same template. Each cluster is thus represented by a single centroid tree.

3.2   Block Correlation

Once each browsed page p is splitted to a set of non-overlapping text fragments, each corresponding to a block id, we begin analyzing pairs of contiguous pages in the browsing history $(p_i \rightarrow p_j)$. Given id_{pi} the block containing the link chosen by the user, and the text content t_{pi} of id_{pi}, we perform a search through the content of the pointed page to find one or more correlated text blocks $\{id_{pj}\}$ by means of a semantic similarity measure [14]. If the similarity between two blocks id_{pi} and id_{pj} is above a given threshold, the tuple:

$$< c(p_i), c(p_j), id_{pi}, id_{pj} > \tag{1}$$

is added to a local knowledge base KB_r, where $c(p_i)$ and $c(p_j)$ are the clusters associated with the two pages p_i and p_j, respectively. The basic assumption of link analysis is that hyperlinks establish relationships between two pages. In our approach, a link from p_i to p_j indicates that there might be some relationship between one block id_{pi} of page p_i and another block id_{pj} of p_j.

3.3   Exploiting the Experience

The last stage exploits this acquired evidence to retrieve text information related to the current user needs. Given a browsing session $\{p_1, p_2, \ldots, p_N\}$ and the acquired experience KB_r, we follow the previous steps in order to obtain the id of the blocks and clusters for each pair of pages $(p_i \rightarrow p_j)$, and the potential text extracted from the blocks.

The relevance of each term in the extracted text is affected by a boosting factor the is linearly dependent with the number of times the tuple $< c(p_i), c(p_j), id_{pi}, id_{pj} >$ is present in KB_r.

---

[1] http://www.w3.org/People/Raggett/tidy/

4   Conclusion

The proposed implicit feedback technique extracts information related to the current user needs exploiting the experience implicitly acquired during a browsing activity. We are currently evaluating the proposed approach with a large set of data collected from real scenarios. In this way, it is possible to collect enough information to represent clusters of Web pages with similar templates and provide measures of relatedness between html blocks. Moreover, we will include in the evaluation different approaches to extract information from Web pages, e.g., advertisement removal techniques. Further work includes better techniques to represent the variation of user activity and interests during different sessions to better represent the user contexts (see [15]).

References

1. Teevan, J., Dumais, S.T., Horvitz, E.: Personalizing search via automated analysis of interests and activities. In: SIGIR 2005: Proceedings of the 28th Annual International ACM SIGIR Conference on Research and Development in Information Retrieval, pp. 449–456. ACM Press, New York (2005)
2. Biancalana, C., Gasparetti, F., Micarelli, A., Sansonetti, G.: An approach to social recommendation for context-aware mobile services. ACM Trans. Intell. Syst. Technol. 4(1), 10:1–10:31 (2013)
3. Biancalana, C., Flamini, A., Gasparetti, F., Micarelli, A., Millevolte, S., Sansonetti, G.: Enhancing traditional local search recommendations with context-awareness. In: Konstan, J.A., Conejo, R., Marzo, J.L., Oliver, N. (eds.) UMAP 2011. LNCS, vol. 6787, pp. 335–340. Springer, Heidelberg (2011)
4. Gibson, D., Punera, K., Tomkins, A.: The volume and evolution of web page templates. In: Special Interest Tracks and Posters of the 14th International Conference on World Wide Web, WWW 2005, pp. 830–839. ACM, New York (2005)
5. Sriram, S., Shen, X., Zhai, C.: A session-based search engine. In: Proceedings of the 27th Annual International ACM SIGIR Conference on Research and Development in Information Retrieval, SIGIR 2004, pp. 492–493. ACM, New York (2004)
6. Daoud, M., Tamine-Lechani, L., Boughanem, M., Chebaro, B.: A session based personalized search using an ontological user profile. In: Proceedings of the 2009 ACM Symposium on Applied Computing, SAC 2009, pp. 1732–1736. ACM, New York (2009)
7. Speretta, M., Gauch, S.: Personalized search based on user search histories. In: Proceeding of the 2005 IEEE/WIC/ACM International Conference on Web Intelligence Proceedings, pp. 622–628 (September 2005)
8. Paranjpe, D.: Learning document aboutness from implicit user feedback and document structure. In: Proceedings of the 18th ACM Conference on Information and Knowledge Management, CIKM 2009, pp. 365–374. ACM, New York (2009)
9. Gasparetti, F., Micarelli, A.: Exploiting web browsing histories to identify user needs. In: Proceedings of the 12th International Conference on Intelligent User Interfaces, IUI 2007, pp. 325–328. ACM, New York (2007)
10. Gasparetti, F., Micarelli, A., Sansonetti, G.: Exploiting web browsing activities for user needs identification. In: Proceedings of the 2014 International Conference on Computational Science and Computational Intelligence (CSCI 2014). IEEE Computer Society, Conference Publishing Services (March 2014)

11. Pirolli, P., Card, S.K.: Information foraging. Psychological Review 106(4), 643–675 (1999)
12. Liu, B., Grossman, R., Zhai, Y.: Mining data records in web pages. In: Proceedings of the ninth ACM SIGKDD International Conference on Knowledge Discovery and Data Mining, KDD 2003, pp. 601–606. ACM, New York (2003)
13. Chawathe, S.S.: Comparing hierarchical data in external memory. In: Proceedings of the 25th International Conference on Very Large Data Bases, VLDB 1999, pp. 90–101. Morgan Kaufmann Publishers Inc., San Francisco (1999)
14. Biancalana, C., Gasparetti, F., Micarelli, A., Sansonetti, G.: Social semantic query expansion. ACM Trans. Intell. Syst. Technol. 4, 60:1–60:43 (2013)
15. Biancalana, C., Gasparetti, F., Micarelli, A., Miola, A., Sansonetti, G.: Context-aware movie recommendation based on signal processing and machine learning. In: Proceedings of the 2nd Challenge on Context-Aware Movie Recommendation, CAMRA 2011, pp. 5–10. ACM, New York (2011)

Proposal on Electronic Application for Writing *Kanji*

Focusing on Producing Sound Based on the Various Handwriting

Namgyu Kang and Koki Ono

Future University Hakodate, 116-2 Kamedanakano, Hakodate, Hokkaido, 041-8655, Japan
kang@fun.ac.jp

Abstract. Chinese character (*Kanji*) is thought as very complexity to person who just started to learn *Kanji* such as a primary schoolchildren or a foreigner. Especially, almost of these beginners are looked like to draw *Kanji* than to write it. It means, almost of the all beginners think *Kanji* is difficult to write. Therefore, in elementary school in Japan, the exercise to write *Kanji* repeatedly using a paper sheet is conducted for primary schoolchildren. However, it was clarified that many primary schoolchild don't like the exercise to write *Kanji* repeatedly is conducting. Moreover, there are many applications to learn *Kanji* in Japan, however almost of all applications are made for a practician to write *Kanji* tidily and quickly. Based previous backgrounds, we address that beginners in learning *Kanji* can get enjoyment of pleasant experience of writing *Kanji*. The purpose of this research is to propose a pleasant handwriting exercise application using each one's handwriting as individuality and sound information. Therefore, experiment to quantify value of each one's handwriting was conducted with 50 Japanese who were from 6 years old to 80 years old. As the results of the analysis, it was clarified that these handwritings as input information are effective to produce a coordinated sounds as output information in an application of electronic device. "*KanjiOn*" was proposed based on the results of the experiment. In using "*KanjiOn*", user writes various *Kanji* many times with various handwritings then they can hear various sound based on the each handwriting. The experiment conducted with 48 participants including primary schoolchildren at *Hakodate Chuo* library. Almost of participants evaluated "*KanjiOn*" is very pleasant application to write *Kanji*, they wanted to use "*KanjiOn*" more. We hope that not only primary schoolchildren but also foreigners who want to learn *Kanji* become to enjoy writing *Kanji* and can understand more *Kanji* by using "*KanjiOn*".

Keywords: Kanji, Application, Sound, Characteristics, Handwriting.

1   Introduce

Chinese character (Kanji) is thought as very complexity to a primary schoolchildren or a foreigner who just started to learn *Kanji*. Especially, almost of these beginners are looked like to draw *Kanji* than to write it. It means, almost of the all beginners think *Kanji* is difficult to write. Therefore, the primary schoolchildren in Japan exer-

C. Stephanidis (Ed.): HCII 2014 Posters, Part I, CCIS 434, pp. 174–179, 2014.
© Springer International Publishing Switzerland 2014

cise to write *Kanji* using a paper sheet repeatedly. However, it was clarified that many primary schoolchild don't like the exercise to write *Kanji* repeatedly. Therfore, there are many applications to learn *Kanji* in Japan, however almost of all applications were made for a practician to write *Kanji* tidily and quickly. Based on the previous backgrounds, the purpose of this research is to propose an electronic application to exercise *Kanji* using each one's individuality of handwriting as input information and to listen a sound information as output information depend on the written each one's handwriting. We aim that the beginners in learning *Kanji* can get enjoyment of pleasant experience of exercising *Kanji* using the proposed electronic application.

2   Investigation

To affirm the current situation of the relationship with primary schoolchildren and exercising *Kanji*, we visited 3 elementary schools in Hakodate-city in Japan, and had conducted an interview with 13 teachers of 3 elementary schools. As a result from the investigation, it was cleared that almost of primary schoolchildren are not interest in exercising *Kanji*. Especially, they don't like writing *Kanji* using the learning material which is printed in a paper. It means the beginners like primary schoolchildren need a new motivating way to write *Kanji*.

As a next step, we had conducted an experiment about a lot of Japanese's handwriting by using some *Kanji* like 犬 (*INU* : means a dog), 猫 (*NEKO* : means a cat), and 鳥 (*Tori* : means a bird). The purpose of this experiment was to extract some objective characteristics as input information for the electronic application from each one's handwriting. This experiment was had conducted with 80 participants who were from 9 years old to 73 years old in Hakodate city.

The results of 80 participants' handwriting were quantified using the method that was used in previous Kang's research about quantification of physical quantity in a design field. As a result of the analysis of quantification, degree of density, largeness, and aspect ratio of the three *Kanji* were extracted as input information on electronic application. The figure 1 shows the results of a participant's handwriting of three letters. And the table 1 shows the results of the quantification of 3 handwritings.

From the analysis, it was clarified that the characteristics of handwriting can be quantified, and the quantified date has a potential as objective input information for new electronic application. The following figure 1 shows that how to quantify the each one's individuality of handwriting as input information for replaying a pronunciation sound as output information on the electronic application.

The pronunciation on the electronic application is sounded based on the quantified degree of density, largeness, and aspect ratio. The figure 2 illustrates the algorithm of replay a pronunciation based on the input information.

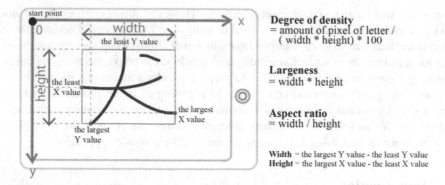

Degree of density
= amount of pixel of letter /
(width * height) * 100

Largeness
= width * height

Aspect ratio
= width / height

Width = the largest Y value - the least Y value
Height = the largest X value - the least X value

Fig. 1. Quantification method from handwriting of *Kanji* on the electronic Application

Table 1. The results of quantification of three different handwritings of *INU*(means a dog)

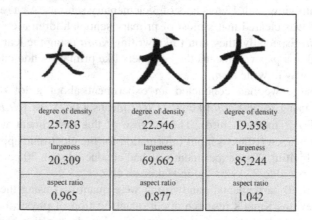

degree of density	degree of density	degree of density
25.783	22.546	19.358
largeness	largeness	largeness
20.309	69.662	85.244
aspect ratio	aspect ratio	aspect ratio
0.965	0.877	1.042

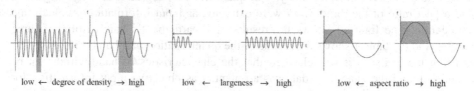

low ← degree of density → high   low ← largeness → high   low ← aspect ratio → high

Fig. 2. Algorithm of replay a pronunciation based on the quantified information

3   Proposal *"KanjiOn"*

"KanjiOn" was proposed based on the results of the previous experiment (Fig.3). The concept of this *"KanjiOn"* is to accelerate the drive for writing *Kanji*. On(音) of the application name means sound. The name *"KanjiOn"* means, a user can enjoy various pronunciation sound depend on the written *Kanji*. Using this *"KanjiOn"*, a user can enjoy and delight from writing *Kanji* with various pronunciation sounds depend on different handwriting of the written *Kanji*.

The figure 4 illustrates the design of the main screen of an example *Kanji* on "*KanjiOn*". A user can write a *Kanji* on the empty big area freely using his/her own finger. In that time, he/she can adjust the weight of line of letter using adjustment lever. Moreover, he/she can erase his/her written letter by the way side using the gray icon. The red icon is for listening a pronunciation sound depending on the handwriting of the written *Kanji*. If he/she mistake to write Kanji rightly, he/her can't listen the pronunciation sound.

Fig. 3. KanjiOn

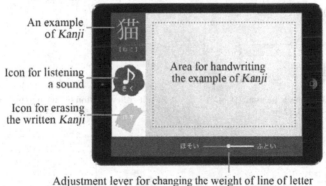

An example of *Kanji*

Icon for listening a sound

Icon for erasing the written *Kanji*

Area for handwriting the example of *Kanji*

Adjustment lever for changing the weight of line of letter
(Thin ━━━●━━━ Thick)

Fig. 4. Each function of *KanjiOn*

4   Evaluation Experiment of *"KanjiOn"*

To verify the efficacy of the "*KanjiOn*", the evaluation experiment was conducted with 30 primary schoolchild and 18 parents of the primary schoolchild at Hakodate *chuo* public library from 11th Mar. to 13th Mar. 2014. Especially, the experiment was conducted using the following different 3 device conditions to clarify the validity of "*KanjiOn*" and effect of sound,; 1) A participant writes *Kanji* using "*KanjiOn*" with sound function ("*KanjiOn*" with sound condition), 2) A participant writes *Kanji* using "*KanjiOn*" without sound function ("*KanjiOn*" without sound condition), and 3)

A participant writes *Kanji* using a paper (paper condition) (Fig. 5). In the experiment, 3 *Kanji*, 舌 (*SITA* : a tongue), 虎 (*TORA* : a tiger), and 牛 (*USHI* : a cow) were requested to write repeatedly and freely for 90 sec. And, the 3 *Kanji* were separated in random order into the each 3 device conditions.

"*KanjiOn*"with sound condition   "*KanjiOn*"without sound condition   paper condition

Fig. 5. There device conditions on evaluation experiment

After using all of the three different device conditions, all participants were requested to evaluate the order of the 3 device conditions based on 'pleasant' and 'wish to use more' using order evaluation method. As the results of order evaluation method of 'pleasant' and 'wish to use more', '*KanjiOn*'' with sound condition' was evaluated highest than other conditions on the not only child participants group but also parents group (Fig. 6).

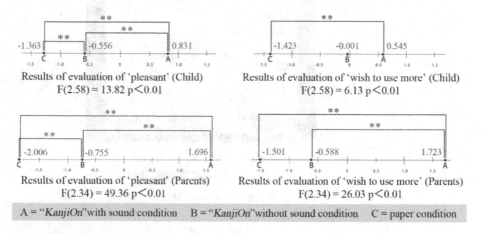

Results of evaluation of 'pleasant' (Child)
$F(2.58) = 13.82$ $p < 0.01$

Results of evaluation of 'wish to use more' (Child)
$F(2.58) = 6.13$ $p < 0.01$

Results of evaluation of 'pleasant' (Parents)
$F(2.34) = 49.36$ $p < 0.01$

Results of evaluation of 'wish to use more' (Parents)
$F(2.34) = 26.03$ $p < 0.01$

A = "*KanjiOn*"with sound condition   B = "*KanjiOn*"without sound condition   C = paper condition

Fig. 6. Results of the evaluation of three device conditions

From the results of behavior protocol analysis, it is cleared that almost of all child participants were more started over to write *Kanji* and used the adjustment lever for changing the weight of line of letter on '*KanjiOn* with sound condition' than '*KanjiOn* without sound condition'(Fig.7). The result means the various pronunciation sounds depend on different handwritings of *Kanji* help to motivate to write *Kanji* repeatedly with different handwriting.

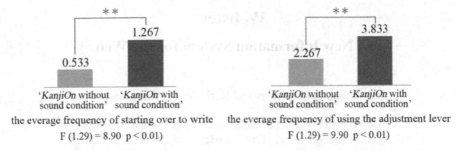

Fig. 7. Results of behavior protocol analysis

5   Conclusion

In this research, we addressed to propose a new electronic application for writing *Kanji* using each one's handwriting and various different pronunciation sounds depend on the handwritings of written *Kanji*. As a result, the following findings were clarified in this research.

Firstly, using each one's individuality of handwriting as input information on electronic application, and to listen a sound information as output information depend on the written each one's handwriting are useful to motivate writing *Kanji*.

Secondly, our *"KanjiOn"* help to motivate to write *Kanji* repeatedly with pleasant. Especially, the various pronunciation sounds help to motivate to write *Kanji* repeatedly with different handwriting.

From these results, it is cleared that users can write *Kanji* with pleasant using *"KanjiOn"* for a long time. We hope that not only primary schoolchildren but also foreigners who want to learn *Kanji* become to enjoy writing *Kanji* and can understand more *Kanji* by using "*KanjiOn*".

Reference

1. Kang, N.K.: The Characteristics of Kansei Quality Evaluation by Design Experience, doctor thesis of Tsukuba Univ., Japan (2006)
2. Ministry of Education, Culture, Sports, Science and Technology, national list of Kanji in common use (2013), http://www.bunka.go.jp/bunkashingikai/soukai/pdf/kaitei_kanji_toushin.pdf
3. Kuribayashi, I.O.: Instruction to raise will of learning *Kanji*. Educational Practice Study 19, 33–38 (2009)

Webster

A New Information System for the Web

Susanna Lederhaas and Karl-Heinz Weidmann

University of Applied Sciences Vorarlberg, Dornbirn, Austria
info@susled.com, karl-heinz.weidmann@fhv.at

Abstract. Webster is a new information system for the Web using it as a huge database and not a huge amount of pages. By concentrating on content and not on authorship, Webster offers a new way to search and browse the Web. Webster shows how the presentation and usage of the Web with new semantic technologies could work without using the metaphor of a page in all its dimensions. The metaphor of a page as well as the history of web design will be discussed in the following to present the concept and the basic ideas of Webster in an understandable way.

Keywords: information system, search engine, semantic technologies, tags.

1 A New Media Changed the World

The Internet had its worldwide breakthrough due to the World Wide Web and the E-Mail. Published in the beginning of the 1990ies the WWW was regularly advanced by its founder Tim Berners-Lee among others. Marc Andreessen developed a first graphic browser, which could be handled by private users. With this development the WWW started to become an important and widespread new medium.

Although the Web started with displaying and connecting scientific publications, it contains nowadays all kinds of data. The Social Web and other developments lead to the term Web 2.0, defined by Tim O'Reilly. But the Web itself did not change it is mainly how we use it. Platforms like Facebook or Wikipedia formed a new way of interacting with the Web using private data as their meat.

The medium Web is new, but there is a strong metaphor, which influences its appearance and media-type: the metaphor of a page. Documents on the Web are called pages and use consciously or unconsciously well known characteristics of print media. This circumstance blocks out a lot of chances and opportunities. The Web is a new way to present and manage information, but by creating pages, some of its chances are missed out. The tool Webster shows how the presentation and usage of the Web could work with new semantic technologies and without using the metaphor of a page in all its dimensions.

2 Metaphors and Mental Models

The first step to do this is to understand how and why the metaphor of a page has evolved. Metaphors make it easier to understand a new media because they contain

C. Stephanidis (Ed.): HCII 2014 Posters, Part I, CCIS 434, pp. 180–185, 2014.
© Springer International Publishing Switzerland 2014

known characteristics. By creating pages on the Web, users are able to inform themselves online like they do offline in a familiar linear way. Hoffmann [1], a web designer and author of several web design books, points out, that also the linguistic similarity caused the strong use of the metaphor of a page. Print designers and web designers design pages. There does not seem to be such a big difference as there is. The metaphor of a page formed a mental model in the minds of the designer as well as the users.

Norman points out how such a mental model emerges: "(…) people form internal, mental models of themselves and of the things and people with whom they interact. These models provide predictive and explanatory power for understanding the interaction. Mental models evolve naturally through interaction with the world and with the particular system under consideration. These models are highly affected by the nature of the interaction, coupled with the persons prior knowledge and understanding. The models are neither complete nor accurate, but nonetheless they function to guide much human behaviour." [2, p. 46]

Mental models are flexible and extendable, which means, that the mental model of the metaphor of a web page is alterable. With this concept in mind the tool Webster was created.

3   Web Design History

Looking at the Web from the design perspective not the technical side, there are several noticeable trends. Those trends show that designers were motivated to form an independent appearance for the Web. In the early beginnings of web design in the mid 1990ies there were three different types of websites online [3]. First-Generation sites are functional and linear like it was used in the very beginnings of web design. Second-Generations sites use more images and colour to create a more lively appearance. And last but not least Third-Generation sites, which Siegel [3] focuses in his book "Creating Killer Web Sites – The Art of Third-Generation Site Design". The usage of strong metaphors is a big part within designing Third-Generation sites. "Examples of this metaphors include galleries, comic strips, television channels, magazines, tabloids, store environments, museums, postcard racks, amusement parks, inside things (computers, human body, buildings, ant farm, and so on), safaris, cities and cupboards" [3, pp. 35–36]. Beside those quite early classifications there are and were a lot of other trends of course. For example the one-page-sites, which have been a trend since about 2009. But the main quality of Siegels [3] classifications is, that it clearly shows, that early web designers were interested in building a whole new online world and experience instead of filling pages of pages with content. This seemed to fade away after the 1990ies where minimalistic design, harmonic colours and typography became more and more important.

Web design has changed in the last twenty years, it has been improved and it matured. Web designers need to be up-to-date: "The web moves fast. Really fast. What is new today, will be a convention in six months time" [4, p. 6]. The history of web design shows that the Web matured but it does not stop to evolve. New technologies enable new possibilities and they shape the online world.

As the web design becomes better in basic aspects of design (like colour, typography and layout) it offers still a lot more opportunities. By using design knowledge about the mentioned basic aspects of design many print designers made websites as well. And they wanted the same control as in print within the media Web: A predefined, stable width and everything should be in the right place. This behaviour worked for a few years until responsive layouts became more and more important. Smartphones and tablets changed the way of looking at things.

But not only the attractive representation of a website should work for mobile users. Little applications (apps) formed and showed a new way to use the Web. Apps often use the Web as a database while they combine static and dynamic content focused on the users interest/request.

4   Web vs. Print

John Allsopp wrote an article, which was published at "A List Apart" that points out that its time to create and treat the Web differently than print media. "What I sense is a real tension between the web as we know it, and the web as it would be. It's the tension between an existing medium, the printed page, and its child, the web. And it's time to really understand the relationship between the parent and the child, and let the child go its own way in the world." [5] The relation between a new and an older media also manifests in other examples. The first TV shows were influenced by the media radio. "Television was at that time often referred to as 'radio with pictures', and that's a pretty accurate description. Much of television followed the format of popular radio at that time. Indeed programs like the Tonight Show, with its variants found on virtually every channel in the world (featuring a band, the talk to the camera host, and seated guests), or the news, with the suited sober news reader, remain as traces of the medium television grew out of. A palimpsest of media past." [5]

The Web was influenced by the print media, "but its time to move on, to embrace the web as its own medium. It's time to throw out the rituals of the printed page, and to engage the medium of web and its own nature." [5] Designers need to think different about the Web and its characteristics. While print media allows full control over colour, widths and positions, control has to be released in a certain amount while doing web design. But this is caused due to an important characteristic of the Web: flexibility instead of rigidity. And this characteristic stands right beside the main ability of the Web: networking.

Semantic technologies might help to use the Web differently than the print media. "The Semantic Web is a Web of actionable information – information derived from data through a semantic theory for interpreting the symbols." [6]. How to use this new ability of the Web and work against the metaphor of a page was the main dispute while creating Webster – a new information system for the Web. Even the inventor of the WWW, Tim Berners-Lee hold a TED-talk [7], where he pointed out his wish to the users that they should share RAW-data. With this data many different mash-ups could be formed. This circumstance would lead to new opportunities, which would not be possible offline. While thinking of the Web as a huge database not a huge amount of pages the idea of Webster was born.

5   Webster in Detail

The WWW offers such a huge amount of data, that it is not possible for the user to get through all of it anymore. The developed tool should help to get an overview of online information about a specific topic. It works like a search engine but it is different to Google for example. Google presents the user a list of relevant links to different web pages, Webster leads the user directly to information. The search term "drive" for example is connected to the "computer drive", "Google Drive" as well as the movie "Drive" from Nicolas Winding Refn in 2011 and a lot more. The algorithm used by Google works best with personal profiles to manage the page rank whereas Webster works also with semantic tags for the single data to put content about the same topic together. Therefore the first screen after typing in the search term in Webster is a selection of tags related to the searched term. In our example those selections would be "Google Drive", "Drive (2011)", the "computer drive" and so on. All this can be realized without stressing the page metaphor further as the first drafts of Webster can show.

Every tap the user makes to select a specific tag forms a new request for the Web extending the search term with the selected topic. This strategy leads to a new experience in searching the Web thinking about data and content not about a specific author in the first place. Different sources are combined and form a so called "Abstract" about a specific topic. The user always gets a chance to easily see where the content comes from and is able to influence the sources of the abstract.

Fig. 1. Different screens of Webster within a specific use case

The tool was created by exploring specific use cases with the search engine Google and using its algorithm as an example. The link list was put into categories with tags, which can already be done by using semantic technologies. The exploration showed that Googles link list shows on the one hand links to pages, which matches exactly to the search term as well as on the other hand content up to something completely different. Lets work with the same search term like before: If the user searches for the

term "drive" and is looking for the movie from Niclas Winding Refn, the search engine will show him information about the plot of the movie, the actors of the movie,
the trailer and in between there are links to pages about Google Drive, a company
called Watt Drive and so on.

This use case showed that using tags could really help to guide the user to the content he really wants. One click in Webster is enough to define the search term again
without any need to type something in again. Every tap is a new request to the Web
using Googles algorithm to manage the results. But how does the user actually see the
content?

The very first tag displayed on the top of the selection is able to extend directly to
show the found content on the Web. Like mentioned before this is called the "Abstract" in Webster and shows a text combined by the machine from different sources
to offer an overview of the most important (decided by the algorithm) content about
the searched term. If the search term is the movie "Drive" the extendable part would
be the plot of the movie followed by the tags "trailer" and "cast". Webster forms a
new way of searching and exploring the Web using semantic technologies.

Fig. 2. The design of Webster showed on a tablet PC

6   Conclusion

Webster is a concept for a search engine, which uses tag annotations to present relevant information for the user. It was designed during a master thesis and stands at the
very beginning. First small usability studies were made; a significant study with a
bigger group is planned.

References

1. Hoffmann, M.: Modernes Webdesign: Gestaltungsprinzipien, Webstandards, Praxis. Galileo Press, Bonn (2010)
2. Norman, D.A., Draper, S.W.: User Centred System Design. Lawrence Erlbaum, NJ (1986)
3. Siegel, D.: Creating Killer Web Sites: The Art of Third-Generation Site Design. Hayden Books, USA (1996)
4. Boulton, M.: A Practical Guide to Designing for the Web. Five Simple Steps, Penarth (2009)
5. Allsopp, J.: A Dao of Web Design (2000), http://alistapart.com/article/dao
6. Shadbolt, N., Hall, W., Berners-Lee, T.: The Semantic Web Revisited. IEEE Computer Society 1541-1672/06 (2006), http://eprints.soton.ac.uk/262614/1/Semantic_Web_Revisted.pdf
7. Berners-Lee, T.: TED Talks: Tim Berners-Lee on the next Web (2009), http://www.ted.com/talks/tim_berners_lee_on_the_next_web.html

Prescriptive Analytics System for Scholar Research Performance Enhancement

Mikyoung Lee, Minhee Cho, Jangwon Gim, Do-Heon Jeong, and Hanmin Jung

Korea Institute of Science and Technology Information (KISTI)
245 Daehak-ro, Yuseong-gu, Daejeon, Korea
{jerryis,mini,jangwon,heon,jhm}@kisti.re.kr

Abstract. We introduce a prescriptive analytics system, InSciTe Advisory, to provide researchers with advice for their future research direction and strategy. It consists of two main parts: descriptive analytics and prescriptive analytics. Descriptive analytics provides results from research activity history as well as the research power index for the designated researcher. Prescriptive analytics suggests a group of role model researchers to the researcher, as well as methods to adopt their best practices. The prescription for the researcher is provided according to 5W1H questions and their corresponding answers. All of the analytical results and their explanations related to the given researcher are automatically generated and saved to a report. This researcher-centric prescriptive analytics framework is expected to be a useful tool to understand the designated researcher from the perspective of prescriptive and descriptive analytics. We evaluated user satisfaction results for InSciTe Advisory and Elsvier Scival by five test users. The result of the evaluation demonstrated that user satisfaction of InSciTe Advisory is 126.5% higher than Scival.

Keywords: Prescriptive Analytics, Descriptive Analytics, Research Performance Enhancement, User Satisfaction Evaluation, InSciTe Advisory.

1 Introduction

Researchers should predict the future and develop appropriate strategies to respond to predictions, in order to strengthen research competitiveness. It is import to identify researchers' competencies and skill level through the analysis of past and present data; based on this identification, the research objective should be defined. We need to determine an optimum methodology to achieve the defined research objective.

In this study, the analysis methods, descriptive analytics and prescriptive analytics, are utilized to provide researchers' future research strategies. Descriptive analytics is the most common and well understood type of analytics, and many analytic tools commonly support this. Predictive analytics endeavors to predict the future, while prescriptive analytics suggests decision options in conjunction with their implications[1]. Prescriptive analytics first emerged in 2013, and was developed based on Gartner group's emerging technology, Hype cycle. Prescriptive Analytics is the third and final phase of business analytics, which includes descriptive, predictive, and pre-

C. Stephanidis (Ed.): HCII 2014 Posters, Part I, CCIS 434, pp. 186–190, 2014.
© Springer International Publishing Switzerland 2014

scriptive analytics[2]. Prescriptive analytics is a set of mathematical techniques that computationally determine a set of high-value alternative actions or decisions, given a complex set of objectives, requirements, and constraints, with the goal of improving business performance. Hitherto, the majority of business intelligence solutions or decision-making support systems have been focused on descriptive investigate to investigate the past or to provide present statistical information, thus showing insufficient performance to support strategic predictive abilities.

To solve this issue, we have been developing an automated technology analytics system, InSciTe Advisory. We have tackled predictive analytics as well as descriptive analytics in the technology domain, and we are now developing an automated prescriptive analytics service. Our goal is to provide researchers with role model recommendations and advice on considering research methods of the role model group. In addition, in order to evaluate the user satisfaction of InSciTe Advisory service, we compared InSciTe Advisory's user satisfaction results with the user satisfaction of the current best information system, Elsevier Scival.

2   Descriptive and Prescriptive Analytics of InSciTe Advisory

InSciTe Advisory is a prescriptive analytics system for scholarly research performance enhancement. The system analyzes several thousand data sources from different categories such as papers, patents, reports, web news, web magazines, and collective intelligence data. The InSciTe Advisory service provides two analytical and advising services, descriptive analytics and prescriptive analytics.

The descriptive analytics service provides an analysis of researcher' present skill level and consists of the researcher activity history service and researcher power index service that analyzes the researcher' multi-dimensional competencies. The researcher activity history service provides information on researchers' activities from past to present, which were analyzed in terms of their scholarly activity, career activity, and industrial activity. On the other hand, the researcher power index service proposes researcher' power index values by analyzing researchers' competencies from the perspective of nine different indexes, which include commerciality, scholarity, influentiality, diversity, durability, technology emergability, partner trend, market trend and supply & demand. This service is used to compare the relative levels between researchers through the power index of researchers, and seek the researcher' role model group (See Fig.1.). Technological characteristics of the role model group, researcher power index, and representative researchers of the group are described[3].

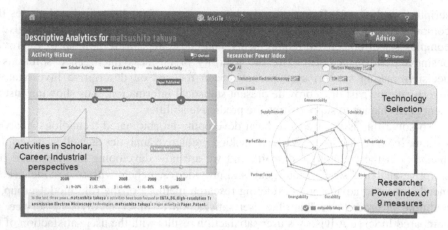

Fig. 1. Descriptive Analytics for Researcher

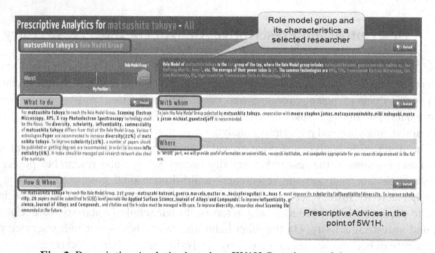

Fig. 2. Prescriptive Analytics based on 5W1H Questions and Answers

The prescriptive service provides strategies and methods for present researchers to adopt the practices of the role model group obtained through the descriptive analytics service. Furthermore, it proposes 5W1H as the method to achieve the optimum objectives based on the analyzed results of the present researcher' competencies (See Fig.2.). 5W1H provides the necessary strategies for determining the aforementioned role model researcher group from the perspective of the following actions taken in regard to the research. These actions include: how, what, with whom the research should be carried out, where, when, and why. As such, the optimized scenarios and predicted results that support the selection of the role model researcher group are provided [4].

3   Evaluation of User Satisfaction

In order to evaluate the usefulness of the InSciTe Advisory system, we decide to compare the user satisfaction of this system to the user satisfaction of the current best information system. We performed a multi-dimensional evaluation to measure user satisfaction from the perspective of the following eight requirements, which can be broadly divided in terms of information service quality and information reliability[5]. The eight requirements include accurateness, completeness, information accuracy, information completeness, information navigability, information individualization, accuracy and fullness.

- Information Service Quality Dimension

— Accurateness: Are the results of the analysis accurate?
— Completeness: Are the work process results error-free and completed clearly?
— Information accuracy: Does the information comply with the information purpose and needs of users?
— Information completeness: Is the provided information free of inconsistencies, and does it promote intuitive understanding of the information?
— Information navigability: Can information be searched easily and quickly, and can the overall overview of the information be easily understood?
— Information Individualization: Can the information be customized according to the user's preferences?

- Information Reliability Dimension

— Timeliness: How accurate is the information at the time the transaction is executed, according to the user's requirements?
— Sufficiency: Does the information reflect the user's requirements and meet the user's expectations sufficiently and completely?

Research by Nielson and Landaur indicated that most HCI problems could be identified through an evaluation of 5~6 test users[6]; therefore, to evaluate user satisfaction, we assembled a group of five test users. This group was comprised of experts who were requested to use the InSciTe Advisory service. Elsevier Scival, the current best information system based on the SCOPUS journal data, was selected as the evaluation target to be compared to InSciTe Advisory. Scival has service models comprised of experts, funding, spotlight, strata, analytics, reviewer, finder, etc.

In the user satisfaction evaluation method, the test users use both systems being compared in the evaluation, and measure the satisfaction score of each evaluation system according to eight items. The score by item includes the following absolute evaluation values: very excellent = 10, excellent = 9, normal = 8, unsatisfactory = 7 and very unsatisfactory = 6. Fig.3. displays the test results; total score of InSciTe Advisory is 75.4 and the total score of Elsevier Scival is 59.6. The user satisfaction of InSciTe Advisory was 126.5% higher than the user satisfaction of Scival.

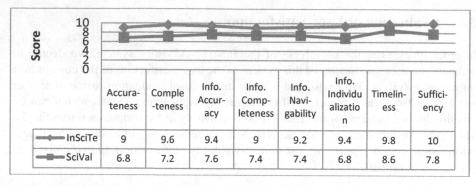

Fig. 3. Evaluation Result

4 Conclusion

The present study described the details of the InSciTe Advisory system, which supports future research direction by analyzing the big data of researcher's past and present work, in order to strengthen the researchers' competencies. InSciTe Advisory provides two main services descriptive and prescriptive analytics services based on the analysis of various researcher-centric data. The analysis service identifies the current research competencies of the researchers, and recommends role model researchers accordingly. Furthermore, the service provides strategies for adopting the best practices of the role model researcher group that is analyzed through the 5W1H method, to enhance the research competitiveness of target researchers. Test results confirmed that the user satisfaction of InSciTe Advisory was 126.5% higher than the user satisfaction of Scival.

References

1. Prescriptive Analytics, http://en.wikipedia.org/wiki/Prescriptive_analytics
2. Gartner Inc.: Hype Cycle for Emerging Technologies (2013), http://www.gartner.com/technology/research/hype-cycles/
3. Song, S.-K., Kim, D.J., Hwang, M., Kim, J., Jeong, D.-H., Lee, S., Jung, H., Sung, W.: Prescriptive Analytics System for Improving Research Power. In: BDSE 2013 (2013)
4. Kim, J., Hwang, M., Gim, J., Song, S.-K., Jeong, D.-H., Lee, S., Jung, H.: Intelligent Analysis and Prediction Model of Researcher's Capability for Prescriptive Analytics. In: AIM 2014 (2014)
5. Jeong, D.-H., Kim, J., Hwang, M., Song, S.-K., Jung, H., Kim, D.-W.: Analytics Service Assessment and Comparison Using Information Service Quality Evaluation Model. International Journal of Information Processing and Management 4(4), 32–43 (2013)
6. Nielsen, J.: Why You Only Need to Test with 5 Users (2000), http://www.nngroup.com/articles/why-you-only-need-to-test-with-5-users/

Customization, Transparency and Proximity: A User-Centered Content Strategy Applied to the Design of a Virtual Library Website

Mireia Leg[1], Mireia Pérez Cervera[2], and Pablo Rebaque-Rivas[1]

[1] Universitat Oberta de Catalunya, Community Initiatives, Barcelona, Spain
{mleg,prebaque}@uoc.edu
[2] Universitat Oberta de Catalunya, Virtual Library, Barcelona, Spain
mperezcerver@uoc.edu

Abstract. We present a case study of the redesign of the organizational presentation and content of the Virtual Library website at the Universitat Oberta de Catalunya (Open University of Catalonia, UOC), based on a user-centered design strategy. The aim of the redesign was to provide users with more intuitive, usable and understandable content (textual content, resources and services) by implementing criteria of customization, transparency and proximity. The study also presents a selection of best practices for applying these criteria to the design of other library websites.

Keywords: usability, findability, user-centered design, library websites, academic libraries, best practices, content strategy, customization.

1 Introduction

Libraries increasingly need to use websites to transmit information and to present their resources and services. This has created a growing awareness of the importance of improving the user experience and raising levels of user satisfaction. As such, there is a growing body of work on the application of user-centered design (UCD) strategies in the creation of library websites [1, 2, 3, 4].

This phenomenon is particularly relevant in the case of virtual libraries, whose websites are the sole means of interaction with users. One such example is the Virtual Library of the Universitat Oberta de Catalunya (Open University of Catalonia, UOC), "the first university in the world [...] that has been built in its entirety from the start on the internet" [5].

In this study we present the successful application of a user-centered design perspective to reconfigure the content structure and information architecture of the Virtual Library website, offering users more intuitive, usable and understandable content (textual content, resources and services) through enhanced customization, transparency and proximity.

The literature makes extensive reference to the usability [1, 2, 3, 4, 6, 7, 8, 9, 10, 11], findability [1,9] and architecture of the information on academic library websites

C. Stephanidis (Ed.): HCII 2014 Posters, Part I, CCIS 434, pp. 191–195, 2014.
© Springer International Publishing Switzerland 2014

[3, 4, 8]. However, we believe that a focus on customization, transparency and proximity gives our case study an extra degree of detail and added value and can serve as a guide to best practice for other institutions looking to implement the same criteria.

2   Methodology

User-centered design refers to a philosophy in which the limitations of the end-user of a product are the focus of each stage of the design process [12]. The broad range of techniques employed at each stage in the UCD process gives the necessary flexibility to adapt to specific requirements and resource availability.

The first months in the design stage of the Virtual Library website were used to gather data on the general requirements. We carried out a benchmarking analysis of major public and university library websites from around the world and identified the key aspects of each, analysing the different solutions adopted for elements such as the home page, navigation, presentation of and access to information, user support, services and functionalities, content and language.

To ensure that we would cater satisfactorily for the needs of our different user profiles, we organized a series of focus groups and interviews with Virtual Library staff, researchers, lecturers and students. To complete the requirements analysis, we also conducted a full study of user consultations and problems reported over the preceding year. The information gathering phase generated a number of ideas for new contents and services and identified the principal information architecture requirements for the redesigned site. To assess the ideal information architecture, we created a map of the site, a data model, and a high-fidelity prototype [13] containing the wireframes of the different library sites examined.

Two usability evaluations of the redesigned site were performed. In both cases, a user test methodology was applied, and a sample of four users was selected for each potential user profile (students, teaching staff, researchers, etc.). The tests comprised a series of questions about the user's profile and pattern of use of the website, a selection of tasks to evaluate effectiveness and satisfaction, and open questions to obtain more detailed feedback.

The first test was conducted with the website at approximately 90% completion and consisted of a global analysis of the design (graphic design, navigation and content structure, content findability, usability and intuitiveness, suitability of tags, etc.). The second test was conducted six months after the launch of the beta version and was used for a detailed usability analysis of some of the most critical sections and functionalities of the website.

Throughout the study period, we monitored and analysed consultations and problems reported by users and examined the usage statistics of the site as a whole and of individual tools and resources.

3   Results and Actions

The results obtained via the different analysis and evaluation methods provided a complete picture of user behaviour and identified the main challenges and problems that the Virtual Library website must address. Notably, the results revealed that users were unaware of many of the resources, tools and services on offer and felt confused by the abundance of tools for accessing information and the sheer volume of information available.

To address these issues, we opted for a clear, uncluttered design; a clear content structure providing concise, contextualized information; and a higher degree of customization, transparency and proximity to users.

For example, to improve the clarity of textual information we used concise, coherently structured texts, written in a familiar style (using the second person singular, avoiding technical terms). Textual information was further clarified by short accompanying videos.

To transmit the values of quality and transparency that form the basis of the redesign, we chose to provide more comprehensive explanations of processes and services, clearly stating the users' rights and duties, outlining the Library's commitment to service, and drafting a series of regulations applicable to all services.

To improve proximity, information on services (and some content types) was expanded to include the names and photographs of the staff responsible, adding a personal element to what is otherwise an entirely virtual service and encouraging feedback between staff and users.

To improve access to different content types, the site was restructured to reflect user needs (article search, database search, take out a loan, obtain an e-document, etc.) rather than the tools that the Library offers (catalogue, link resolver, discovery tool, metasearch engine, etc.). We also introduced a single search box in a prominent position on the every page that offers a simple, centralized means of accessing any resource. This new functionality runs on the discovery tool Summon[1], which can be modified to provide access to resources and contents not originally linked to its unified index, making it highly effective.

The information architecture was customized to display content matching each user profile (students, teaching staff, researchers, etc.), enabling every user to clearly identify the services and resources s/he can access and the corresponding terms of use. In addition, to guarantee the necessary visibility and transparency, the information for each profile is now made available to all users.

4   Conclusions

A new website is a significant change and a considerable undertaking for everyone involved: the architecture must be designed and developed, staff must learn to use a new content management system, and all users will need time to become familiar with the new site. It is important to be aware of these issues and adopt a responsible approach to make the most of the change. At the UOC, the redesign was taken as an

---

[1] Summon, from the firm Serials Solutions, "is built around a single, unified index that returns a single, unified set of results—allowing users to effectively search and navigate across almost all of the library's resources" (Source: Serials Solutions website. http://www.serialssolutions.com/en/services/summon).

opportunity to implement a new approach focused entirely on users and their varying needs. The UCD philosophy was fundamental in achieving this and has been integrated into the working strategy of the entire Virtual Library team.

As is made clear in the Results section, user satisfaction is tied to the concepts of clarity, simplicity, content structure and contextualization, customization, transparency and proximity. These concepts are key factors in the overall usability of the website, enabling users to find and view the desired content in as straightforward a manner as possible. Given that the potential users of a university library present a broad range of needs and varying degrees of knowledge and information skills, designing a website that caters for them all is no easy task. The concept of customization is therefore paramount.

Feedback from users during the information gathering phase made frequent reference to customization. Users are clearly interested in far more advanced customization and would like to be offered content that meets their specific requirements as individuals rather than as members of a particular profile group. To reinforce the point, many users referred to the recommendation function employed by Amazon.

Future work will continue to focus on the customization of the site content. Forthcoming developments will include the creation of shortcuts to customized content for each user profile and the launch of the new "My library" section, where users will be able to manage their various forms of interaction with the Library (doubts and queries, reporting problems, loans, service requests, etc.). We will also continue our efforts to improve access to the digital collection and to increase the transparency and usability of other content and resource management tools offered by the Virtual Library and UOC, as this is a critical part of the user experience.

5   Best Practices

We present a selection of best practices that may of use to other institutions when designing a virtual library website:

— - Customize content. Display the content available to and required by each user, adapting the browsing experience to specific profiles and information needs.
— - Conduct a detailed study of potential site users (information requirements, likely uses of information, behaviour, habits, etc.). This enables information to be organized in a way that reflects specific needs, designing processes that mirror the logic of different patterns of use.
— - Provide content findability solutions adapted to the different user profiles and levels of information skills.
— - Ensure that texts are concise and coherently structured and written in a familiar style, making information on the site easier to read and understand.
— - Prioritize the quality and transparency of processes and services. This ensures that the rights and duties of each party (user and provider) are clearly defined and establishes a trust relationship between the two.
— - Devirtualize the service. Telling users about the team behind a website, service or project creates a trust relationship with the user and encourages mutual feedback.

References

1. Fox, R., Fox, R.: Weaving the digital library web. OCLC Systems & Services 24(1), 8–17 (2008)
2. Newell, P.A., et al.: Collaborating for Change: Leveraging Campus Partnerships to Create a User-Centered Library Website. Internet Reference Services Quarterly 18(3-4), 227–246 (2013)
3. Guo, J., Yan, P.: User-centered information architecture of University Library Website. In: 3rd International Conference on Computer Research and Development, vol. (2), pp. 370–372 (2011)
4. Ward, J.L.: Web site redesign: the University of Washington Libraries' experience. OCLC Systems & Services 22(3), 207–216 (2006)
5. UOC, The leading online University (sub ENG). Universitat Oberta de Catalunya, http://youtu.be/O6eQn-PxS3k
6. Kim, Y.-M.: Users' perceptions of university library websites: A unifying view. Library & Information Science Research 33(1), 63–72 (2011)
7. Mellone, J.T., Williams, D.J.: Applying best practices in web site redesign: the Queens College Libraries experience. OCLC Systems & Services 26(3), 177–197 (2010)
8. Gullikson, S., Blades, R., Bragdon, M., McKibbon, S., Sparling, M., Toms, E.G.: The impact of information architecture on academic web site usability. The Electronic Library 17(5), 293–304 (1999)
9. Blakiston, R.: Developing a Content Strategy for an Academic Library Website. Journal of Electronic Resources Librarianship 25(3), 175–191 (2013)
10. Aharony, N.: An analysis of American academic libraries' websites: 2000-2010. The Electronic Library 30(6), 764–776 (2012)
11. Becker, D.A., Yannotta, L.: Modeling a library website redesign process: developing a user-centered website through usability testing. Information Technology and Libraries 32(1), 6 (2013)
12. Garreta-Domingo, M., Mor, E.: User Centered Design in e-Learning

Twist and Shout: Developing Interactive Annotation for 3D Printers

Linda Lim

Murdoch University, WA, Australia
email2enigma@yahoo.com

Abstract. This short paper encompasses the birth of Project Anno. The researcher investigated the possibility of support for accurate annotation on the output of 3D scanners [14] to enhance the use of 3D printers [12] for use in 3D prototyping. As Project Anno is a work-in-progress, the current system aims to simulate accurate natural user interaction and expects to result in a user's physical movement and voice input being able to operate the system's annotation functions with some degree of precision, nicknamed as the "twist and shout" method by the researcher. In this interactive annotation environment, users can have a natural interactive experience by using their hands to practise accurate control of using the hand in place of a mouse. A description of the solution, closest related work, how Project Anno is novel, how Project Anno's design is iterated upon, and the usability evaluation method of Project Anno are discussed.

Keywords: 3D point clouds, 3D scanners, user annotation, natural user interaction, 3D printers, 3D prototyping.

1   Introduction

The idea of developing interactive annotation for 3D printers [12] was first conceived when the researcher came across the IEEE 3DUI 2014 Contest, where the problem description involves building a system that allows users to annotate 3D point clouds [13] from 3D scanners [14][8]. The challenge of this project is to enable support for accurate labeling of sets of points and authoring of overlapping hierarchies of annotations at varying scales [8]. This project endeavors to possess a set of tools that is versatile enough to meet this challenge. To incorporate annotation precision, the researcher considered the Adobe Illustrator Ruler and Guide [9] concept and the Scalable Vector Graphics [10] concept. As for interactivity, the Interactive Whiteboard [11] concept was considered. To promote Natural User Interaction [3], the Kinect for Windows [2] was considered. Similar examples applying the Interactive Whiteboard [11] concept and Natural User Interaction [3] include ShowMe Interactive Whiteboard [1], Touchless Touch [6], and Ubi Interactive [7]. In terms of 3D prototyping, 3D printing [12] was considered. These considerations contribute towards the solution for developing interactive annotation for 3D printers.

C. Stephanidis (Ed.): HCII 2014 Posters, Part I, CCIS 434, pp. 196–201, 2014.
© Springer International Publishing Switzerland 2014

2   Description of the Solution

Developing interactive annotation for 3D printers [12] was named Project Anno for ease of reference. At this stage of the current version of Project Anno, some constraints were involved. As an enthusiast researcher, budget was the largest constraint followed by development tools (directly related to budget) and manpower (one person involvement). Therefore, the development tools indicated are what the budget permits at this point in time. As for the manpower, the researcher hopes to form a collaboration team for future versions of Project Anno.

2.1   Hardware and Software

The current version of Project Anno was built using both hardware and software. The hardware used consists of two items. The first item is an ASUS All-in-one PC series. The second item is a Kinect for Windows sensor [2] which was used for the development of the user interaction [3].

Microsoft Windows 8.1 was used as the operating system for building Project Anno. Microsoft Visual Studio 2010 was used for coding the applications in C#/C++ to work with the Kinect for Windows sensor [2]. Kinect for Windows SDK v1.8 and Kinect for Windows Developer Toolkit v1.8 were used to build the user interaction [2-3]. Kinect for Windows Runtime v1.8 was used to enable end users to communicate with Project Anno [2]. DirectX SDK was used to enable the compilation of Direct3D-based functions in Project Anno. DirectX End-User Runtime was used to enable end users to operate Direct3D-based functions in Project Anno. XNA Game Studio 4.0 was used to support Kinect's ColorImageStream, DepthImageStream, and SkeletonStream to enable end users to have a natural interaction experience with Project Anno. Speech Platform SDK 11.0 was used to enable user speech recognition when interacting with Project Anno [2].

2.2   Application of Concepts

With reference to the considerations that contribute towards the solution for developing interactive annotation for 3D printers [12], the researcher applied the "snap to grid (snap to pixel)", "snap-to-guide (smart guide)", and "snap to point" from the Adobe Illustrator Ruler and Guide [9] concept, and the versatile "polygon" basic shape from the Scalable Vector Graphics [10] concept, to simulate the accurate annotation of sets of unstructured and unlabeled points at different scales while preserving the vector image shape generated by 3D scanners [14]. In terms of Natural User Interaction [3], the researcher applied motion sensing with the help of the Kinect for Windows [2] to simulate user interaction with the system using a user's physical movement and voice as input. To enhance 3D prototyping, the researcher applied the idea of 3D printing [12] as the final product of annotating 3D point clouds [13] generated by 3D scanners [14] to facilitate the decision-making process in diverse industries, for instance, architecture, construction, dental and medical, education, aerospace, engineering, geographic information systems etc.

2.3   Status Quo of Project Anno

As Project Anno is a work-in-progress, the current system enables users to have a natural interactive experience by using their hands to practise accurate control of using the hand in place of a mouse through a simple exercise routine. This simple exercise routine introduces natural user interaction as another way for human beings to manipulate a system's functions using their physical movement. The objective of this simple exercise routine is to complete all the tasks assigned within a set time frame without instructions. Project Anno expects to result in a user's physical movement and voice input being able to operate the system's annotation functions with some degree of precision. This method of natural user interaction is nicknamed "twist and shout" by the researcher.

2.4   System Architecture of Project Anno

The diagram illustrates Project Anno's system architecture (Fig. 1).

Fig. 1. Project Anno's System Architecture

3   Closest Related Work

The closest related work to Project Anno took some searches before making a final decision on three. There are several projects on interactive whiteboards using the keyboard and the mouse. There are few projects on interactive whiteboards using motion sensors. However, most include user annotations on documents.

3.1   ShowMe Interactive Whiteboard

One closest related work to Project Anno is the ShowMe Interactive Whiteboard [1]. ShowMe Interactive Whiteboard is an iOS application that has a number of features particularly useful for educators. The features include voice recording, assorted brush colors, pause and erase functions, image import from existing library, built-in camera, and web search, upload and share recordings, embed recordings for sharing, unlimited lesson length, and student management using groups function [1].

3.2   Touchless Touch

Another closest related work to Project Anno is Touchless Touch [6]. Touchless Touch is a software that converts any surface into a multi-touch screen, including use as an interactive whiteboard, a standard of 128 touch points, operates with any surface size from 14" to more than 200" (requires more than one sensor), Windows 7 and Windows 8 native touch support, Kinect for Windows, Xbox 360 Kinect, and Open-NI/Prime Sense sensors support, unlimited free trial, and unlimited free upgrades/updates of the licensed software [6].

3.3   Ubi Interactive

Ubi Interactive [7] is another similar example. Ubi Interactive transforms any surface into a touch screen, with no complex setup, no user calibration, no need to develop special applications, simply connect the projector and Kinect to the Windows 8 PC and the Ubi software will callibrate automatically, supports input mode such as finger, hand, or Ubi pen on touch surface, supports touch points from 1-20, supports display size of up to 120", and a 30-day free trial version of the Ubi software [7].

4   How Project Anno Is Novel

Project Anno differs from the three closest related work mentioned in a number of ways. Project Anno aims to apply motion sensing, voice commands, and user annotations on 3D objects, unlike the closest related examples where multi-touch and user annotations are employed. Project Anno also aims to apply 3D scanning [14] capabilities to capture the 3D image before user annotations are carried out on the image and to record user annotations for future references or 3D printing [12]. Project Anno attempts to carry out annotations using a user's physical movement and voice input on the output of 3D scanners [14] to enhance the use of 3D printers [12] for use in 3D prototyping in diverse industries, using the "twist and shout" method nicknamed by the researcher. Project Anno strives to provide 3D scanning [14] and natural user annotation capabilities as a 2-in-1 package so that various industries can benefit from printing annotated versions of a 3D prototype to facilitate the decision-making process. Project Anno is compatible with a large display size when connected to a projector, a Kinect for Windows sensor [2], and a Windows 8 PC or laptop.

5   How Project Anno's Design Is Iterated Upon

A hybrid (Extreme and Scrum [4-5]) development methodology is adopted by the researcher in developing interactive annotation for 3D printers. The Extreme [4] development methodology is employed because Project Anno requires frequent enhancements to system quality and user feedback on system responsiveness, in order to improve productivity, by using checkpoints to introduce new user requirements, to further enhance system efficiency. The Scrum [5] development methodology is also used because Project Anno needs an iterative and incremental approach to achieve an objective, that is to meet the challenge of this project, while being flexible enough to deliver promptly in response to new user requirements. This hybrid development methodology is named ExScrum development methodology (Fig. 2) by the researcher. The researcher will continue with this hybrid development methodology for building future versions of Project Anno.

Fig. 2. ExScrum Development Methodology

6   Usability Evaluation Method of Project Anno

Heuristic evaluation [15] is selected as the usability evaluation method for the development of Project Anno because it is a good way of examining the interface for big and small problems against a set of usability principles called "heuristics", supplementing the method with severity ratings (frequency, impact, persistence) of small problems, by a small group of evaluators, possibly becoming users of Project Anno. To measure the usability of Project Anno, the current version of the system will be examined against the ten usability heuristics [16].

7   Conclusion

This paper explored developing interactive annotation for 3D printers [12]. Hardware and software, application of concepts, status quo of Project Anno, system architecture of Project Anno, ExScrum development methodology, and heuristic evaluation were discussed. The current version of Project Anno comprises a simple exercise routine that introduces natural user interaction as another way for human beings to manipulate a system's functions using their physical movement. Project Anno is still in its infancy and development is continuing towards building a set of tools to carry out annotations using a user's physical movement and voice input, on the output of 3D scanners [14] to enhance the use of 3D printers [12] for use in 3D prototyping in diverse industries, using the "twist and shout" method of natural user interaction.

References

1. Learnbat, Inc. ShowMe Interactive Whiteboard. Version 4.2.2, iTunes (October 15, 2013), http://www.showme.com/
2. Microsoft Corporation. Kinect for Windows (2013), http://www.microsoft.com/en-us/kinectforwindows/
3. Wikipedia. Natural user interface (December 17, 2013), http://en.wikipedia.org/wiki/Natural_user_interface
4. Wikipedia. Extreme Programming (March 5, 2014), http://en.wikipedia.org/wiki/Extreme_programming
5. Wikipedia. Scrum Software Development (March 14, 2014), http://en.wikipedia.org/wiki/Scrum_software_development
6. RobSmithDev. Touchless Touch. Version 4.1 (2012-2013), http://www.touchlesstouch.com/
7. Ubi Interactive Inc. (2013), http://www.ubi-interactive.com/
8. IEEE 3DUI (2014), Contest, http://3dui.org/
9. Adobe Illustrator Ruler and Guide, http://help.adobe.com/en_US/illustrator/cs/using/WS714a382cdf7d304e7e07d0100196cbc5f-631da.html#WS714a382cdf7d304e7e07d0100196cbc5f-6312a
10. Wikipedia. Scalable Vector Graphics (March 13, 2014), http://en.wikipedia.org/wiki/Scalable_Vector_Graphics
11. Wikipedia. Interactive Whiteboard (February 14, 2014), http://en.wikipedia.org/wiki/Interactive_whiteboard
12. Wikipedia. 3D Printing (March 16, 2014), http://en.wikipedia.org/wiki/3D_printing
13. Wikipedia. 3D Point Clouds (February 18, 2014), http://en.wikipedia.org/wiki/Point_cloud
14. Wikipedia. 3D Scanners (March 16, 2014), http://en.wikipedia.org/wiki/3D_scanner
15. Nielsen Norman Group (1998-2014), http://www.nngroup.com/topic/heuristic-evaluation/
16. Nielsen Norman Group. 10 Usability Heuristics for User Interface Design by Jakob Nielsen on January 1 1995 (1998-2014), http://www.nngroup.com/articles/ten-usability-heuristics/

Does the Design Style Influence the Perception of Product Performance Charts?

Che-Chun Liu and Cheng-Hung Lo

Department of Industrial Design Chang Gung University, Taiwan, R.O.C.
259 Wen-Hwa 1st Road, Kwei-Shan Tao-Yuan, 333, Taiwan, R.O.C.
qc131313@hotmail.com, ch.lo@mail.cgu.edu.tw

Abstract. Product performance charts are commonly seen in the product reviews published on the relevant web sites, magazines, and other public media. They are aimed at helping consumers understand the similarities and differences among the gathered products. This study investigates whether the design style influences the perception of the product performance charts. And this paper presents the result of an initial experiment that evaluates three chart types, including bar charts, count charts, and radar charts. The result shows that the participants may evaluate a product differently if presented with different design style. The result of this initial experiment provides some interesting insights. Further investigations that follow will include the dimensional factors and the more in-depth analysis of how a consumer responds to product performance charts.

Keywords: chart design, information visualization, consumer behavior.

1 Introduction

The advances of manufacturing technologies have lowered the thresholds for companies to develop new products. The market availabilities of many products such as consumer electronics have also transited from "large quantity with small variety" to "small quantity with big variety". When a consumer shops for a particular type of products, they may indeed have many (sometimes more than needed) different choices. It should be safely assumed that the consumer wish to select the products that best meet his/her needs. The selection process usually involves evaluating and comparing the specifications and performances of similar products. Product performance charts are commonly seen in the product reviews published on the relevant web sites, magazines, and other public media. These charts transform factual or numeric data about the products to visual forms, which make it easier for a consumer to understand the similarities and differences among the gathered products. The purpose of this study is to investigate whether different types of product performance chart would result in different product choices.

C. Stephanidis (Ed.): HCII 2014 Posters, Part I, CCIS 434, pp. 202–205, 2014.

2   Literature Review

Crilly et al. argued that a consumer used visual references to form the concept of a product [1]. They suggested that the sophistication of the visual references also improved a consumer's impression of a product. Six types of such external visual references were discussed in the study, including Stereotypes, Similar products, Metaphors, Characters, Conventions, and Clichés. We deem the product performance chart as one of the external visual references of a product. There are several recent studies that focus on analyzing the effect of different visualization means on a consumer's behaviors. Drechsler and Natter carried out a series of experiments to investigate how the price chart of a product affected price expectations and purchasing time decisions [2]. They found that the pattern of the price chart, which visualizes the price changes of a product during a period of time, had a significant effect on the behaviors studied. For example, a big variation of the price chart would delay a consumer's purchasing decision. The more illustrative visualization approach such as infographics is studied in Borkin et al. They collected a vast range of infographics and conducted the experiments to evaluate their memorability. They concluded that the memorability of an infographic could provide a good measure of how effective it convey the information [3]. Indeed, as Juan Velasco, the graphics editor of National Geographic Magazine, suggested, infographics are self-explanatory visual interpretations that support a reader to comprehend certain concepts or information quickly and consistently [4]. In our work, we attempt to explore this issue at a more detailed level. We are interested how certain design features or styles influence a consumer's preferences among the similar products.

3   Methodology

In this paper, we present the result from an initial experiment that included three chart types, which are bar charts, count charts, and radar charts. We first produced a data set that contained the hypothesized evaluation credits of 10 similar unknown products. The credits, which were randomly generated, were given to 5 imaginative dimensions to measure the performances of the products. The data set was then used to produce the three included chart types. There are, therefore, 10 charts for each chart type. The experiment was carried out with the 2AFC (Two-Alternative Forced Choice) method, in which the participants are required to choose one between two experiment stimuli in each trial. For each chart type, the 10 charts were presented in pairs. The pairs were the non-repeated combinations selected from the 10 charts. That resulted in a total of 45 pairs form each chart type. The entire experiment is divided into three stages. We presented the 45 pairs as digital slides in each stage. Each participant thus had a total of 135 trials in the experiment. In each trial, the participant indicated which of the two comparison charts stood for a better product. The average percentage of choosing one chart over all others was then taken as an integrated measure of its relative preference. 9 of the tested charts are shown in Figure 1.

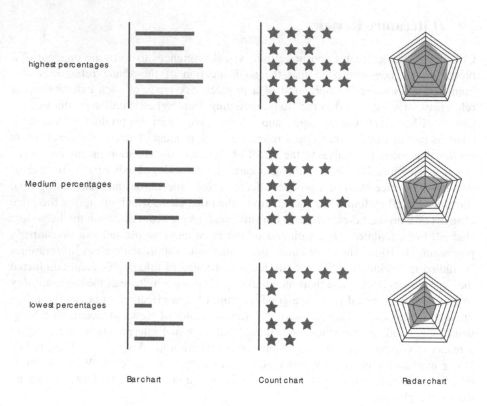

Fig. 1. Excerpted test charts

4　Result and Conclusion

The result is shown in Figure 2. The horizontal axis represents the index number of the charts. The vertical axis represents the average percentage of a chart preferred by the participants. The groups of three bars represent the three chart types, the dark grey for the bar chart, the mid grey for the count chart, and the light grey for the radar chart. At a glance of the chart, the participants exhibit a similar preference across different chart types. Chart 1, 6, 8, and 10 in particular get the highest percentages in all of the three chart types. Despite this similarity, in the radar chart group has the biggest differences in the percentage of chart choices. This indicates that although the three types of chart are created with the same data set, the participants may have a more keen sense of judgment on the evaluations presented with a radar chart. There are also a few minor differences in the preferences among the three types of chart. For example, in the Chart 2 and 3 groups, although they are generated with the same corresponding data, Chart 2 gets less percentage than Chart 3 in the count chart group while the opposite outcome can be observed in the radar chart group. This helps use strengthen the hypothesis that one may evaluate a product differently if presented with different design style. The result of this initial experiment provides some interesting insights. Further investigations that follow will include the dimensional factors and a more in-depth analysis of how consumer respond to product performance charts.

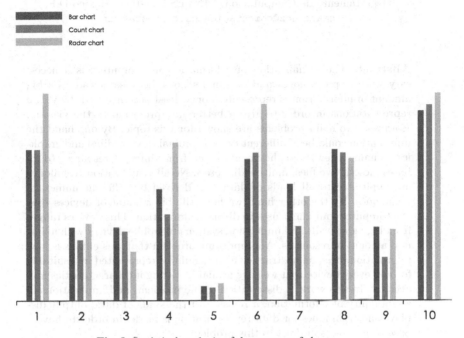

Fig. 2. Statistical analysis of three types of charts

References

1. Borkin, M.A., Zoya Bylinskii, A.A.V., Isola, P., Sunkavalli, S., Oliva, A., Pfister, H.: What Makes a Visualization Memorable? IEEE Transactions on Visualization and Computer Graphics 19(12) (2013)
2. Crilly, N., Moultrie, J., Clarkson, P.J.: Seeing things: consumer response to the visual domain in product design. Design Studies 25(6), 547–577 (2004)
3. Drechsler, W., Natter, M.: Do Price Charts Provided by Online Shopbots Influence Price Expectations and Purchase Timing Decisions? Journal of Interactive Marketing 25(2), 95–109 (2011)
4. The graphics editor of National Geographic magazine Juan Velasco

Implications of Adaptability of Information

Sonia Abigail Martínez Salas and Amilcar Meneses Viveros

Departamento de Computación, CINVESTAV-IPN, México D.F.
smartinez@computacion.cs.cinvestav.mx

Abstract. The visualization of information in computers is a necessary work in professional and personal scopes, because nowadays a big
amount of information is represented, or at least accompanied, by visual
representations in order to give a better interpretation to the viewers.
However, two main problems are shown for this topic. By one hand the
information could be of different types (nominal, text, ordinal and graphics to name a few) and they could come from different resources (data
bases, descriptive files, multimedia, etc.). No all visualization techniques
are applicable to all kinds of data sets derived by different numerical
techniques. By the other hand we have the big amount of devices that
the computer equipment uses to display information. This devices ranges
from big video walls and immersion systems to mobile devices with a limited amount of resources. An important problem that this entails is how
information, been an abstract element ,could be represented in a suitable
form in every device that we have available, taking its characteristics into
account. In this work, a dissertation of the problems and implications of
adaptability of information, a revision of the kinds of data, output displays and techniques for data representation is made, in order to have a
base to propose solutions to this problem.

1 Introduction

The visualization of information is a necessary work in professional and personal
scopes because it is easier for humans to understand images than words and
numbers [1]. That is the reason why nowadays images invades all aspects of our
lives, even making a weather report or a news paper incomplete without images
[2]. It depends on the view of computer graphics that the experience seems as
real as posible, regardless the image or information depicted is from real life or
imagined [2]. Actually, there are factors that can increase the duality of graphics
and user experience, improving the feeling of presence in terms of impressiveness
immersion and natural interaction [3].

Two main problems make the adequate visualization of information difficult.
The first problem is the distinct kinds of data and the different ways in which this
data, can be represented. The second problem is the different kinds of devices
in which an application can display this data.

The amount of available devices is huge and variable, this make the necessity
of adaptation and ubiquitous access to user interphases evident [4]. An ubicuos
application must be able access information from different devices, and show it

C. Stephanidis (Ed.): HCII 2014 Posters, Part I, CCIS 434, pp. 206–212, 2014.

in the best way posible. To know which is an appropriate manner to display information, the device must take into account the features of the host device, and try to use them to make information more attractive and easy to interprete. Some features like the capability to display information in an immersive system and the use of graphics, have shown to get a better representation and interpretation of the presented information than information without this features [5]. Other important features to take into account in this problem are the display's dimensions, contrast, resolution and energetic consume.

Nowadays, a way to develop a cross platform application and access to devices features, is developing *Rich-Client* applications [6], but most of the work done is only oriented to movie devices as smart phones, leaving out other devices.

Scientific visualization have worked with data models and their transformations to obtain an appropriated and understandable graphic representation of the data. However, it does not exist an study verifying whether this transformations are appropriate for all the output devices or analyzing which transformations are better for each one.

In this work ,a dissertation of the problems and implications of adaptability of information is presented. In section 2 a summary of techniques of data representations is presented to know equivalences and transformations between data models. In section 3 we mention different output devices in order to name their important features. In section 4 we talk about the advances in areas like data visualization and hybrid applications developing, as a possible solution to this problem. Section 5 contains an analysis of the things we need to have, as a base or fist approach to solve our problem. Finally our conclusions are shown in section 6.

2   Techniques of Data Representation

There are diferente data types that could be grouped in 3 categories (nominal, aggregated and ordinal) [2]. Nominal data are represented by a set of points, the order in which this points are representen is not important for the data representation. An example of this graphic representations are bars and cake graphs. In aggregated data, an specific order is important to obtain a correct meaning. This data could be represented in histograms or drawing zones, for example. Ordinal data are representations in which the order is important and the represented image is commonly discontinuous. In this case, values can be joined if the image is continuous.

Some transformations between data are easy or direct, as transforming a 3D histogram to 2D taking slices of the fist one. Other easy way to find an equivalent data model is to represent the same information in distinct data models, as histograms or graphics bars. Other transformations request an elaborate algorithm to be done, and usually, they uses more computations, an example of this transformations is the volume render algorithm, which is used to reconstruct 3D models from borders in 2D images. Even if some representation are equivalent, not all of them are interpreted in the same way, works to represent the same things or can be shown in any kind of device.

3   Output Devices

The devices where we need to display our applications is wide and highly variated talking about their features. This devices vary from smart phones and tablets with limited capacities, and small displays, to CAVE systems and big video walls. The minimum features that we need to take into account to obtain a proper display of information are: display dimensions, resolution, contrast, 3D display capability and energetic consume. Resolution and contrast will help os as a range to deduce the level of detail that a graphic must have, the size in which it must be displayed and even the kind of colors to be used. 3D content capability will indicate whether if the output is going to be displayed in two or three dimensions. Finally, energetic consume to decide if a transformation can be done in our device or an external render server. An other thing in which energetic consume will help, is deciding if the information is going to be presented in gadgets of low energy consume, as tabs, or if it is better to use dark colors instead of bright ones.

4   Related Work

4.1   Data Visualization

Scientific visualization studies the effectiveness of displaying different kinds of graphics, trying to make them more real and entendible [2]. One of the main areas where this discipline is used is in data simulation, because of the big amount of information that we need to view in order to understand the events [7].

Transformations between different data models have been studied by scientific visualization to obtain a best representation and interpretation of them. Some works have shown the data models that visualization systems uses and the algorithms that they use to transform them [7] [8]. There are some guides that tell os how to make graphics more entendible, using different models an even telling os where is a good place to put text in them [9], but most of them are oriented only to scientific publications as articles and similar reports.

4.2   *Rich-Client* Applications

Due to the huge amount of devices in which information could be displayed, if we want an application to execute in all of them, there are two ways to achieve it. The first form is to develop a native application for each device, which is complicated due to the big amount of devices and platforms that exists. The other solution is to use some kind of Web client to display information.

In traditional Web applications, the manner in which the contents are distributed between clients and servers is limited [10]. The three kinds of Web clients are Thin, Fat and *Rich-Client* [6]. If we use a Thin client, the device will only be used to display datas. In Fat clients, all the calculus would be executed in the server, what is not adequate for all kinds of devices. The development of open systems have made posible the use of codes which UI adapts to distinct output devices, in this application called *Rich-Client* or hybrid applications, the features of the host device are obtained in order to adapt the application. *Rich-Client* applications have had an evident success in last years, unfortunately, this works have been used mostly for mobile platforms because of it's hight request.

Rich-Client applications have the capability of execute calculus as if they were a native application [11]. They are able to make client processes without a connection with the server, actualizing changes later when a connection is available (this characteristic gives them the name of temporally disconnected applications too) [10]. They are independent of the operative system where they are running in, what avoids to develop a native application for each one. They do not need any installation, what makes it easier to access than native applications, because any user with an actualized Web Browser will be able to use the application in all they'r devices, without using extra storage. If there is not need of an installation, most sporadic users in many devices would use this applications. Finally, and as the most important feature, *Rich-Client* applications can access to device's features [6], allowing each application to decide it's behavior.

5   Adaptability of Information Analysis

Nowadays there is no any support that allow the adequate interaction of data in different devices, using they'r features to make it posible. Fig. 1 shows a possible solution to this problem in which information could be situated in the device or out it. In case the information is not in the device, it must be obtained from an external data server. Information is presented in different data models. This data models can proceed from representation forms, for example, data bases, descriptive files, plane text files or even multimedia. Once the application is executed, it must know in which device is running, obtaining the device's features (dimensions, resolution, contrast, energetic consume, and capability to display 3D content) in order to decide which is the best way to display information in that device.

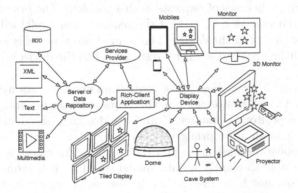

Fig. 1. General infrastructure for adaptability or information

In case the information is not represented in the data model that best fits the device a transformation must be done. In this case mobile devices could not be able to make this computations every time because it would take a considerable battery consume. If this happens, an other evaluation will be whether if the device would make the transformation or if it is better to make it in an external render server. In this scenario, other importan thing to take into account is Web connectivity, to request and sent, information and data models. Once the information is represented in the correct data model in the device, they are going to be displayed and used among user interaction.

All applications are adaptable if they have at least an adaptable element. In this case information is our adaptable element and it is going to be required as a message. Information could be represented in different data models, all of them with different features. A user might ask for an specific data model independently of it's device's features. The way to determine which is the most adequate data model for each device depends on it's features.

Been F the set of features that a device has, information set I will contain different data models to represent information. A message, requesting information, from a device to the data server or repository should include at least F or the specific data model i_s. If the message only contains F, the data repository must decide which representation of the information will fit the most to the device's features F. If it only contains the request model, it will be imposible to know whether the device will be able to display it in an adequate way, so it will just send it without verification. Finally, if the message contains both F and i_s, the data server will verify that i_s is the best way to display information in a device with F features, if it is not, it will send a message to the device, asking whether if it wants that data model anyway.

Whenever the data server does not have information in the specific data model that it is requested, a transformation must be done. The data server must decide, based on F, if this transformation should be done in the device or in an external render server. The data model from where we are going to obtain the new data model, must be the one that makes less computational work, in order to obtain the new one. The data repository will select this model from I.

There are four main cases of requests in this problem. The firs case is the ideal case, when the data server decides that the request data model will be displayed in an appropriated way in the device. The request data model is available in the data server, so it just have to send this data model to the device who will display it.

The second case is when the device request an specific data model, independently of it's device's features F, but the request message contains F. In this case, the data repository evaluates F and decides that the device will not be able to display it in an appropriate way, so it sends an advertisement. Now the *Rich-Client* application must make an other request. An example where the device will not be able to display a data model could be if it requires a 3D data model, but it does not have the specific hardware to display it. In this case, if the device does not provides F, the data repository would not be able to know whether if the device is able to display the requested model, so it would send it, and the client must then realize, that it will not be able to display it and show it's corresponding advertisement.

Third case is when the data server does not have the requested data model i_s, so a transformation must be done. The data server evaluates the features F, deciding that the device will be able to compute this transformation, then it selects the best data model to be transformed from I, and finally it sends this model to the device. In the device the client will make all the computational calculus to obtain the best model that fits it's features and then it displays it.

Fourth is similar third case, but with the difference that now the data server decides that the device will not be able to make the computations itself. In this case, the selected data model is sent to a render server instead of sent to the device. The render server makes the transformation and sends the new data model directly to the device, in order to reduce time and net traffic. An example of devices that could not be able to make a big computation are movie devices, where energetic consume could limit it's performance.

Until now we have been talking about data model transformations of information, without mentioning how the data server or *Rich-Client* application, is going to decide which is the most adequate way to display information in a device, according to it's features F. This evaluation must be done, according to a mapping as Fig. 2 shows, in which the data types are nominal, ordinal and aggregated, and the data representations are the way in which we can represent them, as histograms, drawing zones, etc. Depending on the features of each device, we will know which data representations will fit it well. Taking this into account, we may name some examples of mapping. Tiny and small devices are able to display nominal data in an appropriate way. Ordinal data is preferable to be displayed in devices with normal size display. In devices with small display, but aceptable resolution an contrast, ordinal data can be displayed too.

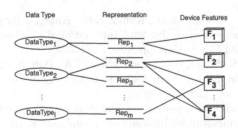

Fig. 2. Mapping to decide which data model is the best representation to a device

6   Conclusions

The representation of information through images is an important aspect nowadays, making indispensable to be sure that images are attractive and can be interpreted by users in an appropriated manner. In order to decide which is the best way to represent information in a device, it's features must be taking into account. A proper way to obtain device's features, to take it as an advantage, is using *Rich-Client* applications. In devices in which energetic consume should be used carefully, any kind of transformation will be executed preferentially in an external render server, unless the cost of transferring data results hight due to it's size. In order to make adaptability or information posible, it is necessary a big infrastructure, and the way that applications are connected to data repositories and render servers must change. Information should be available in data repositories, whose must be provided of specific features, and event artificial intelligence, to decide, or juts verify, the best data model according to each device's features and where transformations must be done, in case it is required. Until now, approaches to solve this problems are only factible using *Rich-Client* applications, to access to device features and decide the system's behavior. Unfortunately, most or the work of this technology is just focused in movie device developing.

References

1. Arteaga, P., Batanero, C., Días, C., Contreras, J.M.: El lenguaje de los gráficos estadísticos. Revista Iberoamericana de Educación Matemática 1, 93–104 (2009)
2. Wright, H.: Introduction to Scientific Visualization, 1st edn., vol. 1. Springer (2007)
3. Nocent, O., Piotin, S., Benassarou, A., Jaisson, M., Lucas, L.: Toward an immersion platform for the world wide web using auto stereoscopic displays and tracking devices. In: Proceedings of the 17th International Conference on 3D Web Technology, pp. 69–72 (2012)
4. Moralez, G.S.: Redistribución semi-plástica mixta: el caso de estudio de un pizarrón compartido. Computer sciences, CINVESTAV-IPN, México D.F. (2009)
5. Raja, D., Bowman, D., Lucas, J., North, C.: Exploring the benefits of immersion in abstract information visualization. In: Proc. of IPT (Immersive Projection Technology) (2004)
6. Hernández, I.M.T., Viveros, A.M., Rubio, E.H.: Analysis for the design of open applications on movile devices. In: 23rd International Conference on Electronics, Communications and Computing, pp. 126–131 (2013)
7. Ni, T., Schmidt, G.S., Staad, O.G., Livingston, M.A., Ball, R., May, R.: A survey of large high-resolution display technologies techniques and applications. In: Vistual Reality Conference, pp. 223–236 (2006)
8. Chi, E.H.: A taxonomy of visualization techniques using the data state reference model. In: IEEE Sympoium on Information Visualization, pp. 69–75 (2000)
9. Kelleher, C., Wagener, T.: Ten guidelines for effective data visualization in scientific publications. Environmental Modelling and Software 26(6), 822–827 (2011)
10. Preciado, J.C., Linaje, M., Comai, S., Sanchez-Figueroa, F.: Designing rich internet applications with web engineering methodologies. In: 9th IEEE International Workshop on Web Site Evolution, 23–30 (2007)
11. Meier, J., Homer, A., Hill, D., Taylor, J., Bansode, P., Wall, L., Boucher Jr., R., Bogawat, A.: Patterns and practices Application Architecture Guide 2.0, 2nd edn. Microsoft Corporation, USA (2009)

Inspiring Viewers of Abstract Painting by a Gaze Based Music Generation

Tatsuya Ogusu[1], Jun Ohya[1], Jun Kurumisawa[2], and Shunichi Yonemura[3]

[1] Waseda University, Global Information and Telecommunication Institute
Bldg. 29-7, 1-3-10 Nishi-Waseda, Shinjuku-ku, Tokyo 169-0051, Japan
[2] Chiba University of Commerce, Faculty of Policy Informatics, Japan
[3] Shibaura Institute of Technology, College of Engineering, Japan
tatsuyaogusu@akane.waseda.jp

Abstract. This paper explores the effectiveness of prompting abstract paintings' viewers' inspiration and imagination by the authors' gaze based music generation system. The authors' music generation system detects the viewer's gaze by a gaze detection equipment. At each of the gaze staying positions in the painting, the color of that point is converted to the sound so that as the gaze moves, music that consists of the converted time series sounds is generated. Experiments using six subjects and six abstract paintings were conducted for the three cases in which the subjects see the abstract paintings without hearing any music, while hearing pre-selected music and while hearing the viewers' gaze based music generated by the authors' system. The experimental results imply that "hearing gaze based music" could stimulate the viewers' inspiration and imagination best, "hearing pre-selected music" second best, and "without music" third best.

Keywords: Abstract Painting, Music, Gaze Behavior, Inspiration.

1 Introduction

In early times, one of the concepts of abstract paintings was to depict music on canvases. For example, Kandinsky left many works that depict the music (e.g. [1]). In recent years, many works that combine audio and visual media by computer have been presented, but there are not many representations that combine paintings and music. The authors have proposed a music generation system that utilizes viewers' gazes [2]. To generate music from paintings, temporal information needs to be extracted from the painting, because music consists of time series sounds. The gaze of a person who sees the painting corresponds to temporal changes in the position in the painting. This property is utilized by the authors' system.

Concerning music composition using still images such as drawings and/or paintings, Xenakis developed a system called UPIC [3], [4], which scans the still image so that lines and points in the image are converted to sounds using a computer. UPIC's algorithm assigns vertical coordinates of the image to pitch and horizontal coordinates to timeline. However, as temporal changes in the position in the still

C. Stephanidis (Ed.): HCII 2014 Posters, Part I, CCIS 434, pp. 213–217, 2014.
© Springer International Publishing Switzerland 2014

image, the horizontal scan might not be very reasonable. Another example of combining paintings and music is Iura's work entitled "map" [5], in which the color pointed by the user's mouse, which is an alternative of the viewer's gaze, is converted to sound. However, to our knowledge, Iura did not implement the proposed system.

This paper explores the effectiveness of the authors' gaze based music generation system. In particular, whether the inspirations the viewers obtained from the abstract painting could be enhanced by this system is studied.

2   Approach

In the authors' music generation system, the gaze of a person who views an abstract painting is detected by a gaze detection equipment such as the Eye Tracker. The gaze tends to stay at certain points in the painting for certain durations. At each of such staying points, color information, specifically, hue, brightness and saturation, is obtained. The hue is converted to a tone row in an octave. The brightness determines the pitch of the octave determined by the hue. The frequency of the saw wave, which is generated by an oscillator, is determined by the pitch determined by the brightness, where the height of the saw wave is determined by the volume of the sound. Normally, saw waves are low-pass filtered; the saturation determines the cut off frequency of the low pass filter. As the gaze moves and stays at different positions, time series sounds, which could be a material of music, are generated.

In general, abstract paintings aim at stimulating viewers' inspiration and imagination, but it is not so easy for many people to interpret abstract paintings that most of those people cannot enjoy viewing abstract paintings. The authors' gaze based music generation system could be able to prompt abstract paintings' viewers to inspire and/or image something more from the paintings than the viewers just see the paintings. To verify this, this paper conducts some experiments as described in the following sections. More specifically, subjects are asked to see abstract paintings under the following three conditions: (1) just see the paintings (without hearing any music), (2) while haring pre-selected music, and (3) while hearing the music generated by the authors' system; then, subjective tests are performed for the three conditions.

3   Experiment-1: Effect of Music

3.1   Method of the Experiment-1

As described in Section 2, when a person sees abstract paintings, his/her inspiration and imagination could be affected by whether music is played or not. The Experiment 1 compares the two cases in which the viewers see abstract paintings, while hearing pre-selected music and without hearing any music. We use six subjects, six abstract paintings, and one music: Stockhausen's "Studie 1 (1953)". The procedure of the Experiment-1 is as follows.

1. Before the experiment, we instruct each of the subjects to express what he/she thinks and how he/she feels, by uttering words so that we can record the words he/she utters.
2. Three of the six abstract paintings are presented to each subject without music, and then the subject's utterances are recorded.
3. The other three paintings are presented to each subject while playing the pre-selected music, and then the subject's utterances are recorded.

3.2   Results of the Experiment-1

As shown in Table 1, it turns out that the contents of the six subjects' recorded uttered words can be classified into the three categories: Category A (concrete ideas), Category B (impression) and Category C (movements). The numbers of uttered words in each of the three categories are shown in Fig. 1, where the ratio of the number of uttered words in that category to the number of all the uttered words is presented. In case of "without music" and "Hearing pre-selected music", there are many uttered words in Categories A and C, respectively.

In addition, the case in which multiple uttered words correspond to a same meaning can be seen; that is, the multiple uttered words are the repetition of the same meaning. Table 2 shows the number of the repetition for the words that were repeated at least once (uttered at least twice) in either "without music" or "hearing pre-selected music". As can be seen in Table 2, the number of the repetition in "hearing music" is much less than "without music". This implies that due to "music", the number of uttered words with independent meanings is increased. In other words, "music" could stimulate viewers' inspiration and imagination.

Table 1. Category of Viewers' Uttered words

Category	Meaning	Example
A	Concrete Idea	This looks like the sun.
B	Impression	Scary. Strange feeling.
C	Movement	Something is falling. Something is bulging

Fig. 1. Number (ratio) of uttered words in each category in "without music" and "with music"

Table 2. Number of repeated uttered words in the Experiment-1

Word	Without music	Hearing pre-selected music
Sun	3	0
Moon	2	0
Hot, Warm	3	0
Heavy, So heavy	1	0
Steps	1	0
City, Concrete jungle	2	0
Cloth's pattern, Curtain's pattern	0	1

4   Experiment-2: Effect of Music Generated by the Authors' Gaze Based System

4.1   Method of the Experiment-2

Similar to the Experiment 1, we compare the two cases in which the viewers see abstract paintings while hearing pre-selected music and while hearing the music generated by the authors' system. We use six subjects, six abstract paintings that are different from the ones used for the Experiment-1, the same music as the one used for the Experiment-1, and the gaze based music generated by the authors' system. The procedure of the Experiment-2 is as follows.

1. Before the experiment, we instruct each of the subjects to express what he/she thinks and how he/she feels, by uttering words so that we can record the words he/she utters.
2. Three of the six abstract paintings are presented to each subject while playing the pre-selected music, and then the subject's utterances are recorded.
3. The other three paintings are presented to each subject while detecting the gaze of the subject and playing the music generated based on the detected gaze.

4.2   Results of the Experiment-2

The contents of the six subjects' recorded uttered words are classified into the three categories defined by Table 1. As opposed to the Experiment-1, the number (ratio) of the uttered words in each category is not significantly different between "hearing pre-selected music" and "hearing gaze based music".

Then, similar to the Experiment-1, the numbers of the repetitions of the same meanings in case of "hearing pre-defined music" and "hearing gaze based music" are listed in Table 3. As can be seen in Table 3, the number of the repetition in "hearing gaze based music" is much less than "hearing pre-selected music". This implies that due to the gaze based music, the number of uttered words with independent meanings is increased. In other words, "gaze based music" could stimulate viewers' inspiration and imagination.

Through the results of the Experiment-1 and Experiment-2, "hearing gaze based music" could stimulate viewers' inspiration and imagination best, "hearing pre-selected music" second best, and "without music" third best.

Table 3. Number of repeated uttered words in the Experiment-2

Word	Hearing pre-selected music	Hearing gaze based music
Bug	1	0
Stationery	2	0
Face, Part of face	7	0
Monster	2	0
Neo-futuristic	1	0
Sun	1	2

5   Conclusion

This paper has explored the effectiveness of prompting abstract paintings' viewers' inspiration and imagination by the authors' gaze based music generation system. Experiments using six subjects and six abstract paintings were conducted for the three cases in which the subjects see the abstract paintings without hearing any music, while hearing pre-selected music and while hearing the viewers' gaze based music generated by the authors' system. The experimental results imply that "hearing gaze based music" could stimulate the viewers' inspiration and imagination best, "hearing pre-selected music" second best, and "without music" third best.

Remaining issues include that we conduct experiments using more subjects and abstract paints so that more solid results can be obtained.

References

1. Wassily Kandinsky - Compositions,
   http://www.wassilykandinsky.net/compositions.php
2. Ogusu, T., et al.: Analysis of Gaze Behaviors of Viewers Who See Abstract Paintings and Proposal of its Application to Music Composition. In: IEICE General Conference, vol. A, p. 254 (March 2012) (in Japanese)
3. Centre Iannis Xenakis, http://www.centre-iannis-xenakis.org
4. Nagashima, Y.: Discussion for PGS (Polyagogic Graphic Synthesizer), Information Processing Society of Japan, SIG Technical Report, 2005-MUS-59 (7) (2005) (in Japanese)
5. Iura, T.: New Creative for Imagery and Music in Digital Media - Expressive Effect through Audio and Visual Interaction. Journal of Kansai University Faculty of Informatics (34) (2011) (in Japanese)

Digital Rhetoric in Collaborative Knowledge-Making

Reading Answers and Super-Answers
to Existential Questions on Quora

Cosima Rughiniş[1], Răzvan Rughiniş[2],
Ştefania Matei[1], and Alina Petra Marinescu Nenciu[1]

[1] University of Bucharest, Department of Sociology, Bucharest, Romania
{cosima.rughinis,stefania.matei,alina.marinescu}@sas.unibuc.ro
[2] University Politehnica of Bucharest, Department of Computer Science, Bucharest, Romania
razvan.rughinis@cs.pub.ro

Abstract. We examine the ways in which answers formulated in the Q&A community Quora are aggregated in a collaborative, computer-mediated body of knowledge. Readers' experiences are shaped by the answer ranking algorithm, a central rhetorical device on Quora. Answer visibility on page is strongly dependent on the number of upvotes, but also on recency and author popularity. Upvotes depend to some extent on wordcount, followers, and use of visual representations, but not on answer's age. This indicates that readers engage with Quora as a body of stratified information, rather than pursuing unlimited diversity of perspectives: engagement seems to be limited to the top answers, which represent, for practical purposes, Quora's persuasive statements.

Keywords: Quora, experiential knowledge, computer supported collaborative knowledge, answer ranking.

1 Introduction

Quora is a Q&A platform that aims to crowdsource experiential knowledge and use the power of social networks in order to provide meaningful answers to a wide variety of questions (Paul, Hong, & Chi, 2012; Wang, Gill, Mohanlal, Zheng, & Zhao, 2013). We look into a specific field of inquiry, examining six questions about "what does it feel like" to have different psychological conditions: depression, schizophrenia, ADHD, bipolar disorder, and OCD. We aim to understand the formulation and aggregation of knowledge on Quora: how do readers encounter this computer mediated, collaborative knowledge? To this purpose, we examine answer popularity and visibility, focusing on the 'super-answers' which stand out through intense reader reactions, in terms of votes and comments.

Quora readers who may want to find out about what does it feel like to have schizophrenia, for example, may reach this topic through the search bar. Once they find the question and click / touch on it, their reading experience will depend on whether

C. Stephanidis (Ed.): HCII 2014 Posters, Part I, CCIS 434, pp. 218–223, 2014.

they are on a desktop or on a mobile device. The mobile app will only display the first answer, and the user has to click a second time on the question to read all answers. Desktop users will see all answers at their first click on the question. By default, answers are ranked through Quora's 'Magic' algorithm. Users have the option to sort answers according to the number of readers' votes or recency (Fig. 1).

Authors may post answers as anonymous, or under their signature – situation in which readers can click on their name to see their profile, which includes the number of followers, of people that they follow, and other metrics of their activity on Quora, as well as a list of recent activities.

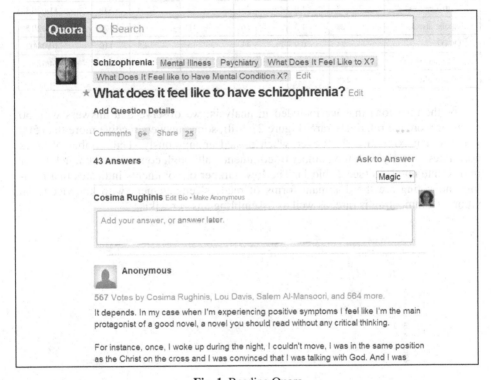

Fig. 1. Reading Quora

The ranking algorithm influences significantly readers' experiences on Quora, especially for questions with large numbers of answers. Many readers will stop after a few answers – or, on mobile devices, maybe after the first one – although reading strategies are diverse, as told by contributors themselves in various places on Quora (Quora Collaborators, 2012). The ranking algorithm is not published, but Quora engineers have clarified some of its principles (Quora Collaborators, 2013), mainly stating that ranking takes into account votes in relation to the number of views the answer has received, and does not take into account recency. In this analysis we attempt to infer some properties of the ranking algorithm, through correlational analysis, and to discuss its consequences for readers' learning experience.

The distribution of upvotes for answers is strongly skewed, as illustrated in Table 1 and Figure 1.

Table 1. Overview of questions and answers included in analysis

What does it feel like [to have] ...	No. of answers	Comments		Upvotes			Date of first published answer [by/mm/did]
		Avg.	Max.	Avg.	Median	Max	
...depression?	87	0.8	21	17	4	393	11/02/01
... ADHD?	52	1.6	12	20	8	200	11/04/26
... schizophrenia?	43	1.9	27	24	4	548	11/02/13
... bipolar disorder?	28	1.3	6	15	6	120	11/02/15
... OCD?	21	0.9	11	16	4.5	119	10/08/02
... to be depressed?	17	0.6	4	12	3	108	14/01/01
Total sample	**248**						

For the questions that we included in analysis, we observe that answers with 30 votes or more are relatively rare (Figure 2). Still, some answers receive more than 500 votes (our maximum is 548) even when posted anonymously. The number of votes correlates strongly with the number of comments, although comments are much lower in absolute numbers (see Table 1). The low number of comments indicates that reading and voting are the dominant forms of readers' engagement with knowledge on Quora. Commenting is rare, as well as assembling answer wikis.

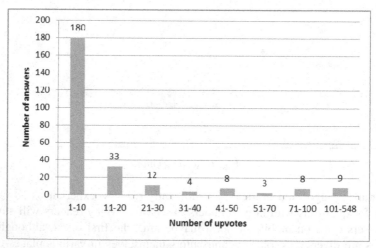

Fig. 2. Distribution of upvotes for answers about psychological conditions

There is a strong relationship between the rank on page (1st, 2nd answer etc.) and the number of upvotes of a given answer (Figure 3). The relationship is not linear, and it can be best estimated by an inverse function. We have thus used *visibility*, computed as *1 / Rank*, as our main dependent variable.

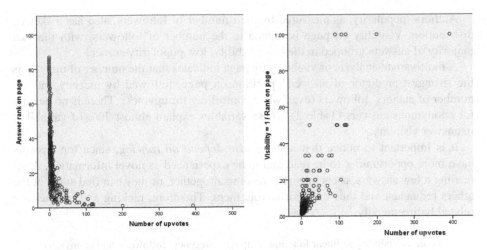

Fig. 3. Relationship between rank on page and number of upvotes or visibility (scatterplot)

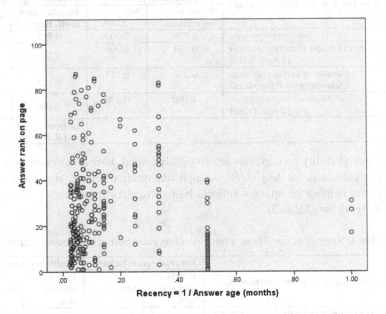

Fig. 4. Relationship between rank on page and answer recency (scatterplot)

Figure 4 indicates that there is a certain relationship between the answer age (measured as number of months since posting) and answer rank. Again, this is not a linear relationship – as illustrated in Figure 4, that plots answer rank against *recency*, measured as *1 / number of months*. A threshold is at a recency of 0.5 – that is, after 2 months of age the spectrum of ranks increases visibly. In our multivariate analysis we used a *binary measure of recency*, distinguishing answers of 2 months and less from those of 3 months and more.

Authors' popularity, as measured by their number of followers, also has a skewed distribution. Visibility on page is related to the number of followers, with the vast majority of answers grouped in the low visibility, low popularity corner.

A multivariate analysis of visibility on page indicates that the number of upvotes is the strongest predictor of answers' position on page, followed by recency and the number of authors' followers (even when controlling for upvotes). There is no penalty for anonymous answers (Table 2). These variables explain almost 70% of variability in answer visibility.

It is important to notice that *upvotes also depend on ranking*, since top answers have more opportunities to be read and to be experienced as novel information. After reading a few answers, users may stop reading altogether, or they can find some of the others redundant and thus may not upvote them. Therefore, ranking and upvotes are related bidirectionally.

Table 2. Visibility as linear function of upvotes, recency, followers, and anonymity

Visibility (defined as 1 / Rank on page) as linear function of...	Bivariate correlations		Multiple regression	
	Pearson correlation	Sig.	Standardized coeff. Beta	Sig.
Number of upvotes	0.790	0.000	0.761	0.000
The answer is recent (2 months or less) (1=yes, 0=no)	0.174	0.006	0.200	0.000
Number of author followers (Anonymous = 0 followers)	0.310	0.151	0.199	0.000
Answerer is anonymous (1=yes, 0=no)	-0.062	0.320	-0.066	0.070
			Listwise N=247 Adj.R Square = 0.693	

Given that visibility and upvotes are so tightly bound, how do answers acquire up-votes? The answer is far less clear, through quantitative lenses, since, unlike page visibility, the number of upvotes reflects human readers' preferences rather than a computer algorithm (Table 3).

Table 3. Number of upvotes as a function of recency, author and answer features

Number of upvotes as a linear function of...	Bivariate correlations		Multiple regression	
	Pearson correlation	Sig.	Pearson correlation	Sig.
Number of months since the answer was updated (at 01.03.14)	0.076	0.232	0.064	0.311
Recency = 1 / Answer age (months)	-0.070	0.269	N/A	N/A
The answer is recent (2 months or less) (1=yes, 0=no)	-0.031	0.627	N/A	N/A
Answerer is anonymous	0.075	0.235	N/A	N/A
Number of author followers (Anonymous = 0 followers)	0.151*	0.015	0.132*	0.038
Wordcount	0.209**	0.001	0.183**	0.004
Answer includes pictures or illustrations	0.145*	0.020	0.143*	0.024
Answer includes links to external documents	0.011	0.255	-0.018	0.776
			Listwise N= 246 Adj.R Square = 0.064	

We do find out, though, that upvotes do not accumulate significantly in time: recency is not associated with votes, no matter how we measure it. Votes depend somehow on the number of followers and wordcount (the higher the better), and also on using pictures or illustrations. Still, these variables only account for 6% of variability in upvotes (Table 3).

2   Conclusions

The fact that upvotes do not increase, on average, with time indicates that answers that lag in the lower regions of the question page will only be read by the most curious or dedicated readers. This also decreases their opportunity to receive upvotes. The typical reader engages with top answers – even more so on mobile devices, where the Quora app privileges the very first answer. Page ranking is strongly linked to the number of upvotes (in a bidirectional relationship, most likely), but also, to some extent, it favors recent answers (up to around 2 months) and popular authors. Popularity also influences upvotes, thus also having a mediated effect on ranking.

Given the strong coupling between answer visibility and votes, and evidence for readers' typical engagement with top answers only, we can conclude that the digital rhetoric on Quora produces a body of stratified knowledge, in which persuasion is clearly differentiated while scrolling down the page.

Acknowledgments. This article has been supported by the research project "Sociological imagination and disciplinary orientation in applied social research", with financial support of ANCS / UEFISCDI with grant no. PN-II-RU-TE-2011-3-0143, contract no. 14/28.10.2011.

References

1. Paul, S.A., Hong, L., Chi, E.H.: Who is Authoritative? Understanding Reputation Mechanisms in Quora. In: Collective Intelligence, pp. 1–8 (2012),
   http://arxiv.org/ftp/arxiv/papers/1204/1204.3724.pdf (retrieved)
2. Quora Collaborators, How often do you agree with the answer ranking on Quora? Quora (2012), http://www.quora.com/Answer-Ranking-on-Quora/
   How-often-do-you-agree-with-the-answer-ranking-on-Quora (retrieved)
3. Quora Collaborators, In:what order are answers to a question displayed in May 2013? Quora (2013), http://www.quora.com/Answer-Ranking-on-Quora/
   In-what-order-are-answers-to-a-question-displayed-in-May-2013 (retrieved)
4. Wang, G., Gill, K., Mohanlal, M., Zheng, H., Zhao, B.Y.: Wisdom in the Social Crowd: An Analysis of Quora. In: International World Wide Web Conference, pp. 1341–1352. ACM (2013), https://www.cs.ucsb.edu/~ravenben/publications/pdf/
   quora-www13.pdf (retrieved)

Measurement Evaluation of Keyword Extraction Based on Topic Coverage

Ryosuke Saga, Hiroshi Kobayashi, Takao Miyamoto, and Hiroshi Tsuji

Graduate School of Engineering, Osaka Prefecture University
1-1, Gakuen-cho, Naka-ku, Sakai-shi, Osaka, Japan
{saga,tsuji}@cs.osakafu-u.ac.jp,
kobayahi@mis.cs.osakafu-u.ac.jp,
aki@kis.osakafu-u.ac.jp

Abstract. This paper proposes a method to measure the performance of keyword extraction based on topic coverage. The answer set of a keyword is required to evaluate keyword extraction by methods such as TF-IDF. However, creating an answer set for a large document is expensive. Thus, this paper proposes a new measurement called topic coverage on the basis of the assumption that the keywords extracted by a superior method can express the topic information efficiently. The experiment using the proceedings of a conference shows the feasibility of our proposed method.

Keywords: keyword extraction, performance evaluation, recall, precision, topic.

1   Introduction

Computerized documents are continuously being generated and used because of the progress of information technology. Furthermore, news articles and magazines from publishers, as well as blogs and tweets in social media, are generated by users daily, and the document set consists of several topics under different genres.

Keyword extraction is one of the most important techniques for comprehending the topics in a document set. Given that these keywords often express topics, we can analogize topics from keywords. The extracted keywords are used not only to determine the topic of documents but also to generate queries for a document set (often called a corpus). Hence, keyword extraction is important in treating a document set.

Keyword extraction can be conducted by several methods, and keyword extraction methods are categorized as supervised or unsupervised. An example of supervised keyword extraction is SVM, which is used for extracting keywords from an answer set [1]. An example of unsupervised keyword extraction is TF-IDF, which uses word frequency in documents [2].

We may choose a keyword extraction method on the basis of performance evaluation. The performance evaluation of a method is based on how well the method extracts keywords or how much the extracted keywords include the answer set. Precision and recall are developed on the basis of these criteria. However, these criteria

C. Stephanidis (Ed.): HCII 2014 Posters, Part I, CCIS 434, pp. 224–227, 2014.
© Springer International Publishing Switzerland 2014

assume that a manually created answer set exists; that is, an answer set needs to be generated for a new document set when evaluating a keyword extraction method. Such tasks require considerable time and effort, particularly for a large document set, such as tweets in social media (i.e., big data). The Mechanical Turk method focuses on creating answer sets; however, this method requires considerable time and resources [4].

Therefore, this paper proposes a measurement, namely, *topic coverage*, to evaluate the performance of a keyword extraction method without an answer set. This measurement is similar to recall except that the proposed method considers the topic.

2   Evaluation of Keyword Extraction Based on Topic Coverage

2.1   Principle and Assumption

Keyword extraction methods are normally evaluated by precision and recall, which have been introduced by several representative books. These methods are based on the contingence table shown in Table 1. For example, precision is calculated as A/(A + B) with the notations in the table, that is, these methods are derived from the correctness and convergence with an answer set assigned by humans.

The proposed method is based on the assumption that *keywords extracted by a superior method can express the topic information efficiently. A better method corresponds to higher topic coverage.* The adequacy of the idea can be proper because keyword extraction itself is used for understanding topics in a document set.

Table 1. Contingence table for recall and precision

	Keywords assigned by humans	Non-keywords assigned by human
Keywords extracted by a method	A	C
Non-keywords extracted by a method	B	D

Thus, if topic coverage is one, the keyword extraction method will cover all topics. If topic coverage is zero, the keyword extraction method will fail to extract keywords from the topic. To implement the proposed method, topic coverage TC is defined as follows:

$$TC = \frac{1}{|T|}\sum_{i \in T} \frac{|E_i \cap M_i|}{|E_i|}, \tag{1}$$

where $|E|$ shows the number of elements of set E, T is the set of topics in the document sets, and E_i shows a set of top j keywords in topic i. For convenience, E_i is called topic keywords in this paper. M_i is a set of top k keywords in topic i extracted by a certain method, such as TF-IDF and RIDF.

2.2   Evaluation of Extracted Keyword

We conducted the following steps to evaluate the performance of the proposed keyword extraction method.

Topic Extraction. The first step in evaluating the performance of a keyword extraction method is topic extraction. In this research, we assumed that each document belongs to a topic and does not belong to more than two topics different from a multi-topic model [5]. Thus, we can employ a clustering method to extract topics. Clustering methods include the k-means, k-medoids, and Girvan–Newman algorithm [6][7][8].

Keyword Extraction from Topics. The second step is extracting topic keywords. For example, we can use the TF-IDF index [5] to extract keywords as follows:

$$TFIDF_{ij} = TF_{ij} \log \frac{N_t}{DF_i} \tag{2}$$

where N_t is the number of documents in topic t, TF_{ij} is the frequency of term i in document j, and DF_j is the document frequency, which is calculated as the number of documents with term i. The j extracted keywords correspond to E_j in Equation (1).

Keyword Extraction by an Evaluated Method and Measurement Calculation. The third step involves extracting keywords that correspond to M_i by using an evaluated method. Hence, k keywords are extracted from each topic i. *Topic coverage* can then be calculated by using M_i and E_i.

3   Experiment

We conducted an experiment to confirm the feasibility and characteristics of the topic coverage. We used 2008 and 2009 NIPS corpuses in this experiment. To verify the proposed measurement, we compared the value of the *topic coverage* with the keywords of abstract in each paper through the correlation between the topic coverage and recall of corpus. If *topic coverage* can be correlated with recall through an answer set, *topic coverage* is useful because it does not require an answer set. The experiment was conducted as follows:

1. N keywords were extracted, and recall for the keywords was calculated.
2. The topic coverage for N keywords in the first step and the correlation between recall and topic coverage were calculated.

Table 2. Correlation between Topic coverage and Recall

# of Topics	Correlation (NIPS in 2007)	Correlation (NIPS in 2008)
7	0.924	0.923
10	0.950	0.933
13	0.978	0.935

We set the number of topics to 7, 10, and 13 in this experiment and calculated the correlations for each topic size to confirm the robustness of this method.

The result of the experiment is shown in Table 2, which shows that topic coverage and recall have high correlation over 0.90. Thus, topic coverage may be used instead of recall.

4   Conclusion

This paper has proposed a new measurement method, namely, topic coverage, to evaluate keyword extraction performance without the use of an answer set. From the experiment, we confirmed that topic coverage and recall have high correlation. However, Keyword extraction from topics depends on the keyword extraction method employed. Thus, the use of preset or prepared keywords as topic keywords, such as in the paper "Keyword Extraction and Performance Evaluation," is better than extracting keywords by a certain method. In the future, the feasibility of this measurement on other corpuses, such as newspaper articles, and its correlation with other measurement will be verified.

Acknowledgement. This research was supported by JSPS KAKENHI Grant Numbers 13370017, 25420448, 23760358.

References

1. Manning, C.D., Raghavan, P., Schütze, H.: Introduction to Information Retrieval. Cambridge University Press (2008)
2. Zhang, K., Xu, H., Tang, J., Li, J.: Keyword Extraction Using Support Vector Machine. In: Yu, J.X., Kitsuregawa, M., Leong, H.-V. (eds.) WAIM 2006. LNCS, vol. 4016, pp. 85–96. Springer, Heidelberg (2006)
3. Salton, G.: Automatic Text Processing: The Transformation Analysis and Retrieval of Information by Computer. Addison-Wesley Publisher (1988)
4. New York Times: Artificial Intelligence, With Help From the Humans (2007), http://www.nytimes.com/2007/03/25/business/yourmoney/25Stream.html (accessed in March 2013)
5. Blei, D.M., Lafferty, J.D.: Dynamic topic models. In: Proceedings of the 23rd International Conference on Machine Learning, pp. 113–120 (2006)
6. Jayabharathy, J., Kanmani, S., Parveen, A.A.: A Survey of Document Clustering Algorithms with Topic Discovery. Journal of Computing 3, 21–28 (2011)
7. Han, J., Kamber, M., Pei, J.: Data Mining: Concepts and Techniques, 3rd edn. Morgan Kaufmann (2011)
8. Newman, M.E.: Detecting community structure in networks. The European Physical Journal B-Condensed Matter and Complex Systems 38, 321–330 (2004)

A Study on Query-by-Any-Word Based Music Retrieval System

Shinji Sako, Ai Zukawa, and Tadashi Kitamura

Nagoya Institute of Technology, Gokiso-cho, Showa-ku, Nagoya, 466-8555, Japan
{s.sako,kitamura}@nitech.ac.jp, aizkw@mmsp.nitech.ac.jp

Abstract. Recently, commercial interest in the field of music information retrieval (MIR) has been growing rapidly. This paper describes a MIR system that accept any Japanese word as query. Previous studies focused on emotion based MIR system generally uses limited words such as major adjectives or kansei words. However, emotion of the music is represented by various words in practice. Music review is a one of good example. Word can also express complicated emotions with which various emotions are mixed. Starting from this point of view, we propose a method for MIR system that is able to find the appropriate music directory from any word as query. There are three main issues in this study. First one is how to mapping music and emotion. We introduce two-dimensional space which can represent emotion and music in a unified space. This space is obtained automatically from the emotion evaluation data of words and music. Second issue is extraction method for musical feature in order to map to the emotion space from given music. In our approach, optimal feature parameters are automatically selected with respect to each axis of the emotion space. Third issue is how to cope with any query word. Our method can find a music pieace corresponding to emotion of any word by measurement of relationship between each basic word for the given query word. A feature point of this approach is the use of co-occurrence probability of words obtained from a large scale of web text corpus. We performed a subjective evaluation experiments using 100 classical musical pieces and 50 Japanese words that are often used in music reviews. The experimental results show that our proposed system can find the correct music piece which matches mostly given query word.

Keywords: emotion based music retrieval system, co-occurrence probability of word.

1 Introduction

The general approach to music retrieval by emotion is used adjective words (e.g. happy, sad and etc.). Sato, et. al. proposed the retrieval method for music works using emotion word [1]. Using the affective value scale of music, they established the relation between music structure and six factors of emotion (positive, negative, affection, strength, frivolousness, and solemnity). Levy and Sandler[2] also proposed a semantic space using high-volume social tags, because tags for music capture sensible attributes grounded in individual tracks. Moreover, Kumamoto and Ota[3] suggested an impression-based music retrieval system with 10 adjective-pairs. It asks users to select one or more pairs

C. Stephanidis (Ed.): HCII 2014 Posters, Part I, CCIS 434, pp. 228–233, 2014.
© Springer International Publishing Switzerland 2014

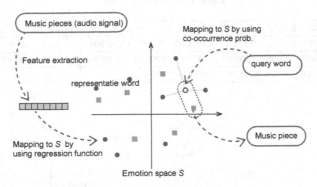

Fig. 1. System outline

and estimate each pairs on a seven-step scale, and outputs musical piece which is suitable for the given word. However, there exists many ways to to represent emotion of music in practive. For example, text of music review consists of many kind of word to represent impression or emotion of music pieces. From this point of view, we proposed the MIR system which can find music piece from any query word. In order to express any words, relation of words is utilized. Emotion space is configured as an indicator of emotion music and words, and some words whose impression is known were mapped in the space. Any query words can be mapped from these words by using similarity of words. Emotion of music is also mapped to the identicle emotion space from music features that are extracted audio signal. We can calculate the distances between music and word in the emotion space.

In section 2, we propose the approach which deals with any words and describe emotion space. Next, section 3 presents how to map query words, and section 4 presents how to map music in the space. Section 5 shows the subjective evaluation experiment. Finally, conclusions and future work are drawn in section 6.

2 Emotion Space for MIR

The outline of our system is shown in Fig. 1. Any music pieces are mapped in the emotion space, and the words whose emotion is already known *representative words*, are also mapped by the similarity. When a query word is given to the system, the position of query word on emotion space is determined using representative words. Then, the Euclidian distances between query word and music pieces in the emotion space is calculated, and the music piece which is the closest to query word is selected as the search result.

2.1 Development of the Emotion Space

In order to set the emotion space, we conducted factor analysis by using an impression of music pieces database[4]. This database contains around 120 subjects who were asked to listen 100 short music pieces and evaluate them at the 7 point scale for the

Table 1. 14 adjective pairs

light – heavy	bright – dark	sad – cheerful	powerful – quiet
calm – violent	dismal – amusing	free – subdued	fast – slow
elegant – rough	lonely – lively	hurried – careless	profound – nimble
relaxed – tense	gorgeous – simple		

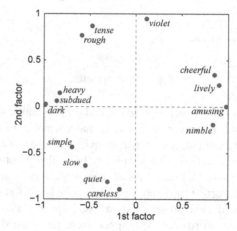

Fig. 2. Emotion space S

adjective-pairs1. Each music clip was segmented in 15 seconds from well-known classical pieces in RWC music database[5], and impression of music was regarded as constant. As a result of further investigation the database,it was found that some subjects with low reliability are included. For example, some subjects did not spent enough time to listen the music. Such kind of outliers are omitted from database in advance. In addition, to get a common emotion space, the data whose values are more than the standard deviation away from the average of all subjects are removed, too.

Factor analysis was conducted on the evaluation scores of 14 adjective pairs. Fig. 1 shows 14 adjective words in the generated emotion space. As the result, 1st factor mainly contains "bright" and "amusing", it means brightness. On the other hand, because 2nd factor mainly contains "violent" and "hurried", it means violence.

3   Mapping Method of the Query Word

It is difficult to assign in advance the position of any word on the emotion space. We propose a method for estimating the position on the emotion space automatically by using the relationship between words. In our approach, the relationship between words is represented by co-occurrence probabilities of words pairs. We used the large scale co-occurrence probability database of Japanese that was developed by ALAGIN project[6]. This database contains co-occurrence probability of half a million headword by using 100 million web text corpus. A co-occurrence probability $C(w_1, w_2)$ of word w_1 and

w_2 is defined as Eq. 1. Where, $F(w_1)$ and $F(w_2)$ means individual word frequencies of word w_1 and word w_2, and $F(w_1, w_2)$ means co-occurrence frequency of w_1 and w_2.

$$C(w_1, w_2) = \frac{F(w_1, w_2)}{F(w_1) + F(w_2)} \tag{1}$$

3.1 Definition of Representative Word

To represent the emotion of any word by the relationship of base words, one possible approach is use of well-known adjective words. However, it seems not realistic to express tens of thousands query word by using small number of words. In practice, a lot of base words are needed in order to cope with various words. In this study, we introduced *representative word* as the base word. The representative words are selected which has high degree of co-occurrence probability with adjective word. It is noted that adjective word were converted to noun form The reason of this, it is considered that noun has a high co-occurrence probability than an adjective.

The position of the representative words r in the emotion space is calculated as in Eq. 2. Where a_i is the adjective word, and N means the number of adjective word.

$$\left[\frac{C(r, a_n)}{\sum_{i=1}^{N} C(r, a_i)} \cdot x_{1a_n}, \frac{C(r, a_n)}{\sum_{i=1}^{N} C(r, a_i)} \cdot x_{2a_n} \right] \tag{2}$$

3.2 Calculate the Position of Query Word

In order to determine the position of the query word, we used representative word closely related to the query word. For given query word w, representative words can be found from 300 word high degree of co-occurrence probability The position of w on the emotion space is calculated as Eq. 3. Where $(r_1, r_2, \ldots, r_M)$ are representative words and M means number of representative word.

$$\left[\frac{\sum_{i=1}^{M} (C(w, r_i) \cdot x_{1r_i})}{\sum_{i=1}^{M} C(w, r_i)}, \frac{\sum_{i=1}^{M} (C(w, r_i) \cdot x_{2r_i})}{\sum_{i=1}^{M} C(w, r_i)} \right] \tag{3}$$

4 Mapping Method of Music Piece

4.1 Mapping Function by Using Regression

We considered that to represent the relationship between the emotion and features with the impression evaluation data as same as Sec. 2 by using multiple regression analysis. An average value of *bright − dark* and *calm − violent* are used as dependent variables of 1st factor and 2nd factor, respectively. It is noted that the mean value should be normalized as $[-1, 1]$, because range of emotion space should be $[-1, 1]$.

Table 2. List of feature parameters

Root mean square energy	Low energy	Roll off	Spectral flux
Spectral centroid	Roughness	Zero crossing	MFCC
Harmonic change	Key clarity	Mode	Tempo

Table 3. Result of evaluation experiment

Mean value of score	Number of sample
1 – 2	0
2 – 3	3
3 – 4	23
4 – 5	24

4.2 Feature Parameter and Variable Selection by Stepwise Procedure

Many studies have been done to extract musical features from audio signal. We used *MIRtoolbox*[7] to extract well-known frame level feature parameters listed in Table 2.

In our experiments, sampling frequency, window size (frame length), and window hop size was 44.1 kHz, 44.66 msec, and 20 msec, respectively. Feature parameters for each music piece are calculated as the mean and variance of all over the frames.

It is assumed that an optimal feature parameter depend on each axis of emotion space. We conducted stepwise procedure to determine optimal feature parameters for each axis independently. Variable selection is made variance ratio F until less than 2 in this experiment. The variable selection process was repeated until variance ratio less than 2. As the result, 16 dimensional and 17 dimensional feature parameters were selected independently in the 1st and 2nd axis, respectively.

5 Experiment

The subjective listening tests were conducted to evaluate this method. It was verified that whether the selected music piece meets the emotion of query word. We selected 50 words as query that can recall certain emotion, and searched music piece from 100 classical music pieces that are same as Sec. 2. Subjects were asked to agree or disagree and write down the number of statements on a 5-point scale (5: Agree, 1: Disagree). 8 subjects were men and women aged 20s. Table 3 shows the results of subjective evaluation. We confirmed that most of subjects agree with the result of query.

We also examined the relationship between the evaluation value of the subjective test and the distance between the (x_{w_1}, x_{w_2}) from the origin on the emotion space. The correlation coefficient between two variables was 0.36. This result implies that accuracy of mapping becomes high when the degree of the emotion is strong. However, some query words failed to mapping the emotion space. The concrete examples of such problem are "pure" and "sleepiness", etc.. We need improve mapping method that is not dependent on a particular word.

6 Conclusion

In this paper, we proposed an emotion based MIR system which is capable to query by any Japanese word. 2-dimensional emotion space that indicates both of any word and music was calculated using SD method and factor analysis. In order to mapping any query words, some words whose emotion is known are selected, and any words are translated into these words. Therefore, the words which are similar to the adjective words are set in the space using the co-occurrence probability. And, the coordinates of any words are decided by these words and the co-occurrence probability. On the other hand, music is located by music feature parameters because impression of music appears in them. When a word is an input to the system, it outputs music which is close to the word in the impression space. Through a subjective evaluation experiment, selected music is suitable for the corresponding input query word Evaluations of several music collections showed that our approach achieves encouraging results in terms of recommendation satisfaction. It was also showed that emotion of music is more complicated, we extend our system which can cope with multiple words or sentence as query. This is direction of our future work.

References

1. Sato, A., Ogawa, J., Kitakami, H.: An impression-based retrieval system of music collection. In: Proc. of 4th International Conference on knowledge-Based Intelligent Engineering Systems & Allied Technologies, pp. 856–859 (2000)
2. Levy, M., Sandler, M.: A semantic space for music derived from social tags. In: Proc. of 8th International Society for Music Information Retrieval Conference (ISMIR 2007), pp. 411–416 (2007)
3. Kumamoto, T., Ohta, K.: Design, implementation, and opening to the public of an impression-based music retrieval system. Transactions of the Japanese Society for Artificial Intelligence 21, 310–318 (2006)
4. Iwatsuki, Y., Sako, S., Kitamura, T.: An estimation method of musical emotion considering individ. In: Proc. of International Conference on Kansei Engineering and Emotion Research (KEER 2012), pp. 456–461 (2012)
5. Goto, M., Hashiguchi, H., Nishimura, T., Oka, R.: Rwc music database: Popular, classical, and jazz music databases. In: Proc. of the 3rd International Society for Music Information Retrieval (ISMIR 2002), pp. 287–288 (2002)
6. NICT MASTAR Project: ALAGIN Language Resources and Voice Resources Site (accessed May 18, 2014)
7. Lartillot, O., Toiviainen, P.: MIR in Matlab(II): A Toolbox for Musical Feature Extraction form Audio. In: Proc. of the 7th International Conference on Music Information Retrieval (ISMIR 2007), pp. 287–288 (2002)

Database Design for Online Psychometric Design (OnPsyD) Tool

Ahmad Ali Salman and Shiny Verghese

Gulf University for Science and Technology, Mishref, Kuwait
ahmad.salman.pl@gmail.com, moncy.s@gust.edu.kw

Abstract. The objective of this poster is to discuss the extensible database design for an Online Psychometric Design (OnPsyD) Tool that will be used for research in Online Psychometrics.

1   Introduction

The Online Psychometric Design (OnPsyD) Tool is an online tool that is being developed for online psychometric research. It is essential to develop the scientific understanding of how presentation-design factors affect people's responses in psychometric measurement and design guidance. In order to facilitate this scientific understanding, the OnPsyD Tool has to be developed on a framework of an extendable software architecture with a good database design.

2   Background

Various research studies demonstrate how usability science, along with other research in HCI, can benefit from the application of psychometrics in our daily life such as assessment, information search, and diagnostics. Because psychometrics models human psychological characteristics, it is important for instruments administered on-line to be sound and standardize in terms of measurement. Very little research exists in online psychometrics that addresses psychometric measurement in human-computer interaction through web applications or mobile applications. The development of the OnPsyD Tool will help collect and facilitate the data that is required for further research in online psychometrics. For this, a strong and extensible database design is the foundation of the OnPsyD tool. The desired database design modelling will involve three aspects: first, a database design that supports the content and hierarchical structure of psychometric questionnaires; second a design that supports storage of an extensible range of design parameters and third, a design that supports the storage of the psychometric data collected from administering the questionnaires online.

3   Database Design

This section discusses details of database design including tables, packages and diagrams. The database design categorizes the database tables into three main groups or

C. Stephanidis (Ed.): HCII 2014 Posters, Part I, CCIS 434, pp. 234–239, 2014.

packages Questionnaires and Question, User Interaction and Layout Options. Fig 2 shows the details diagram with all tables, relations and attributes.

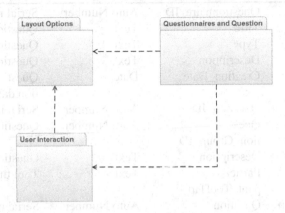

Fig. 1. Shows the packing diagram that shows the overall view of the database design

The following sub section discusses the details of the design and provides detailed explanation for the three database packages - Questionnaires and Question, User Interaction and Layout Options.

3.1   Questionnaires and Question

This group contains tables that comprise of questionnaires. It also provides information regarding questionnaire type and purpose. Furthermore, it includes tables that relate to questions the form the basic building block for all questionnaires.

Question tables contain information about question type, question group, possible answers and to the questionnaires they belong. Question type specifies if the question is close-ended (for example true and false or multiple choice) or open-ended question. Question group specifies the question category like opinion or behavior category. Further, it contains the mapping information for the questions with the possible questionnaire(s).Table 1 shows the tables in Questionnaire and Question package and their attributes.

Table 1.

Table Name	Attribute Name	Data Type	Description
Questionnaire	Questionnaire_ID	Auto Number	Serial numeric key
	Title	Text	Questionnaire Title
	Type	Text	Questionnaire Type
	Description	Text	Questionnaire details
	Creation_Date	Date	Questionnaire Creation date
Question	Question_ID	Auto Number	Serial numeric key
	Question_Group_ID	Auto Number	Question Group ID
	Description	Text	Question details
	Participant_ToolTip	Text	Tool tip participant
Question_Group	Question_Group_ID	Auto Number	Serial numeric key.
	Description	Text	Question group description and details
Questionnaire_Question	Questionnaire_ID	Auto Number	Refer to Questionnaire entry
	Question_ID	Auto Number	Refer to Question entry.
	IsRequired	Boolean	Whether the question is required or not.
Question_Options	Question_ID	Auto Number	Refer to Question entry.
	Option_ID	Auto Number	Serial numeric key.
	Question_Option	Text	Possible answer for the close-ended question.
Input_Method	Method_ID	Auto Number	Serial numeric key.
	Method_Type	Text	Type of close-ended question.
	Remarks	Text	Additional remarks.

3.2 User Interaction

User Interaction group or package holds information for the different users and their interaction with the system. It contains two types of tables - system users and user response.

System user table. This table holds information for different users with their roles in the system. It also contains the basic information required to participate in completing the questionnaire. The user acquires the role of either the system admin or participant. Admin role provides permission to create and modify system components like questionnaires, questions, users and layout (see section 3.3 Layout Options for more information about layout component). The participant role is provided with permission only to participate in the questionnaire(s) assigned by the admin.

User response table. This table contains information about participating user's response to different questions.

Table 2 shows the tables in User Interface package and their attributes.

Table 2.

Table Name	Attribute Name	Data Type	Description
User	User_ID	Auto Number	Serial numeric key
	Role	Text	User role. Admin or Participant.
Admin_User	Name	Text	Admin full name.
	Last_Login	Date	Last login date to the system.
Partici-pant_User	Gender	Text	Participant gender.
	Age_Group	Text	Participant age group.
	Education	Text	Participant education level.
	Professions	Text	Participant job or business.
Us-er_Response_Question	User_ID	Auto Number	Refer to User entry.
	Question_ID	Auto Number	Refer to Question entry.
	Questionnaire_ID	Auto Number	Refer to Questionnaire entry
	Remarks	Text	Additional remarks.
Clo-seEnded_Response	Answer_ID	Auto Number	Refer to Question_Option entry.
	Remarks	Text	Additional remarks.
Ope-nEnded_Response	Answer	Text	Participant answer as text.
	Remarks	Text	Additional remarks
Question-naire_Participant	Participant _ID	Auto Number	Refer to User entry.
	Questionnaire_ID	Auto Number	Refer to Questionnaire entry
	Participan-tion_Date	Date	Completing questionnaire date.
	Remarks	Text	Additional remarks.

3.3   Layout Options

Layout Option package holds information for different questionnaire layout and format options. Currently two types of layout such as position and style is included in this package for both questionnaires and questions.

One table contains information for the component style like color, font-style, font size, etc. This style is adapted by the admin user for different questionnaires and questions. Information about question order within questionnaires is contained in a separate table. The database design for the layout option provides flexibility for the admin user can create multiple questionnaires with different order of questions.

Table 3 shows the tables in Layout Options package and their attributes.

Table 3.

Table Name	Attribute Name	Data Type	Description
Layout	Layout_ID	Auto Number	Serial numeric key
	Font_Family	Text	Text Font Family
	Font_Size	Text	Text Font Size.
	Font_Color	Text	Text Font Color.
	Remarks	Text	Additional remarks.
Question-naire_Layout	Questionnaire_ID	AutoNumber	Refer to Questionnaire entry
	Layout_ID	Auto Number	Refer to Layout entry
	Remarks	Text	Additional remarks.
Question-naire_Instance	Question-naire_Instance_ID	Auto Number	Serial numeric key
	Questionnaire_ID	Auto Number	Refer to Questionnaire entry
	Question_ID	Auto Number	Refer to Question entry
	Layout_ID	Auto Number	Refer to Layout entry
	Questions_Per_Page	Number	Number of Question per page
	Ques-tion_Display_Order	Number	Question order in the page.

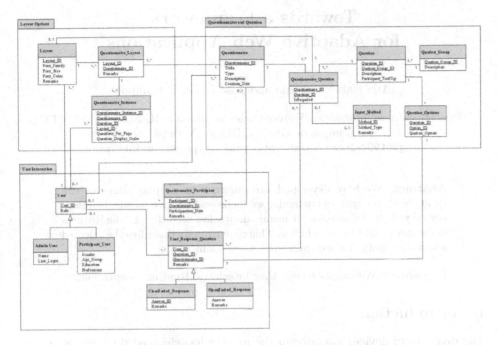

Fig. 2. Detailed Class diagram with all tables, relations and attributes

4   Conclusion

The proposed database system will also allow the definition of online experiments as a sequence in which information is presented and one questionnaire or a set of questionnaires is administered. The functionality will cover both functions of the management of psychometric items, questionnaires, response data and the setup of online administration and experiments, and the actual administration of online experiments. The database modeling further enables data collection from experiments conducted in different (social and geographical) settings. This will help to establish the generalizability of results. Although the focus of HCI has always been on user interaction, the field of HCI recently is contributing to designing new tools and techniques that improve usability. Hence, OnPsyD Tool will be a unique knowledge contribution to the field of HCI and online Psychometrics.

Towards a Framework
for Adaptive Web Applications

Ana Isabel Sampaio and José Creissac Campos

Departamento de Informática/Universidade do Minho & HASLab/INESC TEC
Campus de Gualtar, Braga, Portugal
pg20190@alunos.uminho.pt, jose.campos@di.uminho.pt

Abstract. We have developed a framework to support adaptive elements in Web pages. In particular we focus on adaptive menus. Developers are able to define rules for menu adaptation according to the features of the device and browser in use. This paper briefly describes the selected adaptation patterns and their implementation.

Keywords: Web applications, User interfaces, Runtime adaptation.

1 Introduction

The diversity of devices available in the market has changed the way we access and share information. At the same time, it has created a number of challenges for application developers. It has become more and more important to offer solid user experiences to an increasing number of contexts. Context is an all-encompassing concept that must be understood in relation to a specific purpose [2]. In this particular case, we are mainly interested in how to develop applications that adapt to the diversity of devices mentioned at the start. That is to say that the particular aspects of context we are dealing with are the input-output characteristics of the devices where the applications should run. Of particular relevance, of course, is screen size, but other aspects such as supported interaction modalities must also be considered.

The main motivation for this work stems from an ongoing project on prototyping ubiquitous environments [6]. A framework (APEX) has been developed that is based on building virtual world simulations of the environments. Users are able to interact with the environments both implicitly, through simulated sensors, and explicitly, through interactive devices (e.g., smartphones or public displays). Such devices can be simulated, or actual devices connected to the simulation framework. This, then, begs the question of how to deploy applications that are capable of adapting to different execution contexts. We base our solution on the use of Web applications, and in this paper we explore how to support the adaptation of such applications to different devices.

2 Deploying Applications to Multiple Devices

Two basic approaches can be considered when thinking of deploying an application to a multitude of devices. One is to develop native applications for each

C. Stephanidis (Ed.): HCII 2014 Posters, Part I, CCIS 434, pp. 240–245, 2014.

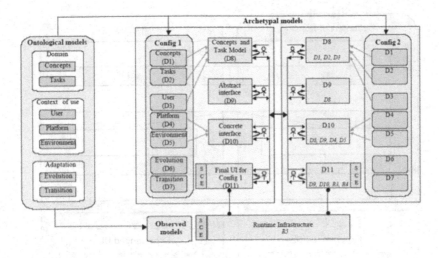

Fig. 1. Cameleon reference framework (from [1])

category of device. Another is to develop Web applications, using the browser as a multi-target runtime platform. In the case of Web applications, we can further opt for performing adaptation on the server side, delivering different versions of the applications based on the platform/browser used, or performing adaptations on the client side (i.e. in the browser). While the former has been the most common approach, technological development is making the latter a viable alternative.

From a methodological perspective, the Cameleon reference framework [1] (see Figure 1) provides the conceptual foundations to reason about this adaptation. The framework proposes a number of abstraction levels from Tasks and Concepts (the Domain), down to the Final User Interface (the code of the running user interface), and posits that these should be adapted to concrete contexts of use, according to an adaptation model. The framework rest on the assumption that a runtime platform is available that supports the dynamic adaptation of the applications according to context.

At the technological side, Responsive Web Design [4] and Progressive Enhancement [3] already offer approaches to support the development of Web applications that adapt to the characteristics of the browser/device they are running on. One characteristic of these applications is the existence of a single code base that is able to provide users with increasingly rich user interfaces (evolution), based on the characteristics of the platform, but also change the structure of the user interface to adapt to different form factors (transition), in response to different platforms. Although a number of patterns and libraries exist that support the implementation of this adaptation, it is still up to developers to implement the adaptation capabilities. The browser, rather than constitute the needed platform for dynamic adaptation, acts as a mostly passive infrastructure that is queried by the application in order to determine information about context.

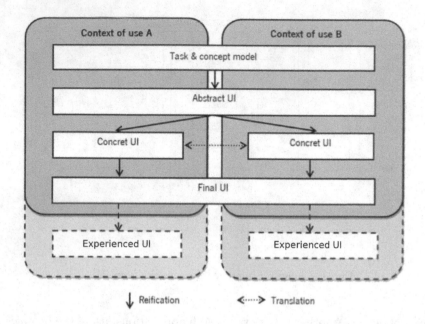

Fig. 2. Multiple concrete models, one final user interface

3   A Framework for Adaptive Web Applications

Mapping the development of a typical responsive Web application to Cameleon, the impact of context is seen mostly at the level of the concrete interface that should be presented. Designers typically draw different mockups depending on the devices/screen size. Using a unified code base means that the different concrete interfaces are merged in a single final user interface (see Figure 2). The logic that governs adaptation, i.e. the adaptation model, is encoded in Cascading Style Sheets (CSS) and JavaScript.

An approach to better support the development of these interfaces is to push as much adaptation as possible into the final interface, and do this in an as automated as possible manner. This can be achieved by introducing adaptation capabilities into the widgets used to create the final interface. Hence, an abstract control will be mapped into a concrete widget, and this widget mapped into an adaptive control that will react to context according to some adaptation rules, to create the User Interface (UI) experienced by the User.

In order to test these ideas we have developed a framework to support adaptive menus. Developers are able to define rules for menu adaptation according to the context of execution (see Figure 3). This can be seen a introducing a further level in the reference framework, detailing how a final user interface adapts to the platform to generate the UI actually provided to the users (what we call Experienced UI in Figure 2).

Fig. 3. Menus (Menu bar: top and left; Select menu: middle right; Off-canvas: right)

3.1 Determining Device Features

Detecting the context of execution, in this case, amounts to detecting features of the device and browser the application is running in. This can be done, either on the server, or directly in the browser. Server side detection explores the user agent string sent by the browser in the HTTP requests. This supports obtaining detailed information about the browser and the device being used. However, it depends on the browser sending the correct user agent string, and (typically) on third party services to obtain the characteristics of the different devices.

Client side detection is performed directly in the browser, and a number of Javascript libraries are available to support it. Modernizr[1] is one such library. Using it, it is possible to query more than 40 features, such as support for HTML5 or CSS3 in the browser, touch or geo-referencing capabilities in the device. Although more limited than server side detection, client side detection it easier to implement (as it does not rely on external services), and does not rely on the browser sending the correct information. Considering this, it was decided to use client side detection, and Modernizr in particular, to support the implementation of the different adaptation patterns described below.

3.2 Adaptation Patterns

A total of five patterns for adaptive menus were identified and implemented. The assumption is that the menu will initially be represented by an unordered list of links. Using CSS (more specifically CSS3) it is then possible to render that menu differently according to the features of the browser. In this case, we are interested in CSS3 support, touch support, and the size of the browser window.

---

[1] http://modernizr.com (last accessed, March 7 2014).

The simplest solution is to create a **Menu bar** at the top of the page, and reflow the options as the page size changes. This is achieved with CSS only, without need for Javascript, but works well for small menus only. For small screen or larger menus, it tends to take to much vertical space, going against the content-first, nav-second principle [7].

A pattern that better supports that principle is the **Footer anchor** menu pattern, In this case, a link (the anchor) is placed at the top of the page. This link points to the menu, which is placed in the footer of the page. Javascript is used in the implementation of this pattern to perform a number of changes in the page: move the menu to the footer; add the anchor at the top; and add a *Back to top* option in the menu to help users navigate the page.

Another option to avoid using too much space with the menu at the top of the page is to render the menu in a **Select** (drop down) component. Navigation is kept at the top of the page and each browser will render the component appropriately. This is particularly useful with complex menus. The pattern is implemented by replacing the list of links with a select element containing the links originally in the list.

A pattern that also supports hiding the menu, but without the need of adding a new component to the page, is the **Toggle menu** pattern. In this case, an icon is used to allow the user to show/hide (i.e. toggle on/off) the menu. The toggling of the menu is achieved through Javascript and CSS, by dynamically adding appropriate classes to the list and its elements. Depending on the class the elements are assigned they will be shown or hidden, as defined in the CSS.

The last implemented pattern is the **Off-canvas menu** pattern. This pattern uses a floating lateral column (typically placed on the left) where the menu is presented. As with the Toggle menu, the Off-canvas menu is accessed through an icon. However, in this case the menu appears from the left (or right) and takes all the hight of the page. How much of the horizontal space is used depends on the window's width. This pattern is commonly used in native mobile applications, so it has the advantage of providing a similar look and feel.

The Off-canvas menu pattern features the more complex implementation of the five patterns, as it requires changing properties, not only of the menu, but also of other elements in the page. This happens because the elements in the page must be moved left (right) when the menu appears. To achieve this, a wrapper is introduced that contains all elements in the page. It is this wrapper that is then slid when the menu appears/disappears. The sliding effect was achieved using CSS3 transitions.

As described, all but the first pattern resort to Javascript in order to carry out runtime changes to the Web page. This is unlike [5] which statically creates all alternative menus in the page, using CSS to select the appropriate menu from the available alternatives by hiding or showing them depending on the viewport. The advantage of runtime adaptation is that the original Web page becomes simpler, featuring the basic version of the menu only (avoiding duplicated menu codification). The drawback is that Javascript is required for the adaptation to work, which adds a delay when the page loads (even if barely perceptible).

4   Conclusions

To support the diversity of devices currently available, two main solutions are possible. Develop different version of the same application for the different deployment contexts, or include adaptations capabilities in a single solution that enables it to react to its deployment context in order to provide the best user experience possible.

In this work we have taken the latter approach and explored how, in a model based user interface design context, we can create adaptable components to support runtime adaptation of the user interface (as opposed to development time translation between contexts). To this end, we have developed a framework consisting of a number of adaptation patterns for menus. Namely: Menu bar, Footer anchor menu, Select menu, Toggle menu, and Off-canvas menu. The framework implements these menus in a mix of JavaScript (using Modernizr to determine browser and device capabilities) and CSS3. The implementation of the patterns was briefly discussed.

Acknowledgments. This work is funded by ERDF - European Regional Development Fund through the COMPETE Programme (operational programme for competitiveness) and by National Funds through the FCT - Fundao para a Cincia e a Tecnologia (Portuguese Foundation for Science and Technology) within project FCOMP-01-0124-FEDER-015095.

References

1. Calvary, G., Coutaz, J., Thevenin, D., Limbourg, Q., Bouillon, L., Vanderdonckt, J.: A unifying reference framework for multi-target user interfaces. Interacting with Computers 15(3), 289–308 (2003)
2. Crowley, J.L., Rey, G., Reignier, P.: Perceptual components for context aware computing. In: Borriello, G., Holmquist, L.E. (eds.) UbiComp 2002. LNCS, vol. 2498, pp. 117–134. Springer, Heidelberg (2002)
3. Gustafson, A.: Adaptive Web Design: Crafting Rich Experiences with Progressive Enhancement. Easy Readers (2011)
4. Markotte, E.: Responsive Web Design. A List Apart (2010)
5. Pietrusky, T.: Responsive menu concepts. Appliness, 9 (December 2012)
6. Silva, J.L., Ribeiro, Ó.R., Fernandes, J.M., Campos, J.C., Harrison, M.D.: The APEX framework: Prototyping of ubiquitous environments based on petri nets. In: Forbrig, P. (ed.) HCSE 2010. LNCS, vol. 6409, pp. 6–21. Springer, Heidelberg (2010)
7. Wroblewski, L.: Mobile First. A List Apart (2011)

An Onomatopoeia-Based Web Music Video Searching System and Its Performance Evaluation

Shizuka Sato[1], Eiichiro Kodama[2], Jiahong Wang[2], and Toyoo Takata[2]

[1] Graduate School of Software and Information Science, Iwate Prefectural University, Japan
[2] Faculty of Software and Information Science, Iwate Prefectural University, Japan
crowz1547@gmail.com

Abstract. In recent years, as use of the Internet became widespread, numerous music videos became available on Web. In Japan, many of these music videos are the CGM (Consumer Generated Media) that are created using a singing synthesis software called Hatsune Miku, and published on YouTube and other similar Web sites. Existing Web sites, however, support only the search methods based on music video title and artist name, which could not be effectively used to search for the unknown music videos such as the CGM ones. This paper presents a system model for effectively searching for the unknown music videos, which is characterized by the use of the onomatopoeia. The system model consists of a music video collecting engine for collecting pairs of music video URL and its tags, an onomatopoeia assigning engine for assigning onomatopoeias to music videos, and an onomatopoeia retriever for presenting users the music video URLs satisfying their onomatopoeia requirements. We have implemented a prototype system of the proposed system model and conducted experiments to study its performance. It has been found that with the proposed system model, a precision ratio of 66.82%, a recall ratio of 56.36%, and an F-measure of 61.14% could be achieved.

Keywords: Onomatopoeia, Web Search, Music Video.

1   Introduction

In recent years, as use of the Internet became widespread, numerous music videos became available on Web. As a result, it becomes more and more important to meet users' requirements for more effectively searching for the music videos. It is found that in Japan, many of these music videos are the CGM (Consumer Generated Media) that are created using a singing synthesis software called Hatsune Miku, and published on YouTube[1] and other similar Web sites.

In this paper, we present a system model for effectively searching for the unknown music videos from Web, which is characterized by the use of the onomatopoeia. An onomatopoeia is a word that sounds like the common sound of the object it is describing, and an example of onomatopoeia is a train being called a choo choo.

C. Stephanidis (Ed.): HCII 2014 Posters, Part I, CCIS 434, pp. 246–251, 2014.
© Springer International Publishing Switzerland 2014

2   Problems of Existing Search Methods

Existing Web sites support only the search methods based on the title and artist name of a music video, which could not be effectively used to search for the unknown Hatsune Miku music videos since users could not know their titles and artist names. Using the existing techniques, users could only use the retrieval keyword "Hatsune Miku" to search for Hatsune Miku music videos, and find their favorite ones by checking the music videos given in the resulting list, which is generally sorted in publishing time order, one by one.

Considering the problem stated above, we think that a more effective search method for the unknown Hatsune Miku music videos is necessary.

3   Related Work

Two existing work are closely related to this research. In paper [2], the subject of searching for sound data from a static sound database with some onomatopoeic words was addressed. In paper [3], the subject of music retrieval from static music database using classic sensitive words was addressed.

For searching for the music videos, it has not been known which one of the sensitive word-based methods and the onomatopoeia-based methods is more effective. In fact, it may be too difficult to give a definite declaration concerning which one is more useful. We do not think these two methods are exclusive, but we think that to meet users' varying requirements, it would be important to investigate the possibility of using solely the onomatopoeia to support the retrieval of music videos.

4   Search for Unknown Music Videos Using Onomatopoeia

The proposed system model for searching for the unknown music videos from Web using the onomatopoeia is given in Fig. 1.

4.1   Music Video Collecting Engine

The *music video collecting engine* is used to collect the pairs of music video URL and its tags from the music video distribution sites such as YouTube [1] and Niconico [4]. Note that music videos in these sites have been assigned some attribute words such as "Hatsune", "Miku" and "Append", which are called the *tags* and are used to describe the music videos and make their retrievals easier. The collected data will be stored in the *target music video database* temporarily, and processed by the *onomatopoeia assigning engine*.

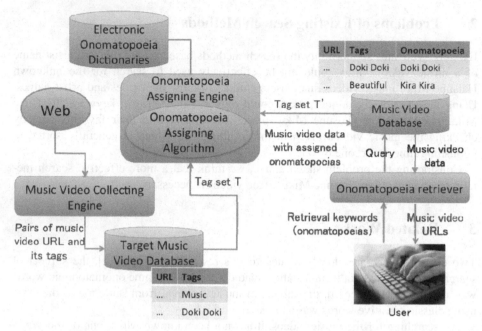

Fig. 1. Onomatopoeia-based Web music video searching system model

4.2   Onomatopoeia Assigning Engine

By applying the tag sets of *target music video data* and the tag sets of *music video data* stored in the *music video database*, onomatopoeia assigning engine assigns onomatopoeias to the target music video data using an *onomatopoeia assigning algorithm* given below. The resulting target music video data will be moved into the music video database. It is assumed that before the algorithm is started, there have been accumulated at least n records in the music video database, where n is a predefined system parameter.

Onomatopoeia Assigning Algorithm

1. Get tag set T of the target music video data to which onomatopoeias will be assigned. Using electronic onomatopoeia dictionaries, onomatopoeias included in T are extracted, and the results are assigned to the target music video data.
2. Get the next record from the music video database, and then get the tag set T' from the record.
3. Calculate the similarity degree of T and T' by the following formula.

$$Jaccard(T,T') = \frac{|T \cap T'|}{|T \cup T'|}$$

4. Repeat steps 2 and 3 for all the music video records, and assign the onomatopoeias of the music video data of the maximal similarity degree to the target music video

data. In the case that the maximal similarity degree is greater than a predefined threshold θ $(0 < \theta < 1)$, the onomatopoeias obtained in step 1 are also assigned to the music video data of the maximal similarity degree.

4.3 Onomatopoeia Retriever

The *onomatopoeia retriever* presents users the music video URLs that satisfy their onomatopoeia requirements by comparing the onomatopoeias provided by users as the retrieval keywords with the onomatopoeias of the music videos.

Figure 2 shows user interface of the search engine. As an example, if the retrieval keyword "TanTan" is entered, we will have the results shown in Fig. 3. Users can enjoy a music video with a browser by clicking the URL.

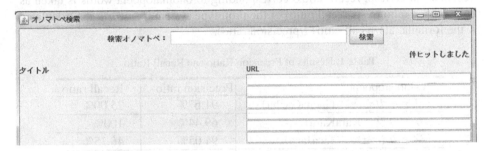

Fig. 2. User interface of the search engine

Fig. 3. Results for retrieval keyword "TanTan"

5   Performance Evaluation

We have implemented a prototype system of the proposed system model and conducted experiments to study its performance in terms of *precision ratio* and *recall ratio*.

Music video data used for the experiments consists of 100 initial music videos and 100 target music videos. The experiment for the precision ratio was conducted with 12 test subjects and 48 onomatopoeia words that have been assigned to the music videos. For each retrieval keyword, the ratio of correct answers, which are judged by the test subjects, included in the searching results of music videos are calculated, and the average of 12 test subjects is taken as the precision ratio.

For the recall ratio, first the music videos corresponding to the 48 onomatopoeia words, which are judged by 5 test subjects, are determined as the correct answers. Music videos are searched using the onomatopoeia words that have been assigned to them, and the ratio of correct answers included in the searching results of music videos is taken as the recall ratio.

A part of the experiment results are shown in Table 1, where the average of the precision ratios (resp. recall ratios) corresponding to onomatopoeia words is taken as the precision ratio (resp. recall ratio) of the prototype system. *F-measure* is calculated by the formula: 2(1/recall ratio+1/precision ratio).

Table 1. Results of Precision Ratio and Recall Ratio

Onomatopoeia	Precision ratio	Recall ratio
ガチャガチャ （GachaGacha）	91.67%	25.00%
カラカラ （KaraKara）	69.44%	100%
ジャカジャカ （JacaJaca）	94.05%	46.15%
シャンシャン （ShanShan）	68.75%	33.33%
タンタン （TanTan）	78.85%	83.33%
ノホホン （NohoHon）	66.67%	50%
ピコピコ （PikoPiko）	57.10%	50%
ビュンビュン （ByunByun）	91.67%	33.33%
フラフラ （FuraFura）	41.67%	100%
ルンルン （RunRun）	75%	0%
ワクワク （WakuWaku）	75%	50%
Average	66.82%	56.36%

6   Conclusion

In this paper we have proposed a new system model for searching for the music videos from Web, which is characterized by the use of the onomatopoeia. We have conducted experiments to evaluate performance of the proposed system model. Experiment results shown that with the proposed system model, a precision ratio of 66.82%, a recall ratio of 56.36%, and an F-measure of 61.14% could be achieved.

References

1. YouTube, http://www.youtube.com
2. Uota, K., Suzuki, K., Pitoyo, H., Hashimoto, S.: Sound Database Retrieved by Onomato-poeia and Sound, Technical report of Electronics, Information and Communication Engineers. HCS 104(446), 19–22 (2004)
3. Ikezoe, T., Hajikawa, Y., Nomura, Y.: Music Database Retrival System with Sensitivity Words Using Music Sensitivity Space. Information Processing Society of Japan Journal 42(12), 3201–3212 (2001)
4. Niconico, http://www.nicovideo.jp/

Document Management and Tracking System for Emergency Response Headquarters

Wataru Sendo[1], Norihisa Segawa[2], Jun Sawamoto[2], Eiji Sugino[2],
Masato Yazawa[3], and Shinji Akitomi[4]

[1,2] Iwate Prefectural University (Graduate School), 152-52 Sugo,
Takizawa, Iwate 020-0693, Japan
g2311021@s.iwate-pu.ac.jp, sega@acm.org,
{sawamoto,sugino}@iwate-pu.ac.jp
[3] Mathematical Assist Design Laboratory, 1058-5 Yoshizawa-cho,
Ota, Gunma 373-0019, Japan
yazawa@mail.wind.ne.jp
[4] Iwate Medical University, 19-1 Uchimaru, Morioka, Iwate 020-8506, Japan
shin-zi@pop12.odn.ne.jp

Abstract. One problem faced by an emergency response headquarters is that emergency response procedures are not adequately documented. This lack of documentation is a major problem in testing preparedness for future emergencies. However, it is difficult to document an emergency response while actually responding to an event. The authors have attempted to resolve this issue by building a content management system with a focus on documentation created during emergency responses and on documentation that can be printed out and attached.

Keywords: Disaster information, content management, operations support, automation, image processing.

1   Introduction

One issue in Japan currently is learning from the lessons of the Great East Japan Earthquake and Tsunami, and verifying that organizations are prepared for any future disasters. One extremely important mission for handling future disasters is verifying the decision-making and action processes and operations of an emergency response headquarters, which are key to an emergency response.

With respect to the verification of the operations at an emergency response headquarters, one current topic is that the minutes of the emergency response meetings are not recorded [1]. Given insufficient documentation, it is unclear at the time an instruction or command is given by the emergency response headquarters, what information that instruction or command was based on. The people involved in emergency response events are working to rectify this problem by creating minutes after the fact, but this relies on human memory, and as such is lacking in reliability.

C. Stephanidis (Ed.): HCII 2014 Posters, Part I, CCIS 434, pp. 252–257, 2014.

One obstacle to documentation in an emergency response headquarters is the sheer amount of work that must be carried out in the initial outbreak stages of an emergency (within the first 72 h). The main responsibilities are gathering and sharing information, linking up with other relevant organizations and authorities, and issuing instructions and commands based on the information gathered. Information gathering often occurs by sending and receiving paper faxes, and sharing information with everyone often involves copying paper documents onto whiteboards or pasting them onto presentation panels. Paper documents created at an emergency response headquarters or gathered from relevant authorities contain information about the state of the affected area or parties that is required for deciding on an appropriate emergency response, and other information about the staffing of the relevant organizations and their emergency response. All of this forms not just the basis for the decision making and orders issued by the emergency response headquarters and the related organizations, but it is also considerably important material for verifying in future whether the response was appropriate on the basis of the information available at the time, and for verifying preparedness for future emergencies.

However, while responding to an emergency, it is difficult to make changes to the created documentation, or to entirely record when information was shared or how widely paper documents were distributed. Further, unlike email or electronic files, copying or sending paper documents (such as via a scanner, by fax, or by hand) does not leave any computer log, making it harder to trace after the fact.

In our research into this problem, we developed a content management and tracking system that can be set up at an emergency response headquarters in the event of a major disaster, such as an earthquake or tsunami.

2   Related Cases

Content management systems are widely used to manage content and versioning for documents created on computers. Well-known content management systems (CMSs) include Alfresco [2] and KnowledgeTree [3]. These systems are web-based, and system users access the server running the CMS via web browsers running on their client machines, using the browser to upload, manage, and otherwise operate on the document content.

Managing documentation by using a web browser from an emergency response headquarters differs from the normal workflow and thus, requires prior training. There is also the possibility of human error leading to failures in documentation management for areas differing from the normal workflow, such as forgetting to upload documentation. It would not be helpful to increase the user workload at an emergency response headquarters, where considerable output is already demanded of workers during an emergency response. What is needed is a system that reduces human error as much as possible, while also not introducing any impediments to user work.

It is also conceivable that paper documents posted and used in decision making at one point in time might have taken down and not used in decision making at a later point in time. A CMS must allow users to not just manage document content and versioning but also print documents and manage them after printing and posting in an emergency response headquarters.

3   System Concept

We built a CMS for recording document content and changes to this content as authored in an emergency response headquarters, and for tracking the status of document sharing within the headquarters over time. Figure 1 shows how a CMS can be used in an emergency response headquarters.

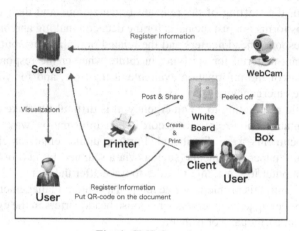

Fig. 1. CMS Overview

When users create documents or print them out for sharing, the CMS starts managing document data in the background. These document data are sent to the server, and making them visible via the web makes it possible to view and verify the information using a web browser. Document data managed by the system are as follows: Document Title, Content, Creator, Created, QR Code Link Document ID, Document Revision ID.

The CMS also adds a QR code to a document when a user prints it. Users can then manage date information for when a document was posted to a whiteboard or taken down again by using a web camera to scan the QR code. The information recorded for paper documents are as follows: QR Code Link, Data Posted, Data Removed(last date confirmed as posted).

The most significant feature of the CMS is that documents are managed automatically without requiring users to even be aware of the process. Users do not have to utilize any specialized tools other than the ones that they regularly use in their work.

These various types of data are also collected in real time, such that workers in areas with a functioning Internet infrastructure can monitor the situation at the emergency response headquarters and possibly help in decision making processes. However, some problems remain in terms of how to manage who can access which information. These issues will be dealt with in the future.

The next section provides a more detailed description of the system configuration and implementation.

4   System Implementation

This system consists of software used by the workers of an emergency response headquarters to create documents (the client), a server for storing the document data, and a web camera for monitoring documents posted within the headquarters.

The client is implemented so that users do not need to know any commands or operations other than those used normally when creating documents. The client software is installed on a MacBook Pro and includes PHP and the PEAR libraries, as well as shell scripts. Users can use Microsoft Office Word 2007 or later to create documents.

Figure 2 shows the processing flow for managing documents, with the client portion marked clearly.

When a user creates and prints a document, the system catches the printing event, and the document data are temporarily saved to the client machine's working directory as a PDF. No commands have yet been sent to the printer. The saved PDF document is then analyzed using the `pdftotext` feature of the open-source XPDF library for analyzing PDF files. A unique QR code identifying the document is then generated and added to the saved PDF. Once the QR code is applied, the print commands are sent to the printer. The PDF document and the URL obtained by reading the QR code are then registered to the server's database. These data are used to link the saved document with any paper copies posted on whiteboards or elsewhere.

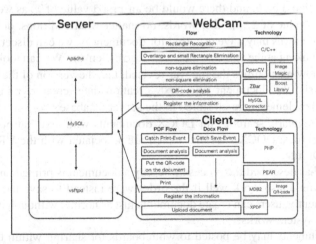

Fig. 2. Document Management Processing Flow

The user next saves the created document. Saving generates a copy of the document in the working directory. Word documents (with the filename extension of `*.docx`) use Office Open XML [4] as the internal data representation of the text and formatting information that make up the document. One notable aspect of this system is that a

Word file can be unzipped to access the collection of the Office Open XML files that make up the document. Analyzing this collection of files makes it possible to get the document text and to get a record of content revisions.

Figure 3 shows the portion of an XML file internal to a Word document that is required to manage document revisions.

```
 4
 5    <w:rsids>
 6        <w:rsidRoot w:val="00A324B3"/>
 7        <w:rsid w:val="001C62C4"/>
 8        <w:rsid w:val="004E6FEF"/>
 9        <w:rsid w:val="00713A0A"/>
10        <w:rsid w:val="00A324B3"/>
11        <w:rsid w:val="00F42583"/>
12    </w:rsids>
13
```

Fig. 3. XML for Managing Revisions

In Figure 3, the rsidRoot element contains a string value that is automatically assigned when a document is first created. The rsid elements contain strings that are automatically assigned when the document is edited to add or delete content. For instance, a given document A would have a random value assigned to the rsidRoot element when the document was created. For example, let us use a value of 0. After document A was edited, the rsidRoot value would still be 0, and a new rsid value—again random in real life, but here let us use 1—would be assigned. Irrespective of the number of times the document may have been revised, the rsidRoot value clearly identifies this document as document A. Now, assume that this document A has new content added and is then saved as document B. In this case as well, the rsidRoot value would be 0, and there would be an rsid value of 1, as well as a newly assigned rsid value of 2. In other words, no matter what additions, deletions, name changes, or file moves may have occurred for document A, we can discern the original document by looking at the value of the rsidRoot element. We can look at the rsid values to see how many times the file was revised, i.e., the version of the file.

After analysis, the document title, text, creation date, creator, rsidRoot, and number of rsid elements are all stored in the server database.

The server regularly searches for DOCX documents with text that matches that of the stored PDF files. DOCX files that match are associated with the URL of the QR code in the PDF file.

This paper has described the process whereby a document is printed and then saved. This system would also work well if the order were instead to save the file and then print. Consequently, users can create documents just as normal without having to worry about how the system works.

Printed documents may be posted to whiteboards for sharing within the headquarters. This system uses a web camera to monitor and record when a document is posted and when it is removed. We used the Buffalo BSW180ABK [5] web camera in the normal video mode for monitoring. To recognize QR codes appearing in the video captured by the web camera, we used C++, the image processing library OpenCV, the barcode and QR code analysis library ZBar, the Boost library, and the ImageMagick library.

The processing flow is shown in the "WebCam" portion of Figure 2.

The first step is to use OpenCV to extract a single frame of the video. Next, we detect any rectangles in the image. In this system, the identifier that we want to recognize is a QR code; therefore, detection excludes any shapes that are not squares or that are too small. We then use ZBar to analyze any barcodes in the collection of found rectangles. If the analysis results in a URL from a QR code that has been detected for the first time, the first and last posting date and time for that document are recorded in the database as the current date and time. If the document has been detected before, the last posting date and time are updated to the current date and time. We can calculate the length of time that a document has been shared within the headquarters by finding the difference between dates and times of the first and last posting. This makes it possible to know that this document was used for emergency response decision making.

Lastly, we process the data stored on the server to make them viewable via the web. For server software, we use the Apache web server, vsftpd for file transfer, and MySQL for the database, and we use the HTML, CSS, PHP. CakePHP framework, and Java-Script as our development languages. The web view shows the stored data along a time axis and provides a search tool and other features.

5   Conclusion

In this paper, we proposed a CMS system built to avoid any impediments to user workflows, as a means of overcoming the difficulties faced in recording documentation in an emergency response headquarters.

In the future, we intend to conduct tests using this CMS in regular daily work and other situations to ascertain whether document content and document postings are correctly managed.

References

1. No Meeting Minutes for Ten Earthquake Response Meetings: Shoddy Document Management. Nikkei. (January 27, 2012), http://www.nikkei.com/article/DGXNASFS2700A_X20C12A1MM0000/ (in Japanese)
2. Alfresco, http://www.alfresco.com/
3. KnowledgeTree, http://www.knowledgetree.com/
4. Office Open XML, http://msdn.microsoft.com/en-us/library/office/aa338205%28v=office.12%29.aspx
5. BSW180ABK, http://buffalo.jp/products/catalog/supply/multimedia/webcamera/60/bsw180a/

Novel Training Techniques for Novice Timetablers

Victoria Smy, Helen Seeby, Esther Winslow, and John Patrick

School of Psychology, Cardiff University, Tower Building, Park Place, Cardiff, CF10 3AT, UK
{smyva,seebyh,winslowe,patrickj}@cardiff.ac.uk

Abstract. This study investigates the efficacy of training in facilitating human-computer interaction during a timetabling task. A computerized feedforward facility highlighted timeslots that could accommodate class requirements, thus integrating relevant constraint information and easing the computational workload of the timetabler. Feedforward training was compared to: metacognitive training that prompted individuals to plan and evaluate their timetabling decisions; a metacognition plus feedforward condition; and a control no training condition. A training and transfer design was used. Results indicated that feedforward training did not improve performance. However, metacognitive training resulted in more classes successfully scheduled and fewer timetabling errors than in control or feedforward conditions. The addition of feedforward to the metacognitive training did not result in additional improvement. Therefore, feedforward training, in its present form, offered no advantage, unlike metacognitive training. Practical advantages of metacognitive training is that it is inexpensive and quick to develop.

Keywords: Timetabling, automated timetabling aid, interface design, human-computer interaction.

1 Introduction

Humans are still the principal developers of timetables in many commercial and educational contexts [1]. Timetabling, as a human-computer interaction task, is a complex form of problem solving, utilizing various cognitive processes such as planning, decision making, monitoring and evaluation. Hoc et al. [1] reported that expert timetablers differ from novices, as experts work with the external representation at the interface to a greater extent whilst formulating partial solutions and novices devote more time to managing constraints before developing a solution. Similarly, Smy and Patrick [2] found that timetabling performance of novices deteriorates, as the number of timetabling constraints increases. Therefore, constraint management appears to be a source of difficulty for the inexperienced person in this HCI task.

The present study aims to examine whether a computerized planning aid, labeled feedforward, may be of benefit when training novice timetablers to manage timetabling constraints. The feedforward aid identifies timetable positions and locations that would satisfy the constraints that restrict the scheduling of a class. As such, constraint integration should become less effortful. Given that such activity preoccupies novices

C. Stephanidis (Ed.): HCII 2014 Posters, Part I, CCIS 434, pp. 258–263, 2014.
© Springer International Publishing Switzerland 2014

[1], such an aid would alleviate cognitive load during training, allowing timetablers to focus on solution planning.

The transfer performance of the feedforward training condition was contrasted to that of a control condition that received no training, and also a metacognition training condition. The metacognition training required timetablers to inspect the constraint information and propose some alternative positions for an unscheduled class. In doing so, the metacognitive groups were instructed to manually generate and vocalize information similar to that automatically generated in the feedforward condition. Whilst some evidence of the beneficial effects of feedforward have been found in the context of faultfinding [3] and e-learning [4], little evidence exists concerning the utility of such a feedforward mechanism within timetabling. In contrast, the beneficial and generic effects of metacognition across multiple contexts are well-documented [i.e., 5-6]. It was expected that both the feedforward and metacognition conditions would perform better than the control group. However, the combination of metacognition plus feedforward was expected to produce the best performance.

2   Methods

2.1   Participants

Forty-three psychology undergraduates participated in the study in return for course credit and were randomly assigned to one of four conditions. All participants were females with an age range of 18-23 years (M=19.33 years, SD=.99).

2.2   Materials

Experimental materials consisted of four timetabling tasks, programmed in Java and presented via two computer screens. The timetabling screen (Fig. 1) contained an empty, five-day timetable with tiles depicting the classes to be scheduled. An information screen displayed resource availability (teachers, classrooms etc.) and class requirements (facilities required or prerequisite classes). It also displayed any applicable timetabling rules. Example rules were;

- Classes are scheduled in chronological order (i.e., Maths I precedes Maths II)
- The required class facilities must be met by the room allocated to that class

Two timetabling tasks were used for training purposes. Both tasks had the same five applicable timetabling rules and 20 classes to be scheduled. However, one task also incorporated the feedforward facility. This facility allowed timetablers to select a class and view any empty timeslots and classrooms that satisfy all of the rules constraining that class (demonstrated in Fig. 1, where the class 'Art' has been selected via a mouse click, and a number of empty timeslots on Tuesday have been highlighted along with the classroom "PP14").

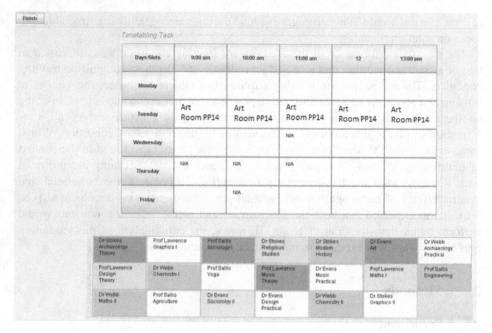

Fig. 1. Timetabling screen, N/As correspond to unavailable timeslots, labeled timeslots correspond to the timeslots selected via feedforward activation

A further timetabling task was used for interface familiarization. The final task, used for testing purposes, contained 20 classes to be scheduled and had seven applicable timetabling rules. No feedforward facility was available.

2.3   Design and Procedure

A between-subjects design was utilized with four levels of the independent variable, training: control (no training); feedforward; metacognition; metacognition plus feedforward. All participants received instruction as to the nature of the timetabling interface and performed a familiarisation task. Every group, excluding the control group, then received training that was limited to ten class placements, so that the timetabling experience received across groups was approximately equal. The training differed across conditions;

- The feedforward group were told that they could select any class and view all empty timeslots and classrooms that could successfully accommodate the class without breaking any rules. They should then select a timeslot for that class.
- The metacognitive group were required to pause before each class placement and propose two timetabling positions for the selected class. They then had to explicitly evaluate these positions, by examining whether they satisfied all applicable timetabling rules. After this they scheduled the preferred timeslot.
- The metacognitive plus feedforward group performed the same process as the metacognitive group. However, before placing their selected class they activated the

feedforward facility, thereby receiving feedback on their constraint satisfaction performance.

All participants then completed a seven rule transfer timetabling task. Here, they were instructed to schedule all classes in the timetable as quickly and accurately as possible.

3   Results

Means and standard deviations for all experimental conditions are displayed in Table 1. These results indicate that groups undergoing metacognitive training produced the best timetables, and did so whilst incurring the fewest errors.

Table 1. Effect of training condition on test performance

Performance on transfer test	Training condition	Mean	SD
Number of classes correctly scheduled	Control	12.30	4.22
	Feedforward	11.18	4.94
	Metacognition	16.91	2.30
	Feedforward & Metacognition	17.18	2.27
Number of errors on final timetable	Control	11.90	7.53
	Feedforward	11.83	9.79
	Metacognition	3.36	3.47
	Feedforward & Metacognition	3.45	3.08
Number of errors during timetabling	Control	24.10	12.36
	Feedforward	15.91	9.84
	Metacognition	9.27	11.15
	Feedforward & Metacognition	5.27	3.50

One-way ANOVAs revealed a significant effect of training on the number of classes successfully scheduled, $F(3, 39) = 7.99$, $MSE = 13.03$, $p < .001$, $f = .78$. Bonferroni comparisons revealed that the feedforward group successfully placed fewer classes than both the metacognition, and the metacognition plus feedforward conditions ($ps < .01$). Likewise, the control condition placed fewer classes successfully than both metacognitive groups ($ps < .05$). There were also significant effects of training on the number of timetabling errors. With regards to errors in the final timetable, $F(3, 39) = 5.92$, $MSE = 43.18$, $p < .01$, $f = .67$, the feedforward group made significantly more errors than both the metacognition, and the metacognition plus feedforward groups ($ps < .05$). Likewise, the control group made more errors than either group involving metacognitive training ($ps < .05$). There was a significant difference in the errors committed during timetabling between conditions, $F(3, 39) = 7.54$, $MSE = 94.11$, $p < .001$, $f = .76$. The number of errors made by the feedforward group did not significantly differ from either metacognition group, or the control group. The control group differed from both the metacognition and metacognition plus feedforward groups ($ps < .01$ and $.001$ respectively). On all measures of timetabling performance, the feedforward group did not differ from the control group.

4   Discussion

The results indicate that having undergone feedforward training, whereby a computerized planning aid integrates relevant constraint information in an attempt to enable greater attention to be paid to solution generation, does not improve performance on a subsequent timetabling task where feedforward information is no longer available. Contrary to expectations, the feedforward group was no more effective at the subsequent timetabling test than their counterparts in the control group, who had no timetabling training. However, feedforward, when accompanied with a metacognitive self-explanation technique, did result in favorable performance on a subsequent timetabling test, although effects were not significantly better than the metacognition only group.

It appears that easing the cognitive load of the timetabler by integrating constraint information, does not encourage the acquisition of timetabling skills. Whilst a feedforward facility may make the timetabling interface easier to navigate, the present study found little evidence that it led to skill acquisition. On the contrary, the effortful processing and integrating of task constraints, and the explicit examination of planning strategies required in the metacognitive training resulted in better performance. Veenman et al. [7] suggested the mechanism through which metacognition exerts its beneficial effects is via prompting individuals to reflect upon, and refine, their performance strategy. Such activity is not explicitly required in the feedforward group and is unlikely to occur spontaneously.

A couple of limitations surrounding the current experimental methodology should be acknowledged. Firstly, the use of a more difficult timetabling task, whereby the scheduling of classes is more constrained than experienced during training, may have diminished any training effects. Secondly, it may be that the amount of feedforward training provided was insufficient to produce a beneficial effect. Finally, training variability was not examined in the present experiment. There is reason to suppose that tackling a diverse range of training tasks may be an important means of improving performance on such cognitive tasks [8]. Further research could examine whether the length, difficulty and variety of training tasks has an effect on timetabling performance.

The results of this study indicate that the provision of a feedforward facility, envisaged to simplify and aid in the planning process during the training of timetabling, does not lead to any strategic improvement in subsequent timetabling performance where the feedforward facility has been removed. In contrast, a metacognitive training procedure, requiring individuals to explicitly state and evaluate their planning strategy, improved subsequent timetabling performance. Given the benefit and ease of developing metacognitive training programs, future research should evaluate how this can best be integrated into the computer interface for training this complex design task.

References

1. Hoc, J., Guerin, C., Mebarki, N.: The nature of expertise in scheduling: The case of timetabling. Human Factors and Ergonomics in Manufacturing & Service Industries 24, 192–206 (2014)
2. Smy, V., Patrick, J.: Some effects of increasing external constraint rules on design performance in a timetabling task. In: Proceedings of the 30th European Conference on Cognitive Ergonomics, pp. 104–107. Edinburgh Napier University, Scotland (2012)
3. Patrick, J.: Training: Research and Practice. Academic Press, San Diego (1992)
4. Baker, D.J., Zuvela, D.: Feedforward strategies in the first-year experience of online and distributed learning environments. Assessment & Evaluation in Higher Education 38, 687–697 (2012)
5. Berardi-Coletta, B., Buyer, L.S., Dominowski, R.L., Rellinger, E.R.: Metacognition and problem solving: A process oriented approach. Journal of Experimental Psychology: Learning, Memory, and Cognition 21, 205–223 (1995)
6. Tajika, H., Nakatsu, N., Nozaki, H., Neumann, E., Murano, S.: Effects of self-explanation as a metacognitive strategy for solving mathematical word problems. Japanese Psychological Research 49, 222–233 (2007)
7. Veenman, M.V.J., Van Hout-Wolters, B.H.A.M., Afflerbach, P.: Metacognition and learning: Conceptual and methodological considerations. Metacognition Learning 1, 3–14 (2006)
8. Holladay, C.L., Quiñones, M.A.: Practice variability and transfer of training: The role of self-efficacy generality. Journal of Applied Psychology 88, 1094–1103 (2003)

Case Study: A Visual Analytics System, Sapientia

Sookyoung Song and Taesung Park

Samsung SDS Seoul, Korea
{sookyoung.song,ts10.park}@samsung.com

Abstract. The visual analytics is increasingly drawing attention according to the fast growing trend of big data. To meet the demands of the times, the project was carried out to make a working prototype of visual analytics system for big data analysis.The visual analytics system 'Sapientia' was planned for providing big data analytics service. By performing user researches to establish user-centered UX strategy, it provides intuitive and convenient UI, which is able to easily control the pipeline of data analysis and also customize the UI depending on the purpose of use.We anticipate that 'Sapientia' will be able to encourage the expansion of big data analysis and also be able to contribute to finding new business opportunities and enhancing the business capabilities of company.

Keywords: Visual Analytics, Data Visualization, Big Data Analytics, Information Design, Case Studies.

1   Introduction

Recently, the importance of visual analytics is increasing by the trends of big data analytics. Visual analytics is one of the most recent methods to extract insights from large-scale data combining the data processing ability of computer and the cognitive reasoning ability of human.

This is a case study for introducing the project 'Sapientia' which is proposed to make a working prototype of visual analytics system for big data analysis. The project goal is to provide a user-centered system for casual users as well as expert users. In this research document, the authors anticipate the contribution to the HCI and UX communities by sharing the experience and knowledge from this project.

2   Sapientia: Big Data Visual Analytics System

The name 'Sapientia' having the meaning of 'wisdom' is the product name as well as the project name to make visual analytics system for big data analysis. This name contains the vision that this system can help customers get insights through the big data analysis so that they can make a wiser decision-making.

The most powerful feature of 'Sapientia' is to provide a variety of methods for data visualization and data analysis. It provides more than 30 data visualization methods not only for structured data but also for unstructured data. And it provides more than

C. Stephanidis (Ed.): HCII 2014 Posters, Part I, CCIS 434, pp. 264–267, 2014.
© Springer International Publishing Switzerland 2014

20 data analysis algorithms through an intuitive UI to control the data analysis process by just drag and drop. The UI was designed to update these methods of data visualization and analysis consistently.

3   Methods Used

To establish user-centered UX strategy, several methods were taken to find user's needs and extract insights.

3.1   Cognitive Walkthrough

The goal of this method is to draw the UX considerations to figure out the usability issues by situations. It was conducted following the steps to analyze the representative visualization solutions and evaluate the scenarios and user goals by the expert heuristics.

- Select four representative visualization solutions
- Define the scenarios and user goals
- Conduct the expert heuristic evaluation

3.2   In-depth Interviews

The goal of this method is to understand the business process and work patterns related to data depending on the various departments. It was conducted through interviews with six business experts performing works related to data analysis and collecting information about the current work situations and opinions about their works.

- Research planning and preparation – user interview and observation scenarios, questionnaires, pilot test
- Conducting user interviews

From the results of researches, the UX considerations and UX Strategy were derived.

3.3   Prototyping

The representative wireframes were drawn referring to the UX strategy.

- Define the main scenarios and screens
- Draw storyboards by the representative wireframes
- Verify the interaction using the interactive prototype by Axure

3.4   User Study

The scenario reviews with expert user and casual user were conducted and user feedbacks were gathered.

- Usability test with eight users
- Collect user feedbacks through demonstrating interactive prototype
- Draw final storyboards applying user feedback

4   UX Concept and UI Design

As the result of user research UX concept was established and finally the consistent UI design was implemented based on the UX concept.

4.1   UX Concept

The four UX directions were set to provide the optimized user experience.

- Intuitive User Interface
- Providing Proactive Interaction
- Considering Collaboration
- Optimizing Interface for Specific Domains

4.2   User Interface

The data pipeline dealing with all the processes of data analysis was designed with the coherent user interfaces. The usability was maximized by providing the domain modes which is customized depending on the use goal and frequency.

- Data analytics pipeline
- Domain specific mode

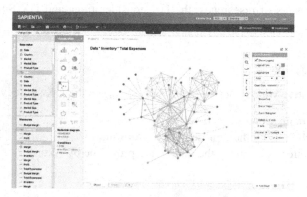

Fig. 1. User interface design for data visualization

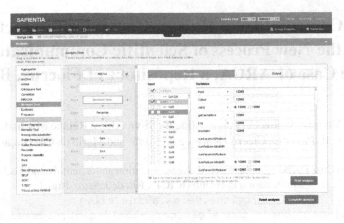

Fig. 2. User interface design for data analysis

5   Conclusion

The visual analytics based on data visualization and data analysis is increasingly gaining its importance with the rising trend of big data analysis. Catching up this trend, a visual analytics system 'Sapientia' was proposed.

We conducted user researches like cognitive walkthrough, in-depth interviews, prototyping, user study to establish user-centered UX strategy. As a result, 'Sapientia' provides the intuitive and convenient user interface to control all the process of data analysis. Also it maximizes the user's convenience by providing customized mode for specific domains.

It is anticipated to be a chance for expanding the users from expert users to casual users and also be a contribution to finding new business opportunities and enhancing the business capabilities of company as well.

References

1. Dill, J., et al.: Expanding the Frontiers of Visual Analytics and Visualization. Springer (2012)
2. Few, S.C.: Now You See It: Simple Visualization Techniques for Quantitative Analysis. Analytics Press (2009)

A Contribution of Human-Computer Interaction to the New Process of Scientific Communication: The Case of ARCA, a Repository of Fiocruz, Brazil

Viviane Santos O. Veiga, Aline da Silva Alves, Rejane Machado,
Denise Nacif Pimenta, Cícera Henrique da Silva, and Maria da Conceição Carvalho

Oswaldo Cruz Foundation, Institute of Communication and Scientific and Technological
Information in Health (ICICT), Rio de Janeiro, Brazil
{viviane.veiga,aline.silva,
rejane.machado,conceição.carvalho}@icict.fiocruz.br,
cicera.silva@globo.com

Abstract. Institutional Repositories (IR) are tools of information and communication technologies (ICTs) which are altering the process of science communication and its impact on society. It aims primarily to improve the scientific communication of institutions internally and externally, maximizing its accessibility, usage and visibility. Literature searches indicate a lack of usability studies about IR involving users in the task of self-archiving, a fundamental process in the change of culture and behavior of researchers, which improves RI adherence and success. Aiming to know more about this question, a usability study with five researchers in accomplishing the task of self-archiving in ARCA is presented. Cooperative evaluation and post-test questionnaires were applied and possible solutions to usability issues were identified and solved. As a result, despite the recognition of the benefits provided by the use of institutional repositories in terms of visibility of their scientific production, usability barriers of the interface have been contributing to the non-adherence. Other barriers identified were language translation of the software; lack of immediate feedback overall, principally in the authorization of deposit; excess of information in the pages, often leading the user to error. By evaluating interfaces and providing solutions to usability problems of repositories, the area of Human-Computer Interaction has greatly aided in perfecting institutional repositories and the process of scientific communication as a whole.

Keywords: Institutional Repository, Usability, Cooperative Evaluation, Self-archiving.

1   Introduction

Institutional Repositories (IR) are tools of information and communication technologies (ICTs) which are altering the process of science communication and its impact on society. It aims primarily to improve the scientific communication of institutions internally and externally, maximizing its accessibility, usage and visibility [1].

C. Stephanidis (Ed.): HCII 2014 Posters, Part I, CCIS 434, pp. 268–273, 2014.
© Springer International Publishing Switzerland 2014

In RIs, self-archiving is generally advocated and is known as the deposit of a digital document in the system by the author or person authorized by him. The autonomy of the author in performing this task of self-archiving of his or hers scientific research sometimes cannot be carried out due to several impeding factors, among them, problems with the usability of the interface [2].

Literature searches indicate a lack of usability studies about IR involving users in the task of self-archiving, a fundamental process in the change of culture and behavior of researchers, which improves RI adherence and success. These studies also aid in understanding the mental model of researchers from different knowledge fields, as adherence to self-archiving may depend on knowledge areas and there is particular resistance from senior researchers to change their behavior of publication [3].

ARCA is the Institutional Repository of the Oswaldo Cruz Foundation (Fiocruz). Fiocruz, a research institute linked to the Brazilian Ministry of Health is one of the most prominent science and technology health institution in Latin America. Launched in 2011, ARCA contains approximately 5.006 digital documents and aims to organize, preserve and disseminate the institutional scientific production of Fiocruz.[4]

In this sense, a usability study with researchers from Fernandes Figueira Institute, a unit at Fiocruz, was conducted in accomplishing the task of self-archiving in ARCA. Cooperative evaluation and post-test questionnaires were applied and possible solutions to usability issues were identified and solved.

2   Method

This work is a descriptive qualitative study which used the technique of cooperative evaluation [5,6] and implementation of post-test questionnaire for data collection. For the evaluation, test scenarios were established relevant to the process of self-archiving in ARCA.

As for the post-test questionnaire, the level of user satisfaction for the task of self-archiving articles in the RI was assessed. Questions concerning the following aspects were evaluated: design of screens, terminology (use of words/terms), messages and information.

A scenario for the tests was elaborated so that the users were able to conduct activities sequentially, enabling the identification of problems in the interaction with the RI interface. A time limit was not stipulated, respecting the individual interaction time of each user. In order to verify any possible problems during the testing and the best ways of formulating the scenario tasks, a pilot test was performed. The pilot test did not identify the need for changes in the test environment and scenario.

With regard to the sample of users, it was composed of six professionals pertaining to the Fernandes Figueira Institute (IFF), a unit of Fiocruz. To ensure the anonymity of participants, these were coded as the following: U-1, U-2, U-3, U-4, U-5. This project was approved by a ethics committee with the registration number of 09673712.8.0000.5241

These users had the following profile: the age ranged from 28 to 56 years old, used computer as a study tool and for daily work. Although they are part of a research institute and accustomed to using various sources of scientific and technical health information systems, most were unfamiliar with institutional repositories as a whole and ARCA in particular.

The library located at the IFF institute was defined as the site for performing the tests, due to the ease of movement of the research participants, apart from the fact that the management of the IFF community in ARCA was also located in this library. repository with role of being the motive to self-archiving at the Institute.

The tests took place in a controlled environment, created specifically for conducting the tests. The Windows platform was utilized with three choices of browsers: Internet Explorer, Mozilla Firefox and Google Chrome. The observations were conducted individually, either during the tests or during the observation of the interaction itself. The equipment that would be used laptop was presented to the participants, stressing that the interaction would be recorded on audio for later analysis. The necessity that user should feel comfortable in performing the tasks was emphasized, making it clear that the focus of the tests was to assess the self-archiving process and not the participants.

3   Data Analysis: Cooperative Evaluation and Post-test Questionnaire

The task of self-archiving in ARCA has two sub-tasks for its completion. The first is the completion of a user profile, in which basic personal information is required. The second activity is the submission of a digital document in the RI, in this case, a research article. This process of upload has a series of steps that must be followed, such as upload of the document, licensing and insertion of metadata identifiers.

3.1   User Registration

In the sub-task of the user registration, after filling in the form with personal information, an email is sent to confirm the registration validity. During this moment of the test, it was observed that the users did not identify the e- mail validation registration. It was then noted that the sender of the email was named "dspace", name of the software used, as noted by some users. This email configuration comes as a default in the system and needs to be customized in order for the user to acknowledge this email. After the confirmation of the registration, users must then finish filling out some data.

Another usability problem then came up. In this screen the user sees a message informing him that, from that moment, the user is appropriately registered and ready to use the system. However, this information is not sufficient. It does not make it clear to the user that he still must enter the system through a login and password. Most users, as they completed the registration process thought they were automatically logged into the system.

Another usability problem then came up. In this screen the user sees a message informing him that, from that moment, the user is appropriately registered and ready to use the system. However, this information is not sufficient. It does not make it clear to the user that he still must enter the system through a login and password. Most users, as they completed the registration process thought they were automatically logged into the system.

Even the most experienced user took a long time to realize that when he finishes the registration he was not automatically logged and several attempts to upload the document into the system were not successful. This difficulty was expressed in statements by the users. Therefore, it was found that the delay in realizing the registration and not being automatically logged in, generated a lot of frustration for the users.

3.2   The Self-archiving Process

In this next sub-task, the user must do the task of self-archiving or uploading the digital document. To do this, the user must login into the system with a password and follow the steps on the screen. However, it was observed that the fields to do login do not clearly state which information should be completed, as noted by some users after mistakenly filling in the login field with their name and not with an e-mail address.

After performing the login starts the upload of the digital document. During this moment, it was identified that some users had difficulty understanding some terms and concepts present in the interface, such as the term "collection", which appeared at the beginning of this sub-task. Even so, throughout the interaction process some users correctly inferred the term, while others felt they understood correctly, and during the post-test questionnaire stated that they had not.

Also in relation to the terms used in the system, it was emphasized that the user U2 clicked the checkbox and stated: "The record consists of more than one file", thinking that he could have uploaded multiple files by the same author into the system. When, in fact, this choice means that the record has more than on file to be uploaded. Normally a record contains just one file to be uploaded and the correct option would be "the record was already published or distributed publicly".

With regard to the design problems identified, the change in font size and colors used were highlighted. Another example of nomenclature and design problems, several users clicked on the button "Save/Cancel" instead of clicking on the "Next" button. User U3, after removing the document and restarting the submission process several times, went to verify whether his upload was available in the RI. He searched for the name of the author and was unsuccessful, finally giving up performing the task.

Also with respect to the nomenclature, user U4 observed: *"I need to see the number of pages"*, when in fact this information is not required at any point in the self-archiving process.

It was found that some users did not understand when the submission process had ended. A user reported that had completed the process, when in fact there has still one step left. This was labeled in the breadcrumb of the self-archiving process as "verify", confusing the users. Another user questioned the timing of the curation, in other words, the time dedicated for the review and inclusion of the data generally inserted by a librarian. The lack of feedback to the users in relation to the existence of this stage prior to publicizing the digital document in the RI, caused confusion in some users. The email confirmation is sent to users only after the librarian has checked the metadata. This important information was not highlighted on the screen. Therefore, the main problem found in the completion of the self-archiving process is the lack of feedback.

4   Recommendations and Conclusions

The present study sought to elucidate relevant aspects regarding the interaction of users in the process of self-archiving in the Institutional Repository of the Oswaldo Cruz Foundation. This task actively involves changing the behavior and culture of Fiocruz researchers in adherence to the repository. The methodology was based on the observation of users using the technique of cooperative evaluation and a post-test questionnaire.

The results demonstrate that, despite the recognition of the benefits provided by the use of institutional repository in terms of visibility of their scientific production, some barriers faced by users of the interface can contribute to the non-adherence of self-archiving the own production in the repository, weakening the proposal of improving the communication and visibility of the scientific output of the institution. Language and nomenclature problems as well as the lack of immediate feedback in the autho-rization for deposit were observed. In certain stages, there was also overloading information on the screens which diverted the focus of the tasks impeding its ac-complishment and demanding more time and effort than necessary, often leading to error. Additionally, the opposite problem, the lack of information on the screens also caused some difficulty for the users. It leads sometimes to the withdrawal of the researcher from finalizing the task.

During the analysis these usability problems were identified and are in the way to being solved, enhancing the user interaction as the registration confirmation, where the person should already be logged into the system. Also, since the IR belongs to a Brazilian institution, the language Portuguese must be used as the default. Also, the word 'login' should be replaced for 'email', if the user has not deposited any document. The button 'accepted deposits' and link to 'see alerts' should not appear before the first deposit. It is recommended that the description page should be filled on one single screen, since the use of breadcrumb featured in the self-archiving process generates the expectation that other metadata are requested. Finally, in the last page of the submission process, it is recommended that the user be informed that the submission process is over by informing something of the type 'deposit Done! Thank you! Also information about data confirmation and the availability of the final document in the IR should also be informed to the user by email.

Cooperative evaluation proved to be effective enabling the verification that, despite having experience in information retrieval in bibliographic databases, users sometimes infer some terms mistakenly. The self-archiving process itself also was not easily understood, making it difficult and even impossible to complete the tasks. Thus, it becomes necessary to perform detailed studies which recognize the specific interaction of this group of users, in order to identify possible barriers that may impair or prevent the use of the system. By evaluating interfaces and providing solutions to usability problems of repositories, the area of Human-Computer Interaction has greatly aided in perfecting institutional repositories and the process of scientific communication as a whole.

References

1. Leite, F.C.L.: Como gerenciar e ampliar a visibilidade da informação científica brasileira: repositórios institucionais de acesso aberto. Ibict, Brasília (2009)
2. BOAI – Budapest Open Access Initiative. Self-Archiving FAQ (2012), http://www.eprints.org/openaccess/self-faq
3. Swan, A., Brown, S.: Open access self-archiving: An author study. Technical Report, External Collaborators, JISC, HEFCE (2005), http://eprints.ecs.soton.ac.uk/10999
4. Arca (Institutional Repository of the Oswaldo Cruz Foundation). (2013), http://www.arca.fiocruz.br
5. Monk, A., Wright, P., Haber, J., Davenport, L.: Improving your human-computer interface: a practical technique. Prentice Hall International (UK) Ltd. (1993)
6. Muller, M.J., Haslwanter, J.H., Dayton, T.: Participatory Practices in the Software Life-cycle. In: Helander, M.G., Landauer, T.K., Prabhu, P.V. (eds.) Handbook of Human-Computer Interaction, 2nd edn., pp. 255–297. Elsevier (1997)

Sentences Extraction from Digital Publication for Domain-Specific Knowledge Service

Mao Ye[1,2,3], Lifeng Jin[2], Zhi Tang[1,2], and Jianbo Xu[2]

[1] Peking University, Beijing, China
[2] State Key Laboratory of Digital Publishing Technology
(Peking University Founder Group Co. LTD.), Beijing, China
[3] Postdoctoral Workstation of the Zhongguancun Haidian Science Park, Beijing, China
xjtuyemao@163.com, {lifeng.jin,zhi.tang,jianbo.xu}@founder.com

Abstract. Digital publication resources contain a lot of useful and authoritative information which is normally organized in small sections such as paragraphs, book sections or chapters. It is important to use the information from digital publication resources for knowledge service. In this paper, concepts in a domain are obtained from encyclopedia. Sections are extracted from e-books and then indexed for searching. The related sections for the important concepts are then found by using full text search technique. SVM is used to classify the related sections and the semantic information is computed for the concept. The sentences are then extracted by dynamically extending the adjacent sentences into sentence group. With the method, the sentences extracted are continuous and the length of the sentences would approximate to a specified length statistically. The method is effective for domain-specific knowledge service.

Keywords: knowledge service, sentence extraction, digital publication.

1 Introduction

Knowledge service [1][2] is a high value-added service which manages knowledge from a variety of resources by searching, organization, analyzing and restructuring. It is an advanced stage of information service to solve users' problems [3]. Digital publication contains a lot of useful and authoritative information which is normally organized in sections. The technique to use the information of the digital publication resources for domain-specific knowledge service is important and useful. Our project is to build a domain-specific knowledge service with the digital publication as source of information. The concepts in the domain are extracted from encyclopedia. Encyclopedia is a kind of digital publication which contains a summary of information from either all domains of knowledge or a particular domain of knowledge in the format of articles or entries. Sentences are extracted from e-books for the important concepts. When users learn the concept, they can review the sentences related with the concept for brief information and read the sections or e-books from which the sentences are extracted for detailed information. To build such a knowledge service system, one important step is to extract sentences for concepts from the digital publication re-

C. Stephanidis (Ed.): HCII 2014 Posters, Part I, CCIS 434, pp. 274–279, 2014.

sources. Some methods to extract sentences or passage are presented in the references [4][5][6][7][8]. However, the sentences obtained by these methods are not continuous which may be difficult to understand. In addition, they don't follow an expected length statistically, which may be not easy for displaying or reading. Furthermore, the sentences extracted don't corresponding to a specific domain, which may not fit the requirement for a domain-specific knowledge service.

2   Sentences Extraction from Digital Publication Resources

After the concepts are extracted from the encyclopedia, sentences will be extracted from the e-books for the important concepts. It is needed that the sentences should be continuous and follow an expected length. The length of the sentence is counted by the character number in the sentence. Let $O = \{o_1, o_2, \cdots, o_n\}$ be the concepts set extracted from the encyclopedia and $X = \{x_i, i = 1, \cdots, n\}$ be the label set of the concepts in the encyclopedia where x_i is the label of the concept o_i. The main process of our approach for extracting sentences is as Figure 1. Firstly, the sections are extracted from the e-books to get the set $D = \{d_i, i = 1, 2, \cdots, z\}$, where d_i is a section. The size of the set D is z which may be very large because there are a lot of sections extracted from the e-books. Secondly, all the sections in the set D are indexed with full text indexing technique. The dictionary used for word segmentation in this step consists of all labels X. To index the sections is necessary for us to find the related sections quickly because the number of the sections is large. Thirdly, the set $D' \subseteq D$ is obtained from the indexed full text library for a concept o_i by searching with its label x_i. D' can be a reduced set if the number of the matched sections still be large. Apply support vector machine to classify the sections in D' to get a class label c_i for each $d_i \in D'$. Support vector machine is an effective method for classification problem [9][10][11]. The domain related sections R are then selected according to its class label. For the concept o_i, obtain the context of the concept in R through the sliding window method. They are the sentences adjacent to the ones in which the label of the concept o_i is displayed. All these sentences are segmented into words and stop words are removed from the result set. Compute the semantic information of the concept and get a vector $W = \{w_1, w_2, \ldots, w_q\}$ which is represented by words' weight, where q is the dimension of the vector. The weight w_i is computed by $\dfrac{t_i}{\sum t_i}$ where t_i is the occurrence frequency of the ith word. Finally the sentences are extracted dynamically by the vector W. The sentences extracted are regarded as the related sentences of the concept O_i. They will be combined with other attributes and values of the concepts for domain-specific knowledge service.

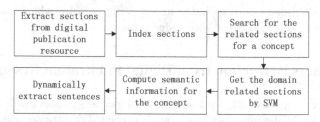

Fig. 1. The main process for extracting sentences

Let E be the expected sentence length to extract from the sections. Let $f(s)$ be the function to compute the length of the sentence s by counting the character number in s. Let m be the initial number of sentences in a sentence group. We will extend the sentence group towards two directions left and right. Let α be the parameter to control the number limit of the sentences which can be extended to the sentence group from a direction. Let $\theta > 1$ be the factor to control the dynamical threshold. Let $W = \{w_1, w_2, ..., w_q\}$ be words' weight for a concept. The detail description to dynamically extracting sentences from a section $r_i \in R$ by W is summarized as the following steps.

Step 1: Split the section r_i to get an ordered list $L_1 = s_1 s_2 ... s_n$ of sentences, where s_i is the ith sentence in L_1.

Step 2: Compute the average weight $\overline{w} = \left(\sum_i w_i \right) / q$.

Step 3: Combine the sentences in the list L_1 to get a sentence group list L_2. Each sentence group $g_i = s_i s_{i+1} ... s_{i+m-1}$ initially consists of m sentences from L_1 in order.

Step 4: Get a sentence group g_i from L_2 and set $k = 1$. Set the weight of g_i by summing up w_i in W for words which the sentence group g_i contains.

Step 5: If $k > \alpha$ or there is no sentence s in L_1 which is on the left side of s_i, go to the next step. Otherwise, compute the weight of the sentence s by summing up w_i in W for words which the sentence s contains. Set the variable $\beta = E / \left(f(g_i) + \dfrac{f(s)}{2} \right)$. If $\beta < 1$, then set $\beta = \beta / \theta$. If $\beta > 1$, then set $\beta = \beta * \theta$. If the weight of the sentence s is less than $\overline{w} / \beta$, then go to the next step. Otherwise, append s to the left side of g_i. Accumulate the weight of the sentence s to the weight of g_i. Set $k = k + 1$ and continue to perform this step.

Step 6: Reset $k = 1$.

Step 7: This step is similar to the step 5. The difference is that this step is to append the right side's sentences to the sentence group g_i. If $k > \alpha$ or there is no sentence s in L_1 which is on the right side of s_i, go to the next step. Otherwise, compute the weight of the sentence s by summing up w_i in W for words which the sentence s contains. Set the variable $\beta = E / \left(f(g_i) + \dfrac{f(s)}{2} \right)$. If $\beta < 1$, then set $\beta = \beta / \theta$. If $\beta > 1$, then set $\beta = \beta * \theta$. If the weight of the sentence s is less than $\overline{w} / \beta$, then go to the next step. Otherwise, append s to the right side of g_i. Accumulate the weight of the sentence s to the weight of g_i. Set $k = k + 1$ and continue to perform this step.

Step 8: Add the sentence group g_i generated to the map M. Go to the step 4 until all sentence groups in L_2 are processed.

Step 9: Sort all the sentence groups in the map M by the weight density in descending order which is computed by $h_i / f(g_i)$, where h_i is the weight of g_i. Select the top N sentences which are the most related sentences for the concept.

3 A Case Study

The concept adopted in the case is the emperor of QinShiHuang (秦始皇) in Chinese history. The aim is to extract the continuous sentences approaching the expected length statistically for the concept in the domain of history. More than 40 thousand e-books are prepared to extract sections which are then indexed in the full text library. The domain-related sections are obtained by searching from the library with the label "秦始皇" and classifying them by SVM. One section obtained is "...秦始皇像 陕西临潼秦始皇陵 战国末年，从诸侯割据向全国统一的趋势已日益明显...公元前238年，他亲理国事，平定嫪毐的叛乱，免除吕不韦的相职，令其徙处蜀郡...终

于建立了中国历史上第一个统一的、多民族的、专制主义中央集权制国家秦朝
。…秦二世胡亥即位后，对人民的剥削和压迫变本加厉…不久，秦朝灭亡。".
The length of the section is 1700 characters. The text of the section describes the emperor Qinshihuang and the events and persons related to him in detail. Apostrophe is used in the above text for simplification. Words and their respective weights computed from the data are listed in the table 1. The field "Words" shows the words which are related with the concept Qinshihuang and the field "Weight" shows the relatedness between them. It is shown from the table that the concept Qinshihuang is described by a group of words and weights.

Table 1. Words and weights for the concept of Qinshihuang

Word	Weight	Word	Weight	Word	Weight
统一	0.059343900	孟姜女	0.012286522	焚书坑儒	0.009829217
皇帝	0.035876643	蒙恬	0.011795061	割据	0.008477700
秦国	0.023221526	秦朝	0.011426465	法律	0.008109104
秦王	0.014252365	史记	0.011426465	方士	0.007494778
丞相	0.014129500	赵高	0.011303600	本纪	0.007371913
匈奴	0.013023713	中央集权	0.010812139	刘邦	0.007249048
李斯	0.012900848	分封	0.010320678	秦汉	0.007003317
…	…	…	…	…	…

The parameters E, θ, α, m are set to 300, 10, 3, 3 respectively. One sentence group extracted from the section is "中国统一的秦王朝的开国皇帝。名政，秦庄襄王之子，十三岁即王位，三十九岁称帝，在位共三十七年。…公元前 238年，他亲理国事，平定嫪毐的叛乱，免除吕不韦的相职，令其徙处蜀郡；并任用尉缭，李斯等人，部署统一全国的战略和策略。" The length of the sentence group is 208 which consists of 6 continuous sentences. It describes the role of Qinshihuang and his relationship with other persons very briefly in history domain. The length of the top 28 sentence groups are listed in the table 2. The field "Id" is the identifier of the sentence groups extracted and the field "Length" shows their length. The average length of them is about 313 which are very close to the expected length of 300.

Table 2. Sentences extracted and their length for the concept of Qinshihuang

Id	Length	Id	Length	Id	Length	Id	Length
1	208	8	356	15	299	22	232
2	379	9	354	16	341	23	334
3	276	10	333	17	296	24	255
4	341	11	303	18	289	25	366
5	379	12	382	19	177	26	180
6	423	13	344	20	344	27	261
7	455	14	303	21	305	28	247

4   Conclusions

Digital publication resources are important for knowledge service because they contain a lot of useful and authoritative information. A method is proposed in this paper to use the information in digital publication resources for domain-specific knowledge service. Sections of e-books can be indexed and the ones related with the domain can be obtained for a concept. Sentences are then extracted to associate with the concepts for knowledge service. Compared with the methods in the references [4][5][6][7][8], the sentences extracted by the proposed methods can match the semantic information of the knowledge concept in the domain. The sentences are continuous and the length of the sentences conforms to a specified length statistically. The case shows the effectiveness of the method. The work described here is a first stage study. The next step in this work is to combine ontology information to improve the relatedness of the sentences with the concepts.

Acknowledgment. The work was funded by China Postdoctoral Science Foundation and Beijing Postdoctoral Science Foundation of China.

References

1. Zhang, Q., Zhang, Q., Peng, X.: Research on Knowledge Service System in Open Innovation Environment. In: 2011 International Conference on Management and Service Science (MASS), pp. 1–4. IEEE Press, New York (2011)
2. Li, G., Song, X.: A New Visualization-oriented Knowledge Service Platform. Procedia Engineering 15, 1859–1863 (2011)
3. Wei, X., Ke, Z., Yatao, L.: Research on an Intelligent Knowledge Service System Based on Internet. In: 2nd International Conference on Education Technology and Computer (ICETC), vol. 2, pp. 506–510. IEEE Press, New York (2010)
4. Alguliev, R.M., Aliguliyev, R.M., Mehdiyev, C.A.: Sentence Selection for Generic Document Summarization Using an Adaptive Differential Evolution Algorithm. Swarm and Evolutionary Computation 1(4), 213–222 (2011)
5. Song, X., Huang, J., Zhou, J.-M., Zhang, H.: A Sentence Selection Method of Query-based Chinese Multi-document Summarization. In: Second Asia-Pacific Conference on Computational Intelligence and Industrial Applications, vol. 1, pp. 224–228. IEEE Press, New York (2009)
6. Ko, Y., Seo, J.: An Effective Sentence-extraction Technique Using Contextual Information and Statistical Approaches for Text Summarization. Pattern Recognition Letters 29(9), 1366–1371 (2008)
7. Wang, D., Zhu, S., Li, T., Gong, Y.: Comparative Document Summarization via Discriminative Sentence Selection. ACM Transactions on Knowledge Discovery from Data 7(1), 1–18 (2013)
8. Salton, G., Singhal, A., Mitra, M., Buckley, C.: Automatic Text Structuring and Summarization. Information Processing & Management 33(2), 193–207 (1997)
9. Cortes, C., Vapnik, V.: Support-vector Network. Machine Learning 20, 273–297 (1995)
10. Fan, R.-E., Chang, K.-W., Hsieh, C.-J., Wang, X.-R., Lin, C.-J.: LIBLINEAR: A Library for Large Linear Classification. Journal of Machine Learning Research 9, 1871–1874 (2008)
11. Chang, C.-C., Lin, C.-J.: LIBSVM: A Library for Support Vector Machines. ACM Transactions on Intelligent Systems and Technology 2(3), 1–27 (2011)

Information Quality Evaluation
of mobile-Government (mGovernment) Services

Ikhlas ZamZami, Murni Mahmud, and Adamu Abubakar

Human Centered Design Group, Department of Information Systems,
Kulliyyah of Information and Communication Technology,
International Islamic University, Malaysia
ikhlas_zamzami23@hotmail.com, murni@iium.edu.my

Abstract. The transactions between the government of a given country and businesses, services, employees' details and roles, the wellbeing of citizens and transactions with other governments is becoming faster and remotely through what is known as an eGovernment system. This system utilizes an information and communication technology platform to perform digital interaction in real time. The mGovernment system is a mobile platform extension of eGovernment, but unfortunately it has drawbacks in terms of gaining citizens' trust and willingness to embark on using the system. Previous studies have attributed this to the state of information quality as well as the privacy and security of transmitted information. This paper focuses on evaluating mGovernment information quality. The quantitative user study of a sample population is based on the assumption that knowledge about reality can be obtained through the eyes of the researcher. The result indicates that the representation format of mGovernment is tied to its information quality, whereas the accessibility, accuracy and relevance of information are also key attributes of mGovernment.

Keywords: mGovernment, Mobile devices, Information quality.

1   Introduction

Mobile communication makes it possible to make voice/video calls, send/receive messages, browse the Internet and makes all sorts of transactions that can be performed on PCs. Mobile devices, specifically mobile phones, are necessarily small in size, and their computational capability is low to deal with huge computational operations. These properties have greatly affected the delivery of certain types of information which may create problems for the user [1]. Therefore, information through mobile devices has to be identified, structured, organized, labeled, specific and straightforward [2]. Conventionally "quality" is regarded as a degree of excellence, which relies on metrics or benchmarks. It is critical that for any aspect of government transactions, information should be presented with a high degree of excellence. However, there are some limitations to the amount and type of information that might be accessed through mGovernment, in addition to the need for presentation of relevant information in real time [3]. It is difficult to understand complicated information on

C. Stephanidis (Ed.): HCII 2014 Posters, Part I, CCIS 434, pp. 280–285, 2014.
© Springer International Publishing Switzerland 2014

small screen mobile devices [4]. Mobile sites are like normal sites but are optimized for mobile phones, meaning that their content has fewer features. Information is an important asset to any organization.Received information quality reflects the quality of information a system produces [5]. Data and information quality is commonly thought of as a multi-dimensional concept with attributes varying   according to an author's philosophical viewpoint. It is the objective of this paper to investigate the information quality of mGovernment through a quantitative user study.

2   mGovernment Information Quality

The adoption and implementation of mGovernment is still at an early stage [6]. Implementation involves the utilization of wireless and mobile technologies, services, applications and devices for improving the benefits of the parties involved [7]. Hypothetically, the benefit of implementing mGoverment will be enormous if the information quality on this platform is high; therefore the state of information quality should be investigated with reasonable measures. As a result, this research measures the quality of information on the mGovernment platform using key criteria used in previous research.

2.1   Variables

This research adopted four main key variables (Accuracy of data, Relevance of data, Accessibility of data, Representation) synthesized from previous research [8] on measuring information quality. These four variables represent an independent or antecedent variable. Independent variables are variables that are presumed to cause change in another variable [9]. In this research, the variables are conceptualized with each one of them comprising some numbers of scale items. Information quality in this study represents the dependent variable, which is the outcome or consequence that the researcher seeks to understand or explain [10]. Information quality in the present study is conceptualized as a multi-dimensional construct with multiple indicators. In this way it is possible to incorporate as many measures as possible.

Accuracy of Information
Several studies have used accuracy as a key, as either the only or one of several key dimensions for measuring information quality. This dimension is used in [8] to measure "the extent to which data are correct, reliable, and certified free of error". In this study accuracy will measure the degree of information on mGovernment that is perceived as actual facts on the ground. Thus the following hypothesis is formulated:

H1: *Information quality is associated with Accuracy of Information*

Relevance of Information
This dimension, according Wang and Strong [8], measures "the extent to which data are applicable and helpful for the task at hand". Therefore this research measures the information on the mGovernment platform that is applicable and helpful for the task at hand.   The following hypothesis is formulated:

H2: *Information quality is associated with Relevance of Information*

Accessibility of Information

This is another key information quality dimension, which measures the degree to which information is available on demand. Wang and Strong [8] describe it as "the extent to which data are available or easily and quickly retrievable". Thus for this study Accessibility of Information measures the extent to which mGovernment make information available on demand. Consequently the following hypothesis is formulated:

H3: *Information quality is associated with Accessibility of Information*

Representation of Information

This dimension dwells on aspects of the format of presentation of information at the right place and at the right time. Wang and Strong [8] measure representation consistency as "the extent to which data are always presented in the same format and are compatible with previous data". Thus this research measures the quality of presentation of information in the mGovernment platform, and the following hypothesis is formulated:

H4: *Information quality is associated with Representation of Information*

Conceptualization and Pilot Test

The research process involves conceptualization of research constructs. Conceptualization is the process of taking a construct and refining it by giving it a conceptual or theoretical definition [11]. A construct is thus a conceptual term used to describe a phenomenon of theoretical interest [12] or "an element of scientific discourse that serves as verbal surrogates for phenomenon of interest" [13]. The present research contains four main independent constructs and one dependent variable; these will be conceptualized so that aggregation of the four independent constructs reflects the dependent instance. Thus a conceptual frame work (see figure 1) is proposed, establishing the relationships among the constructs. Prior to the data collection, a pilot test of the scale items from the main constructs was carried out in order to improve the final version. As a result several scale items were deleted, based on the reliability and validity of the results.   The following scale items were deemed fit for data collection:

Accuracy

- The information provided is accurate
- The information provided is reliable
- The information provided is presented in a consistent format

Relevance

- The information provided is relevant to my needs
- Overall, I find the information provided is useful

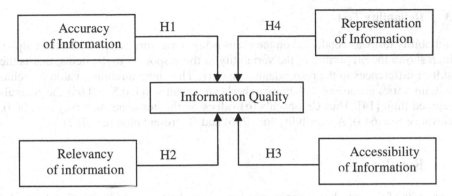

Fig. 1. Conceptual framework

Accessibility

- The information provided is quickly accessible
- The information provided is obtainable
- The information provided is easy to retrieve

Representation

- The information provided is easy to understand
- The information provided is easy to read
- The information provided is easy to find
- The information provided is well organized

A total of 300 questionnaires were distributed in MOHE, MOH and MOMRA in Saudia Arabia. The highest usable response rate was from MOHE (33.9% of 86), followed by MOH and MOMRA (33.1% of 84 respectively). 56.1% respondents were male and 48.4% respondents female. 95% of the respondents were under 40 years of age, and 85% had Bachelors level of education. 42% and 48% had been using a smartphone for 1 to 3 and more than 3 years respectively. Finally, 69% and 26% of the respondents respectively used mobile sites always or regularly.

2.2 Treatment of Data Integrity

The data analysis was undertaken with SPSS version 18.0, in two stages. Inferential statistics were used to determine the influence of correlation, Multiple Regression Analysis on the data in order to test for the relationship between the variables and to determine the difference between the independent and the composite dependent variable. Prior to the reliability and validity tests, treatment of normality was undertaken with the aid of the Explore procedure in SPSS. Normality variables were assessed by either statistical or graphical methods [14]: Kolmogorov-Smirnova and Shapiro-Wilk tests were conducted and the results indicate that the entire variables met the normality assumption.

2.3   Reliability Test

A reliability test was conducted on the items using a measure called Cronbach's alpha, which shows the proportion of the variability in the responses to the items, that is the result of differences in the respondents' answers. The alpha minimum value for reliable items varies according to the researcher's views, although 0.5 to 0.6 is the generally agreed limit [14]. Thus Cronbach's (α) values on the items are Accuracy (α= .663), Relevance (α= .644), Accessibility (α= .756) and Representation (α= .782).

3   Results

The results of the correlation analysis indicate that the values of Pearson's (r) correlation coefficient range from r = 0.530 to r = 0.806. The highest correlation coefficient (r) was obtained from the relationship between the accuracy and relevance of information (r = 0.806). This indicates a very strong and significant relationship between them. Pearson's correlation coefficient (r) between accessibility and relevance of information (r = 0.530) was the lowest, although still significant. In general, the entire Pearson's correlation coefficient (r) was positive and significant. This suggests that the entire construct changes directly affect each other in a positive way, as an increase in one results in an increase in the rest. The finding of multiple regressions based on coefficient results indicate that all variables make a statistically significant contribution. Representation of information (Beta = .36, p = .00 at .05 alpha level) makes the strongest contribution to nformation quality. The next is Accessibility (Beta = .30, p = .00 at .05 alpha level), followed by Accuracy and Relevance of information (Beta = .26, p = .00 at .05 alpha level), (Beta = 18, p =.00 at alpha level). Therefore the regression analysis results suggest that information quality can be highly influenced by all the independent variables. Thus the results of correlation and regression analysis (see Table 1) support the entire four hypothesized relationships posed for this research. As a result, the hypothesized model is fit and satisfied a measure for determining the information quality on mGoverment.

Table 1. Multiple Regression Analysis result

Model 1	Beta	T	Sig	Hypothesis
Relevancy	.184	4.561	.000	Accepted
Representation	.365	7.538	.000	Accepted
Accessibility	.305	8.836	.000	Accepted
Accuracy	.267	6.451	.000	Accepted

4   Conclusion

This study focuses on the information quality of mGovernment. It is a responsibility of any government to serve the wellbeing of its citizens and ensure efficient transactions within the state and with other governments. The study investigated the information quality on mGovernment through a quantitative research approach. It utilized a hypothesis testing approach in order to generalize the outcome. A total of 254 respondents participated in the survey. Their responses were analyzed using statistical analysis tools. The result indicates that the representation format of mGovernment information is a major influence on information quality. Accessibility, accuracy and relevance of information are also key variables supporting the information quality of mGovernment.

References

1. Nielsen, J., Budiu, R.: Mobile Usability. Nilsen Norman Group (2013)
2. Hoober, S., Berkman, E.: Designing Mobile Interface. O'Reilly Media, Inc., Sebastopol (2012)
3. Carroll, J.: What's in IT for me? Taking m-government to the people. In: 19th Bled Econference Evalues, Bled, Slovenia, June 5-7, 2006
4. Singh, R., Sumeeth, M.: Evaluating the readability of privacy policies. In Mobile Environments. International Journal of Human Computer Interactions, 55–78 (2011)
5. Delone, W., McLean, E.: The Delone and McLean model of information systems success: A ten-year update. Journal of Management Information Systems (Spring 2003) 0742-1222/2003
6. Thunibat, A., Zin, N., Ashaari, N.: Mobile government services in Malaysia: Challenges and opportunities. IEEE (2010) 978-1-4244-6716-7/10/
7. Kushchu, I., Kuscu, M.: From e-government to m-government: Facing the inevitable. Mobile Government Lab (2004), http://www.mgovlab.org
8. Wang, R.Y., Strong, D.M.: Source: Journal of Management Information Systems 12(4), 5–33 (1996)
9. Johnson, D., Turner, C.: International business themes and issues in the modern global economy. Routledge, London (2003)
10. Schwab, D.P.: Research methods for organizational studies, 2nd edn. Lawrence Erlbaum Associates, Mahwah (2005)
11. Neuman, W.L.: Social research methods: qualitative and quantitative approaches, 6th edn. Pearson, Boston (2006)
12. Nunnally, J.C.: Psychometric theory, 2nd edn. Mc-Graw Hill, NY (1978)
13. Edwards, J.R., Bagozzi, R.P.: On the nature and direction of relationships between constructs and measures. Psychological Methods 5(2), 155–174 (2000)
14. Hair, J.F., Anderson, R., Black, W., Babin, B.: Multivariate data analysis, 7th edn. Pearson Education, Upper Saddle River (2010)

Data Extraction from DXF File and Visual Display

Han Zhang and Xueqing Li

School of Computer Science and Technology, Shandong University, China
zhanghan800418@mail.sdu.edu.cn, xqli@sdu.edu.cn

Abstract. DXF File is a graph exchanging file for CAD data exchange between other softwares provided by Autodesk Company. The house drawing of Shandong University is designed by AutoCAD software, and the graph information of house is recorded by the DXF file. Based on the DXF file, this paper will conduct an analysis on DXF file and extract the information from it. Then this paper will relate those extracted information with the information of house saved in the database by the automatic information retrieval algorithm and manual information retrieval algorithm. Finally, the information from database can be reclassified into four layers: base graph layer, room name layer, room area layer and room user layer.And those reclassified information will be displayed at the end of CS.

Keywords: parse DXF file, extract information, information retrieval, visualization.

1 Introduction

DXF file is a graph exchanging file for CAD statistics exchange between other softwares developed by Autodesk Company. It is a kind of file format for saving graph and data.

Housing drawings is made by the AutoCAD software, with the information recorded in the DXF files.But the information recorded in the DXF files is not related with the information stored in database.For this reason,this paper proposes two algorithms: the automatic information retrieval algorithm and manual information retrieval algorithm.Based on the two algorithms,we can relate the information recorded in DXF file with the information stored in the database.Then we can visually display more information stored in the database on the end of CS.

2 Related Work

2.1 Analysis of DXF File Structure

The key point to analyzing the DXF file is to know its structure intimately. A complete DXF file is composed of 7 segments, including the followings:

- HEADER SEGMENTS

C. Stephanidis (Ed.): HCII 2014 Posters, Part I, CCIS 434, pp. 286–291, 2014.

- CLASSES SEGMENTS
- TABLES SEGMENTS
- BLOCK SEGMENTS
- ENTITIES SEGMENTS
- OBJECTS SEGMENTS
- THUMBNAILIMAGE SEGMENTS

ENTITIES SEGMENTS includes all the graphic objects (graphic primitives) appeared in the graph, including the reference of block. Thus, this paper will extract all graph information from the segment.

Each segment of DXF file begins with group code "0" and character string "SECTION", and ends with group code "0" and character string "ENDSEC". Each segment is composed of several groups, each of which has a Group Code and a Group Value. The Group Code is used to record the character of data, and the Group Value records the value of data

2.2   Parse of DXF File

By parsing the DXF file structure, two lines of data, one is the group code and another the group value, will be read from the DXF file in the program. According to the value of group code, the corresponding value of group value is recorded. And during the process of the parse, the bound of DXF data elements is also recorded. This is the basis of information retrieval algorithms introduced later.

2.3   Proposed Algorithm

- Automatic information retrieval algorithm

The core concept of automatic information retrieval algorithm can be described as follows:

In the process of parsing DXF file, all text elements will be recorded. Then this paper will divide the text elements into three categories: room number, room area and others. The room number is matched to room number saved in the database.If it succeeds, the bound of room number will be considered as a standard. Then it finds out that all the line elements recorded in the DXF File elements are not contained in the bound. Then all the line elements are divided into horizontal lines and vertical lines. Based on the horizontal lines,this paper can determine the minimum value of Y and maximum value of Y and based on the vertical lines, it can determine the minimum value of X and the maximum value of X.Finally,this paper makes use of the value of X and Y to determine the bound of room

- Manual information retrieval algorithm

The core concept of manual information retrieval algorithm can be described as follows:

The first step is to select the bound manually. In this selected bound, the room number is supposed to be found out. Then this paper will match the room number to room number saved in the database. If it succeeds, the selected bound will be considered as a standard. Then this paper finds out that all the line elements recorded in the DXF File elements are contained in the bound. In this paper all the line elements are divided into horizontal lines and vertical lines. Based on the horizontal lines, this paper can determine the minimum value of Y and maximum value of Y. And based on the vertical lines, this paper can determine the minimum value of X and the maximum value of X. Finally, this paper makes use of the value of X and Y to determine the bound of room.

2.4   Visual Display

Through the above information retrieval, the house information which has been successfully matched should be reorganized. This paper will divide information of house into four layers: base graph layer, room name layer, room area layer and room user layer. The information of different layers is differentiated by color and the visual display at the end of CS. On the basis of different focuses, this can also close different layers to show different house information.

2.5   Outcome of Experiment

The Figure 1 is displayed by AutoCAD software and the figure 2 shows that the house drawing is displayed by our system.

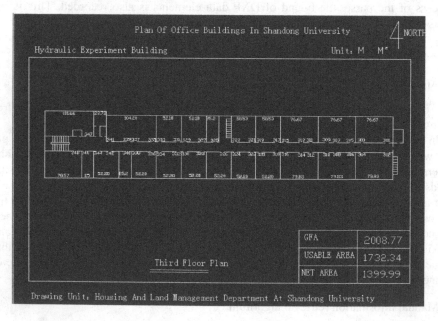

Fig. 1. The original AutoCAD drawings

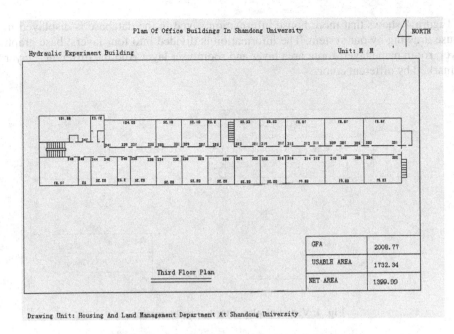

Fig. 2. House drawing displayed by our system

Figure 3 shows that the borders marked by red color are extracted by automatic information retrieval algorithm.

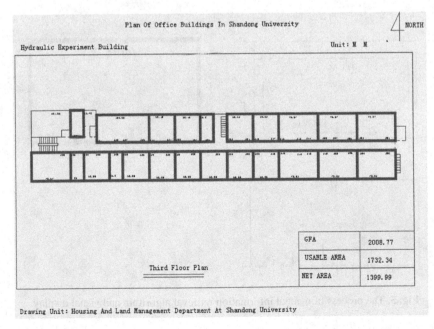

Fig. 3. Result of border extraction by automatic information retrieval algorithm

Figure 4 shows that more house information saved in the database is displayed in house drawing by our system. The information is divided into four layers: base graph layer, room name layer, room area layer and room user layer.And the different   layer is marked by different color.

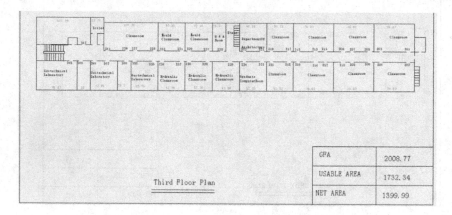

GFA	2008. 77
USABLE AREA	1732. 34
NET AREA	1399. 99

Third Floor Plan

Fig. 4. Visual display after border extraction

We can find upper left corner of the border is not marked correctly.Figure 5 shows the final border by manual information retrieval algorithm and displays more information stored in database about house.

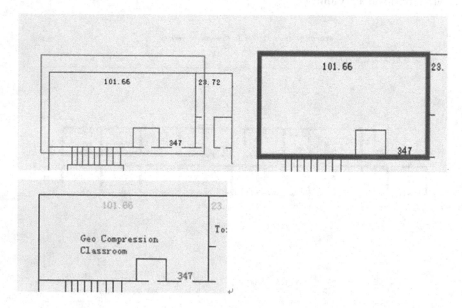

Fig. 5. The process of manual information retrieval algorithm and visual display

3   Conclusion

On the basis of conducting a complete analysis of File DXF and extracting data information of different segments of DXF file, this paper takes advantage of two retrieval algorithms to implement the association between information of house recorded in DXF file and information of house stored in the database. It is possessed of three advantages:

- More service information of the house can be displayed in the drawing, which makes the system more flexible.
- Keep the consistency of the house information in the drawing and the database and make sure the accuracy of the drawing display.
- The user can see through the drawing by the system without additional AutoCAD software.

Cognitive, Perceptual and Emotional Issues in HCI

Real-Time Detection of Erroneous Behavior for a Spindle Exchange Task in IPS²

Michael Beckmann and Ulaş Yılmaz

Department of Psychology and Ergonomics, Chair of Human-Machine Systems,
Technische Universität Berlin, Marchstraße 23, 10587 Berlin, Germany
{michael.beckmann,ulas.yilmaz}@mms.tu-berlin.de

Abstract. The consideration of human factors for Industrial Product-Service Systems (IPS²) is an essential purpose in the SFB/TR29 to prevent errors due to malpractice or human error. These innovative systems, integrating both products and services in industrial applications, are multifaceted and dynamic, providing a challenge to the operators because of their high complexity. On the operational level this requires human operators to handle highly complex technical systems in different environments. At the same time operator errors pose a considerable risk to the overall system robustness. This negative impact on work complexity, resulting in additional costs, can be counterbalanced by a cognitive system which detects erroneous behavior before damage or injury occurs. This article describes a pretest with this recognition system where a spindle dismantling is performed. The task, system setup and an estimate of the performance for real-time use is reported.

Keywords: Cognitive modeling, process simulation, motion capturing, machine learning, error recognition, error prevention.

1   Introduction

Industrial Product-Service Systems (IPS²) [1] involve human operators during their lifecycle and contain technical systems. They belong to the category of socio-technical systems. High flexibility during operation and adaptability to different settings are inherent properties of IPS². In addition, technical systems are adapted to customer requirements. For the technical systems these characteristics result in a modular design and possibly an individual configuration of the system which might change over time. For optimal performance the human operators require a vast amount of knowledge for managing and maintaining these systems without getting any more training time. The added complexity can be addressed by providing additional assistance functions to the human operators to prevent errors which can cause injury, damage or require subsequent processes. To provide these functions a mechanism for recognizing (likely) errors is required.

The field of human factors addresses the human operator with limited resources [2] and optimizes the human well-being and system performance by applying theories, principles and data and other methods to design human-machine systems [3]. Age,

C. Stephanidis (Ed.): HCII 2014 Posters, Part I, CCIS 434, pp. 295–300, 2014.
© Springer International Publishing Switzerland 2014

state of mind, emotions and propensity for common mistakes are examples of these factors. Taking these factors into account and learning from errors of human operators can increase human reliability and performance. One possibility is to provide contextual real-time assistance in case of an error or dangerous situation. The recognition or prediction of these situations by evaluating actual user actions in conjunction with the system state using a normative cognitive model is the focus of this research.

In this paper a pretest for automatically recognizing operator error is presented, using a spindle disassembly task. The framework used in this approach [4] combines motion capturing, additional sensor data to recognize interaction or changes in the environment and cognitive modeling, using ACT-R [5], to simulate and recognize valid user behavior. By comparing simulated actions with real operator-behavior the situation and the state of the human-machine system can be accessed. This evaluation provides the information to warn the human operator in case of a perceived or likely error.

The paper is organized as follows. Section 2 describes the task and the prototype developed for this task, while the preliminary evaluation is presented in Section 3. The article is concluded by a discussion and summary in Section 4.

2   Approach

This chapter describes the task which was executed by three participants as well as the software and hardware architecture.

The primary goal was to test the error recognition using location data and sensor input, as well as to collect data for later training a gesture recognition module. Of interest was the communication between the different subsystems of the prototype and to determine if any additional changes need to be made to achieve the time resolution for real-time error recognition.

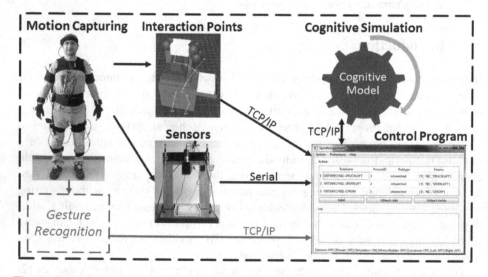

Fig. 1. Setup for the experiment showing the components for the error recognition and their communication

The setup is shown in Figure 1. Erroneous behavior of human operators during the spindle exchange task is detected using motion capturing, gesture recognition and sensory information in combination with a normative cognitive model for simulating the ground truth. Motion capturing provides information about the location of the extremities for locations with possible interactions as well as providing the data for the training of a gesture recognition module. The sensors allow drawing conclusions about state changes in the system. The control program communicates with the ACT-R simulation which then evaluates the observed actions and determines if an error just occurred or is likely to occur.

2.1 Task

The task for the removal of the spindle consists of three parts in sequential order: 1. Preparation, 2. Cable removal, 3. Spindle removal. Tools which can be used for this task are several open ended and Allen wrenches of different sizes which are deposited in a drawer.

The preparation consists of shutting down the power, shutting off sealing air and compressed air in any order. For the cable removal the power and air cables need to be removed in any order. The air cables nuts need to be loosened with an open ended wrench before the removal. The spindle removal consists of fixating the spindle with the left hand, getting the Allen wrench for loosening the two clamp screws with an Allen wrench, loosening the screws after fixating the spindle and depositing the wrench. Afterwards the spindle needs to be fixated with the right hand and can be removed.

Examples for dangerous situations during this task are an improper executed preparation or loosening the screws holding the clamp instead of the screws fixating the spindle inside the clamp.

2.2 Simulation

The simulation is the execution of a normative model of the described task modeled in the cognitive architecture ACT-R. Cognitive architectures incorporate research in the field of cognitive processes, making it possible to represent selected cognitive processes, like memory retrieval, with respect to human parameters, like a maintenance task. ACT-R is a bottom-up approach to human modeling, meaning that each step in the task is subdivided into several rules. Each rule consists of pre- and post-conditions. The pre-conditions determine which rules are allowed to fire, in case these rules represent actions by the human operator. The post-conditions describe changes in the model when the rule is activated. Some of these changes correspond to changes in the real world, in this context called observable changes. In this case the movement of the left and right hand to certain locations, gestures and relevant (automatic) changes in the technical system are all observable changes. When an observable change is detected by the control program a list with allowed changes generated by the simulation is checked. If the change was valid it is accepted by the simulation, which then continues to simulate the task to determine all following changes.

When loosening the fixation of the spindle there is a high risk for dropping the spindle because the human operator can be surprised by the sudden weight (3.5kg).

To provide a preemptive warning, risk-values were added to the ACT-R architecture and assigned to the rules which precede the dangerous interaction. When such a risky interaction is determined as a following change a warning is generated.

Explicitly dangerous interactions which are not covered by a deviation from the task execution, like the interaction with a hot spot which did not cool down fast enough, are modeled in another model as non-interactions.

To account for mix-ups during task execution, i.e. grabbing an open ended wrench of incorrect size for loosening the nuts, the similarity-mechanism of ACT-R is used on the first interaction with the item.

2.3 Motion Capturing and Location Tracking

Motion Capture (MOCAP) technologies are used widely in ergonomics research and film/game industry [6]. The application areas are extending in various directions such as motion tracking and 3D human behavior-modeling. In our study we use an inertial sensor based XSENS motion suit [7] as well as two 5DT Data Gloves 5 Ultra [8] with 14 bend sensors to capture and model operator's body movements.

Once the body movements are captured, these are mapped into a 3D virtual model of the environment. In this environment predefined locations on the micro milling machine, such as the location of electric switch, valves, toolbox, spindle, etc. can automatically be tracked when the hand makes a move into or out of them. A snapshot of the actual system taken from the surveillance camera is shown in Figure 2.

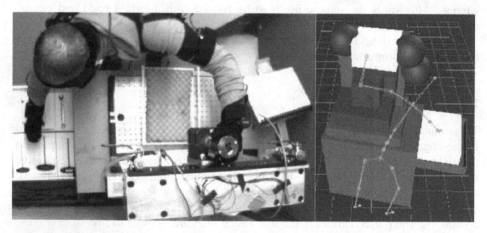

Fig. 2. Operator holding the spindle while reaching for a tool in the tool-drawer as seen by the camera (left) and virtual representation (right)

2.4 Sensors

Sensors such as heat sensors, pressure sensors and cameras, are mostly implemented as an obligatory part of the industrial machines, in order to survey, evaluate and document system behavior. The data is collected using two Arduino Uno and evaluated by the control program.

3   Pretest and Preliminary Evaluation

For the pretest the software was executed on an Intel® Xeon® 3.2 GHz 4 core workstation that had 12 GB of RAM with 64 Bit Windows® 7 operating system and small subroutines on the two Arduino Uno for collecting the sensor data.

For the pretest three participants performed the spindle removal tasks 92 times, of these recordings 72 were useable, mainly due to degradation of the MOCAP data. For tagging the data for the gesture recognition a videos were recorded and referenced using LED markers. Before each task execution the participants assumed a reference position so the 3D environment could be aligned. The data was logged during the task execution without the simulation, because some system interactions could not be determined using the sensors, needing the gesture module. These actions were added to the log files, the log files were then used for online replay using the simulation.

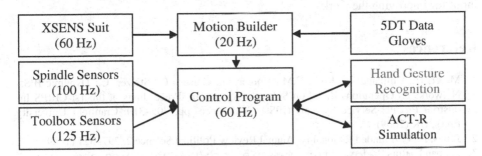

Fig. 3. System components and their working frequencies

For the real-time requirements the data processing frequency of the different components was determined. As illustrated in Figure 3 input devices in our system deliver and process data with varying speeds. The Motion Builder interface by which we capture hand and body movements represents the bottleneck of the system. 20Hz is an acceptable data rate for hand gesture recognition and allows a sufficiently fast response in case of an error. On the other hand, spindle and toolbox sensors trigger data transmission only when the operator performs an action. As a result, our main control program, running at 60 Hz, has enough time to process graphical user interface routines, in addition to the other hardware and software components of the system.

4   Summary and Discussion

This article describes a pretest for a system to detect erroneous behavior in real-time using the example scenario of a spindle exchange task. The system uses a normative cognitive modeling approach for simulating the task with respect to human parameters. The control program evaluates different data sources to determine the actual course of action and reports an error in conjunction with the simulation when an invalid course of action is observed or likely. The down sampling of the data rate in the Motion Builder application was due to a threading issue, making faster responses possible. The biggest problem poses the initial calibration of the MOCAP system which can be seen by the discarded trials.

The next step for the poster representation is to train gesture models on a subset of the collected data and report the performance of the system on the remaining data. Future research is necessary for including information reception (visual), which is assumed by the model but not part of the performance evaluation. Another aspect is the mechanism used for modeling slips which requires additional research for proper warning thresholds.

Acknowledgements. We express our sincere thanks to the Deutsche Forschungsgemeinschaft (DFG) for funding this research within the Collaborative Research Project SFB/TR29 on "Industrial Product-Service Systems – dynamic interdependency of products and services in the production area". We thank our colleagues on continuous input for improving the work.

References

1. Meier, H., Uhlmann, E., Krug, C.M., Völker, O., Geisert, C., Stelzer, C.: Dynamic IPS^2-Networks an Operations Based on Software Agents. In: Proceedings of the 1st CIRPS Industrial Product-Service Systems (IPS^2) Conference, pp. 305–310. Cranfield University Press, UK (2009)
2. Jones, B.D.: Bounded Rationality. Annual Review Political Science 2, 297–321 (1999)
3. Human Factors Society, http://www.hfes.org/web/abouthfes/about.html
4. Beckmann, M., Yılmaz, U., Pöhler, G., Wegerich, A.: Real-time Task Accomplishment Simulation for Error Recognition in IPS^2. In: Shimomura, Y., Kimita, K. (eds.) The Philosopher's Stone for Sustainability, vol. 122, pp. 417–422. Springer, Heidelberg (2013)
5. Anderson, J.R., Bothell, D., Byrne, M.D., Douglass, S., Lebiere, C., Qin, Y.: An integrated theory of the mind. Psychological Review 111(4), 1036–1060 (2004)
6. Bergler, C.: Motion Capture Technology for Entertainment. IEEE Signal Processing Magazine 24(6), 158–160 (2007)
7. XSens MVN Biomech, http://www.xsens.com/products/mvn-biomech/
8. 5DT Data Glove 5 Ultra, http://www.5dt.com/downloads/dataglove/ultra/5DTDataGloveUltraDatasheet.pdf

Inducing Anxiety through Video Material

Tibor Bosse[1], Charlotte Gerritsen[1,2], Jeroen de Man[1], and Marco Stam[3]

[1] VU University Amsterdam, Department of Computer Science,
De Boelelaan 1081, 1081 HV Amsterdam, The Netherlands
{t.bosse,c2.gerritsen,j.de.man}@vu.nl
[2] Netherlands Institute for the Study of Crime and Law Enforcement,
De Boelelaan 1077, 1081 HV Amsterdam, The Netherlands
[3] VU University Amsterdam, Department of Criminology,
De Boelelaan 1077, 1081 HV Amsterdam, The Netherlands
marcotcs23@gmail.com

Abstract. For professionals in various domains, training based on Virtual Reality can be an interesting method to improve their emotion regulation skills. However, for such a training system to be effective, it is essential to trigger the desired emotional state in the trainee. Hence, an important question is to what extent virtual stimuli have the ability to induce an emotional stress response. This paper addresses this question by studying the impact of anxiety-inducing video material on skin conductance, heart rate and subjective experience of participants that watch the videos. The results indicate that the scary videos significantly increased skin conductance and subjective response, while no significant effect on heart rate was found.

Keywords: anxiety and stress, video material, virtual reality.

1   Introduction

For human beings, the ability to cope with negative emotions such as sadness, anger, and fear is important to live a pleasant life. For professionals in domains such as the police, military and public transport, the specific ability to cope with fear (or anxiety) [14] is probably even more crucial. Employees in these domains generally have a higher probability of being confronted with fear-inducing stimuli like aggressive individuals, gun fights, or human casualties. And since the extreme negative emotions experienced in such situations are known to impair cognitive processes like attention and decision making [13, 15], professionals in these domains highly benefit from effective emotion regulation skills. In addition, even if they make optimal decisions from an external perspective, inadequate emotion regulation may increase the risk of developing anxiety related disorders such as Post-Traumatic Stress Disorder (PTSD) [3].

For these reasons, much attention is dedicated to developing appropriate training methods for police officers and military personnel, to learn to cope with extreme circumstances. Such training often uses role-play, where the roles are played by co-students or professional actors. However, an important drawback of these types of training is that they are very costly, both in terms of money and time.

C. Stephanidis (Ed.): HCII 2014 Posters, Part I, CCIS 434, pp. 301–306, 2014.

As an alternative, training based on Virtual Reality (VR) currently receives much attention [2]. The main goal of the STRESS project [18] is to develop an adaptive VR-based environment to train professionals to cope with extreme negative emotions. Trainees will be placed in a virtual scenario, in which they have to make difficult decisions, while negative emotions are induced. By measuring certain physiological states, the system will be able to assess their emotional state at runtime, and to provide adequate feedback, both in terms of suggestions to improve their emotion regulation and decision making, and of runtime adaptation of the scenario.

Despite this promising prospect, the effectiveness of such a system crucially depends on its ability to evoke the desired level of anxiety in the trainee. Therefore, one of the research questions addressed in the STRESS project is to what extent computer generated stimuli trigger an emotional (stress) response in human beings that watch them. As a first step, in [1] the effect of affective pictures on emotional response was investigated. The results pointed out that a set of negatively valenced images triggered a significantly stronger emotional response than neutral or positive images. Moreover, participants that applied emotion regulation strategies (in particular reappraisal [9]) experienced the images as significantly less intense when viewing them again, an effect that persisted six months later.

Nevertheless, there is still a large gap between affective images and affective VR material. Therefore, as a second step, the current paper investigates the effect of affective videos on emotional response. To this end, an experiment has been performed in which participants were asked to watch a variety of video clips while measuring their emotional response via physiological as well as subjective data.

The remainder of this paper is structured as follows. Section 2 provides a brief overview about the relevant literature and a description of the research question. Section 3 describes the experiment performed to measure the impact of affective videos, and Section 4 presents the results. Section 5 concludes the paper with a discussion.

2   Background

Evoking an emotional (stress) response by different types of stimuli has been the focus of many research projects. Various definitions have been used to indicate more or less the same phenomenon. In our research, we use the term *stress response*, which we define as 'a physiological reaction of the autonomic nervous system to a threatening stimulus'.

In the literature, two main indicators of a stress response are reported, namely a change in heart rate and an increased skin conductance. Both these indicators are considered to be part of the physiological stress response [6, 11, 12]. However, some papers conclude that skin conductance is a more stable indicator than heart rate [8, 10, 16]. Findings regarding change in heart rate are less consistent. For example, Craig and Lowery [5] report that directly experienced stress-inducing stimuli may lead to an increased heart rate, while indirect (or vicarious) stimuli may cause a decreased heart rate. Some stimuli based on video material can be considered instances of such vicarious stimuli. Based on these considerations, we hypothesize that video clips with negative (scary) material will lead to an increment in skin conductance, but not necessarily of heart rate. These hypotheses will be tested by an experiment as described in the next section.

3   Method

Thirty participants took part in the experiment, aged between 20 and 64 years old (with an average age of 33), of which 17 people were male and 13 female. Experiments took place in a secluded room at VU University in Amsterdam. Heart rate and skin conductance were measured using Plux wireless biosensors [17].

Each participant watched five different movies in sequence. After each movie, participants were asked to report the emotion they felt and its intensity. The possible emotions were 'relaxed', 'bored', 'interested', 'excited' and 'scared', the intensity was given on a Likert-scale ranging from 0 (not at all) to 5 (very much). Thereafter, a short break of 30 seconds was added. The first movie showed an empty beach for three minutes in order to get the participants in a calm state. The second movie showed a three minute clip from a nature documentary and was used to measure a baseline for both heart rate and skin conductance. The third clip was a collection of scenes from various scary/horror movies and was intended to evoke a stress response. The fourth movie was a different three minute clip from the same nature documentary as before. The final movie was a repetition of the empty beach. These last two movies were shown to see whether heart rate and skin conductance returned to their baseline values.

4   Results

Before considering any possible effects in physiological responses due to the different nature of the clips, it is first checked whether each of the movies indeed evoked the desired emotion. A pairwise comparison of the subjectively reported emotions using a Bonferroni correction showed that each clip evoked a different emotion at the $p < 0.001$ level, except for the 1st and 5th (beach) as well as 2nd and 4th movie (documentary). The beach was found to be relaxing or boring, the documentary interesting and the stressful movie exciting or scary.

To investigate whether heart rate and skin conductance of the participants during the stressful movie differed significantly from the other clips, a repeated-measures ANOVA has been performed. This method is suited to test for significant differences within participants between the two experimental groups they were part of [7].

Figure 1 shows the average heart rate during each movie. As can be seen, there are only small differences between the clips. This is confirmed by the repeated-measures ANOVA which shows no significant differences in the average heart rate ($F(4,116)=1.401$, $p=.238$).

With regard to the skin conductance, the assumption of sphericity has been violated and a Greenhouse-Geisser correction was applied. Figure 2 shows the average values and statistical testing shows the presence of significant differences between the five clips ($F(2.251, 65.285)=27,213$, $p<.001$). As can be seen, the average skin conductance is highest during the stressful movie, with the largest difference in comparison with the two preceding clips. A pairwise comparison reveals almost all differences to be significant at the .05 level. Table 1 shows for each pair the difference in skin conductance and its significance. While there is a significant decrease after the stressful movie, skin conductance remains significantly higher in comparison with the similar clips shown before. This is consistent with the fact that decay of skin conductance level is generally quite slow.

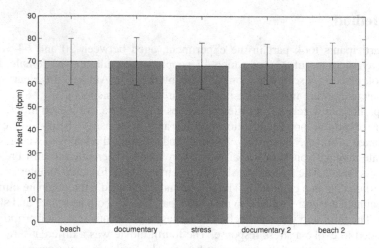

Fig. 1. Average heart rate and standard deviation for each movie

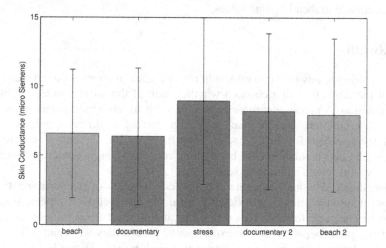

Fig. 2. Average skin conductance and standard deviation for each movie

Table 1. Pairwise comparision of skin conductance differences

	Documentary 1	Stressful	Documentary 2	Beach 2
Beach 1	-18,23	235,01***	161,29***	136,12**
Documentary 1		253.24***	179.53***	155.354***
Stressful			-73.71*	-97.89**
Documentary 2				-24.17
Beach 2				

*** p<0.001; ** p<0.01; * p<0.05

5   Discussion

In this paper, a preliminary exploration has been made regarding the possibilities to induce a stress response through video material. An experiment has been performed in which participants were asked to watch five different video clips while their emotional response was measured via physiological measurements as well as questionnaires. Among the five movies, the third one was composed in such a way that it could be experienced as being stressful, whereas the clip prior to this movie designed to serve as a neutral movie, to determine the baseline level of heart rate and skin conductance of the participants. The results of the measurements showed that the heart rate of the subjects did not differ significantly during the stress film compared to the other four movie clips. Instead, the skin conductance of the participants increased significantly (compared to the other four clips), and the same held for the subjective ratings. Hence, we conclude that it is possible to generate a stress response by means of video material, and that skin conductance is an effective indicator to measure this.

Although this is a promising result, it is only a first step to the accomplishment of our objectives. As mentioned earlier, our final aim is to develop a Virtual Reality-based environment for training of emotion regulation and emotional decision making skills. Hence, as a next step, we will perform similar experiments with actual video game material instead of video clips (comparable to the work of [4]), and compare the results with our current results. After that, we will investigate whether it makes a difference when the participants apply certain emotion regulation strategies while watching video (game) material. When doing this, we will study the impact on participants' emotional stress response, but also on their performance while executing certain domain-specific tasks, such as decision making or communication. This will provide further insight in the possibilities to develop intelligent VR-based training systems using physiological measurements.

Acknowledgements. This research was supported by funding from the National Initiative Brain and Cognition, coordinated by the Netherlands Organisation for Scientific Research (NWO), under grant agreement No. 056-25-013.

References

1. Bosse, T., Gerritsen, C., de Man, J., Treur, J.: Effects of Virtual Training on Emotional Response. In: Imamura, K., Usui, S., Shirao, T., Kasamatsu, T., Schwabe, L., Zhong, N. (eds.) BHI 2013. LNCS, vol. 8211, pp. 21–32. Springer, Heidelberg (2013)
2. Bouchard, S., Guitard, T., Bernier, F., Robillard, G.: Virtual reality and the training of military personnel to cope with acute stressors. In: Brahnam, S., Jain, L.C. (eds.) Advanced Computational Intelligence Paradigms in Healthcare 6. SCI, vol. 337, pp. 109–128. Springer, Heidelberg (2011)
3. Brewin, C.R., Andrews, B., Valentine, J.D.: Meta-analysis of risk factors for posttraumatic stress disorder in trauma-exposed adults. Journal of Consulting and Clinical Psychology 68(5), 748–766 (2000)
4. Brouwer, A.-M., Neerincx, M.A., Kallen, V., van der Leer, L., ten Brinke, M.E.: Alpha Asymmetry, Heart Rate Variability and Cortisol in Response to Virtual Reality Induced Stress. Journal of Cybertherapy & Rehabilitation 4(1), 21–34 (2011)

5. Craig, K.D., Lowery, H.J.: Heart rate components of conditioned vicarious autonomic responses. Journal of Personality and Social Psychology 11(4), 381–387 (1969)
6. Epstein, S., Roupenian, A.: Heart rate and skin conductance during experimentally induced anxiety: the effect of uncertainty about receiving a noxious stimulus. Journal of Personality and Social Psychology 16(1), 20–28 (1970)
7. Field, A.: Discovering statistics using SPSS. Sage, London (2009)
8. Goldstein, M.J., Jones, R.B., Clemens, T.L., Flagg, G.W., Alexander, F.G.: Coping style as a factor in psychophysiological response to a tension-arousing film. Journal of Personality and Social Psychology 1(4), 290–302 (1965)
9. Gross, J.J.: Emotion regulation: affective, cognitive and social consequences. Psychophysiology 39, 281–291 (2002)
10. Khalfa, S., Isabelle, P., Jean-Pierre, B., Manon, R.: Event-related skin conductance responses to musical emotions in humans. Neuroscience Letters 328, 145–149 (2002)
11. Lazarus, R.S., Speisman, J.C., Mordkoff, A.M.: The relationship between autonomic indicators of psychological stress: heart rate and skin conductance. Psychosomatic Medicine 25, 19–30 (1963)
12. Lin, H., Lin, H., Lin, W., Huang, A.C.: Effects of stress, depression, and their interaction on heart rate, skin conductance, finger temperature, and respiratory rate: sympathetic-parasympathetic hypothesis of stress and depression. Journal of Clinical Psychology 67(10), 1080–1091 (2011)
13. Loewenstein, G.F., Lerner, J.S.: The role of affect in decision making. In: Davidson, R., Scherer, K., Goldsmith, H. (eds.) Handbook of Affective Science, pp. 619–642. Oxford University Press, New York (2002)
14. Öhman, A.: Fear and anxiety: Evolutionary, cognitive, and clinical perspectives. In: Lewis, M., Haviland-Jones, J.M. (eds.) Handbook of Emotions, pp. 573–593. The Guilford Press, New York (2000)
15. Ozel, F.: Time pressure and stress as a factor during emergency egress. Safety Science 38, 95–107 (2001)
16. Speisman, J.C., Lazarus, R.S., Mordkoff, A.M., Davison, L.: Experimental reduction of stress based on ego-defense theory. Journal of Abnormal and Social Psychology 68(4), 367–380 (1964)
17. http://www.biosignalsplux.com/
18. http://stress.few.vu.nl

The Influence of Emotions on Productivity in Software Engineering

Broderick Crawford[1,2], Ricardo Soto[1,3], Claudio León de la Barra[1],
Kathleen Crawford[1], and Eduardo Olguín[4]

[1] Pontificia Universidad Católica de Valparaíso, Chile
[2] Universidad Finis Terrae, Chile
[3] Universidad Autónoma de Chile, Chile
[4] Universidad San Sebastián, Chile

{broderick.crawford,ricardo.soto,claudio.leondelabarra}@ucv.cl,
kathleen.crawford.a@mail.pucv.cl,
eduardo.olguin@uss.cl

Abstract. This work presents the relevance of emotions in the software development process. Emotions are an important human factor that must be considered when developing software. Unlike in psychology, where the influence of emotions on industrial productivity is well known, there are few studies reported on its importance in software engineering.

Keywords: Software Engineering, Human Factors, Emotions.

1 Introduction

A software engineering project depends significantly on team performance; software is created by people for people involving human cooperation. A successful collaboration is built on a high level of emotional literacy, without the capacity to develop and hold certain feelings our ability to collaborate with others is not possible.

We can learn to cultivate the emotions that promote collaborative process [23]. Studies have shown that humans are more efficient and creative problem solvers when they are happy [10,20,21]. Considering the importance of human factors in organizational activities, it is especially relevant the research about the influence of emotions in the creation of a software engineering project [3,12,17,8].

2 Fundamental Aspects of Emotions on Productivity

By some researchers of other areas, it is well known the influence of emotions on productivity. Our emotions, positive or negative, not only affect our own job performance - including decision, making, creativity, efficiency, teamwork, negotiation and leadership abilities - but also the emotions and behaviour of coworkers and customers. Positive emotions encourage more creative and generative thinking and they promote exchange of ideas and creation of consensus [8,14].

C. Stephanidis (Ed.): HCII 2014 Posters, Part I, CCIS 434, pp. 307–310, 2014.
© Springer International Publishing Switzerland 2014

Meanwhile, negative emotions are linked to feelings of frustration and discomfort in the workplace. However, it is important to emphasize that new studies have confirmed that the conflict can also bring benefits to innovation and creativity [5,2,13,7].

In [3] Colomo-Palacios mentioned that the emotion is mainly composed of three aspects:

- the experience of conscious feeling of emotion
- the processes that occur in the brain and nervous system
- the observable extensible patterns of emotion

This means that our emotions influence our behavior certainly also in the way we interact with others. Particularly, this could be related to levels of productivity in working groups considering that our overall mood is in effect defined by the number of positive versus negative moments experienced during the course of the day.

3   Tools to Measure Emotional States

Many approaches have tried to give an objective answer to the question of how to measure emotions. Harsher methods are presented as neuroscience and biometric sensors [16,15]. Also, there exist methods associated with social psychology such as questionnaires, surveys and tests.

One of the most popular tools of psychology studies has been called PANAS (Positive and Negative Affect Schedule) [22]. This is an item survey that represents positive and negative affects. Participants must complete it according to the emotions experienced at different times of work, dayly, weekly, monthly or yearly. This type of tool is extremely important to demonstrate as the emotions of the people involved in the creation of a project may affect the development and productivity [1,9,19].

In [3] it was applied a tool of social psychology to measure emotions in software requirements elicitation: the affect grid of Rusell [18]. They concluded that emotions are a factor that must be taken into account when establishing requirements.

Importantly, these tools not only provide the individual sense or feeling of professionals, also at the level of collaborative work and the implications that would bring, for example, detecting and enhancing poor communication between peers in agile software development [6,4].

4   The Impact of Human Factors in Software Quality

The importance of human factors in software engineering is demonstrated by the fact that regardless of the approaches, methods and tools used, the success of the project depends on how well the participants - managers, developers, support personnel, practitioners, experts, customers and users - communicate and collaborate. For this reason in the last years software engineering has had to involve a series of multidisciplinary elements to create its projects. Because agility of changes, projects should have large degrees of adaptation, this certainly involve a number of factors - including emotions of the actors - linked also to the productivity and quality with which these processes are carried out [23,17,11].

5 Conclusions

We considered that emotions are an important factor that must be taken into account when designing any type of project. Furthermore, considering that software engineering is a human capital intense activity, it must be inescapably considered in software projects. The key is to use emotions intelligently, to work for best group results. The role of emotions in the software development process is one of the keys to understand the impact of participants on team productivity and software quality. Our job is to continue investigating on the support tools who will guarantee not only individual results, also a work environment that will make possible great results in common projects.

References

1. Agarwal, A., Meyer, A.: Beyond usability: Evaluating emotional response as an integral part of the user experience. In: CHI 2009 Extended Abstracts on Human Factors in Computing Systems, CHI EA 2009, pp. 2919–2930. ACM, New York (2009)
2. Barsade, S., Gibson, D.: Why does affect matter in organizations?. Academy of Management Perspectives (21), 36–59
3. Colomo-Palacios, R., Casado-Lumbreras, C., Soto-Acosta, P., Garcia-Crespo, A.: Using the affect grid to measure emotions in software requirements engineering. Journal of Universal Computer Science 17(9), 1281–1298 (2011)
4. Crawford, B., de la Barra, C.L., Soto, R., Misra, S., Monfroy, E.: Knowledge management and creativity in software engineering - the foundations of agility. In: Hammoudi, S., Maciaszek, L.A., Cordeiro, J., Dietz, J.L.G. (eds.) ICEIS (2), pp. 265–272. SciTePress (2013)
5. Crawford, B., de la Barra, C.L.: Enhancing creativity in agile software teams. In: Concas, G., Damiani, E., Scotto, M., Succi, G. (eds.) XP 2007. LNCS, vol. 4536, pp. 161–162. Springer, Heidelberg (2007)
6. Crawford, B., León de la Barra, C., Soto, R., Monfroy, E.: Agile software engineering as creative work. In: CHASE, pp. 20–26. IEEE (2012)
7. Crawford, B., Soto, R., León de la Barra, C., Crawford, K., Olguín, E.: Agile software teams can use conflict to create a better products. In: HCI 2014. CCIS, Springer (2014)
8. Fisher, C., Ashkanasy, N.: The emerging role of emotions in work life: An introduction. Journal of Organizational Behavior 21(2), 123–129 (2000)
9. Ganglbauer, E., Schrammel, J., Deutsch, S., Tscheligi, M.: Applying psychophysiological methods for measuring user experience. In: Possibilities, Challenges, and Feasibility. Proc. User Experience Evaluation Methods in Product Development Workshop (2009)

10. Hirt, E.R., Melton, J.R., Mcdonald, H.E., Harackiewicz, J.M.: Processing goals, task interest, and the mood-performance relationship: A mediational analysis. Journal of Personality and Social Psychology 71(2), 245–261 (1996)

11. Khan, I.A., Brinkman, W.-P., Hierons, R.M.: Do moods affect programmers' debug performance? Cognition, Technology & Work 13(4), 245–258 (2011)

12. Kolakowska, A., Landowska, A., Szwoch, M., Szwoch, W., Wrobel, M.: Emotion recognition and its application in software engineering. In: 2013 The 6th International Conference on Human System Interaction (HSI), pp. 532–539 (June 2013)

13. de la Barra, C.L., Crawford, B., Soto, R., Misra, S., Monfroy, E.: Agile software development: It is about knowledge management and creativity. In: Murgante, B., Misra, S., Carlini, M., Torre, C.M., Nguyen, H.-Q., Taniar, D., Apduhan, B.O., Gervasi, O. (eds.) ICCSA 2013, Part III. LNCS, vol. 7973, pp. 98–113. Springer, Heidelberg (2013)

14. Oswald, A., Proto, E., Sgroi, D.: U. of Warwick. Department of Economics. Happiness and Productivity. Warwick economic research papers. Department of Economics, University of Warwick (2008)

15. Paleari, M., Huet, B., Chellali, R.: Towards multimodal emotion recognition: a new approach. In: Proceedings of the ACM International Conference on Image and Video Retrieval, CIVR 2010, pp. 174–181. ACM, New York (2010)

16. Prendinger, H., Ishizuka, M., Nakasone, A.: Emotion recognition from electromyography and skin conductance. In: Proceedings 5th International Workshop on Biosignal Interpretation (BSI 2005), Tokyo, Japan, pp. 219–222 (2005)

17. Ramos, I., Berry, D.M.: Is emotion relevant to requirements engineering? Requir. Eng. 10(3), 238–242 (2005)

18. Russell, J.A., Weiss, A., Mendelsohn, G.A.: Affect Grid: A single-item scale of pleasure and arousal. Journal of Personality and Social Psychology 57(3), 493–502 (1989)

19. Saariluomaand, P., Jokinen, J.P.P.: Emotional dimensions of user experience: A user psychological analysis. International Journal of Human-Computer Interaction 30(4), 303–320 (2014)

20. Seo, M.-G.: The Role of Affective Experience in Work Motivation. Boston College (2003)

21. Seo, M.-G., Bartunek, J.M., Barrett, L.F.: The role of affective experience in work motivation: Test of a conceptual model. Journal of Organizational Behavior 31(7), 951–968 (2010)

22. Watson, D., Clark, L.A., Tellegen, A.: Development and validation of brief measures of positive and negative affect: the panas scales. Journal of Personality and Social Psychology 54, 1063–1070 (1988)

23. Wrobel, M.R.: Emotions in the software development process. In: Proceedings of the 6th International Conference on Human System Interaction (2013)

The Exploratory Study of Emotional Valence and Arousal for Eco-visualization Interface of Water Resources

Yu-Min Fang and Meng-Hsien Sun

Department of Industrial Design, National United University, Taiwan
{FanGeo,M0118005}@nuu.edu.tw

Abstract. This research focuses on the study of the Eco-Visualization Interface for water resource, and explores the different design elements and approaches that affect the user's emotional valence and arousal of eco-visualization interface. Respondents were invited to view the interactive interfaces with 6 different ways to show the volume of consumed water in a certain setting. The surveys were also incorporated with the scales of Self-Assessment Manikin (SAM) and the Questionnaires for User Interaction Satisfaction (QUIS). As statistical results indicated, the interfaces with the best performance were separately those of tropical fish and water droplets with a good conformity with typical design principles. The interfaces with emotional animation brought with positive responses. However, what was noteworthy was a fact that some respondents contended more water would be consumed whenever the interfaces were displayed. Such a response deviated from our original expectation.

Keywords: Eco-Visualization, Emotional Valence, Emotional Arousal, Interface Design.

1 Introduction

Numerous energy-saving expectations and visions had been emphasized, but it is not easy to propose and integrate technological solutions. With the improvement of ubiquitous computing technologies, the development of various kinds of sensors and divergent platforms had been broadly applied. The technologies of human-computer interaction also entered our daily life with such a development trend to help users take good control over the situation of energy consumption by means of ambient display. Ambient display devices could be demonstrated in different ways wherein visual information was applied on most occasions. The applications of images or texts were meant to demonstrate the information in a compressive way. These applications, improving knowledge transparency to increase users' understanding of information, were referred to as information visualization. It was aimed to explore the ways how to unravel the information hidden in environment to provide individuals or groups with eco-feedback in view of the habits purposed for energy saving and carbon reduction.

C. Stephanidis (Ed.): HCII 2014 Posters, Part I, CCIS 434, pp. 311–316, 2014.
© Springer International Publishing Switzerland 2014

For HCI researchers, their researching basis could be used to conduct further exploitation on how about the ways for the most minor details to affect the interaction of eco-feedback and what kinds of media or methods most suitable for their transmission of such a message (such as images or abstract environmental media). These details were critically important because emotional products or systems were used with much more convenience and better fruitful results achievable.   This research focuses on the study of the Eco-Visualization Interface for water resource, and explores the different design elements and approaches that affect the user's emotional valence and arousal of eco-visualization interface.

2   Literatures Review

2.1   The Categorization of Ambient Display Devices

With technique advancement, ambient display devices were never confined to screen display anymore yet there were further featured with more divergent facades in development.   From two points of views proposed by researchers - the internal context and the function between devices and environment (external context), display devices were divided into four categories inclusive of visualization as translation, visualization as augment, visualization as embodiment and visualization as overlap [1].

This research was operated for further categorization with the interactive features of a relationship between objects and human beings and the other relationship between objects and environment separately.   The interactive features arisen from the relationship between objects and human beings were inclusive of three points described as below: (1) It meant that the denotation of the display devices, namely the data and models demonstrated by materials;   (2) the metaphors or implications provoked by the aesthetics of those device designs;   (3) the interaction reacting with the external resources of messages.   The interactive features between objects and environment meant the social and physical messages conveyed therein and even included the environment set by devices themselves.

2.2   The Categories of the Images of Display Devices

Based on aforesaid categorization, the performance types of display devices could be divided into three types – imaging display, augmenting objects, and artificial objects. Because that the imaging display was affected by physical conditions to the least extent, and with the prevalence of platforms for information communication triggered by the raising of smart devices, this research had conducted the further exploitation. According to the analysis on the degree of precision for reproduction from concrete images to abstract images, Pousman and Stasko proposed five groups of formats of information display for environment information [2]. Among these groups, they could be further divided into three different levels.   In accordance with the order from inferior to superior precision, the said five groups were ranked as below: (1) Data index – including measurement tools, maps and photographs; (2) Image – drawings, graffiti, and comics; (3) Image – metaphor; (4) Symbol – linguistic symbols – texts, and numeric; (5) Symbol – abstract symbols (Table 1).

Table 1. The Categories of the Images of Display Devices

Embodiment	Data Index	Including measurement tools, maps, and photographs
	Image	Drawings, graffiti, and comics
		Metaphors
	Symbol	Linguistic symbol - texts and numerics
Abstract		Abstract symbols

2.3 The Influence on Decision Making / Judgment Caused by Emotional Dimensions

In view of the researching dissertation proposed by Odom et al., these researchers used to interview students and know what about their reaction and suggestions toward the methods demonstrated by ecological visualization [3]. The interviewees indicated whenever the data or statistical data of energy were shown, such a phenomenon seemed to cause no encouragement. If these data were shown by means of images or drawings, the effect was more workable. As Froehlich et al. mentioned, taking water resource for example, if the data of water consumption was combined with the images of those local wild animals nearby by the water resource regions, it would probably provoke the altruistic response among users [4]. As Wright et al. contended in their research, emotion could affect the rational cognition and external behaviors of human beings such as the execution of those already-made decisions, learning, and the alternatives for action[5].

3 Questionaire Survey and Data Analysis

3.1 The Collection of the Existing Samples

Samples were selected by means of purposive sampling. This research focused on the exploitation about the visualization of energy in display devices environmentally. As a result, we had collected nine pieces of conceptual, artistic, and commercial objects, featured with the availability for the visualization of water resource, to conduct systematical analysis by scientific literatures review.

3.2 The Categorization of the Displaying Types for the Existing Samples

By reviewing scientific literatures, the summarized categorization methods were meant to conduct analysis on the aforesaid 9 items of devices. The results are shown in the following table 2.

Table 2. Categorization of the Displaying Types for the Existing Samples

		Index	Drawings	Image	Symbols	Abstract symbols
Visualization as Translation	amphi-ro			•	•	
	Eco-Sherdrop		•		•	
	Water-pebble					•
Visualization as Augment	PoorLittle Fish	•				
	Show-me					•
	OneLiter Limited	•				
	isave				•	
Visualization as Embodiment	Eco Drop Shower			•		
Comprehensive Category	Shower calendar			•		

3.3 The Implementation of Interface Designs

During the experimental phases inclined to this research, Adobe FLASH was used to produce six diffident designs of interfaces. Under manual operation, whenever every 500 ml. water was consumed, changes were displayed on the screen.

Table 3. Six Different Deaigns of Experimental Samples

Title	Display Categorization	Image	Imagine Type
Water Meter	Index		By simulating the shape of additionally water meter to indicate water consumption.
Tropical Fish	Drawing		The survival correlation between water consumption and goldfish is meant to indicate water consumption.
Water Droplet	Drawing		By means of the process of elapsing water droplets, it is meant to indicate water consumption.
Ripple	The Drawing of Metaphor		By no means of ripples, it is meant to indicate water consumption.
Text	Linguistic Symbol	節約用水	By no means of alerting texts, it is meant to keep cautious of water consumption.
Lamp	Abstract Symbol		By no means different lighting colors, it is meant to indicate water consumption.

4   Results and Discussions

This study recruited the respondents aging from 18 to 25 among the students of the National United University. There were 31 respondents arranged for this study (12 males and 19 females). Respondents were invited to view the interactive interfaces with 6 different ways to show the volume of consumed water in a certain setting. The surveys were also incorporated with the scales of Self-Assessment Manikin (SAM) and the Questionnaires for User Interaction Satisfaction (QUIS).

The correlation analysis was conducted to explore the correlation of the emotional dimensions between "arousing respondents' interest" and "efficiency for promoting water-saving". Among them, the emotional arousal showed its strong correlation to both the aforesaid items, while weak correlation was found in the item of affective valence. Secondly, both ANOVA (the analysis of variance) and the Duncan's test were conducted to separately make the comparisons for four different items, namely "affective valence", "emotional arousal", "arousing respondents' interest", and "efficiency for promoting water-saving", together with the performance difference among six different displaying ways of interfaces. The affective valence caused by six different interfaces were divided into three groups. Among them, tropical fish and water droplets showed the highest delight and then separately followed by the combination of lamps, water meters and ripples. Textual contents showed the least delight. The combination to show the highest emotional arousal was those of tropical fish and water droplets and then followed by the combination of ripples, lamps and water meters, together with the last one - textual contents. In the items to arouse respondents' interest, the combination of tropical fish and water droplets showed the highest strength and then followed by the combination of ripples, lamps and water meters, along with the last one - textual contents. In view of the item of water-saving efficiency, the highest one was the combination of tropical fish and water droplets and then followed by the combination of the combination of ripples, lamps and water meters. The last one was the item of textual contents.

5   Conclusion and Suggestion

As statistical results indicated, the interfaces with the best performance were separately those of tropical fish and water droplets with a good conformity with typical design principles. The interfaces with emotional animation brought with positive responses. The design of tropical fish gave respondents the feelings of compassion, vigilance, fun and expectation. However, what was noteworthy was a fact that some respondents contended more water would be consumed whenever the interfaces were displayed. Such a response deviated from our original expectation. Secondly, in view of the opinions of respondents toward "ripple interfaces", respondents supposed the connection with water resource showed no equivalent valence. Some respondents contended it was difficult for "lamp interfaces" to be connected with water resource. Therefore, there was no intensive feeling aroused. It could be seen from such results. Whether the interfaces could be effectively connected with the design subjects was exactly the point required for attention the most when designing. Finally, respondents posed negative assessment against the interfaces of water meters and texts.

By means of questionnaire surveys and the review of scientific literatures, a fact could be deduced and it meant the interfaces with different displaying formats would be significantly correlated to emotional dimensions.   After experiment, a fact was found respondents showed more congruent opinions toward identical interfaces in view of emotional arousal.   However, emotional valence showed the totally contradictory opinions among respondents.   For subsequent researches, it was still required for the effort exploring the influence on water-saving behaviors caused by cognitive psychology.   It was further meant to design more well-organized interfaces after professional discussion to take proper control over both positive or negative emotion. Also, in the experiments, actual tasks accompanied with the settings to show the changes of water resources consumed could be further conducted with the tests for emotional valence against "arousing respondents' interest" and "efficiency for promoting water-saving".

Acknowledgement. The authors would like to thank the financial support by the National Science Council of Republic of China under grant number NSC 102-2410-H239-015 and NSC 102-2218-E-239-003.

References

1. Moere, A.V., Offenhuber, D.: Beyond Ambient Display: A Contextual Taxonomy of Alternative Information Display. International Journal of Ambient Computing and Intelligence 12(1), 39–46 (2009)
2. Pousman, Z., Stasko, J.: A taxonomy of ambient information systems: four patterns of design. In: Proceedings of the Working Conference, pp. 67–74 (2006)
3. Odom, W., Pierce, J., Roedl, D.: Social Incentive & Eco--Visualization Displays: Toward Persuading Greater Change in Dormitory Communities. In: Workshop Proc. of OZCHI (2008)
4. Froehlich, J., Findlater, L., Landay, J.: The design of eco-feedback technology. In: Proceedings of the SIGCHI Conference on Human Factors in Computing Systems (CHI 2010), pp. 1999–2008 (2010)
5. Wright, P., Blythe, M., McCarthy, J.: User experience and the idea of design in HCI. In: Gilroy, S.W., Harrison, M.D. (eds.) DSV-IS 2005. LNCS, vol. 3941, pp. 1–14. Springer, Heidelberg (2006)

Saccade Detection and Processing
for Enhancing 3D Visualizations in Real-Time

Ingmar S. Franke, Tobias Günther, and Rainer Groh

Technische Universität Dresden, Department of Computer Science,
Institute of Software- and Multimedia Technology
{ingmar.franke,rainer.groh}@tu-dresden.de

Abstract. We describe the utilization of the visual phenomenon saccadic suppression for masking graphical modifications in real-time 3D visualizations in order to hide disruptive effects from the human visual perception. Consequently, a saccade detection algorithm was implemented, which delivers outcomes at runtime. Furthermore an appropriate plugin for a software framework for 3D visualization (cf. [8]) was developed. A demonstration scene illustrates the performance of our approach regarding saccade detection and processing. Test results revealed that 96,5% of the measured latencies undercut our determined threshold of 30ms.

Keywords: Saccadic suppression, Eye-tracking, Real-time computer graphics.

1 Introduction

The human system of visual perception is constantly scanning the environment and composing the fragments into a mental representation (cf. [1]). During saccadic eye movements the visual perception capability is limited, an effect called saccadic suppression (cf. [2]).

The leading motive of this contribution is the utilization of this effect for several time critical applications in the context of 3D visualizations. In the field of interactive computer graphics, it is often necessary to perform large modifications to the image in order to bring the system status up to date. Immediate, abrupt changes in the graphics could have disruptive effects on the visibility of the 3D scene. The saccadic suppression has proven to be an appropriate solution to mask extensive graphic updates in virtual environments (cf. [3]).

For instance, distracting geometrical changes in a three-dimensional scene (cf. [4]), such as perspective correction (cf. [5]) of graphical objects with unaesthetic distortions, could be masked if the modification is performed during the suppression of the visual cognitive ability (see Fig. 1). To achieve a hiding effect it is necessary to execute the scene manipulations as fast as possible after the start of the saccade because the visual perceptual ability will only be repressed for 50-80ms (cf. [6]).

C. Stephanidis (Ed.): HCII 2014 Posters, Part I, CCIS 434, pp. 317–322, 2014.

Fig. 1. Perspective image. Geometrical difference between Multi- and Mono-Perspective are shown (cp. [5]). This difference is obviously and can mask by using our approach.

2   Real-Time Saccade Detection Algorithm

We describe the implementation of a real-time saccade detection algorithm. Saccadic suppression will reach the highest masking capability 20-30ms after saccade start (cf. [6]). To address that fact we determine the critical threshold for our algorithm at 30ms. During this time all necessary steps in processing should be completed including the manipulation of the 3D scene.

Based on the velocity threshold approach of Kumar et al. (cf. [7]) the algorithm was enhanced with a possibility to compensate the loss of gaze data samples. Furthermore, a plugin for a software framework for 3D visualization (cf. [8]) was developed which allows the user to enter distinct parameters for saccade detection like a velocity threshold in degree per second. For convenient values with different setups the user can input the size, resolution and distance of the display in order to get a correct conversion from gaze angles to screen-pixels (see Fig. 2).

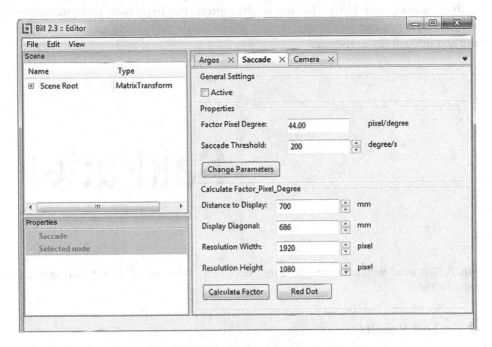

Fig. 2. User interface of the plugin with several parameter options

For eye tracking we used the video-based and head-mounted EyeLink II-System from SR-Research (cf. [9]) with a data rate of 500 gaze samples per second. To achieve a low latency in terms of image refresh rate an ASUS VG278HR monitor was utilized. As a result the images updates were displayed within 7ms in the worst case due to the provided refresh rate of 144 images per second.

3 Demonstration Scene

With a demonstration scene we visualized that it is possible to mask an evident stimulus during a saccade in context of real time visualization systems using our implementation. The users should alternately look at red targets at left and right border of the display to provoke saccades. The rest of the image was blank. Only in the case of a saccade a huge red text appeared.

Almost all eye-tracked users did not perceive the stimulus on the screen while other non-tracked observers could read the message (see Fig. 3). Related psychological works already showed the possibility of masking patterns [10], texts [11] and details in photos [12] during saccadic eye movement. However, it should be noted that this demonstration is an extreme case because the scene manipulation draws more attention of the user than practical applications normally do. In consequence of inattentional blindness even unmasked changes will regularly not be realized by the user in realistic scenarios (cf. [13]). Thus our results represent an impressive performance for saccade detection and processing since it seems nearly impossible to miss the huge red text through inattentiveness.

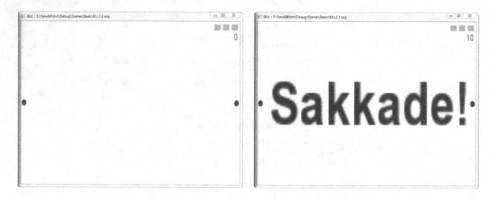

Fig. 3. Test scene with red targets on screen sides (left). "Flashing of the red font" during a saccade (right).

4   Test Results

Test results led to an average latency of 12.61ms for saccade detection. The overall average latency for all processing steps (including the depiction of the modified 3D-scene on the display) was 16,66ms. However, more important are the results of performance in terms of the defined critical threshold of 30ms. In our experiments we noticed that, on average, 96,5% of the latencies undercut this threshold. Thus, in almost all cases the necessary steps for saccade detection and scene manipulation could be concluded in a time span, which guarantees that the user is still in a state of clearly limited visual perception.

The exclusion of blinks as a trigger for saccade detection is still problematic. Due to the high velocity of blinks and the similarly characteristic profile in the beginning it is a huge competition to distinct them from saccadic eye movement within a few milliseconds.

5   Conclusion

We implemented a saccade detection algorithm to utilize the visual phenomenon saccadic suppression for masking graphical modifications in real-time 3D visualizations in order to hide disruptive effects from the human visual perception. Besides a plugin for a 3D visualization software framework and a demonstration scene were developed. Although we already accomplished various performance tests a scientific study is required to confirm the obtained results.

Acknowledgements. The authors like to acknowledge the Unit of Engineering Psychology and Cognitive Ergonomics of Technical University Dresden, and especially Sebastian Pannasch for the technical support with the EyeLink II-System.

This work has been supported by the European Social Fund and the Free State of Saxony (Young Investigators Group CogITo, project no. 100076040). We like to thank the participants of the study and express our gratitude for their numerous comments and helpful insights.

References

1. Holmqvist, K.: Eye Tracking: A Comprehensive Guide to Methods and Measures. Oxford University Press, Oxford (2011)
2. Matin, E.: Saccadic Suppression: A Review and an Analysis. Psychological Bulletin 81(12), 899–917 (1974)
3. Schuhmacher, J., Allison, R.S., Herpers, R.: Using Saccadic Suppression to Hide Graphic Updates. In: Eurographic/ACM SIGGRAPH Symposium on Virtual Environments, pp. 17–24 (2004)
4. Franke, I.S., Pannasch, S., Helmert, J.R., Rieger, R., Groh, R., Velichkovsky, B.M.: Towards Attention-centered Interfaces: An Aesthetic Evaluation of Perspective with Eye Tracking. ACM Transactions on Multimedia Computing, Communications and Applications 4(3), 1–13 (2008)
5. Franke, I.S., Zavesky, M., Dachselt, R.: Learning from Painting: Perspective-dependent Geometry Deformation for Perceptual Realism. In: Fröhlich, B., Blach, R., van Liere, R.J. (eds.) Virtual environments 2007 IPT-EGVE 2007: 13th Eurographics Symposium on Virtual Environments; 10th Immersive Projection Technology Workshop, Weimar, July 15-18, pp. 117–120, Weimar (2007); Eurographics Association in Cooperation with Institute of Computer Graphics & Knowledge Visualization at Graz University of Technology and Institute of Scientific Computing at Technical University at Brunswick
6. Carpenter, R.H.: Movements of the Eyes. Pion Limited (1988)
7. Kumar, M., Klingner, J., Puranik, R., Winograd, T., Paepcke, A.: Improving the Accuracy of Gaze Input for Interaction, p. 65 (2008)
8. Wojdziak, J., Kammer, D., Franke, I.S., Groh, R.: BiLL: An Experimental Environment for Visual Analytics. In: Proceedings of the 3rd ACM SIGCHI Symposium on Engineering Interactive Computing Systems - EICS 2011, Pisa, Italy, p. 259 (2011)

9. SR Research, EyeLink II User Manual: Version 2.14 (2009),
   http://www.sr-research.com (access: March 18, 2014)
10. Bridgeman, B., Hendry, D., Stark, L.: Failure to Detect Displacement of the Visu-al World During Saccadic Eye Movements. Vision Research 15(6), 719–722 (1975)
11. McConkie, G.W., Zola, D.: Visual Information Integrated Across Successive Fixations in Reading? Perception & Psychophysics 25(3), 221–224 (1979)
12. Grimes, J.: On the Failure to Detect Changes in Scenes Across Saccades (1996)
13. Mack, A., Rock, I.: Inattentional Blindness. MIT Press, Cambridge (1998)

Continuous Gaze Cursor Feedback in Various Tasks: Influence on Eye Movement Behavior, Task Performance and Subjective Distraction

Sven-Thomas Graupner and Sebastian Pannasch

Technische Universitaet Dresden,
Engineering Psychology and Applied Cognitive Research, Dresden, Germany
`{sven-thomas.graupner,sebastian.pannasch}@tu-dresden.de`

Abstract. Using gaze as input modality has often been promoted as a method for advanced computer interaction. One important detail in gaze controlled interfaces is the design of optimal feedback. Highlighting the current point of gaze by a gaze contingent cursor represents a simple form of feedback. In an experimental study, we investigated the influence of gaze cursor feedback on eye movement behavior, task performance and subjective distraction. Participants of the study completed three different tasks (gaze typing, reading and image exploration) with five different feedback conditions. No-feedback was implemented as baseline condition and compared with gaze cursor feedback of various spatial precision and temporal delays. A blue, semitransparent small dot served as gaze cursor. The observed findings are discussed in the context of user friendly feedback for gaze based computer interaction.

Keywords: eye tracking, gaze interaction, cursor feedback, eye movements, distraction, gaze typing, reading, image exploration.

1 Introduction

Using gaze as input modality has often been promoted as a method for advanced computer interaction [1]. Although various concepts for gaze interaction have been proposed, the most often used and intuitive concept is that of gaze pointing in conjunction with dwell time based selection [2]. In order to interact with the on-screen interface elements (e.g. buttons), the user has to look at the respective element for a predefined (dwell) time; typically 500-1000 ms. Previous research has focused on various aspects of gaze interaction, such as the optimal dwell time for text entry or the design of appropriate user feedback [2].

A simple form of feedback in gaze based interfaces is a cursor that follows the user's eye position [1]. The gaze cursor provides a direct continuous feedback and might be beneficial to adjust gaze behavior in case of poor eye tracking accuracy. However, there might also be disadvantageous effects due to the continuous movement of the cursor that could distract from the task at hand [1]. Moreover, a gaze cursor might alter gaze behavior itself and influence basic processes of perception and

C. Stephanidis (Ed.): HCII 2014 Posters, Part I, CCIS 434, pp. 323–329, 2014.

cognition. Previous research has examined influences of cursor shape on usability [3] or the temporal delay of the shown gaze cursor on performance in gaze typing [4]. However, the relationship between gaze cursor feedback and its influences on perception and performance are still unknown.

This issue becomes more relevant as cheap and mobile eye tracking devices become available. These systems often come with limitations regarding their spatial precision and temporal resolution, resulting in imprecise and inaccurate gaze position signals. Such noisy signals can be improved by data filtering [5] providing a more stable and exact signal. Applying such forms of filtering, automatically introduces a temporal delay between the point of gaze in real time and the gaze cursor position, which presumably affects performance in gaze based interfaces [2].

Here we investigated influences of gaze cursor feedback on user behavior in three different tasks: dwell time based gaze typing, text reading and exploration of images. We manipulated spatial and temporal characteristics of the gaze cursor behavior in order to simulate eye tracking systems of various precision or effects of data filtering. We analyzed the influences on the control of eye movements, on the task performance, and on the subjective evaluation of distraction caused by the gaze cursor.

2   Method

2.1   Participants

Fourteen subjects, (8 females) participated (age: M=25 years) in the study. All had normal or corrected to normal vision and received a reward of 10€ for their efforts. Informed consent was obtained prior to the test session.

2.2   Apparatus, Stimuli and Procedure

An EyeLink CL (SR Research Ltd.) system served as an eye tracking device. Recording was done monocular (right eye) with a temporal resolution of 250 Hz. A chinrest was used to stabilize the head. A 24" wide screen monitor (BENQ Model XL2420-B, refresh rate: 120 Hz, screen resolution: 1920x1080 pixel) was used to display the experimental tasks and placed at a distance of 68 cm from subjects head.

In the experiment subjects performed three different tasks: gaze typing, reading and image exploration. Each task was run in a separate block, consisting of multiple trials. The order of the tasks was balanced across the participants.

For gaze typing, subjects had to enter a sequence of five numbers on a numeric screen keypad by using gaze. A trial started with a random sequence of five numbers, shown on the left side of the screen for 3 s. Then, a numeric keypad (ten-key type with numbers 0-9) was presented, centrally aligned to the screen. Each number (font size 16) represented the center of a gaze sensitive button (size: 150x150 pixel, clearance: 50 pixel) with a dwell time of 500 ms. In the gaze-over state, the button changed its color to blue, the font size increased to 20 and the font style changed to bold. If the gaze remained on the button for the set dwell time, color changed to light blue for 300 ms and font size increased further to 28; it was registered as a button press and the respective number was entered. Subsequently, the button resumed to its gaze-over status. If the gaze left the button it returned to its original appearance. Once the typing of the five numbers was completed, subjects had to activate a dwell button in the lower left corner of the screen to proceed with the evaluation query. A question appeared, asking to rate the intensity of distraction during the task completion due to the cursor feedback (six-item Likert scale). Subsequently, subjects were able to continue with the next trial. Altogether the gaze typing task contained 50 trials.

In the reading task subjects had to read paragraphs of text for comprehension. A trial started with a central fixation cross (2 s). Then, the paragraph (~160 words, font size: 24) was presented, aligned centrally to screen. After reading the paragraph once, subjects had to activate a dwell button at the lower left corner in order to proceed with the evaluation query. Two questions appeared; one question asked for a certain word in the paragraph and the second question was the same rating as in the gaze typing task. After answering both questions, subjects summed with the next trial.

In the image exploration task subjects' had to explore images of paintings in order to memorize its content. The images (1152x864 pixel) were shown in colors and were centrally aligned to the screen. Each trial started with a fixation cross (2 s), followed by the image presentation for 15 s and was completed by the evaluation query. One question required to judge if a presented image cutout (80x80 pixels) belonged to the previously seen image. The second question was again the distraction rating.

Within the experiment five variations of gaze cursor behavior were implemented and quasi randomly assigned to the trials of each task. A small semitransparent blue dot (size: 20 pixel) served as cursor. A condition without cursor (*no feedback*) served as a baseline. In the *direct* feedback condition the cursor was displayed at the current gaze position on screen with a slight jitter. In the *direct-noisy* condition an error (Gaussian distribution with $M = 0$, $SD = 15$) was added to gaze position signal, creating a noticeably erratic cursor. In the *smoothed* condition the mean value of the last ten samples was used, generating a highly precise cursor with a small temporal delay (40 ms). In the *smoothed-delayed* condition the smoothed signal was further delayed by ~280 ms, creating the impression of dragging the cursor behind. Only the cursor feedback was manipulated, not the gaze input that was used to control the typing task.

2.3   Data Analysis

Subjective ratings of distraction for each task and cursor condition were pooled for each subject. Eye movements and behavioral data were analyzed for the time span while the task was performed. Median of fixation duration, saccadic amplitude and number of short saccades ($<2°$) for each task, cursor condition and subject were aggregated. Task performance for each task was analyzed individually. For gaze typing, we analyzed the time for task completion, total number of errors (missing and erroneous activations) and the number of repeated button activations. For the reading task, we calculated reading time per word, number of regressive saccades (saccades opposite to the reading direction) and percent of correct answers in the word query. For the image exploration task, the percent of correct answers for the cutout recognition was analyzed. All measures were analyzed with repeated measure ANOVAs.

3   Results

The analysis for rating of distraction showed main effects for task, $F(2,26) = 5.68$, $p < 0.05$, and cursor condition, $F(4,52) = 78.7$, $p < 0.001$, and a significant interaction between task and cursor, $F(8,104) = 10.1$, $p < 0.001$. Subjects rated cursor feedback most distracting in the reading task and least distracting during gaze typing (see Figure 1A). The noisy cursor was evaluated most distracting. As reflected by post-hoc pair wise comparisons, all other cursor conditions were significantly different from the noisy as well as from the no feedback condition, ($p < 0.05$). The significant interaction was related to a reversed evaluation in the no feedback condition.

Analysis of fixation duration revealed a main effect for task, $F(2,26) = 8.89$, $p < 0.01$, cursor condition, $F(4,52) = 9.27$, $p < 0.01$, as well as a significant interaction, $F(8,104) = 7.44$, $p < 0.01$. Fixation durations were shortest for reading and longest for gaze typing (see Figure 1B). Cursor feedback generally increased fixation duration (about 10 ms in the reading and 20 ms in the image exploration/gaze typing task). In gaze typing there was an additional increase for the smoothed and delayed condition, which was not observable during reading and image exploration.

No effect of cursor condition was found in the analysis of saccadic amplitudes. Only a main effect of task was observed, $F(2,26) = 91.2$, $p < 0.001$. Saccadic amplitudes were largest in the gaze typing and smallest in the reading task. A more detailed picture was obtained in the analysis of frequency of small saccades, which revealed significant effects for task, $F(2,26) = 92.7$, $p < 0.001$, cursor condition, $F(4,52) = 11.7$, $p < 0.001$, and a significant interaction, $F(8,104) = 3.5$, $p < 0.05$. The frequency of small saccades was higher in the reading task compared to image exploration and gaze typing. Generally, more small saccades occurred in the no feedback compared to the cursor conditions, apart from the smoothed cursor condition (see Figure 1C).

Task performance measures for gaze typing revealed poorest results for the smoothed/delayed cursor condition. Subjects were significantly slower (task completion time) and made more errors (total number of errors, number of repeated activations and number of erroneous entries) with the delayed cursor, all $F > 15$, $p < 0.001$. There were no differences between all other cursor conditions, including no feedback.

For reading we found a main effect for reading time per word, $F(4,52) = 3.7$, $p < 0.05$. Subjects were slower in the no feedback condition (280 ms) and fastest with the smoothed cursor (257 ms). Pairwise testing revealed a significant difference between these two conditions only. A similar finding was observed for frequency of regressive saccades. Again we found a main effect for cursor condition, $F(4,52) = 4.5$, $p < 0.01$. Fewest regressive saccades were made in the smoothed cursor condition, which differed significantly from no feedback and delayed feedback condition

($p < 0.05$, pairwise testing). No significant effect was found concerning the recognition performance of target words, but a similar trend was observed with poorest performance for no feedback and delayed cursor condition.

The analysis of recognition performance for cutouts in the image exploration task revealed no main effect of cursor condition, $F(4,52) = 2.01$, $p = 0.09$. However, the trend was similar as in the reading task, with poorest recognition performance in the no feedback and best performance in direct and noisy feedback condition.

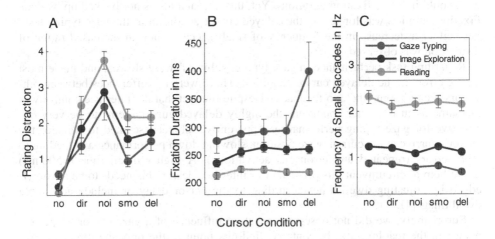

Fig. 1. Effect of cursor feedback on subjective ratings of distraction (A), fixation duration (B) and the frequency of small sized saccades (C) for three different tasks. Larger values in (A) indicate higher level of subjective distraction during the task. Abbreviations cursor condition: no = no feedback, dir = direct, noi = direct and noisy, smo = smoothed, del = smoothed and delayed.

4   Discussion

Our results show that perceived distraction by a gaze cursor is strongest in the reading task; especially the noisy cursor was rated as disturbing. Accordingly, cursor feedback seems not appropriate if an interface contains text or images. For gaze typing, however, a cursor seems less detrimental; it might be even experienced as useful. This raises the question of what to do if mixed contents, i.e. text, images and buttons, are present? No cursor presentation might be one option. Another one is a configuration, with the cursor visible only in the spatial extent of buttons. Consequently, this cursor would switch on and off abruptly when the user moves the gaze across the interface. This might lead to new and probably unwanted effects of distraction [6]. A possible solution would be to replace the rapid on- and offsets by more gradual fading.

The gaze cursor also induces direct effects on the control of eye movements by increasing fixation durations and influencing the frequency of small saccades. Contrary to the rating of distraction this effect was smaller for reading than for image exploration and gaze typing. The feeling of subjective distraction is thus not related to objective effects on behavioral control. Particularly, the highly disturbing effect of a noisy cursor is not reflected in data of fixation duration. Unexpectedly, the frequency of small saccades decreased when a cursor was shown. This might reflect efforts of the visual system to cope with the distracting event by stabilizing the gaze, which, in turn, could increase fixation durations. Yet, this explanation is not backed up by data. Fixation duration was longest in the delayed cursor condition of the gaze typing task, but neither a decrease in the frequency of small saccades nor an increased rating of distraction was observed.

Regarding task performance in gaze typing, subjects' were slowest and made most typing errors in the delayed cursor condition. There were no differences between other cursor conditions (incl. no feedback). Despite the fact that the interface control was the same as in the other conditions the highly delayed cursor seems to be very obstructive for gaze typing performance. Apparently, subjects' seemed to wait for the cursor to arrive at the current gaze position, slowing down performance and leading to more errors (repeated and erroneous activations). A higher dwell time (>500 ms) might help to circumvent this problem. For interface design this needs to be acknowledged by adjusting dwell times according to the cursor delay or include adjustable dwell times [4].

Surprisingly, we did not observe a negative influence of a gaze cursor on performance in the reading task. In contrary, findings point in the opposite direction. According to our results, performance in both tasks, i.e. word and cutout recognition, was poorer for the no feedback compared to the cursor conditions (apart from delayed cursor). Despite the increase in fixation duration, reading time per word and the frequency of regressive saccades decreased, both indicating enhanced reading performance. We are not aware of any theoretical or empirical background that could explain or support these findings. Therefore, further empirical testing is needed for clarification of this surprising effect.

Acknowledgements. This research was supported by grants from the German ministry of education and research (BMBF 16SV5843) to the project FAIR.

References

1. Jacob, R.J.K.: Eye movement-based human-computer interaction techniques: Toward non-command interfaces. In: Hartson, H.R., Hix, D. (eds.) Advances in Human-Computer Interaction, vol. 4, pp. 151–190. Ablex Publishing Co. (1993)
2. Majaranta, P.: Text Entry by Eye Gaze. Dissertation. In: Interactive Technology, vol. 11. University of Tampere, Tampere (2009)
3. Murata, A., Uetsugi, R., Hayami, T.: Study on Cursor Shape Suitable for Eye-gaze Input System. In: Kurosu, M. (ed.) HCII/HCI 2013, Part IV. LNCS, vol. 8007, pp. 312–319. Springer, Heidelberg (2013)

4. Helmert, J.R., Pannasch, S., Velichkovsky, B.M.: Influences of dwell time and cursor control on the performance in gaze driven typing. Journal of Eye Movement Research 2, 1–8 (2008)

5. Spakov, O.: Comparison of eye movement filters used in HCI. In: Proceedings of the Symposium on Eye Tracking Research and Applications, pp. 281–284. ACM, Santa Barbara (2012)

6. Yantis, S., Jonides, J.: Abrupt visual onsets and selective attention: evidence from visual search. Journal of Experimental Psychology: Human Perception and Performance 10, 601–621 (1984)

Easy to Use Driving Behavior Analysis Using DriveLab

Tobias Heffelaar[1], Jorrit Kuipers[2], Jonas Andersson[3],
Leon Wiertz[1], and Lucas P.J.J. Noldus[1]

[1] Noldus Information Technology BV Wageningen, The Netherlands
{T.heffelaar,L.wiertz,L.noldus}@noldus.nl
[2] Green Dino BV Wageningen, The Netherlands
Jorrit@greendino.nl
[3] Smart Eye AB Göteborg, Sweden
Jonas@smarteye.se

Abstract. With the ever increasing computerization in vehicles it becomes essential to assess the impact these technologies have on drivers. DriveLab is an easy to use system for measuring and analyzing driver behavior. Introduced by Green Dino, Noldus Information Technology and SmartEye, it is designed to support researchers' need to quickly record and analyze a driver's behavior. It records common driver performance measures and various (cognitive) workload measures. Using real-time date exchange, data analysis can start immediately after a trial.

Drivelab is built on Green Dino's driving simulator, SmartEye's Smart Eye Pro and Noldus' The Observer XT.

Keywords: Driving Simulator, Driver Performance Measurement, Workload, Human Factors analysis, Systems Integration.

1   Introduction

The number of computer-based technologies in vehicles has increased exponentially over the last thirty years. One of the contributing factors are the high-speed ICT developments, such as miniaturization, in personalized computer technology; most people will carry at least one computational device with them during the day. For new generations of drivers cars are an extension of their plugged-in lives, with iPods and other gadgets (USA Today, 2009).

Parallel to that the automotive industry has significantly increased the number of features in vehicles. They increase comfort (climate control), fuel efficiency (eco drive) and safety (connected car). Despite the aim of a significant number of these systems to support drivers (Advanced Driver Assistance Systems, ADAS), they can also act as a source of distraction, that increases the complexity of driving. Combining this with the fact that distraction plays a role in most (near) accidents [1], it is crucial to ensure newly introduced systems do not add complexity nor increase distraction.

It is common to test the impact of systems on driver performance, distraction and cognitive workload, as a means to ensure new (ADAS) systems do not overload nor

C. Stephanidis (Ed.): HCII 2014 Posters, Part I, CCIS 434, pp. 330–334, 2014.
© Springer International Publishing Switzerland 2014

distract drivers [2]. Preferably in a controlled environment, such as a driving simulator. Numerous proven driver observation methods, such as expert observation, lateral vehicle displacement and eye tracking), are available for driving simulator testing. Often these methods focus on different aspects of a driver's actions. So a multi-method research approach is important for researchers, to get the complete picture. However, in most studies only a small set of behavioral data is recorded, as a significant amount of knowledge is required to apply the individual data collection systems for the methods properly, so combining these techniques in one study is beyond the reach of most researchers. Another hurdle is linking the data from the different systems, which is time-consuming and frequently requiring advanced computer skills. This sometimes leads to controversial results. At the same time the pressure on researchers to produce is increasing.

2   DriveLab

With DriveLab, developed in the Advanced Driver Vehicle Interface in a Complex Environment (ADVICE) project [3], GreenDino, Noldus Information Technology and SmartEye introduce an easy to use, flexible and real-time multimodal driving behavior analysis tool. DriveLab is based on The Observer XT, Noldus' tool for behavioral analysis for over 20 years [4, 5, 6]. It integrates a multi-camera remote 3D eye tracker [7, 8] and a fixed-base medium fidelity driving simulator [9, 10]. Each system has its own strengths and has proven its value in numerous experiments [11 - 14]. The systems are synchronized using the Meinberg NTP client, to ensure accurate synchronization of all systems with a central computer clock [15].

Fig. 1. Driving simulator with eye tracking in action

2.1   Driving Simulator

The driving simulator consists of three screens providing a 140 degrees visual field, and a real-world steering column, seat gearbox and foot pedals. The simulator has a pre-defined set of driving adaptable scenarios that covers all common driving tasks (such as car following, and city driving) in various driving conditions (e.g. day/night, fog). This allows the behavior of other traffic to be adjusted to create busy traffic. The simulator is not only used for generating the test environment it is also a source of driver performance data.

2.2   Noldus Communication Framework

The Noldus Communication Framework (NCF [16]) is an implementation of the Advanced Message Queuing Protocol (AMQP) [17]. It is a system that supports real-time scalable and flexible data exchange between the data acquisitions systems (SmartEye Pro and driving simulator) and the data recording systems (The Observer XT). NCF is an open communication framework, designed to easily extend the system with additional measurement systems such as acquisition of psycho-physiological signals or facial expressions

2.3   The Observer XT

The Observer XT is used for the collection and analysis of behavioral data. It allows integrated analysis and visualization of multimodal data, such as headway a video of the driving environment and gaze events (fig 2). Its data filtering features enables zooming in on specific situations (e.g. approaching a crossing) and driver characteristics (e.g. age and experience of drivers). The package is completed by a keen set of statistics.

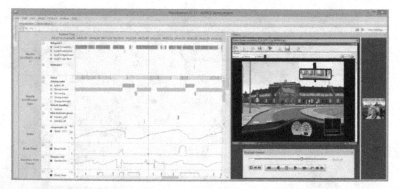

Fig. 2. The Observer XT: integrated display of the driver's main front screen with gaze overlay, gaze events (red colored bars), driving tasks (multi-colored bars), and vehicle parameters (red/green/blue lines)

2.4   SmartEye Pro

The 3-camera eye tracker supports free camera placement for optimal unobtrusive tracking. It uses an open coordinate system, to be used by other systems. The eye tracker has a big head box and a large tracking area, which allows for natural head motion.

3   Conclusion

Combined, these systems provide the most commonly used parameters for detecting distraction and inattention, measuring driver performance, such as speed variations and headway, and multiple cognitive workload measures (such as pupil dilation and steering reversal rate).

A unique feature is the matching of gaze point with other traffic, traffic lights and road signs (objects that move around, varying in size in the virtual environment). The fully automated matching results in Regions of Interest (ROIs) with varying size, location and existence, something which usually requires labor-intensive manual annotation. Additionally the distance at which these RoIs are seen is recorded.

References

1. Dingus, T.A., et al.: The 100-car Naturalistic Driving Study, Phase II – Results of the 100-Car Field Experiment, National Highway Traffic Safety Admin, Report No. DOT HS 810 593 (2006)
2. Chisholm, S.L., Caird, J.K., Lockhart, J., Fern, L., Teteris, E.: Driving performance while engaged in MP-3 player interaction: Effects of practice and task difficulty on PRT and eye movements. In: Driving Assessment 2007: 4th International Driving Symposium on Human Factors in Driver Assessment, Training, and Vehicle Design (2007)
3. ADVICE project: http://www.noldus.com/projects/advice
4. Zimmerman, P.H., Bolhuis, J.E., Willemsen, A., Meyer, E.S., Noldus, L.P.: The Observer XT: A tool for the integration and synchronization of multimodal signals. Behavior Research Methods 41(3), 731–735 (2009)
5. The Observer XT: http://www.noldus.com/observer
6. Grootjen, M., Neerincx, M.A., van Weert, J.C.M., Truong, K.P.: Measuring cognitive task load on a naval ship: Implications of a real world environment. In: Schmorrow, D.D., Reeves, L.M. (eds.) HCII 2007 and FAC 2007. LNCS (LNAI), vol. 4565, pp. 147–156. Springer, Heidelberg (2007)
7. Smart Eye, http://smarteye.se/products/simulator-eye-trackers
8. Se Zhang, Z., Lu, G., Wang, Y., Tian, D., Wu, J.: The Effect of Moving Objects on Drivers' Gaze Point at Unsignalized Intersections with Mixed Traffic. Bridges 10 (2014) 9780784412442-235
9. Dino, G.: Dutch simulators (May 28, 2008), http://www.dutchsimulators.nl
10. Weevers, I., Kuipers, J., Brugman, A., Zwiers, J., Dijk, E.M.A.G., Nijholt, A.: The virtual driving instructor: a multi-based system for driving instruction (2003)
11. Jones, M., Jones, M., Olthoff, T., Harris, S.: The cab technology integration lab: A locomotive simulator for human factors research. In: Proceedings of the Human Factors and Ergonomics Society Annual Meeting, vol. 54(24), pp. 2110–2114. SAGE Publications (2010)

12. Gd Anand, S., Terken, J., Hogema, J.: The effect of cognitive load on adaptation to differences in steering wheel force feedback level. In: Proceedings of the 5th International Conference on Automotive User Interfaces and Interactive Vehicular Applications, pp. 158–164. ACM (October 2013)

13. van Leeuwen, P.M., Happee, R., de Winter, J.C.F.: Investigating the Effect of a Visual Search Task for Simulator-Based Driver Training. In: 7th International Driving Symposium on Human Factors in Driver Assessment, Training, and Vehicle Design, vol. (65) (2013)

14. De Winter, J.C.F., De Groot, S., Mulder, M., Wieringa, P.A., Dankelman, J., Mulder, J.A.: Relationships between driving simulator performance and driving test results. Ergonomics 52(2), 137–153 (2009)

15. Ofli, F., Chaudhry, R., Kurillo, G., Vidal, R., Bajcsy, R.: Berkeley mhad: A comprehensive multimodal human action database. In: 2013 IEEE Workshop on Applications of Computer Vision (WACV), pp. 53–60. IEEE (2013)

16. Bouma, H., Baan, J., Borsboom, S., van Zon, K., Luo, X., Loke, B., Dijk, J.: WPSS: Watching people security services. In: SPIE Security+ Defence, pp. 89010H–89010H. International Society for Optics and Photonics (October 2013)

17. O'Hara, J.: Toward a commodity enterprise middleware. ACM Queue 5(4), 48–55 (2007)

Hand-Held Support for Spatial Awareness
for the Dismounted Soldier

Björn J.E. Johansson, Charlotte Hellgren,
Per-Anders Oskarsson, and Jonathan Svensson

FOI-Swedish Defence Research Agency, Linköping, Sweden
{bjorn.j.e.johansson,charlotte.hellgren,per-anders.oskarsson,
jonathan.svensson}@foi.se

Abstract. This contribution presents a summary of activities performed in an ongoing military research project aiming at investigating the impact of navigational support on spatial awareness. Investigated tasks are e.g. indication of direction to objects beyond visual range with and without navigational support, display size, performance time, and use of GPS device in darkness. The results indicate that the ability to keep track of targets in the terrain without a technical aid is very poor, but with a GPS device targets can be indicated with relatively high precision. Precision on target indication is slightly better with a larger display, it seems possible to indicate as fast as 5 seconds with a GPS device without impairments of precision, and a GPS device can be used for target indication in darkness. Spatial ability measured by PTSOT can discriminate important aspects of spatial ability with direct relevance for navigation and target indication.

Keywords: Spatial awareness, digital maps, navigational support, spatial tests.

1 Introduction

Military forces utilize different kinds of navigational support such as digital maps, handheld GPS devices and electronic compasses. Efforts are taken to develop systems for dismounted soldiers, aiming to support team spatial awareness, target indication and navigation. This contribution presents findings and conclusions drawn from an ongoing Swedish military research project with the focus to explore how hand-held navigational support such as GPS devices, digital maps and electronic compasses impact spatial awareness. The aim has been to explore how technical support can be used to enhance the ability to navigate and to create and maintain a high level of spatial for individual soldiers and, eventually, groups of soldiers in the battlefield. Several nations have ongoing soldier system projects with different levels of ambition, ranging from basic navigation support to fully networked battle management systems for order distribution, blue force tracking and target indication. Several scientific studies have been performed to improve knowledge concerning basic issues such as display type/placement/size and what information should be presented to the solider [1-2], [10], [12], [16]. A common feature of both the development of support

C. Stephanidis (Ed.): HCII 2014 Posters, Part I, CCIS 434, pp. 335–340, 2014.
© Springer International Publishing Switzerland 2014

systems and research in the area is that technology is needed to improve spatial awareness regarding directions and headings. Spatial awareness, or spatial ability, is often described as the ability of maintaining a sense of location and direction while moving about in the environment [19]. Previous research in our group [7-8], [13-14] and other research [3], [9], [11], [15], [17-19], has pinpointed some factors with influence on the ability to navigate and at the same time being aware of the direction to several positions. Since 2010, we have performed several studies with the purpose of investigating different aspects of technical support for spatial awareness, with both military and non-military personnel, both in rural and urban areas, and to some extent during night-op conditions. All studies have been conducted in field settings. A multi-methodological approach has been applied, combining controlled experiments in a natural setting with performance measures, rating questions, free text answers, spatial tests, and focus groups, in order to gain a holistic understanding of the problem. We have thus aimed to get practical experiences in terms of both performance measures and qualitative data, regarding design and applied usage of support systems for target indication and navigation. Below follows brief descriptions of the performed studies, the most important conclusions and a discussion about the implications for the design of hand-held support systems for dismounted soldiers.

2   Performed Studies

The overall purpose of this project is to investigate the possibilities of supporting soldiers' spatial awareness. Presently four studies have been performed.

Three different spatial tests were used to assess spatial ability. SBSOD [5] was used in all studies and PTSOT [6] and the Paper Folding Test [4] was used in the last three studies. PTSOT had highest correlation with precision on target indication. Results on PTSOT were thus used to categorize participants according to spatial ability.

2.1   Study 1 – Navigation and Target Indication in Urban Areas [8]

The purpose of study 1 was to explore if usage of a handheld GPS device during navigation could support spatial awareness during target indication in an urban area.

18 novices participated. They were divided into three groups (between-subjects design), with different amount of information on the GPS map (no targets / three targets / five targets). The participants' task was to by foot navigate to six waypoints with the aid of the GPS device. At each waypoint they should indicate the direction to predefined targets in the terrain. The targets (three or five) were continuously presented on the GPS map for two of the groups during navigation, while the third group had to remember three targets' positions shown on a paper map at the start of the navigation. The GPS device was only used during navigation, i.e. it was not used during the target indication task.

Precision on the indication task was equal whether the positions were presented on the GPS map or not. However, the precision deteriorated during navigation, with significantly lower precision at waypoint 3-6 (30 – 40 degrees deviation) than at the start (average 14 degrees deviation). There was no correlation between precision and SBSOD.

This shows that the ability to maintain target directions during navigation is limited even when using a navigational aid such as a GPS device. However, in this experiment the participants did not use the GPS device when the indication task was performed, which meant that they had to rely on their memory of the target positions, either from the GPS-map or from the paper map.

2.2   Study 2 – Navigation and Target Indication in Wooded Terrain [8], [10]

The purpose of study 2 was to investigate if usage of a handheld GPS device during target indication could enhance precision.

16 novices participated in the study. Their task was to navigate to three waypoints in the terrain using a handheld GPS device. At each waypoint they should point out the direction to five predefined targets in the terrain. There were two conditions, 1) the GPS device was used both for navigation and target indication and 2) the GPS was only used for navigation, i.e. the participants had to remember the target positions from a paper map shown at the start of the navigation. The study had a within subjects design, i.e. all subjects performed both conditions.

Precision on target indication was relatively high when the GPS device was used (average 12 degrees deviation), but poor when it was not used (average 41 degrees deviation). When the GPS device was not used during target indication participants with high spatial ability performed target indication significantly better (average 31 degrees deviation) than those with low spatial ability (average 51 degrees deviation). When the GPS device was used there was no difference between participants with low and high spatial ability. However, the amount of time used for target indication was significantly longer when the GPS device was used.

This indicates that precision on target indication can be considerably increased when a GPS device is used. Also, when target indication is not supported by a GPS device, the precision on target indication decreases throughout navigating and this deterioration is largest for participants with low spatial ability. The increase in target indication time with the GPS device indicates that it may not be appropriate to use in time critical situations.

2.3   Study 3 – Indication of Direction with Digital Map – Effects of Display Size and Time Constraints [13]

Study 2 showed that target indication with a small screen (2.6") without time limit can be performed with relatively high precision. The purpose of study 3 was to investigate how time pressure and display size affect target indication precision.

16 novices participated in the study. Their task was to indicate the direction to symbols shown on a digital map. The symbols were either shown on a small display (3.5" iPhone) or a large display (9.7" iPad). Also, the element of navigation was excluded, so all target indications were performed at the same position. A time limit of 5, 10, 15, or 20 seconds per target was used. The study was performed with within

subjects design, i.e. all participants tested both displays with all five time limits. At each condition they indicated the direction to five symbols.

Precision was significantly higher with the large screen (average 8 degrees deviation) compared to the small screen (average 10 degrees deviation). The time constraints did not affect precision with any of the two display sizes. When the small screen was used, subjects with high spatial ability (according to PTSOT) performed the indication task with higher precision (average 8 degrees deviation) than subjects with low spatial ability (average 12 degrees deviation). When the large screen was used there was no performance difference between participants with high or low spatial ability.

This indicates that precision on an indication task can be slightly higher when a larger screen is used. However, in this experiment this gain in precision was relatively small and must be weighed against the drawback of handling a larger screen in the field. Furthermore, when spatial ability is considered, in this experiment only participants with low spatial ability had lower precision with the small screen.

2.4   Study 4 – Target Designation and Indication with GPS Map in Night-op Conditions [14]

The previous studies showed that target indication supported by a GPS map can be performed with relatively high precision in daylight. Since military units often perform night missions the purpose of study 4 was to investigate target designation and target indication in darkness.

Ten experienced officers participated. Five performed target designation of cardboard figures visible in the terrain, and five made terrain indications from received target information (direction and distance). The tasks were performed both with a GPS device map (2.6" low light screen) and with a standardized verbal target designation protocol. All participants were equipped with night vision goggles. The participants and further eight officers also took part in focus group discussions concerning design and usage of a GPS device in night-op conditions.

Precision on target indication was approximately equal when target information was given either on the GPS device (average 22 degrees) or as verbal target indication (average 25 degrees deviation). For target designation the results of precision are because of data loss more uncertain (11 - 14 degrees deviation). Performance time was longer when the GPS device was used, both for target indication (average 21 s increase) and target designation (average 8 s increase), than using verbal protocol.

The focus group discussions provided important information, e.g. for requirements specification of a potential GPS device, but also for other related soldier systems. The most important conclusions was that it must be possible to place the device freely on the uniform system as well as attached to the forearm (like a wristwatch), it must be rugged, have easily identifiable hardware buttons, a screen that works both in day- and night-ops conditions and present a highly detailed map.

This study indicates that it may be possible to use a GPS device for target indication in night op-conditions. A drawback is that performance time is longer when a GPS device is used. However, this may partly be remedied by training and developing methods of use – and a GPS device will probably not be used in time critical situations.

3   Discussion

There is an obvious need to support spatial awareness with some type of digital navigational device. Firstly, our studies have shown that target indication is improved by use of a GPS map. However, according to study 1 and 2, a necessary condition for this seems to be that the GPS device is actually used during target indication, not only shortly prior to it, for example during navigation. However, the participants in these studies were novices without prior training in using the GPS devices for these kinds of tasks, and targets were not of vital importance. It is therefore possible that training and use of task relevant scenarios can support memorization of direction to positions shown during navigation and thus improve spatial awareness.

Secondly, study 3 showed that time pressure during target indication supported by a digital map in optimal conditions does not affect accuracy even if task time is restricted to 5 seconds. On the other hand, in a more realistic and complex situation time constraints may have a larger influence. Also, a GPS device will most likely not be used in time critical situations. Our results also showed a slight improvement of precision on target indication with a larger screen. This small increase must however be weighed against the drawbacks of carrying, providing power for, and handling a larger display in the field.

Thirdly, study 4 showed that it is possible to use a GPS device for target indication in night op conditions with night vision goggles. The focus groups provided valuable information on a number of critical issues regarding the design of a GPS support device, e.g. the importance of ruggedness, flexibility in placement, ease of use and the need for highly detailed maps.

Finally, it was found that the spatial test PTSOT has high capability to discriminate spatial performance on target indication, a task with high relevance for applied settings. A similar, although lower, relation was also found between the Paper Folding Test and task performance. On the other hand, no relation between task performance and SBSOD was found which is somewhat contradictory to other research [5].

Presently, the aim of the project is to investigate how the gained experiences can be transferred to support platoon and squad leaders' spatial awareness and command on the battlefield by navigational support systems.

References

1. Ashbrook, D., Clawson, J., Lyons, K., Patel, N., Starner, T.: Quickdraw: The Impact of Mobility and On-Body Placement on Device Access Time. In: Proceeding of the CHI 2008 Conference on Human Factors in Computing Systems, pp. 219–222. ACM (2008)
2. Bos, J.C., Tack, D.W.: Visual display alternatives for infantry soldiers – a literature review. Technical report, Defence Research and Development, Toronto, Canada (2005)

3. Downs, R.M.: Maps and mappings as metaphors for spatial representation. In: Liben, L.S., Patterson, A.H., Newcombe, N. (eds.) Spatial representation and behavior across the life span: Theory and application. Academic Press (1981)

4. Ekstrom, R.B., French, J.W., Harman, H.H.: Kit of factor referenced cognitive tests. Educational Testing Service, Princeton, NJ (1976)

5. Hegarty, M., Richardson, A.E., Montello, D., Lovelace, K., Subbiah, I.: Development of a self-report measure of environmental spatial ability. Intelligence 30, 425–447 (2002)

6. Hegarty, M., Waller, D.: A dissociation between mental rotation and perspective-taking spatial abilities. Intelligence 32, 175–191 (2004)

7. Hellgren, C., Hörberg, U., Sandberg, S.: Soldatens Informationshantering. Report No. FOI-R–3325–SE. FOI, Linköping (2011)

8. Hellgren, C., Johansson, B.J.E., Oskarsson, P-A. & Svensson, J.: Gruppens informationshantering – Lägesuppfattning vid Förflyttning. Report No. FOI-R–3561–SE. FOI, Linköping (2012).

9. Ishikawa, T., Fujiwara, H., Imai, O., Okabe, A.: Wayfinding with a GPS-based mobile navigation system: A comparison with maps and direct experience. J. Env. Psy. 28(1), 74–82 (2008)

10. Johansson, J.E.B., Hellgren, C., Oskarsson, P.-A., Svensson, J.: Supporting situation awareness on the move - the role of technology for spatial orientation in the field. In: Comes, T., Friedrich, F., Fortier, S., Geldermann, J., Müller, T. (eds.) The 10th International ISCRAM Conference, Baden-Baden, Germany, pp. 442–451 (2013)

11. Liben, L.S., Myers, L.J., Christensen, A.E.: Identifying Locations and Directions on Field and Representational Mapping Tasks: Predictors of Success. Spatial Cognition & Computation: An Interdisciplinary Journal 10(2-3), 105–134 (2010)

12. Mitchell, K.B., Sampson, J.B., Short, M., Wilson, R.: Display options for Dismounted Infantry: Flexible Display Center Human Factors. Preliminary User Survey. U.S.Army Research Laboratory: Human Research and Engineering Directorate, Aberdeen Proving Ground. MD 21005-5425. Technical Report NATICK/TR-07/007 (2006)

13. Oskarsson, P.-A., Johansson, J.B., Svensson, J., Hellgren, C., Allberg, H.: Invisning med elektronisk karta – Betydelsen av skärmstorlek och tillgänglig tid för invisning. Report No. FOI-R–3685–SE. FOI: Linköping (2013)

14. Oskarsson, P-A., Svensson, J., Allberg, H.: Målangivelse och målutpekning i mörker. Jämförelse mellan att använda GPS och muntliga utgångspunkter. Report No. FOI-R–3803–SE. FOI, Linköping (2013)

15. Prestopnik, J.L., Roskos-Ewoldsen, B.: The relations among wayfinding strategy use, sense of direction, sex, familiarity, and wayfinding ability. J. Env. Psy. 20, 177–191 (2000)

16. Sampson, J.B., Boynton, A.C., Mitchell, K.B., Magnifico, D.S., Dupont, F.J.: User Evaluation of a Soldier Flexible Display Personal Digital Assistant. U.S.Army Research Laboratory: Human Research and Engineering Directorate, Aberdeen Proving Ground. MD 21005-5425. Technical Report NATICK/TR-08/20 (2008)

17. Thorndyke, P.W., Hayes-Roth, B.: Differences in spatial knowledge acquired from maps and navigation. Cog. Psy. 14(4), 560–589 (1982)

18. Waller, D., Montello, D.R., Richardson, A.E., Hegarty, M.: Orientation Specificity and Spatial Updating of Memories for Layouts. J. Exp. Psy.: Learning, Memory, and Cognition 28(6), 1051–1063 (2002)

19. Wolbers, T., Hegarthy, M.: What determines our navigational abilities? Trends in Cog. Sci. 14(13), 138–146 (2010)

Research of Frequency Resolution with fMRI
for a Decoding System from Primary Auditory Cortex

Tatsuya Kaneko[1], Hironobu Satoh[2], Kyoko Shibata[1], and Yoshio Inoue[1]

[1] Kochi University of Technology Miyanokuchi 185, Tosayamada, Kami, Kochi, Japan
[2] Kochi National College of Technology Monobeotsu 200-1, Nangoku, Kochi, Japan
140048z@ugs.kochi-tech.ac.jp,
satoh@ee.kochi-ct.ac.jp,
{shibata.kyoko,inoue.yoshio}@kochi-tech.ac.jp
http://www.kochi-tech.ac.jp,
http://www.kochi-ct.ac.jp

Abstract. The aims of this study are reconstructing audio signal from fMRI (functional magnetic resonance imaging) data measured primary auditory cortex of human and developing brain machine interface. In order to develop a sound decoding system from brain activity, it is necessary to distinguish brain activities which respond to several frequencies of stimuli. In this paper, it is shown that the brain activities have significant differences which respond to semitone-difference stimuli with 3-mm spatial resolution of fMRI.

Keywords: Auditory cortex, Decoding system, Machine learning.

1   Introduction

fMRI is used to measure brain activities and generates structural images of a brain. fMRI generates images with high resolution compered to other functional brain imaging analyses. Previous research1 suggests that neurons which respond to a specific frequency of sound are known in primary auditory cortex. The aim of this study is to reconstruct audio signals from brain activities and to develop a brain machine interface. In order to develop a method of sound decoding from a human brain, brain mapping data that respond to several sound frequencies of stimuli have to be collected. The spatial resolution of fMRI is as large as 3-mm voxel. Therefore, if significant differences are seen between the brain activities which stimulated by semitones of different frequencies, it is capable of being realized to develop a sound decoding system from images generated by fMRI. As a feasible study, the data showed significant differences between brain activities which respond to stimuli by semitones of different frequencies.

2   Methods

On the basis of written informed consent, nine healthy subjects were participated in this experiment. Subjects were in supine position inside the fMRI bore of a

C. Stephanidis (Ed.): HCII 2014 Posters, Part I, CCIS 434, pp. 341–345, 2014.
© Springer International Publishing Switzerland 2014

MAGNETOM Verio 3T (SIEMENS). The functional images were acquired by EPI (echo planer imaging) sequence with 3.0-mm-thick adjacent slices (TR 3000 ms; TE 30 ms; flip angle 90°; field of view 192 × 192 mm).

In this experiment, stimuli were presented to confirm a significant difference between the brain activities which respond to stimuli by semitones of different frequencies.

fMRI gives off driving sound continually and it may adversely affect the brain activities when measuring data. To reduce ill effects of fMRI driving sound, stimuli were selected. Fig.1 shows the result of frequency analysis of fMRI driving sound. As can be seen from Fig.1, the driving sound of fMRI had the lowest intensity in 2kHz band in the audible range (30-15kHz). For this reason, C7 (2097Hz), C#7 (2217.46Hz), D7 (2349.32Hz) and D#7 (2489.02Hz) were selected as the sound stimuli. A pure tone was used for each stimulus. The stimuli were generated by Nuendo6 on a personal computer and were stored 24-bit of quantifying bit number with a sampling frequency of 44.1kHz. Stimuli were presented subjects binaurally with electrostatic headphones connected audio I/O, FireFace UC.

Stimuli were presented subjects in the form of block design (Fig.2) .Block design is one of the experimental designs of fMRI test, which considers the BOLD (blood oxygenation level dependency) signal. current of blood increases active spots in the brain, which is called the BOLD effect. BOLD signal reaches the highest level from four to six seconds and returns a baseline from twenty to thirty seconds after a stimulus. fMRI make brain activities visible by observing the BOLD signal. Every EPIs (echo planar imaging) were taken five seconds after stimulus presentation in order to wait for the BOLD signal reaches the highest level.

In the data analysis we made use of MatLab r2007b (The MathWorks Inc.) and SPM8 (statistical parametric mapping 8) software package[2]. To analyze the data, spatial pre-processing is needed. Images generated by fMRI are not measured at the same time to be exact, however they are generated by many slices of picture. First, images have to be realigned by using a six parameter (rigid body) spatial transformation to analyze on SPM8. Second, fMRI images are normalized into standard space defined by MNI (montreal neurological institute) . The shape of brains are different from each other, it makes possible to compare brain activities of different subjects by normalizing each subject's brains to MNI template image. Finally, the images are smoothed to suppress noise and effects due to residual differences in functional and gyral anatomy during inter-subject averaging with an isotropic 8 mm Gaussian kernel.

The analyses were performed only in auditory cortex by filtering brodmann areas 41 and 42 (Fig.3) on SPM8.

To acquire significant differences, called "contrasts" in SPM analysis, t-tests were performed between four different brain activities, stimulated C7, C#7, D7, D#7.

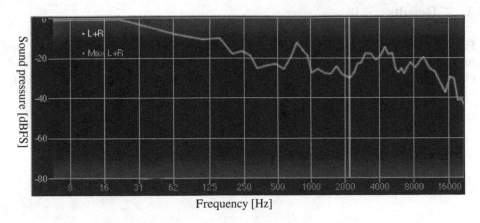

Fig. 1. Frequency analysis of driving sound of fMRI

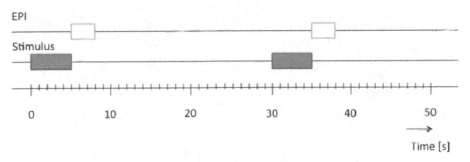

Fig. 2. Experimental design

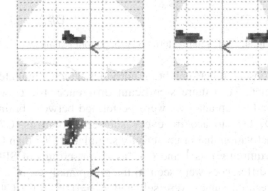

Fig. 3. Brodmann 41-42 area

3 Results

Fig.4 shows group model analyses of the activation patterns in auditory cortex in response to four different stimuli, C7, C#7, D7 and D#7. All tonotopic mappings were obtained contrast to brain activation with no artificial stimuli. The threshold value of t-test was selected as p=0.1.

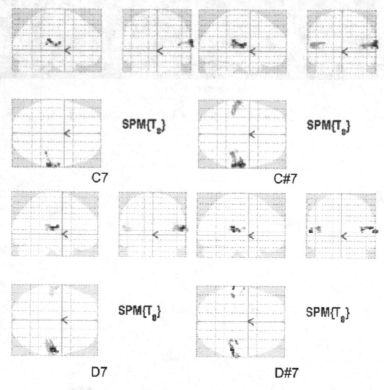

Fig. 4. Activation patterns of group model analyses

Distinctions were observed between brain activities which stimulated by semitones of different frequencies. To acquire significant difference, t-tests were performed. Individual analyses and group analyses were performed between brain activities, C7-C#7, C#7-D7 and D7-D#7 to acquire every subject's contrasts. C7-C#7 indicates significantly higher activation that brain activity stimulated C#7 than C7. In this case, contrasts had been acquired C7 as 1 and C#7 as -1 on settings of SPM8. Fig.5 indicates that significant differences were seen in the group analyses of C7-C#7, C#7-D7 and D7-D#7. The threshold values were selected as p=0.08 in C7-C#7 analysis, and p=0.05 in C#7-D7 and D7-D#7 analyses.

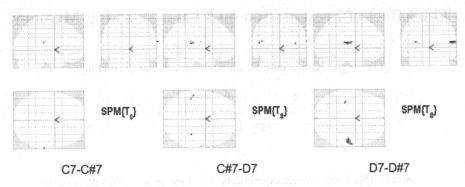

Fig. 5. Significant differences

4   Discussion

Assuming that significant differences are confirmed between brain activities stimulated by semitones of different frequencies, it is feasible to distinguish brain activities and to develop a sound decoding system with spatial resolution of fMRI. As Fig.5 indicates, contrasts were observed between brain activities which stimulated by semitones of different frequencies C7, C#7, D7, and D#7. Thus, fMRI has sufficient spatial resolution to develop a sound decoding system.

5   Conclusion and Perspectives

In group analyses, contrasts were observed between brain activities stimulated by semitones of different frequencies. Threshold value was selected as p=0.08 in C7-C#7 analysis, and as p=0.05 in C#7-D7 and D7-D#7 analyses. Our results demonstrate that the brain activity stimulated by semitones of different frequencies can be distinguished by t-tests. To develop a sound decoding system, the brain mapping data which respond to sound stimuli are required. After measuring brain mapping data, mapping data will be distinguished by machine learning.

References

1. Langers, D.R.M., Backes, W.H., van Dijk, P.: Representation of lateralization and tonotopy in primary versus secondary human auditory cortex. NeuroImage 34, 264–273 (2007)
2. SPM, http://www.fil.ion.ucl.ac.uk/spm/software/spm8/ (accessed at March 21, 2014)

The Effect of Presentation on Visual Working Memory

Dae-Hyun Kim[1], Sang-Hyun Kim[2], and Kwanghee Han[1]

[1] Yonsei University, Seoul, Korea
[2] SK Communications Co., Seoul, Korea
{nagguy,shkimjava}@gmail.com, khan@yonsei.ac.kr

Abstract. This paper reports experiments investigating the effect of presentation on visual working memory (VWM) when set-size increases. The capacity of VWM is limited to approximately four items (Luck & Vogel, 1997) and increasing set-size impairs the performance in visual tasks. Also, the performance in visuospatial tasks was better in the simultaneous presentation than in the sequential presentation. However, it is possible that large set-size in the simultaneous presentation caused overload in visual processing, and also, there is a possibility to increase interference among stimuli.Therefore, we speculated that performance in a simultaneous presentation would show a sharper decrease than in a partitioned presentation, which divides stimuli into two halves in order to reduce visual processing load and interference among stimuli when number of stimuli increases. Thus, the experiments with two types of set-size and two types of presentations (simultaneous and partitioned) were performed.The experiment examined whether a probe item was old or novel after seeing 4 or 8 items that appeared at random locations. These items were displayed either in simultaneous or in a partitioned manner. The results revealed a significant interaction between set-size and presentation. In a small set-size condition, performance was better in the simultaneous presentation than in the partitioned presentation. However, no difference was found between performances for both presentations in the large set-size condition, as it was influenced by the partitioned presentation. The results proposed that the partitioned presentation was more stable method to show items than the simultaneous presentation when set-size is large.

1 Introduction

Vision is one of the most important sensation of humans, and that many related researches have been performed over time. Through these researches, it became known that visual information is processed utilizing a variety of factors, including color and shape (Egeth, Virzi, & Garbart,1984; Friedman-Hill & Wolfe, 1995), spatial positioning (Posner, 1980; McCormick & Klein, 1990), brightness differences (Donk & Theeuwes, 2001; Belopolsky, Theeuwes, & Kramer, 2005) and object motions (Saenz, Buracas, & Boynton, 2003). Vision performs visual processing by utilizing these factors, and such processing is influenced by total number of stimuli. This being that human's capacity of Visual Working Memory (VWM) is limited to approximately 4 items. (Luck & Vogel, 1997). Thus, increase in set-size would impair the

C. Stephanidis (Ed.): HCII 2014 Posters, Part I, CCIS 434, pp. 346–350, 2014.

performance in visual tasks (Duncan & Humphreys, 1989; Trick & Pylyshyn, 1993), and such a VWM with limited storage capacity does not store the exact information of each individual item. Instead, the relational information of an individual item on the basis of global spatial configuration is used for storage (Jiang, Olson & Chun, 2000).

This strategy of VWM supplements its limitation in storage capacity that visual processing possesses. Therefore, the method of presenting the relational information of stimuli has advantages for the visuospatial tasks. This means that accuracy in simultaneous presentation is higher than sequential presentation when same numbers of stimuli are presented (Lecerf & Ribaupierre, 2005).

However, simultaneous presentation is not always the best method. Rather, when the number of stimuli increases, simultaneous presentation needs to process all of the visual information at once and due to limitation in processing loads, the performance diminishes. On the contrary, it may be considered that the method of presenting the information in parts could reduce the load in visual processing which needs to be done at once. Hence, in this study, we would like to verify the hypothesis which the simultaneous presentation is effective in smaller number of stimuli, and partitioned presentation is more effective for the large number of stimuli.

2 Experiment

Experiment was designed to investigate whether a simultaneous presentation was always better than a partitioned presentation. Experiment had 4 conditions of which 2 set-size (small and large), and 2 presentation conditions (simultaneous and partitioned) for experiment participants to perform visual tasks.

If the overload is occurred for simultaneous presentation with large set-size, the performance result in a simultaneous presentation would be better with partitioned presentation with small set-size, however the performance result in a simultaneous presentation will not be better with partitioned presentation with large set-size.

To investigate this assumption, accuracy rates, hit rate, correct reject rate and Pr score were analyzed as a primary dependent variable.

Pr score was the discrimination measure for Accuracy of confident and non-confident recognition. [probability of a hit minus probability of a false alarm] (Lecerf & Ribaupierre, 2005).

Participants performed all conditions with 2 set-size conditions in 2 presentation conditions.

Participants. Seven undergraduate students participated in exchange for course credit. All subjects had normal or corrected-to-normal vision.

Stimuli. Twenty alphabetical characters (excluding A,E,I,O,U,Y) was used. The size of stimulus on the screen was 1.6°x1.6° and was presented as white character in black background of 15°x15° size.

Procedure. 2 different set-size conditions were used. Set with 4 items designated as small, and set with 8 items designated as large. For the small set-size condition, 4 alphabetical characters were selected randomly from 20 characters pool, and did the same for large set-size by randomly picking 8 characters.

2 different methods of presentation was used, as one being presenting all stimuli at once (simultaneous presentation), and the other being partitioned presentation by sequentially showing presentation which is divided into 2 sets. Each stimulus was displayed for 50msec (ex. For the partitioned presentation, 8 stimuli was divided into 2 sets, and that 4 stimuli were displayed in sequential manner for 200msec, and rest 4 stimuli were displayed after that in 200msec)

When participants pressed "Space" key, fixation is displayed for 2000msec and stimuli were displayed in random locations according to conditions. After that blank screen was displayed for 1000msec, display of Probe was followed. (Figure 1.)

All participants were instructed to press 'z' if the Probe is "Old" and '/' if the Probe is "Novel". There were no limitation in the response time, however we have excluded result exceeding 5000msec.

Participants have performed practice trials between 15 to 20 times, and executed 160 trials (40 trials per each condition). Set-size conditions were displayed randomly, and presentation conditions were presented randomly with counterbalanced sequences.

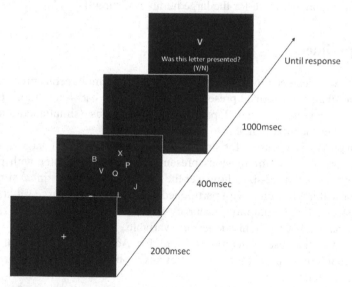

Fig. 1. An example of large set-size and simultaneous condition

3   Result

The experiment data was analyzed in a repeated measure ANOVA.

The accuracy rate was significantly higher in small set-size condition than in large set-size condition. $F(1,6) = 49.743$, $p < .01$. The main effect of set-size conditions in all dependent variables was significant. The main effect of presentation conditions was not significant. $F(1,6) = .763$, $p > .05$. The interaction between set-size and presentation was significant. $F(1,6) = 6.873$, $p < .05$. (Figure 2.)

There was no difference between presentation conditions in hit rate and correct reject rate. $F(1,6) = 1.229$, $p>.05$, $F(1,6) = .795$, $p>.05$, respectively.

The interaction of set-size conditions and presentation conditions in hit rate and correct reject rate was not significant. $F(1,6) = 5.757$, $p>.05$, $F(1,6) = 1.087$, $p>.05$, respectively.

In Pr score, the main effect of presentation conditions was not significant. $F(1,6) = .617$, $p > .05$. However, the interaction of set-size conditions and presentation conditions was significant. $F(1,6) = 9.136, p < .05$.

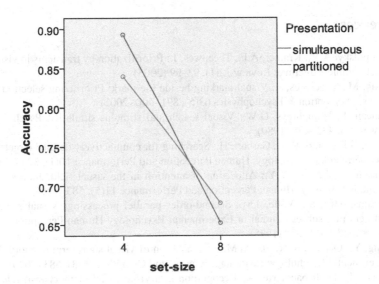

Fig. 2.   Result from Experiment. Total accuracy rate.

4   Discussion

This study confirmed that there is difference in performance per number of stimuli and presentation condition. When the set-size increased, the accuracy decreased, however for partitioned presentation, the decrease in accuracy was smaller than simultaneous presentation. This can be interpreted that simultaneous presentation is better for smaller set-size, but as the set-size gets large, simultaneous presentation is not as good as partitioned presentation, and can be implied that simultaneous presentation is not the best method in all situation.

It can be suggested that there is limitation of how much the information can be processed simultaneously, that presenting large amount of information at once would decrement ability to process, whereas partitioned presentation would reduce amount of information which needs to be processed simultaneously by delaying the process time, in return would increase the overall efficiency of the process.

However, in this study, Hit Rate and Correct reject rate did not showed the meaningful result. This is may be, that the stimuli was displayed at random location, where for partitioned presentation, identification to verify the location information had occurred 2 times which needs of big effort, and may ended up getting penalty.

If the further study fixes the location of stimuli display to reduce such a penalty, partitioned presentation would show more effective results. Despite such penalties, partitioned presentation in large set-size was shown to be effective, meaning that simultaneous presentation is not the best method for all events.

Through further experiments, the effect of partitioned presentation will be investigated through diverse conditions in set-size.

References

1. Belopolsky, A.V., Kramer, A.F., Theeuwes, J.: Prioritization by transients in visual search. Psychonomic Bulletin & Review 12(1), 93–99 (2005)
2. Donk, M., Theeuwes, J.: Visual marking beside the mark: Prioritizing selection by abrupt onsets. . Perception & Psychophysics 63(5), 891–900 (2001)
3. Duncan, J., Humphreys, G.W.: Visual search and stimulus similarity. Psychological Review 96(3), 433–458 (1989)
4. Egeth, H.E., Virzi, R.A., Garbart, H.: Searching for conjunctively defined targets. . Journal of Experimental Psychology: Human Perception and Performance 10(1), 32 (1984)
5. Eriksen, C.W., Yeh, Y.Y.: Allocation of attention in the visual field. Journal of Experimental Psychology: Human Perception and Performance 11(5), 583 (1985)
6. Friedman-Hill, S., Wolfe, J.M.: Second-order parallel processing: Visual search for the odd item in a subset. Journal of Experimental Psychology-Human Perception and Performance 21(3), 531–550 (1995)
7. Jiang, Y., Olson, I.R., Chun, M.M.: Organization of visual short-term memory. Journal of Experimental Psychology: Learning, Memory, and Cognition 26(3), 683 (2000)
8. Lecerf, T., De Ribaupierre, A.: Recognition in a visuospatial memory task: The effect of presentation. . European Journal of Cognitive Psychology 17(1), 47–75 (2005)
9. Luck, S.J., Vogel, E.K.: The capacity of visual working memory for features and conjunctions. Nature 390(6657), 279–281 (1997)
10. McCormick, P.A., Klein, R.: The spatial distribution of attention during covert visual orienting. Acta Psychologica 75(3), 225–242 (1990)
11. Palmer, J.: Attention in visual search: Distinguishing four causes of a set-size effect. . Current Directions in Psychological Science 4(4), 118–123 (1995)
12. Posner, M.I.: Orienting of attention. Quarterly Journal of Experimental Psychology 32(1), 3–25 (1980)
13. Sàenz, M., Buraĉas, G.T., Boynton, G.M.: Global feature-based attention for motion and color. Vision Research 43(6), 629–637 (2003)
14. Trick, L.M., Pylyshyn, Z.W.: What enumeration studies can show us about spatial attention: evidence for limited capacity preattentive processing. Journal of Experimental Psychology: Human Perception and Performance 19(2), 331 (1993)

The Use of EEG to Measure Emotional Response to Tactile Sensation in Evaluation of DSLR Camera Usability

Jung-Yong Kim and Mi-Young Yoon

Department of Industrial and Management Engineering, Hanyang University, Ansan, Korea
miyoungy@hanyang.ac.kr

Abstract. This study explores the possibility of using EEG (electroencephalography) in conducting usability tests of hardware products such as DSLR cameras which require physical contact with hands. Since questionnaire-based usability tests use verbal or lingual expressions about tactile feeling, it is often difficult to precisely indicate the level of the differences. Thus this study took a different approach utilizing EEG technology to directly measure psychophysical responses in order to quantitatively observe the difference in tactile sensation. In the experiment, four different brands of camera with similar market position and outfit design were used. Twenty subjects were asked to complete the same three tasks. They included the primary modes of picture taking: gripping, shuttering, and mode dialing. Among EEG parameters, we chose relative alpha band power (7.5-12.5 Hz) and beta band power (13-30 Hz) on the frontal, parietal, and occipital lobes. Subjects were told to perform the tasks twice, once with closed eyes and again with eyes opened. ANOVA and post-hoc analysis were performed to indicate the differences of alpha and beta band power response of subjects during given tasks. In results, relatively apparent differences were observed in mode dialing in left hemisphere and with open eyes than the others. Such data revealed user's tactile preference among four DSLR cameras although the outcome was not always statistically significant. In conclusion, psychophysical response can be applied to evaluate the subtle tactile stimulation of products along with questionnaire-based tests under certain experimentally-controlled conditions.

Keywords: EEG, tactile, User Experience, usability, psychophysiology.

1 Introduction

Usability test using psychophysiology. Certain scientific fields, such as affective neuroscience, study mechanisms of emotion like pain and pleasure. The same methods applied in these fields could be used in the context of usability tests, as well. do Amaral et al. [1] suggested that specific EEG patterns of the certain emotional states could be analyzed and used for software usability tests. Masaki et al. [2] found that Alpha and Beta power spectrum could be an indicator for measuring users' satisfaction of software interface quantitatively. In addition, Lee et al. [3] used EEG and

C. Stephanidis (Ed.): HCII 2014 Posters, Part I, CCIS 434, pp. 351–356, 2014.
© Springer International Publishing Switzerland 2014

fMRI to discern the brain's reaction between proper and poor design. Their results showed that the human brain responds quicker and stronger to perceptions that stir averse feelings.

Alpha and Beta band power. Wang et al. [4] examined Alpha and SMR signal variation according to haptic stimulations. Nakamura et al. [5] used a frequency range of 4 to 22 Hz for FFT(Fast Fourier Transform) to quantify tactile preference. This is the same range chosen for the current experiment.   The frequency of alpha rhythm is known to be between 7.5 to 12.5 Hz. A brain emitting this frequency is in a state of relaxed wakefulness according to [6]. Uusberg et al. [7] observed that alpha frequency increased when subjects were shown appealing images. These studies show that brains emit particular patterns of signals in the perception of positive sensation. The frequency of beta rhythm typically ranges from 13~30 Hz and indicates a brain in active information processing status. In particular, Beta rhythm can be found from parietal cortex sensory-motor cortex [8]. van Ede et al. [9] studied tactile perception speed and timing using low beta rhythm (mu: 8-12 Hz) and beta rhythm (15-35 Hz) as variables.

The purpose of this work is to explore whether brain responses to subtle tactile stimuli are quantitatively discernible by EEG, specifically in task-based tactile-sensation exercises using four models of camera with similar specs and design.

2   Methods

Hypothesis. In each task (gripping, shuttering, dialing), EEG can be used to detect measurable differences in the brain's response to the tactile sensations of the four models of camera.

Subjects. Twenty healthy volunteers (15 males 5 females; mean age 24.4 ± 3 years) having experience of using camera around 2 ± 2.2 years.

Apparatus. BIOPAC MP 150 (BIOPAC System Inc. USA) was employed to record the EEG measurements of the subjects. The subjects' EEG data were recorded for 15 seconds at a 200 Hz sampling rate under closed- and opened-eye conditions. Electrode locations are based on the International 10-20 System, and six locations were chosen: Frontal lobe (Fp1, Fp2), Parietal lobe (P3, P4), Occipital lobe (O1, O2). Reference electrode is left earlobe. A ground electrode was also affixed to the center of the head (Cz).

For the experiment, four cameras were selected which share similar market positions and exterior designs. Brand logos were covered by black tape so as not to affect subjects' judgment of preference [10].

Experiment design. The study implemented a single-factor, four-repeated-measures-within-subjects experimental design. All participants completed three tasks (gripping, shuttering, and dialing) to with each of the four different brands of camera, one with open eyes and once again with closed eyed. The dependent variables are the relative power spectrum of EEG signals: Alpha band power and Beta band power.

The three chosen tasks are basic to the functioning and of control of a camera for effective physical user interface (PUI) (**Error! Reference source not found.**).

Table 1. Contol task types: basic camera PUI

Task types	Task command
Gripping	Concentrate on the tactile sensation of the camera grip while holding the camera with one's right hand
Shuttering	Concentrate on the tactile sensation of the camera shutter while clicking the shutter button as you would when taking a photo
Dialing	Concentrate on tactile sensation of the camera dialing while rotating the dial with one or two fingers in both clockwise and counter-clockwise directions

Data analysis. The EEG data from six channels were analyzed using TeleScan (LAXTHA Inc.) to calculate power spectrum by fast Fourier transform. Relative Alpha band power was calculated as the range (7.5 -12.5 Hz) divided by a 4-50 Hz spectrum range. Relative Beta band power was calculated as the range (13-30 Hz) divided by a 4-50 Hz spectrum range. We first tried to observe the difference between left and right hemisphere signals and then scrutinize left and right hemisphere signals separately. We regarded data that demonstrated an increase of Alpha power as indicative of a more relaxed user status. Increased Beta power was interpreted as higher levels of concentration and stress in the users.

3 Results

A repeated-measure ANOVA summary (**Error! Reference source not found.**) shows significant main effect results depending on the task, lobe, hemisphere, and presence of visual input, as well as on the type of spectrum being observed (alpha and beta power spectrum). Significant main effects emerged from the data averaging between 5 to 10 seconds (DATA 1). However the data collected from the first 3 seconds and the last 3 seconds (DATA 2) of tactile sensation did not yield significant results. Therefore, we parsed the data and conducted a Bonferroni post-hoc analysis for the Data 1 set only (**Error! Reference source not found.**).

Table 2. Summary of one-way repeated-mesures ANOVA

Hemisphere	Task	Time range	DATA 1 (5-10 sec) Frontal X	O	Parietal X	O	Occipital X	O	DATA 2 (3 sec btw begin and end) Frontal X	O	Parietal X	O	Occipital X	O
		Lobes / Visual Info	X	O	X	O	X	O	X	O	X	O	X	O
Both	Task 1.	Alpha	*											
		Beta												
	Task 2.	Alpha						*						
		Beta												
	Task 3.	Alpha						*						
		Beta	***		*									
Left	Task 1.	Alpha	*											
		Beta												
	Task 2.	Alpha			**		**							
		Beta												*
	Task 3.	Alpha			**		*							
		Beta	**		**		**							
Right	Task 1.	Alpha												
		Beta												
	Task 2.	Alpha												
		Beta												
	Task 3.	Alpha							*					
		Beta	**											

*$p<0.1$, **$p<0.05$, ***$p<0.01$

4   Discussion and Conclusion

- Stimuli like dialing with relatively more complex interaction than shuttering and gripping showed a more significant result.
- Beta power spectrum can be used as a variable to examine levels of cognitive workload for tasks that are relatively complex.
- Left-hemispheric brain signals reacted more strongly than those from the right. This may be associated with the fact that subjects used their right hand to touch and control the cameras.
- More significant differences were recorded between subjects' experience of the four cameras when they kept their eyes open versus when their eyes were closed. This means that subjects are able to form more distinct impressions when the tactile is sensed in conjunction with visual stimulation.
- EEG can be a useful tool for PUI (Physical User Interface) evaluation since it can sense the subtle differences in perception of tactile sensations, although the difference may not always be statistically significant.

Table 3. Summary of post-hoc analysis

			DATA 1 (5-10 sec)					
			Frontal		Parietal		Occipital	
Hemisphere		Visual Info	X	O	X	O	X	O
Both	Task 1.	Alpha	C>A>B>D					
		Beta						
	Task 2.	Alpha						D>C>B>A
		Beta						
	Task 3.	Alpha						A>C>B≒D
		Beta		B>D**, C>D*	B>A**			
Left	Task 1.	Alpha	A>C>B>D					
		Beta						
	Task 2.	Alpha				D>C>A=B		D>A*
		Beta						
	Task 3.	Alpha				C>A>B>D		A≒C>B≒D
		Beta		B>D**	B>A***		B>A*	
Right	Task 1.	Alpha						
		Beta						
	Task 2.	Alpha						
		Beta						
	Task 3.	Alpha						
		Beta		B>D**, C>D*				

">", "<" means significant difference, "≒" or "no mention" is non significance,
*$p<0.1$, **$p<0.05$, ***$p<0.01$

Reference

1. do Amaral, V., Ferreira, L.A., Aquino, P.T., de Castro, M.C.F.: EEG signal classification in usability experiments. Paper Presented at the Biosignals and Biorobotics Conference (BRC), ISSNIP (2013)
2. Masaki, H., Ohira, M., Uwano, H., Matsumoto, K.-I.: A Quantitative Evaluation on the Software Use Experience with Electroencephalogram. In: Marcus, A. (ed.) HCII 2011 and DUXU 2011, Part II. LNCS, vol. 6770, pp. 469–477. Springer, Heidelberg (2011)
3. Lee, H., Lee, J., Seo, S.: Brain response to good and bad design. In: Jacko, J.A. (ed.) HCI International 2009, Part I. LNCS, vol. 5610, pp. 111–120. Springer, Heidelberg (2009)
4. Wang, D., Xu, M., Zhanq, Y., Xiao, J.: Preliminary study on haptic-stimulation based brainwave entrainment: World Haptics Conference (WHC), pp. 565–570. IEEE (2013)
5. Nakamura, T., Ito, S.-I., Mitsukura, Y., Setokawa, H.: A Method for Evaluating the Degree of Human's Preference Based on EEG Analysis: Intelligent Information Hiding and Multimedia Signal Processing. In: Fifth International Conference on IIH-MSP 2009, pp. 732–735. IEEE (2009)
6. Niedermeyer, E.: 9. The Normal EEG of the Waking Adult. Electroencephalography: Basic principles, clinical applications, and related fields 167 (2005)
7. Uusberg, A., Uibo, H., Kreegipuu, K., Allik, J.: EEG alpha and cortical inhibition in affective attention. International Journal of Psychophysiology (2013)

8. Rosanova, M., Casali, A., Bellina, V., Resta, F., Mariotti, M., Massimini, M.: Natural frequencies of human corticothalamic circuits. The Journal of Neuroscience 29, 7679–7685 (2009)
9. van Ede, F., Jensen, O., Maris, E.: Tactile expectation modulates pre-stimulus β-band oscillations in human sensorimotor cortex. Neuroimage 51, 867–876 (2010)
10. McCabe, C., Rolls, E.T., Bilderbeck, A., McGlone, F.: Cognitive influences on the affective representation of touch and the sight of touch in the human brain. Social Cognitive and Affective Neuroscience 3, 97–108 (2008)

Multitasking and Performance under Time Pressure

Hyebeen Lee and Kwanghee Han

Department of Psychology, Yonsei University, Seoul, KOREA
hblee27@gmail.com, khan@yonsei.ac.kr

Abstract. This study is intended as an investigation of relationship between task-switching and time pressure. Task-switching means switching attention from one task to another task. There are two sub-categories: task-switching which is involuntary task-switching, switching task caused by external stimulus, and voluntary task-switching, switching task caused by internal motivation. To investigate whether time pressure makes people do task-switching more frequently and perform task better or not, an experiment was executed. The existence of stopwatch was set as independent variable. The number of task-switching and result of task performance were set as dependent variables. After the experiment, a survey was taken by participants to examine their evaluation on experiment, time pressure, and preference of task-switching. As a result, task-switching occurred more frequently in timer condition when participants were not interested in tasks. Moreover, participants performed tasks better in timer condition when the difficulty level of task was high. These results lead to the conclusion that effect of time pressure varies according to interest in tasks and level of difficulty.

Keywords: multitasking, task-switching, attention, voluntary, time pressure, performance, switching cost.

1 Introduction

People occasionally switch tasks quickly from one task to another or perform more than two tasks at the same time. According to study of Mark, Gonzalez and Harris (2005), every 11 minutes, people switched from one task to another because they were influenced by various disturbances from external environment. Simultaneously executing more than two tasks is called multitasking. Multitasking requires shifting attention from one task to another or performing more than two tasks very quickly one after another. Multitasking, executing many works at the same time seems to be saving time. However, compared to performing one task continually, changing attention from one task to another diminishes task performance (Jersild, 1927), which is called switching cost. Switching cost gets bigger and ability of task performance was impoverished as assignment got more difficult and complex (Rubinstein, Meyer, & Evans, 2001). The reason why switching cost comes into force is that multitasking asks people to switch attention quickly one task to another (Hallowell, 2007). Thus, inefficient result is caused because attention is dispersed in task-switching

C. Stephanidis (Ed.): HCII 2014 Posters, Part I, CCIS 434, pp. 357–362, 2014.

process. To measure multitasking behaviors and switching cost, task-switching test is usually used (Pashler, 2000). Switching cost can be measured by comparing how much time different groups consumes when they perform tasks.

1.1   Multitasking and Voluntary Task-switching

Even though task-switching does cause switching cost, it does not always give rise to "loss". There might be benefits from task-switching process. When categorizing types of multitasking, multitasking can be occurred when one is enforced to do multitasking due to external disruption. This type of multitasking can be triggered by external notification and external stimulus from environment. In this circumstance, external disturbance causes multitasking. The 40 percent of multitasking is occurred involuntarily (Czerwinski, 2004). On the other hands, volitional multitasking is occurred when one deliberately exchanges messages with friends, searches news, and checks email at the same time. It can be occurred by voluntary thinking with no external disturbance. In this case, internal disturbance causes multitasking (Gonzalez & Mark, 2004; Mark, Gonzalez, & Harris, 2005). In other words, one can change task by one's will.

Different from many former studies that are focused on decrease in task performance of involuntary task-switching, recent studies give attention to positive effects of voluntary task-switching. In Lee's article (2013), when people with high multitasking preference voluntarily switched task, they carried out better task performance than those who did not switch task. In this way, despite the same multitasking tasks are performed, if multitasking is volitional, allocating more attention to specific task can derive more effective task-switching behavior and better performance.

Adler and Benbunan-Fich (2013) categorize reasons that cause task-switching into positive reasons and negative reasons. In a circumstance associated with negative reasons, multitasking is occurred because a task is too difficult to solve and causes frustration and exhaustion. In a circumstance associated with positive reasons, multitasking is occurred at the time one reconstructs task for better performance or explores new tasks. Also, a group that performs multitasking caused by negative reasons executes more task-switching and has lower task performance than a group that does multitasking caused by positive reasons. It shows that even people switch tasks voluntarily, aspects of task-switching and level of task performance vary according to cause of induction of multitasking.

1.2   Multitasking and Time Pressure

According to article of Classens (2010), the facts that affect task performance are urgency and importance of task. People prioritize their tasks based on these facts. Urgency of task means how much time remains until deadline. Importance of task correlates with a cost that occurred when task is not accomplished by deadline. Both facts are related to time so that the time is the important element in task performance. A mental state, perceiving lack of time, is called time pressure (Ackerman & Gross, 2003; Gunthorpe & Lyons, 2004). In study of Adler and Benbunan-Fich, effect on task-switching varies according to characteristics of cause of induction. In this paper, time pressure can be treated as another key ingredient of cause of induction. Thus, experiment is executed to explain how time pressure effects on task-switching. More voluntary task-switching behavior is anticipated when people perceive lack of time or have too many tasks to fulfill. Moreover, in study of Ackerman (2003), a group of students that feel more time pressure and have less free time got better grades and predicted future success better than a group of students that feel less time pressure. Therefore, when people perform tasks, better results are expected in high time pressure condition.

2   Research Method

In order to investigate time pressure makes people to do more voluntary task-switching and fulfill their task better, level of time pressure was considered as independent variable. There was a digital stopwatch next to computer in high time pressure condition, while there was no watch in low time pressure condition. Dependent variables were both number of task-switching and result of task performing. Moderator variables were degree of level of difficulty and interest of tasks. Undergraduate students who take psychology as major or electives (27 males, 23 females, mean age = 22.7) participated in the experiment. All participants were fluent in Korean and they got credits as rewards. 50 participants were randomly allocated to experimental group and control group. Participants were asked to accomplish three tasks in 20 minutes and their task-switching numbers were counted by a Visual Studio 2010 program. The three tasks were composed of tabs which made participants free to move one task to another. Participants performed three tasks in 20 minutes and they were asked to deliberately execute all tasks. Three tasks were numerical reasoning problems, Sudoku problems, and wordsearch problems. Participants performed tasks by using number keys of keyboard and mouse. An example of numerical reasoning problems is shown in Figure 1.

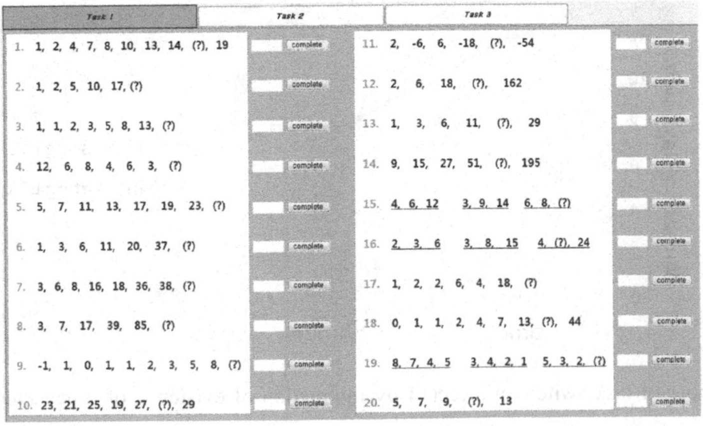

Fig. 1. Numerical reasoning task (One of three tasks in experiment)

After finishing 20 minutes of task, 15 questions of survey were given to subjectively evaluate each task. These questions were 7-point scale and measure level of difficulty and interest of tasks. To control the effect on relationship between voluntary multitasking and time perception caused by ordinary multitasking preference, measurement item used in Pierro's study (2012) was given. Questions to measure effect of time pressure were presented in two categories. Firstly, four questions about ordinary time pressure were given. To evaluate subjective perception about time pressure and time-consuming behavior, measurement item used in study of Lin and Wu (2005) were presented. Moreover, to measure time pressure, participants were asked to answer 7 scale questions about nervousness, pressure, anxiety, and tension.

3   Results and Discussion

Since the number of voluntary task-switching means the number of participants switch task during 20 minutes, it was measured by the number of tab buttons clicked. The task performance ability was measured by the number of questions participants got correct out of 83 questions which consisted of 20 numerical reasoning problems, 43 sudoku problems, and 20 wordsearch problems. As a manipulation check, mere existence of timer caused people feel more time pressure during task session than no-timer condition, $t(48) = 2.13$, $p < .05$. Also, participants in timer condition significantly got more tasks right than those in no timer condition, $t(48) = 1.68$, $p < .05$. According to degree of both level of difficulty and interest in tasks, moreover, time-pressure differently affected aspects of task-switching and task performance. When participants had low interest in tasks, people in timer condition (Ye = 12.01) performed more task-switching than those in no-timer condition (Ye = 7.37), $F(1, 46) = 6.90$, $p < .05$ (Figure 2). It seems that they switched their attention from one task to another for exploring another task.

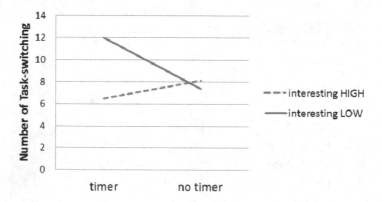

Fig. 2. Number of task-switching affected by interaction of existence of timer and interest in task

Also, the fact arousing curiosity was that if participants thought the level of difficulty was considerably high, people in timer condition (Ye = 57.02) accomplished tasks better than those in no-timer condition (Ye = 41.08), $F(1, 46) = 6.82$, $p < .05$ (Figure 3). This shows that time pressure affected positively because motivations to resolve the tasks were increased when they were performing high level tasks.

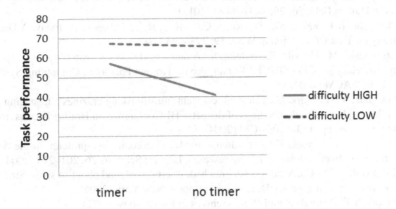

Fig. 3. Task performance affected by interaction of existence of timer and level of difficulty

4   Conclusion

Finally, through the interest in tasks and level of difficulty, time pressure affected frequency of multi-tasking and degrees of task performance. Since there are lack of research papers that explain time pressure which causes multi-tasking, this result has significance. These days people constantly do multitasking because they don't want to get left behind in the limitless competition. There are also lots of stimulus provided by intimate smart phones and tablet PCs which make people do multitasking constantly. Although switching cost is generated and people constantly get disturbances when they switch task in multitasking environment, benefits from task-switching can be bigger than loss from intentional task-switching under some conditions. Therefore, whether multitasking is voluntarily or not, result of multitasking can be positive or negative according to cause of multitasking induction. Through the time pressure experiment in this paper, characteristics of task and interest of task can change aspects of multitasking. Moreover, according to level of difficulty, task performance can be changed under time pressure. From the practical point of view, it can be applied to learning and working fields. When program designers design programs such as education programs, task performance can be maximized by customizing programs. For instance, on the basis of survey about interest of tasks and level of difficulty, there is a way to utilize stopwatch in next education process.

References

1. Ackerman, D.S., Gross, B.L.: Is time pressure all bad? Measuring the relationship between free time availability and student performance and perceptions. Marketing Education Review 13, 21–34 (2003)
2. Adler, R.F., Benbunan-Fich, R.: Self-interruptions in discretionary multitasking. Computers in Human Behavior 29, 1441–1449 (2013)
3. Claessens, B.J., Van Eerde, W., Rutte, C.G., Roe, R.A.: Things to do today. A Daily Diary Study on Task Completion at Work 59, 273–295 (2010)
4. Czerwinski, M., Horvitz, E., Wilhite, S.: A diary study of task switching and interruptions. In: Proceedings of the SIGCHI Conference on Human Factors in Computing Systems, pp. 175–182. ACM (2004)
5. González, V.M., Mark, G.: Constant, constant, multi-tasking craziness: managing multiple working spheres. In: Proceedings of the SIGCHI Conference on Human Factors in Computing Systems, pp. 113–120. ACM (2004)
6. Gunthorpe, W., Lyons, K.: A predictive model of chronic time pressure in the Australian population: Implications for leisure research. Leisure Sciences 26, 201–213 (2004)
7. Hallowell, M.D.: Crazy busy–overstretched, overbooked, and about to snap! Strategies for coping in a world gone ADD. Ballantine Books, New York (2006)
8. Jersild, A.T.: Mental set and shift. Archives of Psychology (1927)
9. Lee, S.M., Lee, J.H., Han, K.H.: Cognitive Cost and Benefit from Voluntary Task Switching in Multitasking. Korean Journal of Cognitive Science 24, 71–93 (2013)
10. Lin, C.H., Wu, P.H.: How to deal with conflicts? The effect of consumers' subjective time pressure on product attitude judgment and choice. The Journal of American Academy of Business 6, 219–224 (2005)
11. Mark, G., Gonzalez, V.M., Harris, J.: No task left behind?: examining the nature of fragmented work. In: Proceedings of the SIGCHI Conference on Human Factors in Computing Systems, pp. 321–330. ACM (2005)
12. Pashler, H.: Task Switching and Multitask Performance. In: Monsell, S., Driver, J. (eds.) Attention and Performance XVI I I: Control of Cognitive Processes, pp. 277–307. MIT Press, Cambridge (2000)
13. Pierro, A., Giacomantonio, M., Pica, G., Kruglanski, A.W., Higgins, E.T.: Locomotion and the preference for multi-tasking: Implications for well-being. Motivation and Emotion 37, 213–223 (2013)
14. Rubinstein, J.S., Meyer, D.E., Evans, J.E.: Executive control of cognitive processes in task switching. Journal of Experimental Psychology: Human Perception and Performance 27, 763–797 (2001)

Influence of High-resolution 4K Displays on Psychological State During Content Viewing

Kiyomi Sakamoto[1], Seiji Sakashita[1], Kuniko Yamashita[2], and Akira Okada[2]

[1] R&D Division, Panasonic Corporation, 3-1-1 Yagumo-nakamachi, Moriguchi City,
Osaka 570-8501, Japan
{sakamoto.kiyomi,sakashita.seiji}@jp.panasonic.com
[2] Department of Human Life Science, Osaka City University, 3-3-138 Sugimoto,
Sumiyoshi-ku, Osaka, 558-8585 Japan
{yamasita,okada}@ life.osaka-cu.ac.jp

Abstract. We experimentally investigated the influence of high-resolution images on viewers' psychological state while viewing content at 4K and 2K on a 65-inch 4K TV. Their scores for "presence," "relaxed," "natural," "liked," "comfortable" and "precise" when viewing 4K scenic content were significantly higher than those for 2K content. Our results suggest that, when using a large (65-inch) screen, viewing 4K scenic content affords greater psychological refreshment and lower stress than when viewing similar material at 2K resolution.

Keywords: Emotional states, psychological measurements, high resolution 4K TV, TV viewing.

1 Introduction

Bigger and higher-definition screens and longer TV viewing times due to changing TV viewing styles, which are becoming more diverse due to broadening content, such as video games and Web pages in addition to conventional TV programs, make it increasingly necessary to consider the effects of these changes on visual fatigue and health. To develop TVs that keep visual fatigue to a minimum and to be able to propose optimum TV viewing conditions, these factors need to be investigated in addition to the conventional focus on image quality and presence. In modern society, people are exposed to different levels and types of stress that have major effects on them both physiologically and psychologically, making it increasingly important to reduce stress. The physiological and psychological relaxation effects caused by exposure to scenes of nature are attracting growing research interest, and several studies have been carried out on the beneficial effects of short walks in the forest and of viewing rose blooms [1]. High-definition TV technology, such as for 4K TV and 8K TV, continues to progress, but it is also important to ensure that HDTV has no negative impact on visual or general health by minimizing any visual fatigue or stress that might be caused by very high image quality and presence. We therefore explored and evaluated the influence of high-resolution 4K displays on psychological state during content viewing.

C. Stephanidis (Ed.): HCII 2014 Posters, Part I, CCIS 434, pp. 363–367, 2014.

2   Methods

Subjects. Ten adults aged in their 20s participated in this experiment.

Measurements: The following items were investigated.
Participants' psychological state, reported on a scale of 3 to –3 for 21 items, including "stressed–relaxed," "presence–no presence," "comfortable–uncomfortable," and "like–dislike." These psychological items were defined in the light of the results of pilot experimental interviews and those of our prior studies (Table 1).

Apparatus

1. The display device was a 65-inch 4K TV (Panasonic TH-L65WT600).
2. The viewing distance was set at 1.5H (120 cm). Screen-to-eye distance was defined in relation to screen height (H). The recommended viewing distance for the 4K TV, defined as 1.5 times the display's height for a 65-inch display, was 120 cm.
3. Test room illumination was set at 200 lx to simulate the average light level of a Japanese living room, based on JIS standardization.

Procedure: The participants engaged in TV viewing of five types of video content: three types with scenic content, including nature scenes and urban built-environment scenes, and two types of close-up of food and material content, including jewel, watch, fur and glass; etc. Each program comprised 2 minutes of 4K and 2 minutes of 2K content. After viewing each program, the participants gave a subjective assessment of their psychological state ("stressed–relaxed," "presence–no presence," "comfortable–uncomfortable," "like–dislike," etc.), on a score of 3 to –3 (Figure 1) (Table 1). To eliminate the order effect, the order of content and 4K or 2K resolution in the program were made different for each participant.

Statistical analysis: A paired t-test was performed to statistically analyze the influence of the high-resolution 4K displays on the subjects' psychological state while viewing different types of content. The level of significance was set at $p = 0.05$.

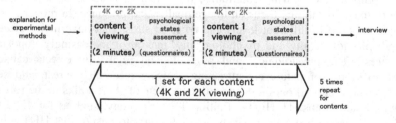

Fig. 1. The process of the viewing test using five types of content

Table 1. Subjective assessment items

Subjective assessment items (including 21 items)
Qualitative assessment of high resolution
"sharp focus–no sharp focus,"
"precision–lack of precision,"
"precise–coarse,"
"natural–artificial,"
"looks like a real object–doesn't look like a real object,"
"clear–not clear,"
"realistic–not realistic,"
"dynamic–static,"
"feeling of depth–no feeling of depth"
"high quality–low quality,"
Emotional assessment of high resolution
"presence–no presence,"
"feeling of invigoration–no feeling of invigoration,"
"feeling of congruity– feeling of incongruity"
"impact–no impact,"
"good–bad,"
"comfortable–uncomfortable,"
"enjoyable–boring,"
"relaxed–stressed,"
"like–dislike,"
"aroused–sleepy,"
"no visual fatigue–visual fatigue"

3   Results and Discussion

The results showed that the scores for "presence," "relaxed," "natural," "liked," "comfortable" and "precise" when viewing 4K scenic content, including nature scenes and urban built-environment scenes, were significantly higher than those for 2K scenic content (Figure 2). The participants may have felt as if they were viewing a real scene through a window when viewing 4K high-definition content on a large-screen TV. Conversely, when viewing close-up images of material content at 4K, only the score for "precise" was significantly higher than the corresponding scores for close-up images of material content at 2K, and the score for "natural" of 4K content tended to be higher than that for 2K (Figure 3). No significant differences were observed between the scores for 4K and 2K for food content. It is possible that these results were caused by a sense of incongruity on the part of the subjects due to the much greater size of the displayed items than the same items in real life.

In brief, the positive scores for the majority of the psychological indices for 4K were significantly higher than those for 2K. Our results suggest that, when using a large (65-inch) screen, viewing 4K scenic content affords greater psychological refreshment and reduced stress than when viewing similar content at 2K resolution.

Further investigations will be needed to gain a more precise picture of the influence on psychological state of high-resolution 4K displays.

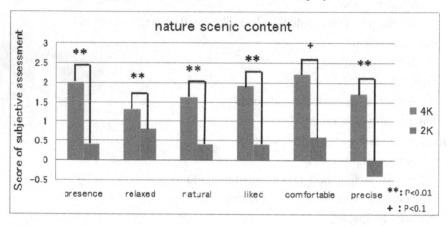

Fig. 2. Mean scores of subjective assessments at 4K and 2K when viewing nature scenes. (Eight participants)

A higher score indicates a more positive evaluation.
**: $p < 0.01$, +: $p < 0.1$
X-axis (subjective assessments at each resolution)
Y-axis (score of subjective assessments)

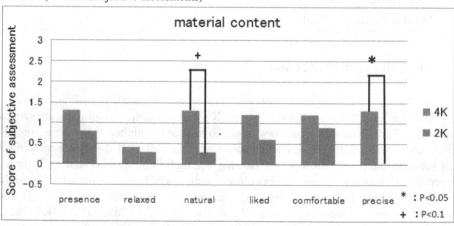

Fig. 3. Mean score of subjective assessment at 4K and 2K when viewing close-up images of material content (Eight participants)

A higher score indicates a more positive evaluation.
*: $p < 0.05$, +: $p < 0.1$
X-axis (subjective assessments at each resolution)
Y-axis (score of subjective assessments)

References

1. Komatsu, M., Matsunaga, K.: The physiological and psychological relaxing effects on medical staff of viewing rose flowers. Japanese Journal of Physiological Anthropology 18(1), 1–7 (2013)
2. Ishibashi, K., Kitamura, S., Kozaki, T., Yasukouchi, A.: Inhibition of Heart Rate Variability during Sleep in Humans By 6700 K Pre-sleep Light Exposure. Journal of Physiological Anthropology 26(1), 39–43 (2007)
3. Ishibashi, K., Ueda, S., Yasukouchi, A.: Effects of Mental Task on Heart Rate Variability during Graded Head-Up Tilt. Journal of Physiological Anthropology 18(6), 225–231 (1999)

Combining Human and Machine Capabilities for Improved Accuracy and Speed in Visual Recognition Tasks

Amir Schur and Charles Tappert

Seidenberg School of CSIS, Pace University
1 Martine Ave., White Plains, NY 10606, USA
amirschur@aol.com, ctappert@pace.edu

Abstract. This study investigated methods of enhancing human computer interaction in applications of pattern recognition where higher accuracy is required than is currently achievable by automated systems, but where there is enough time for a limited amount of human interaction. On a flower identification task, methods were explored to improve the accuracy of human-only and machine-only recognition by employing human-computer interaction. Human involvement in the feature extraction process, especially in color selection, was found to be most beneficial.

Keywords: Human-computer interaction, visual object recognition, pattern classification, feature extraction.

1 Introduction

In various areas of pattern recognition, particularly in visual recognition tasks, there is generally a trade-off between accuracy and speed. Having the task performed manually by an expert usually results in high accuracy but takes a significant amount of time to accomplish. Performing the task automatically by machine usually can be done rapidly but the accuracy level is often low. The visual recognition task areas can be facial recognition, hand-writing recognition, etc. While research can focus on how to create a tool to assist an expert or on how to create a better automated tool, another way of improving automated tools is by employing human assistance in tasks where the time required is still deemed acceptable. This study, therefore, investigates the employment of human assistance in the feature extraction process of an automated visual pattern recognition task.

This study uses a java-based software tool called IVS (Interactive Visual System) which was developed from the CAVIAR model in which humans and machines interact to identify flowers [1]. IVS can operate on handheld devices or a code simulator run on laptop/desktop machines (Figures 1 and 2).

C. Stephanidis (Ed.): HCII 2014 Posters, Part I, CCIS 434, pp. 368–372, 2014.
© Springer International Publishing Switzerland 2014

Fig. 1. IVS tool: a) in the field, b) close-up of handheld with attached camera

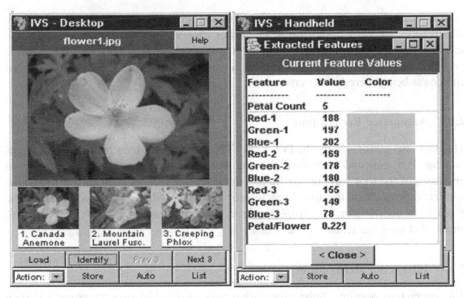

Fig. 2. IVS simulator: a) original image and top three recognition choices, b) interactive screen with feature selection

The CAVIAR model performs the usual visual pattern recognition tasks of segmentation, feature extraction, and classification. Feature extraction is performed primarily by the machine while the segmentation and classification processes are interactively performed by the human and the machine. A parametric segmentation procedure fits a "rose curve" to the flower object and the rose curve parameters can be adjusted by the human. After the machine classifier produces a list of ordered choices, the human reviews the choices to make the final decision, which is usually correct when the correct flower is in the top three choices. The current study, however, explores more deeply the employment of human input in the feature extraction process – for example, the degree to which items of human assistance improve system performance in terms of recognition speed and accuracy is measured.

2   Experiment 1 – Manual, Automated, Interactive Recognition

This experiment was conducted in three parts: human-only flower recognition (manual recognition), machine-only flower recognition (automated recognition) and human-assisted automated flower recognition (interactive recognition). Three testers (participants) were used in the three recognition tasks, and an experiment coordinator monitored the activities and recorded the results. For identification in each of the three parts of the experiment, thirty flower images, each of a different flower, were selected from a database of 535 images from 131 flower species.

2.1   Manual Recognition

In the manual task, the testers used a flower guidebook to assist them in the identification process. The top three flower choices and the time to identify the selected flowers were recorded. The experiment coordinator reviewed the answers provided by the participants against the answer key and identified the recognized choices as being correct or incorrect.

2.2   Automated Recognition

This task was performed by the IVS tool. The three testers loaded the flower images into the IVS tool and performed the automated feature extraction and recognition processes of the tool without any human input/feedback. For each flower image the application presented the top three selection choices which were recorded by the experiment coordinator. Each of the three testers performed the task separately to ensure that the same result was obtained.

2.3   Interactive Recognition

The interactive portion of the recognition task allows the user to provide certain feature input: petal count (the number of flower petals), petal color 1 (the most dominant color of the petal), petal color 2 (the second most dominant color of the petal), and stamen color. Additionally, the user can crop the image of the flower to eliminate possible confusion with other flowers and the background. Finally, the user can draw an outline around a petal to help the application segment a petal shape.

The interactive identification task was further divided into three subtasks, each evaluating human assistance with a different set of features. Interactive A evaluated human assistance in providing only the petal count feature (1 feature) with the user inputting the petal count after the application performed its automated feature extraction. Interactive B added petal colors (primary and secondary) and stamen color to the petal count feature (total of 4 features), and Interactive C added the cropped flower area (total of 5 features). The IVS process was that the user could always input or modify the machine's automated activity. Thus, the testers provided human input through the selection of feature data, using the action menu to select and input the feature data being evaluated, and then performed automated identification.

2.4   Results of Experiment 1

Table 1 presents a summary of the results of the experiment. Manual recognition took the longest time and provided rather low accuracy results. Automated recognition was fast but the least accurate. Although all of the human-assisted tasks yielded higher accuracy than the fully automated task, the only interactive task that performed significantly better than the human-only (manual) task was Interactive B where color recognition and petal count were performed with human assistance. Adding the cropping of the flower actually decreased recognition accuracy.

Table 1. First experiment results: 3 testers, 30 flower images

Test Type	Percent Accuracy (Top 3)			Average Accuracy	Average Time (sec)
	Tester 1	Tester 2	Tester 3		
Manual	40.0%	36.7%	20.0%	32.2%	173
Automatic	13.3%	13.1%	13.3%	13.3%	56
Interactive A petal count	13.3%	16.7%	16.7%	15.6%	44
Interactive B plus colors	63.3%	60.0%	30.0%	51.1%	41
Interactive C plus flower area	40.0%	36.7%	40.0%	38.9%	44

3   Experiment 2 – Color Recognition

Motivated by the results of the first experiment, a second experiment was performed to focus on human assistance in the color recognition processes (primary and secondary color of the petal and the stamen color), letting the machine perform the shape/contour recognition processes. This experiment used 20 flower images from different species and 15 testers. The results of the experiment are shown in Table 2. Recognition accuracy in the top three choices ranged from 60 to 95% with an average of 74%, and recognition time from 43 to 63 seconds with an average of 54 seconds. This is a significant improvement in accuracy results over those in experiment 1, while maintaining an acceptable recognition time.

Table 2. Second experiment results: 15 testers, 20 flower images

Tester	1	2	3	4	5	6	7	8	9	10	11	12	13	14	15
Accuracy (Top 3)	70%	90%	95%	85%	75%	70%	70%	70%	75%	70%	75%	60%	75%	60%	70%
Avg Time (sec)	57	62	43	55	63	47	54	55	48	49	52	54	48	58	61

4   Conclusions

This study reveals that there is room for improvement in human-machine interaction in the feature extraction process. Human assistance in color recognition on an automated flower recognition tool showed a significant increase in accuracy while maintaining an acceptable time to accomplish the task. Assistance in other areas did not significantly increase the accuracy level, and actually decreased it when including human assistance in the shape recognition process (Interactive C). For areas where human assistance doesn't show performance increase, the approach of using automated features should not be changed. Correctly combining human and machine strengths is the approach advocated. In this study shape/contour recognition by machine combined with human input on color seems to provide the best accuracy while maintaining a reasonable time to complete the task.

Improvement of limitations is a desired goal. In this case, the human's ability in shape/contour recognition can probably not be improved. Rather, we should further explore how to improve automated capabilities in color recognition. We want to know the limit of machine capability in color only recognition.

References

1. Evans, A., Sikorski, J., Thomas, P., Cha, S.-H., Tappert, C., Zou, G., Gattani, A., Nagy, G.: Computer Assisted Visual Interactive Recognition (CAVIAR) Technology. In: 2005 IEEE International Conference on Electro-Information Technology, Lincoln, NE (May 2005)

Perception of Parallelism in Perspective Images

Sebastian Walther[1], Ingmar Franke[1], Sebastian Pannasch[2], and Rainer Groh[1]

[1] Chair of Media Design, Technische Universität Dresden, Dresden, Germany
{sebastian.walther2,ingmar.franke,rainer.groh}@tu-dresden.de
[2] Applied Cognitive Research, Technische Universität Dresden, Dresden, Germany
pannasch@psychologie.tu-dresden.de

Abstract. This contribution presents a study in which subjects are shown perspective views of simple shapes. The subject's task was to decide whether the shape's outlines were parallel to each other or not. It was observed that the subjects were strongly misled by perspective depth cues. Real parallels in orthographic projections were rarely detected. In contrast a minor convergent alignment of the outlines like in a linear perspective projection were perceived as parallel.

Keywords: Linear Perspective, Reverse Perspective, Visual Perception, Parallelism, Projection.

1   Introduction

The rediscovery of the linear perspective in the early renaissance marks one of the most important steps for the evolution of western art and culture. This procedure of projection has become the norm for most realistic looking images. No matter where linear perspective dominates painting, photography, motion pictures or computer graphics. Linear perspective images are two-dimensional presentations of a spatial environment. Parallels of the three-dimensional space are shown in a linear perspective image with a convergent alignment towards a vanishing point.

The permanent use of the linear perspective in most pictorial media, and thus its constant impact on the human system of perception, has a significant effect on the way one expects a representation of its environment to be in linear perspective. It is often discussed that an observer needs to learn how to read a perspective image before it appears natural [1], [2]. Without a doubt, the linear perspective is a powerful and deceitful illusion [3] and it may be a good and solid representation of the three-dimensional environment [4]. However, the linear perspective is only one way to project the three-dimensional space onto a flat surface and it is not the ultimately 'right' way to do it [2], [5-8]. Further research indicates the strong impact of the adaption to the linear perspective. It even influences the perception of the real world [6-8]. On closer examination, it is necessary to discuss possible side-effects of this progress and it is beneficial to achieve a comprehensive understanding of the linear perspective's effect on

C. Stephanidis (Ed.): HCII 2014 Posters, Part I, CCIS 434, pp. 373–378, 2014.

the human system of perception. This is also valid for the field of human-computer interaction since linear perspective dominates virtual three-dimensional worlds and is even the most common projection system in virtual reality systems.

This contribution is focused on the human sensation of parallelism in mathematical accurate and abstract images. In the following section an experimental approach is described.

2   Description of the Study

Judgments on parallelism in the three-dimensional space are often inaccurate or wrong [9-13]. While the detection of parallelism is relatively well reviewed for spatial environments, it is widely unclear how subjects judge parallelism on plane images which show three-dimensional scenes. In [14] it is supposed that the apparent convergence of parallels in linear perspective pictures is used by observers as a cue to construct a spatial comprehension of the pictured three-dimensional space.

The goal of the presented study is to find the circumstances under which parallels of three-dimensional objects appear also parallel in the two-dimensional images of these objects. Three projection systems are used to render images of geometric objects with parallel properties. The linear perspective maps parallel properties to convergent lines. The reverse perspective projection creates divergent lines out of parallels and the orthographic projection preserves all parallel properties. It is supposed that parallels in an orthographic projection are not always perceived as parallels.

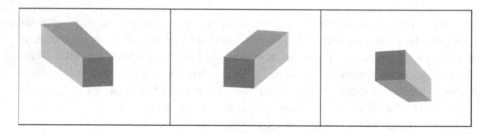

Fig. 1. Three examples of the presented computer generated stimuli. Shown is a cuboid object in different orientations. The field of view of the virtual camera is set to -12° angular degree (left - reverse perspective), to 0° angular degree (mid - orthographic projection) and to 20° angular degree (right - linear perspective).

The subjects were requested to determine whether particular lines in an image were parallel to each other or not. By pressing one of two specified keys on a normal keyboard the subjects logged their decision and the following image was presented. The images were presented in random order on a 22inch computer screen aligned as a frontoparallel plane. Although there was no time limit for pressing a key, the subjects were asked to decide fast and the response time was measured. 23 subjects (10 women, 13 men) without visual impairment took part. The relevant lines for which the decision was made spread in each case from the middle of the screen to one of its edges (figure 1). The lines were actually the depth lines of objects which were shown with different degrees of perspective distortion. One of the three basic shapes (square, circle or equilateral triangle) formed the base area for the three used objects (cuboid, cylinder, prism). With the base area in the middle of the screen and the spatial orientation towards one of the screen edges, the object's justification brings to mind an arrangement similar to the often used cavalier or cabinet projection. Overall 204 images were shown to each subject (three objects, four rotations and 17 different degrees of perspective distortion). The perspective distortion was controlled by the field of view of the virtual camera and its distance to the object. The stimuli images were screenshots created with a self programmed plugin for BiLL (Bildsprache Live Lab - an openGL based framework for viewing and manipulating virtual scenes which is developed at Technische Universität Dresden) [15].

3   Results

For the analysis of the data a one-factored variance analysis (ANOVA) (17 different angles of field of view) with a Bonferroni correction as post-hoc test was applied. For every angle of the field of view there were 12 repetitions of rating (three different objects each with four spatial orientations).

As depicted in figure 2, most images (94.20%; 260 out of 276) with a field of view of 10° angular degree were rated as parallel. Except for the two nearby measurements 8° (86.96%; 240 out of 276) and 12° (86.23%; 238 out of 276) this is a significant difference to all the other angles, $p < .03$. These ratings are surprisingly high in comparison to images where the lines were actual parallel. Less than one out of five of these images were rated as parallel and therefore correct (18.11%; 50 out of 276). The commonness of misjudgment is very clear for the angles of degree between 8 to 12. Nearly no misjudgment was to be observed for images in reverse perspective. Only every fiftieth image was rated as parallel (2.11%, 35 out of 1656).

In additional examinations we could suspend the assumption that the grade of knowledge about perspective projections influenced the subject's ratings. Also there was no significant difference for the ratings of the three objects nor the four object rotations. However, there was a noticeable difference in the mean reaction time. It took the subjects significant more time to make a decision for linear perspective images (2500ms) than for reverse perspective images (1052ms).

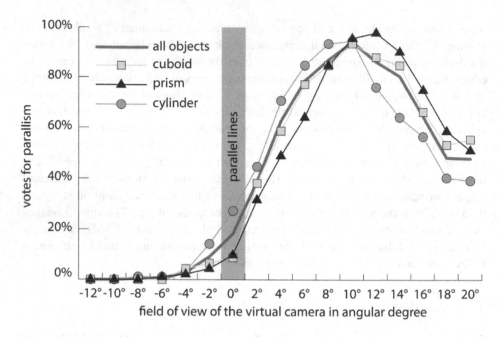

Fig. 2. The subject's perception of parallelism for all three objects over the used values of the computer generated image's field of view

4   Discussion

The misjudgment on the perception of parallelism was consistent and similar for every spatial orientation. That is why we assume that the subjects were clearly misled by the three-dimensional impression of the stimuli. The images were interpreted as illustrations of three-dimensional objects like cuboid or cylinder. In difference, another possible interpretation of the stimuli as flat and separated shapes, should have led to a discrepancy. The effect of perceived depth in the image is to return to the rare depth cues like linear perspective. In addition, the effective mapping of the actual flat stimuli to a well understood representation of a three-dimensional object seems to play an important role. As known, the illusion of linear perspective is successful because the human perception system is well trained in mapping flat images to equivalent spatial ideas of the shown scene [2-3]. As described in the previous section, nearly every image (94.2%) which showed an object under the field of view of 10° angular degree, was rated as parallel. The clearness of this result seems to be caused by the illusion of seeing a spatial object due to the perspective presentation. Only in rare occasions the lines in reverse perspective pictures were rated as parallel. This result seems to support the theory of an adaption to the linear perspective [1-2], [7]. That means that there could be an awareness, when viewing pictures with a spatial impression: depth parallels need to converge towards a vanishing point. In the case of the study this awareness could be an explanation for the consequent misjudgment of the subjects. Figure 3 shows the obviousness of this misjudgment.

It seems that it was more 'easy' for the subjects to except parallelism for pictures in reverse perspective. The decisions were significant faster and mostly correct. It should be more likely to detect parallels on an object where you know that it has clearly parallel structures (like the cuboid). So maybe the 'odd' representation in reverse perspective prevented the detection of the a e.g. cuboid-like structure. Due to the experience of the subjects with linear perspective, the perspective distortion in reverse perspective is against the expectance. Therefore it could have been more easy for the subjects to make the right decision against parallelism.

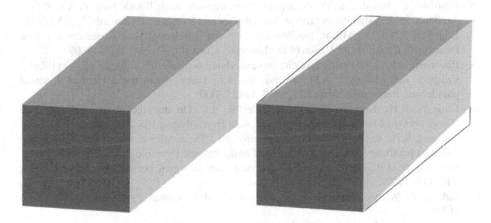

Fig. 3. Comparison between a cuboid in orthographic projection with real parallel lines (left) and a cuboid in linear perspective with perceived parallel lines (right). The black outline depicts the difference to real parallelism.

5   Conclusion

In this paper we discussed the effect of the frequent usage of linear perspective for drawing, photography, moving pictures and computer graphics. In study, we asked 23 subjects to determine, whether or not outlines of shapes are parallel to each other. The shapes were part of spatial seeming and simple objects like a cuboid, a cylinder and a prism. All the images were created with different degrees of perspective distortion. As expected, apparent parallels in an image does not have to be perceived as parallel. The subjects detected parallels very often in slightly linear perspective images, where the seeming parallels were actual not parallel at all (figure 3). These findings seem to support the thesis, that the adaption of the human perception system to linear perspective images influences the visual perception [6-8].

Acknowledgements. This work has been supported by the European Social Fund and the Free State of Saxony (Young Investigators Group CogITo, project no. 100076040).

References

1. Willats, J.: Art and representation / new principles in the analysis of pictures (1997)
2. Gregory, R.L.: Eye and brain / the psychology of seeing (1998)
3. Talbott, S.L.: The Future Does Not Compute: Transcending the Machines in Our Midst. O'Reilly, Associates, Inc (1995)
4. Franke, I.S., et al.: Towards Attention-centered Interfaces: An Aesthetic Evaluation of Perspective with Eye Tracking. . ACM Trans. Multimedia Comput. Commun. Appl. 4, 18:1–18:13 (2008)
5. Panofsky, E., Wood, C.S.: Perspective as symbolic form. Zone Books, New York (1991)
6. Arnheim, R.: Inverted Perspective in Art: Display and Expression. Leonardo 5, 125 (1972)
7. Edgerton, S.Y.: The Mirror, the Window, and the Telescope: How Renaissance Linear Perspective Changed Our Vision of the Universe. Cornell University Press (2009)
8. Rauschenbach, B.V.: Perspective pictures and visual perception. Leonardo, 45–49 (1985)
9. Cuijpers, R.H., Kappers, A.M., Koenderink, J.J.: Large systematic deviations in visual parallelism. Perception-London 29, 1467–1482 (2000)
10. Cuijpers, R.H., Kappers, A.M.L., Koenderink, J.J.: On the role of external reference frames on visual judgements of parallelity. Acta Psychologica 108, 283–302 (2001)
11. Cuijpers, R.H., Kappers, A.M.L., Koenderink, J.J.: The metrics of visual and haptic space based on parallelity judgements. Journal of Mathematical Psychology 47, 278–291 (2003)
12. Derȩgowski, J.B., Parker, D.M.: Convergent and divergent perspective. Perception 21, 441–447 (1992)
13. Indow, T.: Alleys in visual space. Journal of Mathematical Psychology 19, 221–258 (1979)
14. Saunders, J.A., Backus, B.T.: Both parallelism and orthogonality are used to perceive 3D slant of rectangles from 2D images. J. Vis. 7, 7 (2007)
15. Wojdziak, J., Kammer, D., Franke, I.S., Groh, R.: BiLL: An Experimental Environment for Visual Analytics. In: Proceedings of the 3rd ACM SIGCHI Symposium on Engineering Interactive Computing Systems, pp. 259–264. ACM (2011), doi:10.1145/1996461.1996533

ESTER

Eye-Tracking Science Tool and Experiment Runtime

Jan Wojdziak[1], Dietrich Kammer[2], Andreas Stahl[2], and Rainer Groh[2]

[1] GTV – Gesellschaft für Technische Visualistik mbH
[2] Technische Universität Dresden, Department of Computer Science,
Institute of Software- and Multimedia Technology

Abstract. We introduce ESTER, an interactive 3D real-time (Eye-tracking) Science Tool and Experiment Runtime for investigating visual attention by means of the aggregation and representation of three-dimensional gaze paths and positions.

Keywords: eye-gaze tracking, stereoscopic imaging, 3D visualization, real-time, user studies.

1 Introduction

3D visualization is widely recognized as a crucial aspect in communication of spatial information. The widespread usage of 3D graphics engines and the development of 3D formats consequently results in a variety of systems ranging from information visualization systems to computer-aided design (CAD) tools as well as computer games and entertainment. However, the success and further progress of 3D applications inherently depends on visualizing content in a user-centered way. User-Centered Design is an approach to user interface design in which the needs, wants, and limitations of users are given extensive attention. Our consideration is focused on analyses and investigations of 3D interfaces, which assist the user in perceiving spatial information as effectively and efficiently as possible [3]. A necessary requirement to achieve this aim is the provision of a visual experiment creation tool to investigate the visual attention of users interacting with virtual three-dimensional objects and scenes.

2 Eye-Tracking in Stereoscopic Projected Virtual Scenes

Stereoscopic projection is a well-established technology that exploits the fact that our visual system consists of two eyes [10]. Recently, 3D visualization using stereoscopic projection is gaining increased attention [2, 10]. In addition, the usage of eye-tracking systems facilitates the correct detection of eye positions and furthermore the calculation of 3D gaze positions in a virtual scene, whereby we can effectively simulate the real-world experience of depth perception in virtual worlds [11].

C. Stephanidis (Ed.): HCII 2014 Posters, Part I, CCIS 434, pp. 379–383, 2014.

However, the detection of the gaze position in three-dimensional virtual environments still lacks methods and techniques to process and depict information about the visual attention of the user.

Researching attention-based 3D visualizations as well as perceptual bias towards stereoscopic 3D visualizations in human-computer interaction requires interactive computer systems [9]. To this end, an extensible component-oriented software framework was implemented to record and give feedback about the visual attention of the user [4]. The framework was developed based on standard components: OpenSceneGraph [5] and wxWidgets [8]. Additionally, the framework uses a modern approach to extensible component-based software engineering in C++, by using an implementation of the OSGi standard [7], the Open Service Platform [1].

The Eye-tracking Science Tool and Experiment Runtime (ESTER) is developed based on this software foundation. On the one hand, ESTER visualizes a three-dimensional scene in an interactive real-time environment (see Fig. 1) and renders the virtual world stereoscopically using NVIDIA 3D Vision [6] shutter glasses. On the other hand, a stereoscopic eye-gaze tracking setup is used to detect the intersection points of gaze rays of the user with the observed virtual world [11]. To achieve this, the visual attention and eye movements are recorded with up to four cameras for high accuracy and tolerance of head motion.

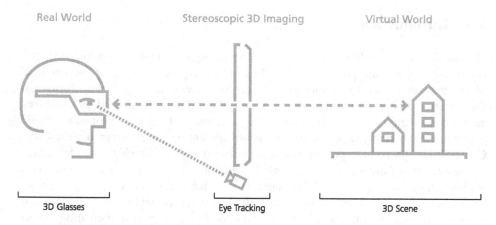

Fig. 1. Conceptual structure of ESTER for stereoscopic and eye-tracking based 3D visualizations of virtual scenes

2.1   Science Tool

The software framework ESTER provides a graphical experiment creation environment for scientists as well as interface and interaction designer. The features in ESTER have been designed to address many of the research needs that have been encountered when working with three-dimensional scenes in interactive environments. This ranges from simple experiments in which a static scene is shown that is explored by the user, to more sophisticated experiments in which the user interacts with virtual three-dimensional worlds.

The creation of experiments is achieved by an intuitive hierarchical experiment interface, which features building conceptual blocks (see Fig. 2). The functionality of the editor window supports the realization of simple as well as complex experimental procedures. Furthermore, custom JavaScript code can be added to extend experiments when required. Additionally, the editor window of ESTER provides a built-in 3D visual stimulus creation to compose primitives, textures, and lights into a virtual scene, with support for a multitude of import data formats. As a science tool for creating eye-tracking experiments, ESTER supports a variety of eye-tracking devices, performing camera set-up, calibration, and validation. ESTER also contains a real-time preview window that visualizes the currently selected three-dimensional scene as it is presented during the experiment. (see Fig. 2).

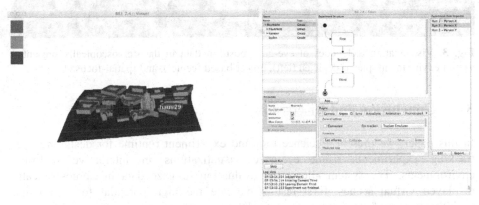

Fig. 2. Preview window of ESTER showing a virtual 3D scene (left) and Editor Window of ESTER showing the active experiment's configuration

2.2   Experiment Runtime

In order to improve visual analysis of gaze data in stereoscopically displayed virtual scenes, we propose a set of eye-gaze visualization techniques: *planar-depicted*, *object-based*, and *spatial-focused*. By providing different kinds of depicting eye-gaze data, visual attention can be depicted in different ways whereas a combination of these techniques has the potential to considerably facilitate usability studies in interactive 3D applications.

Comparable to the visualization of 2D eye-tracking data, ESTER provides a visualization method, which is a 2D planar representation of 3D fixation data (see Fig. 3 left). This kind of visualization can be used to analyze the visual attention of the user in principle due to the ambiguous representation, which results from 3D data depiction on a 2D layer.

To investigate a subject's attention towards individual scene elements, an object-based visualization method is integrated. This technique highlights objects that are focused using a representative color (see Fig. 3 center). This visualization technique is especially helpful to a supervising experimenter, because it allows the rapid identification of objects that are currently looked at by the subject.

With the spatial-focused visualization technique, we introduce a new gaze visualization of eye-tracking data for facilitating detailed inspection of visual attention of virtual worlds (see Fig. 3 right). Fixation data is visualized as spheres in the virtual world and allows the depiction of fixation locations in spatial coordinates. Compared to the previous techniques, the spatial-based attention visualization is the most complex approach due to the transformation of real eye fixation and saccades into virtual world coordinates. Thereby, the virtual depth position of user fixations are recordable and presentable.

Fig. 3. Visualization techniques of eye-gaze position data in the stereoscopically presented virtual environment: planar-depicted (left), object-based (center), and spatial-focused (right).

3   Conclusion and Discussion

In this paper, we present a science tool and experiment runtime for designing eye-tracking experiments using eye-gaze visualizations in interactive real-time environments. The system allows the evaluation of gaze data in stereoscopically displayed virtual scenes. First results indicate the high potential for facilitating usability studies of 3D user interfaces for HCI researchers and practitioners. However, visual gaze analysis of virtual worlds is still in an early stage and therefore offers much potential for further development. Using this system, interaction and interface designer can investigate 3D visualizations and interfaces relating to expectations concerning usability. This is achieved by the real-time representation of the visual attention inside the virtual scene and the evaluation of gaze behavior by recording and playing back the registered eye movements of subjects for usability studies.

4   Future Work

Prospectively, the hardware setup and the software framework comprising ESTER will be used for all steps required in regular user studies – from preparation, to live data recording, and finally data play back and analysis. Additionally, it is necessary to systematically compare the efficacy of the planar, object-based and spatial visualization technique to analyze their relative efficiency. Therefore, several parameters of the visualization methods have to be estimated in empirical studies. Furthermore, the creation of user studies using ESTER as a design tool and experiment runtime has to be validated by empirical studies of the system itself. Also, the improvement and optimization of the visualization techniques in the con-text of the evaluation of user data is needed. For example, it is highly desirable to represent data from several users at once for comparison purposes. In addition, possibilities to combine various auxiliary data, such as fixation duration, pupil radius, or viewing directions, have to be investigated.

References

1. Applied Informatics, http://www.appinf.com/index.html
2. Bourke, P.: Omni-Directional stereoscopic fisheye images for immersive hemispherical dome environments. In: Computer Games, Multimedia and Allied Technology, pp. 136–143 (2009)
3. Jokela, T., et al.: The standard of user-centered design and the standard definition of usability: analyzing ISO 13407 against ISO 9241-11. In: Proceedings of the Latin American Conference on Human-Computer Interaction, pp. 53–60 (2003)
4. Kammer, D., et al.: A component-oriented framework for experimental computer graphics. Elsevier - Comput. Stand. Interfaces 34(1), 93–100 (2012)
5. Kuehne, B., Martz, P.: OpenSceneGraph Reference Manual v2.2. Skew Matrix Software and Blue Newt Software (2007)
6. NVIDIA, http://www.nvidia.com/object/3d-vision-main.html
7. OSGi Alliance: OSGi Service Platform Release 4, Version 4.1. OSGi Alliance, San Ramon, CA, USA (2007)
8. Smart, J., et al.: Cross-platform GUI programming with wxWidgets. Prentice Hall (2006)
9. Stellmach, S., et al.: 3D Attentional Maps: Aggregated Gaze Visualizations in Three-dimensional Virtual Environments. In: Proceedings of the International Conference on Advanced Visual Interfaces, pp. 345–348. ACM, New York (2010)
10. Su, C.-H., et al.: A real-time robust eye tracking system for autostereoscopic displays using stereo cameras. In: IEEE International Conference on Robotics and Automation, Proceedings, ICRA 2003, vol. 2, pp. 1677–1681 (2003)
11. Weber, S., et al.: Eye tracking in real world and virtual environments: Algorithms for determining gaze position in 3D space. In: Proceedings of the17th European Conference on Eye Movements (2013)

Naïve Physics in Vehicle Steering Control

Xin Xu, Guy Wallis, and Steven Cloete

Centre for Sensorimotor Performance, School of Human Movement Studies,
The University of Queensland, QLD 4072, Australia
{x.xu1,gwallis,s.cloete}@uq.edu.au

Abstract. Wallis and colleagues have reported that drivers have a surprisingly limited understanding of the relation between steering movements and vehicle heading [1-3]. They suggest that popular models based on wholly open-loop or closed-loop control fail to capture a driver's true behavior. One limitation of Wallis et al.'s studies has been that they were all conducted on a straight road. Because of the tendency of passenger vehicles to self-center their steering wheels, it is possible that the effects which they report are due to drivers not actively centering the steering wheel, but simply releasing it. This report describes an experiment conducted on a circular road, which required a non-zero steering wheel angle to be actively selected by the driver at all times. Despite this added requirement, the results were highly consistent with previous experiments carried out on a straight road [1-3], confirming that the errors are due to the drivers' poor understanding of basic vehicle dynamics.

Keywords: lane-changing, ADAS, driving simulation.

1 Introduction

One of the major areas of current interest in motor vehicle technology is to develop advanced driver assist system (ADAS), which monitor numerous aspects of driver behavior and warn or in some cases actually intervene to help prevent accidents. However, a problem besetting such technology is that we do not have a full understanding of how humans control motor vehicles and hence the details of the behavior such technology should assist. Obviously, these unknowns could result in unforeseen consequences. For instance, a common task in daily driving behavior is lane changing. Current models largely fail to capture the nuances of how humans execute even such a basic maneuver, which could result critical errors that might themselves lead to dangerous or even fatal situations. These fatal errors could be corrected if an ADAS accurately predicts both what a driver intends and how he/she intends to do it. However, as mentioned above, such correction is based on current, limited understanding of a driver's behavior when changing lanes. Unsurprisingly, the scientific world has been making efforts to model such behavior, resulting in two widely accepted models being disproven. One is the open-loop model that suggests drivers can change lane without visual feedback [4-6]. Another is the closed-loop model which argues drivers rely on continuous visual feedback [7-16]. Till recently,

C. Stephanidis (Ed.): HCII 2014 Posters, Part I, CCIS 434, pp. 384–389, 2014.

academics on this lane-changing topic have been largely polarized according to these two models. However, in a more recent work in Wallis' lab, suggests that neither model captures the true control mechanisms employed [1-3]. Participants in Wallis' driving simulation experiments demonstrated the ability to change lane nearly perfectly with very limited visual feedback, lasting no more than 100ms, if presented during a critical time window [2]. However, drivers did make a systematic error when changing lane without vision at all. These errors were all due to the drivers completely omitting the second phase of this bi-phasic manoeuver [1-3]. These results appear inconsistent with either the open-loop or closed-loop model. However, the experiments reported were all carried out on a straight road in a driving simulation, hence the possibility arises that the tendency of a steering wheel to re-center itself may impact the drivers' behavior and render the result only true in the specific case that passive release of the wheel which results in the vehicle following the form of the road (straight), if not the true heading. Therefore, it is reasonable to assume different results might happen if subjects are required to change lane on a circular road, which requires a non-zero steering wheel angel at all times and hence that the drivers actively select a steering-wheel response at all times. This paper reports an experiment of lane changing on a circular road, carried out on a computer driving simulation with a force-feedback steering wheel. The results indicate that subjects made exactly the same characteristic mistake reported in previous experiments on straight roads, which suggests that the re-centering of the steering wheel is not the source of the error in either experiment. Instead, the results point to the presence of a fundamental misconception of the impact of a steering wheel on vehicle heading, which is normally compensated for through the use of appropriately timed, brief periods of visual feedback gathered during the maneuver.

2   Method

Experiments were carried out on a circular road with two lanes. A set of counter-balanced experiments were designed according to different conditions, such as the radius of the circular road (105m vs. 55m), the starting lane (inner lane vs. outside lane), and the direction in which the vehicle travelled (counterclockwise vs. clockwise). The combinations of all these conditions were as follows:

Table 1. Combinations of all conditions in this experiment

Radius	105m				55m			
Starting Lane	Inner Lane		Outside Lane		Inner Lane		Outside Lane	
Direction	Counter-	Clock-	Counter-	Clock-	Counter-	Clock-	Counter-	Clock-

Fig. 1. The virtual environment of this driving simulation. Left – aerial view, showing the roads of different radius Right – typical scene viewed from the vehicle driver's seat.

All subjects were required to complete two lane-changing tasks with and without visual feedback. The lane-changing task with vision was to test whether subjects could change lane at all, and also provide an opportunity to familiarize them with the driving simulation. The simulation was developed on an SGI ONYX3200 computer using custom software based on OpenGL and SGI Performer libraries. A typical scene in this simulation is illustrated in figure 1.

All subjects went through all these eight combinations and repeated them seven times for each combination described in table 1. Hence each subject conducted fifty-six trails in total. A total of fourteen subjects with current Australian driving license were tested although two were excluded from the analysis because they were unable to complete the task in the allotted 45 minutes. The procedure of each trail was described as following:

1. Trial starts with full visual feedback.
2. Subjects drive freely to familiarize.
3. Around 10 seconds elapse and then a red bar is displayed on the screen as a trigger to ask subjects to change lane.
4. Around 10 seconds after step 3, the screen is turned to black with a red bar on top of the screen as a trigger to ask subjects to change lane back into the lane they just came from.
5. Around 10 seconds after step 4. The current trial ends without letting subjects know their performance for lane changing without visual feedback, and a new trial with a different condition begins from step 3.

All these steps are preprogramed in the simulator and executed automatically.

3   Results

The data of the results were divided into two groups according to the direction of lane changing manoeuver, such as changing to the left lane from the right lane (Group 1) and changing to the right lane from the left lane (Group 0). If participants did lane-changing tasks successfully, then the vehicle's final heading after changing lane, either from left to right or right to left, should be consistent with the direction of the road. Otherwise, the final heading will deviate from the road, either over-steer to the left or over-turn to the right. Furthermore, to demonstrate a systematic error, the error of subjects' final heading should be consistent with the direction of the lane-changing task, such as over-turn to the left when subjects changed lane from right to left. The analysis of the final heading does show a systematic error, suggesting subjects produced an error that was directly comparable to that described in earlier studies using straight roads.

A paired-samples t-test was conducted to compare final heading error at 6.750 seconds, which we found is sufficient for most subjects to complete the manoeuver, after subjects were required to change lane from left to right and from right to left. There was a significant difference in the final heading errors for changing lane from left to right (M = -31.51, SD = 17.37), and from right to left (M = 34.21, SD = 19.55) conditions; t (11) = -6.75, p < .001, CI.95 -87.17, -44.28. Therefore, we reject the null hypothesis that there is no difference in final heading error between changing lane from left to right and from right to left. Further, Cohen's effect size value (d = 3.55) suggested a large practical significance.

With the given condition that negative M represents the angle of over-steer to the right while the positive M represents the angle of over-steer to the left, these results suggest subjects made a systematic error when they were asked to change lane without visual feedback on a circular road, in a manner consistent with studies conducted on a straight road.

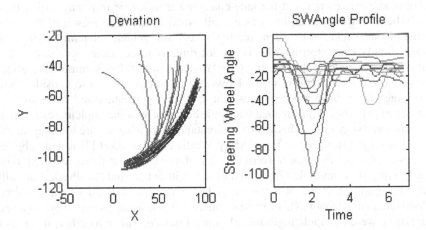

Fig. 2. Left - Deviation from road, Right - changes of steering wheel angle through the lane-changing maneuver without vision across twelve subjects from a single trial under a single combination of conditions (large radius, counter-clockwise, change from right to left)

Figure 2 reveals the behavior of twelve subjects when they were required to change lane from right to left. All the red lines in the left panel of figure 2 represent the actual trajectory travelled by subjects, while the blue lines are the expected path that subjects should follow in a correct lane-changing manoeuver. The different colorful lines on the right side of figure 2, which represent the changes of steering wheel angle, indicate that all of them only carried out the first phase of a lane-changing manoeuver, completely omitting the returning phase. Taken together, it is clear that most subjects over-steer to left, compared to the expected path, due to the fact that none of them completed a correct bi-phasic lane-changing maneuver.

Additionally, an interesting found in these results is that compared to previous study conducted on a straight road [1-2], the average heading errors reported here are considerably larger. In the study carried out in 2002 [1], 4 to 6 degrees of heading errors were reported in both direction of lane-changing. Likewise in Wallis et al. (2007) no more than 10 degrees of heading errors (regardless of different vehicle speeds) were reported [2]. However, as shown above, the average heading errors in this paper are -31.51 and 34.21 degrees. The reason of this significant difference may due to that different approach of calculating final heading errors that was applied. The study in both 2002 and 2007 asked subjects to release their steering wheel when they felt they complete the required manoeuver. This paper uses a fixed time for all subjects and calculated their heading errors based on that time. Despite the difference, final heading errors in both direction of lane-changing in aforementioned the three studies were all found to show the same trend and in each case the amplitude of the effect was comparable for both left and right lane changes.

4   Conclusion

The results reported here are consistent with the hypothesis that drivers employ a 'turn-and-see' approach to multiphase steering movements. [1-3].Without visual information, subjects carried out the lane-changing manoeuver in a way which they intuitively believe was correct, but was actually incomplete. The reason of this may due to the physical relation between steering wheel and vehicle's lateral position. In all modern family cars, steering wheels do not directly affect lateral position of the car, but rather the angle of the steering (front) wheels which has a cumulative effect on heading and in turn lateral position. However, all subjects seem to consider they could change the vehicle's lateral position by simply rotating-and-releasing the steering wheel [3]. They didn't realize that their behavior was incomplete, resulting in a significant over-steer error. This wrong understanding is what we are terming 'naïve physics'. A similar phenomenon reported by Wallis et al. in 2009 [3] tested subjects on tri-phasic steering movement (obstacle avoidance). The authors reported how subjects produced a multiple-phase maneuver without visual feedback but still omitted one phase, resulting in a bi-phasic lane-changing, instead of the required obstacle-avoidance behavior. This can be explained if one assumes that subjects acted as though they were manipulating a lateral control device. Taken together, this paper suggests the reason that subjects omitted one phase in both lane-changing and obstacle-avoidance tasks is neither because of re-centering of the steering wheel or because of the inability of a person to do a multiple-phase manoeuver without visual feedback, but is strongly related to this misconception i.e. 'naïve physics'.

The significance of these results is that they confirm that the heading error is not due to the vehicle wheels' self-centering, but due to the 'naïve physics' internalized by drivers. Therefore, in terms of the development of ADAS for monitoring and regulating lane-changing, one should consider the crucial moments at which feedback is being used which will inform the how and when a system detects errors and the timing and form of warnings or indeed, steering corrections.

Acknowledgements. The author Xu-Xin of this paper receives his fellowship from China Scholarship Council.

References

1. Wallis, G., et al.: An Unexpected Role for Visual Feedback in Vehicle Steering Control. Current Biology 12(4), 295–299 (2002)
2. Wallis, G., Chatziastros, A., Tresilian, J., Tomasevic, N.: The role of visual and non-visual feedback in a vehicle steering task. Journal of Experimental Psychology: Human Perception and Performance 33, 1127–1144 (2007)
3. Cloete, S., Wallis, G.: Limitations of feed-forward control in multiple-phase steering movements. Experimental Brain Research 195, 481–487 (2009)
4. Senders, J.W., et al.: The attentional demand of automobile driving. Highway Research Record (195), 15–32 (1967)
5. Godthelp, J.: Precognitive control: open- and closed-loop steering in a lane-change manoeuvre. Ergonomics 28(10), 1419–1438 (1985)
6. Hildreth, E.C., et al.: From vision to action: experiments and models of steering control during driving. J. Exp. Psychol. Hum. Percept. Perform. 26(3), 1106–1132 (2000)
7. Land, M., Horwood, J.: Which parts of the road guide steering? Nature 377(6547), 339–340 (1995)
8. Fajen, B., et al.: A Dynamical Model of Visually-Guided Steering, Obstacle Avoidance, and Route Selection. International Journal of Computer Vision 54(1-3), 13–34 (2003)
9. Fajen, B.R., Warren, W.H.: Behavioral Dynamics of Steering, Obstacle Avoidance, and Route Selection. Journal of Experimental Psychology: Human Perception and Performance 29(2), 343–362 (2003)
10. Wilkie, R., Wann, J.: Controlling steering and judging heading: Retinal flow, visual direction, and extraretinal information. Journal of Experimental Psychology: Human Perception and Performance 29(2), 363–378 (2003)
11. Salvucci, D.D., Gray, R.: A two-point visual control model of steering. Perception 33(10), 1233–1248 (2004)
12. Wilkie, R.M., Wann, J.P.: The Role of Visual and Nonvisual Information in the Control of Locomotion. Journal of Experimental Psychology: Human Perception and Performance 31(5), 901–911 (2005)
13. Land, M.F., Lee, D.N.: Where we look when we steer. Nature 369(6483), 742–744 (1994)
14. Wilkie, R.M., Wann, J.P.: Driving as Night Falls: The Contribution of Retinal Flow and Visual Direction to the Control of Steering. Current Biology 12(23), 2014–2017 (2002)
15. Robertshaw, K.D., Wilkie, R.M.: Does gaze influence steering around a bend? Journal of Vision 8(4) (2008)
16. Kandil, F.I., et al.: Driving is smoother and more stable when using the tangent point. Journal of Vision 9(1) (2009)

Multimodal and Natural Interaction

UCF Smart Mailbox: Reinforcing Communications in the Neighborhoods

Anastasia Angelopoulou[1], Konstantinos Mykoniatis[1], Karen Carlson[2], and Si-Jung Kim[2]

[1] Modeling & Simulation Graduate Program, University of Central Florida, Orlando, FL 32816, USA
{kmykoniatis,aangelopoulou}@knights.ucf.edu
[2] Digital Media - School of Visual Arts and Design, University of Central Florida, Orlando, FL 32816, USA
karenjcarlson@gmail.com, sjkim@ucf.edu

Abstract. Commonplace objects are being redesigned with digital functionality. Near invisible networks of radio frequency identification tags (RFID) are being deployed on almost every type of consumer product, and the "Ambient intelligence" promises to form a global network of physical objects as ubiquitous as the worldwide web itself. This diverse global network, "the internet of things" (IoT), provides digital connectivity on top of existing infrastructure and items. Nascent "smart object" developments like the presented "UCF Smart Mailbox," not only reformulate our relationship with the objects themselves, but they can also support social relationships that contribute to the sustainability of the society.

Keywords: Arduino, mailbox, sensors, audio, physical interaction, neighborhood, communications, temperature, notifications.

1 Introduction

In February 2013, the United States Post Office made a historic announcement: Saturday delivery will cease by August [1]. This follows a downward trend in mail so sharp that some speculate that paper mail be obsolete in the future. We look to the mailbox: the symbol of residential communication for two centuries, and ask a simple question: how can a mailbox be used to support communication between neighbors and strengthen community?

The answer lies in new media technology, the very technology often blamed for the breakdown of community in the 21st century neighborhood. "As the Internet further reduces the burden of distance, it may further degrade the role of the parochial realm; ties across the street may become increasingly rare as ties at a distance become ever more accessible" [2]. Digital technologies, while uniting people across distances, can also be used to reinforce place-based communities.

Urban planning and digital media practitioners have joined forces in the past several years to recast public spaces with tools and technologies to promote

C. Stephanidis (Ed.): HCII 2014 Posters, Part I, CCIS 434, pp. 393–398, 2014.

information sharing, community pride and play [3]. Examples of experimentation abound. Consider Mouna Andraos and Melissa Mongiat's "21 Swings", an urban installation in Montreal, Canada, where swinging generates a melody, but one that is best experienced communally, when many swings are engaged [4]. Imagine how many dreary bus stops could be improved with a musical swing installation: where people aren't shutting out the world by listening to music from their ipods and earbuds, but making music together, by moving their bodies.

Another whimsical application of digitally augmented public space is the Piano Staircase in Berlin, Germany, by Volkswagon. The stairs are painted like a piano and music sounds as they are stepped on. The designers of this installation had more than music in mind. They wanted to create an incentive for people to use the stairs, instead of the escalator, by making the stairs more fun. They were able to increase stair usage by 66% [5].

While the bulk of urban digital projects have focused on public places, some have concentrated on the domain of the neighborhood. Digital devices join a long line of technology blamed for the breakdown of community, including the air conditioner and television. Now smart phones and social media fulfill our communication needs without real time interaction or geographic proximity.

Can digital experiences draw people back outside and into communication patterns with their neighbors? This is the goal of The Smart Mailbox. Can the mailbox become its owners face and voice in a faceless community? Apostol et al. in "From Face-Block to Facebook or the Other Way Around," provide more fodder for our discussion: "We wish to employ the technology developed for such online communities to bring communities back to the "barn-raising"-type of collective action that could encourage participation, increase the feelings of solidarity and social capital, and lead to building community identity" [6]. As electronic mailboxes continue to innovate at rapid pace, physical mailboxes have changed little in the last century. Sensors implanted into everyday objects are changing the way we interact with our homes, transforming them into smart communicators [7]. Why should the mailbox be left behind?

We are not the first to ask this question. Denzil Ferraira, a computer science student at the University of Oulu in Finland created SmartMail: a digital physical mail. Using an ArduinoDuemilanove and a photosensitive sensor, he developed an electronic notification reporting "you've got mail" for physical mail [8].

2   Prototype Design Description and Implementation

This section describes the design process of the UCF Smart Mailbox, including the implemented algorithms, the hardware architecture and the prototype implementation. The UCF Smart Mailbox system is able to play a Personal Message that the owner wants to share with the community and also to record a message from the neighbors. If a message is recorded, the system notifies the owner for the recorded message. More specifically, a Twitter notification is sent to the owner via email. Twitter notifications about the outdoor environment's temperature and receiving a new mail are sent as well.

Software. Several algorithms were developed, such as for playing an audio file and recording a message. The mailbox plays an audio message if a person is detected near the mailbox (distance less than 1m). Another algorithm waits for input in order to allow the message recording. While the user presses the recording button, a message is being recorded. An LED turns on to indicate that a recording takes place. When the button is released, a Twitter notification is sent to the owner and the LED turns off to indicate that the recording is over. Algorithms for providing information about the temperature and the changes in light conditions were also implemented. The overall behavior of the UCF Smart Mailbox system is described using a UML diagram. The UML use case diagram (Fig. 1) illustrates the events that occur in order for the UCF Smart Mailbox owner to leave and/or receive messages from the neighbors.

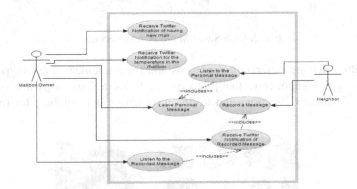

Fig. 1. UML Diagram for the UCF Smart Mailbox System

Hardware Architecture. The configuration of the hardware consists of a Rugged audio shield mounted on the Arduino board. A speaker and a microphone are connected on the Rugged Audio Shield for playing and recording a message, respectively. An XBee shield is placed on top of the Rugged Audio Shield. A proximity sensor and a force sensitive sensor are connected to the Xbee shield as inputs. Two XBees were used to send and receive signals for all the Twitter notifications. An LED is used to indicate that the message is recorded. A temperature sensor and a photocell provide information about the temperature and the changes in light conditions. The architecture diagram (Fig. 2) illustrates an internal view of the system architecture in order to understand the different components of the UCF Smart Mailbox's components and how they interact.

Prototype. The UCF Smart Mailbox prototype has been developed to give neighbors a geography-based tool for communication and interaction. The Mailbox exhibits the following functionalities:

- Proximity-triggered message broadcast
- Push button-triggered recording device for leaving a message
- Notification to owner via digital social network Twitter that a message has been delivered
- Notification to owner via digital social network Twitter that physical mail has been delivered
- Notification to owner of temperature at mailbox

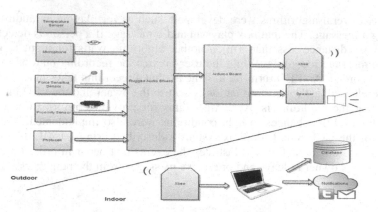

Fig. 2. UCF Smart Mailbox Architecture

Fig. 3 illustrates the different components and the implemented prototype. Except from the visual components, the prototype includes a Twitter-python script for sending the Twitter notifications and storing information in a database for future data manipulation.

Fig. 3. UCF Smart Mailbox Components & Prototype Representation

3   Pilot Testing and Results

The Smart Mailbox prototype was initially tested with 12 Central Florida community members. The participant population was all between the ages of 18-35 and included an equal number of males and females. Quantitative and qualitative data was collected in the form surveys. The experimenters also took notes during user-mailbox interaction to document usability issues. The experimental process consisted of three steps:

- Step One (Baseline Survey): Participants were asked to fill out a pre-demo survey about their residential status and communication patterns with neighbors.
- Step Two (Exposure to Mailbox): Participants were given verbal instructions from the experimenters about the Smart Mailbox. They were instructed to approach the mailbox, listen to the broadcast and leave a message for the mailbox owner.

- Step Three (After Exposure): After using the Smart Mailbox, participants were asked to complete the second survey. This survey assessed usability, feature set preference on the part of users and user projection about how they believed the Smart Mailbox may influence their neighborhood communication patterns.

After the collection and the cleaning of the raw data, we applied basic statistics to analyze the data. More specifically, the analysis included descriptive statistics such as mean, median, mode, and min/max, computing means (averages) and standard deviations, computing proportions and percentages, and drawing histograms or pie charts.

Mailbox Impact on Meeting New People. Users predict the Smart Mailbox will improve the likelihood of meeting new people in the next month. We compared the likelihood of meeting new people with and without using the Smart Mailbox, resulting in an average rating of 4.36 vs. 2.80 on a scale of 1-5. Males were more likely to rate the Smart Mailbox's potential to improve relationships, than females. Females averaged 3 (a few times a month), males averaged 4 (a few times a week). Users also predict they will walk around the neighborhood more if it had Smart Mailboxes (Fig. 4).

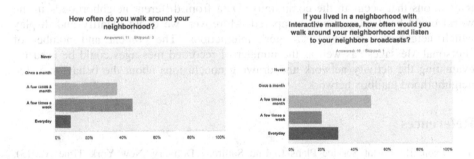

Fig. 4. Results about likelihood of walking around the neighborhood more

Feature Popularity. Ability to leave a message, hear a message and be notified when you receive mail all received equal average rating of 2.2 on a **scale** of 1-5 (1 being most useful, 5 being least useful). Ability to receive a temperature reading was the least popular feature and received a rating of 3.4.

Usability. While gender was not a focus of our study, we did collect demographic information that included gender. Males and Females rated most questions the same, however males found the Smart Mailbox significantly easier to use than females. On a scale of 1-5 (5=easy, 1=Difficult) males averaged 4.333 and females averaged 2.666. It would be interesting to see if this is repeated with a larger sample size.

Sociability Correlation to Type of Housing. We predicted that the type of housing a user lived in may influence their baseline level of sociability as well as their predictions about how the Smart Mailbox would influence their sociability. We did not have a large sample size, but can see from pilot data that single family home dwellers are more likely to know their neighbors and communicate with them than dorm and apartment dwellers. This may be explained by the temporary status of apartment and dorm living vs. the more permanent or 'settled' nature of single-family home dwellers. We did not ask whether single-family home dwellers owned their homes. That may be a question for a future survey. Perhaps owners are more likely to invest time and energy in getting to know their neighbors.

4   Conclusions and Future Work

A larger phase experiment could be conducted in the future to see if networked interactive mailboxes improve a community's sense of cohesiveness. We could track inter-community interactions and relationships before and after the installation to understand how the mailbox facilitates neighborliness. In the future, the UCF Smart mailbox system will integrate an identification and tracking module that will allow interaction with the users only if they carry an RFID tag. Future work may include transforming the recorded WAV messages to byte array, transmitting them to the receiver XBee, converting the byte array to WAV file and saving them in the database in order for the user to listen to them on a computer or a portable device. Future plans may also include the implementation of a blog/website to display and analyze the interactions that occur in the community. Data from different neighborhoods in the world could be displayed and compared. Moreover, we could identify and display which neighborhoods have "stronger" interactions. The content and number of "Personal Messages" as well as the number of recorded messages could be used for evaluating the activity network and drawing conclusions about the behavior of the neighborhood mailbox network.

References

1. Nixon, R.: Postal Service Plans to End Saturday Delivery. New York Times (2013), http://www.nytimes.com/2013/02/07/us/postal-service-plans-to-end-saturday-delivery.html?_r=0 (retrieved on February 27, 2013)
2. Hampton, K.: Neighborhoods in the Network Society the e-Neighbors study. Information, Communication & Society 10(5), 714–748 (2007)
3. Klaebe, H.G., Adkins, B.A., Foth, M., Hearn, G.N.: Embedding an ecology notion in the social production of urban space. In: Handbook of Research on Urban Informatics: The Practice and Promise of the Real-time City, pp. 179–194 (2009)
4. Andraos, M., Mongiat, M.: 21 Balançoires (2012), http://www.dailytouslesjours.com/project/21-balancoires/ (retrieved on February 27, 2013)
5. Volkswagon: Piano Staircase. The Fun Theory (2009), http://www.thefuntheory.com/ (retrieved on February 20, 2013)
6. Apostol, I., Antoniadis, P., Banerjee, T.: From Face-Block to Facebook or the other Way Around? In: Proceedings of Sustainable City and Creativity, Promoting Creative Urban Initiatives, Naples (2008)
7. Chan, M., Estève, D., Escriba, C., Campo, E.: A review of smart homes—Present state and future challenges. Comp. Methods and Programs in Biomedicine 91(1), 55–81 (2008)
8. Ferreira, D.: SmartMail-digital physical mail, http://www.denzilferreira.com/smart-mail/ (retrieved on February 22, 2013)

Sound Design in Interactive Environments

Luiz Roberto Carvalho and Alice T. Cybis Pereira

Federal University of Santa Catarina, Brazil
{semprecarvalho,acybis}@gmail.com

Abstract. As message transmitters, all acoustic signals - natural or constructed - are perceived as having specific information. However, a little amount of research has been directed to the study of what is heard by people about the world around them and how it occurs, especially with regard to its interrelationship with interactive environments applications. Based on the universe of hypermedia, this study aims to explain the main applications of sound in a broad perspective with regard to its features of content, form and function, which are manifested through the use of dialogue, ambience and sound effects.

Keywords: sound design, game sound, dynamic audio, interactive sound.

1 Hearing and Experience: A Sound Design Perspective

When hearing, memories are aroused and their meanings associated with the auditory event. Jekosch (2006) suggests that the listener has an acquisition system of sounds and meaning, or, in technical terms, a lexical set of sounds. This lexical set contains invariant auditory resources, such as the shape of the sound (like the typical sound caused by a hammer hitting metal), its contents of experience (strong sound of something crashing into another), and their inter-relationships of functions (use the blow of the hammer to forge the metal). These lexical items are important aspects of information that is used in order to obtain the associative meaning of the corresponding sound. Based on the individual stored meanings, a satisfactory correspondence between perception data, experience data and expectation will attach meaning to the sound event. So, to hear certain types of sound, systems of meanings are activated and used as a reference, being the auditory stimulus a signal carrier that associates these memorized events. As a result, a meaning is assigned to the sound stimulus. Such associations and meanings are also activated when an unknown sound is heard: the perceived characteristics of what is heard are correlated with an internal system of meanings, that contains all that was experienced by the individual, and this new information is then seized.

A significant scope for improvement in the field of sound design is given when the sound is analyzed in a broad perspective with regard to its features of content, form and function. The central question, then, focuses on pointing out how listeners process the acoustic events when they´re taken as information carriers. This question can be systematically examined making specific use of modern paradigms of psychoacoustics

C. Stephanidis (Ed.): HCII 2014 Posters, Part I, CCIS 434, pp. 399–403, 2014.

and semiotics. Jekosch (2006) suggests a new direction of research that understands and interprets the perceived auditory events as carriers of meaning, and calls it Semioacoustics, defined as the science of auditory signs.

Except for a few studies (BALLAS, 1993; GAVER, 1993 *apud* SUSINI et al., 2006), little research has been directed to investigate what is heard by individuals in the world and how this occurs. However, most part of studies have focused in the perception of sound attributes in terms of location, such as size and shape, leaving an empty space regard to sound and its properties related to emotional responses.

The perceived sounds in everyday life have emotional connotations which precede their cognitive interpretation, and these connotations influence how individuals perceive them. According to Tractinsky, Adi & Ikar (2000), studies have shown that emotional system modifies the operating level of the cognitive system. Emotions enable rapid decision-making, while cognition allows us to interpret and understand it. Thus, measuring the emotional quality of a product can provide access to the characterization of their function in terms of sound design. A systematic approach to affective reactions to sounds should increase the ability to predict human responses to products with sound properties.

2   Sound in Interactive Environments: Speech, Ambience and Sound Effects

Jekosch (2006) states that, in principle, each acoustic event can be perceived as a signal sending system by which certain information is transmitted. This is a well-established fact when it concerns sounds made by the human voice, through the spoken language. However, other types of sounds - such as music or sound effects - emitted by digital devices also communicate. In this context, the importance of sound is in the ability to capture the user´s attention at different levels. Tong and Wong (2006) argue that without the use of sound into interactive systems, the impact of a narrative is significantly reduced, and it may even become incomprehensible.

Jorge (2002) uses the term soundtrack to define all perceived sounds by the human ear. The soundtrack is a mix of different elements that can be divided into dialogue, ambience and sound effects. Apart from Jorge (2002), Serafin (2004) and Moses (2010) define that the acoustic events that occur in interactive systems can also be divided as follows:

a)   Dialogue, representing the sounds that express the spoken language;
b)   Ambience, divided into background music and sound environment;
c)   Sound Effects, also called by *Foley sounds*.

Iuppa & Borst (2010) say that to create a realistic interface, an especial attention must be given to sounds. If there is not a basic level of music and background sounds in the interactive environment, an insufficient atmosphere will be perceived by users. The soundtrack can provide an environment for the narrative context of the application, and its elements can serve to guide users and improve their overall experience.

In dialogues, human speech is intended to be informative. The background music sets the mood and pace of the narrative, being connected to emotional interpretation, and thus causing distinct reactions in the users. Ambient sound is the sound of natural background of a given environment. The sound effects are brief and have the function to highlight some point of the message by increasing its impact.

When individuals express themselves through speech, the attention is explicitly given to the words that are said, but also clings implicitly on how these words are spoken. Thus, the meaning is not exercised solely by verbal content, but also the vocal qualities that are imposed during the speech. Van Leeuwen (1999) divided human voice and classified it into different properties, which carry culturally formed communicative meanings, namely:

a)   tension: tight or tense;
b)   roughness: hoarse or guttural (being more associated with men, harsher tones);
c)   aeration: aerated or intimate (in Western cultures generally more airy voices are considered less authoritarian);
d)   sonority: expansive or mild;
e)   pitch: high or low (in terms of frequency spectrum, how high or low this voice may be);
f)   vibration: which tension level (in terms of vocal cords vibrationa, associated to the technical term *vibrato*).

Among all the items that compose the soundtrack, music can be considered one of the key elements to establish mood inductions. Music is categorized not only by its structure, but by the abstraction of events and cultural, social and psychological experiences, as well as by its subjective processes. Ilari (2006) suggests that music is a social phenomenon that has maintained traditional roles and own meanings in different societies throughout history: in Western world, the music has specific functions in human activities such as dancing, storytelling, celebrating special dates, praying, entertaining, and also selling products. These and the many other functions of music in everyday life are clearly related to interpersonal relationships and, based on this premise, regarding to species' evolution, the music plays an important role. According to the author, to the African Yorubas, for instance, the use of music implies the idea of kinship, religion, politics and economics. As for Brazilian Capoeiras, music is associated with body movement, a ritual of freedom.

According to Martinez (2000), music refers to a variety of acoustic and non-acoustic objects, and may be associated with other forms of expression, belonging to visual and verbal fields. Forms such as dance, theater, multimedia and hypermedia itself constitute languages that canalize their meanings through the two main human senses, hearing and vision, which are the main aesthetic senses. The efficiency of these aesthetic forms of expression - that make music their base or share it with their properties in various types of connective structures - is the way they process complex signs, addressing the two main human senses and enabling a wealth of meaning and interpretation.

To Parker & Heerema (2008), the sound effects have multiple functions, being frequently used as a confirmation feedback to a requested activity. To this end, sound effects need to be representative of the sounds that are part of the things in the world, since the metaphorically represented objects in interface resemble the real objects. Another important function of the sound effects is to add a sense of reality and presence to an ambient.

Using volume levels it is possible to classify which sounds are important and which are less – this is the dynamic volume control that is mentioned in Gibson (1997). A constant balance between all sound effects does not direct any focus to a narrative particular aspect, but nevertheless, when a sound abruptly changes its volume, attracts attention, ie, becomes more important. Tong and Wong (2006) indicated that it is possible to use parameters of equalization to make a sound become "closer" to the user. Accentuating the frequencies around 3.000 Hz in a dialogue will result in a much more clearer and audible sound. The playback speed of a sound can also change its property. For a rhythmic sound, like the sound of an automobile engine ignition, reducing its time will result in a feeling of losing potency. On the other hand, by increasing its speed, there is a impression of a strong structure. By changing the speed of the sound, a different interpretation about the amount of power produced by the engine is achieved.

As pointed out, the sound in interactive environments is mainly comprised of three elements: dialogue, ambience and sound effects. However, McKee (2006) suggests that silence, or almost no sound, also need to be part of any considerations about sound in interactive systems. The silence was, until recently, the default setting for any interactive web display, given that its reproduction was very fragmented and the methods to insert sound files were also very complex. However, in recent years, such conditions have changed, and silence is no longer necessarily the default setting of interactive environments. Being able to hear sound, it is also possible to hear silence, ie, its use become purposeful. Silence is no longer a default, but a choice, and hypermedia designers need to make a conscious use of this element. Perceiving silence is complex, it involves listening to an absent presence – the silence legitimizes their break and the sound legitimate the silence in such a way that there is not a split between them - hence the importance of silence in all discussions about sound. Silence should not be considered in isolation, but as an important and integral element of sound, whose relationship with the other elements, such as dialogue, ambience and sound effects, must be promptly investigated .

3   Final Considerations

In terms of perception, these sound synthesis parameters are difficult to estimate with high accuracy. Interactive processes give rise to an equivalent perception that only corresponds to an approximate factual physics reality. Especially where interaction is a key issue, the sound design should consider the most advanced requirements of the user experience design to achieve tangible results. However, there is still a relative absence of analysis tools with sufficient functional and aesthetic potential to extract relevant information about the impact of sound in the context of interactivity.

Sound design applied to interactive environments is a relatively new area in the academic field, yet not sufficiently able to develop strong theories without a substantial empirical research, which will examine the practice of audio productions in this area. So, it is important to proceed with the discussion of audio into objects and interactive systems, as a way to evidence the need of a new group of knowledge that will point out the important role played by sound into interactive systems.

By showing the sound structures present in an interactive system, there is a relevant starting point to designing sounds in hypermedia in a consistent and systematic manner. Interactive environments mobilize distinct perceptual modes and quickly transform our symbolic structures and signification systems. Proposing more organic ways to organize the user cognitive structure becomes indispensable.

References

1. Gibson, D.: The Art of Mixing. MixBooks, Michigan (1997)
2. Ilari, B.: Música, comportamento social e relações interpessoais. In: Psicologia em Estudo, vol. 11(1), Maringá (January/April 2006)
3. Iuppa, N., Borst, J.: Terry. End-to-end game development: creating independent serious games and simulations from start to finish. Elsevier, Massachusetts (2010)
4. Jekosch, U.: Sound Perception and Sound Design. In: 2nd ISCA/DEGA Tutorial & Research Workshop on Perceptual Quality of Systems, Deutschland, Berlin (2006)
5. Jorge, R.P.: Edição de som: algumas perspectivas. Caleidoscópio: Revista de Comunicação e Cultura. Lisboa, Portugal: Departamento de Ciências da Comunicação, Artes e Tecnologias da Informação da Universidade Lusófona de Humanidades e Tecnologias (ULHT), vol. 2(2) (2002)
6. Martinez, J.L.: Semiótica da música na multimídia e hipermídia computadorizada. Projeto de pesquisa vinculado ao Programa de Pós-Graduação em Comunicação e Semiótica e a Faculdade de Comunicação e Artes do Corpo da PUC-SP. Ago, (2000), Disponível em: http://www.pucsp.br/~cos/rism/projet-j.htm (acesso em: November 22, 2012)
7. Mckee, H.: Sound matters: Notes toward the analysis and design of sound in multimodal webtexts. Computers and Composition 23(3), 335–354 (2006)
8. Moses, L.: Sound Design. EventDV 23(1), 37 (2010)
9. Parker, J.R., Heerema, J.: Audio Interaction in Computer Mediated Games. International Journal of Computer Games Technology 2008, Article ID 178923, 8 pages (2008)
10. Serafin, S.: Sound Design to Enhance Presence in Photorealistic Virtual Reality. In: Proceedings of the 2004 International Conference on Auditory Display, Sidney, Australia, July 6-9 (2004)
11. Susini, P., et al.: Closing the Loop of Sound Evaluation and Design. In: 2nd ISCA/DEGA Tutorial & Research Workshop on Perceptual Quality of Systems, Deutschland, Berlin (2006)
12. Tong, K.-P.M., Wong, K.-W.: Schematic interface of sound creation for computer animators. Journal of Zhejiang University. China, Science 7(7) (2006)
13. Tractinsky, N., Adi, S.-K., Ikar, D.: What is Beautiful is Usable. Interacting with Computers 13, 127–145 (2000)
14. Leeuwen, V.: Theo. Speech, music, sound. Macmillan, London (1999)

Virtual Dressing System for Fashion Coordination Using Parallel Retrieval Interactive Tabu Search

Shoya Domae[1], Hiroshi Takenouchi[2], and Masataka Tokumaru[2]

[1] Graduate School of Kansai University
3-3-35 Yamate-cho, Suita-shi, Osaka 564-8680, Japan
[2] Kansai University, 3-3-35 Yamate-cho, Suita-shi, Osaka 564-8680, Japan
{k220958,toku}@kansai-u.ac.jp, takenouchi_hiroshi@yahoo.co.jp

Abstract. We implemented a virtual dressing system that presents fashion coordination recommendations to users based on their likes and dislikes using parallel interactive tabu search (ITS). Parallel ITS operations were implemented via user hand movements tracked by a Kinect sensor. Our proposed system automatically generates numerous fashion coordination recommendations that consist of four components, namely jackets, shirts, pants, and socks. Users choose multiple fashion coordination that they likes while trying on clothes virtually. In this study, we performed evaluation experiments with real users to demonstrate the efficacy of our proposed system. Experimental results show that our proposed system successfully presented fashion coordination based on user likes and dislikes.

Keywords: Virtual dressing system, Parallel ITS, Kinect sensor.

1 Introduction

When customers choose clothes at apparel stores, they often try these clothes on to ensure proper size and an acceptable appearance, which can be a laborious and task for customers. To address this problem, researchers have developed several virtual dressing systems that produce images of users virtually trying on clothes[1]–[3]. More specifically, researchers have developed virtual dressing systems using the Kinect sensor and suGATALOG to coordinate the user's clothes using their own wearing image[1][2]. These systems can reduce user evaluation load for choosing clothes; however, these systems tend to have the problem in which users must choose from a large number of clothes and options.

Therefore, we implemented a virtual dressing system for fashion coordination to recommend fashion coordination that the user likes from a number of clothes using parallel interactive tabu search (ITS)[4]. In our simulation results, we confirmed that parallel ITS was able to retrieve the user's likes and dislikes efficiently from each user's complex sensitivity space[4]. Until now, the effectiveness of parallel ITS for real users has not been demonstrated. Therefore, we

C. Stephanidis (Ed.): HCII 2014 Posters, Part I, CCIS 434, pp. 404–409, 2014.

implemented a virtual dressing system for fashion coordination using parallel ITS. In our proposed system, we implemented parallel ITS operations in which the user manipulates the system with his or her hands using a Kinect sensor. The user chooses multiple fashion coordination that he or she likes and dislikes from a large number of fashion coordination while trying on clothes virtually. In this study, we performed evaluation experiments with real users to demonstrate the effectiveness of our proposed system.

2 Virtual Dressing System for Fashion Coordination

2.1 Parallel ITS

Parallel ITS uses Tabu Search (TS) as an Evolutionary Computation (EC) algorithm. TS is a local search method which retrieves a local neighborhood of the current optimum candidate solution and generates new candidate solutions. In parallel ITS, a user chooses candidate solutions that he or she likes and dislikes from the presented candidate solutions. Parallel ITS generates multiple retrieval paths and retrieves candidate solutions in the complex sensitivity space. Therefore, parallel ITS can retrieve the user's likes and dislikes space.

Figure.1 shows the schematic of parallel ITS. In the first generation, parallel ITS randomly generates initial candidate solutions and presents them to the user. The user chooses candidate solutions that he or she likes and dislikes. The candidate solutions that the user likes and dislikes generate multiple retrieval paths; these retrieval paths are positive TS (PTS) and negative TS (NTS) paths, respectively. Each PTS and NTS path generates neighboring candidate solutions. In addition, parallel ITS randomly generates candidate solutions and presents them to the user.

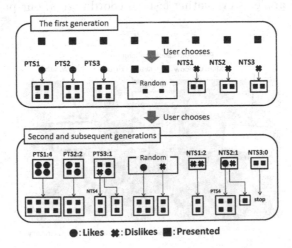

Fig. 1. Schematic of parallel ITS

In the second and subsequent generations, the user chooses candidate solutions that he or she likes and dislikes from candidate solutions generated by the PTS and NTS paths and those randomly generated. The PTS and NTS paths generate neighboring candidate solutions. Parallel ITS regards the number of neighboring candidate solutions that the user chooses as the evaluation value of the PTS and NTS paths. The PTS and NTS paths generate neighboring candidate solutions using the ratio of the evaluation values. Parallel ITS presents the candidate solutions generated by the PTS and NTS paths and those randomly generated to the user. Parallel ITS repeats these steps until the final generation.

2.2   Proposed System

Figure.2 shows the proposed system. As shown, the main window displays presented candidate solutions and the virtual user trying on clothes. The "good" window displays fashion coordinations that the user likes, whereas the "bad" window displays that the user dislikes.

We implemented the parallel ITS operation such that the user manipulates our proposed system with his or her hands using via a Kinect sensor. First, the user stands in front of the main window. Our proposed system automatically generates numerous fashion coordination consisting of four components, namely jackets, shirts, pants, and socks; these are presented to the user. Next, the user chooses multiple fashion coordination that he or she likes and dislikes from the presented fashion coordination while he or she is virtually trying on. To do so, the user manipulates our proposed system by moving his or her right hand from side to side. The center of the presented candidate solutions are virtually tried on. The user then chooses whether he or she likes (or dislikes) the fashion coordination by moving his or her left hand to the right (or the left). These actions move the fashion coordination to the "good" window or the "bad" window. Finally, when the user completes evaluating fashion coordination, our proposed system

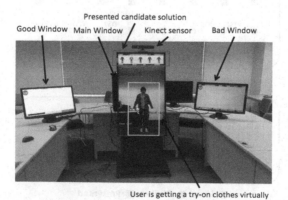

Fig. 2. Virtual Dressing System for Fashion Coordination

proceeds to the next generation by putting his or her right hand down. The user repeats these operations until the last generation.

2.3 Fashion Coordination Design

Figure.3 shows the gene coding for our fashion coordination design. We make fashion coordination design from the the Marvelous Designer[5]. Each component has eight or sixteen designs, which are expressed by 3 or 4 bits in coding. As observed in the figure, our proposed system can generate $32,768(=2^{15})$ different patterns.

3   Evaluation Experiment

3.1   Outline of the Experiment

We performed evaluation experiments with real users to demonstrate the efficacy of our proposed system. Eleven university students, all in their 20s, were the subjects of our experiments. The subjects were instructed to use our proposed system to choose what they would prefer wear clothes during winter.

Table 1 shows the parameters of parallel ITS. Subjects evaluated fashion coordination for five generations. After the experiments, the subjects evaluated the satisfaction levels of resulting fashion coordination and the efficacy of our proposed system through a 4-stage evaluation. In addition, we examined the number of candidate solutions that the user chose in every generation.

3.2   Experimental Results

Figure.4 shows the number of chosen candidate solutions. "like" is the number of candidate solutions that the user liked and "dislike" is the number of candidate solutions that the user disliked. The number of chosen candidate solutions

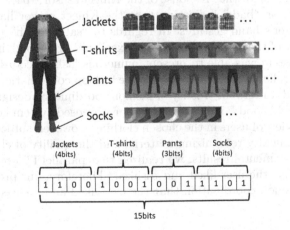

Fig. 3. Gene coding for our fashion coordination design

Table 1. Parallel ITS Parameters

Gene length	15 bits
Generations	5
Candidate solutions in the first generation	20
Tabu list	8
Neighboring range	1 bit

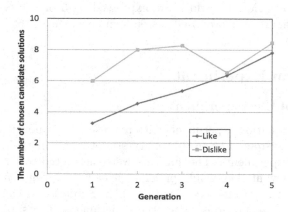

Fig. 4. Chosen candidate solutions

increased as the generations proceeded. Therefore, the number of candidate solutions that the user liked and disliked also increased as the generations proceeded. As a result, parallel ITS could retrieve fashion coordination that the user liked and disliked.

Figure.5 shows survey results. In regards to the "usability" of our proposed system, 55% of the subjects answered "good," indicating that our proposed system is easy to use. As for the "response of the Kinect sensor," 64% of the subjects answered "poor" or "bad," indicating that the Kinect sensor had difficulty in recognazing a user's hand gestures. In regards to "satisfaction" (after the fifth generation), 73% of the subjects answered "excellent" or "good," indicating that our proposed system was able to present numerous fashion coordination to the user, because parallel ITS was able to retrieve fashion coordination that the user liked and disliked. In term of "reality of fashion coordination design," 55% of the subjects answered "good," indicating that our proposed system could express a realistic virtual view of users in the chosen clothing; however, subjects also stated that they had difficulty recognizing material and the quality of clothes.

From our experimental results, we realized that parallel ITS retrieved candidate solutions that the user liked and disliked. Therefore, our proposed system could present fashion coordination that the user liked and disliked.

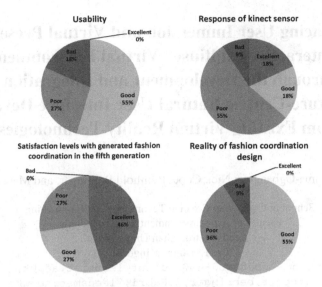

Fig. 5. Survey results

4   Conclusion

In this paper, we presented a virtual dressing system for fashion coordination using parallel ITS. We performed evaluation experiments with real users to demonstrate the efficacy of our proposed system. The experimental results implied that our proposed system was able to present fashion coordination that the user liked and disliked because parallel ITS retrieved candidate solutions that the user liked and disliked. In our future work, we aim to increase the types and variety of clothing presented to users.

Acknowledgments. This work was supported by MEXT.KAKENHI(24500264).

References

1. Ioannis, P., Kostas, K.: Augmented Reality Platforms for Virtual Fitting Rooms. The International Journal of Multimedia and Its Applications 4(4), 35–46 (2012)
2. Sato, A., Watanabe, K., Yasumura, M., Rekimoto, J.: suGATALOG: Fashion coordination system that supports users to choose everyday fashion with clothed pictures. In: Kurosu, M. (ed.) HCII/HCI 2013, Part V. LNCS, vol. 8008, pp. 112–121. Springer, Heidelberg (2013)
3. Cecilia Garcia, M., Erdal, O.: Human Friendly Interface Design for Virtual Fitting Room Applications on Android Based Mobile Devices. Journal of Signal and Information Processing 3(4), 481–490 (2012)
4. Domae, S., Takenouchi, H., Tokumaru, M.: Parallel Retrieval Interactive Tabu Search. In: 14th International Symposium on Advanced Intelligent Systems 2013, T3f-2, pp. 35–46 (2013)
5. Marvelous Designer, http://www.marvelousdesigner.com/

Enhancing User Immersion and Virtual Presence in Interactive Multiuser Virtual Environments through the Development and Integration of a Gesture-Centric Natural User Interface Developed from Existing Virtual Reality Technologies

Chika Emma-Ogbangwo, Nick Cope, Reinhold Behringer, and Marc Fabri

School of Computing Creative Technology and Engineering
Faculty of Arts, Environment and Technology
Leeds Metropolitan University,
Leeds, United Kingdom
c.emma-ogbangwo2888@student.leedsmet.ac.uk,
{n.cope,r.behringer,M.Fabri}@leedsmet.ac.uk

Abstract. Immersion, referring to the level of physical or psychological submergence of a user within a virtual space relative to that user's consciousness of the real-world environment, has predominantly been established as an indispensable part of interactive media designs. This is most prevalent in *Virtual Reality* (VR) platforms, as their applications are typically reliant on user believability. With a wide variation of possible methodologies for the enhancement of this feature, the collectively recognised paradigm lies on the emphasis of naturalism in the design of the virtual system [7].

Though widely used by some specialised VR applications [4] such concepts are yet to be fully explored in the more contemporary virtual systems such as Social Immersive Virtual Environment (SIVE).

The focus of the study described in this paper are the techniques being developed to enhance user immersion, virtual presence and co-presence in a SIVE application, through the design and integration of a VR-based *Natural User Interface* (NUI) that allows users to naturally and intuitively interact with the virtual environment and other networked users through the utilisation of full body gesture controls. These gestural controls prioritise the emulation of the alternate equivalent of such real-wold interactions, whilst also providing an interface for the seamless and unobtrusive translation of the user's real-world physical state into the virtual environment through intuitive user to virtual avatar proprioceptive coordination.

1 Introduction

With the increasing advancement in digital computing technologies comes an equivalent increase in the processing resources available to Virtual Environment (VE) developers, consequently resulting in its increase in complexity. For SIVE

C. Stephanidis (Ed.): HCII 2014 Posters, Part I, CCIS 434, pp. 410–414, 2014.
© Springer International Publishing Switzerland 2014

applications, however, there is a need for the inclusion of additional subsystem that effectively translates the user's real-world physical state upon their actualised virtual representation, consequently leading to the introduction of a *Natural User Interface (NUI)* paradigm for the sustainability of user immersion and virtual presence. While there have been a significant number of studies utilising the NUI design concept [4], an invariably high number of such studies are typically focused on its integration within the more specialised VR applications, with virtual systems such as the SIVE platform still utilising conventional 2D UIs. Notable limitations of such 2D UIs are in the form of a disconnection between performed user actions and its resulting effects on the reactive VE. In SIVE applications, these limitations are significantly more prevalent as certain UI functionalities, particularly those required for inter-user communication, cannot be effectively adapted to such UI due to the obvious limitation of their implemented technologies.

Mitigating such limitations is the primary focus of this study, as it seeks to utilise the NUI design concepts within a SIVE application, intuitively adapting its immersive VR technologies for the development and integration of an NUI architecture that allows for seamless and unobtrusive user virtual interaction, perception, embodiment and inter-user communication, within a perceptively shared immersive virtual space. Its approach primarily seeks to focus on the emulation of natural real-world interaction and communication paradigms within its SIVE's Interaction, Perception, and Embodiment UIs.

2   Related Works

While the integration of the NUI design concept in VR and other immersive applications can be considered as being relatively new, a significant number of studies have been done in this area with their respective scope ranging from the focus on a single component within the UI to the development of multimodal architectures. Among these studies include *HandNavigator* device [10] and *Piivert* device [3], with [10] focusing on kinesthetic virtual interaction, [3] combining the Ray-Casting technique with a finger gesture UI. The implementation of the hybrid UI concepts is a relatively common methodology in immersive VR development, as illustrated by *EyeMotion* interface [8], which integrated gaze tracking technology with a gesture recognition and mouse input interface.

With regards to user virtual navigation, methodologies for UI integration can generally be classified as either Position Tracking Interfaces, or User Controlled Interfaces. Notable work done on position tracking in immersive VR include *Redirection Technique* [12], which constituted the dynamic adjustment of the user's translational and rotational movements within the VE in order to compensate for the limited available real-world space. Other methodologies from related studies include *Immersive Navidget* [9], and the *Step WIM interface* [11]. Though typically not prioritised by most NUI developers, there has, however, been some notable work done on the immersive embodiment UI, with some methodologies developed by previous studies including haptic user *kinesthetic interface* [1], *Puppet UI* concept [6], and proprioceptive embodiment UI [5], which utilised the Vicon motion tracking system.

3   Research Methodology

Considering the limitations of the methodologies employed in the current state of the art, this study's approach to the integration of the NUI concept within a VR SIVE application (developed via Crytek's *CryEngine 3 SDK*) focuses on emphasising the emulation of natural real-world interaction and communication paradigm within the VE, through an unobtrusive gesture-centric user control interface.

3.1   The Interaction UI

Gesture sequences configured in the Interaction UI utilise a combination of single and two-handed virtual interaction technique, while position translational gestures implements a series of static user leg gestures that natural depict the intended direction of movement. For user perspective viewpoint control, however, the interaction UI implements a hybrid architecture, consisting of a hand motion tracking and head tracking system respectively. Through the Kinect device, the hand tracking system incorporates a series of static hand gestures that naturally depict the intended direction of viewpoint orientation, while the alternate head tracking system makes use of NaturalPoint Inc's *TrackIR 5* (6DOF) and *Trackclip Pro* head tracking device, for viewpoint orientation control.

3.2   The Embodiment UI

Utilised for the visualisation of avatar Non-Verbal Communication (NVC) features within the SIVE, the embodiment UI comprises of the *Autonomous Non-Verbal Communication (ANVC)* system, the *Motor Spatial Mapping (MSM)* system, and the avatar *Lip-Sync Emulation (LSE)* system. Consisting of a series of static (MSM) and dynamic (ANVC) gesture libraries, synchronously tracked and recognised, the MSM and ANVC systems allowed for natural user to avatar motor channel proprioceptive coordination, and the LSE system used for the visualisation of avatar lip-syncing functionalities.

3.3   Designing the GMA API

Written in C# programming language, and developed via Microsoft Visual Studio 2012's .NET Framework, the GMA API is a custom designed software application created and implemented for the purpose of interfacing the NUI's immersive VR technology with a target SIVE platform. Interfaced with the NUI's VR technology and the SDK's SIVE application through *Open Sound Control (OSC)* networking, the GMA is utilised in the integration of the interaction UI's gesture-based VE interaction and navigation interface, the embodiment UI's ANVC, MSM, and LSE sub-systems, and the perception UI's user *crossConnection* system. In order to achieved precise gesture recognition the GMA consist of three independently developed interrelated APIs comprising of the *GMASynthesiser*, the *GMARecognizer.dll* class libraries, and the *GesturePak API*.

3.4   Research Testing and Evaluation

While this study is currently part of an ongoing research, its intended methodology for evaluation would require three distinct VR setups, including the *NUI HMD-Based VR* (for *Discrete Evaluation* data), the *NUI Desktop-Based* VR (used for *Experiment Control* data), and the *Desktop VR* (for analysis *Baseline* data). Testing procedures would involve the engagement of participants through multiple *Virtual Scenarios (VS)*, consisting of VS1, VS2, and VS3, incorporated for the evaluation of immersion, interface usability, virtual presence and co-presence, through a communicative, natural interactive and contemporary IVE virtual scenarios respectively. Adopting the triangulation methodology, quantitative data being measured would be the participants' *Heart Rate Variation (HRV)* values, critically evaluated via a proposed *Response Expectancy (RE)* concept, which would seek to correlate expected changes in participants' HRV values to its actual changes relative to the current state of the SIVE. Supporting qualitative analysis would utilise Presence Evaluation and Immersive Tendency Questionnaires and interviews.

4   Conclusion

This study presents a gesture-centric NUI architecture that aims at emphasising natural virtual interaction and inter-user communication within a SIVE application, for the purpose of enhancing its user immersive quality. To achieve this, the GMA API was developed and utilised in the integration of a multi-tiered UI architecture consisting of a multimodal *Interaction UI*, a proprioceptive *Embodiment UI* and an immersive *Perception UI*. While the study is currently part of an ongoing research, critical evaluation of the developed NUI architecture would adopt a triangulation methodology, implementing quantitative measures via a proposed *RE HRV* concept, and qualitative measures done through suitable *ITQ* and *PQ* templates.

References

1. Ahn, S.J.: Embodied Experiences in Immersive Virtual Environments: Effects on Pro-Environmental Attitude and Behaviour (2011), http://vhil.stanford.edu/pubs/2011/ahn-embodied-experiences.pdf (accessed March 13, 2014)
2. Banos, R.M., et al.: Immersion and Emotion: Their Impact on the Sense of Presence (2004), http://www.itu.dk/~khhp/Konceptudvikling/Banos,%20R%20M,%20mfl%20-%20Immersion%20and%20Emotion%20Their%20Impact%20on%20the%20.pdf (accessed March 17, 2014)
3. Berthaut, F., Hachet, M., Desainte-Catherine, M.: Piivert: Percussion-based Interaction for Immersive Virtual Environments (2010), http://www.researchgate.net/profile/Martin_Hachet/publication/224129938_Piivert_Percussion-based_interaction_for_immersive_virtual_environments/file/504635156a0986c566.pdf (accessed March 12, 2014)

4. Deller, M., Ebert, A., Bender, M., Hagen, H.: Flexible Gesture Recognition for Immersive Virtual Environments (2006), http://www.researchgate.net/publication/4247845_Flexible_Gesture_Recognition_for_Immersive_Virtual_Environments/file/72e7e51a5f0769ba3b.pdf (accessed February 03, 2014)
5. Dodds, T.J., Mohler, B.J., Bulthoff, H.H.: Talk to the Virtual Hands: Self-Animated Avatars Improve Communication in Head-Mounted Display Virtual Environments) (2011), http://www.plosone.org/article/fetchObjectAttachment.action?uri=info%3Adoi%2F10.1371%2Fjournal.pone.0025759&representation=PDF (accessed March 13, 2014)
6. Eirik, F., Xin, L.: The Puppet UI: Tools for Nonverbal Communication in Virtual Environments (2007), http://www.thoughtbird.com/portfolio/puppetui/puppetui_paper.pdf (accessed March 13, 2014)
7. Hillaire, S., Lecuyer, A., Cozot, R., Casiez, G.: Using an Eye-Tracking System to Improve Camera Motions and Depth-of-Field Blur Effects in Virtual Environments (2008), http://people.rennes.inria.fr/Anatole.Lecuyer/vr08_hillaire.pdf (accessed February 03 2014)
8. Jimenez, J., Gutierrez, D., Latorre, P.: Gaze-based Interaction for Virtual Environments (2008), http://giga.cps.unizar.es/~diegog/ficheros/pdf_papers/final.pdf (accessed March 12, 2014)
9. Knodel, S., Hachet, M., Guitton, P.: Navidget for Immersive Virtual Environments (2008), http://iparla.inria.fr/publications/2008/KHG08a/paper.pdf (accessed March 13, 2014)
10. Kry, P.G., et al.: HandNavigator: Hands-on Interaction for Desktop Virtual Reality (2008), http://www.cs.mcgill.ca/~kry/pubs/hn/hn.pdf (accessed March 12, 2014)
11. LaViola, J.J., et al.: Hands-Free Multi-Scale Navigation in Virtual Environments (2001), http://cs.brown.edu/~jjl/pubs/i3d01_laviola.pdf (accessed March 13, 2014)
12. Suma, E.A., et al.: A Taxonomy for Deploying Redirection Techniques in Immersive Virtual Environments (2012), http://ict.usc.edu/pubs/A%20Taxonomy%20for%20Deploying%20Redirection%20Techniques%20in%20Immersive%20Virtual%20Environments.pdf (accessed March 12, 2014)

FlexiWall: Interaction in-between 2D and 3D Interfaces

Ingmar S. Franke, Mathias Müller, Thomas Gründer, and Rainer Groh

Chair of Media Design, Technische Universität Dresden, 01062 Dresden, Germany
{ingmar.franke,mathias.mueller,thomas.gruender,
rainer.groh}@tu-dresden.de

Abstract. Elastic displays offer new ways to interact with multi-dimensional data by using the deformation of the surface as a tool to explore, filter, structure, or manipulate data. While a large number of prototypes exist, a general concept for using this promising technology in real-world application domains has not been established. In this paper, we introduce a framework about elastic displays and their applications with reference to the interaction techniques they provide. We investigate the data applicable to elastic displays and the appropriate interaction techniques. Using this approach, it is possible to identify strengths and weaknesses of this technology regarding specific scenarios, to find commonalities to traditional user interfaces and to explore novel concepts for interaction.

Keywords: Elastic Displays, Haptic Interaction, Natural Interaction.

1 Introduction

Devices with elastic displays have the potential to establish novel user interfaces by extending traditional multi-touch technology with an additional interactive dimension. We can utilize the deformation of the display in addition to the touch capabilities of the surface. Over the last years, several hardware prototypes have demonstrated the power of this technology by analyzing specific use cases. However, there is a need for a general model, which describes the strengths and weaknesses of elastic displays, regardless of the specific hardware. The additional capabilities of this technology require a careful application design. Especially the consideration of specific features of the technology is necessary to provide a significant benefit compared to traditional devices. We investigate different types of applicable data structures and describe possible mappings of suitable interaction techniques. Using this model, it is possible to define the abilities and potential issues of elastic displays regarding specific application domains.

2 Related Work

Recently, researchers have started to focus on interactive surfaces other than rigid ones [1, 2]. While there is a considerable body of work in the literature regarding malleable

C. Stephanidis (Ed.): HCII 2014 Posters, Part I, CCIS 434, pp. 415–420, 2014.
© Springer International Publishing Switzerland 2014

displays [3, 4] and actuated displays [5, 6], the knowledge about elastic displays that feature only temporary deformations is scarce [7, 8]. One of the first elastic displays presented is the *Khronos Projector* by Cassinelli and Ishikawa [9]. It is a vertical installation of a deformable tissue that is used to fast-forward to a certain position in a video when pressed. With the *Deformable Workspace*, a comprehensive system for manipulating virtual 3D objects on vertical elastic displays is available [10]. Other examples allow varying haptic feedback are *MudPad* [11] and *GelForce* [12].

The DepthTouch [13] is one of the first published systems that exhibited a tabletop system with an elastic display. The Obake display is a similar prototype devised at MIT media lab that demonstrates various interactions with a silicone based screen [14].

Fig. 1. Flexible visualization interface: Utilizing the deformation of the surface for exploration of complex data structures

3   Framework

The list of related reveals a growing interest in elastic displays. However, the field lacks a general model which is needed to analyze applicable interaqction paradigms or design systems for productive use. When developing elastic displays, the interface needs to be carefully designed. What are the design guidelines? What are the weaknesses and what are suitable application domains? Our approach starts with identifying suitable data structures for 3D or 2.5D elastic displays. Subsequently, we relate interaction techniques to the data structures and create a toolset for interacting with elastic displays. The goal is to use the specified tools to explore the opportunities of elastic displays regarding concrete scenarios. Accordingly, we can define the strengths and weaknesses of the technology in the same context.

3.1   Data

Spindler et al. investigated three dimensional data structures in their work with *PaperLenses* and distinguished between volumetric, layered, zoomable, and temporal information space [15]. We concentrate on a simplified data-driven point of view and distinguish three fundamental data structures suitable for elastic displays. The first type of data is **zoomable data (2D)** (Fig. 2-A). The category contains two-dimensional data structures, which are variable in their level of detail. They are explored in zoomable user interfaces and imply gigabit images or applications like google earth. The second is **volumetric data (2.5D)**, which features slices of a three dimensional structure like a MRT, CT, or range images (Fig. 2.-B). Furthermore, volumetric data also includes layer based data structures, like maps or videos. We discarded the distinction between "real" volumetric data and layered data as both types use the same structural foundation, differing only regarding the density of data layers used and the continuity of values throughout the data volume. Being equal from a data perspective, a distinction may become reasonable when incorporating a semantic perspective: As data may vary substantially over the different layers, this influences the presentation of and the interaction with the data. The third category is called **three dimensional data (3D)** (Fig. 2- C). The category comprises real three dimensional scenes which are not structured in layers or slices. In contrast to volumetric data, the main purpose is not exploring the layers, creating several data views or analyzing relationships, but to model 3D space interactively to influence virtual entities in the scene or the scene parameters themselves. Examples include the reproduction of physical effects like gravity simulation, or 3D modeling of surfaces and volumes.

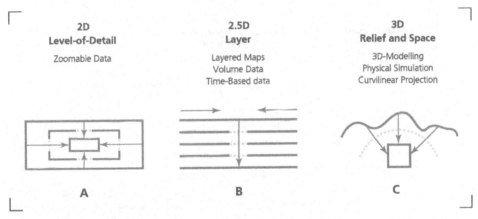

2D
Level-of-Detail

Zoomable Data

2.5D
Layer

Layered Maps
Volume Data
Time-Based data

3D
Relief and Space

3D-Modelling
Physical Simulation
Curvilinear Projection

A   B   C

Fig. 2. Classification of data types: High-resolution 2D data (A), layered data, including volume data (B), real 3D scenes (C)

3.2 Interaction Techniques

Originating from multi-touch techniques, the same actions on a planar surface are applicable to elastic displays, following similar interaction paradigms. The difference appears while exercising pressure. This does not necessarily restrict interaction to pushing into the surface but also includes pulling the surface towards the user. Basically, we can distinguish three groups of techniques regarding interaction with an elastic surface:

1. Using the fingers to model the surface, which can be related to traditional multi-touch technologies as touch extended by a third dimension (Fig. 3-A).

2. Using planar Tangibles as lenses or slicing shapes could be emulated on rigid touch-surfaces with tangibles and the additional specification of translation in depth and amount of applied rotation (Fig. 3-B).

3. The use of arbitrary Tangibles or forms has no direct equivalent on traditional devices. Instead, a 2D profile could be generated using tangibles. Its rotation and the manual reconstruction of the surface relief are additional parameters needed to achieve results comparable with elastic displays (Fig. 3-C).

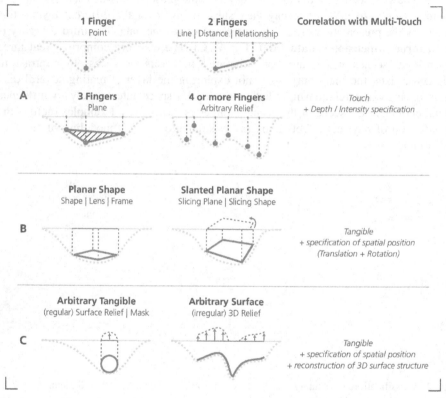

Fig. 3. Interaction techniques related to multi-touch: Fingers (A), the use of simple (B) and complex shapes (C)

Regarding the touch interaction with the elastic surface, one finger defines a point in space, like a 3D cursor. The use of a second finger as a pointer allows to define a line in the interaction space, to specify a spatial distance or a spatial relation (Fig. 3.-A). Additionally, a plane can be formed using three fingers, allowing the user to intersect interaction and data space. This intersection can be parallel to the non-bent surface or it generates a slant plane if one or more fingers are used as pointers to another height. Considering additional fingers and collaborative use, there are additional possibilities like forming complex reliefs by using different amounts of pressure at different locations. Of course, the user is not constrained by using his or her hands and fingers for interaction. Tangibles allow spanning complex polygons inside the interaction space. Planar rectangles or circles may be used to intrude a region to generate slanted or non-slanted intersecting planes (Fig. 3-B). The concept of shapes can be extended to arbitrary shapes (Fig. 3-C), which can be used to model complex reliefs into the surface. This particular interaction technique is a specific feature of an elastic display as it is difficult to achieve similar results on rigid surfaces. Additionally, Tangibles may be used to prevent the surface from restoring its initial state when changing the applied pressure. This relates to the concept of *Gravibles*, which could be used to save the current state [8].

4   Conclusion

Elastic displays have the potential to create novel interaction methods between the user and the application through deforming the display. Increasing usability or efficiency significantly may not be reached by simply replacing traditional multi-touch interaction methods with those provided by elastic displays. In order to take advantage of their capabilities, application interfaces have to be carefully designed. This paper introduces a framework, which covers the classification of suitable data types and a collection of possible interaction techniques. The framework should support further investigations of capabilities, issues, and application domains for elastic displays. However, there remain several research questions, e.g. whether traditional gestures on flat surfaces can be easily translated to gestures on arbitrary surfaces or how users adapt to the technology, how they perceive the extended interaction space and what are the interaction metaphors. With the proposed framework, we have laid the groundwork for further investigations.

Acknowledgements. This work has been supported by the European Social Fund and the Free State of Saxony (Young Investigators Group CogITo, project no. 100076040).

References

1. Alexander, J., Brotman, R., Holman, D., Younkin, A., Vertegaal, R., Kildal, J., Lucero, A.A., Roudaut, A., Subramanian, S.: Organic experiences (re)shaping interactions with deformable displays. In: Ext. Abstracts CHI 2013, pp. 3171–3174. ACM (2013)
2. Steimle, J., Benko, H., Cassinelli, A., Ishii, H., Leithinger, D., Maes, P., Poupyrev, I.: Displays take new shape: an agenda for future interactive surfaces. In: Ext. Abstracts CHI 2013, pp. 3283–3286. ACM (2013)
3. Follmer, S., Johnson, M., Adelson, E., Ishii, H.: deForm: an interactive malleable surface for capturing 2.5D arbitrary objects, tools and touch. In: Proc. UIST 2011, pp. 527–536. ACM (2011)
4. Sato, T., Takahashi, N., Matoba, Y., Koike, H.: Interactive surface that have dynamic softness control. In: Proc. AVI 2012, pp. 796–797. ACM (2012)
5. Leithinger, D., Ishii, H.: Relief: a scalable actuated shape display. In: Proc. TEI 2011, pp. 221–222. ACM (2010)

6. Riedenklau, E., Hermann, T., Ritter, H.: An integrated multi-modal actuated tangible user interface for distributed collaborative planning. In: Proc. TEI 2012, pp. 169–174. ACM (2012)
7. Bacim, F., Sinclair, M., Benko, H.: Understanding touch selection accuracy on flat and hemispherical deformable surfaces. In: Proc. GI 2013, pp. 197–204. Canadian Information Processing Society (2013)
8. Gründer, T., Kammer, D., Brade, M., Groh, R.: Towards a design space for elastic displays. In: CHI 2013 Workshop: Displays Take New Shape (2013)
9. Cassinelli, A., Ishikawa, M.: Khronos projector. In: ACM SIGGRAPH 2005. ACM (2005)
10. Watanabe, Y., Cassinelli, A., Komuro, T., Ishikawa, M.: The deformable workspace: A membrane between real and virtual space. In: Proc. TABLETOP 2008, pp. 145–152 (2008)
11. Jansen, Y., Karrer, T., Borchers, J.: MudPad: tactile feedback for touch surfaces. In: Ext. Abstracts CHI 2011, pp. 323–328. ACM (2011)
12. Vlack, K., Mizota, T., Kawakami, N., Kamiyama, K., Kajimoto, H., Tachi, S.: GelForce: a vision-based traction field computer interface. In: Ext. Abstracts CHI 2005, pp. 1154–1155. ACM (2005)
13. Peschke, J., Göbel, F., Gründer, T., Keck, M., Kammer, D., Groh, R.: DepthTouch: an elastic surface for tangible computing. In: Proc. AVI 2012, pp. 770–771. ACM (2012)
14. Dand, D., Hemsley, R.: Obake: Interactions with a 2.5D elastic display. In: Proc. UIST 2013 Adjunct, pp. 109–110. ACM (2013)
15. Spindler, M., Stellmach, S., Dachselt, R.: PaperLens: Advanced magic lens interaction above the tabletop. In: Proc. ITS 2009, pp. 69–76. ACM (2009)

The Design Process of Wearable Computers for Extending the Performer's Expression

Yu-I Ha and Yi-Kyung Kim

GSCT, KAIST, 291 Daehak-ro, Yuseong-gu, Daejeon 305-701, Republic of Korea
{yuiha,clarakkim}@kaist.ac.kr

Abstract. This research proposes a new process of designing wearable computers, which combines interaction design methodology and actual stage costume design processes. The performing arts have achieved an extension of space and time on stage and the enhancement in expressivity by introducing a new technology to theater, resulting in the strengthened "liveness" of performance. Performers, considered as the primary medium of performance communication by showing their characters, lively on stage, are the most important factor in achieving "presence", which is the key aesthetic concept in performing arts. From this perspective, liveness is re-mediated and strengthened by the performer's capabilities of expression, and wearable computer technology can further extend the performer's expression, thereby creating a new media effect on stage. However, literature on performing arts lacks an adequate study of the design processes of wearable computers to help actual performers understand them. This study provides artists an understanding of this process and presents a new method of design that integrates interaction design and stage costume design. This new process is applied to the design and construction process of costumes using wearable computer technology in a live performance work, 『The *Pieces of Me* 』. Through this case study, artists can understand the concept of wearable computer technology more easily and potentially engage with wearable computers with a deeper understanding.

Keywords: Wearable computer, interaction design, performer's expression, design process, performing arts.

1 Introduction

"Presence", the aesthetic concept representing the key value of performing arts may consist of the existence of performers, the key members, and above all, liveness is understood as the most important feature forming presence. Thus, the performer's lively expression of characters or specific and clear revelation of interactive actions taken among them can be a standard that strengthens liveness of the performance and forms presence.

Theater has always used the cutting-edge technology of the time to enhance the "spectacle" of productions [1]. But this has been used as a form of visual images presenting a spectacle on the stage. Yet, as mentioned above, since performing arts mediate contents of production through performers, extension of their expression

C. Stephanidis (Ed.): HCII 2014 Posters, Part I, CCIS 434, pp. 421–426, 2014.

using wearable computer technology can be closely related to the strengthening of liveness of the performance.

A wearable computer is a computer that is subsumed into the personal space of the user, controlled by the user, and has both operational and interactional constancy, i.e. is always on and always accessible [2]. This can get the intention to use and the context of the surrounding environment in a place closest to the user's body and allows him or her to carry out computing capabilities in any kinds of environments, which can double the intimacy among human, computer and environment. When a computer is worn, the user's surroundings and state can be recognized. Context-sensitive applications can then be designed to exploit the intimacy among them [3]. Wearable devices are a new way to manage information. In addition, they can extend human cognitive and physical functions. Therefore, introducing wearable computers to performing arts in particular performers are put up as major representation media can extend their bodies, which may have great impacts on the development of new representations and methods of interactions, and it is expected that they will dramatically change the ways of communications between objects on the stage and help create effects of new media.

However, in the field of wearable computer, preceding studies have mostly dealt with special fields such as military, medicine and aerospace or have been carried out from the perspective of costume studies related to wearability, and their focuses have been brought to the development of smart devices that can directly be involved in the user's real life. In contrast, there is a lack of studies on the method of introducing wearable computers to performing arts, the method of optimizing the technology or the effectiveness of the new media.

Thus, this study seeks to propose a methodology of introducing wearable computers for the extension of performers' expression through the convergence of the actual stage costume design process and interaction design methodology. Through this, it will discuss what roles a wearable computer can play in strengthening vividness of performance by mediating performers' bodies and bringing about changes in the method of interaction, and aims to help artists understand the processes of application of the technology.

2   Methodology

This study aims to extend performer's expressiveness through the introduction of a new process of designing wearable computer. Thus, it will introduce wearable computer technology to stage costumes to help creative expression of characters and interactions among them by mediating performer's movements with a new form, and for this, it will propose a design process reflecting interaction design methodology and stage costume production process that facilitate the interaction between human and services, and characteristics of performing arts and the technology.

2.1   Process of Stage Costume Design

Stage costume design process, requiring close consultation with the production crew, unlike the general fashion design process: 'Determining a concept - Design –

Production' necessitates a study on the process of the overall performance production, which was summed up in Youngsam Kim [4] as the following five stages: 'Pre-production, Rehearsal, Production Week and Preview, Run and Post-production'. In addition, Suh, Ji-Sung [5] classified the process into seven steps, focusing on the original costume design process, and Lee, Ji-Seon [6] summarized the stage costume work process based on three steps of 'Preparation, Production and Performance' and summarized tasks by each process.

Stage costume design should be completed through the analysis on the work, participation in practice process and discussions with the production crew and go through several processes of modifications considering performers' activities. Thus, stage costume design process can be summarized and proposed combining three perspectives in the above cases as follows.

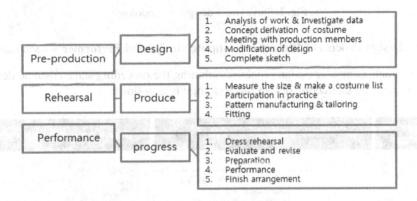

Fig. 1. Process of stage costume design

2.2   Interaction Design Methodology

Since interaction design comprehensively includes all activities that take place between men and the environment surrounding them, it is important to understand the user's needs accurately. Among interactive design techniques, crucial are a method of focusing on understanding of design context and discovering needs through a user survey and a method of evaluating the proposed design and improving it [7]. In particular, contextual design methodology [8], which collects and analyzes data to understand the users' real needs and is helpful for agreement on effective design method, is appropriate for understanding the users' needs and the structure of experience, which is summarized as seven steps: Contextual inquiry / Interpretation / Data Consolidation/ Visioning / Story boarding / User environment design / Prototyping.

On the other hand, since introducing wearable computers to stage costumes requires actual production, it is necessary to look into the prototype production design process that integrates interactive elements as well. This study refers to 'interactive design process and prototype method' proposed by Steve Gill [9] to form a design methodology that can quickly respond to the demands for correction by the director or performers.

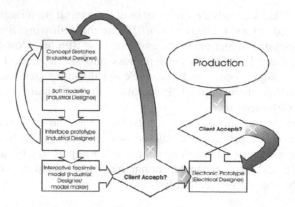

Fig. 2. Steve Gill's design methodology

2.3   Design Process of Wearable Computer to Extend Performer's Expressions

The wearable computer design process combining the preceding stage costume design process with the interaction design methodology is as follows:

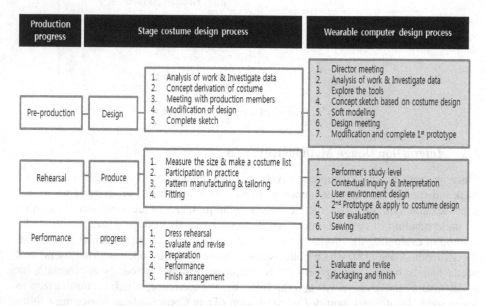

Fig. 3. New process of designing wearable computers

In the design step, as costume design sketch has been accomplished, the final agreement should be made among the staff members regarding that, so this is a step that requires intimate and ongoing consultation between the wearable computer designer and the costume designer. At this time, a technology that stimulates the performers' expression can be designed if a lucid interpretation of the producer's intent to introduce the technology precedes.

Second, the production step provides performers with a time to learn the technology that gives them the opportunity to apply that in various forms and find a method to extend their expressions. Then, they should understand the form of the use by asking contextual questions and should come up with the best method of representation by modifying and supplementing the work. Then, based on the newly arranged scenarios, the second prototype is completed and applied to the costumes, and the performers wear them and have a rehearsal so that the errors occurring in the actual application are corrected to complete the finished costumes.

Lastly, correction of errors that might occur during the performance and final completion of the work are included in the wearable computer design process in performing arts.

3   Application and Conclusion

The wearable computer design process for the extension of performer's expressions proposed in this study has been actually applied to the process of designing wearable costumes in a performance, 『 The *Pieces of Me* 』. Performers who had learned the prototype produced according to the design process provided the following feedback: "There are several interactive motions in the work, and all motions and times of approach differ, so it is difficult to reflect the intention of the proposed technology." Accordingly, choreography were analyzed and the numbers, times and angles of the interactive motions were analyzed to complete wearable costumes through the steps like modifying the Codes to increase the LED output speed of the wearable costumes.

Fig. 4. Wearable costumes in 『*The Pieces of Me*』

Consequently, the performer could variously explore patterns of movement and relation with objects, audiences and space using wearable technology, and they show their purpose of movement more clearly and intuitively.

Since the proposed design process was organized to reflect unique situations according to the production step of performing arts, it would be able to help artists who work on the boundaries between art and technology understand the methodology and procedure of both sides, when they would design wearable computer technology to the performing arts.

Reference

1. Dixon, S.: Digital performance: a history of new media in theater, dance, performance art, and installation, p. 40. MIT Press (2007)
2. Mann, S.: Definition of Wearable Computer. In: ICWC 1998, Fairfax. VA (1998)
3. Bilinghurst, M., Starner, T.: Wearable devices: new ways to manage information. Computer 32(1), 57–64 (1999)
4. Kim, Y.: A study on the production system of stage costume for theatre 'Picasso's Women'. The Research Journal of the Costume Culture 19(1), 83–95 (2011)
5. Suh, J.-S.: A Study on the Production of Performing Costume of Musical 'The Sword of Fire'. Chung-Ang University, Doctorate thesis (2006)
6. Lee, J.-S.: A Study on the Systematic Stage Costume Design Process – Focusing on the Musical Dracula. Sangmyung University, Master's thesis (2009)
7. Kim, C.-W., Nam, T.-J.: Interaction Design Technique to Enhance the ludic Value of Everyday Products – with Emphasis on the Application and Design Development of Imaginary Creature-Based Narratives. Journal of Korean Society of Design Science 87(23-1), 111–122 (2010)
8. Beyer, H., Holtzblatt, K.: Contextual design. Interactions 6(1), 32–42 (1999)
9. Gill, S.: Developing information appliance design tools for designers. Personal and Ubiquitous Computing 7(3-4), 159–162 (2003)

Development the Hand Color Detection System for Hand Gesture Front of the Face

Yukinobu Hoshino, Hiroomi Okada, and Keita Mitani

Kochi University of Technology
Tosayamada-cho, Kami-city, Kochi, 782-8502, Japan
hoshino.yukinobu@kochi-tech.ac.jp,
165051f@gs.kochi-tech.ac.jp, keita.mitani.kut@gmail.com

Abstract. In recent years, Intuitive style operations and the user-friendly operations are necessary for the future computer interaction. HMD and camera devices are usually used on those style systems and research. For beginner operators, HMD is easy devices at anywhere and anytime. But there are some problems. Especially, the hand detection is difficult. The hand area has specific dynamic colors. It is not robust for illumination change and individual difference of flesh color. For those problems, our research selects the color distribution of hand area for the gesture operations. Our method renews color distributions dynamically about hand areas by the characteristic tracking. This method has robustness at illumination change and individual difference of flesh color. In addition, this method runs only processing of tracking area. It cuts calculation cost. The implementing the proposal method has an advantage at real time.

Keywords: HMD, User interface, Cognitive exercise therapy, Hand color detection.

1 Introduction

Intuitive style operations and the user-friendly operations are necessary operations for the future computer interaction as UI. Because these techniques are possible to work the hand gesture using the hand detection techniques. HMD and camera devices are usually used on those style systems and research. Our proposed system has the same approach. For beginner operators, HMD is easy devices at anywhere and anytime. But there are some problems. Especially, the extracting hand area is not robust. The hand area has specific dynamic colors. It is not robust for illumination change and individual difference of flesh color. This problem has been solved by many approaches. Muto's method used the brightness gradient [1][2]. This method is learning a specific area and SVM makes clusters by the brightness gradient. Higashiyama's method uses the pattern matching processing for the 3-D model [3]. Muto's method is robust to illumination change of use of brightness gradient. Higashiyama's method has a low calculation cost. This method detects to pattern matching process. But there are some problems

C. Stephanidis (Ed.): HCII 2014 Posters, Part I, CCIS 434, pp. 427–433, 2014.

about those methods. Mutou's method needs big calculation costs. Because the brightness gradient is the local characteristic values, there are complex calculations on many tiny areas. The Higashiyama's method cannot recognize many hand figures. Because the template sample can not support all hand figures. Our proposal is supporting those problems and doesn't use color templates and/or figure templates. Our research selects the color distribution of hand area at gesture operations [4]. The method dynamically renews color distributions about hand areas by the characteristic tracking. This method has robustness at illumination change and individual difference of flesh color. In addition, this method runs only processing of tracking area. It cuts calculation cost. The implementing the proposal method has an advantage at real time.

2   The proposed method

We describe the state of the operation target at the beginning. The next, we explain the proposed hand detection method. Left of Fig.1 representing the state of the target operation. Fig.2 shows the hand detection algorithm for the hand gesture interface.

Fig. 1. Operating target (left) and Hand detection (right)

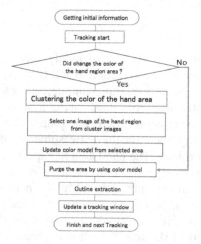

Fig. 2. The hand detection algorithm

2.1   Getting Initial Information

The first step, we set a getting window area and shot one image. The color information is gotten as the initial information. Initial information is different by skin color extraction environment. Therefore, a proposal algorithm always takes first. This method makes it possible to follow with change in skin color caused by individual differences. Also, this method will be robust to the dynamics of the illumination light. The screen is shown in Fig.3.

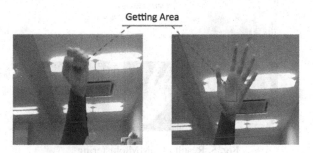

Fig. 3. Getting initial information

2.2   Color Changing of the Hand Region Area

This section describes the determination of the color change of the hand area. If system algorithm wants to track robustly the hand region, then the hand region must keep a color information density above a certain level in the follow-up window. At this time, a change in the color distribution is generated about the hand region of the palm or back of the hand by the Camera's dynamic range. There are same cases lots. When this case, the color information density of the hand region is altered to rough as shown in Fig.4. So the tracking window area has low density in this case.

For the algorithm, the focus point is this nature. If the density of the hand area of the window in the tracking becomes below a certain value, then the algorithm to update the color model. This algorithm was about 0.4 density threshold.

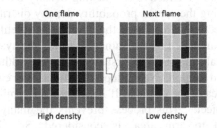

Fig. 4. The color information density on 1st and 2nd flames

2.3   Changing the Color of the Hand Region Area

The hand region is made up of a number of colors among orange, flesh color, yellow, red, and white. Those are depending on a changing illumination. Thus, the algorithm system encloses in a rectangular hand area. The system makes clusters with the color distribution in that rectangle.

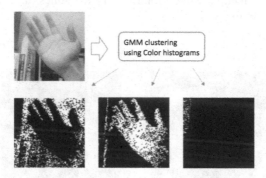

GMM clustering
using Color histograms

Fig. 5. Result of GMM clustering

Dynamic clustering execution gives the region extraction robust to "individual differences", "illumination changes" and "color disturbances". We have set three-classes as a number of hand region classes. The reason is that area of the hand is a small area. Clustering the subject is a two-dimensional UV histogram of the YUV color space. Gaussian Mixture Model (GMM) was used as the clustering algorithm.

2.4   Following Up the Hand Area

The mean-Shift method was used to hand region tracking technique. The system algorithm sets the initial position and is taken the initial color and position information. After that, tracking is started using your mean-Shift method from that position. Color and Motion likelihood estimation's map is used to mean-Shift method. Tracking density distribution must correspond to the dynamic motion. The likelihood estimation's map is the most effective as tracking density distribution. However, the basic mean-Shift are using the spatial probability density distribution. We do not use the color likelihood directly but also used the cumulative likelihood of colors. This is the color likelihood accumulated by the sampling time. The system also must prevent many tracking other small objects. The first step is to track other objects that exist in the around of the hand region. Next step, the algorithm calculates the collision detection of the hand area of the original. If it's not already collision, this object is not tracked the original object.   This process prevents the many wrong tracking. The hand area is included to arm area, is considered. So, the system algorithm successively updates to the shape of the hand region-tracking window of mean-Shift. Tracking is a process the list below.

1. Getting Initial position
2. Createing Various likelihood map
3. Execution of Mean-Shift
4. Collision detection
5. Update Tracking window

2.5   Update of tracking window

Tracking using a mean-Shift Method is enabled. Space probability distribution by dense likelihood map that has been synthesized plays a major role. However, there are other problems in the follow-up of the hand area. If short-sleeved image, distribution is widespread. In the next frame, local value of the density is uniform or 0. Distribution is multimodal. Distribution of part of the elbow and the palm becomes multimodal. Angle of the elbow is changed after this extreme. Distribution of a peak is disappearing in this case. The reason for this is due to the characteristics of the likelihood map, which is combined with the characteristics of the mean-Shift Method.

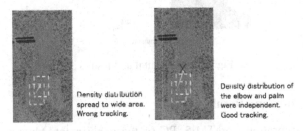

Density distribution spread to wide area. Wrong tracking.

Density distribution of the elbow and palm were independent. Good tracking.

Fig. 6. the untraceable case by mean-Shift method

A basic Mean-Shift method uses a spatial probability density of the tracking window to track objects. However, our likelihood contains the color and movement. That is using the spatial probability density distribution due to the likelihood map. Therefore, it is a problem that the motion likelihoods cause. See Fig.5 In addition, we solved this problem by changing the shape hand region window of mean-Shift method. See.Fig.6.

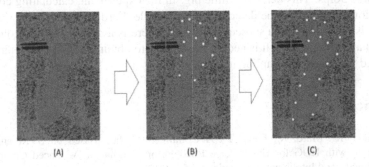

(A)   (B)   (C)

Fig. 7. changing the shape hand region window

2.6   Segmentation

Our algorithm uses a binary region segmentation using Graph Cut method finally. As a result, the system will merge each class. And segmentation of the perfect hand region is established. This study uses color likelihood in that hand region window, which created from the color information in Graph Cut.

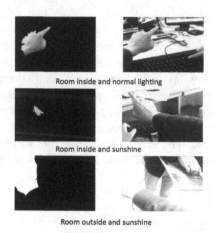

Room inside and normal lighting

Room inside and sunshine

Room outside and sunshine

Fig. 8. Experimental and results

2.7   Experimental and Results

We use Intel Corporation CoreTMi5, PC of the experiment. Memory size is 8GB. Moving point camera was used front of the eyes of the camera Wrap920 of Vuzix Corporation. Language is C++ and OpenCV.

3   Conclusion

Algorithms in this study depend on the clustering results of GMM. Processing speed was average 56fps. This delay is a little big. In the experiment, calculating cost of the other regions is large. So the detection was unstable. Further, the influence of the re-sampling is propagated to a subsequent frame. There is a danger that the color model generated as wrong model. It is necessary in order to obtain a robust result that we are considered for a new re-sampling method.

References

1. Shimada, K., Muto, R., Endo, T.: A Combined Method Based on SVM and Online Learning with HOG for Hand Shape Recognition. Journal of Advanced Computational Intelligence and Intelligent Informatics 16(5) (2012)

2. Mutou, R., Simada, K.: T. Endou Hand Shape Recognition based on SVM and online learning with HOG: the institute of electronics, information and communication engineers, IEICE Technical Report, pp.459-464 (2010)
3. Kazuhiro, H., Satoshi, O., Yu, W., Shigeru, N.: Finger Character Recognition Using 3-Dimensional Template Matching. IEEJ. Transactions on Electronics, Information and Systems
4. Okada, H., Hosino, Y.: Development of virtual gadgets using the HMD. In: Proceedings of Shikoku-section Joint Convention, Record of the Institutes of Electrical and Related Engineers, CD-ROM (2012)

An Omnidirectional Virtual Desktop Environment Using HMDs and Its Evaluation

Kento Kaneko[1], Makio Ishihara[2], and Kazumasa Yamazawa[2]

[1] Graduate School of Computer Science and Engineering, Fukuoka Institute of Technology,
3-30-1 Wajiro-higashi, Higashi-ku, Fukuoka, 811-0295, Japan
mfm13006@bene.fit.ac.jp
[2] Fukuoka Institute of Technology,
3-30-1 Wajiro-higashi, Higashi-ku, Fukuoka, 811-0295, Japan
{m-ishihara,yamazawa}@fit.ac.jp

Abstract. This manuscript attempts to expand work space with the basic idea of omnidirectional virtual desktops. HMDs are used to expand work space. Users wear the HMD and look around to see it. Application windows can be placed all around the user virtually and their positions are represented in the world coordinate system. Their positions are transformed in the HMD coordinate system then these windows are shown on the HMD screen. Our system requires less room to work as compared with multi-display systems that take up much more room. From a pilot experiment in target search tasks, the result showed that users tended to look for the target in a spiral way and locate them in about 19 seconds.

Keywords: Omnidirectional virtual desktops, HMDs, augmented reality, evaluation, user interface.

1 Introduction

In an environment of desktops and laptops, computer screens are the one of important components for user interface. They often influence usability of those computers. Especially the size of computer screens is a major factor in usability. Larger computer screens (or work space) improve the performance of computer work because users can put more relevant documents and icons on the screen at a time to come across quickly. It is now around 24~27 inches for desktops. As regards the size of computer screens, A. Kimura et al. [1] expanded work space with large displays. They designed their large display systems to organize work and view medical images. Larger displays however take up more room to be put. To expand the work space, this manuscript employs head mounted displays or HMDs, which require less room to work, and conducts a pilot experiment in performance of our prototype.

2 Omnidirectional Virtual Desktop

This manuscript attempts to expand work space with the basic idea of omnidirectional virtual desktops as shown in Fig. 1. HMDs are used to expand work space. A HMD

C. Stephanidis (Ed.): HCII 2014 Posters, Part I, CCIS 434, pp. 434–439, 2014.

used in our system is a video-mixed type equipped with a built-in head tracker. Users wear this HMD and look around to see work space. The orientation of the user's head is traced by that head tracker and work space synchronously goes around before the user's eye. The user feels as if he/she was in a spherical computer screen. The user can still do his/her daily routine in it using a mouse and a keyboard as he/she usually does on the usual desktop.

Fig. 2 shows a brief demonstration of our system. This user wears the HMD to get in an omnidirectional virtual desktop environment. Fig. 3 shows images of that user's view. In the figure, (a) he runs a notepad and places it in the center and then (b) he looks to the right side to use a calculator.

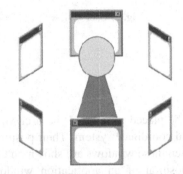

Fig. 1. An omnidirectional virtual desktop

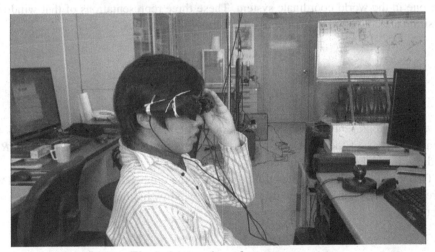

Fig. 2. An overview of our system

(a) The user runs a notepad.   (b) The user uses a calculator.

Fig. 3. User's views

3   System Design

3.1   How it Works

Application windows can be placed all around the user virtually and their positions are represented in the world coordinate system. Their positions are transformed in the HMD coordinate system then these windows are shown on the HMD screen.

Let (w_u, w_v) be the position of an application window on the HMD screen, $w(w_x, w_y, w_z)$ be the one in the HMD coordinate system, and $W(W_x, W_y, W_z)$ be the one in the world coordinate system. These three representations of that window's position are converted each other by the following equations.

$$w^T = R \cdot W^T \tag{1}$$

$$(w_u, w_v) = \frac{-f}{w_z}(w_x, w_y) \tag{2}$$

, where f represents the focal length of the HMD screen and R represents the rotation matrix of the HMD. In our system, f is the constant of 192 dpi and R is updated by the head tracker in real time.

The above equations updates the position of the application window on the HMD screen (Fig. 4) whenever if the user drags that window by the mouse or the user looks around.

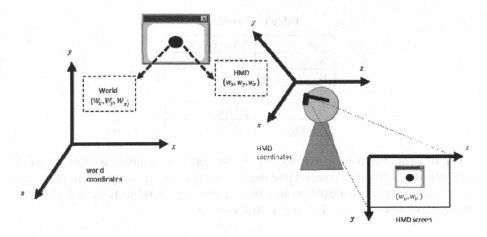

Fig. 4. Three coordinate systems and coordinate transformation

3.2   Hardware

A HMD used in our system is shown in Fig. 5. This HMD is a glasses-like device that has a stereo camera and a head tracker. The spec is specified below.

Fig. 5. A HMD used in our system

- HMD:Vuzix Wrap920AR
  Twin high-resolution 640 x 480 LCD displays
  31-degree diagonal field of view
  Two discrete VGA (640 x 480) video cameras
- 6-axis head-tracking sensor: Razer Hydra
  Ultra precise sensor for 1mm and 1 degree tracking

4   Pilot Experiment and Results

A pilot it in performance of our system was conducted. There were four subjects with the ages of 23~24. All were right-handed. Each subject was asked to look at the specified start position and search a target, which was shown at a random position on the omnidirectional virtual desktop. The elapsed time to locate the target and the angular movement of the subject's head were recorded. Table 1 shows the elapsed time.

Table 1. Elapsed time

Subject	Time (sec)
A	19.46
B	11.88
C	20.69
D	27.08
Average	19.78

Fig. 6. shows the angular movement of the subject's head during the task. The red circle represents the start position and the red star does the target position. From the figure, all the subjects looked around in a spiral way, it subjects A and C did it counter clockwise and the others did it clockwise.

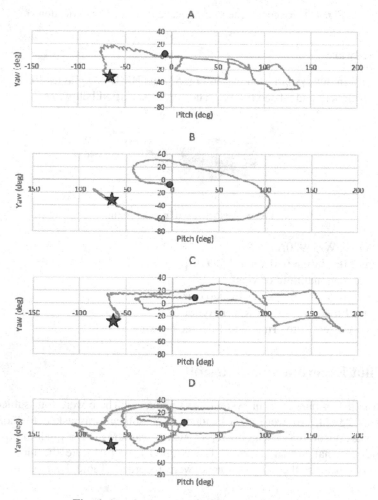

Fig. 6. Angular movement of the subject's head

5   Conclusions

In this study, an omnidirectional virtual desktop system was designed and implemented with HMDs. The user wore the HMD and got in the surrounding work space. Our system required less room to work as compared with multi-display systems that took up much more room. From a pilot experiment in performance of our system, it was shown that users tended to look for targets in a spiral way and locate them in about 19 seconds. In the future work, we are going to conduct further experiments in common tasks such as manipulation of mouses and application windows.

References

1. Kimura, A., Shibata, F., Tsuruta, T., Sakai, T., Oniyanagi, M., Tamura, H.: Design and Implementation of Minority-Report-Style Gesture Interaction with Wide-view Electronic Working Space. IPSJ Journal 47(4), 1327–1339 (2006)

Evaluation of a Hear-Through Device

Anders Kalsgaard Møller, Pablo Faundez Hoffmann, Flemming Christensen,
and Dorte Hammershøi

Aalborg University, Department of Electronic Systems, Aalborg, Denmark
{akm,pfh,fc,dh}@es.aau.dk

Abstract. A solution for recreating the natural sound reception of the
open ear while wearing earphones exists. It is achieved by mounting microphones on the outside of earphones, and simultaneously record and playback the sound. The solution could potentially be used for augmented audio
applications. Due to practical limitations, such as the size of the earphones
and microphones, it is not possible to record the sound in the ideal position. This paper presents work on finding the best position of a microphone
with the purpose of reproducing as much of the spatial information as possible. The results from measurements with an artificial ear show that all
spatial informations can be reproduced up to around 5-6 kHz. Above this
frequency deviations in the reproduced sound, compared to the natural,
is introduced. A method to evaluate how the deviations in the reproduced
sound affect the listening experience is also proposed.

Keywords: augmented reality, augmented audio, virtual reality, binaural recordings, hear-through.

1 Introduction

In augmented audio applications natural sounds are mixed with virtual sounds.
The virtual sound could potentially be played through earphones but when wearing earphones the earphones will to some degree block the ear canals and dim
the sounds from the listener's surroundings. By mounting microphones on the
outside of the earphones and simultaneously record and playback the sound, the
natural sound reception of the open ear can be recovered.

A device which can simultaneously record and reproduce the sound surrounding the user is presented in this paper and will be referred to as a hear-through
device. The hear-through device consist of a pair of earphones AKG328 Blue
and two MEMS microphones(Analog Device, ADMP504). The earphones and
the microphone is connected to an Arduino Due board with a codec shield used
to handle the recording, playback, and equalizing.

The recordings done by the hear-through device is based on the principles of
the binaural recording technique. According to Møller [1] the complete auditory
experience can be preserved by recording and reproducing the sound pressure
at each eardrum exactly as it were. Hammershøi and Møller [2] concluded that
recordings at the blocked entrance to the ear canal also include all the spatial
information and is therefore a more suitable place for making binaural recordings.

C. Stephanidis (Ed.): HCII 2014 Posters, Part I, CCIS 434, pp. 440–445, 2014.
© Springer International Publishing Switzerland 2014

Even though the earphones and microphones available today are quite small it is not possible to record the sound exactly at the blocked entrance to the ear canal but instead in a position sticking a bit out from the ideal position.

In [3] a method is presented for measuring the transfer functions for the ideal position, at the blocked entrance to the ear canal, and the position of an in-ear device respectively. The in-ear device consisted of an earphone with a build-in microphone. Later [4] continued the work with several different types of earphones.

The principles of a hear-through device have previously been described and tested [5] and potential applications have been described in [6]. The work included the design of a hear-through device and a small-scale usability evaluation. The usability evaluation revealed some issues to the listener experience such as the sound of the listeners own voice and annoying noise levels. The general impression of the audio quality was however good.

The hear-through device offers new options as a tool for HCI-applications where the real sound environment is combined with computer-generated sound. This could for instance be used for a museum guide where the user receive information about the attraction when moving close to it or in other ways offer options for interaction with the attraction. The augmented audio could also be combined with other modalities like vision to create an augmented reality that immerse the user into an intriguing environment.

Before adding a virtual sound it is however important to be able to reproduce the natural sound environment or at least be able to measure to what degree this can be accomplished. If the natural sound can't be reproduced correct it might compromise the experience of the augmented reality.

In this paper the work on a hear-through device is described. The work include finding the optimal position of the microphones and earphones for reproducing the spatial information and it include an subjective evaluation of the auditory experience created using the hear-through.

2   Method

This section describe the method used to find the optimal position of the microphone on the earphone.

2.1   Setup

The measurements to find the optimal position of the earphone were performed in an anechoic room. The measurement system used in this method consisted of 25 loudspeakers distributed on a half sphere with 22.5 degree angular difference between the loudspeaker positions. The sphere was attached to a baffle with a hole in the middle with room for an ear to stick out (either an artificial ear or a human ear). The loudspeakers suspension construction was wrapped in acoustically absorbing material in order to minimize reflections from the setup. In Figure 1 the setup is presented.

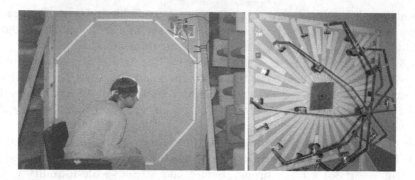

Fig. 1. The front and back of the baffle used in the setup (Source: [3])

2.2   Measurements

A custom-built measurement system was used to play Maximum Length Sequence noise through each of the loudspeakers, one at a time, and compute the impulse responses.

One measurement was conducted with a MEMS microphone(Analog Devices, ADMP504) attached to the blocked ear canal of the artificial ear. Another eight measurements were conducted with the same microphone attached in different positions on the AKG328 Blue earphones. Figure 2 shows the microphone positioned on the earphone and on the blocked entrance to the ear canal.

Another series of measurement were conducted using five human subjects. The subjects were placed in a chair with their ear sticking out of the baffle. For each subject, a measurement with the microphone attached to the blocked ear canal and three measurements with the microphone positioned at selected positions on the earphone, were conducted.

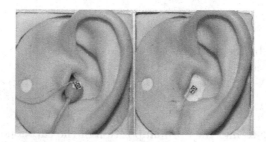

Fig. 2. To the left a microphone placed on the earphone in the artificial ear. To the right a microphone placed at the blocked entrance to the ear canal.

3   Results

Figure 3 shows the amplitude response of the transfer function with the artificial ear. The amplitude response for each direction is very similar up to around 5-6 kHz where they start to separate. This was the best result observed out of the eight positions measured with the artificial ear. The position of the microphone on the earphone is the same as on Figure 2.

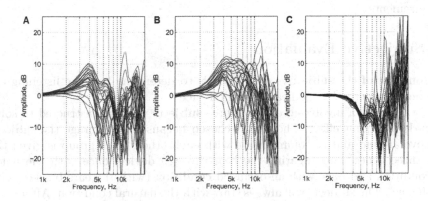

Fig. 3. Amplitude response of transfer function measurement conducted with the artificial ear. (A) Microphone placed at the blocked entrance to the ear canal. (B) Microphone placed on a selected position on the earphone. (C) Difference between blocked entrance to the ear canal and earphone.

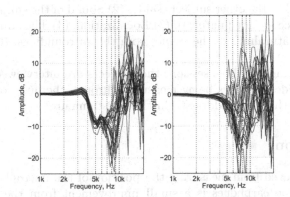

Fig. 4. Amplitude response of transfer function measurement conducted with human ears. Each plot represents the difference between a measurement at the blocked entrance to the ear canal and a position on the earphone. The two plots represent two different subjects with the microphone placed at two different positions.

In the measurements with the human ears the position of the microphone on the earphones is also compared with the position at the blocked entrance to the ear canal. Figure 4 presents two selected subjects with the microphone placed at a different position for each subject. On the plot to the left the amplitude response for each direction are very similar up to around 5-7 kHz where they starts to separate. This was the best case out of all the measurements with the human subjects. On the plot to the right the amplitude response for each direction start to separate around 4 kHz. This was the tendency in most of the measurements.

4   Subjective Evaluation

The purpose of the subjective evaluation is to determine how the listening experience is affected by the hear-through device.

The evaluation involves groups of three subjects who are instructed to solve a puzzle in a joint effort. The task is chosen because it encourage the subjects to move around and to communicate with each other. Each group is given the task three times, once wearing the hear-through device, once with the natural condition and once with an occluded condition (with the ears blocked with earphones). The subjects will always start with the natural condition. After completing the puzzle together in the natural condition the subjects continue with either the occluded condition or the hear-through condition. The order of these two conditions is balanced. After the second and third session the subjects are asked to answer a questionnaire with six questions. In each question the subjects are asked to rate the session they just completed compared to the natural condition. The subjects are instructed to answer the questions on continuous scales. The questions address the following topics: (1) Communication (ability to understand what the other subjects said). (2) Sound of the subjects own voice (If their own voice sounded natural). (3) Localization. (4) The annoyance due to noise. (5) The naturalness of the sound from the surroundings. (6) The overall sound quality.

After completing the three sessions the subjects are interviewed to elucidate other issues besides the ones being measured through the questionnaire and to further describe the issues addressed in the questionnaire.

5   Discussion

The results achieved from measuring the position of the microphone placed on the AKG328 Blue earphones is a small improvement from the measurement conducted in [3] and at least comparable to the measurements conducted in [4]. The AKG328 earphones can therefore be considered a good choice for the hear-through device. The earphones are quite small and allow the microphone to be placed very close to the ideal position at the blocked entrance to the ear canal. The results from measuring the ears of the human subjects showed that some variation from ear to ear is added. This could both be due to the different geometry of the pinna and due to the different fit in the ear canal. The optimal position of the microphone could not be decided based on the small group of subjects and further measurements will have to be conducted.

The hear-through's representation of the spatial information deviate from the natural acoustics of the listeners surroundings. The deviations are however frequency dependent, and are minor in the frequency range of human speech. It remains uncertain to which degree the listening experience is affected by this, if at all. This is evaluated in the ongoing experiment.

References

1. Møller, H.: Fundamentals of Binaural Technology. Applied Acoustics 36, 171–218 (1992)
2. Hammershøi, D., Møller, H.: Sound transmission to and within the human ear canal. J. Acoust. Soc. Am. 100 (1996)
3. Christensen, F., Hoffmann, P.F., Hammershøi, D.: Measuring directional characterstics of in-ear recording devices. Audio Engineering Society Convention 134 (2013)
4. Hoffmann, P.F., Christensen, F., Hammershøi, D.: Quantitative assessment of spatial sound distortion by the semi-ideal recording point of a hear-through device. In: Proceedings of Meeting on Acoustics, vol. 19 (2013)
5. Riikonen, V., Tikander, M., Karjalainen, M.: An augmented Reality Audio Mixer and Equalizer. Audio Engineering Society Convention 124 (2008)
6. Lokki, T., Nironen, H., Vesa, S., Savioja, L., Härmä, A., Karjalainen, M.: Application Scenarios of Wearable and Mobile Augmented Reality Audio. Audio Engineering Society Convention 116 (2004)

Proposal for an Interactive 3D Sound Playback Interface Controlled by User behavior

Ryuichi Nisimura, Kazuki Hashimoto, Hideki Kawahara, and Toshio Irino

Wakayama University, 930 Sakaedani, Wakayama 640-8510, Japan
nisimura@sys.wakayama-u.ac.jp

Abstract. Our study introduces an interactive 3D sound playback interface system that is controlled by the user's behavior. It consists of an Android terminal, stereo headphone, and Nintendo Wii Balance Board. Traditional binaural audio systems can only deal with simple fixed playback conditions. On the other hand, our system assumes that the user is continuously moving. When a user who is riding on the Wii Balance Board moves his/her body, binaural sounds during playback are generated according to changes in his/her center of gravity. To implement the system, we have prepared a set of twenty-four acoustic signals for embedding into the system. If the user's center of gravity corresponds with one of the twenty-four regions, an acoustic signal recorded in advance corresponding to that region is reproduced for the user. We experimentally evaluate how accurately a user can judge the position of a sound source. Experimental results prove the proposed system yielded significantly higher locational accuracy than the original binaural system.

Keywords: Binaural stereo sound, Wii balance board, Interactive sound interface.

1 Introduction and Overview of the Proposed System

We have developed an interactive 3D sound playback system that is controlled by user movement. Figure 1 shows an overview of the system. It consists of an Android terminal (main controller), stereo headphones, and a Nintendo Wii Balance Board[1] (for detecting the position of a user's center of gravity). Communication is via Bluetooth wireless connection.

Binaural recording is a method of recording audio signals using two microphones. It is meant to produce the sensation of a 3D acoustical space during headphone playback. Traditional binaural audio systems, used primarily for high-fidelity recording of natural sounds, are equipped for simple, fixed playback conditions, and are insensitive to the user's movements. In this paper, we propose a new binaural system that is sensitive to continuous motion by the user. By shifting his/her center of gravity over the Wii Balance Board, the user controls the perceived location of the binaural sound source. For example, when the user moves to the left, the perceived sound source moves to his/her right.

C. Stephanidis (Ed.): HCII 2014 Posters, Part I, CCIS 434, pp. 446–450, 2014.

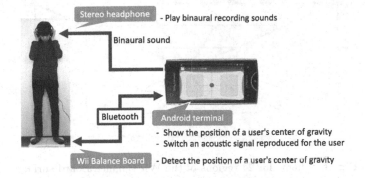

Fig. 1. Overview of the proposed system

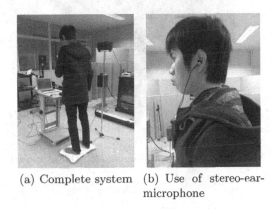

(a) Complete system   (b) Use of stereo-ear-microphone

Fig. 2. Setup for binaural recording with a stereo-ear-microphone

To implement our system, we first used a stereo-ear-microphone (Roland CS-10EM[1]) to binaurally record a set of twenty-four acoustic signals for embedding. Figure 2 shows the setup of these binaural recordings.

If the user's center of gravity corresponds with one of the twenty-four regions of the Wii Balance Board surface (Fig. 3), the acoustic signal corresponding to that region is reproduced for the user. The system can switch seamlessly between signals via look-ahead processing and triple buffering which enable switch between the signals without gaps in playback.

2   Evaluation of the Proposed System

We experimentally evaluated how accurately a user could judge the position of a sound source using our system. Figure 4 provides a snapshot of our experiment.

---

[1] http://www.roland.com/products/en/CS-10EM/

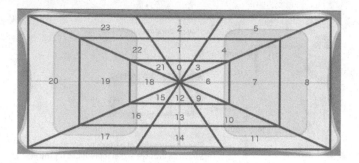

Fig. 3. Scheme for 24 regions of the Wii Balance Board surface

Fig. 4. A snapshot of our experiment using the proposed system

For the test signals, two kinds of sounds were used; a simple beep, and a submarine sonar pulse. Each signal was recorded at each of the 24 board positions, and the resulting 48 embedded signals were played back in random order for test listeners (a group of 15 students).

To measure how accurately participants could estimate the position of the sound source, we asked them to select from eight candidate positions for the sound source; (1) Left front, (2) Front, (3) Right front, (4) Left, (5) Right, (6) Left back, (7) Back, and (8) Right back. They attempted to identify the position of the sound source as they listened to the binaural signals and shifted their bodies freely on the Will Balance Board.

We also conducted exit interviews with the test participants, to get a better indication of how intuitive the interface seemed to them. We asked the participants to answer the following questions on a five-point scale:

Q1) How confident did you feel about your location estimates? (1: not confident – 5: very confident)
Q2) How much delay did you perceive delay during sound reproduction? (1: a lot of delay – 5: little or nodelay)
Q3) To what degree did the reproduced sounds seem natural? (1: not at all – 5: very much)

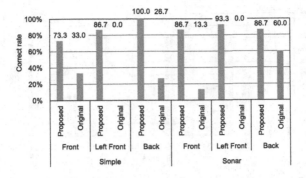

Fig. 5. Comparison of sound source location accuracy between the proposed system and a traditional binaural sound system

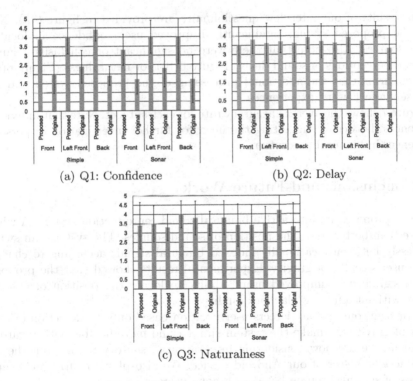

(a) Q1: Confidence   (b) Q2: Delay

(c) Q3: Naturalness

Fig. 6. Results for interview questions

Figure 5 shows the location accuracy rates for the proposed system and for a traditional system, in which user motion causes no shift between signals. The bars indicate the average accuracy rate for the 15 test participants. Note that the proposed system yielded significantly higher locational accuracy than the original binaural system.

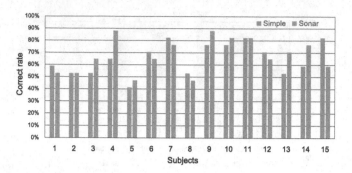

Fig. 7. Correct rates of for each subject in using the proposed system

The results of our interview questionnaire are provided in figure 6(a). Note that the proposed system significantly improved user confidence in locating sound sources. Also note that there were no significant or conclusive changes in users' perceptions of sound delay (Figure 6(b))) or naturalness (Figure 6(c)). This confirms that the additional processing of the proposed system did not adversely affect users' experiences.

Figure 7 shows the average accuracy rate for each subject. Note that individual differences did occur, suggesting the need for further investigation of personal differences in binaural perception.

3   Conclusions and Future Work

We have proposed an interactive binaural sound reproduction system in which the user can better sense the position of sound sources. The system can switch seamlessly between locationally indexed binaural signals according to changes in the user's center of gravity. Experimental results showed that the proposed system significantly improved users' ability to locate the position of a sound source, without affecting playback quality.

At present, our system detects user position based only on detection of their center of gravity. To make the system simpler and more flexible with regard to movement, we are now considering integration of sensory input from the on-board accelerometer of our Android device. We also plan to carry out deeper analysis of spatial listening behavior among users.

References

1. Nintendo, Wii Balance Board Operations Manual (2008),
   http://www.nintendo.com/consumer/downloads/wiiBalanceBoard.pdf

Micro-pose for Gesture Recognition
with Bodily-Pose Decomposition

Jae-wan Park, Su-yong Park, and Chil-woo Lee

Dept. of Electronics and Computer Engineering, Chonnam National University,
Gwang-ju, Korea
{cyanlip,qkrtndyd12}@naver.com, leecw@jnu.ac.kr

Abstract. Because a pose is implemented with static configuration of bodily joints expressing an abstract meaning of human intention, a gesture can be thought as a sequential combination of specific poses of human body. Therefore we can understand the meaning of a gesture if we can analyze the arrangement of the poses in spatiotemporal space. In this paper we propose a novel gesture recognition algorithm in which a pose is decomposed into micro-poses that are constructed with a small number of bodily joints. A micro-pose is a smallest unit of joints which can include a physical mean of body. To obtain the location of body joint MS Kinect is used and the information extracted from the micro-poses is finally applied to code matrix as the code book of the Bag-of-Words to understand the meaning of the gesture.

Keywords: Micro-pose, pose estimation.

1   Introduction

We can think a human gesture as a typical combination of bodily poses in temporal space and also a pose is implemented with static configuration of bodily joints expressing an abstract meaning of human intention. That means that we can understand the meaning of a gesture if we can analyze the spatiotemporal configuration of the joints of human body. In this paper we propose an algorithm which adopts the novel approach of "divide and conquer" for pose decomposition in gesture recognition.

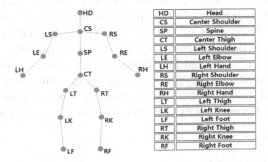

HD	Head
CS	Center Shoulder
SP	Spine
CT	Center Thigh
LS	Left Shoulder
LE	Left Elbow
LH	Left Hand
RS	Right Shoulder
RE	Right Elbow
RH	Right Hand
LT	Left Thigh
LK	Left Knee
LF	Left Foot
RT	Right Thigh
RK	Right Knee
RF	Right Foot

Fig. 1. Human body structure with sixteen principal joints

C. Stephanidis (Ed.): HCII 2014 Posters, Part I, CCIS 434, pp. 451–456, 2014.

As we know, human body has a very complicated and articulated 3D structure of bodily joints as shown in Fig.1. So, we suggest an approach using decomposition of large set of whole bodily joint into general case of a small set of some specific joints. We call that configuration of small joint set micro-pose. If we utilize this micro-pose for pose recognition the whole process of the recognition becomes straightforward because we can make use of simple combination of micro-pose instead of complex matching process in huge search space.

In most case, pose recognition method usually can be divided into two approaches. The first approach uses appearance information of human body such as silhouette and edge. We call this approach "appearance base method" and the implementation of the method is very simple since we can obtain sufficient information if we find distinctive patterns from the appearance for a specific gesture. However, it sometimes cannot produce robust result because we cannot assume general pattern for the specific pose since the appearance is changed according to view direction and different person.

In the second approach, we call it "model based approach", the location of joints of body structure is used for recognition. In this case, we may face to solve the problem of estimating accurate locations of the joints which need much computational cost, so it was very difficult to implement algorithms in real-time. Consequently for the practical application, we used to attach some markers on the dominant joints of body.

And body part based method can be used Cardboard People [1], Pictorial Structure [2] and Poselets [3] for body representation. These recognizing method can be represented as rigid body set of the constellation. Namely, they connect the close body joints with straight lines. And they can use the connected body-joints as a tree structure. This body part based models should need two principal elements. The first one is that each body part has been combined to the space of real image, and the second is that connection of body joints has to be arranged with hierarchical system.

In this paper, we analyze features of the poses consisting of gestures according to the body part based method, and we recognize the gestures with code matrix as the code book of the Bag-of-Words.[4].

2   Micro-pose for Gesture Recognition

From the topology of the fig.1 we firstly derive the micro-poses for limbs; MP1 and MP2 are assigned to the joints connecting left and right shoulder to each hand, and MP3 and MP4 are also assigned to the joints connecting left and right thigh to each foot respectively. These MPs are used for display the deformation for limbs. In this paper, in order to configure micro-pose group, we use sixteen principal joints.

For the rotation of arms and legs around bodily axis we consider another four Micro-Poses as shown in fig.2 (e, f, g and h). As the same with the previous MPs, they are also joint groups which connect principal joint of limbs to the center of a body. These four MPs are used for dominant rotation of arms and legs.

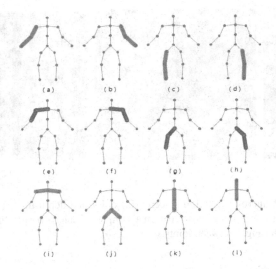

Fig. 2. The joint group used for Micro-poses

Practical shape of the MPs is decided by the angle between two joints around the center joint and the angle can be used as feature vector for pose recognition. For instance, fig.3 shows the three feature vectors projected onto X-Y, Y-Z, and Z-X plane respectively.

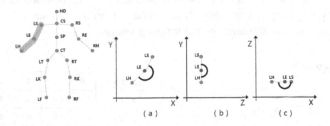

Fig. 3. Feature Vectors for Micro-pose Groups ((a) definition of the angle in X-Y plane (b) definition of the angle in Y-Z plane (c) definition of the angle in Z-X plane)

3   Gesture Recognition

In this paper, we use MS KINECT[5] to obtain the 3D information of bodily joints. As described in section 3, we take twelve micro-poses for measuring the feature vector and the information is converted to symbols which represent a pose of trained image, and finally we can understand the meaning of the temporal gesture with code matrix as the code book of the Bag of words.

In the paper, we select 11 gestures of upper body as the recognition subject and those gestures are composed with 24 poses. To segment the micro-poses from the poses, we insert real-time training data more than 20 times for each pose. Fig.4 (a, b) show the procedure of the training.

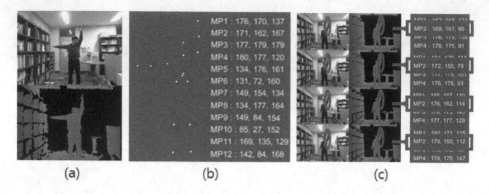

Fig. 4. Examples of micro-pose training scene ((a) color and depth image, (b) an example of joint feature vectors for a micro-pose, (c) an example of micro-poses; 'lift left hand.' The numbers represent the angle between joints.)

In the training process, the user can watch his/her own pose through a monitor and if he/she feels any discomfort on the pose he/she can change the pose. If the user makes an appropriate pose the system capture the data and it flush the twelve micro-poses into a file. Actually the micro-poses means angle difference among three specific joints.

Fig.4(c) shows an example of extracting a micro-pose from several input images. We use some different images for a micro-pose since real 3D position of bodily joints for the pose is very rugged even though the same person tries to make the same pose. Therefore we use multiple images as the training image.

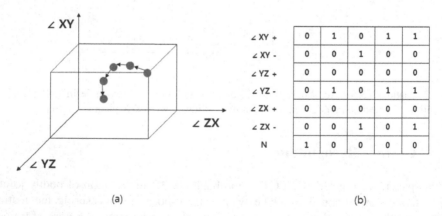

(a)   (b)

Fig. 5. Code matrix generation ((a) variation of the three dimensional angle values from a micro-pose, (b) code matrix generation using variation)

Fig.5 shows code matrix generation using variation of the three dimensional angle values. In the Fig.5(a), when we learn some micro-poses if angle is increased in the X-Y plane, ∠XY is increased one degree in the Fig.5(b).

The feature vectors of the micro-pose are consisted of angle between joints. We set the number of pose and micro-pose according to when is to recognize gesture.

	0	1	2	3	4	5	6	7	8	9	10	11	12	13	14		T
∠XY +	0	21	0	20	0	20	0	0	21	0	20	0	0	0	0		0
∠XY -	0	0	0	0	19	0	0	0	0	19	0	0	19	0	0		0
∠YZ +	0	20	2	19	20	17	0	0	20	20	17	0	20	0	0		0
∠YZ -	0	0	0	0	0	0	0	0	0	0	0	0	0	0	0	.....	0
∠ZX +	0	19	0	20	17	19	0	0	19	17	19	0	17	0	0		0
∠ZX -	0	0	0	0	0	0	0	0	0	0	0	0	0	0	0		0
N	22	1	18	1	1	2	22	22	1	1	2	0	1	22	22		22

Learned code matrix as the micro-poses of gesture A   Learned code matrix as the micro-poses of gesture B

∠ XY +	1	0	1	0	1
∠ XY -	0	0	0	1	0
∠ YZ +	1	0	1	1	1
∠ YZ -	0	0	0	0	0
∠ ZX +	1	0	1	1	1
∠ ZX -	0	0	0	0	0
N	0	1	0	0	0

User's code matrix as the micro-pose of a gesture

Fig. 6. Example of learned code matrix as the micro-poses

So, in this paper, we define the ten body gestures. And then, in order to generate micro-pose code matrix, we executed twenty-two learning by each micro-pose. The method which to learn pose is as follow Fig.6. In the Fig.6, the learned code matrix is compared with learned micro-pose's code matrix of gestures by using the Euclidean Distance.

To measure similarity using the Euclidean Distance, code matrixes are compared by applying as follow equation 1. In equation 1, n is number of valid column and m is number of valid row. And we estimate most similar to learned code matrix when the code matrix has maximum values by calculating similarity of the distance between the values.

$$\sum_{i=1}^{12} \sum_{j=1}^{n \times m} (Value_{Learned\ cm} \times Value_{User's\ cm}) \tag{1}$$

4   Conclusion

In this paper, we propose a unique algorithm which can identify the meaning of sequential bodily motion as a gesture by estimating deformed shapes of joints.

We call that micro-pose. The contribution of the approach is that we can reduce degree of freedom of articulated motions of a whole body since the variation of the pose is decomposed into small piece of joint combination. And the micro-poses are converted into symbols which are suitable for making use of code matrix as the code book of the Bag-of-Words.

The weak point of our approach is that gesture model is strictly limited to some gestures which have big variation of body shape. We think this defect comes from manual classification of gestures when we make the code book of model gesture. In the near future, we can make up the weakness by adopting automatic classification of model by using a clustering algorithm based on similarity measurement.

Acknowledgment. "This research was supported by the MSIP(Ministry of Science, ICT and Future Planning), Korea, under the ITRC(Information Technology Research Center) support program (NIPA-2014-H0301-14-1014) supervised by the NIPA(National IT Industry Promotion Agency)".

References

1. Ju, S.X., Black, M.J., Yaccob, Y.: Cardboard people: A parameterized model of articulated image motion. In: FG (1996)
2. Felzenszwalb, P.F., Huttenlocher, D.P.: Pictorial structures for object recognition. IJCV 61(1), 55–79 (2005)
3. Wang, Y., Tran, D., Liao, Z.: Learning hierarchical poselets for human parsing. In: CVPR 2011, pp. 1705–1712 (2011)
4. Jurie, F., Triggs, B.: Creating efficient codebooks for visual recognition. In: ICCV, vol. 1, pp. 604–610 (2005)
5. Shotton, J., Fitzgibbon, A.W., Cook, M., Sharp, T., Finocchio, M., Moore, R., Kipman, A., Blake, A.: Real-time Human Pose Recognition in Parts From Single Depth Images. In: CVPR (2011)

Gestures for Interaction between the Software CATIA and the Human via Microsoft Kinect

Juan Carlos Rodríguez Esquivel[1], Amilcar Meneses Viveros[2], and Nicolas Perry[3]

[1] Maestría en Diseño Interactivo y Manufactura, CINVESTAV-IPN, México, D.F.
jcrodriguez@cinvestav.mx
[2] Departamento de Computación, CINVESTAV-IPN, Mexico D.F.
amilcar.meneses@google.com
[3] Arts et Métiers ParisTech, Bordeaux - I2M - CNRS UMR 5295 - FR-33405 Talence, France
n.perry@i2m.u-bordeaux1.fr

Abstract. CAD systems are very useful tools in the industry, because they help design processes and new product development. However, it requires new mechanisms of interaction to provide greater usability of these tools. This usability can be provided through new interaction devices such as Kinect. We describe a methodology to find a series of gestures makes by the hands for control a CAD system with Kinect sensor of Microsoft. These gestures must be easy to remember for the user of the system and they don't should represent a cognitive load to make the design's experience most interactive.

Keywords: Kinect, Gestures, Interaction, Cognitive Load.

1 Introduction

One of the most demanding works in the world is the mechanical designer because it requires being in front of a computer for many hours several days a week. The mechanical designer uses the CAD systems for accomplish his work.

One of the most popular CAD systems in companies such as automotive and aviation is the software CATIA, develop by Dassault Systèmes. CATIA help us to design and develop new products [1][4]. But this system can cause problems by the use of a keyboard or a mouse after a workday and is also known that sitting in front of the computer could harm us by the lack of body movements. And also, sometimes this system may not be as easy to use for novice users.

The main idea in this document is to look for the right gestures to use in MOCAP system, in this case the Kinect sensor, to help users of CATIA in the design and management of parts and assemblies. These gestures will make correspond a task or a command in software, reducing the cognitive load when the user learns and remember the gestures.

2 Gestures for Communication

The gestures define the communication between humans. Finding a series of gestures to define an action or task is difficult because in the world exist several ways to say or

C. Stephanidis (Ed.): HCII 2014 Posters, Part I, CCIS 434, pp. 457–462, 2014.
© Springer International Publishing Switzerland 2014

do a thing, depending on the language and the culture of the people. We can have an infinite number of gestures to interact, but many of them may not be identified or remembered [5][6][7].

One important task is to find the bridge in communication between the humans to perform gestures and then, translate these gestures to a Human-Computer communication, so that they can be expressed naturally and can be remembered easily [2][3][5]. Also these gestures can't confuse the computer or do something that has not referred to do in the development of the tasks. Computer-Human interaction is also handled by the feedback that should exist with an Augmented Reality system and human for have a more natural interaction.

The augmented reality help us to supplement the interaction giving the feeling of manipulating a physical piece and not a virtual piece in 2D like the conventional systems.

3   Gestures Definition

In a study conducted in 1955 by George A. Miller, a professor at Harvard University, talks about the limits of human ability to process information. Miller found that the ability of humans to store items in your short term memory is between 5 and 9 elements, ie, 7, plus or minus two, because these processes are provided by our biological limitations delivering the nervous system characteristic of every human being, because every human being processed information differently. Thus one of the main objectives in the design of interfaces that the number of gestures used by the user are less than nine.

The proposed methodology to the system is the use to the state machines, based on the proposed work by Carrino, S., Caon, M et al. [3]. The idea is to find the gestures in a series of actions to be taken should take some order. Carrino proposes using finite state automata to study the changes of states in the system in which the interaction take place [3]. The states of the automaton are the states of the system. Transitions in the automaton are given by gestures that the user uses to interact with the system. Thus, the interface designer can verify that the nine gestures are not exceeded in every state of the system.

Then to define gestures in CATIA, we must first define their states and the set of actions and tasks that change the system state.

States / interactive entities defined for the project:

- Program closed: the CATIA software is closed and we are in the Windows environment.
- Open program, no file display: the CATIA program is open, but we are in the welcome screen without any open file.
- Viewing and editing: we have an open file or a new file for the part to make or change
- Close piece, Save: we are in the save screen.
- Close Program: shutdown screen and return to the Windows environment.

The functional gestures that were handled in the project are:

- Move: Move the cursor around the screen.
- Rotation: Rotate Part / Assembly in CATIA.
- Zoom +: zoom in the part/assembly.
- Zoom -: zoom out the part/assembly.
- Select/left click: choose a piece/action.
- Drag: move a piece around the screen.
- Undo.
- Special case functional gesture 8
  - This is the gesture that will change status , this is due to the different steps that have to be done to open a document and look between the user's files . This will depend on what state we are and shall consist of the combination of some past functional gestures.

Table 1. Set of states and functional gestures for deterministic finite-state automaton

States:	Functional gestures:
a. Program closed. b. Open program. c. Viewing and editing. d. Close piece, Save. e. Close Program.	1. Move. 2. Rotation. 3. Zoom +. 4. Zoom -. 5. Select/left click 6. Drag. 7. Undo. 8. Special combination

We found that the deterministic finite automata which describes the use of CATIA has 5 different states and 8 funcional gestures (alphabet). The set of states Q = {a, b, c, d, e} and the alphabet Σ = {1,2,3,4,5,6,7,8}. Table 1 shows the description of the states and of the elements of the alphabet. The transition function is expressed in the figure 1.

The number of functional gestures taken based on the work of Miller on the ability to process information and learning these. In what states gestures and giving us a total of 8, within the limits of human capacity are proposed. The functional gestures were defined using surveys to find frequently used commands under the CATIA software environment.

To find the gestures we are developed two principal ideas:

- The gestures should be easy to remember
- The gestures should be natural, i.e. these gestures should be easy to do, the user will don't make any effort.

The gestures were found on the observation of daily life of people and their way of doing routine things because in everyday life that can make for some aspects similar to the worked within the CATIA environment.

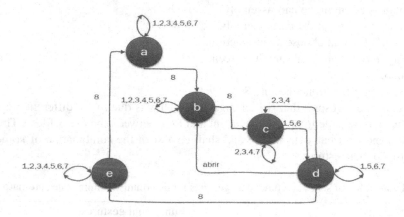

Fig. 1. Finite States Machine of the project, in which we can see the 5 states a,b,c,d,e and we can find the functional gestures defined by the numbers

Table 2. Gestures - functions relationship

Function	Gesture
Move Left hand or right hand takes control of the mouse to scroll the screen, as if it was moving the hand to grasp an object.	
Undo Both hands are downward as if you were crushing or removing something opposite.	
Select Place the mouse pointer with the hand in the point / piece desired and leave the hand in this position for 3 seconds.	

Table 2. (*continued*)

Drag Do the gesture to select, and then, with the piece selected, down both wands to activate the movement to the piece.	
Zoom + Joining both hands at the stomach, and then hands them away horizontally.	
Zoom – Put your hands up to the stomach (hands should be away), and then bring them closer horizontally.	
Rotation We started holding the piece (place both hands at the stomach and make a gesture of pressure), then move one hand to the point where you want to rotate and wait 3 seconds. Will now rotate with one hand.	

4   Conclusions

You can make the state characterization of the CAD systems such as CATIA. This allows knowing the transitions between them, ie actions or tasks that they change state. With the characterization of finite automaton system is possible to identify the number of actions and tasks for state changes. These actions and gestures em tasks are mapped in the case of MOCAP devices, such as Kinect. You can have the control of the state transitions to prevent over nine gestures are associated with a system status. It has been observed that these gestures do not handle all tasks in CATIA, so you can opt for multimodal gestures.

References

1. Lee, K.: Principles of CAD/CAM/CAE Systems. Addison-Wesley Longman Publishing Co., Inc., Boston (1999)
2. Miller, G.A.: The Magical Number Seven, Plus or Minus Two, Some Limits on Our Capacity for Processing Information (1955)
3. Carrino, S., Caon, M., et al.: Functional Gestures for Human Environment Interaction (2013)
4. Gillet, P.: Conception assistée par ordinateur, CAO (1994)
5. von Hardenberg, C., Berard, F.: Bare-Hand Human-Computer Interaction (2001)
6. Karam, M., Schraefel, M.C.: A taxonomy of Gestures in Human Computer Interaction
7. Jacko, J.A.: Human-Computer Interaction Handbook: Fundamentals, Evolving Technologies, and Emerging Applications, 3rd edn. CRC Press, Inc., Boca Raton (2012)

NIRS-Based BCIs: Reliability and Challenges

Megan Strait and Matthias Scheutz

Tufts University, Medford MA 02155, USA

Abstract. Previously we contributed to the development of a brain-computer interface (Brainput) using functional near infrared spectroscopy (NIRS). This NIRS-based BCI was designed to improve performance on a human-robot team task by dynamically adapting a robot's autonomy based on the person's multitasking state. Two multitasking states (corresponding to low and high workload) were monitored in real-time using an SVM-based model of the person's hemodynamic activity in the prefrontal cortex. In the initial evaluation of Brainputs efficacy, the NIRS-based adaptivity was found to significantly improve performance on the human-robot team task (from a baseline success rate of 45% to a rate of 82%). However, failure to find any performance improvements in an extension of the original evaluation prompted a reinvestigation of the system via: (1) a reanalysis of Brainput's signal processing on a larger NIRS dataset and (2) a placebo-controlled replication using random (instead of NIRS-based) state classifications [1].

The reinvestigation revealed confounds responsible for the original performance improvements and underscored several challenges for NIRS-based BCIs in general. Specifically, it revealed the original performance improvements were due to a disparity in difficulty between experimental conditions of the original evaluation (i.e., the task being easier in the adaptive versus the baseline condition). Moreover, the reinvestigation showed Brainputs model of user multitasking (trained on the n-back task) generalized to neither the human-robot team task (the classifications showed systemic violations of basic hemodynamic principles) nor to other workload-inducing tasks (classifications of brain activity while users performed arithmetic were better than chance for only 1/4 of the subject population). Hence, in in an effort to identify ways forward, we first summarize the methods and results of this reinvestigation and then explore the challenges for achieving more reliable NIRS-BCIs.

1 Introduction

Brain-computer interfaces (BCIs) have been gaining traction in the field of human-computer interaction (HCI) for various application domains (e.g., [2,3]). Functional near infrared spectroscopy (NIRS, also referred to as fNIRS and fNIR), in particular, has been described as a suitable modality for BCIs given that it is relatively portable and reasonably robust to user movement [2]. Despite these useful characteristics, however, the reliability of these NIRS-based BCIs remains relatively unexplored [4,1]. Hence, here we summarize a reinvestigation

C. Stephanidis (Ed.): HCII 2014 Posters, Part I, CCIS 434, pp. 463–468, 2014.

of a NIRS-based passive BCI system, Brainput [5], of whose development the authors were part. Brainput was designed to react to fluctuations in cognitive workload by adapting a robot's level of autonomy, and in its initial evaluation, the passive NIRS-based adaptivity was found to significantly improve performance on a human-robot team task. However, when we attempted a follow-up extension, we did not find the improvements that we had observed originally. Hence, we set out to systematically evaluate the reliability of NIRS-based BCIs through a two-part reinvestigation of Brainput (first, via a reanalysis of Brainput's signal processing on a large NIRS dataset, followed by a placebo-controlled replication using random state classifications) which revealed confounds in the original study responsible for the initial performance improvements [1]. The goal of this experience report is to illustrate, in addition to the utility of the replication, some of the challenges and limitations involved as well.

2   Motivation

We previously participated in the development of the NIRS-BCI, Brainput, with the aim of classifying a user's multitasking state during a human-robot team task [5]. We hypothesized that brain-based adaptive autonomy would improve task performance. A two-probe NIRS instrument was used to image subjects' (N=11) prefrontal cortex while subjects explored a simulated environment with two robots to find a target location. The task ran until both robots found the goal location (success), or until five minutes had elapsed (failure). During the task, Brainput used classification of subjects' NIRS data to dynamically adapt the autonomy of one of the robots according to the subject's level of workload. The initial results showed that the brain-based adaptivity substantially improved performance (82% of subjects successfully completed the task) versus a baseline (no adaptivity) of 45%. Moreover, *mal-adaptive autonomy* (enabling of autonomy during low workload) caused performance to significantly worsen (18% success), indicating that the autonomy must be appropriately timed for it to be effective in human-robot teams. Inspired by these initial findings, we employed Brainput in an extension of the original protocol to test whether the performance improvements would persist with real robots (versus simulated robots in simulated environments as used originally). We replaced one of the two previously-simulated robots with a real robot in a real environment, but both were still controlled by the system architecture used in [5]. Here we expected to see the same performance improvements as we did originally; however, the results showed *no* performance improvement (for either simulated or real robot) from baseline performance. Given the nearly identical setups, these results suggested some degree of unreliability of the Brainput system.

3   Reinvestigation

Suspecting the Brainput classifier to have limited extensibility to larger populations (i.e., N=24 in the extension versus N=11 in the original investigation), we conducted a reanalysis of Brainput's signal processing using a larger NIRS dataset, followed by a placebo-controlled replication of the original study [1] – the methods and results of which we summarize here.

Reanalysis of signal processing. Here we investigated two questions: (1) whether the original performance improvements persist over a larger sample and (2) whether the improvements generalize across variants of the same type of task. We obtained a larger NIRS datasest (N=40) consisting of low and high workload PFC samples induced by an arithmetic-based variant of the n-back task [4]. We preprocessed the data and trained the Brainput classifier on samples of each workload class (low, high), mirroring the procedure we used originally (see [5]), and then ran ten-fold cross-validation to predict model performance. Between subjects, the average classification accuracy was 54.5% ($SD = 14.3\%$). While the overall accuracy was statistically significant, only 10/40 subjects showed individual accuracies significantly above chance [1]. Moreover, Brainput's performance on this dataset was substantially lower than than what was found originally (68.4%). This discrepancy may have been due to the differences either in sample size (N=40 vs. N=3) and/or task (numeric vs. alphameric). Regardless, the lower overall performance was particularly worriesome in that the human-robot team task differed substantially from the alphameric task used to train the classifier in the original evaluation [5]. That is, if the classification schema does not extend well to a variant of the same type of task (numeric vs. alphameric n-back task), then it suggests that it might not generalize to more realistic applications (such as human-robot interaction tasks).

As Brainput's performance on the novel dataset differed so substantially from its preliminary evaluation, we revisited the original dataset (from [5]) to investigate Brainput's behavior during the human-robot team task. Using the logs of the realtime classifications, we constructed plots of the robot's autonomous behavior (autonomy-disabled vs. autonomy-enabled) over the course of the task (see Figure 1). Enablement of the robot's autonomy corresponded to classification of the NIRS data as *branching* (high workload), whereas disablement indicated the participant was experiencing *low* workload. Here we expected the behavior to show prolonged periods of autonomy enabled/disabled, but we found instead rapid classification-switching. This rapid oscillation between classifications was even more worriesome than Brainput's performance on the novel dataset. Specifically, the rapid sub-second oscillations were inconsistent with basic hemodynamics – that task-related hemodynamic changes occur over a period of several seconds [1]. These results thus indicated the Brainput classifier was not the primary factor contributing to performance improvements on the human-robot team task in [5], but rather, indicated the presence of a placebo effect or confounding factor (e.g., the mere presence of robot autonomy) in the protocol.

Placebo-controlled replication. To understand the performance improvements observed in [5] despite the unrealistic behavior of Brainput's classification, we performed a placebo-controlled replication of the original protocol ([5]), with the only modification being that the *cognitive state classifications from Brainput were replaced by random classifications* (generated based on the classification distributions from the original study). This design allowed us to explicitly mea-

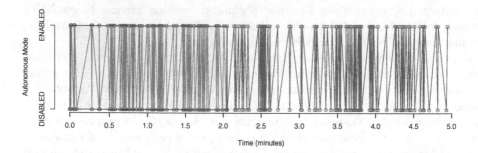

Fig. 1. Example classification log of *autonomy* toggling. Each line indicates a switch in autonomy (e.g., enabled to disabled). Figure reproduced from [1] with permission.

sure effects due to *autonomy* of the robot separate from Brainput's accuracy in recognizing multitasking states. Here we expected (random) *adaptive* and (random) *maladaptive* conditions to have equal effects on performance given that the adaptivity was drawn randomly from the *same* underlying classification distribution. Instead we found similar patterns of task success accross this placebo-replication and [5]. Specifically, subjects succeeded (in both experiments) more often at locating the goal location with the autonomous robot in the *adaptive* condition than in the *maladaptive* condition. This was surprising because the random classifications should have caused the success rates across the *adaptive* and *maladaptive* conditions here to be equal, given that the two conditions themselves were equal in all aspects in this replication.

Hence it was not Brainput that yielded the performance improvements observed initially, as, in the absence of the brain-based adaptivity, we still achieved these improvements. This result thus indicated a confound in the execution of the two conditions (adaptive vs. maladaptive). Upon inspection of the logs from this replication, we discovered a serious confounding factor: the goal location in the environment co-varied with the task condition. Specifically, the robot had significantly further to travel in the *maladaptive* condition (18.4m) than in the *adaptive* condition (9.4m). Hence, the task was strictly more time-consuming in the *maladaptive* condition. As success was determined by the team's ability to locate the goal in 5 min., it is clear that the coordinates of the goal location relative to the robot affected rate of success. Since no aspects of the underlying system were changed aside from the classification approach (from NIRS-based to random) in this placebo-controlled replication of [5], this affected the original study as well. Review of the logs from the original evaluation ([5]) confirmed that the goal locations in the adaptive versus maladaptive conditions of the original study were the same as what we found in this replication.

4 Discussion

4.1 Implications

Due to finding null results in an extension of [5], we were motivated to conduct a reinvestigation of the Brainput framework. We first revisited Brainput's signal processing to test the its extensibility to a novel dataset. There we found its classification approach to perform worse than expected (effective for only 25% of subjects), indicating low efficacy for a general population. Moreover, in looking at Brainput's realtime behavior (plots of the classification logs from [5]), we found that its behavior did not follow basic hemodynamic principles. With unrealistic behavior and worse-than-expected classification accuracy, we then revisited the original evaluation of Brainput's efficacy via a placebo-controlled experiment to find what was responsible for the performance improvements observed in [5]. There, by successful replication of the original performance improvements – despite the absence of NIRS-based adaptivity – we identified a confound within the experimental design. In analyzing logs from the replication and the original study, we found a disparity in starting locations between the experiment conditions (i.e., the robot was 2x closer to the target location in the adaptive versus maladaptive condition), which resulted in the task being easier in the *adaptive* condition. These results indicate that further work is necessary to achieve a robust framework for NIRS-BCIs.

4.2 Challenges

This reinvestigation from [1], as well as the limitations to the interpretation of results, highlight several challenges for NIRS-based BCIs. Here we discuss three. First, questions of generizability were raised: whether results from small samples extend to larger populations, as well as whether models trained on one workload-induction strategy (e.g., the n-back task) extend to other workload-based variants (e.g., human-robot team tasks) [6]. As many NIRS studies are underpowered (e.g., [5]) and all BCIs must necessarily be trained on labeled data (i.e., *not* unconstrained and asynchronous tasks such as human-robot interactions), these questions are highly relevant to HCI. In particular, successful deployment of a BCI depends on how well it works within a general population and also how well the training tasks model the more realistic target tasks.

Second, although the reinvestigation revealed low reliability of the Brainput framework, subjective reports indicate some utility of the brain-based adaptivity [1]. This suggests that the current ways in which we measure and interpret the success or efficacy of a BCI may not capture its full or true utility. For instance, although Brainput's classification accuracy on the novel dataset was only slightly above chance level (55%), that minor improvement in understanding (and adaptive response to) the user's cognitive state may be sufficient to improve a interactions with a robot. Lastly, efforts to disseminate the results of this reinvestigation questionned what is an appropriate forum for (failures in) replication. While this is not unique to NIRS-BCIs, the reliability of signal processing is an orthogonal endevor to developing effective interactions between people and computer systems. Hence it is not comparable to applications of NIRS-BCIs in terms of novelty. It is, however, complimentary in that the utility of NIRS-based BCIs is dependent on the robustness of the methods used to extract meaningful information from noisy signals. Thus, while growing accessibility of brain-based sensors allows for researchers to approach signal processing as a black box, it is important to consider how we can facilitate discussion on both fronts (novel applications and signal processing methods) as they are both invaluable to the advancement of NIRS-BCIs. Publication, in particular, allows discussion, feedback, and improvement of the work, but without a clear venue for replication, progress for NIRS-BCIs will be slowed.

5   Conclusions

NIRS-based BCIs have received considerable attention as a tool for HCI. However, in this series of reinvestigations of the Brainput NIRS-BCI, we found significant limitations of its efficacy. First, we found when we increased our sample size from 3 to 40, Brainput's performance was only effective for 1/4 of the population. Moreover, we observed that Brainput's realtime behavior (rapid state-switching) is not in accordance with basic hemodynamic principles (slow changes). Further investigation identified a major confounding factor (different goal locations) in our original evaluation of the system, which was likely responsible for the performance improvements (not the NIRS-based adaptive autonomy). Hence, it is important that we revisit our NIRS-BCI frameworks to consider the reliability of our systems. We hope that this systematic reinvestigation and discussion of related challenges will lead towards more robust NIRS-BCIs.

References

1. Strait, M., Canning, C., Scheutz, M.: Reliability of NIRS-based BCIs: a placebo-controlled replication and reanalysis of Brainput. In: Alt.CHI (2014)
2. Canning, C., Scheutz, M.: Function near-infrared spectroscopy in human-robot interaction. Journal of Human-Robot Interaction 2, 62–84 (2013)
3. Strait, M., Scheutz, M.: Building a literal bridge between robotics and neuroscience using functional near infrared spectroscopy. In: Human-Robot Interaction (HRI) Workshop on Bridging Robotics and Neuroscience (2014)
4. Strait, M., Canning, C., Scheutz, M.: Limitations of NIRS-based BCI for realistic applications in human-computer interaction. In: BCI Meeting (2013)
5. Solovey, E., Schermerhorn, P., Scheutz, M., Sassaroli, A., Fantini, S., Jacob, R.: Brainput: enhancing interactive systems with streaming fNIRS brain input. In: CHI, pp. 2193–2202 (2012)
6. Brouwer, A.-M., van Erp, J., Heylen, D., Jensen, O., Poel, M.: Effortless passive bCIs for healthy users. In: Stephanidis, C., Antona, M. (eds.) UAHCI 2013, Part I. LNCS, vol. 8009, pp. 615–622. Springer, Heidelberg (2013)

Prediction of the Input Accuracy of the Hiragana BCI

Hisaya Tanaka

Kogakuin University, 1-24-2, Nishi-shinjuku, Shinjuku-ku, Tokyo, Japan
hisaya@cc.kogakuin.ac.jp

Abstract. In this study, we provide an index of classification for BCI-processing. We named the index a discrimination rate. A discrimination rate is the percentage of the LDA classifier, which was able to accurately determine P300. Based on the experimental results, we found that the correct answer rate is changed in proportion to the discrimination rate. Particularly, there was a statistical significance in less than 75% and more than 80% (p<0.01). In addition, the correct answer rate also increases with expression of P300.

Keywords: Index of Classification, LDA, P300.

1 Introduction

We have been studying the BCI system based on requirements for ALS patients in the past [1, 2]. In the case of our brainwave measurement with the BCI, training data with the BCI is measured at first, then training with linear discrimination analysis (LDA) is applied as offline processing, and an online experiment is conducted by using a discriminator adjusted with LDA. The weakness of this method is that adjustment of the discriminator might be unsatisfactory depending on the training data. For this reason, averaging was applied to the training data to confirm expression of P300 in the past. However, the shape of P300 has individual differences and confirming P300 only is not sufficient as analysis of training data, leading to possible hindrance in precision of online experiments. In this study, therefore, a hit rate for discrimination of training data ("discrimination rate") is introduced as a new index in offline processing in order to clearly determine whether or not adjustment of a discriminator with LDA is sufficient for online experiments, to conduct evaluation and experiments.

2 BCI System

2.1 Hiragana BCI

The principle of BCI's operation is indicated in Figure 1. Letters arranged in a 6x10 matrix are presented in the display, a row and column randomly flickers as visual stimuli, and brainwaves are recorded for each column and row in synchronization. When the flickering of the matrix is repeated several times, the averaged waveform of

C. Stephanidis (Ed.): HCII 2014 Posters, Part I, CCIS 434, pp. 469–474, 2014.

the brainwave corresponding to each stimulus is recorded in the memory within the computer. Since the P300 component induced with attention to specific letters is observed in this waveform, the row and column with strong response is detected and the intersecting letter can be assumed as the letter to which the subject was paying attention.

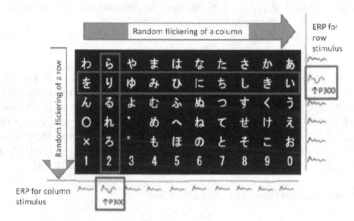

Fig. 1. Principle of BCI's operation (6x10 letter board)

2.2 LDA Processing Method

Since the level of attention has an influence on P300, individual differences occur in amplitude and latency. It is therefore necessary to measure the amount of characteristics by subject and adjust the discriminator to make it suitable for the subject. Training data was measured in advance in this study and the discriminator is adjusted for each subject by using LDA. LDA is one of discriminant analyses and is an analysis method to obtain a linear function that can best discriminate between two groups. The general formula is expressed in the Formula 1. X_i, a_i and a_0 represents a dependent variable, independent variable, regression coefficient, and constant term, respectively. In the case of BCI, the independent variable represents training data and the dependent variable represents discriminant scores. The regression coefficient and constant term are obtained by applying LDA to training data. This regression coefficient and constant term become the amount of characteristics, with the linear discriminant function as the discriminator.

$$Z = a_1 X_1 + a_2 X_2 + \cdots + a_n X_n + a_0 \tag{1}$$

The amount of characteristics in a BCI is obtained as follows. First, the sampling frequency of training data goes through the process of downsampling from 256Hz to 64Hz, followed by a band-pass filter between 0.1Hz and 60Hz. Next, data that respond to each stimulus is extracted from the filtered data. Data is extracted at the data length of 100ms before stimulus and 700ms after stimulus, i.e., the total data length of 800ms, and is comprised of 45 potential data in the 800ms length. Once data is extracted, a moving average is conducted on each data, followed by downsampling. The 45 potential data in 800ms are thinned out to 15 with downsampling. After downsampling, a data vector is created for LDA. This data vector becomes the actual independent variable. A discriminator of LDA is created in accordance with the data vector. The discriminator becomes a 121-dimensional linear discriminant function consisting of 120 regression coefficients and one constant term, totaling 121 parameters. Online analysis is conducted by using the discriminator created. This discriminator is established, so that the threshold for the dependent variable Z is divided into 1 or -1 as a discriminant criterion. If the discriminant score of measured data is one or more, it is determined that there is sufficient P300 response; and if it is -1 or less, it is determined that there is no P300 response at all.

2.3   Analysis of Training Data

Figure 2 is a flow chart of the experiment. A traditional BCI experiment had a flow of offline processing including training data measurement, LDA processing and confirmation of P300 components, followed by online processing. In the case of P300 Speller, accuracy in communication improves by conducting BCI training that matches the individual. However, poor training data causes less precision of LDA-adjusted discriminator, leading to an increase in false positives. Low precision of a discriminator causes problems for online experiments, and it is not possible to conduct valid BCI evaluation. It is therefore necessary to confirm precision of training prior to online experiments to determine whether or not sufficient training is conducted. If the training results were poor, training can be repeated to achieve sufficient precision of the discriminator to move onto online experiments. However, precision of training had been confirmed only with ERP analysis in the past. ERP analysis is a method to plot the waveform after the process of averaging to measured data and to count the number of P300 expressions with visual confirmation. The criterion for judging P300 expression is approximately $5\mu V$ of positive reaction at approximately 300ms latency. In other words, training is confirmed with ERP confirmation, while precision of the discriminator is not confirmed. In this study, therefore, a hit rate for discrimination of training data (discrimination rate) is introduced as a new index to confirm precision of the discriminator. The discrimination rate [%] in this study means precision of data discrimination with the LDA-adjusted discriminator. Accurate discrimination means that discriminant scores are positive values at the time of target stimuli and negative values at the time of non-target stimuli. Positive discriminant scores less than one are also considered as successful discrimination at this time. Negative discriminant scores are treated in the same manner. The discrimination rate is obtained in accordance with the proportion of the counts of accurate discrimination in all stimuli.

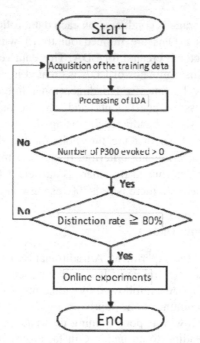

Fig. 2. Flow chart for BCI experiment proposed in this study offline processing includes data measurement up to branching

3   Experiment

3.1   Evaluation Method

The discrimination rate is evaluated by using the value of discrimination rate [%], presence of P300 component, and average correct answer rate [%] in online experiments. The correct answer rate is determined with the number of letters in the letter string detected against the input letter string intended. In the case that intention to mean "o-na-ka-ga-i-ta-i" is detected with "o-na-ka-ga-u-ta-i," for example, the correct answer rate is 5/6=83.3%. Subjects included a total of ten healthy college students: eight males and two females. All subjects operated the BCI for the first time. Subjects participated in the experiment after receiving full explanation on the operation method of the BCI and then practiced. Electrodes were arranged at eight locations including Fz, Cz, Pz, P3, P4, Oz, PO7 and PO8 according to the international 10-20 system [5]. The reference electrode was A1 at the earlobe and the ground electrode was Fpz. The monopolar lead was adopted as a lead method. Highpass filter, lowpass filter and notch filter were set at 0.6Hz, 30Hz and 50Hz, respectively. The brainwave at each electrode was amplified with a biosignal amplifier (g.USBSamp by g.tec). Amplified brainwaves were recorded, analyzed and processed with g.BCIsys developed by using the numerical analysis software MATLAB by MathWorks. The experiment was conducted in a sitting position at rest. One letter was gazed at out of the letters arranged on the 8x8 matrix presented on the monitor (EIZO FlexScanHD2452) established in front of subjects.

The screen was presented on the monitor by operating a notebook PC (Vostro 1320). After that, tasks for offline processing were conducted. For this task, a total 30 stimuli, i.e., 15 times each for one row and one column, were given for one-letter entry. In regards to stimulus onset asynchrony (SOA), the duration of flashing (Flashtime) and extinction (Darktime) is fixed at the rate of 4:3 by setting the stimulus interval at 140ms. LDA is applied after that, and an online experiment (BCI experiment) is conducted in accordance with the discriminator obtained. For the online experiment, a total of 20 stimuli, i.e., 10 times each for one row and one column, is given for one-letter entry. The stimulus interval is not changed. In this experiment, a six-letter word is entered by using the copy-spelling method where letters to be entered are pre-set as a letter-entry task.

4   Discrimination Rate and Correct Answer Rate

The discrimination rate at this time was less than 80% for all 10 subjects. Therefore, we also obtained a discrimination rate in regards to the data measured in our previous studies. The experimental method was the same as this experiment, while a 5x5 letter board was used in the tasks for offline analysis. An 8x8 letter board was used in regards to tasks for online analysis. Data for five healthy people in their 20s was used including two males and three females. Figure 3 shows the results of discrimination rate and correct answer rate for all subjects. The horizontal axis represents the discrimination rate for training data [%] and the vertical axis represents the correct answer rate for online experiments [%].

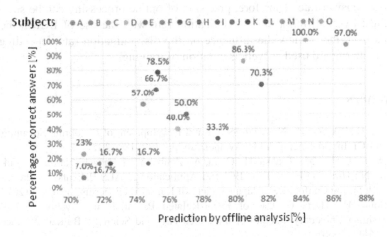

Fig. 3. Scatter diagram of discrimination rate and correct answer rate (for 15 subjects)

When the discrimination rate is compared with the correct answer rate, the discrimination rate tends to be higher if the average correct answer rate is higher, and vice versa. In other words, we can assume that the discrimination rate bears a proportional relationship to the correct answer rate. When the data on subjects are divided into three sections including less than 75%, between 75% and 80%, and 80%

or more, the average correct answer rate was 22.8±3.1[%], 53.7±3.5[%], and 88.4±1.8[%] in the case of less than 75%, between 75% and 80%, and 80% or more, respectively. A significant difference was recognized as a result of one-tailed t-test in regards to the average correct answer rate for less than 75% as well as 80% or more (p<0.01). A significant difference was also recognized between 75% an 80% as well as 80% or more (p<0.01). 70% to 80% accuracy in communication with a BCI tends to be considered as passing scores. In consideration of the results on the discrimination rate and correct answer rate at this time, 80% or more of a discrimination rate for training data is considered as one indication for offline processing.

5   Summary

A discrimination rate was introduced as a new index to discriminate a target for online processing of BCI in this study to conduct evaluation and experiments. As a result, a significant difference was successfully confirmed when a t-test was conducted in regards to the average correct answer rate in two sections of discrimination rate: less than 75% and 80% or more (p<0.01). A significant difference was also confirmed in two sections: between 75% and 80% as well as 80% or more (p<0.01). Based on this above, a higher discrimination rate is considered to be relating to a higher correct answer rate in online processing. It was also found that the correct answer rate is higher if P300 expression can be confirmed at the same time. However, it seems important to achieve a higher discrimination rate in order to further improve the correct answer rate. Therefore, precision of online processing can be successfully maintained by confirming the discrimination rate with the use of BCI in the future. We plan to further review the influence on the discrimination rate depending on the size of a letter board used as well as duration of training.

References

1. Inada, H., Tanaka, H.: Need Survey for and Development of Pictogram-Scanning Method for a BCI. In: Proceedings of HI Symposium, pp. 179–182 (2011)
2. Kawano, R., Ito, M., Tanaka, H., Otera, A., Zenba, Y., Takahashi-Narita, K., Fukuda, M., Asai, N.: Hiragana Entry-Type BCI and Application to ALS Patients. In: Proceedings of the 8th Spring Conference of Japan Society of Kansei Engineering, pp. 8–12 (2013)
3. Nittono, H., Hori, T.: Use of Event-Related Potentials in Psychological Research, Hiroshima University, Faculty of Integrated Arts and Sciences, Bulletin Science Edition 26, 15-32 (2000)
4. Farwell, L.A., Donchin, E.: Talking off the Top of Your Head: Toward a Mental Prosthesis Utilizing Event-Related Brain Potentials, Electroen-ceph. Clin. Neurophysiol. 70, 510–523 (1988)
5. Jasper, H.H.: The Ten-Twenty Electrode System of the International Federation. The International Federation of Society for Electroencephalography. Recommendation for the Practice of Clinical Neurophysiology. p.8

Implementation of an Emotional Virtual Creature with a Growth Function Model

Masataka Tokumaru

Kansai University
3-3-35 Yamate-cho, Suita-shi, Osaka 564-8680, Japan
toku@kansai-u.ac.jp

Abstract. In this study, we developed an emotional virtual creature that grows according to a growth function model influenced by user input. Our preceding study proposed a growth model for emotions based on changes in the network structure of a self-organizing map. We applied a multilayer perceptron neural network to generate more sophisticated emotional expressions using growth functions. This model generated behavior similar to affective change, as described in behavioral genetics. Based on the growth model for emotions, we propose a virtual creature with which a user can interact using a tablet computer. This creature resembles a bouncing ball and changes color depending on its emotion. The user can pet or tap the creature, play with it using some items, and provide it food. The creature's actions and emotional expressions are influenced by a various stimuli from the user. We implemented the virtual creature using an Apple iPad and confirmed that the creature grew and learned various emotional expressions through user interaction.

Keywords: Entertainment robot, Emotional model, Tablet computer.

1 Introduction

Recent technological advances have expanded the market for entertainment robots with artificial intelligence (AI). As a result, many models for robot emotions have been proposed [1]–[5]. Several emotional models for artificial neural networks (ANN) have been developed. The models focus on emotional recognition, control, and expression. Generally, these emotional models use a simplified emotion- generation algorithm, and users quickly lose interest in simple systems. Although some models have attempted to generate more complex expressions, no previous studies have considered the growth of a robot.

Our preceding study proposed a growth model for emotions that focuses on two approaches [2]. The first approach increases the emotions as robots grow using a self-organizing map (SOM) [6], which is a type of ANN. SOMs are used for data mining, clustering, and pattern recognition. A SOM is a single-layered ANN that uses an algorithm for competitive learning, which does not require a teaching signal. Based on this structure, the model can classify an input that has not been learned. The network learns unknown external stimuli continually and classifies similar input (emotions) even if an input is unknown.

C. Stephanidis (Ed.): HCII 2014 Posters, Part I, CCIS 434, pp. 475–479, 2014.
© Springer International Publishing Switzerland 2014

The second approach changes time-series of emotion in a network's behavior using a working memory system. An emotion is affected by previous emotional conditions. Therefore, creatures remember previous emotional conditions for a specific period. Our growth model for emotions uses a multilayer perceptron (MLP) ANN to implement the changes in expressiveness and the development of emotions affected by previous emotional conditions.

Our previous study indicated that this emotion model was more suitable for producing a robot with growth functions based on a psychological model using numerical simulations. However, we did not develop any actual robots or applications using this model.

Based on our growth model for emotions, we propose a virtual creature that can communicate with users by means of tablet computers. We implemented our emotional growth model for robots in an iPad application.

2   Emotion Growth Model

In this model, we propose a robot that can communicate with users through an "emotion" function. Many emotional models handle emotions from a psychological perspective [7]; therefore, we discuss emotional development from this perspective. Our emotion model is based on genetic psychology and the concept of working memory [8].

Figure 1 illustrates the structure of the emotional growth model in [2]. We built the model based on two ideas. First, we attempted to identify similar emotions and to increase the number of emotions that can be expressed. Our model uses a SOM and an ANN. With the SOM structure, the network repeatedly learns new data and classifies similar emotions for each input. In addition, to increase the number of types of emotion that can be expressed, we changed

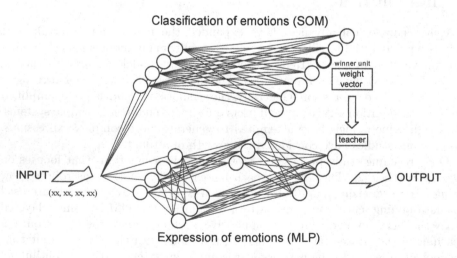

Fig. 1. Structure of the Emotional Growth Model

the number of connections between the neurons that constitute the SOM. The output units express emotions. The number of additional emotions that can be expressed as output is determined by the number of units. This structure enables the model to develop more complex emotions, which we refer to as "the evolution of network." In addition, to depict the stages of emotional development, we define a simplified version of the emotion differentiation model proposed by Bridges [9]. We call the branching structure of this emotion model the "emotion tree."

Develop realistic emotions using only an SOM network is difficult because the emotions that actual creatures develop are influenced by previous emotions, but SOM networks are not influenced by time-series inputs. Therefore, we used a multilayer perceptron (MLP) ANN to model the influence of previous emotional states on emotional changes, and the resulting model can generate complex emotions. We consider this to be a model of short-term "working memory." Using the MLP structure, the network can express emotions that have been affected by previous emotions. By combining the two networks described above, we have built a model that generates more realistic emotions for robots.

3   Application

We have implemented a virtual creature with the emotional growth model described above in an iPad application. This virtual creature (character) has an emotional growth model with two inputs and two outputs. These inputs depict the character's internal states, such as pleasure and arousal, which are two axes of the circumflex model of affect proposed by Russell [10]. The coordinate value of the outputs in the circumflex model presents the character's current

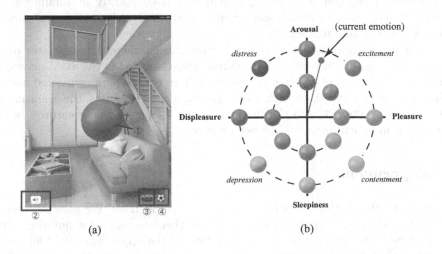

(a)   (b)

Fig. 2. Application of Virtual Creature with the Emotional Growth Model

emotional expression towards the user. In addition, the character has two physiological desires—appetite and sleep drive. These two desires strengthen with time and are reduced when satisfied. The two desires affect and change the degrees of pleasure and arousal. As the character's appetite is satisfied by eating food, the degree of pleasure increases and arousal slowly decreases. Then, the sleep drive gets stronger, because the character wants to sleep on a full stomach; its sleep drive is reduced by sleeping.

Figure 2 presents the GUI of the application and the correspondence between the character's emotions and colors. The object in Figure 2(a) that is marked (1) and resembles a ball is the character. It can move around the screen slowly or quickly. The button (2) is for quitting the application. Icon (3) represents food and icon (4) represents a ball. Users interact with the character by touching the screen. If they want to provide it some food, they drag and drop the food icon (3) anywhere on the screen. To play with it character, they drag and drop the ball icon (4). If the character is satisfied, it moves to catch the ball. When the users play with the character for long, the character's pleasure increases but its arousal slowly decreases owing to fatigue. Its desire for both food and sleep grows stronger. In contrast, leaving the character alone for a long time makes it disappointed and its pleasure decreases slowly. In addition, its pleasure also decreases when its sleep is disturbed.

The character expresses its emotions through simple colors and action patterns. It always expresses emotion within a range marked by eight cardinal emotions: arousal, excitement, pleasure, contentment, sleepiness, depression, displeasure, and distress. These emotions are arranged on the circumflex model of affect hues illustrated in Fig.2(b). Each emotion has a single hue, within which there is a gradient of intensity. When the creature's emotion is strong, its color is more vivid. The hue and intensity of the color of the creature are selected according to the output values of the MLP NN.

The size of the character changes slightly and constantly in simulation of breathing. This movement is faster when it is aroused and pleased, and slower when it is sleepy and displeased.

At the beginning of user interaction with the character, it expresses only simple emotions, because only a few neurons are connected in the SOM network. The number of types of emotion increases as more neurons are connected and it gains experience interacting with users. Through these features, the application allows users to interact with the character as they do with real creatures, in an interaction in which users act like pet owners.

4   Experiment

We experimented with the application using an Apple iPad. We gave 29 college subjects two types of applications and asked them to answer a questionnaire about their impressions of the characters. One of the applications had an inexperienced character that expressed only simple emotions when first interacting with users. The other application had an experienced character that had an

SOM classifying internal states into eight emotions and a learning ANN. The two versions of the characters were visually indistinguishable.

The questionnaire survey showed that several subjects realized that the inexperienced character was growing and beginning to express a variety of emotions during interaction. Some subjects answered that they felt the inexperienced character seemed abandoned, carefree, or insubordinate. In contrast, they considered the experienced character simple and amenable.

In the experiment, subjects interacted with the two characters without time restriction. The operational log shows that almost all subjects interacted with the inexperienced character longer and more often than the experienced character. This result indicates that an unfledged and primitive creature attracts users strongly.

References

1. Sumitomo, H., Tokumaru, M., Muranaka, N.: Study on an Emotion Generation Model for a Robot Using a Chaotic Neural Network. In: Yang, H.S., Malaka, R., Hoshino, J., Han, J.H. (eds.) ICEC 2010. LNCS, vol. 6243, pp. 502–504. Springer, Heidelberg (2010)
2. Harata, M., Tokumaru, M.: An emotion generation model with growth functions for robots. Journal of Advanced Computational Intelligence and Intelligent Informatics 17(2), 335–342 (2013)
3. Kubota, N., Nojima, Y., Baba, N., Kojima, F., Fukuda, T.: Evolving pet robot with emotional model. In: Proceedings of IEEE Congress on Evolutionary Computation, pp. 1231–1237 (2000)
4. Ogata, T., Sugano, S.: Emotional Communication Between Humans and the Autonomous Robot which has the Emotion Model. In: Proceedings of 1999 IEEE International Conference on Robotics and Automation, pp. 3177–3182 (1999)
5. Miwa, H., Okuchi, T., Itoh, K., Takanobu, H., Takanishi, A.: A New Mental Model for Humanoid Robots for Human Friendly Communication. In: Proceedings of the 2003 IEEE International Conference on Robotics and Automation, pp. 3588–3593 (2003)
6. Kohonen, T.: The self-organizing map. Proceedings of the IEEE 78(9), 1464–1480 (1990)
7. Robert, P.: Emotion. A Psychoevolutionary Synthesis. Harper & Row (1980)
8. Miller, G.A.: The Magical Number Seven, Plus or Minus Two: Some Limits on our Capacity for Processing Information. Psychological Review 63(2), 81–97 (1956)
9. Bridges, K.M.B.: Emotional development in early infancy. Child Development 3(4), 324–334 (1932)
10. Russell, J.A.: A circumplex model of affect. Journal of Personality and Social Psychology 39(6), 1161–1178 (1980)

Using Depth Information for Real-Time Face Detection

Sun-Hee Weon, Sung-Il Joo, and Hyung-Il Choi

Department of Media, Soongsil University, Seoul, Korea
{nifty12,sijoo82,hic}@ssu.ac.kr

Abstract. This paper proposes a method for real-time face detection. The proposed method is to use depth information to detect faces in a manner that performs robustly even in response to changes of lighting and face sizes. And we use the depth difference features in depth image and apply this to the boosting algorithm for training and recognition. The depth difference features that this study proposes to use enable dynamic changes to be made to the window according to the face size. The conventional method of face detection was to define the size of the face to be detected in advance, and complete scanning for all the possible sizes. By contrast, this new method requires only a single scan to detect faces of all sizes, since it uses the central depth value to predict size based on 2nd polynomial model. These detected depth difference features are performed training and recognition step with boosting algorithm[1]. The boosting classifier performs recognition by connecting strong classifiers that are constituted by weak classifiers.

Keywords: Face detection, depth, depth difference feature, real-time.

1 Introduction

Research on image-based face detection can be broadly categorized into the knowledge-based method, feature-based method, template-matching, and appearance-based method. In this study, real-time face detection is performed by improving the boosting classifier, which is one of the appearance-based methods, and applying this to depth images. The depth difference features used in this study consist of improved MCT features. The use of these MCT features was proposed by Fröba[3]. Because of the MCT features used by Fröba express local features, they perform very strongly in response to changes in lighting, and the modified AdaBoost classifier with the cascade structure reduces the false positive rate and thereby improves face detection performance. However, when compared to the method for face detection proposed by Viola and Jones[2], which uses Haar-like features combined with the AdaBoost classifier, the MCT feature is at a relatively disadvantage. The MCT feature uses a fixed mask and performs detection using the shape while down-scaling the image, and this results in a relatively slower detection speed in comparison to the Haar-like feature, which extracts the feature by changing the mask size to ensure that strong detection performance in response to changes in the face size occurring in the input image. This paper uses depth images and depth difference feature to perform face

C. Stephanidis (Ed.): HCII 2014 Posters, Part I, CCIS 434, pp. 480–483, 2014.

detection in a manner that overcomes the problems posed by lighting effects and occlusion. This paper is organized as follows. Section 2 gives a detailed explanation regarding the depth difference features in depth image, and Section 3 presents the results of experiments in real-time system. Section 4 gives the conclusions and the future directions for research.

2   Face Detection

In this study, face detection is performed using depth images, by generating depth difference features consisting of local feature structures that have been improved over the conventional MCT features. Conventional MCT features expressed local feature by using a window kernel of a fixed size, regardless of the size of the image. For this reason, there was a disadvantageous requirement to change the image size instead of adjusting the window kernel when detecting faces of every possible size. Moreover, there was a relatively small number of features, because the features are generated using the relations among locally neighboring pixels. In a color image, the interior facial components such as the eyes, nose and mouth have clearly distinguishable differences in terms of their brightness values, and therefore Haar-like features that utilized these elements demonstrated strong results. In the case of depth images, however, such features within the face are not as clearly distinct, and therefore it is impossible to use the common features that were used in color images. Table I shows the algorithm for extracting depth difference features[4,5].

Table 1. Depth difference feature[4,5]

Input :

   I : input image

   N_x, N_y : the number of blocks in x and y axis

Definition :

   $Step_x = I_{width} / 2N_x, Step_y = I_{height} / 2N_y$

   $block_{width} = I_{width} / N_x, block_{height} = I_{height} / N_y$

   $End_x = 2N_x - 1, End_y = 2N_y - 1$

Algorithm :

   $i \leftarrow 0$

   For $x = 0, ..., End_x$

      For $y = 0, ..., End_y$

         $ROI = RECT(x \times Step_x, y \times Step_y, block_{width}, block_{height})$

         $Fv[i] = Depth_c - Area(ROI) / (ROI_w \times ROI_h)$

         $i \leftarrow i + 1$

      End

   End

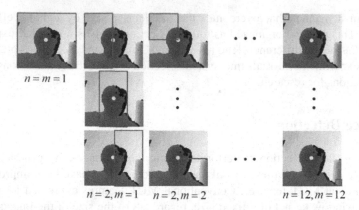

$n = m = 1$

$n = 2, m = 1$ $n = 2, m = 2$ $n = 12, m = 12$

Fig. 1. The examples of depth difference feature extraction

The conventional method of face detection was to define the size of the face to be detected in advance, and complete scanning for all the possible sizes. By contrast, this new method requires only a single scan to detect faces of all sizes, since it uses the central depth value to predict size. Although there can be individual differences in face size, the sizes are generally similar and the dispersion is not large. Therefore, the 2nd polynomial model is used to predict the region size based on the central depth value[4,5]. Figure 1 shows an example of the process of changing the block's size in order to extract the depth difference features. The red rectangle means the block that is segmented using the algorithm in Table I. The yellow dot is the central point of the face region in the training image, and means the location from which the depth value is acquired in order to obtain the difference between the block and the mean, for the purpose of feature extraction.

These detected depth difference features are performed training and recognition step with boosting algorithm. The boosting classifier performs recognition by connecting strong classifiers that are constituted by weak classifiers.

3   Experimental Results

Tests were conducted in an environment equipped with Intel(R) Core2 Quad CPU 3.20GHz and 8G RAM, and the depth images with a size of 320x240, obtained from Microsoft Kinect sensor. To implement training, a training sample database is prepared consisting of face images and non-face images. In this study, the training data was collected by segmenting the region according to the size that was determined using the 2nd polynomial model at various distances. Non-face images were extracted randomly from depth images that did not contain a face. Figure 2 shows that the results of face detection in real-time system with depth image.

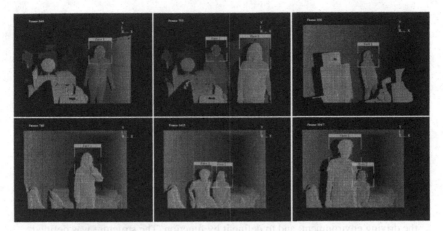

Fig. 2. The results of face detection in real-time system

4   Conclusions

This paper proposed a method of using depth difference features from depth images to enable speedy and accurate real-time face detection. To ensure strong performance in response to changes such as changes in face size or rotations, depth difference features applying the 2nd polynomial model. Furthermore, by using depth images that are not affected by changes in lighting, this study further demonstrated its potential for serving as the groundwork for actual user recognition technology. From now on, we will be needed to research methods to detect the bodies of users for the purpose of user recognition.

Acknowledgments. This research was supported by the Seoul R&BD Program(SS110013) and Basic Science Research Program through the National Research Foundation of Korea(NRF) funded by the Ministry of Science, ICT & Future Planning(2013R1A1A2012012).

Reference

1. Freund, Y., Shapire, R.E.: A short introduction to boosting. Journal of Japanese Society for Artificial Intelligence 14(5), 771–780 (1999)
2. Viola, P., Jones, M.: Rapid object detection using a boosted cascade of simple features. In: Proceedings of IEEE Conference on Computer Vision and Pattern Recognition, vol. 1, pp. 511–518 (2001)
3. Fröba, B., Ernst, A.: Face Detection with the Modified Census Transform. In: Proceedings of the Sixth IEEE International Conference on Automatic Face and Gesture Recognition (FGR 2004), pp. 91–96 (2004)
4. Joo, S.I., Weon, S.H., Hong, J.M., Choi, H.I.: Hand detection in depth images using features of depth difference. In: Proceedings of the International Conference on Image Processing, Computer Vision, and Pattern Recognition (IPCV 2013), vol. 2, pp. 823–834 (2013)
5. Joo, S.I., Weon, S.H., Choi, H.I.: Real-time Hand Region Detection based on Cascade using Depth Information. KIPS Transactions on Software and Data Engineering 2(10), 713–722 (2013)

A Study on Methods of Multimodal Interaction in Vehicle Based on Wheel Gestures and Voices

Seungmin Yang and Younghwan Pan

Graduate School of Techno Design, Kookmin University, Seoul, Korea
eqmark@gmail.com, peterpan@kookmin.ac.kr

Abstract. This study was aimed to investigate the multimodal interaction providing wheel gesture and voice inputs together- that is suitable for car driers in the driving environment, and to define it by function. The structure was defined first of the wheel gesture-voice multimodal interaction, followed by discussion on the resulting wheel gesture and voice interaction respectively. Next, multimodal interaction set was extracted to practically use after mapping the two interactions with the in-vehicle functions, and verify it through interviews with experts. This allowed the deriving of a specific set for multimodal interaction based on the wheel gesture and voice in the vehicle, which is expected to be used as a basis for future research on the multi interaction interface that can take advantage of the gesture and voice in a driving environment.

Keywords: Vehicle, Multimodal interaction, Gesture, Voice.

1 Introduction

1.1 Research Background and Objectives

The most important thing while driving is the level of competitive tasks that take away driver's visual attention from the driver's front lobe, or Primary Visual Attention Lobe (PVAL) [5]. The competing tasks with PVAL for visual attention include reading a map or tuning the radio dial while driving [1].

Currently, motor companies are running the projects to find a new way to solve these problems, among which they are actively studying on the interaction utilizing the gesture and voice in driving environment. Currently, motor companies are running the projects to find a new way to solve these problems, among which they are actively studying on the interaction utilizing the gesture and voice in driving environment. Previous studies have confirmed that the multimodal interaction combined with gesture and voice is the most appropriate interaction method for the driving environment. However, there are limitations that disturbance factors are found in the gesture due to the driving, device operation and hand movements during conversation, and that disturbance factors are found in the voice due to the in-vehicle noise or conversation with passengers. In addition, multimodal interaction is required that can be flexibly used depending on circumstances because cases occur when a variety of input methods may be necessary depending on the changing conditions within the vehicle from

C. Stephanidis (Ed.): HCII 2014 Posters, Part I, CCIS 434, pp. 484–489, 2014.
© Springer International Publishing Switzerland 2014

time to time. Therefore, the purpose of this study was to propose the wheel gesture-voice multimodal interaction set bases on the mapping of wheel gesture and voice interaction that can be used while operating specific functions in the vehicle.

1.2   Previous Research

Previous studies have performed experiments to find out the best combination of non-contact gesture and voice recognition for interaction of vehicle information systems operations; according to the results, the way of voice commands to operate and gesture to maneuver amounts showed the highest satisfaction and efficient in terms of time or error [2].

Other studies have defined the functions to be able to manipulate using wheel gesture and one hand space gesture in the vehicle and proposed, among those, the suitable interaction schemes utilizing wheel gesture for the operation of the functions. Wheel gesture refers to the ability to operate the functions not directly related to the driving by the operator in the vehicle with his two hands holding the steering wheel. Of these, audio, radio, heater and air conditioner were selected as the objects of functional operation, and underwent mapping with the gesture to derive the final wheel gesture interaction set [3].

2   Structure of Wheel Gesture-Voice Multimodal Interaction

Input interaction is defined as the type of the input other than input devices, and is divided by five interactions of instruction word, four-way, cursor, touch and intelligent interaction [4]. This study has defined the multimodal interaction as the input method for the instruction words.

Figure 1 shows the structure of the multimodal interaction set utilizing the voice and gesture in the vehicle. It is the structure that the user commands the functional operation using the gesture and the voice and accordingly the car outputs the command by operating the function.

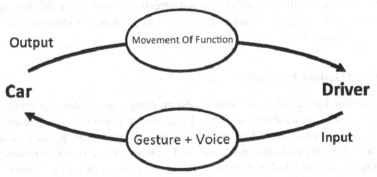

Fig. 1. Structure of Wheel gesture-Voice Multimodal Interaction

All possibilities will be open without precluding limited use assuming that easy-to-use input method may vary depending on the situation of the driver in the vehicle environment.

Therefore, the user may use gesture and voice separately or together in the functional operation through the Wheel gesture-Voice multimodal Interaction. These two can operate each function independently by respective interaction alone without interdependence.

3   Classification of Wheel Gesture-Voice Multimodal Interaction

As shown in Figure 2, the functional operation process in the vehicle is composed of function selection (ON), detailed function selection (Adjustment of Level), after a certain period of time, and function selection (OFF), with each structure that the result being recognized by the user through feedback in each phase [3].

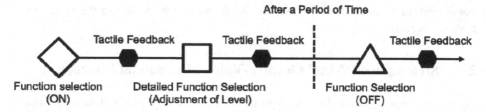

Fig. 2. TASK analysis of operation of ordinary function of the driver (Source : Kang, 2012, p.50)

Among these, what require the input interaction are the function selection (on), detailed function selection (numeric control), and function selection (off). This study has mapped and defined the wheel gesture and voice interaction that can be used each individual stage, has limited the range of functions that can be operated to radio, audio, heater and air conditioner which are not directly related to the driving, and have premises to receive voice feedback step by step to prevent the interference with the forward visual conditions.

3.1   Wheel Gesture Interaction

The selection of the function via wheel gesture comprises of the repetitive input of Left Hand Index Raise as shown in Table 1 and the confirmation of the selected function by voice feedback. Next, fine adjustment of the numerical quantity such as the strength of the heater and air-conditioner and volume of the radio and audio can be made using Right Hand Index Raise and the change of the radio and audio channels and the temperature control of the heater and air-conditioner can be made by Left Hand Index Raise and Left Hand Thumb Twist. In addition, the function could be finished by using Hand Spread [3].

Table 1. Wheel gestures (Source : Kang, 2012, p.59)

WHEEL GESTURES					
Left hand Index raise (Selection)	Left hand Index raise	Left hand Thumb twist	Right hand Index raise	Right hand Thumb twist	Hand spread

3.2   Voice Interaction

The voice interaction was defined based on the classification criteria for the gesture interaction. The function can be operated by the voice operation using instruction words intuitively recognizable when the function required is definite. For example, the radio is turned on by the user intuitively with the combination of words 'Radio' and 'on.' When compared with the wheel gesture interaction, voice interaction can be executed in one step thanks to the direct selection of the desired function

3.3   Wheel Gesture-Voice Multimodal Interaction Set

Table 2. Wheel gesture-Voice Multimodal Interaction Set

FUNCTION	INTERACTION	COMMANDS					
Radio	Name	Turn on	Channel Up	Channel down	Volume up	Volume down	Turn off
	Gesture						
	Voice	"radio on"	"channel up"	"channel down"	"volume up"	"volume down"	"radio off"
Audio	Name	Turn on	Channel Up	Channel down	Volume up	Volume down	Turn off
	Gesture						
	Voice	"audio on"	"channel up"	"channel down"	"volume up"	"volume down"	"audio off"
Heater	Name	Turn on	Temperature up	Temperature down	Strength up	Strength down	Turn off
	Gesture						
	Voice	"heater on"	"temp up"	"temp down"	"strength up"	"strength down"	"heater off"
Air conditioning	Name	Turn on	Temperature up	Temperature down	Strength up	Strength down	Turn off
	Gesture						
	Voice	"aircon on"	"temp up"	"temp down"	"strength up"	"strength down"	"aircon off"

Wheel gesture-Voice Multimodal Interaction Set includes both wheel gesture and voice interaction, which have the same goal of operating specific functions. Therefore, the operation of the function can be performed by the two ways independently or interchangeably. For example, the radio can be turned on by using voice interaction "radio on," turned up by the input of Left Hand Index Raise, and turned down by the input of Right Hand Thumb twist.

4   Expert Interview

4.1   Method and System

Expert interview was conducted to verify for the effectiveness to the users of the function operation of the four tasks (radio, audio, heaters, air conditioners) using Wheel gesture-Voice Multimodal Interaction Set as discussed in this study.

Experts were composed of a total five people including two ordinary drivers (1 male / 1 female each) of 10 or more years of driving experience and three UX design majors (2 males / 1 female) of 5 or more years of driving experience; Full instruction was given to them on the vehicle function operation process and defined Wheel gesture-Voice Multimodal Interaction Set, for their sequential assessment according to the operation process and collection of qualitative results.

4.2   Findings

Results were derived from interviews with experts that Wheel gesture-Voice Multimodal Interaction Set provides higher driver's forward vision concentration compared to the existing traditional button or touch interaction thanks to no interference with driver's vision. On the other hand, it was confirmed that increased kinds of functions accordingly makes it   difficult to learn and remember the gesture or voice instruction words.

5   Conclusion

This study has defined a Wheel gesture-Voice multimodal interaction that can flexibly use tasks because a variety of input methods are required that do not interfere with the driver's field of view according to the ever-changing driving situation. The interaction includes a concrete Set that can be used independently or together depending on the intended use and situation of the driver.

Further research is necessary to expand the four limited functionality discussed in this study up to the different areas of the vehicle, and additional research is needed about the output methods for the input interaction.

Reference

1. Dingus, T.A., Antim, J.F., Hulse, M.C., Wierwille, W.: Human Factors issues associated with in-car navigation system usage. In: Proceedings of the 32nd Annual Meeting of the Human Factors Society, pp. 1448–1453 (1988)
2. Kim, H., Park, S.H.: The Effects of Operation Types on Interacting with Voice and Non-Touch Gestures in In-vehicle Information Systems. Journal of Korean Society of Design Science 25(2), 93–101 (2012)
3. Kang, M.S.: Gesture Interaction Design for Cars (2012)
4. Pan, Y.H.: A Study on Structuring and Classification of Input interaction. Journal of the Ergonomics Society of Korea 31(4), 494–496 (2012)
5. Wickens, C.D., Lee, J.D., Liu, Y.D.: Gordon Becker and Sallie E. An Introduction to Human Factors Engineering, 2nd edn. Pearson Education (2004)

Algorithms and Machine Learning Methods in HCI

Using the Bee Colony Optimization Method to Solve the Weighted Set Covering Problem

Broderick Crawford[1,2], Ricardo Soto[3,4],
Rodrigo Cuesta[3], and Fernando Paredes[5]

[1] Universidad San Sebastián, Chile
[2] Universidad Finis Terrae, Chile
[3] Pontificia Universidad Católica de Valparaíso, Chile
[4] Universidad Autónoma de Chile, Chile
[5] Escuela de Ingeniería Industrial, Universidad Diego Portales, Chile
broderick.crawford.l@gmail.com,
ricardo.soto@ucv.cl,
rodrigo.cuesta.a@mail.pucv.cl,
fernando.paredes@udp.cl

Abstract. The Weighted Set Covering Problem is a formal model for many practical optimization problems. In this problem the goal is to choose a subset of columns of minimal cost covering every row. Here, we present a novel application of the Artificial Bee Colony algorithm to solve the Weighted Set Covering Problem. The Artificial Bee Colony algorithm is a recent Swarm Metaheuristic technique based on the intelligent foraging behavior of honey bees. Experimental results show that our Artificial Bee Colony algorithm is competitive in terms of solution quality with other recent metaheuristic approaches.

Keywords: Weighted Set Covering Problem, Artificial Bee Colony Algorithm, Swarm Intelligence.

1 Introduction

The Weighted Set Covering Problem (WSCP) has many applications, including those involving routing, scheduling, stock cutting, electoral redistricting and others important real life situations [14]. Different solving methods have been proposed in the literature for the Weighted Set Covering Problem. Exact algorithms are mostly based on Branch-and-Bound and Branch-and-Cut techniques [2,15,4], Linear Programing and Heuristic methods [6]. However, these algorithms are rather time consuming and can only solve instances of very limited size. For this reason, many research efforts have been focused on the development of metaheuristics to find as result good or near-optimal solutions within a reasonable period of time. An incomplete list of metaheuristics for the WSCP includes Genetic Algorithms [1,3], Simulated Annealing [5], Tabu Search [7], Cultural Algorithms [11,10] and Ant Colony Optimization [8]. For a deeper comprehension of most of the effective algorithms for the WSCP in the literature, we refer the

C. Stephanidis (Ed.): HCII 2014 Posters, Part I, CCIS 434, pp. 493–497, 2014.
© Springer International Publishing Switzerland 2014

interested reader to the survey by [6]. In this paper we present the metaheuristic Artificial Bee Colony that is relatively new in the area to solve the WSCP.

2 Artificial Bee Colony Algorithm

ABC is one of the most recent algorithms in the domain of the collective intelligence. Created by Dervis Karaboga in 2005, who was motivated by the intelligent behavior observed in the domestic bees to take the process of foraging [17]. ABC is an algorithm of combinatorial optimization based on populations, in which the solutions of the problem of optimization, the sources of food, are modified by the artificial bees, which function as operators of variation. The aim of these bees is to discover the food sources with major nectar. In the ABC algorithm, the artificial bees move in a space of multidimensional search choosing sources of nectar depending on its past experience and its companions of beehive. Some bees fly and choose food sources randomly without using experience. When they find a source of major nectar, they memorize his position and forget the previous one. Thus, ABC combines methods of local search and global search, trying to balance the process of the exploration and exploitation of the space of search. Although, the performance of different optimization algorithm is dependent on applications some recent works demonstrate that the Artificial Bee Colony is more rapid than either Genetic Algorithm or Particle Swarm Optimization solving certain problems [21,20,22].

For more details of ABC we refer the reader to [16]. The pseudocode of Artificial Bee Colony is like that:

Algorithm - ABC pseudo-code

1 **Begin**
2   Initialize the food sources
3   Evaluate the nectar amount of food sources
4   **While** remain interations **do**
5   Phase of Workers Bees
6   Phase of Onlookers Bees
7   Phase of Scout Bees
8   UpdateOptimum()
9   **End While**
10   Return BestSolution
11 **End**

3 Weighted Set Covering Problem

In the WSCP matrix formulation we define a $m \times n$ matrix $A = (a_{ij})$ in which all the matrix elements are either zero or one. Additionally, each column is given a non-negative cost c_j. We say that a column j covers a row i if $a_{ij} = 1$. Let x_j a binary variable which is one if column j is chosen and zero otherwise. The WSCP can be defined formally as *minimize* (1) *subject to* (2). The goal in the

WSCP is to choose a subset of the columns of minimal weight formally using constraints to enforce that each row is covered by at least one column.

$$f(x) = \sum_{j=1}^{n} c_j x_j \tag{1}$$

$$\sum_{j=1}^{n} a_{ij} x_j \geq 1; \qquad \forall i = 1, ..., m \tag{2}$$

$$x_j \in \{0, 1\}; \qquad \forall j = 1, ..., n \tag{3}$$

4   Experimental Results

The ABC algorithm has been implemented in C in a 2.5 GHz Dual Core with 4 GB RAM computer, running windows 7. ABC has been tested on standard non-unicost SCP instances available from OR Library[1]. ABC was executed 30 times on each instance, each trial with a different random seed. In comparison with very recent works solving WSCP - with Cultural algorithms [11] and Ant Colony + Constraint Programming techniques [12] - our proposal performs best than the WSCP instances reported in those works.

Table 1 shows the detailed results obtained by the algorithm. Column 2 reports the optimal or the best known solution value of each instance. The third and fourth columns show the best value and the average obtained by our ABC algorithm in 30 runs (trials). The last column shows the Relative Percentage Deviation (RPD) value over the instances tested with ABC. The quality of solutions can be evaluated using the RPD, its value quantifies the deviation of the objective value Z from Z_{opt} which in our case is the best known cost value for each instance. This measure is computed as follows:

$$RPD = (Z - Z_{opt})/Z_{opt} \times 100 \tag{4}$$

Examining Table 1 we observe that ABC is able to find the optimal solution consistently, i.e. in every trial. ABC is able to find the best known value in all instances with a RPD of 0,00%.

5   Conclusion

We have presented an Artificial Bee Colony Algorithm for the Weighted Set Covering Problem. The promising results of the experiments open up opportunities for further research. Our approach could also be effectively applied to other combinatorial optimization problems. The use of Autonomous Search (AS), AS represents a new research field, and it provides practitioners with systems that are able to autonomously selftune their performance while effectively solving

---

[1] At http://people.brunel.ac.uk/~mastjjb/jeb/info.html

Table 1. Experimental results - Instances with Best Known Solution

Instance	Optimum	Best value found	ABC Avg	RPD (%)
NRE.1	29	29	29	0
NRE.2	30	30	30	0
NRE.3	27	27	27	0
NRE.4	28	28	28	0
NRE.5	28	28	28	0
NRF.1	14	14	14	0
NRF.2	15	15	15	0
NRF.3	14	14	14	0
NRF.4	14	14	14	0
NRF.5	13	13	13	0
NRG.1	176	176	176	0
NRG.2	154	154	154	0
NRG.3	166	166	166	0
NRG.4	168	168	168	0
NRG.5	168	168	168	0
NRH.1	63	63	63	0
NRH.2	63	63	63	0
NRH.3	59	59	59	0
NRH.4	58	58	58	0
NRH.5	55	55	55	0

problems. Its major strength and originality consist in the fact that problem solvers can now perform self-improvement operations based on analysis of the performances of the solving process [13,19,9]. Furthermore, we are considering to use different preprocessing steps from the OR literature, which allow to reduce the problem size [18].

References

1. Aickelin, U.: An indirect genetic algorithm for set covering problems. Journal of the Operational Research Society 53, 1118–1126 (2002)
2. Balas, E., Carrera, M.C.: A dynamic subgradient-based branch-and-bound procedure for set covering. Operations Research 44(6), 875–890 (1996)
3. Beasley, J., Chu, P.: A genetic algorithm for the set covering problem. European Journal of Operational Research 94(2), 392–404 (1996)
4. Beasley, J.E., Jornsten, K.: Enhancing an algorithm for set covering problems. European Journal of Operational Research 58(2), 293–300 (1992)
5. Brusco, M.J., Jacobs, L.W., Thompson, G.M.: A morphing procedure to supplement a simulated annealing heuristic for cost- and coverage-correlated set-covering problems. Annals of Operations Research 86, 611–627 (1999)
6. Caprara, A., Toth, P., Fischetti, M.: Algorithms for the set covering problem. Annals of Operations Research 98, 353–371 (2000)
7. Caserta, M.: Tabu search-based metaheuristic algorithm for large-scale set covering problems. In: Doerner, K.F., et al. (eds.) Metaheuristics: Progress in complex systems optimization. Springer (2007)

8. Crawford, B., Castro, C., Monfroy, E.: A New ACO Transition Rule for Set Partitioning and Covering Problems. In: SoCPaR, pp. 426–429 (2009)
9. Crawford, B., Castro, C., Monfroy, E., Soto, R., Palma, W., Paredes, F.: A hyperheuristic approach for guiding enumeration in constraint solving. In: Schütze, O., Coello Coello, C.A., Tantar, A.-A., Tantar, E., Bouvry, P., Del Moral, P., Legrand, P. (eds.) EVOLVE - A Bridge Between Probability, Set Oriented Numerics, and Evolutionary Computation II. AISC, vol. 175, pp. 171–188. Springer, Heidelberg (2012)
10. Crawford, B., Lagos, C., Castro, C., Parede, F.: A Evolutionary Approach to Solve Set Covering. In: ICEIS, vol. 2, pp. 356–363 (2007)
11. Crawford, B., Soto, R., Monfroy, E.: Cultural algorithms for the set covering problem. In: Tan, Y., Shi, Y., Mo, H. (eds.) ICSI 2013, Part II. LNCS, vol. 7929, pp. 27–34. Springer, Heidelberg (2013)
12. Crawford, B., Soto, R., Monfroy, E., Castro, C., Palma, W., Paredes, F.: A hybrid soft computing approach for subset problems. Mathematical Problems in Engineering 2013(716069), 1–12 (2013)
13. Crawford, B., Soto, R., Monfroy, E., Palma, W., Castro, C., Paredes, F.: Parameter tuning of a choice-function based hyperheuristic using particle swarm optimization. Expert Systems with Applications 40(5), 1690–1695 (2013)
14. Feo, T.A., Resende, M.G.C.: A probabilistic heuristic for a computationally difficult set covering problem. Operations Research Letters 8(2), 67–71 (1989)
15. Fisher, M.L., Kedia, P.: Optimal solution of set covering/partitioning problems using dual heuristics. Management Science 36(6), 674–688 (1990)
16. Karaboga, D.: Artificial bee colony algorithm. Scholarpedia 5(3), 6915 (2010)
17. Karaboga, D., Basturk, B.: A powerful and efficient algorithm for numerical function optimization: artificial bee colony (abc) algorithm. J. Global Optimization 39(3), 459–471 (2007)
18. Krieken, M.V., Fleuren, H., Peeters, M.: Problem reduction in set partitioning problems. Discussion Paper 2003-80, Tilburg University, Center for Economic Research (2003)
19. Monfroy, E., Castro, C., Crawford, B., Soto, R., Paredes, F., Figueroa, C.: A reactive and hybrid constraint solver. Journal of Experimental and Theoretical Artificial Intelligence 25(1), 1–22 (2013)
20. Zhang, Y., Wu, L.: Optimal multi-level thresholding based on maximum tsallis entropy via an artificial bee colony approach. Entropy 13(4), 841–859 (2011)
21. Zhang, Y., Wu, L.: Artificial bee colony for two dimensional protein folding. Advances in Electrical Engineering Systems 1(1), 19–23 (2012)
22. Zhang, Y., Wu, L., Wang, S., Huo, Y.: Chaotic artificial bee colony used for cluster analysis. In: Chen, R. (ed.) ICICIS 2011 Part I. CCIS, vol. 134, pp. 205–211. Springer, Heidelberg (2011)

Modeling Manufacturing Cell Design Problems: CP vs. MH

Broderick Crawford[1,3], Ricardo Soto[1,2], Gustavo Zuñiga[1], Eric Monfroy[4], and Fernando Paredes[5]

[1] Pontificia Universidad Católica de Valparaíso, Chile
[2] Universidad Autónoma de Chile, Chile
[3] Universidad Finis Terrae, Chile
[4] CNRS, LINA, Université de Nantes, France
[5] Escuela de Ingeniería Industrial Universidad Diego Portales, Chile
{ricardo.soto,broderick.crawford}@ucv.cl,
gustavo.zuniga.m@mail.pucv.cl,
eric.monfroy@univ-nantes.fr,
fernando.paredes@udp.cl

Abstract. The manufacturing cell design problem aims at organizing a manufacturing plant in cells that contain machines processing parts from a same family for a given product. The purpose is to minimize the flow of parts among cells so as to increase productivity while reducing costs. This paper focuses on comparing metaheuristics and constraint programming –from a modeling standpoint– when used to solve this problem.

Keywords: Constraint Programming, Metaheuristics, Manufacturing Cell Design.

1 Introduction

The manufacturing cell design problem (MCDP) is a classic optimization problem from group technology. It aims at organizing a manufacturing plant in cells that contain machines that process similar parts for a given product. The purpose is to minimize the flow of parts among cells so as to increase productivity while reducing costs. During the last years, this problem has been tackled with different techniques which can be organized into two main groups: complete search and approximate methods. Complete search methods explore the whole set of potential solutions in order to reach a solution. These methods may be unsuitable once the problem size increases, since it is not possible to explore the complete combinatorial space in a limited period of time. In this context, approximate methods are more appropriate since they attempt to examine only promising regions of the search space. In the first group we can find approaches devoted to the MCDP based on the classic linear programming [12], goal programming [13,14], constraint programming [20], and Boolean satisfiability [19]. The second group is mainly composed of metaheuristics (MH), such as tabu search [9], simulated annealing [22], particle swarm optimization [6], genetic algorithms [21], and some hybridization of them [8,11].

C. Stephanidis (Ed.): HCII 2014 Posters, Part I, CCIS 434, pp. 498–502, 2014.

This paper focuses on comparing metaheuristics and constraint programming –from a modeling standpoint– when used to solve this problem. This paper is organized as follows: We firstly present the mathematical model representing the MCDP, we provide then the discussion about the contrasts of metaheuristics with respect to constraint programming when modeling this problem. Finally, we give the conclusions and future work.

2 Modeling the MCDP

The optimization model for the MCDP is stated as follows. Let:

- M, be the number of machines,
- P, the number of parts,
- C, the number of cells,
- i, the index of machines $(i = 1, \ldots, M)$,
- j, the index of parts $(j = 1, \ldots, P)$,
- k, the index of cells $(k = 1, \ldots, C)$,
- $A = [a_{ij}]$ the $M \times P$ binary machine-part incidence matrix,
- M_{max}, the maximum number of machines per cell.

  The goal of the objective function is to minimize the number of times that a given part must be processed by a machine that does not belong to the cell that the part has been assigned to. Let:

$$y_{ik} = \begin{cases} 1 \text{ if machine } i \in \text{ cell } k; \\ 0 \text{ otherwise;} \end{cases}$$

$$z_{jk} = \begin{cases} 1 \text{ if part } j \in \text{ family } k; \\ 0 \text{ otherwise;} \end{cases}$$

The mathematical model is as follows:

$$\texttt{minimize} \sum_{k=1}^{C} \sum_{i=1}^{M} \sum_{j=1}^{P} a_{ij} z_{jk} (1 - y_{ik})$$

Subject to

$$\sum_{k=1}^{C} y_{ik} = 1 \quad \forall i, \qquad \sum_{k=1}^{C} z_{jk} = 1 \quad \forall j, \qquad \sum_{i=1}^{M} y_{ik} \leq M_{max} \quad \forall k,$$

3 Discussion

We have modeled and solved this problem via CP, Boolean satisfiability (see details in [19]) and different metaheuristics (Tabu Search [7], Artificial Fish Swarm [10], Cuckoo search [23], and Electromagnetism [24]). Several computer science students have participated in these projects, and after this experience we can highlight two important points.

– The CP paradigm has an important advantage w.r.t metaheuristics. In CP, there is no need to design a specific procedure to solve the given problem, the user rather models the problem and a search engine finds a result. In practice, when problems are solved using metaheuristics a specific algorithm must be designed and implemented according to some pre-established patterns. After the experience gained on the aforementioned projects, students may take about 1 month in studying the metaheuristic and then another month to implement the solution. In the context of CP, students may take 1 month in studying CP but only 2 weeks in implementing the solution.

– On the other side, metaheuristics have also an important advantage w.r.t. CP. After implementation, an experimentation phase is required in order to tune the solvers to reach the optimum. This phase requires a high expertise in both contexts, metaheuristics and CP. However, due to the metaheuristics is built from the scratch by the student, he naturally domains better its implementation so it is easier to modify, tune and experiment with it. This is not the case of CP, where the student uses a toolkit which is normally a black-box that provides some kind of configuration but does not provide the full control. It also exists the possibility of exploring the source code of the toolkit, but this is really a hard task as common solvers includes several code lines, most of them hard to handle and as a consequence hard to successfully modify according to our requirements.

4   Conclusion

In this paper, we discussed the main differences between metaheuristics and constraint programming when used for solving the manufacturing cell design problem. In CP, it suffices to encode the mathematical model in the language of the solver, while when metaheuristics are used it is necessary to implement a specific algorithm to solve the problem. On the other side, an experimentation phase may be easier to face off when metaheuristics are used since the user has the full control of its implementation, which is not the case when CP is used.

A continual research direction is about facilitating the user modeling and experimentation phases, for instance to propose easy-to-use modeling languages [18], modeling techniques [1], and modeling features [17,15,2]. The resolution of this problem via CP in conjunction with autonomous search [16,4,5,3] may be also an interesting direction to follow.

Acknowledgements. Ricardo Soto is supported by Grant CONICYT/ FONDE-CYT/INICIACION/11130459, Broderick Crawford is supported by Grant CONI-CYT/FONDECYT/REGULAR/1140897, and Fernando Paredes is supported by Grant CONICYT/FONDECYT/REGULAR/1130455.

References

1. Chenouard, R., Granvilliers, L., Soto, R.: Model-Driven Constraint Programming. In: Proceedings of the 10th International ACM SIGPLAN Conference on Principles and Practice of Declarative Programming (PPDP), pp. 236–246 (2008)
2. Chenouard, R., Granvilliers, L., Soto, R.: High-Level Modeling of Component-Based CSPs. In: da Rocha Costa, A.C., Vicari, R.M., Tonidandel, F. (eds.) SBIA 2010. LNCS, vol. 6404, pp. 233–242. Springer, Heidelberg (2010)
3. Crawford, B., Castro, C., Monfroy, E., Soto, R., Palma, W., Paredes, F.: Dynamic Selection of Enumeration Strategies for Solving Constraint Satisfaction Problems. Romanian Journal of Information Science and Technology 15(2), 106–128 (2012)
4. Crawford, B., Soto, R., Castro, C., Monfroy, E.: Extensible CP-based autonomous search. In: Stephanidis, C. (ed.) Posters, Part I, HCII 2011. CCIS, vol. 173, pp. 561–565. Springer, Heidelberg (2011)
5. Crawford, B., Soto, R., Montecinos, M., Castro, C., Monfroy, E.: A framework for autonomous search in the ecl^{i}ps^e solver. In: Mehrotra, K.G., Mohan, C.K., Oh, J.C., Varshney, P.K., Ali, M. (eds.) IEA/AIE 2011, Part I. LNCS, vol. 6703, pp. 79–84. Springer, Heidelberg (2011)
6. Durán, O., Rodriguez, N., Consalter, L.A.: Collaborative particle swarm optimization with a data mining technique for manufacturing cell design. Expert Systems with Applications 37(2), 1563–1567 (2010)
7. Glover, F., Laguna, M.: Tabu Search. Kluwer Academics Publishers (1997)
8. James, T., Brown, E., Keeling, K.: A hybrid grouping genetic algorithm for the cell formation problem. Computers and Operations Research 34(7), 2059–2079 (2007)
9. Lozano, S., Díaz, A., Eguía, I., Onieva, L.: A one-step tabu search algorithm for manufacturing cell design. Journal of the Operational Research Society 50(5) (1999)
10. Neshat, M., Sepidnam, G., Sargolzaei, M., Toosi, A.: Artificial fish swarm algorithm: a survey of the state-of-the-art, hybridization, combinatorial and indicative applications. In: Artificial Intelligence Review, pp. 1–33 (2012)
11. Nsakanda, A., Diaby, M., Price, W.: Hybrid genetic approach for solving large-scale capacitated cell formation problems with multiple routings. European Journal of Operational Research 171(3), 1051–1070 (2006)
12. Purcheck, G.F.K.: A linear - programming method for the combinatorial grouping of an incomplete set. Journal of Cybernetics 5, 51–58 (1975)
13. Sankaran, S.: Multiple objective decision making approach to cell formation: A goal programming model. Mathematical Computer Modeling 13, 71–77 (1990)
14. Shafer, S.N., Rogers, D.F.: A goal programming approach to cell formation problems. Journal of Operations Management 10, 28–34 (1991)
15. Soto, R.: Controlling search in constrained-object models. In: Kuri-Morales, A., Simari, G.R. (eds.) IBERAMIA 2010. LNCS, vol. 6433, pp. 582–591. Springer, Heidelberg (2010)
16. Soto, R., Crawford, B., Monfroy, E., Bustos, V.: Using autonomous search for generating good enumeration strategy blends in constraint programming. In: Murgante, B., Gervasi, O., Misra, S., Nedjah, N., Rocha, A.M.A.C., Taniar, D., Apduhan, B.O. (eds.) ICCSA 2012, Part III. LNCS, vol. 7335, pp. 607–617. Springer, Heidelberg (2012)
17. Soto, R., Crawford, B., Monfroy, E., Paredes, F.: Syntax Extensions for a Constrained-Object Language via Dynamic Parser Cooperation. Studies in Informatics and Control 21(1), 41–48 (2012)

18. Soto, R., Granvilliers, L.: The Design of COMMA: An Extensible Framework for Mapping Constrained Objects to Native Solver Models. In: Proceedings of IEEE ICTAI, pp. 243–250 (2007)

19. Soto, R., Kjellerstrand, H., Duran, O., Crawford, B., Monfroy, E., Paredes, F.: Cell formation in group technology using constraint programming and boolean satisfiability. Expert Syst. Appl. 39(13), 11423–11427 (2012)

20. Soto, R., Kjellerstrand, H., Gutiérrez, J., López, A., Crawford, B., Monfroy, E.: Solving manufacturing cell design problems using constraint programming. In: Jiang, H., Ding, W., Ali, M., Wu, X. (eds.) IEA/AIE 2012. LNCS, vol. 7345, pp. 400–406. Springer, Heidelberg (2012)

21. Venugopal, V., Narendran, T.T.: A genetic algorithm approach to the machine-component grouping problem with multiple objectives. Computers & Industrial Engineering 22(4), 469–480 (1992)

22. Wu, T., Chang, C., Chung, S.: A simulated annealing algorithm for manufacturing cell formation problems. Expert Systems with Applications 34(3), 1609–1617 (2008)

23. Yang, X.-S., Deb, S.: Cuckoo search via lévy flights. In: World Congress on Nature & Biologically Inspired Computing (NaBIC), pp. 210–214. IEEE (2009)

24. Zhang, C., Li, X., Gao, L., Wu, Q.: An improved electromagnetism-like mechanism algorithm for constrained optimization. Expert Syst. Appl. 40(14), 5621–5634 (2013)

Self-adaptive Systems: Facilitating the Use of Combinatorial Problem Solvers

Broderick Crawford[1,2], Ricardo Soto[3,4], Eric Monfroy[5], and Franklin Johnson[6]

[1] Universidad San Sebastián, Chile
[2] Universidad Finis Terrae, Chile
[3] Pontificia Universidad Católica de Valparaíso, Chile
[4] Universidad Autónoma de Chile, Chile
[5] CNRS, LINA, Université de Nantes, France
[6] Universidad de Playa Ancha, Chile
broderick.crawford.l@gmail.com,
ricardo.soto@ucv.cl,
eric.monfroy@univ-nantes.fr,
franklin.johnson@upla.cl

Abstract. New methods in Combinatorial Problem Solving can solve larger problems in different domains. They also became more complex, which means that they are hard to use and fine-tuning to the peculiarities of a given problem, limiting its use to a small set of experts, and instead black-box solvers with automated search procedure are needed for its broad applicability. Autonomous Search Systems represent a new research field defined to precisely address the above challenge. The main goal of this paper is to review recent works on this kind of Self-adaptive Systems from the standpoint of the actual requirement for solvers.

Keywords: Self-adaptive Systems, Autonomous Search Systems, Combinatorial Problem Solvers.

1 Introduction

An Autonomous Search (AS) system should provide the ability to modify its internal components (heuristics, inference mechanisms, etc.) when exposed to changing external forces and opportunities. As corresponds to an instance of Self-adaptive Systems with the objective of improving its problem solving performance by adapting its search strategy to the problem at hand. Autonomous search is particularly relevant to the Constraint Programming community, where much work has been conducted to improve the efficiency and usability of constraint solvers. AS provides to a system the ability to change its components in order to improve its problem solving performance. AS can be defined as search processes that integrate control in their solving process either by self adaptation or by supervised adaptation [18]. This control allows an AS system to improve its solving performance by modifying and adjusting itself to the problem at hand. In more detail, the notion of control is present when the parameters or heuristics

C. Stephanidis (Ed.): HCII 2014 Posters, Part I, CCIS 434, pp. 503–508, 2014.

are adjusted online, i.e., when the constraint solver is running. Different methods such as control encoding, control variable and value selection, and evolving heuristics have been proposed to provide control during solving [18].

Concerning the control, in self adaptation, techniques are tightly integrated with the search process and usually require some overhead. The algorithm is observing its own behavior in an online fashion, modifying its parameters accordingly. This information can be either directly collected on the problem or indirectly computed through the perceived efficiency of individual components. Because the adaptation is done online, there is an important trade-off between the time spent computing process information and the gains that are to be expected from this information. Therefore we can consider that the most appropriate strategy depends on the set of computed states and changes during solving. Supervised adaptation works at a higher level. It is usually external and its mechanisms are not coupled with the search process. It can be seen as a monitor that observes the search and analyzes it. Then it modifies the components of the solver (or requires the solver to modify its components) in order to adapt it. Supervised adaptation can use more information, e.g., learning-based knowledge.

2   Recent Advances in Constraint Solving

In recent years different efforts of research have been conducted in order to improve the efficiency of solvers. These improvements often rely on new heuristics, adjustement of parameters and heuristics before/during solving and/or hybridization of solving techniques. Diverse domains of research such as parameter setting in evolutionary computing, reactive search, and hyperheuristics have tackled this challenge using different terms and concepts. However, they have common principles and purposes that respond to similar needs.

2.1   Parameter Setting in Evolutionary Computing

The first domain is evolutionary computing, where parameter setting [25] constitutes a major issue and the taxonomy proposed by Eiben et al. [13] may be recalled. Methods are classified depending on whether they attempt to set parameters before the run (tuning) or during the run (control). The goal of parameter tuning is to obtain parameter values that could be useful over a wide range of problems. Such results require a large number of experimental evaluations and are generally based on empirical observations. Parameter control is divided into three branches according to the degree of autonomy of the strategies. Control is deterministic when parameters are changed according to a previously established schedule, adaptive when parameters are modified according to rules that take into account the state of the search, and self-adaptive when parameters are encoded into individuals in order to evolve conjointly with the other variables of the problem.

2.2   Reactive Search

In [2], Reactive Search is characterized by the integration of machine learning techniques into search heuristics. Basically, reactive search allows an internal flexibility of the solver taking into acount, by learning the past history of the search process. Moreover, an escape mechanism allowing the restart of the system from a new random point is used when the system shows no improvement. In [30] a framework for adaptive enumeration strategies and meta-backtracks for a propagation-based constraint solver has been extended in order to trigger some functions of a solver, or of a hybrid solver to respond to some observations of the solving process. Being able also simply design adaptive hybridisation strategies by just changing some rules of its update component.

2.3 Hyperheuristics

Finding the best configuration of heuristic algorithms is strongly related to the recent notion of Hyperheuristics [5,6,8,10,9]. Hyperheuristics are methods that aim at automating the process of selecting, combining, generating, or adapting several simpler heuristics (or their components) to efficiently solve computational search problems. Hyperheuristics are also defined as *heuristics to choose heuristics* [7] or *heuristics to generate heuristics* [1]. Hyperheuristics that manage a set of given available basic search heuristics by means of search strategies or other parameters have been widely used for solving combinatorial problems.

3   Autonomous Search Mechanisms

A classification of basic search processes has been proposed by Hamadi et al. [18]. It tries to differentiate offline tasks from online processes, tuning (adjustment of parameters and heuristics before solving) from control.

Table 1. Autonomous mechanisms and their strategies

Mechanism	Strategy
Tuning before solving [13,25]	Preprocessing [26]
	Parameter tuning on preliminary experiments [23,36,32]
	Component setting [16,4,41,21,22]
Control during solving	Control encoding [19]
	Evolving heuristics [14,17,11]
	Controlling variable ordering and variale selection in search heuristics [28,3,12,29,20,33]
	Controlling evaluation function [31,38]
	Parameter control in metaheuristics algorithms [2,24,34,24,37,39,40,27,15]

As mentioned before, AS has been indeed investigated for many years, across many different areas and under different names. In [18], the way that autonomous mechanisms have been used in the literature are identified. Table 4.1 summarizes the autonomous mechanisms. Autonomous mechanisms are classified in offline tasks (tuning) and online processes (control).

4　Conclusion

This paper has reviewed approaches, methods and challenges in the new field of Autonomous Search systems. The aforementioned approaches are mainly focused on sampling and learning good strategies after solving a problem or a set of problems. We state that an interesting research direction is how we can provide an autonomous solver with an early replacement ("on the fly") of bad-performance strategies without waiting the entire resolution process or an exhaustive analysis of a given class of problems.

References

1. Bader-El-Den, M., Poli, R.: Generating SAT local-search heuristics using a GP hyper-heuristic framework. In: Monmarché, N., Talbi, E.-G., Collet, P., Schoenauer, M., Lutton, E. (eds.) EA 2007. LNCS, vol. 4926, pp. 37–49. Springer, Heidelberg (2008)
2. Battiti, R., Brunato, M.: Reactive Search Optimization: Learning while Optimizing. In: Handbook of Metaheuristics, 2nd edn., Springer (2010)
3. Boussemart, F., Hemery, F., Lecoutre, C., Sais, L.: Boosting systematic search by weighting constraints. In: de Mántaras, R.L., Saitta, L. (eds.) ECAI, pp. 146–150. IOS Press (2004)
4. Boyan, J.A., Moore, A.W.: Learning evaluation functions to improve optimization by local search. Journal of Machine Learning Research 1, 77–112 (2000)
5. Burke, E.K., Hyde, M., Kendall, G., Ochoa, G., Ozcan, E., Qu, R.: A survey of hyper-heuristics. Technical Report NOTTCS-TR-SUB-0906241418-2747, School of Computer Science and Information Technology, University of Nottingham, Computer Science (2009)
6. Burke, E.K., Kendall, G., Hart, E., Newall, J., Ross, P., Schulenburg, S.: Hyper-heuristics: An Emerging Direction inModern Search Technology. In: Handbook of Meta-heuristics, pp. 457–474. Kluwer (2003)
7. Cowling, P., Soubeiga, E.: Neighborhood structures for personnel scheduling: A summit meeting scheduling problem (abstract). In: Burke, E., Erben, W. (eds.) Proceedings of the 3rd International Conference on the Practice and Theory of Automated Timetabling (2000)
8. Cowling, P.I., Kendall, G., Soubeiga, E.: Hyperheuristics: A tool for rapid prototyping in scheduling and optimisation. In: Cagnoni, S., Gottlieb, J., Hart, E., Middendorf, M., Raidl, G.R. (eds.) EvoWorkshops 2002. LNCS, vol. 2279, pp. 1–10. Springer, Heidelberg (2002)
9. Crawford, B., Castro, C., Monfroy, E., Soto, R., Palma, W., Paredes, F.: A hyper-heuristic approach for guiding enumeration in constraint solving. In: Schütze, O., Coello Coello, C.A., Tantar, A.-A., Tantar, E., Bouvry, P., Del Moral, P., Legrand, P. (eds.) EVOLVE - A Bridge Between Probability. AISC, vol. 175, pp. 171–188. Springer, Heidelberg (2012)

10. Crawford, B., Soto, R., Monfroy, E., Palma, W., Castro, C., Paredes, F.: Parameter tuning of a choice-function based hyperheuristic using particle swarm optimization. Expert Systems with Applications 40(5), 1690–1695 (2013)
11. Dahmani, N., Clautiaux, F., Krichen, S., Talbi, E.-G.: Self-adaptive metaheuristics for solving a multi-objective 2-dimensional vector packing problem. Applied Soft Computing 16, 124–136 (2014)
12. Eén, N., Sörensson, N.: An extensible sat-solver. In: Giunchiglia, E., Tacchella, A. (eds.) SAT 2003. LNCS, vol. 2919, pp. 502–518. Springer, Heidelberg (2004)
13. Eiben, A.E., Hinterding, R., Michalewicz, Z.: Parameter control in evolutionary algorithms. IEEE Trans. Evolutionary Computation 3(2), 124–141 (1999)
14. Epstein, S.L., Freuder, E.C., Wallace, R.J.: Learning to support constraint programmers. Computational Intelligence 21(4), 336–371 (2005)
15. Fialho, Á., Costa, L.D., Schoenauer, M., Sebag, M.: Extreme value based adaptive operator selection. In: Rudolph, et al. (eds.) [15], pp. 175–184
16. Fukunaga, A.S.: Automated discovery of local search heuristics for satisfiability testing. Evolutionary Computation 16(1), 31–61 (2008)
17. Goualard, F., Jermann, C.: A reinforcement learning approach to interval constraint propagation. Constraints 13(1-2), 206–226 (2008)
18. Hamadi, Y., Monfroy, E., Saubion, F.: What is autonomous search? Technical Report MSR-TR-2008-80, Microsoft Research (2008)
19. Hansen, N.: Adaptive encoding: How to render search coordinate system invariant. In: Rudolph, et al. (eds.), pp. 205–214
20. Hu, B., Raidl, G.: Variable neighborhood descent with self-adaptive noeighborhood-ordering. In: Proceedings of the 7th EU/MEeting on Adaptive, Self-Adaptive, and Multi-Level Metaheuristics (2006)
21. Hutter, F., Hamadi, Y.: Parameter adjustment based on performance prediction: Towards an instance-aware problem solver. Technical Report MSR-TR-2005-125, Microsoft Research, Cambridge, UK (December 2005)
22. Hutter, F., Hamadi, Y., Hoos, H.H., Leyton-Brown, K.: Performance prediction and automated tuning of randomized and parametric algorithms. In: Benhamou, F. (ed.) CP 2006. LNCS, vol. 4204, pp. 213–228. Springer, Heidelberg (2006)
23. Hutter, F., Hoos, H.H., Stützle, T.: Automatic algorithm configuration based on local search. In: AAAI, pp. 1152–1157. AAAI Press (2007)
24. Khichane, M., Albert, P., Solnon, C.: An ACO-based reactive framework for ant colony optimization: First experiments on constraint satisfaction problems. In: Stützle, T. (ed.) LION 3. LNCS, vol. 5851, pp. 119–133. Springer, Heidelberg (2009)
25. Lobo, F.G., Lima, C.F., Michalewicz, Z. (eds.): Parameter Setting in Evolutionary Algorithms. SCI, vol. 54. Springer (2007)
26. Marques-Silva, J., Sakallah, K.A. (eds.): SAT 2007. LNCS, vol. 4501. Springer, Heidelberg (2007)
27. Maturana, J., Saubion, F.: A compass to guide genetic algorithms. In: Rudolph, et al. (eds.), pp. 256–265
28. Mazure, B., Sais, L., Grégoire, É.: Boosting complete techniques thanks to local search methods. Ann. Math. Artif. Intell. 22(3-4), 319–331 (1998)
29. Mladenovic, N., Hansen, P.: Variable neighborhood search. Computers & OR 24(11), 1097–1100 (1997)
30. Monfroy, E., Castro, C., Crawford, B., Soto, R., Paredes, F., Figueroa, C.: A reactive and hybrid constraint solver. Journal of Experimental and Theoretical Artificial Intelligence 25(1), 1–22 (2013)
31. Morris, P.: The breakout method for escaping from local minima. In: AAAI, pp. 40–45 (1993)

32. Nannen, V., Smit, S.K., E. Eiben, Á.: Costs and benefits of tuning parameters of evolutionary algorithms. In: Rudolph, et al. (eds.), pp. 528–538
33. Puchinger, J., Raidl, G.R.: Bringing order into the neighborhoods: Relaxation guided variable neighborhood search. J. Heuristics 14(5), 457–472 (2008)
34. Randall, M.: Near parameter free ant colony optimisation. In: Dorigo, M., Birattari, M., Blum, C., Gambardella, L.M., Mondada, F., Stützle, T. (eds.) ANTS 2004. LNCS, vol. 3172, pp. 374–381. Springer, Heidelberg (2004)
35. Rudolph, G., Jansen, T., Lucas, S., Poloni, C., Beume, N. (eds.): PPSN 2008. LNCS, vol. 5199. Springer, Heidelberg (2008)
36. Smit, S.K., Eiben, A.E.: Comparing parameter tuning methods for evolutionary algorithms. In: IEEE Congress on Evolutionary Computation, pp. 399–406 (2009)
37. Thierens, D.: An adaptive pursuit strategy for allocating operator probabilities. In: Verbeeck, K., Tuyls, K., Nowé, A., Manderick, B., Kuijpers, B. (eds.) BNAIC, pp. 385–386. Koninklijke Vlaamse Academie van Belie voor Wetenschappen en Kunsten (2005)
38. Thornton, J.: Constraint Weighting Local Search for Constraint Satisfaction. PhD thesis, Griffith University. Australia (2000)
39. Whitacre, J.M., Pham, Q.T., Sarker, R.A.: Credit assignment in adaptive evolutionary algorithms. In: GECCO, pp. 1353–1360. ACM (2006)
40. Wong, Y.-Y., Lee, K.-H., Leung, K.-S., Ho, C.-W.: A novel approach in parameter adaptation and diversity maintenance for genetic algorithms. Soft Comput. 7(8), 506–515 (2003)
41. Xu, L., Hutter, F., Hoos, H.H., Leyton-Brown, K.: Satzilla: Portfolio-based algorithm selection for sat. J. Artif. Intell. Res (JAIR) 32, 565–606 (2008)

Using the Firefly Optimization Method to Solve the Weighted Set Covering Problem

Broderick Crawford[1,2], Ricardo Soto[1,3], Miguel Olivares-Suárez[1],
and Fernando Paredes[4]

[1] Pontificia Universidad Católica de Valparaíso, Chile
[2] Universidad Finis Terrae, Chile
[3] Universidad Autónoma de Chile, Chile
[4] Escuela de Ingeniería Industrial, Universidad Diego Portales, Chile
{broderick.crawford,ricardo.soto}@ucv.cl,
miguel.olivares.s@mail.pucv.cl,
fernando.paredes@udp.cl

Abstract. The Weighted Set Covering Problem is a formal model for many practical optimization problems. In this problem the goal is to choose a subset of columns of minimal cost covering every row. Here, a Binary Firefly Algorithm has been developed to tackle the Weighted Set Covering Problem. Firefly Algorithm is a recently developed population-based metaheuristic inspired by the flashing behaviour of fireflies. Experimental results show that our approach is competitive solving the problem at hand.

Keywords: Weighted Set Covering Problem, Firefly Algorithm, Swarm Intelligence.

1 Introduction

The Weighted Set Covering Problem (WSCP) has many applications, including those involving routing, scheduling, stock cutting, electoral redistricting and others important real life situations [14]. Different solving methods have been proposed in the literature for the Weighted Set Covering Problem. Exact algorithms are mostly based on Branch-and-Bound and Branch-and-Cut techniques [2,15,5], Linear Programing and Heuristic methods [7]. However, these algorithms are rather time consuming and can only solve instances of very limited size. For this reason, many research efforts have been focused on the development of meta-heuristics to find as result good or near-optimal solutions within a reasonable period of time. An incomplete list of metaheuristics for the WSCP includes Genetic Algorithms [1,3], Simulated Annealing [6], Tabu Search [8], Cultural Algorithms [12,10] and Ant Colony Optimization [9]. For a deeper comprehension of most of the effective algorithms for the WSCP in the literature, we refer the interested reader to the survey by [7]. In this paper we present the metaheuristic Firefly Algorithm that is relatively new in the area to solve the WSCP.

C. Stephanidis (Ed.): HCII 2014 Posters, Part I, CCIS 434, pp. 509–514, 2014.
© Springer International Publishing Switzerland 2014

2 Firefly Algorithm

The Firefly Algorithm (FA) is an algorithm inspired by the social behavior of fire-flies. For more details of FA we refer the reader to [16,17]. The pseudo code of the firefly-inspired algorithm was developed using the following rules: All fireflies are unisex and are attracted to other fireflies regardless of their sex. The degree of the attractiveness of a firefly is proportional to its brightness, and thus for any two flash-ing fireflies, the one that is less bright will move towards to the brighter one. Finally, the brightness of a firefly is determined by the value of the objective function. For a maximization problem, the brightness of each firefly is proportional to the value of the objective function. In the original FA, the result of applying a movement (gen-erating the new dimension value of the firefly) is probable to be a real number, to fix this for WSCP we occupy the following binarization rule:

$$x_i^k(t+1) := \begin{cases} 1 \text{ if } rand < T(x_i^k(t+1)) \\ 0 \text{ otherwise} \end{cases} \tag{1}$$

where $rand$ is a uniform random number between 0 and 1, $x_i^k(t+1)$ is the value resulting from the traditional FA movement and $T(x)$ is the binary transfer function. A transfer function defines the probability of changing a position vector elements from 0 to 1 and vice versa. Transfer functions force firefly bits to move in a binary space. In this work the transfer function used is $T(x) = |\frac{2}{\pi}\arctan(\frac{\pi}{2}x)|$. Algorithm 1 shows the pseudo code of FA.

Algorithm 1: Pseudo code of Binary FA for WSCP

---

1 **Begin**
2   Initialize parameters
3   Evaluate the light intensity I determined by $f(x)$ Eq. 2
4   **while** $t < MaxGeneration$ **do**
5   **for** $i = 1 : m$ (m fireflies) **do**
6   **for** $j = 1 : m$ (m fireflies) **do**
7   **if** $(I_j < I_i)$ **then**
8              $movement$ = calculates value according to FA movement Eq.
9   **if** (rand() < arctan($movement$)) **then**
10                $fireflies[i][j] = 1$
11   **else**
12                $fireflies[i][j] = 0$
13   **end if**
14   **end if**
15   Repair solutions
16   Update attractiveness
17   Update light intensity
18   **end for** j
19   **end for** i
20        $t = t + 1$
21   **end while**
22   Output the results
23 **End**

3   Weighted Set Covering Problem

In the WSCP matrix formulation we define a $m \times n$ matrix $A = (a_{ij})$ in which all the matrix elements are either zero or one. Additionally, each column is given a non-negative cost c_j. We say that a column j covers a row i if $a_{ij} = 1$. Let x_j a binary variable which is one if column j is chosen and zero otherwise. The WSCP can be defined formally as *minimize* (2) *subject to* (3). The goal in the WSCP is to choose a subset of the columns of minimal weight formally using constraints to enforce that each row is covered by at least one column.

$$f(x) = \sum_{j=1}^{n} c_j x_j \tag{2}$$

$$\sum_{j=1}^{n} a_{ij} x_j \geq 1; \qquad \forall i = 1, ..., m \tag{3}$$

$$x_j \in \{0, 1\}; \qquad \forall j = 1, ..., n \tag{4}$$

4   Experimental Results

The performance of Binary FA was evaluated experimentally using WSCP test instances from OR-Library of Beasley [4]. The algorithm was coded in C in NetBeans IDE 7.3 with support for C/C++ and run on a PC with a 1.8 GHz Intel Core 2 Duo T5670 CPU and 3.0 GB RAM, under Windows 8 System. In all experiments, the binary FA is executed 50 generations, and 30 times each instance. We used a population of 25 fireflies. The parameters γ, β_0 are initialized to 1. These parameters were selected empirically after a large number of tests showing good results but may not be optimal for all instances. Table 1 shows the results obtained with the 65 instances. Column "Opt." reports the optimal or the best known solution value of each instance. Columns "Min.", "Max." and "Avg." reports the minimum, maximum, and average of the best solutions obtained in the 30 executions.

Table 1. Computational results on 65 instances of WSCP

Instance	Opt.	Min.	Max.	Avg.	Instance	Opt.	Min.	Max.	Avg.
4.1	429	481	482	481.03	B.4	79	98	99	98.03
4.2	512	580	580	580.00	B.5	72	87	87	87.00
4.3	516	619	620	619.03	C.1	227	279	279	279.00
4.4	494	537	537	537.00	C.2	219	272	272	272.00
4.5	512	609	609	609.00	C.3	243	288	288	288.00
4.6	560	653	653	653.00	C.4	219	262	262	262.00
4.7	430	491	492	491.07	C.5	215	262	263	262.07
4.8	492	565	565	565.00	D.1	60	71	71	71.00
4.9	641	749	750	749.03	D.2	66	75	75	75.00
4.10	514	550	550	550.00	D.3	72	88	88	88.00
5.1	253	296	297	296.03	D.4	62	71	71	71.00
5.2	302	372	372	372.00	D.5	61	71	71	71.00
5.3	226	250	250	250.00	NRE.1	29	32	33	32.03
5.4	242	277	278	277.07	NRE.2	30	36	36	36.00
5.5	211	253	253	253.00	NRE.3	27	35	35	35.00
5.6	213	264	265	264.03	NRE.4	28	34	34	34.00
5.7	293	337	337	337.00	NRE.5	28	34	34	34.00
5.8	288	326	326	326.00	NRF.1	14	17	18	17.03
5.9	279	350	350	350.00	NRF.2	15	17	17	17.00
5.10	265	321	321	321.00	NRF.3	14	21	21	21.00
6.1	138	173	174	173.03	NRF.4	14	19	19	19.00
6.2	146	180	181	180.07	NRF.5	13	16	16	16.00
6.3	145	160	160	160.00	NRG.1	176	230	231	230.03
6.4	131	161	161	161.00	NRG.2	154	191	191	191.00
6.5	161	186	186	186.00	NRG.3	166	198	198	198.00
A.1	253	285	285	285.00	NRG.4	168	214	214	214.00
A.2	252	285	286	285.07	NRG.5	168	223	223	223.00
A.3	232	272	272	272.00	NRH.1	63	85	86	85.07
A.4	234	297	297	297.00	NRH.2	63	81	82	81.03
A.5	236	262	262	262.00	NRH.3	59	76	76	76.00
B.1	69	80	81	80.03	NRH.4	58	75	75	75.00
B.2	76	92	92	92.00	NRH.5	55	68	68	68.00
B.3	80	93	93	93.00					

5   Conclusion

We have presented a Binary Firefly Algorithm for the Weighted Set Covering Problem. As can be seen from the results obtained the metaheuristic behaves in a good way in almost all instances. This paper has demonstrated that Binary FA is an alternative to solve the WSCP, although its scope of action is continuous optimization. An interesting research direction to pursue in future work about the integration of Autonomous Search in the solving process, which in many cases has demonstrated excellent results [11,13].

Acknowledgements. Broderick Crawford is supported by Grant CONICYT/ FONDECYT/1140897. Ricardo Soto is supported by Grant CONICYT/FONDECYT/ INICIACION/11130459. Fernando Paredes is supported by Grant CONICYT/ FONDECYT/1130455.

References

1. Aickelin, U.: An indirect genetic algorithm for set covering problems. Journal of the Operational Research Society 53, 1118–1126 (2002)
2. Balas, E., Carrera, M.C.: A dynamic subgradient-based branch-and-bound procedure for set covering. Operations Research 44(6), 875–890 (1996)
3. Beasley, J., Chu, P.: A genetic algorithm for the set covering problem. European Journal of Operational Research 94(2), 392–404 (1996)
4. Beasley, J.E.: A lagrangian heuristic for set-covering problems. Naval Research Logistics (NRL) 37(1), 151–164 (1990)
5. Beasley, J.E., Jornsten, K.: Enhancing an algorithm for set covering problems. European Journal of Operational Research 58(2), 293–300 (1992)
6. Brusco, M.J., Jacobs, L.W., Thompson, G.M.: A morphing procedure to supplement a simulated annealing heuristic for cost- and coverage-correlated set-covering problems. Annals of Operations Research 86, 611–627 (1999)
7. Caprara, A., Toth, P., Fischetti, M.: Algorithms for the set covering problem. Annals of Operations Research 98, 353–371 (2000)
8. Caserta, M.: abu search-based metaheuristic algorithm for large-scale set covering problems. In: Doerner, K.F., et al. (eds.) Metaheuristics: Progress in complex systems optimization. Springer
9. Crawford, B., Castro, C., Monfroy, E.: A New ACO Transition Rule for Set Partitioning and Covering Problems. In: SoCPaR, pp. 426–429 (2009)
10. Crawford, B., Lagos, C., Castro, C., Parede, F.: A Evolutionary Approach to Solve Set Covering. In: ICEIS, vol. 2, pp. 356–363 (2007)
11. Crawford, B., Soto, R., Castro, C., Monfroy, E.: Extensible CP-based autonomous search. In: Stephanidis, C. (ed.) Posters, Part I, HCII 2011. CCIS, vol. 173, pp. 561–565. Springer, Heidelberg (2011)
12. Crawford, B., Soto, R., Monfroy, E.: Cultural algorithms for the set covering problem. In: Tan, Y., Shi, Y., Mo, H. (eds.) ICSI 2013, Part II. LNCS, vol. 7929, pp. 27–34. Springer, Heidelberg (2013)
13. Crawford, B., Soto, R., Monfroy, E., Palma, W., Castro, C., Paredes, F.: Parameter tuning of a choice-function based hyperheuristic using particle swarm optimization. Expert Systems with Applications 40(5), 1690–1695 (2013)

14. Feo, T.A., Resende, M.G.C.: A probabilistic heuristic for a computationally difficult set covering problem. Operations Research Letters 8(2), 67–71 (1989)
15. Fisher, M.L., Kedia, P.: Optimal solution of set covering/partitioning problems using dual heuristics. Management Science 36(6), 674–688 (1990)
16. Yang, X.-S.: Nature-Inspired Metaheuristic Algorithms. Luniver Press (2008)
17. Yang, X.-S.: Firefly algorithms for multimodal optimization. In: Watanabe, O., Zeugmann, T. (eds.) SAGA 2009. LNCS, vol. 5792, pp. 169–178. Springer, Heidelberg (2009)

A Better Understanding of the Behaviour of Metaheuristics: A Psychological View

Broderick Crawford[1,2], Ricardo Soto[3,4], Claudio León de la Barra[3], Kathleen Crawford[3], Fernando Paredes[5], and Franklin Johnson[6]

[1] Universidad San Sebastián, Chile
[2] Universidad Finis Terrae, Chile
[3] Pontificia Universidad Católica de Valparaíso, Chile
[4] Universidad Autónoma de Chile, Chile
[5] Escuela de Ingeniería Industrial, Universidad Diego Portales, Chile
[6] Universidad de Playa Ancha, Valparaíso, Chile
broderick.crawford.1@gmail.com,
{ricardo.soto,claudio.leondelabarra}@ucv.cl,
kathleen.crawford.a@mail.pucv.cl,
fernando.paredes@udp.cl,
franklin.johnson@upla.cl

Abstract. This paper aimed to show the idea that concepts and methods from Creative Problem Solving can also be useful in dealing with developing Metaheuristics. A dynamic approach based on Divergent and Convergent Thinking can be used to understand the modus operandi and behaviour of this kind of optimization solvers.

Keywords: Creative Problem Solving, Metaheuristics, Divergent Thinking, Convergent Thinking.

1 Introduction

In Operations Research, Metaheuristics are useful when finding the best solution of a optimization problem is computationally very expensive using global optimization methods. The key is to provide a way of finding a good enough solution in a fixed amount of time.

Metaheuristics, as the sufix says, are upper level heuristics. They are intelligent strategies to design or improve general heuristic procedures with high performance [10,8,9]. They are iterative procedures that smartly guide a subordinate heuristic, combining different concepts to suitably explore and operate the search space. Over time, these methods have also come to include any procedures that employ strategies for overcoming the trap of local optimality in complex solution spaces, especially those procedures that utilize one or more neighborhood structures as a mean for defining admissible transitions from one solution to another, or to transform solutions in a constructive process.

To get good solutions, any Metaheuristic must establish an adequate balance between two overlayed process: Diversification and Intensification. Diversification is a mechanism that forces the search of solutions into unexplored areas of

C. Stephanidis (Ed.): HCII 2014 Posters, Part I, CCIS 434, pp. 515–518, 2014.

the search space. Intensification is a mechanism that explores more throughly the portions of the search space that seem promising in order to make sure that the best solution is in these areas.

In Psychology, Creative Problem Solving has two key concepts: Divergent and Convergent Thinking. Divergent thinking (creative thinking) starts from a common point and moves outward into a variety of perspectives. It generates something new or different. It involves having a different idea that works as well or better than previous ideas. Convergent thinking (critical thinking) is cognitive processing of information around a common point, an attempt to bring thoughts from different directions into a union or common conclusion.

The focus of this work is on studying the links between Psychology and Operations Research when solving problems. We believe that these preliminary notes can inspire new view points in optimization solvers development.

2   Creative Problem Solving

In [18] Rubinstein stated that the most creative human problem solvers have an unusual capacity to integrate the two modes of conscious functions of the two brain hemispheres, and move back and forth between the holistic and sequential, between intuition and logic, between the fuzzy field of a problem domain and a clear specific small segment of a field.

Such people can be outstanding artists and scientists because they combine the strong attributes of both. We refer to reader to prominent references in Creative Problem Solving are [14,20,21,5,6] for more extensive coverage of this topic.

During a Creative Problem Solving process it is convenient to start with Divergent thinking to produce as many ideas or solutions as possible and thereafter to switch to Convergent thinking to select the most promising ideas. The terms Divergent and Convergent thinking were coined by a psychologist in [12].

By other side, Diversification and Intensification are components that appear in many Metaheuristics. These concepts emerge with Tabu Search (TS) Metaheuristic [11]. Diversification generally refers to exploration, the ability to visit many and different regions of the search space, whereas Intensification refers to the exploitation of the accumulated search experience to obtain high-quality solutions within promising regions.

3   How Metaheuristics Work?

A Metaheuristic is formally defined as an iterative generation process which guides a subordinate heuristic by combining intelligently different concepts for exploring and exploiting the search space, learning strategies are used to structure information in order to find efficiently near-optimal solutions [17].

As aforementioned, the two forces that largely determine the behaviour of a Metaheuristic are Intensification and Diversification. A unifying view on Intensification and Diversification was proposed in [2], recomending that every Metaheuristic approach should be designed with the aim of effectively and efficiently exploring a search space. The search performed by a Metaheuristic approach should be smart enough to both intensively explore areas of the search space with high quality solutions, and to move to unexplored areas of the search space when necessary. The right balance between Intensification and Diversification is needed to obtain an effective Metaheuristic. This balance should rather be dynamical, it should not be fixed or only privileging one direction.

Autonomous Search (AS) systems represent a new research field defined to address the challenge of fine-tuning Metaheuristics [13]. An AS system should provide the ability to modify its internal components (heuristics, inference mechanisms, etc.) when exposed to changing external forces and opportunities. AS corresponds to an instance of Self-adaptive Systems with the objective of improving its problem solving performance by adapting its search strategy to the problem at hand. AS can be defined as search processes that integrate control in their solving process either by self adaptation or by supervised adaptation [4,3,7].

Other very promising research direction in order to improve the performance of Metaheuristics is the hybridization of Metaheuristics [1,19,16,16,15].

4   Conclusion

Diversification and Intensification are components that appear in many Metaheuristics. The relations with Divergent and Convergent thinking should be considered, since benefits may accrue by analysing and combining concepts and methods originating from Psychology.

For example, uncertainty is present in most instantations of Metaheuristics using randomness, then a predisposition to tolerate and to deal with uncertainty may be gained from creativity, in particular from Divergent thinking and Convergent thinking.

References

1. Blum, C.: Hybrid metaheuristics in combinatorial optimization: A tutorial. In: Dediu, A.-H., Martín-Vide, C., Truthe, B. (eds.) TPNC 2012. LNCS, vol. 7505, pp. 1–10. Springer, Heidelberg (2012)
2. Blum, C., Roli, A.: Metaheuristics in combinatorial optimization: Overview and conceptual comparison. ACM Comput. Surv. 35(3), 268–308 (2003)
3. Crawford, B., Soto, R., Castro, C., Monfroy, E.: Extensible CP-based autonomous search. In: Stephanidis, C. (ed.) Posters, Part I, HCII 2011. CCIS, vol. 173, pp. 561–565. Springer, Heidelberg (2011)
4. Dahmani, N., Clautiaux, F., Krichen, S., Talbi, E.-G.: Self-adaptive metaheuristics for solving a multi-objective 2-dimensional vector packing problem. Applied Soft Computing 16, 124–136 (2014)
5. De Bono, E.: Six Thinking Hats. Little, Brown Book Group Limited (1985)
6. De Bono, E.: Serious Creativity: Using the Power of Lateral Thinking to Create New Ideas. HarperBusiness (1992)
7. de la Barra, C.L., Crawford, B., Soto, R., Monfroy, E.: Adaptive and multilevel approach for constraint solving. In: Stephanidis, C. (ed.) HCII 2013, Part I. CCIS, vol. 373, pp. 650–654. Springer, Heidelberg (2013)

8. Derigs, U., Voss, S.: Meta-heuristics: Theory, Applications and Software. Annals of operations research. Kluwer Academic Publishers (2004)
9. Gendreau, M., Potvin, J.: Handbook of Metaheuristics. International Series in Operations Research & Management Science. Springer (2010)
10. Glover, F., Kochenberger, G.: Handbook of Metaheuristics. International series in operations research & management science. Kluwer Academic Publishers (2003)
11. Glover, F., Laguna, M.: Tabu Search. Number v. 1 in Tabu Search. Springer, US (1998)
12. Guilford, J.: The nature of human intelligence. McGraw-Hill series in psychology. McGraw-Hill (1967)
13. Hamadi, Y., Monfroy, E., Saubion, F.: An Introduction to Autonomous Search. In: Hamadi, Y., Monfroy, E., Saubion, F. (eds.) Autonomous Search, p. 11. Springer (2012)
14. Marakas, G.M., Elam, J.J.: Creativity enhancement in problem solving: Through software or process? Management Science 43(8), 1136–1146 (1997)
15. Monfroy, E., Castro, C., Crawford, B., Figueroa, C.: Adaptive hybridization strategies. In: Chu, W.C., Wong, W.E., Palakal, M.J., Hung, C.-C. (eds.) SAC, pp. 922–923. ACM (2011)
16. Monfroy, E., Castro, C., Crawford, B., Soto, R., Paredes, F., Figueroa, C.: A reactive and hybrid constraint solver. J. Exp. Theor. Artif. Intell. 25(1), 1–22 (2013)
17. Osman, I., Laporte, G.: Metaheuristics: A bibliography. Annals of Operations Research 63(5), 511–623 (1996)
18. Rubinstein, M.: Tools for thinking and problem solving. Prentice-Hall, Incorporated (1986)
19. Talbi, E.-G. (ed.): Hybrid Metaheuristics. SCI, vol. 434. Springer, Heidelberg (2013)
20. Vidal, R.V.V., Vangundy, A.B., Pfeiffer: 101 activities for teaching creativity and problem solving. European Journal of Operational Research 172(3), 1067–1068 (2004)
21. Vidal, R.V.V.: Creativity for problem solvers. AI Soc. 23(3), 409–432 (2009)

Easy Modeling of Open Pit Mining Problems via Constraint Programming

Broderick Crawford[1,3], Ricardo Soto[1,2], Carolina Zec[1],
Eric Monfroy[4], and Fernando Paredes[5]

[1] Pontificia Universidad Católica de Valparaíso, Chile
[2] Universidad Autónoma de Chile, Chile
[3] Universidad Finis Terrae, Chile
[4] CNRS, LINA, Université de Nantes, France
[5] Escuela de Ingeniería Industrial, Universidad Diego Portales, Chile
{ricardo.soto,broderick.crawford}@ucv.cl,
carolina.zec.s@mail.pucv.cl,
eric.monfroy@univ-nantes.fr,
fernando.paredes@udp.cl

Abstract. The open pit mining problem aims at correctly identifying the set of blocks of a given mine to be extracted in order to maximize the net present value of the production. During the last years, different techniques have been proposed to solve mining problems, which range from the classic mathematical programming to more recent ones such as the metaheuristics. In this paper we illustrate how this problem can easily be solved by a relatively modern and declarative programming paradigm called constraint programming.

Keywords: Constraint Programming, Metaheuristics, Manufacturing Cell Design.

1 Introduction

Open pit mining is a mineral extraction technique in which the orebody is reached by opening a large ground surface along a mine. The orebody is commonly discretized and modeled as a set of blocks. The goal of the classic open pit mining problem is to correctly identify the blocks of the mine to be extracted in order to maximize the net present value of the production. There exist varied versions of the problem, that mainly consider different kinds of constraints related to the distribution of blocks along the mine, to the production planning, and to the processing plant and mining capacity. During the last thirty years, different techniques have been proposed to solve mining problems. Some examples are the classic linear and mathematical programming [4,10,1], and metaheuristics such as the genetic algorithms [19,8].

In this paper, we focus on solving open pit mining problems (OPMP) via Constraint Programming (CP). CP is a programming paradigm for the efficient solving of constraint-based and optimization problems that has successfully been

C. Stephanidis (Ed.): HCII 2014 Posters, Part I, CCIS 434, pp. 519–522, 2014.

employed in several application domains, different examples can be found in rostering [15], manufacturing [18], games [12,13] and in engineering design [11]. In CP, a problem is modeled by representing the unknowns of the problem as variables and the relations among them as constraints. This mathematical model is then encoded in the language of a CP search engine, which is responsible for search a result. In this paper we illustrate how this problem can easily be modeled by using CP, in particular via the MiniZinc modeling language [9]

From a user perspective, solving problems via CP has an important advantage with respect to metaheuristics: there is no need to design a specific algorithm to solve the problem, the user only models the problem and the solver provides a result. In this paper, we illustrate how this problem can easily be solved by using CP, in particular via the MiniZinc modeling language [9].

2   Modeling the OPMP in CP

CP provides an important feature to the user: there is no need to design a specific algorithm to solve a given problem, the user only models the problem and the search engine search for a result. This can clearly be contrasted to the use of metaheuristics, where the user must implement practically from scratch a new algorithm following some pre-established patterns. In CP, it suffices to encode the mathematical model in the language of the solving engine. In the following we illustrate how the OPMP can easily be solved by using the CP paradigm. For space reasons we consider only the objective function and a single constraint, the complete model can be seen in [2].

The objective function aims at maximizing the total profit from the mining process in a given period of time, where t is the time period index and T is the number of time periods considered; n is the block index and N is the total number of blocks. C_n^t is the net present value obtained from mining block n in time t; and x_n^t is a binary decision variable which is set to 1 if the block is mined and 0 otherwise.

$$\text{maximize } Z = \sum_{t=1}^{T} \sum_{n=1}^{N} C_n^t x_n^t \tag{1}$$

The corresponding MiniZinc code is shown below, which is a straightforward mapping from the mathematical definition of the objective function. A z value captures the double summation which is then launched via the solve maximize instruction.

```
1. var int: z = sum(n in 1..N,t in 1..T)
2.             (C[n,t] * x[n,t]);
3. solve maximize z;
```

The total tons of material to be exploited are restricted by processing and mining capacities. The total material mined, involving ore and waste must respect the given upper bound as stated in Eq. 2; where To_n is amount of ore in block n, Tw_n is amount of waste in block, and MC_{max}^t is the maximum material, including waste and ore, to be mined in period t.

$$\sum_{i=1}^{n} (To_n + Tw_n)x_n^t \leq MC_{max}^t \qquad t \in (1, 2, ..., T) \qquad (2)$$

```
1. constraint
2.    forall(t in 1..T) (
3.       sum(n in 1..N)
4.          ((To[n] + Tw[n]) * x[n,t]) <= mcmax[t]
5.    );
```

3 Conclusion

In this paper, we have illustrated how the OPMP can be modeled by using the CP paradigm. In CP, it suffices to encode the corresponding mathematical model in the solver language in contrast to metaheuristics that require to implement a specific algorithm to solve the problem.

A continual research direction in CP is about facilitating the user modeling and experimentation phases, such as for instance to propose easy-to-use modeling languages [17,3] and modeling features [16]. The use of autonomous search [14,6,7,5] for solving this problem will be an interesting direction to pursue as well.

Acknowledgements. Ricardo Soto is supported by Grant CONICYT/ FONDE-CYT/INICIACION/11130459, Broderick Crawford is supported by Grant CONI-CYT/FONDECYT/REGULAR/1140897, and Fernando Paredes is supported by Grant CONICYT/FONDECYT/REGULAR/1130455.

References

1. Boland, N., Dumitrescu, I., Froyland, G., Gleixner, A.: LP-based disaggregation approaches to solving the open pit mining production scheduling problem with block processing selectivity. Computers & Operations Research 36(4), 1064–1089 (2009)
2. Caccetta, L., Hill, S.: An application of branch and cut to open pit mine scheduling. Journal of Global Optimization 27(2-3), 349–365 (2003)
3. Chenouard, R., Granvilliers, L., Soto, R.: Model-Driven Constraint Programming. In: Proceedings of the 10th International ACM SIGPLAN Conference on Principles and Practice of Declarative Programming (PPDP), pp. 236–246 (2008)
4. Chicoisne, R., Espinoza, D., Goycoolea, M., Moreno, E., Rubio, E.: A New Algorithm for the Open-Pit Mine Production Scheduling Problem. Operations Research 60(3), 517–528 (2012)

5. Crawford, B., Castro, C., Monfroy, E., Soto, R., Palma, W., Paredes, F.: Dynamic Selection of Enumeration Strategies for Solving Constraint Satisfaction Problems. Romanian Journal of Information Science and Technology 15(2), 106–128 (2012)
6. Crawford, B., Soto, R., Castro, C., Monfroy, E.: Extensible CP-based autonomous search. In: Stephanidis, C. (ed.) Posters, Part I, HCII 2011. CCIS, vol. 173, pp. 561–565. Springer, Heidelberg (2011)
7. Crawford, B., Soto, R., Montecinos, M., Castro, C., Monfroy, E.: A framework for autonomous search in the ecl^{i}ps^e solver. In: Mehrotra, K.G., Mohan, C.K., Oh, J.C., Varshney, P.K., Ali, M. (eds.) IEA/AIE 2011, Part I. LNCS, vol. 6703, pp. 79–84. Springer, Heidelberg (2011)
8. Denby, B., Schofield, D.: Open-pit design and scheduling by use of genetic algorithms. Transactions of the Institution of Mining and Metallurgy, Section A: Mining Industry 26, A21–A26 (1994)
9. Nethercote, N., Stuckey, P.J., Becket, R., Brand, S., Duck, G.J., Tack, G.R.: MiniZinc: Towards a Standard CP Modelling Language. In: Bessière, C. (ed.) CP 2007. LNCS, vol. 4741, pp. 529–543. Springer, Heidelberg (2007)
10. Ramazan, S.: The new Fundamental Tree Algorithm for production scheduling of open pit mines. European Journal of Operational Research 177(2), 1153–1166 (2007)
11. Soto, R.: Controlling search in constrained-object models. In: Kuri-Morales, A., Simari, G.R. (eds.) IBERAMIA 2010. LNCS, vol. 6433, pp. 582–591. Springer, Heidelberg (2010)
12. Soto, R., Crawford, B., Galleguillos, C., Monfroy, E., Paredes, F.: A hybrid ac3-tabu search algorithm for solving sudoku puzzles. Expert Syst. Appl. 40(15), 5817–5821 (2013)
13. Soto, R., Crawford, B., Galleguillos, C., Monfroy, E., Paredes, F.: A Pre-filtered Cuckoo Search Algorithm with Geometric Operators for Solving Sudoku Problems. The Scientific World Journal, Article ID 465359 (2014)
14. Soto, R., Crawford, B., Monfroy, E., Bustos, V.: Using autonomous search for generating good enumeration strategy blends in constraint programming. In: Murgante, B., Gervasi, O., Misra, S., Nedjah, N., Rocha, A.M.A.C., Taniar, D., Apduhan, B.O. (eds.) ICCSA 2012, Part III. LNCS, vol. 7335, pp. 607–617. Springer, Heidelberg (2012)
15. Soto, R., Crawford, B., Monfroy, E., Palma, W., Paredes, F.: Nurse and Paramedic Rostering with Constraint Programming: A Case Study. Romanian Journal of Information Science and Technology 16(1), 52–64 (2013)
16. Soto, R., Crawford, B., Monfroy, E., Paredes, F.: Syntax Extensions for a Constrained-Object Language via Dynamic Parser Cooperation. Studies in Informatics and Control 21(1), 41–48 (2012)
17. Soto, R., Granvilliers, L.: The Design of COMMA: An Extensible Framework for Mapping Constrained Objects to Native Solver Models. In: Proceedings of IEEE ICTAI, pp. 243–250 (2007)
18. Soto, R., Kjellerstrand, H., Duran, O., Crawford, B., Monfroy, E., Paredes, F.: Cell formation in group technology using constraint programming and boolean satisfiability. Expert Syst. Appl. 39(13), 11423–11427 (2012)
19. Zhang, M.: Combining genetic algorithms and topological sort to optimize open-pit mine plans. In: Proceedings of the 15th Mine Planning and Equipment Selection, pp. 1234–1239 (2006)

A Creation of Music-Like Melody by Interactive Genetic Algorithm with User's Intervention

Shimpei Koga[1] and Makoto Fukumoto[2]

[1] Graduate School of Engineering, Fukuoka Institute of Technology,
3-30-1 Wajiro-higashi, Higashi-ku, Fukuoka, 811-0295, Japan
mfm13007@bene.fit.ac.jp
[2] Fukuoka Institute of Technology,
3-30-1 Wajiro-higashi, Higashi-ku, Fukuoka, 811-0295, Japan
fukumoto@fit.ac.jp

Abstract. We have recently proposed Interactive Genetic Algorithm (IGA) creating music piece with user's intervention. IGA is one of interactive evolutionary computation and is known as effective method to optimize certain pattern suited to each user's feelings. The user's intervention is expected to accelerate the optimization. In the intervention method, the user operates the music melody by changing keys of some music notes in each of music melodies. In general IGA, solution candidates are presented to the users, then the users subjectively evaluate them. In the IGA with user's Intervention, after the presentation, the users can operate the individual when the users want to. After finishing the operation, the user input the fitness value of the presented solution candidate to the IGA system. This study focuses on improving the proposed IGA to create more music like melody. With the improvements, pattern of music melody is lengthened and is attached music chord.

Keywords: interactive evolutionary computation, music melody, genetic algorithm, intervention.

1   Introduction

Music is one of important media types and is often used in our daily life. Recently, music pieces are easily created by development of information technology. However, it is still difficult for beginners to create music pieces suited to each user's preference and feelings. Psycho-physiological effects of music are widely believed, and higher effects of music pieces are expected if we could obtain n the music pieces suited to each of the user.

Interactive Evolutionary Computation (IEC) is known as an effective approach that reflects user's preference and feelings to media contents [1]. IEC is one of applications of evolutionary computations and reflects user's preference and feelings to created contents. IEC generally accepts user's subjective evaluation as fitness value in evolutionary algorithms and searches optimal patterns of media contents suited to each user's preference and feelings which is considered as indefinite functions.

C. Stephanidis (Ed.): HCII 2014 Posters, Part I, CCIS 434, pp. 523–527, 2014.

As examples of the previous IEC studies, IEC methods creating sign sounds suited to user's feelings were proposed [2, 3]. In most of the IECs, Genetic Algorithm (GA) is employed as evolutionary algorithm. Interactive type of GA is called IGA, and some previous studies proposed IGA for composing music pieces. Recent IEC studies often employed other new evolutionary algorithms with expectations of higher performance in searching solutions.

However, in these previous IEC approaches creating music and sound contents, the users just evaluated the presented contents from the IEC system and could not actively concern with the created music and sound contents. Only with the subjective evaluation by the user, IEC is difficult to change strange sounds in the contents because the search in IEC is a stochastic approach. Additionally, good individuals obtained from IEC are often corrupted in general IEC. User's operation is also expected to amend the corruption by employing elitism strategy simultaneously.

To resolve this problem, we have proposed IGA creating music melody with user's intervention [4] by referring to a previous IEC study with user's intervention [5]. In the intervention process in the IGA, the user directly operates the music melody by changing keys of some music notes in each of music melodies. Previous some IEC studies have proposed intervention methods [6-9], however, few studies have proposed direct operation for individuals in IEC.

This study focuses on proposing IGA with the user's intervention to create more music like melody: created music melodies in our previous study [4] were constructed with only eight successive music notes. As improvements, pattern of music melody is lengthened and is attached music chord. By such improvements, dimension of problem becomes large. IGA with the intervention is expected to help search in the case with larger dimensions.

2   Interactive Genetic Algorithm and User's Intervention in It

2.1   Interactive Genetic Algorithm

GA imitates evolution of natural creatures for finding optimal solution in a certain problem. Search of GA begins with creating solution candidates, which are called GA individuals. In most of GA, values of individuals in initial population are defined in random value in a certain range. The individual is evaluated with problem function, and fitness value of the individual is calculated. To create the individuals in next generation, parents of them are selected from current solution candidates. The selection is performed based on fitness value of individuals. Gene of offspring is made by crossover of parents' genes. Mutation changes part of the gene of individual with constant probability. These steps are repeated until a new population is created [10].

IGA expands GA by obtaining user's subjective evaluation as evaluation value for each of solution candidates. IGA is suitable for the problem including human factors that is hard to represent as a numerical formula. Therefore, IGA is applied in various fields including art, medical engineering, and kansei engineering [1].

2.2   Flow of the Proposed IGA Creating Music Melody with User's Intervention

Most of conventional IGA methods employed subjective evaluations for individuals in GA: change in GA individuals by user's operation as active intervention was not major method and was applied only for visual contents. Our proposed method, the user intervenes in the GA individuals for melody creation [4]. The intervention refers to the user's operation that is direct change in key of some music notes.

Fig. 1 shows a flow chart of the proposed IGA creating music melody with the user's intervention. In general IGA, solution candidates are presented to the users, then the users subjectively evaluate them. In the proposed IGA for creating music melody, after the presentation, the users can operate the solution candidate when the users want to.

In the operation of the user's intervention on music melody, the presented music melody from the IEC system is changed its part of key of music notes. The change is performed by the user's operation. After finishing the operation, the user listens to the operated music melody and inputs the fitness value of it.

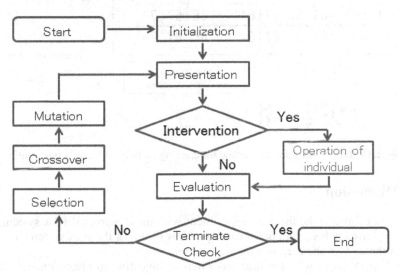

Fig. 1. Flow chart of IGA with user's intervention

3   Proposed Method: IGA Creating Music Like Melody with User's Intervention

This study focuses on improving the IEC creating music melody with the user's intervention [4]. In the improvement, music melody is designed as more music like melody that is long melody having larger number of music notes and has music chord.

Fig. 2 shows a scheme of the improved IGA. Conventional IGA [4] accepts user's operation by means of moving key of music note with drag-and-drop. However, the created music melody is constructed from only eight successive music notes. General music melody is longer and is decorated with various sounds as different music parts.

We propose IGA with the user's intervention for creating more music like melody. To create more music like melody, solution candidate is augmented in two ways. First is lengthening music melody. Sixteen music notes are used to construct music melody. Increase of music notes makes difficult to search optimal solution in evolutionary computation. The user's intervention is expected to ease this problem. Second is attaching music chord. The music chord is known as creating atmosphere of music, and general music pieces have music chord progression. The music chord progression is predefined by user's selection.

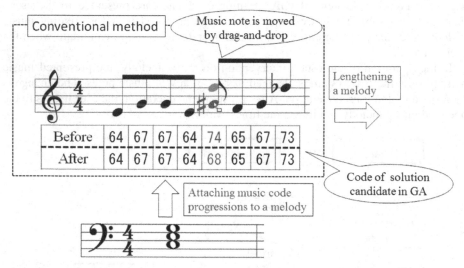

Fig. 2. Outline of the proposed method for creating melody with user's intervention

4   Discussion

We have not finished the listening experiment with the constructed IGA system, thus we have discussion here with presumable patterns of use of the IGA system. We have two hypotheses how the user uses the IGA system.

First hypothesis is with the user has obvious objective to create music melody. Such kind of user aggressively operates the music melody as the intervention. Some of them intervene on the music melody in early generations. They might finish the use of the IGA system in several generations.

Second hypothesis is with the user has No obvious image of objective music melody. They will rely on stochastic search of the IGA system and intervene on the music melody after passing several generations. The intervention of the user is considered as a little adjustments of music melody. In such case, in creation of music melody in initial generation, music melody should be pre-adjusted previously to the chord progression based on music theory.

5   Conclusion

This study proposed the IGA creating music like melody with the user's intervention. The proposed IGA is augmented from our previous method by increasing number of music notes and by attaching music chord progression. With the improvements, the proposed IGA is expected to reflect user's preference and feelings than our previous study.

We have a plan to conduct listening experiments to investigate efficacies of the proposed method. By comparing created music melody through several generations and music melody in the initial generation, we can show the efficacy of the proposed method. Furthermore, it is need to show that the proposed IGA overcome conventional methods with comparing experiment. Developing an efficient interface seems to help effective search. The interface that keeps and visualizes the created music melodies from the proposed IGA system must be needed for the users to easily evaluate and create the music melodies [11].

Acknowledgements. This work was supported in part by Ministry of Education, Culture, Sports, Science and Technology, Grant-in-Aid for Young Scientists (B) and Grant from Computer Science Laboratory, Fukuoka Institute of Technology.

References

1. Takagi, H.: Interactive Evolutionary Computation: Fusion of the Capabilities of EC Optimization and Human Evaluation. Proceedings of the IEEE 89(9), 1275–1296 (2001)
2. Miki, M., Orita, H., Wake, S.H., Hiroyasu, T.: Design of Sign Sounds using an Interactive Genetic Algorithm. In: Proc. IEEE International Conference on Systems, Man and Cybernetics, pp. 3486–3490 (2006)
3. Ogawa, S., Fukumoto, M.: System of Generating Sign Sounds using Interactive Genetic Algorithm. The Transactions of the Institute of Electrical Engineers of Japan C, A publication of Electronics, Information and System Society 131(3), 698–699 (2011) (in Japanese)
4. Koga, S., Inoue, T., Fukumoto, M.: A proposal for Intervention by User in Interactive Genetic Algorithm for Creation of Music Melody. In: Proc. 2013 International Conference on Biometrics and Kansei Engineering, Tokyo, pp. 129–132 (2013)
5. Ono, S., Nakayama, S.: Two-Dimensinal Barcode Decoration Using User-System Cooperative Evolutionary Computation. Information Processing Society of Japan 5(3), 14–25 (2012) (in Japanese)
6. Bush, B.J., Sayama, H.: Hyperinteractive Evolutionary Computation. IEEE Transactions on Evolutionary Computations 15(3), 424–433 (2011)
7. Unemi, T.: Simulated breeding-A framework of breeding artifacts on the computer. Kybernetes 32, 203–220 (2003)
8. Takagi, H.: Active user intervention in an EC search. In: Proc. 5th JCIS, pp. 995–998 (2000)
9. Hayashida, N., Takagi, H.: Visualized IEC: Interactive evolutionary computation with multidimensional data visualization. In: Proc. IECON, pp. 2738–2743 (2000)
10. Holland, J.H.: Adaptation in Natural and Artificial Systems: An Introductory Analysis with Applications to Biology, Control and Artificial Intelligence, The University of Michigan Press, Ann Arbor (1975)
11. Unehara, M., Onisawa, T.: Interactive Music Composition System-composition of 16-bars musical work with a melody part and backing parts. In: IEEE International Conference on System, Man and Cybernetics, pp. 5736–5741 (2004)

Proposal of a User Authentication Method Using Near-Infrared Card Images

Hiromitsu Nishimura

Kanagawa Institute of Technology,
1030, Shimo-ogino, Atsugi, Kanagawa, 243-0292, Japan
nisimura@ic.kanagawa-it.ac.jp

Abstract. Personal authentication alongside card use is implemented in a wide range of situations such as use in financial institutions or swiping a card key. However, card authentication systems have several issues, the largest of which concerns usage by another person as a result of theft or forgery. PINs (personal identification number) are a countermeasure for such crimes, but there is a limit to the number of digits that can be memorized, making it difficult to achieve robust authentication. Bio data like veins and fingerprints are also used, but resistance to the registration of such personal data is high. In this research, a means was devised to obtain human behavioral data for card authentication that is provided more freely by registering customers. The method involves using an image of the card owners swiping style for authentication. This paper also describes a newly devised authentication method for cards that applies a near-infrared transmission filter as a countermeasure for illicit peeking.

Keywords: User Identification, Card Image, Near-Infrared Camera.

1 Introduction

Bankcard authentication is performed through means such as passwords and signatures. Passwords are a series of a few digits of alphanumeric characters; therefore, the limit of human ability to memorize a high number of digits makes attainment of robust security difficult. Hotel card keys and magnetic ID cards are frequently authenticated merely by possession, and are quite vulnerable to theft. As a means to realize high security authentication of such cards, systems which combine vein or fingerprint authentication2 with use of the card have been devised. However, resistance to registering such personal bio data on computer systems remains high.

This research focused on the motion of swiping a contactless ID card over the reading apparatus at the time of usage. From image data obtained while swiping the card, the information printed on the card surface and the manner in which the card was gripped were acquired to create a user authentication method. Behavioral data such as gripping style will likely be provided more freely than conventional bio data. In addition, we designed a new card that has near-infrared transmission film on one side to serve as a countermeasure for illicit peeking of the swiped surface.

C. Stephanidis (Ed.): HCII 2014 Posters, Part I, CCIS 434, pp. 528–532, 2014.

2   Proposed User Identification System

A conventional card, such as a credit card, which has a signature on the back, was envisioned for the design. A near-infrared transmission film was applied to the signed surface so that the signature was invisible under visible light. The reading for authentication employed an inexpensive web camera that could photograph near-infrared light.

2.1   ID Card Design

In this research, the back of the ID card was designed to have three zones: the Grip Marker, Corporate Logo, and Signature.

The Grip Marker zone refers to printed markers that enable determination of finger locations when the card is gripped. These round markers were 8 mm in diameter, according to the approximate width of an adult finger, and arranged randomly along the top and bottom of the card. The Corporate Logo zone was reserved for space to print an established logo for a company or school organization. Exploiting the accuracy of this design can aid in forgery prevention. The Signature zone is like the signature box found on a credit card. Upon receipt, the user signs in this space.

The card user receives a card with the Grip Marker and Corporate Logo zones printed, and signs his or her signature in the Signature zone. Subsequently, as shown in the upper right of Fig. 2, film that appears black under visible light and transmits only near-infrared light is applied so that the information shown on the back is invisible under visible light.

Fig. 1. Details of ID card design

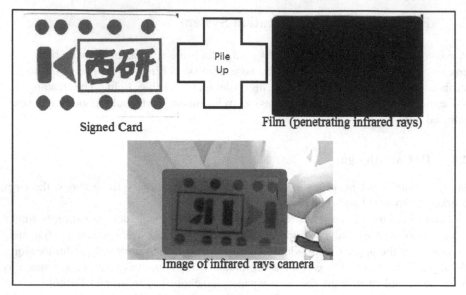

Fig. 2. Devised ID card

2.2   System Environment

In addition to the card surface, the same near-infrared transmission film was applied to the front of the camera lens. Images of cards illuminated with indirect near-infrared LED lighting held approximately 15 cm in front of the camera were photo-graphed and collected, and used in the performance evaluation of the proposed method. Photo samples were collected for 50 subjects gripping an identical card in the same way 10 times, and gripping another person's card in various ways 10 times. This sample data was used for the test described in Section 3 below.

Collected images were in the format shown on the left of Fig. 3. The authentication performance evaluation was conducted by manually cropping the image to just the card's area, as shown on the right of Fig. 3.

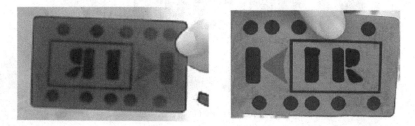

Fig. 3. Image sample of gripping card

2.3   Algorithm of Image Comparison

Image similarity algorithms for authentication include NN and SVM, which have high reported performance. In this research, however, image similarity was computed in the simplest manner as the difference between two images, based on a numerical value for the percentage of pixels of the reference image detected in the target image.

We considered this simple image comparison technique to provide a sufficient basis on which to assess the effectiveness of the proposed method, as it is able to detect differences between images of a card held by the registered user and images of the same card held by another person.

3   Evaluation Experiments

For 18 subjects, listed along the x-axis in Fig. 4, a single pattern was registered, and similarity to swiping patterns made by the same subject with the same card (denoted by the circles) and similarity to swiping patterns made by other persons who have

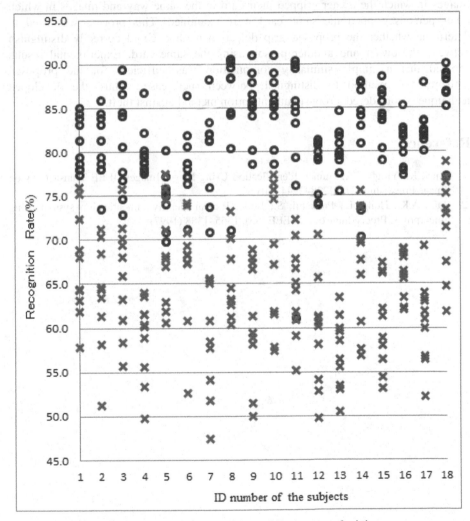

Fig. 4. Comparison of 10 persons' different way of griping

"stolen" the card (denoted by 'x' marks) are plotted. The results show that the proposed method can distinguish the difference between swiping patterns of the owner and other persons with high precision.

4   Conclusion

We developed a card authentication method that utilizes the owners individual swiping motion of the card, and devised a new countermeasure in which near-infrared film was applied to the back of the card and the images of the card swipe were acquired by a near-infrared camera. Styles of gripping the card were distinguished by photographing multiple round markers printed on the card. Differences between images in which the owner gripped their card in the same way and images in which other persons gripped the same card were examined. This process was used to determine whether the proposed grip detection method could correctly distinguish between the owner and another person using the same card. Experimental results showed that a simple similarity computation was sufficient for the proposed authentication method to distinguish between such cases. Thus, the developed technique is considered a robust authentication method against theft.

Reference

1. Ajay, K., Yingbo, Z.: Human Identification Using Finger Images. IEEE Transactions on Image Processing (21), 2228–2244 (2012)
2. Jain, A.K., Hong, L., Pankanti, S., Bolle, R.: An identity-authentication system using fingerprints. Proceedings of the IEEE (85), 1365–1388 (1997)

Human Factor Quantitative Analysis
Based on OHFAM and Bayesian Network

Mei Rong[1], Min Luo[1], Yanqiu Chen[1], Changhua Sun[2], and Yanyang Wang[3]

[1] China Academy of Civil Aviation Science and Technology, Beijing, China
{rongmei,luomin,chenyq}@mail.castc.org.cn
[2] Civil Aviation Administration of China, Beijing, China
ch_sun@caac.gov.cn
[3] Beihang University, Beijing, China
wangyanyang@buaa.edu.cn

Abstract. Occurrence Human Factors Analysis Model is developed for China civil aviation based on the Human Factors Analysis and Classification System (HFACS) and the actual operation conditions and characteristics of China civil aviation to enhance the classification, analysis and utilization of safety information. In addition, to generate a model which can provides quantitative analysis supportive in aviation incident analysis, a human factor analysis model based on OHFAM and Bayesian network is established. This model constructed by combing hill-climbing search method with CH score function is a Bayesian network which uses three layers nodes to represent causality between human factors and incidents. The specific impact degree of human factors on aviation incidents is represented by conditional probability parameters of the model. It is useful in aviation incident analyses and deductions.

Keywords: Occurrence Human Factors Analysis, Human factor quantitative analysis, Bayesian networks, Civil aviation safety, incident analysis.

1   Introduction

Statistic information of aviation accidents investigation shows that nearly 80% accidents were caused by human factors [1], and we also have got the point that we should not only concern about human error, but more in-depth study on the organization and management factors. According to Reason model, the failures of all levels interact and lead to disastrous consequences; the failures are the "holes" of system at different levels [2]. Human Factors Analysis and Classification System（HFACS）is developed based on Reason model [3], this model helps to define the "holes of cheese model". However, the existing human factors analysis model cannot fully meet China's actual needs. Therefore, we develop a model named "Occurrence Human Factors Analysis Model (OHFAM)" for China civil aviation human factors analysis and use the model to analyze the 180 crew caused incidents from 2001 to 2010 in China.

However, All these analysis models includes the OHFAM can hardly provide a more detailed and quantitative analysis [4]. This paper based on Bayesian network

C. Stephanidis (Ed.): HCII 2014 Posters, Part I, CCIS 434, pp. 533–539, 2014.
© Springer International Publishing Switzerland 2014

theory, employed the layer structure of OHFAM, developed human factor quantitative analysis model. By using this model to analyze civil aviation incidents statistic data, detailed impact degree of every human factor to incidents is derived as Bayesian network parameters to help diagnose civil aviation incidents.

2   Occurrence Human Factors Analysis Model

The OHFAM has five layers including "Unsafe Behavior", "Preconditions for Unsafe Behavior", "Department Management", "Organizational Influence" and "Government Supervision". The model clarifies its sub-categories of factors (as shown in Fig. 1) and gives various items as the expression of each factor.

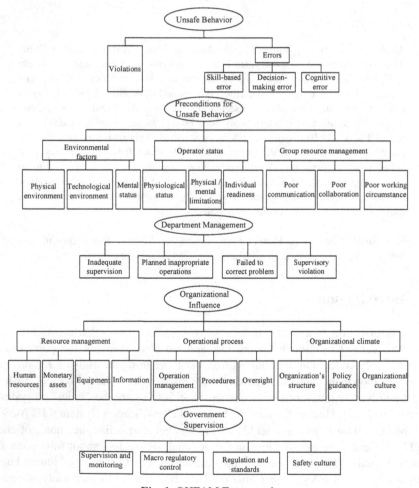

Fig. 1. OHFAM Framework

3   Bayesian Network

A Bayesian network is a binary group (S, P) in which S stands for a directed acyclic graph and the node of the graph stands for stochastic variable, the edge between nodes stands for the dependency relationship between the variables [5]. P is conditional probability distribution $p(x_i \mid \pi(x_i))$, which stands for the strength of dependency relationship among nodes. $\pi(x_i)$ is the set of parent nodes of x_i. A simple Bayesian network contains 5 nodes is described in Fig.2.

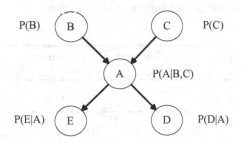

Fig. 2. A simple Bayesian network

The first step to construct a Bayesian network is to distinguish the key variables and its possible values of the domain in which the model will be built, and use nodes to stand for the variables, then to determine the dependency and independency relation between the nodes and express it in a graph. The final step is to calculate the ration part's probability parameter of the Bayesian network [6].Network construction is also called Bayesian network structure learning if both network structure and parameter are unknown. Generally, structure learning contains two steps: model selection and model optimization. Model selection refers to evaluate different model structure while model optimization is a searching process which aiming at searching the best model structure under the given sample data.

Given a data set $D = (D_1, D_2, \cdots, D_m)$, the good and bad of a specific network structure S can be measured by a score function. Bayesian network theory provides many kinds of score functions among which the most common used are CH score and BIC Score. Model optimization is a process of searching the best structure for the given sample data. The most common used searching algorithm in Bayesian network theory are K2 and hill climbing.

4   Human Factor Quantitative Analysis Model Based on OHFAM and Bayesian Network

The OHFAM, as is shown in Fig.1, has five layers. The layer 1 "Unsafe Behavior" is dominant factor while layer 2 to 5 are recessive factors.

Human Factor Quantitative Analysis model we developed is based on Bayesian network theory and adopted the layered structure of OHFAM. In this paper, only layer 1 and layer 2 of OHFAM are employed to build the Human Factor Quantitative Analysis model, it contains three layers.

The Fig.3 shows the structure of a Bayesian network analysis model. The network analysis model has three layers: preconditions for unsafe behavior, unsafe behavior, and incidents. In the network, each node stands for a variable which use two possible values, 1 or 0, to represent whether the factor or incidents happened. A parameter is a conditional probability between two nodes in different layer, for example, the parameter of *edge(Precondition3,Behavior2)* is *P(B2/P3)* which stands for the probability of happing *Behavior2* on condition of happing *Precondition3*.

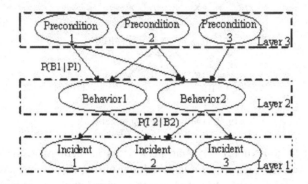

Fig. 3. Bayesian network human factor quantitative analysis model

Nodes in unsafe behavior precondition layer contains precondition nodes like: poor visibility, lack of cross validation, etc. Unsafe behaviors nodes like: misjudge on flight posture, violate flight rules, improper bias correction, etc.

As for Bayesian network theory, direct connection (edge) from nodes of layer 3 to layer 1 or within a layer is possible to generate in construction process. However, to combine Bayesian network theory with OHFAM, we changed the network search algorithm to confine the result network within a layered Bayesian network model which has no cross-layer or reverse connections.

Using the incidents database of China civil aviation, and taking the analysis results of the 180 crew caused incidents from 2001 to 2010 by OHFAM as the sample data of Bayesian network's structure learning and parameter learning, four networks are constructed by collocating K2 and hill climbing searching method with BIC and CH score functions. The agreement degree of each network compared with the actual data is calculated and listed in table 1.

Table 1. Compare of Different Algorithm Collocation

Algorithm collocation	Accuracy	Complexity	Note
K2+CH	87%	Middle	This collocation has a large searching scope, each behavior and premise will be searched.
K2+BIC	23%	Simple	The accuracy of the network result under this collocation is bad because the contradictory of the two algorithms, so it's not a good construct collocation.
Hill Climbing +CH	98%	Complex	The result network is extremely complex because hill climbing algorithm calculates each network structure many times to get a more accurate network.
Hill Climbing +BIC	93%	Middle	The punish function in BIC score limited the complexity of the network.

5   Human Factor Quantitative Analysis

In this paper, network constructed under hill-climbing method and CH score is analyzed as an example for its accuracy, part of it is picked out and shown in Fig.4. (The whole network contains over 130 nodes and over 400 edges.)

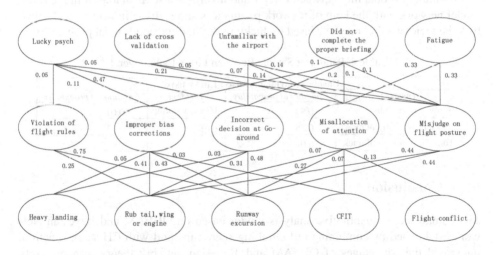

Fig. 4. Part of model network constructed by hill-climbing and BIC

According to the conditional probability parameter of the network, analyst can find out which human factors are the most possible ones that cause the specific incident. It is also available to know which incidents may occur as well as the probability of occurrence if a particular unsafe behavior has happened. Table 2 lists the incidents caused by incorrect decision at go-around (unsafe behavior) and the conditional probability.

Table 2. Parameter Sample Between Layer 1 and Layer 2

Unsafe behavior: Incorrect decision at go-around			
Incident	*Conditional probability*	*Incident*	*Conditional probability*
Heavy landing	0.03	Runway excursion	0.48
Rub tail, wing or engine	0.31	Touch ground out of track	0.18

Table 3 lists the unsafe behaviors that maybe caused by fatigue (preconditions for unsafe behavior) and the conditional probability. The sum of all conditional probabilities caused by one particular node can be more than 1 because the results are not mutually exclusive to each other; they may happen at the same time.

Table 3. Parameter Sample Between Layer 2 and Layer 3

Preconditions for unsafe behavior : Fatigue			
Unsafe Behavior	*Conditional probability*	*Unsafe Behavior*	*Conditional probability*
Misjudge on flight posture	0.33	Improper landing, taking off decision	0.33
Misallocation of attention	0.33	Crude and fierce operation	0.33

Conditional probability between layer 1 and layer 3 is also available from the result model network with the help of network parameters and statistic information. Table 4 lists the incidents that maybe caused by lucky psych and the conditional probability.

Table 4. Parameter Sample Between Layer 1 and Layer 3

Unsafe behavior premise : Lucky psych			
Incident	*Conditional probability*	*Incident*	*Conditional probability*
Runway excursion	0.52	Heavy landing	0.01
Rub tail, wing or engine	0.35	CFIT	0.01
Touch ground out of track	0.09		

6   Conclusion

The human factor quantitative analysis model based on OHFAM and Bayesian Network established by combining hill climbing search method with CH score function, integrated the advantages of OHFAM and Bayesian network theory, can precisely reflect the causality between human factors and civil aviation incidents. The model uses conditional probability to represent the exact impact degree of human factors on incidents which is useful for incidents analysis and risk evaluation.

References

1. Guopeng, L.: Analysis of Accident Resulted from Human Factors in Safety Management. Journal of Civil Aviation University of China 27(4), 18–21 (2009)
2. Reason, J.: Human Error. Cambridge University Press, Cambridge (1990)

3. Wiegmann, D.A., Shappell, S.A.: A Human Error Approach to Aviation Accident Analysis: The Human Factors Analysis and Classification System. Ashgate Publishing (2003) ISBN-13: 978-0754618737
4. Huiying, Z., Yuan, N.: Reasoning and Analysis of Bayesian Network in Machine Learning. Modern Machinery 2 (2012)
5. Lianwen, Z., Haipeng, G.: Bayesian network introduction. In: Structure Learning, pp. 172–191. Science Press, Beijing (2006)
6. Cao, W., Lin, X.: Flight turnaround time analysis and delay prediction based on Bayesian network. Computer Engineering and Design 32(5), 1770–1773 (2001)

An Improved Error Diffusion Algorithm Based on Laplacian Transform and Adaptive Median Filter

Xiaoguo Shi and Xueqing Li

Department of Computer Science and Technology, Shandong University
Jinan, 250101, China
rockworldto@hotmail.com, xqli@sdu.edu.cn

Abstract. In this paper, we propose an error diffusion algorithm that produces higher visual quality results while preserving fine texture details and high contrast present in the original images. Based on the analysis of the Laplacian kernel, we get an edge-enhanced image with the Laplacian transform. Next, we use the adaptive median filter to remove noises and preserve sharpness in the edge-enhanced images. Besides, error diffusion(E-D) by Stucki is adopted to get our halftoning results. Multiple experiments show that our method is superior to the improving mid-tone E-D especially in preserving texture details and contrast. Combined good visual properties with fast speed, our method has significantly improved the user perception and may be applied to most real-world applications.

Keywords: Halftoning, Laplacian transform, Error diffusion, Adaptive median filter, User perception.

1 Introduction

Halftoning refers to converting a continuous-tone image into a pattern of black and white dots. For high practical value, halftoning techniques have been continuously studied for several years [1]. Typical algorithms such as ordered dithering [2], Floyd-Steinberg E-D [3], and dot-diffusion [4] have been widely applied into the fields of printing devices and image display. Although ordered dithering has the fastest speed, its poor quality can't meet the needs of many practical applications.

Analoui et al.[5] first introduced a model based halftoning using direct binary search. It is a typical iterative algorithm to obtain the minimal difference between the halftone image and human visual perception via a HVS model. More recently, the high-profile structure-aware halftoning has been introduced by Pang et al. [6]. Although excellent results are generated, these methods can't be applied into real-world applications due to a large amount of computing time.

At present, researchers mainly focus on improving existing halftone algorithm. For instance, many methods have been proposed to improve E-D algorithm in aspects such as threshold optimization, diffusion coefficients and processing paths. Stucki [7] improved E-D by extending the distribution range to second-level unprocessed neighbors(neighbors of neighbors). Ostromoukhov [8] put forward intensity-dependent variable diffusion coefficients in order to remove patches of regular structure. To break regularities near critical intensity levels, Zhou and Fang [9] further developed this

C. Stephanidis (Ed.): HCII 2014 Posters, Part I, CCIS 434, pp. 540–545, 2014.
© Springer International Publishing Switzerland 2014

method by introducing intensity-dependent noise. Howerver, blurred texture details and poor contrast are two big drawbacks for methods of this type.

Contrast is a topic often neglected, though not inevitably. To preserve the contrast as well as texture details to the original images, we present an improved E-D algorithm based on the Laplacian operator [10] and adaptive median filter [11]. To begin with, the original image is processed with the Laplacian operator, then we obtain an edge-enhanced image. Next, adaptive median filter acts on edge-enhanced images with fine contrast to remove noises and preserve sharpness. Finally, error diffusion by Stucki [7] is run to get the final halftoning results.

To verify the performance of our method, we applied it to various types of images. Simulation results show that our algorithm preserves fine visually sensitive texture details with an ideal contrast especially for the weak texture regions. Our method has successfully improved the user experience due to its good visual perception and fast speed.

2   Our Approach

As shown in Figure 1, we present an overview of our improved E-D algorithm based on the Laplacian operator [10] and adaptive median filter [11] in this section. In the following parts,we analyze our approach in detail.

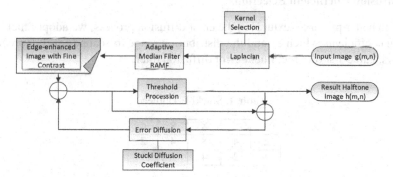

Fig. 1. Schematic representation of the architecture of our method. Please refer to Section 2 for the meaning of all terms.

2.1   Original Image Enhancement

We assume that $g(m, n)$ is an original grayscale image. The Laplacian transform [10] of $g(m, n)$ is defined as

$$\nabla^2 g(m, n) = \partial^2 g(m, n)/\partial m^2 + \partial^2 g(m, n)/\partial n^2 \qquad (1)$$

After the original grayscale image $g(m, n)$ is processed with the Laplacian transform, we get an edge-enhanced result $e(m, n)$ which is defined as follows:

$$e(m, n) = \begin{cases} g(m, n) - \nabla^2 g(m, n) & C(m, n) < 0 \\ g(m, n) + \nabla^2 g(m, n) & C(m, n) > 0 \end{cases} \tag{2}$$

where $C(m, n)$ is the center coefficient of Laplacian transform. Experimental results show that the edge-enhanced effect in $e(m, n)$ changes with different Laplacian kernels. We will further analyze Laplacian kernels in Section 3.1.

2.2 Adaptive Median Filter

To smooth noise in the reconstructed continuous tone image and reduce distortion around the object edge, we process $e(m, n)$ with the $RAMF$ (ranked-order based adaptive median filter [11]), which has variable window size for removal of impulses while preserving sharpness.

$$e'(m, n) = |ifft\{fft[e(m, n)] \cdot RAMF\}| \tag{3}$$

where fft is the Fourier transform and $ifft$ is the inverse Fourier transform.

2.3 Diffusion Coefficient Selection

In order to better preserve textures in the error diffusion process, we adopt Stucki's [7] diffusion coefficients which extend the distribution range to second-level unprocessed neighbors. Table 1 shows the Stucki error diffusion filter.

Table 1. Stucki E-D filter

		X	8	4
2	4	8	4	2
1	2	4	2	1

3   Results and Analysis

In this section, we analyze the Laplacian kernel to archive an satisfactory edge-enhanced image firstly. Then the performance of our method is evaluated with visual comparison. In our work, we test our algorithm with the set of images[Figure 2,3,4] already shown in Pang's paper [6]. This test set comprises a wide range of important natures: smooth tone gradation, rich details of various contrasts and visually identifiable textures.

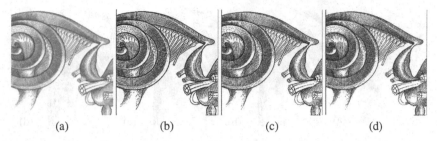

(a)   (b)   (c)   (d)

Fig. 2. Image "snail shaped organ" with the resolution of 384×399. Edge-enhanced images with different Laplacian kernels. (a) Original image; (b) kernel = [-1 -1 -1; -1 9 -1; -1 -1 -1]; (c) kernel = [0 -1 0; -1 5 -1; 0 -1 0]; (d) kernel = [1 -2 1; -2 5 -2; 1 -2 1];

3.1 Laplacian Kernel Analysis

In our algorithm, the Laplacian kernel is required to control the edge-enhanced effect. Figure 2 illustrates that how results produced by our method can be influenced by the Laplacian kernel. Experiments show that satisfactory results including subjective and objective evaluations can always be obtained when kernel = [1 -2 1; -2 5 -2; 1 -2 1]. Therefore, we test our algorithm with the above Laplacian kernel in the following parts.

3.2 Visual Comparison

Figures 3 and 4 visually compare our results to those of Folyd-Steinberg E-D, Stucki's method [7] and the improving mid-tone E-D [9]. Compared to these methods, our results better reproduces the range of contrasts and texture details. In addition, our method preserves fine texture details and clear lines especially for the low contrast and weak texture regions. However, the other three methods all lose the structure of textures more or less in the same areas. It represents that our algorithm performs excellent in structure preservation. In Figure 4, we leave out the result of Folyd-Steinberg E-D because of space, since this method has been undeniable outperformed by the improving mid-tone E-D.

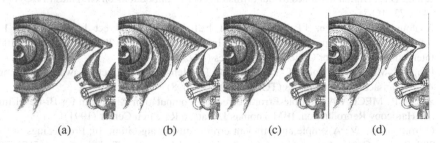

(a)   (b)   (c)   (d)

Fig. 3. Halftoning images with different algorithms. (a) Floyd-Steinberg E-D; (b) Stucki's method; (c) Improving mid-tone E-D; (d) Our method;

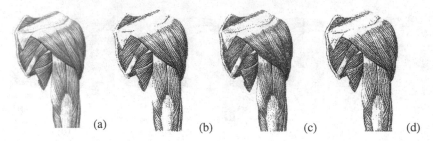

(a)   (b)   (c)   (d)

Fig. 4. Image "arm" with the resolution of 200×307; (a) Original image; (b) Stucki's method; (c) Improving mid-tone E-D; (d) Our method;

4   Conclusion

In this paper, we have presented an error diffusion algorithm based on the Laplacian transform and adaptive median filter. Results in the experiment show that our method combines texture details and contrast successfully. Compared to the well-known halftoning algorithms [3] [7] [9], our algorithm outperforms these approaches and presents both fine texture details and high contrast.

Due to its excellent user experience, our method has successfully enhanced the user perception for the regions with low contrast and weak textures. Meanwhile, the visually pleasing halftone images are more easily identified by the human eyes, especially in the field requiring a color quantization algorithm.

References

1. Ulichney, R.: Digital halftoning. MIT Press (1987)
2. Bayer, B.E.: An optimum method for two-level rendition of continuous-tone pictures. In: SPIE Milestone Series MS, vol. 154, pp. 139–143 (1999)
3. Floyd, R.W., Steinberg, L.: Anadaptivealgorithm forspatial greyscale. Proceedings of the Society for Information Display 17(2), 7577 (1976)
4. Knuth, D.E.: Digital halftones by dot diffusion. ACM Transactions on Graphics (TOG) 6(4), 245–273 (1987)
5. Analoui, M., Allebach, J.P.: Model-based halftoning using direct binary search. In: SPIE/IS&T 1992 Symposium on Electronic Imaging: Science and Technology, pp. 96–108. International Society for Optics and Photonics (1992)
6. Pang, W.-M., Qu, Y., Wong, T.-T., Cohen-Or, D., Heng, P.-A.: Structure-aware halftoning. ACM Transactions on Graphics (TOG) 27(3), 89 (2008)
7. Stucki, P.: MECCA-A Multiple-Error Correction Computation Algorithm for Bi-Level Image Hardcopy Reproduction. IBM Thomas J. Watson Research Center (1991)
8. Ostromoukhov, V.: A simple and efficient error-diffusion algorithm. In: Proceedings of the 28th Annual Conference on Computer Graphics and Interactive Techniques, pp. 567–572. ACM (2001)

9. Zhou, B., Fang, X.: Improving mid-tone quality of variable-coefficient error diffusion using threshold modulation. ACM Transactions on Graphics (TOG) 22(3), 437–444 (2003)
10. Rosenfeld, A., Kak, A.C., Kak, A.: Digital Picture Processing. Computer Science and Applied Mathematics, vol. 1. Academic Press, New York (1982)
11. Hwang, H., Haddad, R.A.: Adaptive median filters: new algorithms and results. IEEE Transactions on Image Processing 4(4), 499–502 (1995)

Bag of Features Based on Feature Distribution Using Fuzzy C-Means

Yuki Shinomiya[1] and Yukinobu Hoshino[2]

[1] Graduate School, Kochi University of Technology, Tosayamada, Kochi, Japan
175055t@gs.kochi-tech.ac.jp
[2] Associate Professor, Kochi University of Technology, Tosayamada, Kochi, Japan
hoshino.yukinobu@kochi-tech.ac.jp

Abstract. The object recognition is an important research area about computer vision. In the object recognition, the BoF (Bag of Features) is kind of generally technique and this is based on "bag of words". The BoF is a frequency histogram, is made from the local features of an image. This is not based on the feature distribution on the frequency histogram and this technique is using k-means and k-nearest neighbor. Therefore, our approach used the FCM (Fuzzy C-Means). The reason is a frequency histogram based on feature distribution for improving the recognition accuracy. The FCM uses another process about a frequency histogram than k-means and k-nearest neighbor. The FCM is a clustering method using fuzzy theory. This method allows variations of a local feature to make two or more clusters. The belonging level of each cluster is fuzzy membership. We discuss about our methods compared to the BoF's results. There results is made from two proposal method and one basic method. Finally, we compare about which category recognition.

Keywords: Object recognition, Scale-Invariant Feature Transform, Bag of Features, Fuzzy C-Means, k-Nearest Neighbor.

1 Introduction

The object recognition is an important research area about computer vision, because it is included in various applications. The object recognition is used to the image retrieval, facial expression recognition and drive assist [1, 2], and the object recognition is important technique for the human-computer interaction. In the object recognition, BoF is kind of generally technique and represented. We discuss to using the FCM clustering, k-means and k-nearest neighbor. In this paper, BoF was represented by FCM clustering and pooling. The reason is a frequency histogram based on feature distribution for improving the recognition accuracy. In addition, we show about which category recognition.

C. Stephanidis (Ed.): HCII 2014 Posters, Part I, CCIS 434, pp. 546–550, 2014.

2   Experiment and Method

2.1   Bag of Features

In the object classification, BoF is kind of generally technique and this is based on "bag of words". The bag of words is a frequency histogram, is made from the words of the sentences. The BoF is frequency histogram, is made from the local features of an image. In this experiment, local feature extractor was used SIFT (Scale-Invariant Feature Transform). SIFT is an algorithm to detect keypoints and describe luminance gradients. This algorithm is calculated from the local area of the image. The advantages of using SIFT are invariant to scale, rotation, illumination and moving viewpoint [2, 3]. SIFT features from each learning images are clustered by k-means, the centers of each cluster are "visual words". After that, SIFT features from each testing images are pooled to a k-means classes SIFT features nearest visual word by k-nearest neighbor. In this experiment, the number of visual words is 500.

2.2   Fuzzy C-Means

FCM is a clustering method using fuzzy theory. This method allows variations of local features to make two or more clusters. The belonging levels of each clusters are fuzzy membership. In equation (1), x_i is SIFT features, c_j is the cluster vector, u_{ij} is the belonging level. m is a fuzziness parameter and the cluster edge is ambiguous by increases m.

$$u_{ij} = \left(\sum_{k=1}^{C} \left(\frac{\|x_i - c_j\|}{\|x_i - c_k\|} \right)^{\frac{2}{m-1}} \right)^{-1} \tag{1}$$

By basic representing method, if x_i is presented in the median of some clusters, x_i is voted to an either cluster. Therefore, BoF is represented by FCM clustering and membership pooling. Our methods are the max pooling method and the threshold pooling method. Max pooling is to vote a max membership, and threshold pooling is to vote memberships larger than the threshold. In max pooling, if x_i is presented in the median of some clusters, x_i is voted a low membership to an either cluster. By membership pooling, the votes are weighted. In addition, in threshold pooling, x_i is not voted to clusters of low belonging level. In threshold pooling, the BoF are represented by memberships larger than 0.02.

2.3   k-Nearest Neighbor

The k-Nearest Neighbor is an algorithm to retrieve images from the database. The k-parameter is a constant. That is recognized assigning the label, which is more frequent among from the k-samples of nearest query BoF.

2.4   Experiment Design and Evaluation Method

The dataset was used Caltech101 that was composed 102 categories from 9,145 images [4]. In addition, Background and Face categories are removed because much the same category exists. The evaluation method was used Recall. Recall is given by equation (2) and it is the matched retrieved images with respect to the number of relevant images.

$$Recall = \frac{relevant\,images \cap retrieved\,images}{relevant\,images} \tag{2}$$

3   Results and Discussion

Fig. 1. shows the average recall curve and the black line shows the uniform distribution. Fig. 2. shows the top five images about which category are easily recognition.

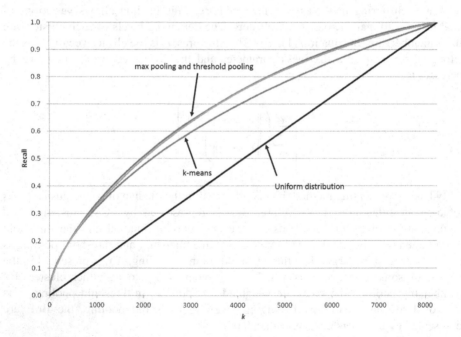

Fig. 1. Average Recall

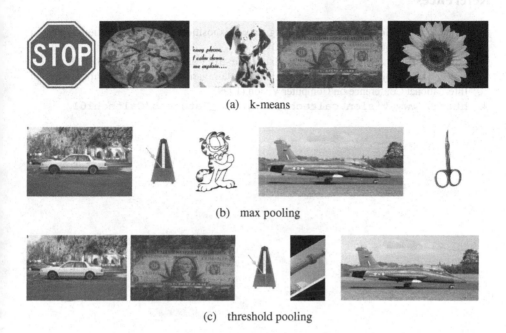

(a)   k-means

(b)   max pooling

(c)   threshold pooling

Fig. 2. easily recognition category by each method

Max pooling and threshold pooling are more effective than k-means. These are shows approximately the same accuracy. That is not improved by increasing the vote. Additionally, k-means and max pooling represents the same space complexity, so max pooling can increase the accuracy in the same complexity as the basic method. However, recognition results in each pooling method were different. These shows

4   Conclusion and Future Work

In this paper, we proposed max pooling and threshold pooling by FCM, and these were more effective than basic pooling method to object recognition. In addition, recognition results in each pooling method were different. In future work, we will optimizing m for several object recognition application and verify recognition accuracy about another image representing method using FCM.

References

1. Sujatha, K.S., Vinod, B.: Soft Clustering Based Exposition to Multiple Dictionary Bag of Words. Journal of Computer Science (2012)
2. Fujiyoshi, H.: Gradient-Based Feature Extraction -SIFT and HOG. In: CVIM (2007)
3. Lowe, D.G.: Object recognition from local scale-invariant features. In: Proceedings of International Conference on Computer Vision (1999)
4. http://www.vision.caltech.edu/Image_Datasets/Caltech101/

Exploring the Large-Scale TDOA Feature Space for Speaker Diarization

Yi Yang and Jia Liu

Tsinghua National Laboratory for Information Science and Technology
Department of Electronic Engineering, Tsinghua University, Beijing, P.R. China
{yangyy,liuj}@mail.tsinghua.edu.cn

Abstract. Using Time-Delay-Of-Arrival (TDOA) features has been proven greatly beneficial to the conventional acoustic feature-based speaker diarization systems by linking the speakers with their localization information. However, most state of-the-art speaker diarization systems depend on (relatively) limited distant microphones, which might not be sufficient in completely exploring the spatial information of speakers. In this study, the feature space spanned by TDOAs from (up to) 64 distant microphones is explored for the purpose of improving the performance of speaker classification, as an important branch of speaker diarization. Additionally, observing the intrinsic correlations of the high-dimensional feature space spanned by large-scale TDOAs, we compare several dimensionality reduction algorithms to explore an effective low-dimensional representation of TDOAs. Experimental results of speaker classification show consistent improvements when expanding the TDOA feature space by increasing the number of distant microphones. Furthermore, dimensionality reduction with the manifold information has been proven to be necessary for large-scale TDOAs.

Keywords: Speaker diarization, time-delay-of-arrival, dimensionality reduction, regularization.

1   Introduction

Using Multiple Distant Microphones (MDM) [1] has been proven effective in improving the performance of Speaker Diarization(SD) [2] which aims to find out "who spoke when" in audio recordings. The underlying reason is that the spatial features, namely Time Delay of Arrival (TDOA), convey the discriminative information of speaker locations, which offers different aspects of speaker identity information from the conventional acoustic features. Therefore, plenty of works are concentrated on the applicability of TDOA features [1, 3, 4, 5], all of which have consistently proven TDOA features to be complementary to the acoustic features.

Nevertheless, most previous speaker diarization systems maximally make use of sixteen microphones. Meanwhile, there are rarely papers discussing the relationship between the number of microphones and the system performance. Triggered by these two observations, we design an experiment which records the audio signals with

C. Stephanidis (Ed.): HCII 2014 Posters, Part I, CCIS 434, pp. 551–556, 2014.
© Springer International Publishing Switzerland 2014

large-scale (64) distant microphones (LSDM) for the purpose of speaker diarization, by which how the classification performance varies from the number of microphones could be investigated.

In this paper, a series of eigenvalue decomposition (EVD) based dimensionality reduction methods [7] with various regularization terms are evaluated to characterize the correlational information of TDOA features for the purpose of enhancing the discriminative power. This paper is organized as follows. In Section 2, we describe how to record the speech data with 64 distant microphones, following by the section introducing the derivation of TDOAs. Section 4 analyzes the properties of TDOA feature space and then present several specified regularized dimensionality reduction methods for the data. Experimental results on our corpus are shown in Section 5 and this paper is concluded in Section 6.

2   Audio Recording by Large-Scale Distant Microphones (LSDM)

2.1   The 64-microphone Audio Recording System

Fig. 1 is a multiple microphones device which we design as 64-channel elements and select part of asymmetric elements to compose one LSDM system. The 64-channel digital signals are collected with PXI-4496 multi-channel collection board produced by National Instruments.

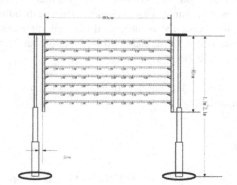

Fig. 1. The 64-channel multiple microphones device

2.2   Derivation of Large-Scale TDOA Feature Space

TDOA features are computed for all couples of distant microphones (in this paper there are in sum $\frac{64*63}{2} = 2016$ TDOA features) by the conventional Generalized Cross Correlation with PHAse Transform (GCC-PHAT) algorithm [8]. The following equations show the procedure of computation. Firstly, for i-th and j-th microphones, the Fourier representations of the snapshots ($x_i[n]$ and $x_j[n]$) should be derived as $x_i(f)$ and $x_j(f)$, with which the GCC-PHAT could be defined by:

$$G_{PHAT}(f) = \frac{X_i(f)[X_j(f)]^*}{|X_i(f)[X_j(f)]^*|} \tag{1}$$

in which the operator $[X(f)]^*$ denotes the complex conjugate of $X(f)$. The TDOA feature of such pair of microphones is estimated by $\hat{d}_{PHAT}(i,j) = \text{argmax}_d(\hat{R}_{PHAT}(d))$.

The feature vector consists of $\frac{N*(N+1)}{2}$ TDOA features.

3 Regularized Dimensionality Reduction for Correlated TDOAS

Suppose there are n training samples, each of which is composed of $D = 2016$ TDOA features as $\vec{x}_i, i = 1,2,\ldots,n$. Each sample is assigned by a class label $y_i \in \{1,2,\ldots,C\}$ for C different speakers. As introduced in the first section, the feature space of $\vec{x}_i$ is highly correlated and abound in the data redundancy. Therefore, the dimensionality reduction will be addressed. The graph-based dimensionality reduction [9] is perhaps the most commonly-used approach which has been proven effective in various pattern classification tasks, including the MDM systems with TDOA features [8]. The basic idea is to find out the projection $W \in R^{D \times d}, d < D$ with which the low-dimensional representation $\vec{z} = W^T\vec{x}$ keeps the most discriminative information in the original high-dimensional feature space. The general optimization problem is to maximize the following objective function:

$$\vec{W} = \text{argmax}_W \frac{\text{tr}(W^T S^b W)}{\text{tr}(W^T((1-\alpha)S^w + \alpha I)W)} \tag{2}$$

where S^b and S^w stand for the between-class and within-class scatter matrices [10]. They describe the separability among different classes and the class compactness, respectively.

3.1 Design of Scatter Matrices and Regularization Terms

The fundamental idea to capture such data structures is to design the scatter matrices by $S^w = \frac{1}{2}\Sigma_{ij} w_{ij}(\vec{x}_i - \vec{x}_j)(\vec{x}_i - \vec{x}_j)^t$ and $S^w = \frac{1}{2}\Sigma_{ij} w_{ij}(\vec{x}_i - \vec{x}_j)(\vec{x}_i - \vec{x}_j)^t$, where the operator $\vec{x}^t$ refers to the transpose of the vector $\vec{x}$. Two weights, namely w_{ij} and b_{ij}, are expected to describe the connectivity between two data points $\vec{x}_i$ and $\vec{x}_j$, which formulate the within/between-class affinity graphs. Such subtleties could be well captured by connecting a limited number of neighbors. This can be realized by setting w_{ij} and b_{ij} as 1 if $\vec{x}_i / \vec{x}_j$ is one of nearest neighbors of $\vec{x}_j / \vec{x}_i$, which results in two scatter matrices S^w_M and S^b_M [11].

In the view of Bayesian interference, the theoretical assumption of this regularization term is that the each row vector of the projection matrix T conform to a multivariate Gaussian distribution with the identity covariance matrix whose variance is controlled by the smoothness parameter α. Observing these facts, we investigate the manifold regularizer to model the subtleties and protrusions over the entire training sets regardless of the speaker identity. This means that the inherent data structures of TDOA features are expected to be explored. The calculation of this regularizer is similar with that of within-class scatter matrix (Eq. 3.1). Symbolized by R_M, the regularizer is derived by $R_M = \frac{1}{2}\sum_{ij} r_{ij}(\vec{x}_i - \vec{x}_j)(\vec{x}_i - \vec{x}_j)^t$. If $\vec{x}_i$ and $\vec{x}_j$ are neighbors, r_{ij} is set as 1, otherwise 0.

3.2   Compared Dimensionality Reduction Algorithms

Since we have reviewed several ways of estimating between-class scatter matrix, within-class scatter matrix, and the regularizer with different interpretations on the TDOA feature space, we compare several ways of derivation T of by defining S^b, S^w and R: LDA with L2-norm regularization, LDA with manifold regularization, LDA without regularization, manifold dimensionality reduction with L2-norm regularization, manifold dimensionality reduction without regularization.

4   Experimental Setup

Our data contain 50 different speakers. The evaluation method is the average pair-wise identification error rate of all possible pairs of speakers. There are in total 5000 samples segmented from the recorded speech signals, in which each speaker (class) has the same number of points. We choose 3000, 1000, and 1000 samples consisting of the training, developing, and testing sets: the projection T is trained by the training samples and the relevant parameters (e.g. the size of neighbors and the smoothing parameters) are tuned by the samples from the developing set. The performance is mainly measured by the average identification error rate for all pairs of speakers.

5   Experimental Results and Discussions

5.1   Experimental Design

To answer two research questions raised in the first section of this paper, we design two experiments. One is to explore the relationship between the identification rate and the number of used microphones. To realize this, we randomly select N; $8 < N \leq 64$ microphones and evaluate the performance of using the TDOA features solely and TDOA+MFCC features. We repeat these two steps 10 times for each possible N and compute the average rate. The other experiment is to explore whether the dimensionality reduction on the large-scale TDOA features is indispensable. Moreover, we compare the approaches mentioned in Section 3.3 to investigate the best way to exploit the structural information of TDOA feature space among these methods.

5.2 Relationship between the Number of Microphones and Speaker Identification Rate (Error Rate)

To find out the relationship between N and the identification rate, we compare the average error rate using different numbers of microphones from 9 to 64 Fig. 2 shows the result. Obviously, the performance in both cases (TDOA only and TDOA+MFCC) is approximately enhanced when N goes larger, which definitely indicates that adopting more distant microphones benefits the speaker identification. Moreover, the improvement in both cases strongly suggests that additional discriminative power from spatial information with more microphones is also helpful to the system with acoustic features.

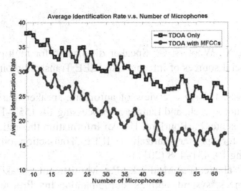

Fig. 2. Performance using different numbers of microphones based on TDOA and features merged by TDOA and MFCCs

Table 1. Performance comparison among five approaches

Methods	Error Rate
No Dim-Reduction	18.4%
LDA without Regu.	17.0%
LDA with L2-Norm Regu.	16.6%
LDA with Manifold Regu.	16.3%
Manifold Dim-Reduction without Regu.	15.2%
Manifold Dim-Reduction with L2 Norm Regu.	15.3%

5.3 Dimensionality Reduction of TDOA Feature Space

As mentioned in Section 3.3, several dimensionality reduction algorithms are evaluated with 64-microphone TDOA features. Since in the previous experiment we found that the merged feature vector outperforms the TDOA feature vector, in this part, we compare the different reduction algorithms by combining the reduced features and MFCCs, which yields the results shown in Table 1.

6   Conclusions and Future Works

In this paper, we designed a novel experiment which collected the data from (up to) 64 distant microphones, which makes it possible to answer several meaningful research questions about MDM-based speaker classification, as an important component of speaker diarization. In the near future, we will design and experiment the evaluation of the large-scale distant microphone system on the speaker diarization system.

Acknowledgements. Thanks to NSFC (61105017) agency for funding.

References

1. Pardo, J., Anguera, X., Wooters, C.: Speaker diarization for multiple-distant microphone meetings using several sources of information. IEEE Transaction on Computers 56, 1212–1224 (2007)
2. Tranter, S., Reynolds, D.: An overview of automatic speaker diarization systems. IEEE Transaction on Audio, Speech, and Language Processing 14, 1557–1565 (2006)
3. Vijayasenan, D., Valente, F., Bourlard, H.: An information theoretic combination of mfcc and tdoa features for speaker diarization. IEEE Transaction on Audio, Speech, and Language Processing 19, 431–438 (2011)
4. Vijayasenan, D., Valente, F., Motlicek, P.: Multistream speaker diarisation through information bottleneck system outputs combination. In: Proceeding of International Conference of Acoustics, Speech and Signal Processing, pp. 4420–4423 (2011)
5. Vijayasenan, D., Valente, F., Bourlard, H.: Multistream speaker diarization of meetings recordings beyond mfcc and tdoa features. Speech Communication 54, 55–67 (2012)
6. Evans, N., Fredouille, C., Bonastre, J.: Speaker diarization using unsupervised discriminant analysis of interchannel delay features. In: Proceeding of International Conference of Acoustics, Speech and Signal Processing, pp. 4601–4604 (2009)
7. Yan, S., Xu, D., Zhang, B., Zhang, H.J., Yang, Q., Lin, S.: Graph embedding and extension: A general framework for dimensionality reduction. IEEE Transaction on Pattern Analysis and Machine Intelligence 29, 40–51 (2007)
8. Anguera, X., Wooters, C., Hernando, J.: Speaker diarization for multi-party meetings using acoustic fusion. In: 2005 IEEE Workshop on Automatic Speech Recognition and Understanding, pp. 426–431. IEEE (2005)
9. Niyogi, X.: Locality preserving projections. In: Neural Information Processing Systems, vol. 16, p. 153 (2004)
10. Fisher, R.A.: The use of multiple measurements in taxonomic problems. Annals of Eugenics 7, 179–188 (1936)
11. Chen, H.T., Chang, H.W., Liu, T.L.: Local discriminant embedding and its variants. In: Computer Vision and Pattern Recognition, vol. 2, pp. 846–853 (2005)

Virtual and Augmented Environments

An Indoor Navigation System Using Signpost Metaphor for Smartphone Environments

Daiki Aono[1] and Makio Ishihara[2]

[1] Graduate School of Computer Science and Engineering, Fukuoka Institute of Technology,
3-30-1 Wajiro-higashi, Higashi-ku, Fukuoka, 811-0295, Japan
mfm13001@bene.fit.ac.jp
[2] Fukuoka Institute of Technology, 3-30-1 Wajiro-higashi, Higashi-ku, Fukuoka,
811-0295, Japan
m-ishihara@fit.ac.jp

Abstract. This manuscript introduces an indoor navigation system that uses signpost metaphor. A signpost is usually installed at each fork of a path and tells people which fork they should take. Our system locates the user's position by reading visual markers, which represent signposts. After that, it retrieves floor maps from the database and allows the user to turn around seeing labels from the perspective of the user's position, which are overlaid on the real world. It also navigates the user's way not only at the signpost but also between signposts by allowing the user to move around in the corresponding virtual world. From an experiment in usability, our system demonstrated good results for indoor navigation.

Keywords: Indoor navigation, signpost metaphor, augmented reality, virtual reality.

1 Introduction

In recent years, there have been various navigation applications or just apps available for smartphone environments. For example, Google Maps and NAVITIME are popular Android apps. Navigation apps are generally designed for outdoor use because the global positioning system or GPS is available to help them locate the user's position. In contrast, indoor navigation is still challenging due to the lack of ways to locate the user's position in buildings. Recently, various researches about indoor navigation are reported. For example, T. Matuszka[1] built an indoor navigation system using augmented reality or AR and a pedometer. This system locates the user's position using by their step counts and it works well in small areas. The accuracy however becomes worse when it works in larger areas. M. Kanbara[2] built an indoor navigation system that locates the user's position using invisible markers. This system has an infrared camera that captures the ceiling. Invisible markers are stuck on the ceiling and they are read by that camera then the system locates the user's position. The problem with this system is to need to stick more invisible markers in larger areas. This manuscript takes an approach of using signpost metaphor for indoor navigation to work in large areas.

C. Stephanidis (Ed.): HCII 2014 Posters, Part I, CCIS 434, pp. 559–562, 2014.

2   Signpost metaphor

To locate the user's position in buildings, our app uses the metaphor of signposts. A signpost is usually installed at each fork of a path and tells people which fork they should take. Our app performs a series of signposts to navigate the user's way through buildings.   Fig. 1(A) shows a signpost. In our app, a signpost is represented by a visual marker as shown in Fig. 1(B).

(A) A signpost in Fukuoka Institute of Technology   (B) A visual marker representing a signpost

Fig. 1. Signpost metaphor

3   An Indoor Navigation System using Signpost Metaphor

3.1   Outline

Multiple visual markers are stuck point by point in the building and each of them has an identification number indicating its own position. The user puts his/her smartphone's camera over the maker to capture it and then our app locates the user's position by decoding its identification number. After that our app retrieves floor maps from the database and allows the user to turn around seeing labels from the perspective of the user's position, which are overlaid on the real world. The user's facing direction is tracked by the built-in compass. Fig. 2 shows a screenshot of our app.

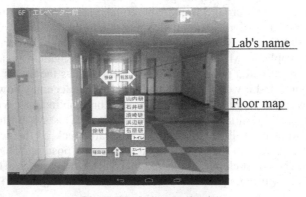

Fig. 2. Our indoor navigation

Our app navigates the user's way not only at the signpost but also between sign-posts by allowing the user to move around in the corresponding virtual world as shown in Fig. 3. The user goes forward/backward in the virtual world by moving his/her finger up/down on the touch screen.

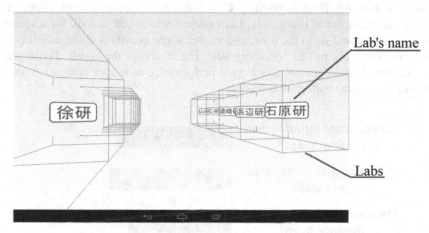

Fig. 3. The virtual world for between-signposts navigation

3.2   Switching between AR Mode and VR Mode

This system has two modes. One is AR mode and the other is VR mode. The system in Fig. 2 is in AR mode and the one in Fig. 3 is in VR mode. When the system starts, it is in AR mode. If the user lowers down and holds the smartphone, the system switches from AR mode to VR mode, and the system switches back to AR mode if the user raises up and holds the smartphone. Fig. 4 shows these two modes and transitions between them.

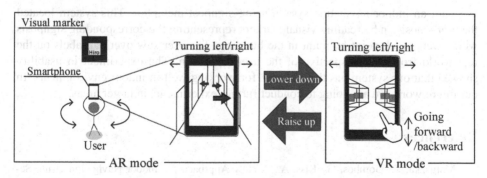

Fig. 4. AR mode and VR mode

4   Usability

We conducted an experiment in performance. Subject were nine people with the ages of 21~23. They had an experience of using smartphones. They used our indoor navigation system on 6th floor in building C of Fukuoka Institute of Technology. Two visual marker were set at two points. Each subject was asked to look for a specified professor's office and go to the door, and answer some questions about usability on a scale from 1(strongly no) to 5(strongly yes). Fig. 5 shows the result. These graphs show that our system demonstrates a good performance in indoor navigation and the basic idea of signpost metaphor is feasible.

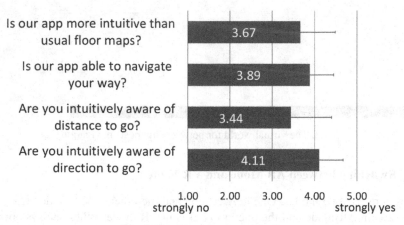

Fig. 5. Results of the experiment

5   Conclusions

We built an indoor navigation system using signpost metaphor. This system located the user's position by reading visual markers representing the corresponding signposts which were stuck point by point in the building. The user saw overlaid labels on the real world from the perspective of the user's position. The experiment in usability showed that our system has the potential for working well in indoor environments. In our future work, we are going to conduct further experiments in larger areas.

References

1. Matuszka, T., Gombos, G., Kiss, A.: A New Approach for Indoor Navigation Using Semantic Webtechnologies and Augmented Reality. In: Shumaker, R. (ed.) VAMR 2013, Part I. LNCS, vol. 8021, pp. 202–210. Springer, Heidelberg (2013)
2. Kanbara, M., Nagamatsu, A., Yokoya, N.: User Localization with Invisible Marker for Large Indoor Area and Its Applications, IEICE Technical Report, MVE2009-54 (2009-2010)

Validity of Driving Simulator for Agent-Human Interaction

Yutao Ba, Wei Zhang, and Gavriel Salvendy

Department of Industrial Engineering, Tsinghua University, Beijing, 100084, China
bb0438@163.com, zhangwei@tsinghua.edu.cn, salvendy@purdue.edu

Abstract. Drivers of intelligent agent in the virtual environment offer researchers a great opportunity to study interaction between drivers in the safe, controlled, replicable and low-cost simulator environment. However, the validation for the effectiveness of agent drivers upon human drivers is required. The present study aimed to evaluate the validity of agent-human interaction in a simulator, compared with human-human interaction on real roads. 20 male participants were recruited to watch eight scenarios concerning interactive driving behaviors and signal usage, which were presented in the forms of both realistic films with human drivers and virtual graphic scenes with agent drivers. Participants' attitude, emotions and visual attention were recorded. The relative validity was established for all measurements. This result suggested that medium fidelity simulator with agent drivers could provide the effective values to evaluate the human-human interaction mirrored these values obtained on real road.

Keywords: validity, intelligent agent, driving simulator, vehicle signals.

1   Introduction

1.1   Agent-Human Interaction in Driving Simulator

From the last decade, intelligent agents with autonomous behaviors have received large amounts of interest in various research areas (Bonabeau 2002). Concerning driving safety research, agent-based drivers in the virtual environment could simulate the driving behaviors (e.g. following, merging or overtaking) as human drivers conduct on the real roads (Ehlert and Rothkrantz 2001, Bonabeau 2002, Doniec *et al.* 2008). This advantage provides researchers a great opportunity to study the effect of other vehicles on the driver's visual perception, cognitive process and according behaviors in the safe, controlled, replicable and low-cost simulator environment. However, a key component of requirements for such agent-human interaction study is the validation for the effect of agents upon human (Hudlicka 2003). In other words, does a driver feel real while interacting with agent drivers in the specific virtual scenarios, in comparing with his/her daily driving surrounded by other human drivers?

C. Stephanidis (Ed.): HCII 2014 Posters, Part I, CCIS 434, pp. 563–569, 2014.
© Springer International Publishing Switzerland 2014

1.2   Validity of Driving Simulator

The previous validation studies concerning driving simulators proposed two levels of validity: physical validity and behavioral validity (Blaauw 1982, Yan et al. 2008, Wang et al. 2010). Physical validity refers to the physical correspondence of the simulator's components, layout, and dynamics with its real world counterpart. Therefore, a moving-base, high-fidelity driving simulator was often assumed to have greater physical validity than a fixed-base, low-fidelity simulator. Behavioral validity refers to the consistency of drivers' responses in simulator and it on real roads. No level of physical validity is useful to human factors research if behavioral validity cannot be established. Absolute behavioral validity is established when the numerical values in simulator and on road are basically the same. Relative behavioral validity requires that the effects of controlled factors are of the same direction and with similar magnitude (or significance) in the two test environments. The relative behavioral validity is the minimum requirement for simulator to reflect the actual response in realistic driving.

As a part of research of driver-driver interaction (Ba and Zhang 2012, Ba et al. 2013), the primary purpose of the present study was to validate the agent-human interaction in specific driving scenarios with communicational signals (e.g. hazard lights, turn signals and horn). The drivers' attitude, emotions and visual attention were measured to evaluate the effects of signals on drivers' cognitive states and visual perception. To compare the difference of these effects in stimulator and on the real road, two types of stimuli were presented: realistic films with human drivers and virtual graphic scenes with agent drivers.

2   Methodology

2.1   Participants

Twenty male drivers (from 20 to 29 years old) were recruited from a university population thorough campus Online Bulletin Board. All participants were required to have a minimum of three years of active driving experience and more than 20,000 kilometers' total driving distance. Participants were required to sign an institutionally approved informed consent form before experiment and were provided with RMB 100 Yuan (about 15 U.S. dollars) after experiment.

2.2   Film of Human Drivers and Medium Fidelity Graphic Scene of Agent Drivers

Consistent with the task protocol proposed in previous study (Ba et al. 2013), this experiment contained eight common scenarios that subject interacted with another vehicle, labeled as signaling vehicle: 1) signaling vehicle in front is parked (Hazard Lights); 2) signaling vehicle in front is traveling at low speed (Hazard Lights); 3) signaling vehicle in front is staring and intending to enter the subject's lane (Turn Signal); 4) signaling vehicle in front is stopping into the park lane (Turn Signal);

5) signaling vehicle behind is moving left to overtake subject's vehicle (Turn Signal); 6) signaling vehicle is merging from left lane (Turn Signal); 7) Signaling vehicle is overtaking after subject's vehicle yield the way (Horn); 8) Signaling vehicle is requesting   subject vehicle to move out of the way (Horn).

Each scenario included two paired scenes, signal-use scene and none-signal scene. In none-signal scene, signaling vehicle conducted the same behaviors as it did in the paired signal-use scenes, e.g. signaling vehicle was parked with hazards lights in signal-use scene versus signaling vehicle was parked without any signal in none-signal scene. To validate the agent-human interaction in simulator, each scene was presented in two types of stimuli, realistic film with human driver and medium fidelity graph with agent driver (Fig. 1). Thus, eight scenarios totally included 32 scenes (8 human signal-use, 8 agent signal-use, 8 human non-signal and 8 agent non-signal).

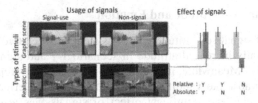

Fig. 1. Illustration of independent variables and establishment of validity

2.3   Measurements

Participant's attitude towards the signaling vehicle was measured by a validated five-point scale based on the Theory of Planned Behavior. A five-point version Self Assessment Manikin was used to measure drivers' emotion states, which included three independent dimensions: pleasure, arousal and dominance. Participants' visual attention towards the signaling vehicle was measured via a SMI IVIEM XTM head-mounted gaze tracker. The fixation was defined as the duration (longer than 80ms) of continuous gaze points on the signaling vehicle.

2.4   Procedure

During the experiment, participant was settled in the driver's seat of a fixed-base simulator. Eye tracker was then calibrated following the manufacturer's instructions. All 32 scenes were presented in the flat screen in front of simulator (3.2×2.5m, 3m from driver's seat) with different random sequences for each participant. During watching, participants' fixations were recorded by eye tracking system. After each scene, there was a short break to let participant rate attitude and emotion.

3   Analysis and Results

3.1   Statistic Methods

Two independent variables were signals (signal-use vs. non-signal) and stimuli types. Dependent variables included attitude, emotion states (pleasure, arousal and dominance) and visual attention (total fixation time, fixation duration and fixation frequency). Repeated-measure General Linear Model was applied to test the validity of agent drivers' effect in simulator. When the main effect of signals was in the same direction with significance for both stimuli types, the relative validity was established. When relative validity was established and no significant main effect of stimuli types was reported, the absolute validity established (illustrated in Fig. 1). The results for all independent variables of eight scenarios are showed in Table 2.

3.2   Cognitive states - Attitude and Emotion

The main effects of signals on attitude was consistent between two stimuli types in all scenarios, significantly increased attitude in scenario 1-7 and significantly decreased attitude in scenario 8. Meanwhile, no significant difference was reported between two stimuli types. Thus absolute validity was established for the effect of agent drivers' signals on the attitude. The significant effect of signals was also demonstrated for pleasure and arousal in all scenarios and the direction of effect was consistent for both stimuli types. Signals significantly increased pleasure in scenario 1-7 and significantly decrease attitude in scenario 8. Arousal was increased in all scenarios. However, the significant main effect of stimuli types was reported in scenarios 4, 5, 6 and 7 for pleasure, and in scenario 3, 4, 5, 6 and 7 for arousal. Thus, only relative validity established for the effect of agent drivers' signals on pleasure and arousal. As to the emotional dimension of dominance, the main effect of signals was not statistically distinguishable in scenario 1, 2, 3, 7 and 8. The definition of validity could be not suitable for these cases. Therefore, we only analyzed the validity in scenario 5 and 6. The signals in realistic films significantly decreased the dominance in scenario 5 and 6. The notable reduction also reported for graphic stimuli. Because of the main effect of stimuli types, only relative validity was established for the effect of agent drivers' signals on dominance.

Table 1. Significance of main effects and validity

Scenarios	Effects of signals in realistic films ($F_{1,19}$)						
	AT	PL	AR	DO	FT	FD	FF
1	35.35**	14.65**	21.53**	2.51	18.31**	10.85**	0.37
2	63.38**	36.65**	7.86*	1.18	35.11**	14.78**	1.05
3	68.26**	57.28**	5.54*	2.88	44.87**	19.55**	1.12
4	24.56**	46.54**	4.65*	3.61	48.98**	8.15*	0.89
5	53.24**	37.16**	6.07*	6.89*	33.29**	23.51**	6.39*
6	61.54**	48.55**	4.55*	11.60**	8.93**	9.55**	8.19*
7	16.87**	11.23**	23.11**	2.55	17.54**	19.55**	8.14*
8	9.53**	8.99**	16.53*	3.59	8.03*	4.65*	11.05**

Table 1. (*continued*)

	AT	PL	AR	DO	FT	FD	FF
Effects of signals in graphic scenes ($F_{1,19}$)							
1	48.45**	16.78**	18.48**	1.15	16.53**	12.55**	0.56
2	71.21**	34.12**	7.51**	3.14	6.14*	11.23**	0.08
3	74.55**	81.55**	5.65**	3.58	5.51*	16.52**	0.32
4	53.21**	31.94**	6.77*	4.89*	4.43*	9.15**	0.12
5	61.81**	45.94**	6.68*	7.11*	5.14*	11.25**	4.34*
6	71.58**	39.65**	7.74*	6.68*	9.55**	13.54*	5.56*
7	18.55**	18.15**	11.15*	3.11	69.66**	48.21*	3.48*
8	9.87**	8.18**	13.58*	0.85	11.59**	17.56*	5.52*
Effect of stimuli types ($F_{1,19}$)							
1	2.67	0.42	1.91	2.88	15.85**	2.53	0.12
2	1.13	0.04	0.59	6.89*	25.13**	0.72	4.89*
3	2.63	0.89	6.38*	8.04*	43.65**	4.15*	9.15**
4	1.85	3.74*	5.81*	2.54	38.77**	2.17	6.75*
5	3.42	7.16*	6.29*	5.45*	38.12**	0.21	8.95**
6	2.32	6.45*	5.95*	6.55*	5.57*	0.84	1.26
7	1.14	7.86*	4.48*	3.31*	45.55**	9.54**	1.35
8	0.77	1.55	3.21	2.55	4.15*	0.35	9.68**
Validity(Relative/Absolute)							
1	Y/Y	Y/Y	Y/Y	-	Y/N	Y/Y	-
2	Y/Y	Y/Y	Y/Y	-	Y/N	Y/Y	-
3	Y/Y	Y/Y	Y/N	-	Y/N	Y/N	-
4	Y/Y	Y/N	Y/N	-	Y/N	Y/Y	-
5	Y/Y	Y/N	Y/N	Y/N	Y/N	Y/Y	Y/N
6	Y/Y	Y/N	Y/N	Y/N	Y/N	Y/Y	Y/Y
7	Y/Y	Y/N	Y/N	-	Y/N	Y/N	Y/Y
8	Y/Y	Y/Y	Y/Y	-	Y/N	Y/Y	Y/N

AT-attitude, PL-pleasure, AR-arousal, DO-dominance, FT-total fixation time, FD-fixation duration, FF-fixation frequency. * $p<0.05$, ** $p<0.01$

3.3   Visual Attention- Fixation Time, Fixation duration and Fixation Frequency

The signals of both stimuli types significantly increased participants' total fixation time towards the signaling vehicle in all scenarios. However, the significant difference was reported between two stimuli types in all scenarios. Thus the relative validity was obtained for the effect of agent drivers' signals on the total fixation time. As to the fixation duration, the signals of both stimuli types significantly increased participants' fixation duration in all scenarios. The significant main effect of stimuli types was obtained in scenario 3 and 7. This indicated that only relative validity established for upon fixation duration. When considering the fixation frequency, it should be emphasized that the significant difference between non-signal scenes and signal-use scenes only established in scenario 5, 6, 7 and 8, where the signaling vehicles appeared in the region out of the road ahead. Among these scenarios, significant difference between two stimuli types was demonstrated in scenario 5 and 8. Thus, we only achieved the relative validity for the effect of agent drivers' signals on the fixation frequency.

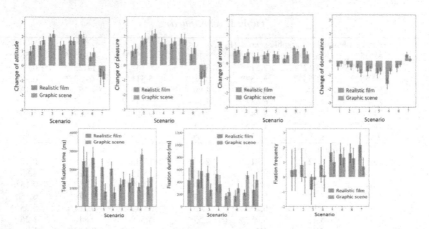

Fig. 2. Effect of signals upon independent variables (Mean±SD) across two stimuli types

4   Discussion and Conclusion

In summary, the relative validity was obtained for all of selected measurements. As to the variable of attitude, we can even achieve the absolute validity for the graphic stimuli of agent drivers. Although the significant difference between two proposed stimuli types existed for the variables of emotional states and visual attention .These gaps did not harm the change tendency of these variables induced by signals. Therefore, agent-human interaction with signals in driving simulator could produce the validated effects on participants' cognitive state and visual perception as it in the situation of human-human interaction on real roads.

Reference

1. Ba, Y., Zhang, W.: An empirical approach for driver-driver interaction study: Attributes, influence factors and framework. Advances in Usability Evaluation, 404 (2012)
2. Ba, Y., Zhang, W., Yang, Y., Salvendy, G.: Interpersonal signal processing during interactive driving scenarios. Working paper (2013)
3. Blaauw, G.J.: Driving experience and task demands in simulator and instrumented car: A validation study. Human Factors: The Journal of the Human Factors and Ergonomics Society 24(4), 473–486 (1982)
4. Bonabeau, E.: Agent-based modeling: Methods and techniques for simulating human systems. Proceedings of the National Academy of Sciences of the United States of America 99(3), 7280–7287 (2002)
5. Doniec, A., Mandiau, R., Piechowiak, S., Espié, S.: A behavioral multi-agent model for road traffic simulation. Engineering Applications of Artificial Intelligence 21(8), 1443–1454 (2008)
6. Ehlert, P.A., Rothkrantz, L.J.: Microscopic traffic simulation with reactive driving agents. In: Proceedings of the Intelligent Transportation Systems, pp. 860–865. IEEE (2001)

7. Hudlicka, E.: To feel or not to feel: The role of affect in human–computer interaction. International Journal of Human-Computer Studies 59(1), 1–32 (2003)
8. Wang, Y., Mehler, B., Reimer, B., Lammers, V., D'Ambrosio, L.A., Coughlin, J.F.: The validity of driving simulation for assessing differences between in-vehicle informational interfaces: A comparison with field testing. Ergonomics 53(3), 404–420 (2010)
9. Yan, X., Abdel-Aty, M., Radwan, E., Wang, X., Chilakapati, P.: Validating a driving simulator using surrogate safety measures. Accident Analysis & Prevention 40(1), 274–288 (2008)

CamouFAB: Real-Time Generation of Camouflage Pattern Using Optic Fiber Display

Woon Jung Cho[1], Jin-Hee Yang[2], Hannah Kim[1], Dong-Hyun Kang[3], Min Sun Kim[1],
Ja Hyung Lee[1], Yong-Jun Kim[3], Joo-Hyeon Lee[2], and Kwanghee Han[1,*]

[1] Cognitive Engineering Lab. Department of Psychology, Yonsei University, Korea
{Chrischo,khan}@yonsei.ac.kr, trinityhkim@gmail.com,
kimmin0414@hanmail.net, 4585452@naver.com
[2] Department of Clothing & Textile, Yonsei University, Korea
{sjinnie7,ljhyeon}@yonsei.ac.kr
[3] Department of Mechanical Engineering, Yonsei University, Korea
{kangtong13,yjk}@yonsei.ac.kr

Abstract. This study attempted to develop CamouFAB, which uses flexible plastic optic fiber (POF) to display camouflage patterns. Previously developed CamouLED system which uses light emitting diodes (LED) array to present camouflage patterns has limitations in that it is inflexible thus is difficult to be applied to combat uniforms. This study shows a further research to expand the CamouLED system to development of a new military uniform, using photonic technology which can change its color according to background. Like CamouLED, a camera receives background image and camouflage patterns are generated by the real-time patterning program. The generated patterns are then displayed on an 8 x 8 optic fiber display instead of LED display. An 8 x 8 flexible optic fiber patch was made by embroidered fabric with high luminance and controlling module was connected to each pixel of optic fiber bundle. This study concludes with an implication that the use of flexible POFs instead of an LED display would broaden the system's application and use.

Keywords: active camouflage, flexible plastic optic fiber, camouflage patterning algorithm, adaptive pattern, real-time patterning.

1 Introduction

Active camouflage and adaptive camouflage are camouflage technologies which can blend an object into its surroundings with panels or coatings which are able to alter their appearance, color, luminance and reflective properties. Active camouflage has been anticipated to have the potential to reach perfect concealment in visual detection [1]. In addition to military strategies and weapons, new combat uniforms which have efficient camouflage ability are needed in today's combats. To respond to these needs, we previously developed CamouLED, a real-time patterning technique [2].

* Corresponding author.

C. Stephanidis (Ed.): HCII 2014 Posters, Part I, CCIS 434, pp. 570–573, 2014.

CamouLED is a new technique which uses a light emitting diodes (LED) array to present patterns generated by real-time pixel-maker program. The input backgrounds are read by a CMOS sensor type camera and the output patterns are extracted and presented on an 8 x 8 LED array. The patterning algorithm processes images received by the camera and then these signals are converted into analog ones, which are sent over to an LED controlling module [3].

Although these new strategies fit well to the concept and definition of active camouflage, CamouLED was not enough for a perfect concealment or camouflage for combat uniforms. The current study developed a system called CamouFAB, which used optic fiber to improve the real-time generation of camouflage patterns. With photonic technology able to change uniform's colors along with the background, we developed a new type of military uniform.

2 Development of Flexible Plastic Optic Fiber Patch

Previously, we developed a prototype of photonic clothing which changes color using optic fiber [4]. In this prototype, three colors, red, green, and blue, were included and only one color could be displayed at a time (Fig. 1). Photonic clothing is a smart clothing within which various kinds of digital devices and functions could be contained for prospective everyday life [5].

Fig. 1. A sample of the previously developed photonic clothing [4]

From this point, we reached to the idea that when photonic clothing made of optic fibers and CamouLED are combined, the concept of chameleonic military uniform that can dynamically change its colors will be available. To achieve this, firstly we developed flexible optic fiber using embroidery method which has higher luminance than weaving method. The structure of optic fiber display patch is based on the previous research [5]. It compared luminance of four fabric display structures which have different light transmitting paths and directions that attempted to optimize expression of red, green and blue colors. Unilateral II embroidery fabric structure showed higher luminance. Thus it was chosen to develop optical fiber patch display (Fig. 2), which actively changes its color reflecting the properties of surrounding environment (Fig. 3).

Fig. 2. A sample of an 8 x 8 flexible plastic optic fiber patch

Fig. 3. A sample of flexible plastic optic fiber display (color off)

3   CamouFAB: Replacing LED Display with Flexible Plastic Optic Fiber Display

Identical with CamouLED, as an input device, CamouFAB uses a CMOS camera to read the background scene [3]. Once an image is received through the camera via a CCD image sensor, it is processed by the real-time pixel-maker program. The program contains two types of strategies, color combination strategy (Average, Main, Mosaic) and pattern arrangement strategies (Arranged, Random) which can be combined to make six pattern strategies. The program also includes pattern strategy preset and parameter (target size, array size, number of colors, seed size, threshold)

Fig. 4. A developed sample of flexible plastic optic fiber display (color on)

control functions. Thus once an image is loaded and the pattern strategy is selected, the program extracts colors to be used for camouflage according to the selected strategy and creates a digital pattern [2, 3].

However, there are two changes which differentiate CamouFAB from CamouLED. First, the processed digital signal is converted into an analog signal and is instead sent over to an 8 x 8 optic fiber patch display. Second, in the previous CamouLED system, one pixel was mapped to one light source. However, in the current CamouFAB system, one pixel is made of several optic fiber bundles. In order to display the camouflage pattern on the optic fiber patch, the connection between the controlling module and the bundle was shortened as much as possible.

4 Conclusion

This study applied the previously developed real-time patterning system, CamouLED to the concept of combat uniform that uses an optic fiber patch display. Future researches are needed to improve fine details of the CamouFAB system, specifically the patterning algorithm and the controlling module for more effective adaptive camouflage.

Acknowledgement. This work has been supported by the Low Observable Technology Research Center program of Defense Acquisition Administration and Agency for Defense Development.

References

1. Adventure and Surplus. Active Camouflage
2. http://www.surplusandadventure.com/shop/home/product-information/camouflage/active-camouflage.html
3. Cho, W.J., Ahn, W., Kim, M.S., Park, J., Kim, S., Han, K.-H.: Making pixel patterns automatically for camouflage – using color information from their background. In: Stephanidis, C. (ed.) Posters, Part II, HCII 2011. CCIS, vol. 174, pp. 98–101. Springer, Heidelberg (2011)
4. Cho, W.J., Seo, H.-K., Kim, H., Lee, J., Kang, D.-H., Kim, M.-K., Han, K.-H.: CamouLED: Real-time generation of pixel pattern for camouflage. In: Stephanidis, C. (ed.) HCII 2013, Part II. CCIS, vol. 374, pp. 699–703. Springer, Heidelberg (2013)
5. Cho, W.J., Jung, D.H., Tae, E., Hyun, J., Kim, S.H., Han, K.H.: Does changing colors in the cloth affect emotions? In: 6th International Conference of Cognitive Science Effects of Changing Color on Emotion, Focusing on Photonic Clothing (2008)
6. Yang, J.H., Cho, H.S., Park, S.H., Lee, J.H.: A Study on the Luminescence effects of POF-woven Fabric Display by Method of Weaving. Korean Journal of the Science of Emotion and Sensibility 16(4), 517–526 (2013)

Robust Real-Time Shadows
for Dynamic 3D Scenes on the Web

Tim Nicolas Eicke[1], Yvonne Jung[2], and Arjan Kuijper[1,3]

[1] Technische Universität Darmstadt, Germany
[2] University of Applied Sciences Fulda, Germany
[3] Fraunhofer IGD, Darmstadt, Germany

Abstract. The authentic display of shadows by modern video games has long become a matter of course. On the web however, this is somewhat different: the rendering of three dimensional scenes in the browser has only in recent years been on the rise. At best, shadows have only played a minor part in that development, despite their importance regarding recognition of spacial relationships in human vision and general increase of a scene's authenticity. An important part in the development of web-based 3D is played by the open-source JavaScript framework X3DOM, as it provides an approach for the integration of declarative 3D in HTML5. However the framework too only offers rudimentary shadow rendering techniques that hardly meet today's demands. This work tackles this issue by first examining existing shadow mapping techniques for their suitability in the web context and based on that developing and implementing a concept for the enhancement of shadow display in X3DOM.

1   Motivation

The presentation of interactive 3D scenes on the Web was the first widespread development of WebGL. The reason for this is that WebGL enables the representation of such scenes without having to make special demands on the hardware and software configuration of a terminal. Such created 3D scenes can thus be represented both on smartphones, tablets or desktop PC with the use of conventional browsers. Plug-ins or other additional software need not be installed. Based on this technology, the in JavaScript implemented, open-source framework X3DOM [1] provides declarative 3D in HTML5. Analogous to the integration of SVG for 2D graphics, X3DOM extends in a declarative way the HTML DOM to additional (X)3D objects. Using these DOM objects a web developer can define complete 3D scenes and determine the runtime behavior, without having to resort to low-level JavaScript or WebGL programming [2].

As the X3D standard [3], X3DOM provided until now only limited opportunities to present different lighting situations. Shadows existed only in rudimentary form, although faithful representation of shadows by modern video games is standard. In addition, for the visual perception of virtual 3D scenes shadows play an important role, because they not only increase the authenticity of virtual worlds, but also help in the classification of spatial events. For this reason, we developed the concept for the integration of high-quality shadows in X3DOM in this paper. Both general shadow mapping problems, as well as Web-specific limitations are taken into account. We will also

C. Stephanidis (Ed.): HCII 2014 Posters, Part I, CCIS 434, pp. 574–578, 2014.

present the results of practical implementation. The approach is now part of X3DOM –
see `http://www.x3dom.org/` and [4]. Online demos can be seen on
`http://x3dom.org/docs/dev/tutorial/shadows.html`.

2 Background

Shadow mapping [5,6] denotes a widely used method for shadows in 3D scenes. For
each fragment it is checked whether it is visible by a light source. If this is not the case,
the corresponding fragment is shadowed. The calculation is done in two steps:

1. *Shadow pass*: The scene is rendered from the viewpoint of the light source and the
   depth information stored in a texture (*shadow map*).
2. *Shadow Rendering*: The scene is rendered from the viewpoint of the camera. The
   distance to the light with is compared the corresponding value of the shadow map
   for each fragment (*shadow test*). If the distance is greater than the value stored in
   the shadow map, the observed fragment is shadowed.

X3DOM is based on the WebGL graphics library [7]. This enables it to display
hardware-accelerated 3D graphics in the browser without any additional extensions.
Compared with the latest versions of Direct3D and OpenGL, which are mainly in focus in the development of modern shading methods, WebGL is limited. The graphics
library only supports Shader Model 2.0 and allows only the programming vertex and
fragment shaders. With WebGL only one render target can also be addressed per rendering step. To extend the functionality of WebGL, it is possible to use WebGL extensions.
However, the applicability of the extensions depends on these systems - not all WebGL
-enabled devices support all extensions. In particular, mobile devices are often limited
in this respect [8,9]. In the design and implementation of a shadowing process on the
web these limitations must therefore be considered.

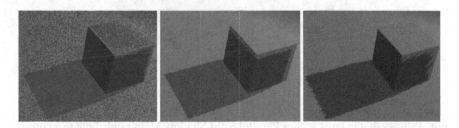

Fig. 1. Shadow-Mapping problem cases. From left to right: surface acne, light leaking, and
aliasing.

In addition to these system-specific constraints also the conceptual weaknesses of
shadow mapping are to be considered [6,10,11].
One of these vulnerabilities is known as *bias problem*: due to the shadow mapping
a larger spectrum of depth values is imaged to a single shadow map texel, the shadow

test can provide locally incorrect results. There will be shred shadow on surfaces that should be unshaded (Surface Acne, Fig. 1, left).

By summation of bias on the shadow map values this problem can be circumvented in some situations. Then however, surfaces, which should actually be completely shaded, partially lie in the light (Light Leaking, Fig. 1, middle).

Another problem concerns *aliasing*: Discretization which takes place through the projection of the scene on the shadow map can make itself felt at the shadow edges by unsightly effects levels (Fig. 1, right).

All the above artifacts should be avoided in the best possible representation of shadows.

3   Real Time Shadows in the Web Browser

We solve these problems via Variance Shadow Maps [10], where besides depth information also the square depth followed by a Gaussian filter [12] are stored. Details on the implementation can be found on http://x3dom.org/docs/dev/tutorial/shadows.html and in [4].

Parallel Split Shadow Maps (PSSM) were included to improve the shadow map sampling and thus increase the quality of shadow representation. Since this strength can be used especially in large scenes, such a scene is considered for the visual observation of the PSSM implementation (Fig. 2).

Fig. 2. PSSM Test scene from the perspective of (directional) light source

Fig. 3 shows that in large scenes Parallel Split Shadow Maps contribute to a considerable increase of the shadow quality. This scene (about 107,000 triangles) was combined with a directional light source for testing. Fig. 4 shows the results of the test series.

3.1   Comparison with *three.js*

Besides X3DOM there are plenty of other frameworks that allow the display of 3D content in a web browser using WebGL. One of the best known and most extensive alternatives here is the JavaScript library *Three.js* [13]. Compared to X3DOM this is,

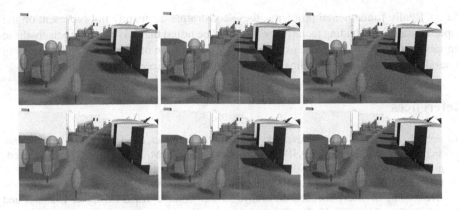

Fig. 3. PSSM results for one, three, and six cascades. Top row: unfiltered. Bottom Row: 5×5 Gauss filter.

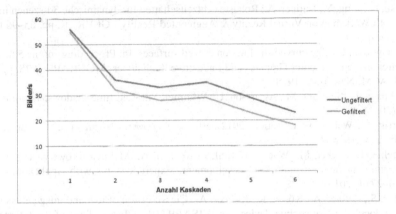

Fig. 4. Graphical representation of the frame rates with Parallel Split Shadow Maps.

however, a completely different operating concept. Instead of defining the scene – and thus the shadow behavior – *declaratively* in HTML, the scene description is given here *imperatively* using JavaScript.

4 Summary

Results show that despite the limitations, the WebGL compared to OpenGL 4.* or Di-rect3D brings high quality shadows mechanisms that are quite applicable. However, in detail some adjustments are needed. As an example, in this case the special treatment for case of lack of support floating point textures, or relatively complex analysis for point lights are mentioned. The lack of support for geometry shaders, and the fact that only one render target per render step may be addressed, leads in some cases to the fact that only the most naive and with regard to the performance least favorable cal-culation technique can be applied (eg in the implementation of parallel Split Shadow

Maps). Really fundamental problems, these constraints ultimately not represent on the implementation of shading techniques. It should be noted that it is due to precisely these limitations that WebGL can be used on such a wide range of platforms and systems in general - and thus have a significant contribution to the success of the technology.

References

1. Behr, J., Jung, Y., Keil, J., Drevensek, T., Eschler, P., Zöllner, M., Fellner, D.W.: A scalable architecture for the HTML5/X3D integration model X3DOM. In: Spencer, S. (ed.) Proceedings Web3D 2010, pp. 185–193. ACM Press, New York (2010)
2. Limper, M., Jung, Y., Behr, J., Sturm, T., Franke, T., Schwenk, K., Kuijper, A.: Fast, progressive loading of binary-encoded declarative-3d web content. IEEE Computer Graphics and Applications 33(5), 26–36 (2013)
3. Web3D Consortium: Extensible 3d, X3D (2011), http://www.web3d.org/x3d/specifications/
4. Eicke, N., Jung, Y., Kuijper, A.: Robuste echtzeitschatten für dynamische 3d-szenen im web. In: 10th Workshop on Virtual Reality & Augmented Reality - GI VRAR, pp. 85–96 (2013) (in German)
5. Williams, L.: Casting curved shadows on curved surfaces. In: Proceedings of the 5th Annual Conference on Computer Graphics and Interactive Techniques, SIGGRAPH 1978, pp. 270–274. ACM, New York (1978)
6. Eisemann, E., Schwarz, M., Assarsson, U., Wimmer, M.: Real-time shadows. Taylor & Francis (2011)
7. Marrin, C.: WebGL specification (2012), https://www.khronos.org/registry/webgl/specs/latest/
8. Engelke, T., Becker, M., Wuest, H., Keil, J., Kuijper, A.: Mobilear browser - a generic architecture for rapid ar-multi-level development. Expert Systems with Applications 40(7), 2704–2714 (2013)
9. Ettl, A.S., Zeilner, A., Köster, R., Kuijper, A.: Classification of text and image areas in digitized documents for mobile devices. In: VISAPP 2013 - Proceedings of the International Conference on Computer Vision Theory and Applications, Barcelona, Spain, February 21-24, vol. 2, pp. 88–91 (2013)
10. Donnelly, W., Lauritzen, A.: Variance shadow maps. In: Proceedings of the 2006 Symposium on Interactive 3D Graphics and Games, I3D 2006, pp. 161–165. ACM, New York (2006)
11. Zhang, F., Sun, H., Xu, L., Lun, L.K.: Parallel-split shadow maps for large-scale virtual environments. In: Proceedings of the 2006 ACM International Conference on Virtual Reality Continuum and its Applications VRCIA 2006, pp. 311–318. ACM, New York (2006)
12. Kuijper, A., Florack, L.M.J.: Understanding and modeling the evolution of critical points under gaussian blurring. In: Heyden, A., Sparr, G., Nielsen, M., Johansen, P. (eds.) ECCV 2002, Part I. LNCS, vol. 2350, pp. 143–157. Springer, Heidelberg (2002)
13. MrDoob: three.js, javascript 3d library (2013), http://threejs.org

An Immersive Virtual Reality Museum via Second Life

Extending Art Appreciation from 2D to 3D

Yu-Chun Huang[1] and Sooyeon Rosie Han[2]

[1] Department of Design, Tatung University, Taipei, Taiwan
ych@ttu.edu.tw
[2] College of Environment Design, University of California, Berkeley, USA
rosie.han@berkeley.edu

Abstract. This research is going to demonstrate a virtual museum via second life, the visitors can have the chance to more profoundly experience the masterpieces. By extending 2D paintings to 3D world, users can be not only more adaptively perceive the expression of painting but also intuitively interact with the 2D famous painting in 3D world. Also this kind of art appreciation can play a profound contribution to the art education especially for children. By using game-like navigation around the virtual art gallery, children can receive deeper impression and be more interested in this immersive art museum than traditional one.

Keywords: Virtual Reality, Human-Computer Interaction.

1 Introduction

In 1973, with the development of computer, the term—HCI (human-computer interaction) began to emerged into our life. HCI involving the study, planning and design of the interaction between people (users) and computers, causes great impact in different fields (Card et al., 1986). On the other hand, cyberspace, as the information space has been dubbed by William Gibson in his 1984 novel—Neuromancer (Ace Books, New York), has become accessible in the 1990s through the World Wide Web. Cyberspace has quickly become more than just another means of communication: online shopping, online education...etc have become part of our everyday lives (Kalay, 2006).

Mitchell (1995) mentioned that as our bodies morph into cyborgs, the buildings that house them are also transforming. Gradually, telecommunication systems replace circulation systems, and the digital information decomposes traditional building types. Physical world gradually merges with virtual world. Our physical living environment is evolving with the development of virtual space. Therefore virtual space has become an important issue in the end of 20th century.

The virtual space can be separated into two categories: simulation space, which is generated by computer and represented through devices like computer monitor, head-mounted display, VR cave (Iovine, 1995; Kalawsky, 1993; Mitchell, 1995); the other

C. Stephanidis (Ed.): HCII 2014 Posters, Part I, CCIS 434, pp. 579–584, 2014.

is cyberspace, where we communicate with others from all over the world (Wertheim, 1999). Simulation space is often used for observation and evaluation of landscape by city planners, designers, engineers, developers, and administrators (Soubra, 2008; Dawood et al., 2009; Yabuki et al., 2011).

In 1999, Philip Rosedale established Linden Lab. He combined these two features of virtual space and made "Second Life (SL)" [1], which is a developing computer hardware allowing people to immerse in a virtual world. In SL, users (called Residents) can interact with each other through avatars. They can socialize, participate individual and group activities and create 3D artifacts, buildings, and social spaces where people interact [2].

Given the features of SL as a social interface allowing multi-users to participate daily activities as well as real life, SL became popular and was used for education (Boulos et al., 2007), science evaluation, and arts fields, such as the virtual museum and art gallery (Urban, 2007; Zhu, 2007). On the other sides, regarding to the web museums, visitors have become accustomed to clicking on images displayed in their browser or retrieve pre-written textual descriptions of cultural heritage objects (Sumption, 2006). Therefore in order to create a more accessible and convenient virtual museum, researchers have built the virtual museum in SL, such as "The Bayside Beach Galleria Museum of Contemporary Art [3] (Urban, 2007)", "A Virtual Gallery (Oberlander et al., 2008)".

2   Problem and Objective

However, the art displays of those museums I mentioned above were just copied from traditional museum and re-build it into SL. Sometimes it is not as easy as traditional museum for user to get used to it. Users have to learn how to control the SL interface and recognize the orientation in the virtual world and then navigate in SL. On the other sides, in the art display of physical museum, visitors always stand in front of the wall to appreciate 2D painting, also in virtual museum, visitors have to control their avatars to appreciate 2D painting. It is difficult for users to perceive the same feelings that artists would like to express. Therefore the concept of this research is to represent a more immersive virtual museum by extending 2D painting to 3D painting via SL. By using SL platform, visitor is able to break limitations of physical world to soar, jump, swim or become a goliath to navigate around the museum. In this museum, users are able to get into the paintings; it means the 2D painting can be visualized in 3D world (see Fig 1). And every individual painting can be properly connected with each other through story telling. There are two different themes in this museum: the European Art and the Asian Art. In this research, we are going to present Asian Art gallery as an example of extending 2D painting to 3D painting.

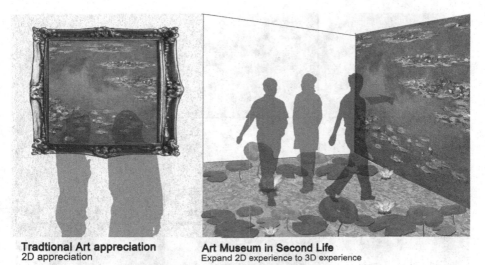

Tradtional Art appreciation
2D appreciation

Art Museum in Second Life
Expand 2D experience to 3D experience

Fig. 1. Comparison of art appreciation

3   Implementation

In order to create a more immersive way to appreciate arts, we collected some important paintings from Asian Art, and used the narrative way to connect it. Therefore the methodology can be divided into three parts: the first step, artwork selection from famous museums; the second step, scenario demonstration; the third step, framework of virtual museum.

Fig. 2. Art collections: a) Chinese painting—"Landscape: tea sipping under willows"; b) Chinese painting—"Moonlit Pavilion in the Mountains"; c) Buddha painting—"Buddha Enthroned on a Mat of Kusa Grass"; d) Japanese painting—"Murasaki Shikibu"; e) Chinese painting—"The Peach Festival of the Queen Mother of the West"; f) Chinese painting—" Hell Story: mirror of retribution".

Fig. 3. Scenario demonstration: A) User walked to the willows and appreciated painting—*"Landscape: tea sipping under willows"*. *And she sat down around the tea table to virtually experience Chinese tea*; B) She got into the landscape and appreciated the second Chinese painting—"Moonlit Pavilion in the Mountains". And then she follow the paths and climbed to the pavilion; D) she found a Chinese table, chair, and two paintings, one is on the table and the other is on the wall. As to the painting on the wall—"Murasaki Shikibu" which displayed a Japanese woman lying on the riverside and enjoying the moonlight; E) Suddenly the virtual world turned to the night time. She wanted to get into this Japanese painting; F) After clicking the left button of the painting, she suddenly transferred herself to the riverside; G) she clicked the left button and transferred her to the needle mountain and lava hell, H) The bridge implied, people who have done many bad things before die, they cannot safely go across the bridge; H) Finally she meet the Buddha painting—"Buddha Enthroned on a Mat of Kusa Grass" after passing the bridge.

Scenario Demonstration of Asian Art Museum

This gallery includes five different styles painting: landscape painting, portrait painting, flower-and-bird painting, hell painting, and Buddha painting. Also, the classification is followed by Chinese traditional water painting. The scenario of this virtual museum was described as below.

The virtual museum began from a Chinese painting—"Landscape: tea sipping under willows" (fig 2a). Visitor controlled the avatar and walked to the willows to sit on the virtual tea table and enjoy sipping tea with other avatars (fig 3A). And then she got into the landscape and appreciated the second Chinese painting—"Moonlit Pavilion in the Mountains" (fig 2b). Subsequently he recognized a Chinese garden behind the painting and a paths connecting to the pavilion of hill (fig 3B). Therefore she walked into the garden paths and climbed up to the pavilion (fig 3C). After arriving to the pavilion hill, she found a Chinese table, chair, and two paintings, one is on the table (fig 2e) and the other is on the wall (fig 3D). The painting on the wall— "Murasaki Shikibu" (fig 2d) displayed a Japanese woman lying on the riverside and enjoyed the moonlight (fig 3E). Suddenly the virtual world turned to the night time. She wanted to experience the same scene from Japanese painting. After she clicked the left button of the painting, she suddenly transferred herself to the riverside (fig 3F). The hell painting—"Hell Story: mirror of retribution" (fig 2f) which was hung on the roof attracted the user to get into it. Hence she clicked the left button and transferred her to the needle mountain and lava hell (fig 3G). And then she found a bridge in front of her. She tried to keep safely going across a bridge (fig 3H). The bridge implied, people who have done many bad things before die, they cannot safely go across the bridge. At the same time the user safely go across the bridge, but there are many other users who fall down the needle mountain. Finally the user met the Buddha painting—"Buddha Enthroned on a Mat of Kusa Grass" (fig 2c, fig 3I) and a big golden Buddha was appearing in front of her.

4   Conclusion Remarks

Through the scenario demonstration of the virtual museum, the visitors had the chance to more profoundly experience the masterpieces. By extending 2D paintings to 3D world, users can be not only more adaptively perceive the expression of painting but also intuitively interact with the 2D famous painting in 3D world.

This kind of art appreciation can play a profound contribution to the art education especially for children. By using game-like navigation around the virtual art gallery, children can receive deeper impression and be more interested in this immersive art museum than traditional one. Although there are some contributions on the child education, however, the interface of SL is still another problem, which people have to learn how to use it before controlling it. Sometimes, it is not easy to use for most beginners. On the other sides, this research just creates a new form of art display in virtual museum via SL. In the future, if we can combine more intuitive HCI interface, such as "body sensor" into this virtual space, it would become more accessible and adaptable for every visitors.

References

1. Dawood, N., Benghi, C., Lorenzen, T., Pencreach, Y.: Integration of Urban Development and 5D Planning. In: Proceedings of the 9th International Conference on Construction Applications of Virtual Reality, Sydney, Australia, pp. 217–228 (2009)
2. Boulos, M.N.K., Hetherington, L., Wheeler, S.: Second Life: an overview of the potential of 3 - D virtual worlds in medical and health education. Health Information & Libraries Journal 24(4), 233–245 (2007)
3. Iovine, J.: Step into Virtual Reality. Windcrest/McGraw-Hill (1995)
4. Kalawsky, R.S.: The Science of Virtual Reality and Virtual Environments. Addison-Wesley (1993)

5. Kalay, Y.E.: The impact of information technology on design methods, products and practices. Design Studies 27(3), 357–380 (2006)
6. Mitchell, W.J.: City of Bits:Space, Place and the Infobahn. The MIT Press, Cambridge (1995)
7. Myers, B.A.: A Brief History of Human Computer Interaction Technology. ACM Interactions 5(2), 44–54 (1998)
8. Oberlander, J., Karakatsiotis, G., Isard, A., Androutsopoulos, I.: Building an adaptive museum gallery in Second Life. In: Proceedings of Museums and the Web, Montreal, Quebec, Canada (2008)
9. Soubra, S.: Combining Virtual Environments and Simulations to Meet Sustainability Challenges of the Construction Sector. In: Proceedings of the 8th International Conference on Construction Applications of Virtual Reality, Kuala Lumpur, Malaysia, pp. 42–57 (2008)
10. Sumption, K.: Search of the Ubiquitous Museum: Reflections of Ten Years of Museums and the Web. In: Trant, J., Bearman, D. (eds.) Museums and the Web 2006: Proceedings, Archives & Museum Informatics, Toronto (2006), http://www.archimuse.com/mw2006/papers/sumption/sumption.html (published March 1, 2006)
11. Urban, R.J.: A second life for your museum: 3D multi-user virtual environments and museums. Archives & Museum Informatics (2007)
12. Wertheim, M.: The Pearly Gates of Cyberspace: A History of Space from Dante to the Internet. W.W. Norton & Company, New York (1999)
13. Yabuki, N., Miyashita, K., Fukuda, T.: An invisible height evaluation system for building height regulation to preserve good landscapes using augmented reality. Automation in Construction 20, 228–235 (2011)
14. Zhu, Q., Xiang, K., Hu, S.: Design an Immersive Interactive Museum in Second Life. In: Second Workshop on Digital Media and its Application in Museum & Heritages, pp. 264–267 (2007)
15. Second Life, http://www.secondlife.com
16. Terms of Service I Second Life, http://secondlife.com/corporate/tos.php
17. The Bayside Beach Galleria Museum of Contemporary Art, http://wiki.secondlife.com/wiki/Third_Party_Viewer_Directory

Handling of Virtual Cloth

Shigeru Inui, Yuko Mesuda, and Yosuke Horiba

ShinshuUniversity, Faculty of Textile Science and Technology, Tokida. 3-15-1, Ueda,
Nagano, 386-8567, Japan
{inui,12st115c,horiba}@shinshu-u.ac.jp

Abstract. In this study, manipulations of virtual cloth model were examined for draping. Cloth was mechanically formalized and modeled. Motion of real human hand is detected by a sensor and the motion is utilized for handling of the cloth model. Cloth manipulations to hold, release and attach were realized. When the cloth model is handling, "coarse model" and fast dynamic calculation method is used and when the cloth is at rest, "precise model" and precise static calculation method is used. When the cloth model is stopped from dynamic regime, the model of the cloth is switched from "coarse" to "precise". When the model is started to move from static regime, the model of the cloth is switched from "precise" to "coarse".

Keywords: virtual draping, real-time, hand gesture, cloth manipulation.

1 Introduction

Draping is one of a design method for clothing. Draping is a method to design paper patterns by putting cloth on dummy surface and forming the shape of clothing. Though draping has many advantages such as it is possible to make clothing fit for each person, it costs much time and money. As it is possible to decrease the costs drastically by virtualizing draping processes, some methods of virtual draping are proposed. Real time cloth handling is important for virtual draping. Some methods have been proposed[1-3], and mouse is utilized for handling of virtual cloth. The method of handling virtual cloth by the motion of real human hands is more realistic than by mouse manipulation. We examined handling methods by the motion of real human hands.

2 Model and Sensor

2.1 The Cloth Model and the Object Model

In our study, the virtual cloth model for handling consists of particles and springs. The particles are aligned in a reticular pattern, and neighboring particles are connected by crosswise, longitudinal and diagonal spring. Other rigid virtual objects consist of particles but the particles are not connected by spring and the objects are not deformed.

C. Stephanidis (Ed.): HCII 2014 Posters, Part I, CCIS 434, pp. 585–589, 2014.

2.2 Dynamic Calculation

Inner force in the cloth, collision force with other objects and the gravity force act on each particle of the cloth model and the forces are calculated. The forces are summed, the summed up forces are integrated by leap-frog method and each position of the particle in the next step is obtained [4].

2.3 Collision Reaction and Collision Detection.

To calculate collision force, collision between cloth model and virtual object has to be detected. When the distance between cloth model and other virtual object is less than predefined threshold, collision is detected, and then collision force acts on the repulsive colliding particle in the cloth model.

3   Manipulation of Cloth Model

In this study, the virtual cloth model is handled by motion of real human hand. Motion of human hand in the real world is detected by a sensor, and Kinct is used for the sensor. In Kinect, a camera and sensors are equipped and three-dimensional coordinate of the joints of human body can be acquired. The coordinates of joints are updated every one-thirty second and motion of human body can be acquired. Here, some fundamental manipulation of cloth for draping are realized with the acquired human body motion.

3.1 Manipulation to Hold and Release Cloth Model

The manipulation to hold cloth model is realized to move one or two particles in the cloth model coordinating the movement of real human hands. The position of the particles is constrained to the movement of real human hands. To release the cloth model, the restriction between the particles and the motion of real human hands is canceled. The cancellation is triggered by a key operation.

3.2 Manipulation to Attach Cloth Model

The manipulation to attach the cloth model is to put handling cloth model on a virtual object. The manipulation to attach the cloth model is triggered by a key operation, some nodes in the cloth model are fixed on the nearest virtual object and the restriction between the particles and the motion of real human hands is canceled. When the cloth model is attached to a virtual object, collision between the cloth model and the object is detected and collision reaction is processed.

3.3   "Coarse" or "Precise" Model

To manipulate virtual cloth in real time, it is desirable that the cloth model is simple as much as possible. On the other hand, to predict the precise shape of real cloth by simulation, it is desirable that the cloth model is detailed model as much as possible. The cloth model is a trade-off between response and precision. For this reason, a mechanism is introduced in which a simple cloth model is applied when the model is manipulated and a precise model is applied when the model is at rest.

A coarse mesh is utilized for the cloth model when cloth model is handled. Cloth is modeled by mass and spring model, and the shape of virtual cloth is calculated by integration of motion equation. The model is called "coarse model". A precise mesh is applied for the cloth model when the virtual mesh is not handled. Cloth is modeled as continuum, and the shape of the virtual cloth is calculated by minimization of energy of the model. The model is called "precise model".

3.4   Switching Models

While the cloth model is handled, the position of the hands of operator is detected by sensor, and the coordinate of the nodes of the cloth model is updated according to the movement of the hands of the operator. The handling of the virtual cloth model by real human hands is realized by the technique. The "coarse model" is applied in the situation above. Handling of virtual cloth is finished when some nodes of the model are fixed or the model is laid on other virtual object. When handling is finished, the model of the virtual cloth is switched from "coarse model" to "precise model". The shape of the "precise model" is obtained from the "coarse model", and the precise calculation is started from the shape as the initial shape. On the other hand, when the virtual cloth is at rest, the "precise model" is applied. When handling of the virtual cloth is started, the cloth model is switched from the "precise model" to the "coarse model" for real time calculation. When the cloth model is attached to a virtual object, collision between the cloth model and the object is detected and collision reaction is processed.

4   Result and Discussion

Manipulation to hold or release was started from the initial condition in which one of the nodes or both nodes of upper end of the cloth model were fixed. It is possible to hold any point of the virtual cloth model, and after that the shape of the cloth model is changed coordinating the motion of real human hands. It is confirmed that the cloth model falls off after cancellation of the restriction between two nodes or one node at the edge of the cloth model and the motion of real human hands shown in figure 1. It is also confirmed that the cloth model is attached to a virtual object. Some gap was observed between the cloth and the object model. The gap was decreased to increase iterations of mechanical and collision calculation.

The "coarse model" is the model of lattice-shaped mesh model. To make the "precise model" from the "coarse model", edge of the unit lattice is divided and new lattice nodes are created in every unit lattice by proportional division. The "coarse model" of the virtual cloth is shown in the left side of figure 2, and the "precise model" made from the "coarse model" is shown in the right side of figure 2. The "precise model" is a triangular mesh divided from a lattice-shaped mesh. The "coarse model" is made by picking up for example every three nodes form the nodes of the lattice of the "precise model".

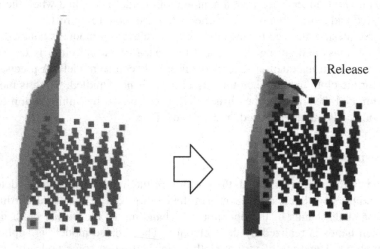

Fig. 1. The small cubes are the nodes of a virtual object. The left side shows that virtual cloth is holding by two corner nodes and the right side shows that one of the nodes is released.

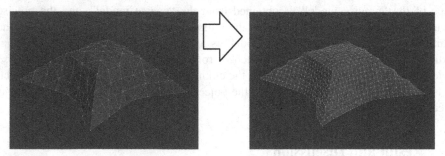

Fig. 2. The mesh of the left side is 10 by 10 lattice structure of "coarse" model. The mesh of the right side is 30 by 30 lattice structure of "precise" model made from the "coarse" model.

5   Conclusion

In this study, manipulations of virtual cloth model were examined for draping. Cloth manipulations to hold, release and attach were realized. It is necessary to extract other manipulations for draping, and other manipulations such as to fold or cut the cloth model should be realized. Then, it is expected to construct a draping system combining those manipulations.

Acknowledgments. This work was partly supported by Grants-in-Aid for Scientific Research (No. 23240100, 24220012) from the Ministry of Education, Science, Sports and Culture and Grants for Excellent Graduate Schools, MEXT, Japan.

References

1. Meng, Y., Mok, P.Y., Jin, X.: Interactive Virtual Try-on Clothing Design Systems. Computer-Aided Design 147, 310–321 (2010)
2. Igarashi, T., Hughes, J.F.: Clothing Manipulation. In: UIST and I3D Reprise session, ACM SIGGRAPH, p. 697 (2003)
3. Mesuda, Y., Inui, S., Horiba, Y.: Cutting Method for Cloth Handling. In: Proceedings of 1st International Symposium on Affective Engineering, pp. 145–151 (2013)
4. Harada, T., Koshizuka, S.: Real-time Collision Computation Between Cloth and Highly-tessellated Models. Transaction of Information Processing Society of Japan 48, 1829–1837 (2007)

Haptic Display of Representing Roughness

Manabu Ishihara

Dept. of Innovative Electrical and Electronic Engineering,
Oyama National College of Technology, Tochigi, Japan 323-0806
ishihara@oyama-ct.ac.jp

Abstract. In this study, we examined methods of sensing roughness with haptic displays. We used a PHANToM DeskTop-E Device (Sensable Technologies) as our haptic device. Representation of paper quality applies to dictionaries, notebooks and other everyday items, not just calligraphy and washi paper(Japanese paper). In contrast, the discrimination thresholds were $Z_{0.75} = 1.0$ [N] for dynamic friction and $Z_{0.75} = 0.25$[N] for static friction. In the case of PHANToM DeskTop-E, we showed that we made a large range of the comparison friction.

Keywords: haptic device, virtual reality ,static friction, dynamic friction, PHANToM DeskTop-E.

1   Introduction

As a result of recent advances in three-dimensional (3D) video technology and stereo sound systems, virtual reality (VR) has become a familiar part of people's lives. Concurrent with these advances has been a wealth of research on touch interface technology [1], and educators have begun exploring ways to incorporate teaching tools utilizing touch properties in their curriculums [5,6]. However, when used as teaching tools, it is important that a touch interface provide a "feel" that is as close to reality as possible. This will make replacing familiar teaching tools with digital media incorporating VR seem more attractive.

For example, various learning support systems that utilize virtually reality (VR) technology [7] are being studied. Examples include a system that utilizes a stereoscopic image and writing brush display to teach the brush strokes used in calligraphy [8,9], the utilization of a robot arm with the same calligraphy learning system [10], a system that uses a "SPIDAR" haptic device to enable remote calligraphy instruction [11], and systems that analyze the learning process involved in piano instruction [12] or in the use of virtual chopsticks[13].

Additionally, since it is a basic rule of pen-drawn characters that even a slight displacement of the pen tip is impermissible, pen-drawn character reproductions must be within 1 mm tolerances and will appear out of balance if drawn too long or too short. In response, support system ems for penmanship instruction and similar applications on tablet PCs have been developed [14], and associated re-search indicates that both the curriculum and content are important factors for creating VR

C. Stephanidis (Ed.): HCII 2014 Posters, Part I, CCIS 434, pp. 590–595, 2014.

materials [5]. Penmanship instruction systems and similar applications using interactive haptic devices connected to networks have been devised, and various experiments have been performed into their usage [15].

We use PHANToM Omni device and obtained satisfac-tory results [16]. It is interesting to compare the results of this study with the former information [17]. In the main cause for the error is machine friction. We used PHANToM DeskTop-E device as a substitute for PHANToM Omni. We changed PHANToM Omni to PHANToM DeskTop-E with improve the accuracy.

Teaching calligraphy, for example, normally requires a paper medium for output. The smoothness of the paper medium will change depending on the paper quality. Accordingly, in this study, we examined methods of sensing roughness with haptic displays. Representation of paper quality applies to dictionaries, notebooks and other every-day items, not just calligraphy and washi paper (Japanese paper). We believe our experimental results provide elements of the basic information necessary for haptic devices to represent such roughness.

2   Experiment

In this study, we used a PHANToM DeskTop-E Device (Sensable Technologies) as our haptic device. It was attached to a control computer (CPU: Intel® Core™i5-4430[3.00GHz], RAM:8.GB, OS:64bit) running Open Haptics™ toolkit v3.0 as the control program [2].

We began by modeling images of the surface texture for notebook and other paper types using friction experiments. When creating friction via the haptic display, it was first necessary to determine what level of friction was discernible.

3   Experiment Overview

We conducted both dynamic and static friction experiments, during which we measured the threshold for frictional force and points of subjective equality. Five male test subjects, approximately 20-21years of age, participated in both experiments.

3.1   Experimental Method

The constant method for measurement was used. During the experiment, each test subject was presented with two stimuli to compare. They then comparatively scaled their subjective impression of the stimuli as "Rough", "Equal", or "Smooth".

3.2   Type of Stimulus

The stimulus on which comparisons were based was called the standard stimulus (SS). For frictional forces, the SS was limited to one type of stimulus with a fixed range of physical quantities. The stimulus used for comparison with the SS was called the comparative stimulus (CS). A number of CS types were prepared in incremental quantities centered on the stimulus quantity of the SS. The friction used were 0.8-3.2[N] for dynamic and static friction (SS = 2.0), with seven types of stimuli prepared for each. Stimulus allocation is shown in Tables 1.

Table 1. Friction stimuli

Stimulus	S_1	S_2	S_3	S_4	S_5	S_6	S_7
Friction [N]	0.8	1.2	1.6	2.0	2.4	2.8	3.2

3.3   Experiment Procedure

Measurements were performed using one test subject at a time. The subject was seated in front of the PHANToM unit and given the pen component to hold. They then followed instructions displayed by the computer and moved their arm to draw a straight line on the model board using an arbitrary amount of force. Subjects were then asked to evaluate a total of 70 randomly presented stimuli combinations comprising seven combinations, including an SS pair, each shown 10 times. As the PHANToM only guarantees forces up to 7.9(kg-m/s2) (7.9[N])[2], the unit was restricted because the application of normal force greater than this level would not register.

4   Results and Discussion

A probabilistic model was introduced to analyze the experimental data. Data parameters were estimated using maximum likelihood[3].

4.1   Results

Frequency distributions of the measurements are shown in Tables 2 and 3. Si (i = 1,...,7) was the SS.

Parameter values for the data in Tables 2(a) and (b) were derived using maximum likelihood to obtain the results in Tables 3 and 4. Here μ is the average, σ is the distribution, c is the decision criterion, and $Z_{0.75}$ is the normal deviation with a cumulative probability of 0.75 at normal distribution. The upper and lower thresholds are $\mu + Z_{0.75}$ and $\mu - Z_{0.75}$, respectively.

These results yield Figures 1 and 2 the horizontal axis gives the exhibited stimulus values, or friction coefficients, and the vertical axis gives the likelihood or proportion of judgment. The small circles represent data values. A green   star means the SS was judged to be stronger (Si < S4), a red square means the values were judged to be equal, and a filled in blue circle means the CS was judged to be stronger (Si > S4). The curve is the probability of the judgment from parameter values derived from the experimental data.

Table 2. Example of Friction Experiment

	(a) Dynamic				(b) Static		
Comparative	Category			Comparative	Category		
Stimulus	$S_4<S_i$	$S_4=S_i$	$S_4>S_i$	Stimulus	$S_4<S_i$	$S_4=S_i$	$S_4>S_i$
S_1	8	9	33	S_1	0	0	50
S_2	9	9	32	S_2	0	3	57
S_3	10	11	29	S_3	0	18	32
S_4	15	24	11	S_4	16	24	10
S_5	30	11	9	S_5	42	8	0
S_6	30	9	11	S_6	47	3	0
S_7	31	9	10	S_7	47	3	0

Table 3. Parameter Values for Dynamic Friction Experiment

μ	Σ	c	$Z_{0.75}$	$\mu+Z_{0.75}$	$\mu-Z_{0.75}$
2.0142	1.4906	0.50768	1.0054	3.0196	1.008

Table 4. Parameter Values for Static Friction Experiment

μ	σ	c	$Z_{0.75}$	$\mu+Z_{0.75}$	$\mu-Z_{0.75}$
1.9623	0.36814	0.25358	0.24831	2.2106	1.714

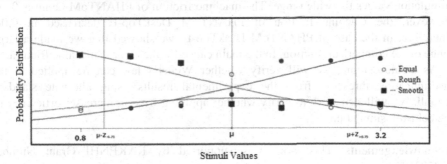

Fig. 1. Analysis Results for Dynamic Friction Experiment

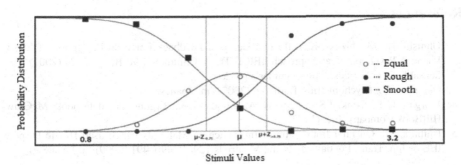

Fig. 2. Analysis Results for Static Friction Experiment

4.2   Discussion

From the results in section-4.1, it can be seen that if a friction of 2.0 is taken as the SS for dynamic friction, the point of subjective equality is $\mu = 2.01$. If a friction of 2.0 is taken as the SS for static friction, the point of subjective equality is $\mu = 1.96$. The margin of error between SS and point of subjective equality is small, indicating that the experiment contains few errors made by individuals. In contrast, the discrimination thresh-olds were $Z_{0.75} = 1.00$ for dynamic friction and $Z_{0.75} = 0.25$ for static friction.

5   Conclusion

In this study, we used haptic displays to measure points of subjective equality and the threshold of friction, an ele-ment of touch. However, because the force displayed by PHANToM units is the touch force transmitted through the hand holding a pen, the results provide deep sensory char-acteristics, not skin sensation, and are much larger than the frictional forces sensed by actual human hands[4]. Never-theless, a haptic display like this system is thought to be usable way of duplicating surface roughness for notebook pages or other similar materials when quantifying basic operating characteristics, such as writing in, touching and turning pages. The threshold of the dynamical friction coef-ficient of the PHANToM DeskTop-E has to make a stimulation values the wide range. The machine friction of PHANToM Omni is 0.26. However, the machine friction of PHANToM DeskTop-E decreased in 0.06. Therefore, In the case of PHANToM DeskTop-E, we showed that we made a large range of the comparison friction. In the main cause for the error is machine friction.

As a future topic, we will verify whether Weber's law can be applied to the discrimination threshold from the experimental results using alternate standard stimuli. We will also work to verify whether applying friction increases efficiency of the collision simulation.

Acknowledgements. This work was supported by KAKENHI Grant Number 25350369.

References

1. Ohnishi, H., Mochizuki, K.: Effect of Delay of Feedback Force on Perception of Elastic Force: A Psychophysical Approach. IEICE Trans. Commun. E90-B(1), 12–20 (2007)
2. Sensable OpenHaptics™ programmer's guide
3. Okamoto, Y.: Psychometrics. Baifukan (2007) (in Japanese)
4. Morgan, C.T., Cook, J.S., Chapanis, A., Lund, M.W.: Ergonomics data book. McGraw-HillBook Company, Inc. (1972)
5. Ishihara, M.: On First Impression of the Teaching Materials which used Haptic Display. IEE of Jpn. Trans. Fundamentals and Materials 129(7), 490–491 (2009) (in Japanese)

6. Ishihara, M.: " Assessment of paper's roughnessfor haptic device". In: Proceedings of Forum Information Technology 2011, K-032 Hokkaido, Jpn., (September 2011) (in Japanese)

7. Hirose, M.: Virtual Reality. Sangyo Tosho (1993) (in Japanese)

8. Yoshida, T., Muranaka, N., Imanishi, S.: A Construction of Educational Application System for Calligrapy Master based on Virtual Reality. IEEE of Jpn. Trans. Electronics, Information and Systems 117-C(11), 1629–1634 (1997) (in Japanese)

9. Yoshida, T., Yamamoto, T., Imanishi, S.: A Calligraphy Mastering Support System Using Virtual Reality Technology and its Learning Effects. IEEE of Jpn., Trans. Fundamentals and Materials 123-A(12), 1206–1216 (2003) (in Japanese)

10. Henmi, K., Yoshikawa, T.: Virtual Lesson and Its Application to Virtual Calligraphy System. TVRSJ 3(1), 13–19 (1983) (in Japanese)

11. Sakuma, M., Masamori, S., Harada, T., Hirata, Y., Satou, M.: A Remote Lesson System for Japanese Calligraphy using SPIDAR. IEICE of Jpn., Technical Report, MVE99-52, pp. 27–32 (October 1999) (in Japanese)

12. Otsuka, G., Sodeyama, G., Muranaka, N., Imanishi, S.: A Construction of a Piano Training System based on Virtual Reality. IEEE of Jpn., Trans. Electronics, Information and Systems 116-C(11), 1288–1294 (1996) (in Japanese)

13. Yamaguchi, Y., Kitamura, Y., Kishino, F.: Analysis of Learning Process of Virtual Chopsticks. IEICE of Jpn., Technical Report, MVE2001-3, pp.11–16 (June 2001) (in Japanese)

14. Muranaka, N., Tokumaru, M., Imanishi, S.: The penmanship (script learning) support system: Education effect of the animation model for pen strokes. IEICE of Jpn., Technical Report, ET2005-115, pp.151–156 (March 2006) (in Japanese)

15. Ishihara, M.: Prototype of Haptic Device and Pen Tablet Collaborative Work System. Journal of Computing 3(8), 51–54 (2011)

16. Ishihara, M.: Empirical Study Regarding Re-presenting Roughness with Haptic Devices. In: Proceedings of 2013 IEEE 2nd GCCE, Chiba, Japan, pp. 471–473 (October 2013)

17. Ishihara, M., et al.: Characteristic of Representing Roughness with Haptic Devices. In: Proceedings of ICEE 2014, Jeju, Korea (in Press, 2014)

Fishing Metaphor for Navigation in CAVE

Makio Ishihara[1] and Yukio Ishihara[2]

[1] Fukuoka Institute of Technology, 3-30-1 Wajiro-higashi, Higashi-ku, Fukuoka,
811-0295, Japan
m-ishihara@fit.ac.jp
http://www.fit.ac.jp/~m-ishihara/Lab/
[2] Kyushu University, 3-1-1, Maidashi, Higashi-ku, Fukuoka, 812-8582, Japan
iyukio@redoxnavi.med.kyushu-u.ac.jp
http://hyoka.ofc.kyushu-u.ac.jp/search/details/K004222/english.html

Abstract. This manuscript proposes a navigation method with fishing
metaphor for large translations and specifies its design, and shows a brief
demonstration. From the demonstration, it was shown that the fishing
metaphor has a better performance and the potential for providing large
translations with intuitive ways.

Keywords: fishing metaphor, navigation, CAVEs, immersive environments, virtual reality.

1   Introduction

A CAVE is a computer system that is capable of immersing users into stereo
virtual spaces. CAVEs are usually used for volumetric data to be visualized and
examined, such as meteorology, magnetic field, tornados, tidal waves, and human
brain activity. For example, K. Dmitriev et al. [1] built a CAVE system for interactive rendering of the car interior. Their system computed global illumination
depending on the user's position and orientation in real time, and displayed the
result with stereo projection. The user could check how the illumination would
be as he/she looked around in the car. In the research field of human factors, N.
Elmqvist et al. [2] discussed how users formed their cognitive map of the virtual
world using the guided navigation method on both usual desktops and a CAVE.
The findings showed that users would form the cognitive map accurately when
they were guided on a predefined tour through the world while being able to
control the speed and deviate locally from the tour.

As regards user interface of CAVEs, a common device is a wand. A wand is a
handheld input device with some buttons (usually three buttons) and a joystick.
The position and orientation of the wand is tracked by a magnetic sensor and
they are used to design the user interface. The user might push forward the
joystick while pointing the wand where to go. Despite giving the user a simple
navigation way, it is reported that manipulation of the wand distracts the user's
attention from the contents. T. Tiainen et al. [3] conducted several experiments
in recalling contents in virtual shops. Subjects in a group were navigated by an

C. Stephanidis (Ed.): HCII 2014 Posters, Part I, CCIS 434, pp. 596–601, 2014.
© Springer International Publishing Switzerland 2014

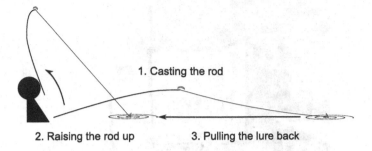

Fig. 1. Fishing metaphor

operator through a virtual shop and the others were navigated by themselves using the wand. The result showed that users could remember more about the products when navigation was done by an operator.

The user interface should be so intuitive and natural that users could concentrate on their main objectives in the virtual world. M.C. Cabral et al. [4] proposed a gesture interface. Their system enabled users to use hand gestures in order to change views and navigate themselves through the virtual world. Some experiment in usability showed that hand gesture was very important to improve the sensation of immersion but it was not good at performing pointing tasks. Taking pointing tasks into consideration, D.F. Keefe et al. [5] built a cave painting system. Users put a tracked pinch glove on and drew paintings using a tracked brush in 3D immersive space. From several demonstrations of paintings, it was shown that the system had a better performance in pointing tasks, so that users would draw such sensitive and sentient paintings.

When it comes to translation/transportation ways, the painting system uses an intuitive way for small translations. Users put a tracked pinch glove on the non-dominant hand and grab the world by pinching together the thumb and the ring finger, and then drag it around by moving the hand. For large translations, the system uses a map based interface. Users draw a trail of paint on a small scale map of the world using the tracked brush then they move along the trail. This requires extra transitions between the virtual world and the small scale map. The work mentioned above [3][4] uses the walk-through for small translations.

This manuscript proposes a navigation method with fishing metaphor for large translations and specifies its design, and shows a brief demonstration.

2   Fishing Metaphor

This manuscript employs fishing metaphor for quick access in a wide range of space. The basic idea of fishing metaphor is shown in Fig. 1. To begin fishing, people cast the rod to position the lure at their target on the water. When a fish is on the hook, they raise the rod up to pull the lure back and retrieve the line as they lower the rod. Thus these acts of casting and raising the rod cause changes

Top:Screens and projectors Left:3D glasses Right:A wand

Fig. 2. Our CAVE system

in distance of the lure from the fisher. We expect without difficulty users could indicate a nearby /distant point by these acts, where they want to move.

3 Navigation Interface in CAVE

3.1 Our CAVE Environment

Fig. 2 (top) shows a CAVE in our laboratory. It has three projection screens, onto which three projectors project stereo perspective views of the virtual space in a synchronous manner. The user wears stereo glasses to see the depth of the virtual space and manipulates a 3D mouse called a wand to point and fly around. The 3D glasses and the wand are shown in Fig. 2 (left) and (right), respectively. Their position and orientation in the CAVE coordinates are tracked in real time. Fig. 3 specifies the measurements of the CAVE and the gyro sensor coordinate system to express the wand's angular position.

Using the wand, the user navigates his/her way through the virtual space. By default, pushing the joystick forward, the user moves or flies in the direction that the wand points, and pushing it to the left, the user turns left. The common methods of navigation include walking and flying. They are good for users viewing the virtual space and examining the volumetric data while moving around in the nearby space. But it is not suitable for quick access to distant points.

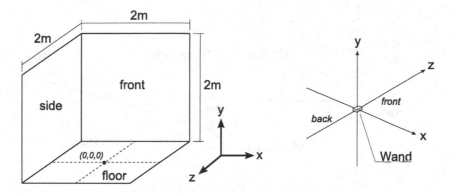

Fig. 3. Measurements of our CAVE and the axes of rotation of the wand

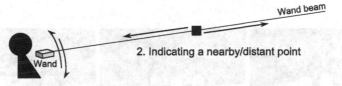

Fig. 4. Manipulation of the wand based on the fishing metaphor

3.2   Settings of Fishing Metaphor

Fig. 4 shows a schematic diagram that illustrates how the fishing metaphor is implemented. Refer to Fig. 1. The wand functions as the rod and a black square does as the lure, which represents where to go. When the user presses and holds the middle button of the wand, the wand beam is frozen, allowing the user to raise up/lower down the wand to indicate the point to go. After finishing indicating the point, the user releases the button then he/she starts moving smoothly to the indicated point. When the user raises up and holds the wand, the black square will come close depending on the angular position of the wand, and when the user lowers down and holds the wand, the black square will go away.

Fig. 5 defines several parameters from the fishing metaphor. The applicable range of rotation angle of the wand is from -25 up to +25 degrees and the applicable range of distance from the point to go is from 0 up to 90 meters. These parameters should be determined considering human factors and the size of the expected virtual world. In this manuscript, they were determined empirically.

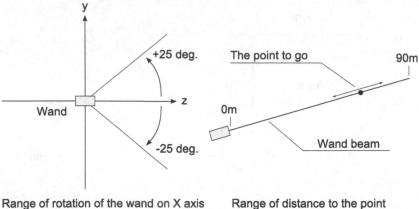

Range of rotation of the wand on X axis   Range of distance to the point

Fig. 5. Parameters from fishing metaphor

Left:Putting the wand in nutral position. Middle:Raising it up. Right:Lowering it down

Fig. 6. Brief demonstration

3.3 Demonstration

Fig. 6 shows some screenshots of our prototype. The virtual world used in this demonstration was 162 meters wide and 162 meters tall. There were a town of small houses, roads, trees, windmills, and a small lake in the virtual world. A nearby/distant point to go is indicated by the orange cube. In (left) the user puts the wand in neutral position and raises it up in (middle), lowers it down in (right).

4 Conclusions

This manuscript proposed a navigation method with fishing metaphor for large translations and specified its design, and showed a brief demonstration. From the demonstration, it was shown that the fishing metaphor has a better performance and the potential for providing large translations with intuitive ways.

References

1. Dmitriev, K., Annen, T., Krawczyk, G., Myszkowski, K., Seidel, H.: A CAVE system for interactive modeling of global illumination in car interior. In: Proc. of VRST 2004, pp. 137–145 (2004)
2. Elmqvist, N., Tudoreanu, M.E., Tsigas, P.: Evaluating motion constraints for 3D wayfinding in immersive and desktop virtual environments. In: Proc. of CHI 2008, pp. 1769–1778 (2008)
3. Tiainen, T., Kaapu, T., Ellrnan, A., Roberts, D.: Effect of navigation task on recalling content: the case of occasional users in restricted, cave like virtual environment. In: Proc. of 11th IEEE Symposium on Distributed Simulation and Real-Time Applications, pp. 209–216 (2007)
4. Cabral, M.C., Morimoto, C.H., Zuffo, M.K.: On the usability of gesture interfaces in virtual reality environments. In: Proc. of CLIHC 2005, pp. 100–108 (2005)
5. Keefe, D.F., Feliz, D.A., Moscovich, T., Laidlaw, D.H., LaViola, J.J.: CavePainting: a fully immersive 3D artistic medium and interactive experience. In: Proc. of the 2001 Symposium on Interactive 3D Graphics (I3D 2001), pp. 85–93 (2001)

Sound Clay: An Immersive Art Form by Sculpting Clay and Sound

Hyunsoo Kim and Changhoon Park

Dept. of Game Engineering, Hoseo University,
165 Sechul-ri, Baebang-myun, Asan, Chungnam 336-795, Korea
hyunsookim@imrlab.hoseo.edu, chpark@hoseo.edu

Abstract. This paper attempts to show the fourth generation of the immersive art forms - Immersive Art - Interactive art platforms that artists and designers serve audience to make their own art through this art platform. The user not only participated in media art, but also they can make their own art. This paper will focus on demonstration all of the above. Therefore we introduce the art form 'Sound Clay' on the border of Immersive Art. An audience can deform clay and refine transforming sound simultaneously in the immersive environment. Thus, this study provides an exciting opportunity to advance our knowledge of user experience design in the media art. Our second goal is to develop a range of techniques that support intuitive 3D modeling interactions based on free-form sculpting operations like those used when working with modeling clay.

Keywords: Virtual clay, three-dimensional modeling, augmented reality, head-mounted display, hand tracking systems, interactive art, sound generating systems

1   Introduction

1.1   The Next Generation of Interactive Media Art

The advances in science and technology have been always reflected in art. From a few years ago, arts shifted gradually from traditional forms towards new media types. The current development in digital media arts involves a significant amount of new carriers in not only new materials, but also in perusing technology, resulting in new dynamic and interactive forms [1, 2].

Looking into the development of public arts, especially the introduction of interactivity, based on the work of Edmonds, Turner and Candy [3], Wang, Hu and Rauterberg defined three generations of art and generative technology according to the carrying material, technology and interactivity [2]: 1) Static forms: there is no interaction between the art artifact and the viewer, and the artifact does not respond to its context and environment. 2) Dynamic forms: the art artifact has its internal mechanism to change its forms, depending on time or limited to reacting to the changes in its environment such as temperature, sound or light. The viewer is

C. Stephanidis (Ed.): HCII 2014 Posters, Part I, CCIS 434, pp. 602–606, 2014.

however a passive observer and has no influence on the behavior of the artifact. 3) Interactive forms: the viewer has an active role in influencing the dynamic form of the art object. The input from the viewer can be gesture, motion, sound as well as other human activity that can be captured by the artifact's sensorial layer. When interactivity is introduced, the "dialog" between the viewer and the perceived dynamic form of the artifact can always vary depending on the difficult-to-predict behavior of the human viewer.

This paper attempts to show the fourth generation of the immersive art forms - Immersive Art - interactive art platforms that artists and designers serve audience to make their own art in the immersive environment. The user not only participated in media art, but also they can make their own art. Through this platforms, they can concentrate this art more deeply and more time in the immersive environment [4]. Then artists and audience can communicate each other to refine unique art forms.

In this paper will give an account of the art form 'Sound Clay' on the border of Immersive Art. An audience can deform clay and refine transforming sound simultaneously in the immersive environment. Thus, this study provides an exciting opportunity to advance our knowledge of user experience design in the media art.

To conform above definition of Immersive Art, Sound Clay uses many devices to make immersive environment. In this virtual environment, an audience can deform clay easily, and can listen to altered sound each of clay. This system will be an electronic musical instrument, then through get together all of the processes, they can make own music.

1.2   Intuitive 3D Modeling for Laymen

3D Graphic artists, industrial designers, researchers and those of many other disciplines perform creating and capturing 3D models using 3D modeling applications, such as Autodesk's 3dsMax or Maya. But current 3D modeling applications perform surface modeling using a range of input devices including keyboard, mouse and tablets. Manipulation techniques are based around mathematical operations to alter surface shape and require extensive training to master. It takes time to get used to seeing a 3 dimensional model in a 2 dimensional monitor. Also, it is difficult to fabricate a 3 dimensional model using 2 dimensional input devices such as a mouse, or a tablet [5].

Our second goal is to develop a range of techniques that support intuitive 3D modeling interactions based on free-form sculpting operations like those used when working with modeling clay. By using the clay sculpting metaphor for the interaction technique design, we endeavored to leverage people's pre-existing understanding of physical clay modeling properties [6].

2   Sound Clay System

Three devices are used to implement this tool. Imagine pushing the keyboard and mouse aside, and reaching into a truly 3 dimensional modeling environment with both your hands through Leap Motion. And using the Vuforia from Qualcomm for augmented reality, it enables one to see that model on the marker from many angles through webcam on the Head Mounted Display (HMD).Finally, wearing Oculus Rift. One of next generation HMDs, It offers environment that engrosses you in the model by making you think you're seeing it in real life.

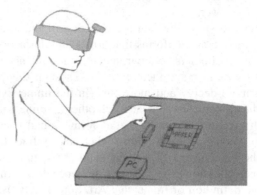

Fig. 1. System overview

Table 1. System specifications

Name	Type	Version	Usage
Apple iMac	Hardware		Personal computer
Microsoft LifeCam Studio	Hardware		Tracking marker
Leap Motion	Hardware		Tracking hands
Oculus Rift	Hardware	For developer	Head Mounted Display
Unity Engine	Software	4.0	Game Engine
Qualcomm Vuforia SDK	SDK	2.5.8	Augmented reality

3   Hand Gestures for Deforming Clay

It provides four gestures, classified by how to deal with a model with both hands. It's the same sort of idea as making a doll out of clay. First, trim the general appearance by molding it with your palms. Second, knead it with your hands. Last of all, take out specific portion by hold and take it up with your thumb and index finger. An audience more easily and instinctively fabricates the model by doing these four gestures.

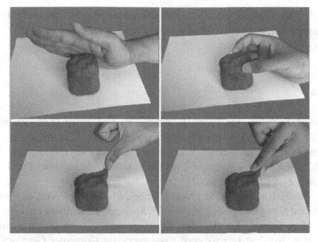

Fig. 2. Four hand gestures for deforming virtual clay

Fig. 3. Prototype view

4   Conclusion

In Immersive media art a Sound Clay is now reaching beyond Interactive media art. In this art space, deforming virtual clay using real hands becomes simultaneously-generated sound. I have argued that in order to make physical and sound interactions in fully immersive augmented environment.

The Sound Clay project also showed the possibility to provide fully immersive augmented environment for deforming clay and sound using HMD, hand tracking device, and AR marker.

References

1. Hu, J., Wang, F., Funk, M., Frens, J., Zhang, Y., Boheemen, T.V., Zhang, C., Yuan, Q., Qu, H., Rauterberg, M.: International Conference in Culture and Computing 2013, Department of Industrial Design, Eindhoven University of Technology, The Netherlands School of Digital Media, Jiangnan University, China, Paticipatory Public Media Arts for Social Creativity, pp. 179–180 (2013)
2. Wang, F., Hu, J., Rauterberg, M.: New Carriers, Media and Forms of Public Digital Arts. In: Culture and Computing 2012, pp. 83–93. Springer, Heidelberg (2012)
3. Edmonds, E., Turner, G., Candy, L.: Approaches to interactive art systems. In: Proceedings of the 2nd International Conference on Computer Graphics and Interactive Techniques in Australasia and South East Asia 2004, pp. 113–117. ACM, Singapore (2004)
4. Özkul, D.: Impacts of The Immersive Interface Design Model on Image- Spectator Interaction in New Media, M.A. Thesis submitted to the Bilkent University, Communication and Design
5. Thomas Massie, A.: tangible goal for 3D modeling 3D Modeling. In: Computer Graphics and Applications, pp. 62–65. IEEE
6. Sheng, J., Balakrishnan, R., Singh, K.: An interface for virtual 3D sculpting via physical proxy. In: GRAPHITE 2006, pp. 213–220 (2006)

Five Features for Modeling Augmented Reality

Sha Liang and Chris Roast

Communication & Computing Research Centre, Sheffield Hallam University,
Howard Street, Sheffield S1 1WB, UK
liangshaahu@gmail.com, C.R.Roast@shu.ac.uk

Abstract. Augmented reality is growing rapidly and supports people in different fields such as education, design, navigation and medicine. However, there is limited discussion about the characteristic features of augmented reality and what is meant by the term. This paper presents five different features: changeability, synchronicity and instant, antecedent, partial one to one and hidden reality. The explanation of each of these features is given follow a consistent structure. The benefits of generating features and future work are described.

Keywords: augmented reality, features, technology.

1   Introduction

Augmented reality (AR) technology combines virtual information with the real environment in real-time performance [1]. Due to the development of the mobile devices, AR is growing rapidly and is becoming popular through in a variety of areas [2]. However, because of the broad meaning for this term, it is not exactly clear what is meant or intended when people use AR. Some of the sources use a very general meaning for it, whereas others mean something very specific and narrow [3]. Section two will explicitly outline the existing research concerning the features of augmented reality. Section three presents five different features and briefly summaries the meanings of them using a lightweight diagrammatic notation. The benefits of developing our understanding through such features are then described in term of how they will be used in future work.

2   Related Work

There is relatively little literature examining the nature of augmented reality, what the term means and how it should be used. The term of AR was coined by Caudell and Mizell [4] as an enabling technology used to 'augment' the visual field of the user with information necessary in the performance of the current task. Azuma [5] defined AR as a system that has the following three characteristics: combines real and virtual, interactive in real time, registered in 3D. However, AR is not limited to our sense of sight, and it could potentially apply to any of the senses, including hearing, touch and

C. Stephanidis (Ed.): HCII 2014 Posters, Part I, CCIS 434, pp. 607–612, 2014.

smell. We can speculate further as to whether tools such as, memory aids represent augmentations to other human capabilities (like cognition). Establishing meanings and identifying boundaries to concepts is a common and important activity much research and AR should benefit from the same.

3   Features

This paper introduces the five features of augmented reality, followed by an explanation of each to initiate establishing the characteristics of the concept. The features have been arrived at from reviewing existing AR research and critical reflection by the authors. The format of explaining the AR features is based upon Borcher's approach [6], which describes a formal model of pattern languages to reduce ambiguity. The structure of this model is simplified in this paper. The explanation of features consists of the following items:

- Title: a short and memorable phrase.
- Problem: the major issue that the feature addresses.
- Definition: a brief summary of the meaning of features.
- Description: a detailed explanation of AR features including examples.
- Diagram: a diagram summarizing the main idea in a graphical way.

3.1   Changeability

Problem: How should virtual information be generated?

Definition: Virtual information born of the real-world information can be changed during an AR event.

Description: With respect to an augmented reality system, virtual information is superimposed on a view of the real world [3]. A key aspect of augmented reality is that the virtual information can be changed dynamically, while the real-world information does not. For example, Wikipedia World is an AR application providing users with the locations of stations, hotels and more [7]. When users use the app and move around, the virtual information bubble will pop up automatically. An icon visually indicating, say, a real-world station, can be clicked more Wikipedia information will be about the station will be presented. This additional information replaces the previous virtual bubble. The content of virtual information has been changed easily and completely. As opposed to the virtual information, the real station has not changed. The feature of changeability is captured by the following diagram (see Fig. 1).

Diagram

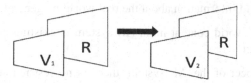

Fig. 1. Feature of Changeability

Letter R represents the real-world information and V the virtual information overlaid on the real-world content. The arrow expresses that the V_1-R augmented reality system is transferred to V_2-R because of an effect of changeability.

3.2 Synchronicity and Instant

Problem: How should the virtual and real content be connected?

Definition: Changing the real content will result in the synchronic and instantaneous transformation of the virtual counterpart.

Description: Due to the changes of the real-world content, an AR virtual counterpart has to be updated synchronously and instantaneously. For example, Word lens [8] is an AR translation application that scans and foreign text and displays the test translated in real time. Once the user changes his or her point of view to another word, the displayed translation on the device changes rapidly in the same time. If the process of generating virtual information is delayed for a long time, viewers are unable to obtain the useful information. However, the time lags can exist because of the inherent information processing. Synchronicity and instant is captured by the following diagram (see Fig. 2).

Diagram

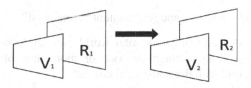

Fig. 2. Synchronicity and instant

V_1-R_1 augmented reality system presents that the virtual content V_1 is the overlay of real-world content R_1. If changing the real-world content from R_1 to R_2, the virtual content has to be transformed from V_1 to V_2 in this process. This corresponding transformation is synchronous and instantaneous.

3.3   Antecedent

Problem: How should information about the real world be generated?

Definition: The real-world content in an AR system is existing or happening before the virtual counterpart.

Description: In respect of the AR system, there is no restriction on what the real-world content is, which might be visual (e.g. photo, object, building and etc.), auditory or even tactile information. However, the process of augmenting them follows a particular order. Going back to the Wikipedia World example [7], the virtual station bubble displayed on the device is based on the fact that there is a real station nearby the users. In other words, the prerequisite of creating the bubble is that the real-world content, the railway station, exists in the physical world first. If the virtual content is created before the real-world content, the virtual element is meaningless because it has no real world interpretation (see Fig. 3).

Diagram

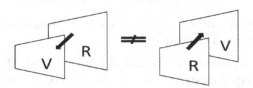

Fig. 3. Feature of Antecedent

The left diagram shows the V-R augmented reality system that the real-world information is antecedent and the virtual content is overlaid. The right diagram illustrates the "R-V" system, which is not an AR system because the virtual information exists at first.

3.4   Partial One to One

Problem: How should the virtual and real content be matched?

Definition: There is one and only one real-world content to correspond with the virtual content. However, there might be one or more than one piece of virtual information to correspond with the real-world content.

Description: A key aspect to augmented reality is that the relationship between virtual and real-world content is one-to-one. Word lens [8] translator could display a translated word '¡Hola!' in Spanish when the AR device scanned the real word 'Hello!' in English. The meaning of one-to-one relationship is that the virtual content '¡Hola!' should only present the real content 'Hello!' and not another physical word. However, AR translator could also render the English word 'Hello!' into different foreign language, such as '你好!' in Chinese, 'Bonjour!' in French and so on. That means the real content can be augmented to lots of virtual content. The term 'Partial one to one' describes this AR feature (see Fig. 4).

Diagram

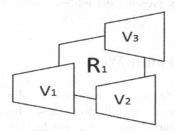

Fig. 4. Partial one to one

The left diagram $V_1 V_2 V_3$ - R_1 augmented reality system summarizes the real-world content R_1 could match the different virtual content V_1, V_2, V_3. However, it is not AR if more than one real-world contents correspond with the virtual content V_1.

3.5 Hidden Reality

Problem: How is the real content hidden by virtual content?

Definition: In an AR system, generating the virtual information will often result in the obstruction of real-world information.

Description: While users look through the virtual content, the real content will be more or less hidden. For example, Word lens [8] AR translator generates the virtually translated words, which replace the real-world words. Users have to remove the AR device if they need to see the original words. They cannot see both the virtual and real content simultaneously. While in such cases it is possible to try alternatives, such as whether the virtual content could be overlaid on the less important information. It still depends on the specific conditions to judge the difference between important and unimportant information, and intrinsic risk of AR is that the virtual occludes some of reality (see Fig. 5).

Diagram

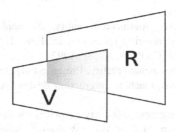

Fig. 5. Hidden Reality

In this diagram, the virtual information V partially obstructs the real-world information R. The shadow presents the hidden real-world content because of the generating virtual content.

4   Conclusion and Future Work

This paper presented five features of augmented reality based upon a simplified model of pattern language. Specifically, these features are: changeability, synchronicity, antecedent, partial one to one and hidden Reality. These features of augmented reality might bring benefits to AR developers and research by providing a more explicit basis on which to articulate AR requirements, issues and technologies. For example, according to the feature of hidden reality, designers could begin to consider the appropriate position to display the virtual content. Partial one to one might bring the potential clues for developers to create different kinds of virtual content corresponding with one piece of real-world information. Understanding the meaning of AR is still the foundation of ongoing PhD research. Our hope is that this paper serves as to innovate, refine and prototype potential solutions using AR for enhancing older population's experience in the future.

Acknowledgements. We are grateful to thank our supervisor team member, Luigina Ciolfi and Elizabeth Uruchurtu for their insightful comments on an earlier draft.

References

1. Liarokapis, F., De Freitas, S.: A Case Study of Augmented Reality Serious Games. In: Ebner, M., Schiefner, M. (eds.) Looking Toward the Future of Technology-Enhanced Education: Ubiquitous Learning and the Digital Native, pp. 178–191. IGI Global Press (2010)
2. Papagiannakis, G., Simgh, G., Magnenat-Thalmann, N.: A survey of mobile and wireless technologies for augmented reality systems. Computer Animation and Virtual Worlds 19(1), 3–22 (2008)
3. Craig, A.B.: The Understanding of augmented reality: Concepts and Applications. Morgan Kaufmann, Waltham (2013)
4. Caudell, T.P., Mizell, D.W.: Augmented reality: An application of heads-up display technology to manual manufacturing processes. In: Proc. Hawaii Int'l Conf. on Systems Sciences, pp. 659–669. IEEE CS Press, Kauai (1992)
5. Azuma, R.T.: A survey of augmented reality. Presence 6(4), 355–385 (1997)
6. Borchers, J.O.: A pattern approach to interaction design. AI & Society 15(4), 359–376 (2001)
7. Madden, L.: Professional Augmented Reality Browsers for Smartphones: Programming for junaio, Layar and Wikitude, p. 29. John Wiley & Sons, Chichester (2011)
8. Word lens on the iTunes App Store (2012), https://itunes.apple.com/ca/app/word-lens/id383463868?mt=8

Augmented Reality Applications Assisting Maintenance Activities in Extreme Environments: HCI Issues

Vasileios-Marios Mantzios[1], Theodoros Apostolopoulos[1], and Olga Beltramello[2]

[1] Department of Informatics
Athens University of Economics and Business 76, Patission Str., 10434 Athens, Greece
[2] ATLAS Experiment
CERN, Route de Meyrin 385, 1217, Geneva, Switzerland
{vmantzios,tca}@aueb.gr, olga.beltramello@cern.ch

Abstract. Maintenance of complex technology artifacts in hazardous environments can be a risky and demanding procedure. Operators need to be both efficient and meticulous in their activities in order to ensure the quality of their maintenance activities and the effectiveness of the limited time spent in the hazardous environment. Thus, an intuitive AR informative system could improve the operators' efficiency during their presence in the hazardous environment. What are the Human-Computer Interaction implications that arise in such applications?

Keywords: augmented reality, extreme environments, personal safety system, human-computer interaction, assistive information systems, exploitation.

1 Motivation

The European Organization for Nuclear Research (CERN) is broadly known across the Globe for its unique physics projects probing the fundamental structure of the universe. In order to deal with such unique objectives and nuclear physics matters, the world largest and most complex scientific instruments are being utilized in day-to-day demanding assignments. These instruments include the Large Hadron Collider (LHC) and the four discrete detector that are lying in the trajectory of LHC. In a typical experiment, the LHC accelerates two beams of protons or heavy ions traveling in opposite directions in extremely high speed. These opposite travelling beams collide at the four detector locations, including the ATLAS[1] detector. This detector is a complex construction which is about 45 meters long, more than 25 meters high, and about 7,000 tons heavy. The operational efficiency of ATLAS and the rest physics detectors is degraded due to the aforementioned collisions of protons, thus maintenance and upgrade activities have to take place periodically at all sites in order to restore and evolve the operational ability of the complex electronics and information systems that are exposed in the beam. These maintenance activities are

---

[1] The ATLAS experiment, http://atlas.ch/

C. Stephanidis (Ed.): HCII 2014 Posters, Part I, CCIS 434, pp. 613–618, 2014.

very complicated operations executed by highly trained and experienced technicians, and can last from one month, to that long as two years. During the maintenance or upgrade operations, the operators are exposed to radiations that has been developed while the accelerator was operating and experiments were executed in the detectors caverns.

The radiations of a radioactive environment are the followings: α (alpha), β (beta) and γ (gamma). This radiation can be very harmful for the operators' health, but unfortunately, it has not yet been discovered a wearable layer that can protect human being (and consequently operators) from gamma radiation. Thus, from a practitioner point of view, the only feasible way for operators to ensure their protection is to monitor the cumulative radiation that each operator absorbs, so that he will stop exposing his self in the hazardous environment once a safety limit has been reached. However, this approach limits the operational timeframe of each user while in the detectors caverns. The aforementioned limitation in conjunction with the enormous number of complex steps that a maintenance routine consist of, emerges the increasing need for a Safety System that will be able to assist operators during their maintenance activities or (possibly) emergent evacuation incidences.

Which would be the operators' requirements for such a system and which are the human-computer interaction implications? A functional characteristic of such a system is that the final artifact should be a lightweight, wearable device that will be easy to start or stop intervening in the maintenance activities. Furthermore, the appropriate information should be displayed in a way so that it does not distract the users from their challenging workload and does not involve the use of their hands, as they need them for the difficult maneuvers in the scaffoldings and the actual activities.

Augmented Reality (AR) applications with Head Mounted Displays (HMDs) could provide operators with the sufficient informative content in order to aid them in their step-by-step maintenance process and assist them in an emergency evacuation plan.

The EDUSAFE[2] project in which the author is involved, has an objective to develop an AR assistive system for maintenance operators in extreme environments. This system aims to improve the operator's performance, by providing maintenance and radiation information and (if feasible) to function as an assisting tool for navigation during an emergent cavern evacuation. While we are at the face of designing the platform, questions arise regarding human-computer interaction in extreme environments.

2   Human-Computer Interaction Issues

The system under development in the project could be classified in the family of mobile and collaborative augmented reality applications, since it will be a wearable device used in known but hazardous environment and will also help in the visual communication of the operator with his supervisor at the safe control room. Because

---

[2] Education in Advanced VR/AR Safety Systems for Maintenance in Extreme Environment, http://edusafe.web.cern.ch/edusafe/site.php

of the environment problematic and the current technology limitations, there are numerous HCI issues to be studied in the view of this project.

2.1 Visual Display Technique

Since the specific application is targeting difficult operations in extreme environments, the operators should be able to work and interact with the system with free hands. Therefore, the proposed display device is on the category of Head Mounted Displays (HMDs). Furthermore, the utilized technique could not be a video see-through device, as functionally wise it is not easy to force the operators to rely their lives on a screen without having direct visual contact with the environment. Thus, the most suitable AR technique for demanding operations in extreme or hazardous environments would be the Optical See-through which utilize a pair of AR glasses with advanced optics so that graphics content can be projected on them and thus, the surrounding reality will be augmented. Currently, for this technique there is a technical limitation that could mitigate the user acceptance of such application; the displaying area is significantly smaller than the human viewing area. For instance, there could be a radioactive hotspot that is in the viewing area of the operator, but the radiation information cannot get augmented on it because it is out of the HMD displaying range.

Another HCI issue regarding the use of AR HMDs is the user fatigue and eye strain that narrows the effective operating timeframe of the user. There is a study claiming that monocular or stereo binocular displays (each eye sees its own image) can cause significantly less discomfort, both in eyestrain and fatigue, than non-stereo binocular displays [15].

2.2 Tracking and (Auto)Calibration

Computer vision algorithms efficiency in such industrial environments that are full of shiny objects and have similar patterns and layouts can be extremely challenging without preparing first the environment with any kind of markers or sensors. On the other hand, this kind of functionality in a safety system could bother users with additional and in some times annoying extra actions. Thus in the view of the project that the author participates, the HCI impact of different computer vision techniques will be measured and will be develop the most suitable one for industrial and extreme environments.

2.3 Depth Perception

One difficult registration problem is the accurate depth perception. Stereoscopic displays could help, but additional problems including accommodation-vengeance conflicts or low resolution and dim displays cause objects to appear further away than their real position [16]. Some depth perception problems can be reduced by rendering objects with correct occlusion. [17] Furthermore, it has been stated that consistent registration plays a vital role in users' depth perception, and this could be achieved by accurately determining the eyepoint location as the eye rotates. An analysis of various eyepoint locations to use while rendering an image concluded that the eye's center of rotation yields the best position accuracy. However, the center of the pupil entrance yields higher angular accuracy [18].

2.4   Augmented Object and User Eyes Position

Since it is difficult to ensure a firm installation and a continuous correct position of the HMD towards the user's eyes, it is difficult to ensure the constant accurate pose of the augmented information with regards to the target objects and the current vision range of the user. Thus, specific eye tracking algorithms and devices will be implemented during the project so that the position of the augmented content is always recalibrated in the vision range of the user based on the current position of his eyes. Furthermore, the augmented content may not fit in the real environment because of difference in the actual distance of operator and augmented point. This issue could also get handled with specific eye tracking techniques in order to understand the user's current focus based on the eyes convergence.

2.5   Overload and Over-Reliance from Content and UI

Since the system is positioned as an assistive system for use in extreme environments, the augmented content as well as the user interface should compose a user experience that will be intuitive and helpful for the users. Thus, decisions regarding the kind and the amount of the provided information and the suitable representation of it have to be taken so that the user interface of the system in extreme environments will be smooth. Furthermore, there are important issues regarding the user interaction with the system that have to be handled as in an extreme environment the alternatives are fairly narrow. For instance, no touch interaction can occur as operators need to utilize specific gloves that are not touch equipment friendly. Tangible interfaces, speech recognition or even physical button utilization could be the optimal for such applications in extreme environments.

2.6   Connections and Communication

In our project, the system technical architecture involves a number of connections and interfaces between the modules (wired and wireless). From HCI point of view, there are numerous concerns about the usability and efficiency of such a system. We need to build an assistive system that will be compact and lightweight without complex wires and heavy units and at the same time it will not compromise in the system efficiency due to unwanted wireless transmission delays. Delay causes more registration errors than all other issues combined. For close range tasks (as the maintenance procedures), a rule of thumb is that one millisecond of delay causes one millimeter of error [19]. More importantly, delay can reduce task performance significantly [15].

3   Other Applications

In order to identify similar applications and exploitation potential of such a system in other industries, we need first to define the term "extreme environment" which is difficult. For the purpose of this paper, we will consider an environment as extreme when the operations in that field might induce mental or physical load or if the environment encapsulates hazards. Hazardous could be considered an environment that potentially can threat the surrounding biota and consequently could harm the human being if it is exposed in this environment beyond a specific amount of time without any protection layers. Given the presence of radiation at CERN detectors caverns, this working environment could be considered as hazardous. Other extreme environments include space, nuclear power plants, disaster scene, underwater, mining and so on.

Applications for such environments have already been developed or explored in the past trying to provide added value in the corresponding operations. The use of AR systems for nuclear power plant maintenance has been investigated in terms of navigation and environmental dose rates visualization [8]. The impact of gravity environments while using a head-mounted AR system has also been investigated [7]. An AR navigation system to aid fire brigade officers during a fire incident has been developed and tested in terms of usability [5]. Another work can be found in marine applications where an AR system for professional divers was developed in order to increase their capability to detect, perceive, and understand elements in underwater environments [6]. Although aircraft and train maintenance are not considered as operations in typical extreme environments, the fact that very complex work has to be performed in very short timeframes with high impact on potential failure, could let us treat them as extreme conditions due to mental overload. In this view, a framework applicable for the industrial maintenance and repair tasks was presented. The system was tested with various controlled settings [10]. Similarly, an AR system prototype for aircraft maintenance was developed to train and support maintenance operators [11]. Such AR systems have been proven to be useful through evaluations in the in-vitro condition. On the other hand, there are also systems designed and tested for real use-case scenarios. For instance, an AR system for military mechanics working in an armored personnel carrier has been developed. In this application, the space for tracking equipment was significantly limited [12, 13]. EDUSAFE application will be more in this category.

Acknowledgments. The PhD research of the first author is part of the aforementioned EDUSAFE project. This project consists of 12 fellows from 9 different Institutes and Organizations that are supported by a Marie Curie Initial Training Network Fellowship of the European Commission's FP7 Program, under contract number PITN-GA-2012-316919-EDUSAFE. We would like to thank each and every member of this project for their contribution to its challenging goal, and especially N. S. Lakshmiprabha and Y. Itoh.

References

1. van Krevelen, D.W.F., et al.: A Survey of Augmented Reality Technologies, Applications and Limitations. The International Journal of Virtual Reality 9(2), 1–20 (2010)

2. Zhou, F., et al.: Trends in augmented reality tracking, interaction and display: A review of ten years of ISMAR. In: Proceeding ISMAR 2008 Proceedings of the 7th IEEE/ACM International Symposium on Mixed and Augmented Reality Pages, pp. 193–202 (2008)
3. Malkawi, A.M., et al.: A new paradigm for Human-Building Interaction: the use of CFD and Augmented Reality. Automation in Construction 14(1), 71–84 (2005)
4. Service on the Atlas Tile Calorimeter drawers, http://cds.cern.ch/record/1321857?ln=en (accessed July 2013)
5. Steingart, D., et al.: Augmented cognition for fire emergency response: An iterative user study. In: 1st International Conference on Augmented Cognition (2005)
6. Morales, R., et al.: An underwater augmented reality system for commercial diving operations. In: OCEANS 2009, MTS/IEEE Biloxi-Marine Technology for Our Future: Global and Local Challenges, pp. 1–8. IEEE (2009)
7. Markov-Vetter, D., et al.: Verifying sensorimotoric coordination of augmented reality selection under hyper-and microgravity. International Journal of Advanced Computer Science 3(5) (2013)
8. Ishii, H., et al.: Augmented reality applications for nuclear power plant maintenance work. In: Proceedings of the International Symposium on Symbiotic Nuclear Power Systems for 21st Century (ISSNP), Fukui Prefectural Wakasa Wan Energy Research Center (2007)
9. Neumann, U., et al.: Cognitive, performance, and systems issues for augmented reality applications in manufacturing and maintenance. In: Proceedings IEEE 1998 Virtual Reality Annual International Symposium, pp. 4–11. IEEE (1998)
10. Schwald, B., et al.: An augmented reality system for training and assistance to maintenance in the industrial context (2003)
11. De Crescenzio, F., et al.: Augmented reality for aircraft maintenance training and operations support. IEEE Computer Graphics and Applications 31(1), 96–101 (2011)
12. Henderson, S., et al.: Exploring the benefits of augmented reality documentation for maintenance and repair. IEEE Transactions on Visualization and Computer Graphics 17(10), 1355–1368 (2011)
13. Henderson, S., et al.: Evaluating the benefits of augmented reality for task localization in maintenance of an armored personnel
14. Mackay, W.E.: Augmented reality: dangerous liaisons or the best of both worlds? In: Proceedings of DARE 2000 on Designing Augmented Reality Environments, pp. 170–171 (2000)
15. Ellis, S.R., et al.: Factors Influencing Operator Interaction with Virtual Objects Viewed via Head-Mounted Seethrough Displays: Viewing Conditions and Rendering Latency. In: Proc. Virtual Reality Ann. Int'l Symp (VRAIS 97), pp. 138–145. IEEE CS Press, Los Alamitos (1997)
16. Drascic, D., Milgram, P.: Perceptual Issues in Augmented Reality. In: Proc. SPIE, Stereoscopic Displays VII and Virtual Systems III, vol. 2653, pp. 123–134. SPIE Press, Bellingham (1996)
17. Rolland, J.P., Fuchs, H.: Optical Versus Video Seethrough Head-Mounted Displays in Medical Visualization. Presence: Teleoperators and Virtual Environments 9(3), 287–309 (2000)
18. Vaissie, L., Rolland, J.: Accuracy of Rendered Depth in Head-Mounted Displays: Choice of Eyepoint Locations. In: Proc. SPIE AeroSense 2000, vol. 4021, pp. 343–353. SPIE, Bellingham (2000)
19. Holloway, R.L.: Registration Error Analysis for Augmented Reality. Presence: Teleoperators and Virtual Environments 6(4), 413–432 (1997)

"Form Follows Function" – Investigating Interactive Physical Objects in Virtual Environments

Mathias Müller[1], Katarina L. Maurer[1], Anja Knöfel[1], Ingmar S. Franke[2],
and Rainer Groh[1]

[1] Chair of Media Design, Technische Universität Dresden, 01062 Dresden, Germany
{mathias.mueller,anja.knoefel,rainer.groh}@tu-dresden.de
[2] Gesellschaft für Technische Visualistik, Dresden, Germany
ingmar.franke@visuativ.com

Abstract. Controlling the available degrees of freedom in virtual environments often represents a challenge for the design of 3D user interfaces. Based on the concept of Tangibles and their natural affordances for spatial interaction, we conducted a study to investigate how users intuitively use physical objects in Virtual Environments. The results reveal a wide range of different approaches. This specifically relates to the utilization of an object's surface or edges for different functions or as representation of elements in the virtual world. The findings of the study have several implications on further research directions regarding tangible objects in Virtual Environments.

Keywords: 3D User Interfaces, Tangible Interaction, Virtual Reality.

1 Introduction

Without constraining the interaction, the available degrees of freedom in three-dimensional virtual environments make it difficult to execute tasks efficiently and precisely. Within the last decades different technologies were developed and tested in this context, for example gesture or speech. The use of natural gestures and movements in virtual environments has several disadvantages, such as the lack of haptic feedback [1] and the restricted interaction space. A different approach incorporates the concept of Tangible User Interfaces (TUI) [2]. Apart from providing haptic feedback, physical objects offer intuitive affordances [3]. Previous research has shown that using Tangibles for interaction can increase the performance of specific tasks [4]. At the same time, carefully designed TUIs can enhance the comfort of interaction [5]. By consulting principles of interaction from the real world, the required mental effort for operations in the virtual environment can be reduced [6]. The gained benefit from applying real-world-principles can be improved by extending objects with additional digital capabilities to increase their power and versatility [6]. Therefore digital augmented physical objects provide a method to bridge the gap between real and virtual environments [7]. By carefully designing tangible interfaces their natural affordances can be utilized to guide the user and facilitate the interaction.

C. Stephanidis (Ed.): HCII 2014 Posters, Part I, CCIS 434, pp. 619–624, 2014.
© Springer International Publishing Switzerland 2014

2   Study Description

In order to evaluate how affordances of basic geometric objects are perceived and utilized, we conducted a Wizard-of-Oz experiment with novice users (cf. **Fig. 1**). Three different objects – a cube, a sphere, and a cylinder – in three different sizes were provided in random order to examine how the participants use them to solve particular orientation and navigation tasks.

During the experiment, the participants stood in front of a large screen, showing a realistic virtual environment. They were instructed to perform one of the following basic orientation and navigation tasks:

- "look 90 degrees to the right"
- "look up"
- "turn around"
- "walk three steps forward"
- "walk three steps to the right"
- "turn to the left and walk three steps in this direction"
- "walk backwards"
- "lift yourself approximately 3 meters upwards"
- "select the bridge near the tower"
- "teleport to the selected location"

The corresponding action in the virtual environment was presented as a scripted sequence, initiated by the experimenter. Afterwards the participants had to demonstrate how they would use the object to execute the default task. Therefore, the presentation of the intended outcome of the task and the task execution were separated steps, because the objects lacked built-in functionality.

Fig. 1. Objects used in the study (left) and study setup (right): Participants use a tangible object to interact with a natural virtual environment projected onto a large screen

Between the blocks, which contained three sizes of one object, the participants had to rate the suitability and describe advantages and disadvantages of the different sizes of the object from their point of view. At the end of the study they were asked to evaluate the three different shapes in comparison and specify which object they preferred for the interaction scenario. The final questionnaire also included questions about desired additional technical capabilities and general comments on the study. 18 participants (10 male) between 19 and 42 years, averaging at about 26 years (SD: 4.99) took part in the study. Two thirds had previous experience with video games, mainly using PC for gaming (9 users), followed by Tablet or smartphones and consoles (6, respective 5 participants, due to the possibility to give multiple answers). However, all of them had experience using a PC and the vast majority stated being familiar with tablets or smartphones (16 participants, 89%).

3   Results

The quantitative results include a preference for sphere and cylinder. Rating the suitability for the given object between 0 (worst) and 10 (best), the sphere obtained an average rating of 7.44 (SD: 1.76), the cylinder was rated 7.22 in average (SD: 2.3) whereas the cube received generally worse ratings (mean: 4.53, SD: 2.44, Fig. 2).

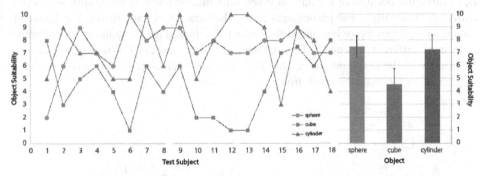

Fig. 2. Rating of object suitability

The object preference judgments show a similar picture. The sphere received an average rating of 7.33 (SD: 1.61), closely to the cylinder (mean: 7.17, SD: 2.38). Averaging at 4.78 (SD: 2.44), the cube did not receive a high rating regarding object preference (Fig. 3).

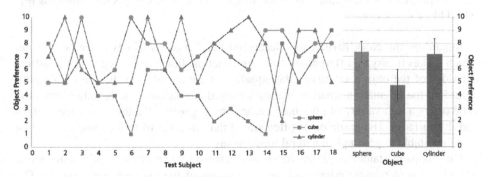

Fig. 3. Rating of object preference

These values are confirmed by the answers to the question which objects the participants could imagine to be using in a comparable setting. 13 participants voted for the sphere, 13 for the cylinder, whereas only 3 would use the cube in a similar scenario (multiple answers possible).

4   Observations

The observations of the participants during the study and the video-analysis of the experiment indicate a relation between object shape and interaction technique. Provided with a realistic scenario, some participants associated the object axes and surfaces of the cube with the spatial axes respectively with the spatial planes. The cylinder was commonly interpreted as a physical representation of the user in respect to the virtual environment. Therefore the participants used the cylinder similar to a pawn in a board game (Fig. 4). It was stated that the shape of the cylinder simplifies deriving a direction because of the natural given information about horizontality and verticality. Additionally some participants noted the straightforward distinction between lateral surface and top or bottom surface which facilitated the assignment and remembrance of different functions. The statements of the participants indicated that the familiarity of the shape due to its similarity to tools such as pointers, joysticks, pens or gear shifts facilitate the utilization.

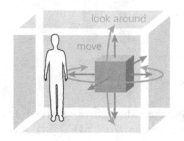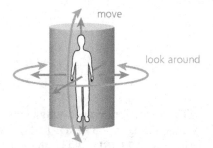

Fig. 4. Relations between object shape and usage in an immersive scenario: The axes of the cube are projected on the spatial axes of the virtual environment, whereas the cylinder is perceived like a simple pawn

Regarding the cube, participants described the discrete surfaces as an advantage, which makes it easy to differentiate between functionalities associated with the different sides of the object. However, the equality of the surfaces leads to an ambiguity regarding the orientation which sometimes caused confusions. On the other hand, the cube offers a rich variety of possible interactions, regarding the use of vertices, edges and the surfaces. The participants often stated that, in contrast to the sphere, the cube wasn`t suitable to accomplish natural movements.

One frequent statement about the sphere refers to the positive haptic sensation it provides due to missing edges and the naturalness of the executed movements. The shape provides a flexible usage, as its shape does not infer a specific amount of applicable functions. The continuity of the surface allows continuous movements.

However, the sphere did not provide any clues about the current orientation, causing confusion among some participants. In contrast to the other objects, the shape of the sphere causes an inherent instability. Therefore many participants recommended a fixation of the object.

5   Discussion

On a general level, the observed interaction techniques can be divided into five basic forms:

1. *Walking* - The participants moved in front of the projection, holding the object in their hands. This implies that the shape of the object did not have any significant influence.
2. *Moving* - The object was moved relative to the body to execute an action.
3. *Steering* - The participants used small object-specific movements, such as tilting, rolling or sliding the object. The position of the object relative to the body or to the projection had no significant influence.
4. *Touching* - The surface of the object was used for interaction.

A common behaviour was a mixture of *Moving* for orientation and *Steering* for navigation. However, the observations imply a strong influence of the object shape, its size and the structure of the virtual environment on the type of interaction used: The specific interaction tasks are determined by the structure of the virtual environment (e.g. in an interactive visualization of the solar system an orbital navigation could be used, which incorporates completely different interaction tasks). On the other hand, the size of the object determines which interaction type may be used. Smaller objects are more likely to be used in conjunction of the first two types, whereas the surface is more frequently utilized when interacting with larger objects. The shape and its haptic sensation are another important factor, which explains why the cube was rated significantly worse regarding performance or suitability, despite of the numerous possibilities it offers.

The cube can be characterized as **static** and rather **abstract**. These characteristics stand in conflict with the immersive setting of the user in the study. In a more abstract or mathematical tasks, such as CAD or 3D-modelling, the cube may receive a higher rating. In contrast, the sphere can be described as **dynamic** and **organic**. However, this dynamism has some disadvantages. This could be addressed with a fixation, which may increase the stability and hence reduce the insecurity of the user regarding the orientation. The cylinder represents a combination of both types, as it incorporates both dynamic (when rolling) and static (standing on its ground surface) aspects. Its **anthropomorphic** form induces a congruency between the structure of the environment and the interaction device. Therefore, the cylinder represents a suitable instrument for operating in an immersive, real-world setting.

6   Future Work

The observations during the study reveal a large bandwidth of interaction techniques even with comparatively simple objects. Extending the capabilities of physical objects with additional sensors and actuators reveals potential for improvements regarding the range of functions provided. Additional sensors and simple changes to the original shapes could provide additional and unambiguous affordances for the user. Augmenting an object with digital contents seems a promising approach to fix disadvantages of the basic object shape. One example could be projected markers on a sphere which allows a dynamic orientation of the object.

Further research directions include exploring the user's mental models in virtual environments in context with Tangibles. As the structure of the presented environment has a strong influence on the use of the objects, comparing the use of primitive bodies in different scenarios could enhance the understanding of how users perceive objects and use affordances in a specific context.

Acknowledgements. This work has been supported by the European Social Fund and the Free State of Saxony (Young Investigators Group CogITo, project no. 100076040). We like to thank the participants of the study and express our gratitude for their numerous comments and helpful insights.

References

1.   Norman, D.A.: Natural User Interfaces Are Not Natural. Interactions 17(3), 6–10 (2010)
2.   Ishii, H., Ullmer, B.: Tangible Bits: Towards Seamless Interfaces between People, Bits and Atoms. In: Proceedings of the ACM SIGCHI Conference on Human Factors in Computing Systems, CHI 1997, pp. 234–241. ACM Press, New York (1997)
3.   Norman, D.A.: The Design of Everyday Things. Basic Books, New York (2002)
4.   Patten, J., Ishii, H.: A Comparison of Spatial Organization Strategies in Graphical and Tangible User Interfaces. In: Proc. DARE 2000, pp. 41–50. ACM Press, New York (2000)
5.   Fitzmaurice, G.W., Buxton, W.: An Empirical Evaluation of Graspable User Interfaces: Towards Specialized, Space-Multiplexed Input. In: Proc. CHI 1997, pp. 43–50. ACM Press, New York (1997)
6.   Jacob, R.J.K., Girouard, A., Hirshfield, L.M., Horn, M.S., Shaer, O., Solovey, E.T., Zigelbaum, J.: Reality-Based Interaction: A Framework for Post-WIMP Interfaces. In: Proc. CHI 2008, pp. 201–210. ACM Press, New York (2008)
7.   van den Hoven, E., Frens, J., Aliakseyeu, D., Martens, J.-B., Overbeeke, K., Peters, P.: Design Research & Tangible Interaction. In: Proc. TEI 2007, pp. 109–115. ACM Press, New York (2007)

Virtual Reality Based Learning Aid to Understand Projection and Section of Solids in Architectural Graphics

Maulishree Pandey[1], Vikas Luthra[1], Pradeep G. Yammiyavar[1], and Anita P. Yammiyavar[2]

[1] Department of Design, Indian Institute of Technology Guwahati
{maulishree,l.vikas,pradeep}@iitg.ernet.in
[2] Department of Architecture, Royal Group of Institution
anitabpy@gmail.com

Abstract. This paper presents a learning tool set in immersive virtual reality to aid students in learning the subject of engineering/architectural graphics. Current instruction methods do not use 3D objects to teach the subject. This hinders student's ability to manipulate and interact with objects and understand the projections produced. Our tool allows students to observe 3D simulations of geometric objects and manipulate them in a virtual environment to closely understand the nature of the projections.

Keywords: Virtual Reality, Architectural Graphics /Engineering Drawing, Projection of solids, Section of solids, learning tool.

1 Introduction

Spatial reasoning is known to be a fundamental and essential skill for architects, designers and engineers. One of the few courses common to the three fields but of utmost importance is that of engineering graphics or technical drawing. It is taught to the students in their first semester of undergraduate studies. Through this course, students learns to develop the ability to think spatially and formally represent the spatial operations in the 2D plane of paper. Most students face difficulty at understanding and learning fundamentals in this course. These are mainly to do with mental visualizations and spatial manipulations.

To enhance students' learning at the subject, we have designed a tool which makes use of the virtual reality (VR) technology. Virtual environments can capture and convey enough social cues such as body language, interactive props, and the look and feel of 'real' surroundings to convince some part of the participants' brains that they are physically in this other world. Our aim is to develop small capsules in virtual reality environment of topics like projection and section of solids that will help students understand these topics effectively by moving around objects visibly instead of just turning them inside their imagination.

C. Stephanidis (Ed.): HCII 2014 Posters, Part I, CCIS 434, pp. 625–630, 2014.

2   Related Work

Different approaches have been used to aid in instruction of architectural graphics/engineering drawing. Some of them include use of animated content[1],development of physical models[2],use of computer graphics simulation tools[3] etc. Results of experimental studies based on these approaches show positive impact on the spatial abilities as well as performance of students. These approaches also highlights the importance of three-dimensionality in instruction material and providing the students with an experiential medium to learn architectural graphics. However the interaction with 'content' in these approaches is still minimal. Thus using virtual reality for our prototype provides with the opportunity of more interaction with the contents as well as "direct manipulation" of solid objects which are visible. Students can view 3D objects from multiple viewpoints or zoom in/out the objects. This potentially deepens the learning effect when the students are actively constructing new knowledge [4]

Many other learning tools to support spatial abilities in engineering design have also been made [5]. Mengshoel et al. [6, 7] have developed the Visual Reasoning Tutor (VRT), an instructional system which exploits the missing view problem as a mechanism to develop the visual reasoning abilities of students. In missing view problems, students create 3D solid objects from two 2D projections by applying operations inverse to orthographic projection. Osborn and Agogino [8] developed an interface that provides an environment allowing the user to interactively explore any arbitrary position of a given object using direct manipulation. Also, it provides the capability to demonstrate standard orthographic and axonometric views with animation.

Virtual reality has been a popular choice for designing learning tools that enhance and/or aid in 3D visualization. Both desktop and immersive VR based applications have been made to familiarize students with 3D learning content in various subjects [9, 10, 11, 12] .The use of virtual reality technology as aid in instruction have also increased due to the unique affordances that it offers in enhancing learners' cognitive skills [13]. Apart from that research also shows that constructivist principles are fundamental and underlying our understanding of learning in a virtual reality environment [14,15,16,17,18]

3   Primary Research

We conducted contextual user research with first, third and fifth semester architecture students at the Architecture Department, of an institution, and first semester design and engineering students of Indian Institute of Technology Guwahati. Backed with literature on learning and cognition models [18, 19], we identified that students' initiation into architectural graphics is not smooth. In current teaching method student has to first learn to imagine, then understand the rules of engineering graphics in order to be able to manipulate 3D images into projections on the 2D surfaces. For a large number of students this is difficult to master as they try to understand spatial manipulation through analyses rather than synthesis. This is also a major deviation from their previous academic experience, wherein they were thinking mainly in terms of coordinates and 2D shapes like lines, circles, planes, etc. Problem lies in visualizing changes in orientations, positions and scale of objects. This is especially evident for complicated objects, and topics like projections, sections and intersections of solids, regeneration of solids, etc.

Fig. 1. User Research in Classroom's Context

Given the need, requirements of the solution are -

1. From the student point of view: as mentioned before, the students have to cope with two realities, the objects and their projections. It is a pedagogical target to decrease the conceptual distance between them, as part of the learning process. The student has to became the observer of the object positioning himself at different points of view and has to be able to establish the connection between the Orthographic Projection and the object and backwards, being able to see the reversibility of the process.
2. From the teacher point of view: although Architectural Graphics/ Engineering Drawing is based on clear conventions, which should create a very easy learning environment, difficulties arise due to the lack of 3D perception of the students.
3. Constructivist Learning: Learning in the course of engineering drawing requires a practical component of 'learning by doing', aligned with constructivist learning Models. Thus, one of the main tasks and challenges is to create environments in which the learner can interact meaningfully with a set of 'real-life' challenges.

4   Prototype

For our prototype, we used Vizard, a virtual reality toolkit that allows virtual reality simulation of geometric objects, real-life objects, avatars, etc. by means of Python scripting. The simulations can be viewed on the computer screens or one could use the head-mounted displays to make the experience more immersive. The toolkit includes a full body motion-sensor device that makes interactions possible with the 3D simulations. Within the subject of Engineering Graphics, the topics of projection and section of solids are difficult for both instructors and students, to explain and grasp respectively. Our prototype tackles these two topics. To this end, we have simulated hexagonal square pyramids and prisms, which are commonly encountered geometric objects in the instructional material. Projections of the simulations are mapped on vertical, horizontal and profile planes. The simulations can be manipulated i.e. scaled, moved and rotated freely along the three axes of rotations using

- Gestures, when the student is wearing a HMD for an immersive learning environment
- Keyboard and mouse, for use of tool on desktops, laptops or computer screens

Changes to the simulations and their projections are updated simultaneously. The conventions followed in engineering graphics for projection lines and labels are used in the prototype.

5   Pilot Testing

The informal testing of the prototype was conducted with six students (four males and two females), who completed the engineering graphics course previous semester. A pre-questionnaire was designed to gather biographical information familiarity with gestural interfaces, computer gaming etc. The major aim of this pilot testing is to:

- To identify some of the major usability errors in our prototype.
- To gain the qualitative feedback about the tool being developed.
- To gauge initial attitude of students towards using this tool for learning.

After pilot testing, we would be conducting an experiment with first semester students to measure the learning effectiveness and acceptance of this tool. For this, we have prepared a questionnaire partly based on Technology Acceptance Model (TAM) (20, 21) widely used in technology acceptance studies. As per TAM, acceptance of a system is represented by intention to use, which in turn is determined by the user's attitude toward using the system. The attitude is determined by users' perceptions of the usefulness and ease of use. Apart from the questions related to TAM, we also incorporated parameters for motivation to learn, effectiveness of the content and perceived engagement. We validated the above questionnaire in our pilot testing to identify ambiguous, irrelevant, similar and misleading questions.

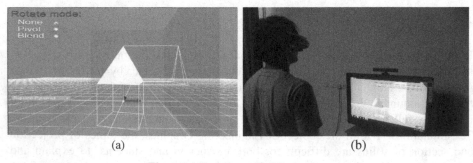

(a)   (b)

Fig. 2. (a) Prototype. (b) Pilot testing.

6   Discussion and Conclusion

All six students in the pilot study were appreciative of the tool's capability as a learning aid for the mentioned topics. They found the tool useful in visualizing and understanding the projections as the geometric objects were manipulated dynamically. Students were comfortable with the feedback provided for projections lines, labeling and positioning of solid. With regard to the interface, two subjects mentioned difficulty in rotational control and understanding angular feedback. With regard to the questionnaire, students' test results suggested few questions to be redundant for our future experiment. We have now reworked the number of questions to 22 from initial 25.

Initial results from the pilot testing suggest that the tool can be employed as an effective instructional aid in engineering graphics. However, a comprehensive empirical study needed to be carry out in future for strengthening out our claims.

7   Future Work

We would be conducting a controlled experiment with first semester students to measure the effectiveness of the prototype as a learning tool. Experimental group would be taught projection and sections of solids using our system while the treatment group would be taught the topics through the conventional classroom method. Post the teaching session(s), both groups would be given a quiz on the topics. Scores, time taken per question, correctness of answers and other such parameters would be used to analyze the effectiveness of the tool against the classroom teaching methods.

Acknowledgement. We would like to acknowledge all the participating students and faculty from Indian Institute of Technology, Guwahati and Royal School of Architecture, Guwahati for helping in our data collection as well as providing their inputs.

References

1. Halim, L., Yasin, R.M., Ishar, A.: CAMED: An Innovative Communication Tool in Teaching Engineering Drawing. WSEAS Transactions on Information Science & Applications 9(2) (2012)
2. Upadhye, S.N., Shaikh, S.M., Yalsangikar, T.B.: New Teaching Method To Teach Projection & Development of Solids. International Journal of Engineering 2(2) (2013)
3. Sun, X., Suzuki, K.: Evaluation of educational effects of the solid simulator. . Journal for Geometry and Graphics 3(2), 219–226 (1999)
4. Hanson, K., Shelton, B.E.: Design and development of virtual reality: analysis of challenges faced by educators. Educational Technology & Society 11(1), 118–131 (2008)
5. Contero, M., Naya, F., Company, P., Saorin, J.L.: Learning support tools for developing spatial abilities in engineering design. International Journal of Engineering Education 22(3), 470 (2007)

6. Mengshoel, O.J., Chauhan, S., Kim, Y.S.: Intelligent critiquing and tutoring of spatial reasoning skills. . AI EDAM-Artificial Intelligence for Engineering Design Analysis and Manufacturing 10(3), 235 (1996)
7. Hubbard, C., Mengshoel, O.J., Moon, C., Kim, Y.S.: Visual reasoning instructional software system. Computers & Education 28(4), 237–250 (1997)
8. Osborn, J.R., Agogino, A.M.: An interface for interactive spatial reasoning and visualization. In: Proceedings of the SIGCHI Conference on Human Factors in Computing Systems. ACM (1992)
9. Kaufmann, H., Dieter, S., Michael, W.: Construct3D: a virtual reality application for mathematics and geometry education. Education and Information Technologies 5(4), 263–276 (2000)
10. Kaufmann, H., Schmalstieg, D.: Designing immersive virtual reality for geometry education. In: Virtual Reality Conference, pp. 51–58. IEEE (2006)
11. Petersson, H., Sinkvist, D., Wang, C., Smedby, Ö.: Web-based interactive 3D visualization as a tool for improved anatomy learning. Anat. Sci. Ed. 2, 61–68 (2009), doi:10.1002/ase.76
12. Wrzesien, M., Alcañiz Raya, M.: Learning in serious virtual worlds: Evaluation of learning effectiveness and appeal to students in the E-Junior project. Computers & Education 55(1), 178–187 (2010)
13. Dalgarno, B., Lee, M.J.: What are the learning affordances of 3-D virtual environments? British Journal of Educational Technology 41(1), 10–32 (2010)
14. Chittaro, L., Ranon, R.: Web3D technologies in learning, education and training: motivations, issues, opportunities. Computers & Education 49, 3–18 (2007)
15. Tax'en, G., Naeve, A.: A system for exploring open issues in VR-based education. Computers & Graphics 26, 593–598 (2002)
16. Virvou, M., Katsionis, G.: On the usability and likeability of virtual reality games for education: the case of VR-ENGAGE. Computers & Education 50(1) (2008)
17. Shih, Y.-C., Yang, M.-T.: A collaborative virtual environment for situated language learning using VEC3D. Educational Technology & Society 11(1), 56–68 (2008)
18. Huang, H.M., Rauch, U., Liaw, S.S.: Investigating learners' attitudes toward virtual reality learning environments: Based on a constructivist approach. Computers & Education 55(3), 1171–1182 (2010)
19. Von Glasersfeld, E.: An exposition of constructivism: Why some like it radical, pp. 229–238. Springer (1991)
20. Mayer, E.R.: Multimedia Learning: Guiding Visuspatial Thinking with Instructional Animation. In: Shah, P., Miyake, A. (eds.) The Cambridge Handbook of Visuspatial Thinking, pp. 477–508. Cambridge University Press, New York (2005) ISBN 978-0-521-00173-0
21. Davis, F.D.: Perceived usefulness, perceived ease of use, and user acceptance of information technology. MIS Quarterly, 319-340 (1989)
22. Davis, F.D., Bagozzi, R.P., Warshaw, P.R.: User acceptance of computer technology: a comparison of two theoretical models. Management Science 35(8), 982–1003 (1989)

Guidance System Using Augmented Reality for Solving Rubik's Cube

Jaebum Park and Changhoon Park

Dept. of Game Engineering, Hoseo University,165 Sechul-ri, Baebang-myun, Asan,
Chungnam 336-795, Korea
ppp4542@imrlab.hoseo.edu, chpark@hoseo.edu

Abstract. This paper proposes a guidance system to help to solve the Rubik's cube. For the puzzle to be solved, each face must be returned to consisting of one color. But the problem is quite difficult because there are 4.3252x1019 different states that can be reached from any given configuration. Our system use augmented reality technology to recognize the placement of each square and provide intuitive and easily understandable guidance for solving procedure.

Keywords: Rubik's Cube, Guidance System, Augmented Reality, Immersive, Intuitive, Solving Algorithm.

1   Introduction

Rubik's Cube is a 3-D combination puzzle invented in 1974 by Erno Rubik of Hungary. In a classic Rubik's Cube, each of the six faces is covered by nine stickers, each of one of six solid colors. The puzzle is scrambled by making a number of random twists. For the puzzle to be solved, each face must be returned to consisting of one color. There are 4.3252x1019 different states that can be reached from any given configuration[1].

The problem is quite difficult. In Rubik's cubers' parlance, a memorized sequence of moves that has a desired effect on the cube, is called an algorithm. Many algorithms are designed to transform only a small part of the cube without interfering with other parts that have already been solved, so that they can be applied repeatedly to different parts of the cube until the whole is solved. Some algorithms do have a certain desired effect on the cube but may also have the side-effect of changing other parts of the cube[1].

Augmented reality (AR) is a live, copy, view of a physical, real-world environment whose elements are augmented by computer-generated sensory input such as sound, video, graphics or GPS data. A major strength of AR systems is their intuitive depiction of information, where the user perceives virtual and real objects as coexisting in the same space. At a glance, the user naturally recognizes the content of the information (i.e., an object's location, size, shape, color and maybe its movement)[2]. In this paper, a series of solution steps will be provided by using AR technology.

C. Stephanidis (Ed.): HCII 2014 Posters, Part I, CCIS 434, pp. 631–635, 2014.
© Springer International Publishing Switzerland 2014

2   AR-Based Guidance System

In this paper, we propose a guidance system to help to solve the Rubik's cube using augmented reality technology. The system consists of iPad, 2x2x2 cube and iPad Stand. The size of iPad is appropriate considering cube size, camera distance, and arm's length. 2x2x2 cube is used because the size of square is bigger than classic 3x3x3 cube. The size of square is closely related to the recognition rate and speed when augmented reality works. And we need a mount in order to use both hands for manipulating cube.

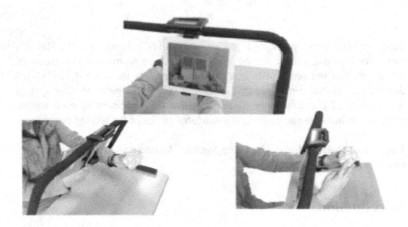

Fig. 1. System Overview

Table 1. System specifications

Name	Type	Version	Usage
1. iPad2	Hardware		Personal computer
2. i-Cozy	Hardware		iPad Stand
3. 2 x 2 x 2 Cube	Hardware		Rubik's Cube
Unity Engine	Software	4.0	Game Engine
4. Qualcomm	SDK	2.5.8	Augmented reality
5. Vuforia SDK			

Our system uses Unity3D as its underlying development platform and rendering engine. Unity3D is a cross-platform game engine with a built-in IDE. It is used to develop video games for web plugins, desktop platforms, consoles and mobile devices. Unity3d is a very flexible engine that was used for generating and integrating richer 3D graphic.

For augmented reality, we use a Mobile AR SDK called Vuforia developed by Qualcomm that supports iOS, Android and Unity 3D. It uses Computer Vision technology to recognize and track planar images and simple 3D objects, such as boxes, in real-time. The virtual object then tracks the position and orientation of the image in real-time so that the viewer's perspective on the object corresponds with their perspective on the Image Target, so that it appears that the virtual object is a part of the real world scene.

Vuforia provides Application Programming Interfaces (API) in C++, Java, Objective-C, and the .Net languages through an extension to the Unity game engine.[3] In this way, the SDK supports both native development for iOS and Android while also enabling the development of AR applications in Unity that are easily portable to both platforms. The Vuforia AR Extension for Unity enables vision detection and tracking functionality within the Unity IDE and allows developers to create AR applications and games easily. Figure 2 shows how Virtual buttons work only with image targets.

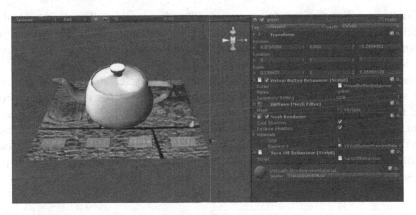

Fig. 2. Vuforia AR Extension for Unity and Virtual Buttons demo

Vuforia uses computer vision technology to recognize 2D and 3D image targets. An image target or 'Trackable" is an image that the Vuforia SDK can detect and track. In the system, a special kind of predefined markers called Frame Markers is used. Vuforia provides 512 predefined Frame Markers where each marker has an unique code of binary pattern around the border of the marker image. Decoding a Frame Marker takes relatively little processing power. In the system, we designed Frame Markers for 24 square with 6 different colors of 2x2x2 cube like the Figure 3.

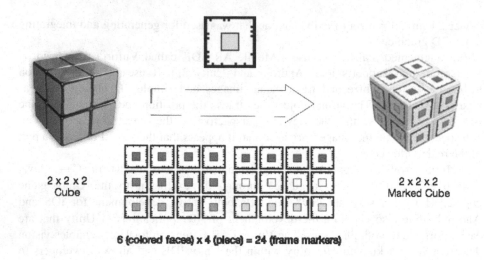

Fig. 3. Frame Markers and 2x2x2 Cube

Our system has three main processes. First, it recognize the placement of each square. If recognition is successes, colored planes are augmented to show the result of recognition. It then figures out the shortest path to solving the puzzle. And, a series of solution steps is provided like the below figure.

Face names are very simple to understand and they let user know which face to turn while reading cube notation. Now if user hold his or her cube strait in front of face, the face of the cube directly in front of user is called the F face, which stands for Front. The cube faces on the right and left side of the cube are the R and L faces. The face on top is U for Up face. The bottom is D for Down face. And the back face is B for Back. Therefore, there are 12 kinds of solution step. These step will be displayed by using AR technology.

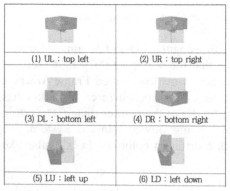

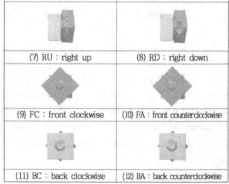

Fig. 4. 12 kinds of solution step

3   Conclusion

In this paper, we proposed a guidance system to help to solve the Rubik's cube. Augmented reality technology is applied to recognize the placement of each square and provide intuitive and easily understandable guidance for solving procedure. Our system has three main processes. First, it recognize the placement of each square. If recognition is successes, colored planes are augmented to show the result of recognition. It then figures out the shortest path to solving the puzzle. And, a series of solution steps is provided like the below figure.

Fig. 5. Display of step-by-step instruction and the result

References

1. Rubik's Cube, http://en.wikipedia.org/wiki/Rubik's_Cube
2. Augmented Reality, http://en.wikipedia.org/wiki/Augmented_reality
3. Włodzimierz, K., Wojciech, S., Łukasz, C.: Rubik's Cube Reconstruction from Single View for Service Robots. Machine Graphics & Vision International Journal 15, 451–459 (2006)
4. Korf, R.: Finding optimal solutions to rubik's cube using pattern databases. In: Proceedings of the National Conference on Artificial Intelligence (AAAI 1997), pp. 700–705 (1997)
5. Demaine, E.D., Demaine, M.L., Eisenstat, S., Lubiw, A., Winslow, A.: Algorithms for Solving Rubik's Cubes. In: Demetrescu, C., Halldórsson, M.M. (eds.) ESA 2011. LNCS, vol. 6942, pp. 689–700. Springer, Heidelberg (2011)

BilliARt - AR Carom Billiards

Exploration of an AR Framework

Ignace P. Saenen[1], Steven De Bock[1], Elhassan Abdou[1], Peter Lambert[1],
Rik Van de Walle[1], Tim Vets[2], Micheline Lesaffre[2], Michiel Demey[2],
and Marc Leman[2]

[1] Ghent University - iMinds - Multimedia Lab,
G. Crommenlaan 8 bus 201, B-9050 Ledeberg - Ghent, Belgium
`ignace.saenen@ugent.be`
[2] Ghent University - iMinds - IPEM,
Sint-Pietersnieuwstraat 41, B-9000 Ghent, Belgium
`tim.vets@ugent.be`

Abstract. This paper presents a framework for processing visual and auditory textures in an augmented reality environment that enables real-time artistic creativity without imposing predefined interaction rules or constraints. It integrates multiple problem domain knowledge in sonification, real-time rendering, object tracking and object recognition in a collaborative art installation using a familiar Carom Billiard game table, motion tracking cameras, a table-top digital projector and a digital audio installation. A demonstrator was presented at a 10-day annual innovation exhibition in Belgium and was perceived as innovative, intuitive and very easy to interact with.

Keywords: Augmented Reality, Framework, Sonification, Visualization, Object Tracking, Art Installation

1 Introduction

Augmented Reality (AR) environments superimpose or replace real world experiences by artificial information. This paper approaches AR as an artistic tool using a familiar game setting as a collaborative creativity platform. The goal was to integrate animated textures in visual and auditory modalities so that they jointly provide a unified experience.

AR systems typically combine several problem domains [1]. Based on our underlying framework, we implemented an AR application around a Carom Billiard table in a project named BilliARt. It features a dynamic system in which generative music and visual textures emerge from the interaction of the participants with the Carom Billiard table. Cues, shots and the movement of multiple balls translate into properties for textural changes that affect the overall experience in response to the enhanced audio-visual feedback.

The culturally established and familiar game Carom Billiard was chosen as a platform for unlocking generative art principles to a broad audience in an interactive way. Instantaneous recognizability of a common situation where people

C. Stephanidis (Ed.): HCII 2014 Posters, Part I, CCIS 434, pp. 636–641, 2014.

interact with each other is brought into effect by the game. However, the game rules are not mandatory and participants can freely interpret the new interactions effectuated by the enhanced audio-visual feedback. BilliARt was conceived as a collaborative interactive musical and visual gaming instrument, and presented at a 10-day annual innovation exhibition [2] in Belgium (Figs. 1 and 2). After interacting with the installation, participants were asked questions about their experience and the visual as well as auditory qualities of the installation.

Fig. 1. BilliARt at the Jaarbeurs 2013   **Fig. 2.** event detection and feedback

Chapter 2 briefly outlines specific AR challenges, followed by Chapter 3 that describes our AR framework and implementation in more detail. An overview of the user experiences is presented in Chapter 4 and we conclude in Chapter 5.

2   Challenges

To correctly superimpose relevant artificial information, a correct world representation is of key importance, so that avoiding or removing discrepancies in the representation is an important technical challenge. BilliARt uses *object recognition* to uniquely identify objects by appearance, state or position, and *object tracking* to identify object state changes over time. Tracking multiple objects simultaneously requires a *multi-object tracking* approach [3].

Sensors and actuators need calibration, and an additional two-second calibration phase after startup is required to correctly project generated visuals on the world.

System latency is preferably reduced below a human-perceivable threshold. For AR systems, this is typically in the order of a number of milliseconds, see also [4].

In the next section, we discuss how these challenges were addressed for the BilliARt system.

3   Overview of BilliARt

3.1   Components

The main game loop [5] updates all subsystems such as the input manager, object recognition, visualization and sonification components, and produces 60 visual frames and 44.100 audio samples per second asynchronously, see Fig. 3.

3.2   Object Tracking

A critical subcomponent of the AR billiards system is the tracking of the billiard balls and cues. To this end, a low-cost and scalable OptiTrack [6] motion capture system with 100Hz infrared cameras is chosen in the demonstrator. Infrared reflecting strips are used to capture 3D coordinates of an object's position. Objects that are not balls are tagged with 3 strips, making Carom Billiard cues easy to identify.

The detection of balls presents a challenge. A first attempt was to cover balls with reflective strips. Because ball movement rotates strips in and out of view of the cameras, 3 strips are largely insufficient. Other disadvantages are non-optimal ball rotations due to the inequalities introduced on the ball surface, and OptiTrack reporting multiple objects for each ball appearing and disappearing during movement. A better result is achieved by covering the balls with an IR reflective dye over the entire ball surface. OptiTrack then reports a single marker per ball, while trajectory smoothness during ball movement is retained. Ball and cue classification is achieved by filtering on marker size and height of the markers.

3.3   Object Recognition

When there are multiple objects, OptiTrack does not uniquely link a marker to an object. We used the following heuristic to resolve this issue: each detected marker of a given frame is compared to all markers of the previous frame. Objects are then uniquely identified by iteratively selecting the marker pair that has the least squared distance in position, velocity and acceleration vectors. While this worked well for our purpose, an alternative algorithm is given in [3,7].

3.4   Visualization

We visualize particle-based effects and motions in real-time. Calculating new particle positions at 1/60 Hz on the CPU scales badly in terms of memory and performance complexities. Because there are no inter-dependencies between particles, latency can be reduced by storing and calculating particle behavior on the graphics hardware (GPU), thus taking advantage of the GPU's Single Instruction Multiple Data parallel execution architecture. Hardware rendering interoperability eliminates the need for costly memory transfers between the CPU and GPU. Every 16.667 ms, a new image is projected on the table surface.

Figure 4 shows a sample visualization: particles [8] are manipulated by the positions of the balls, here represented as metaballs. *OpenGL* is used for 3D rendering [9] and *CUDA* is used to compute the visuals on the GPU.

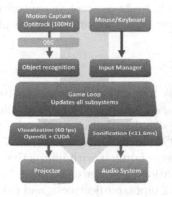

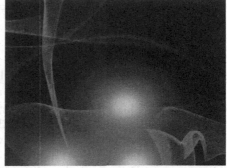

Fig. 3. BilliARt framework   **Fig. 4.** visualization sample

3.5   Sonification

JackAudio. A virtual sound device with virtual jack in- outputs and associated memory buffers is emulated by JackAudio's client/server, see [10] and [11]. When the JackAudio server moves audio content from an input to an output buffer of 2 connected virtual jacks, it is processed by a digital signal processor (DSP). The audio sample period (44100Hz) and the sample buffer-size (512 samples) require that DSP processing time takes at most 11.6ms to avoid invalidating the output buffer, audible as static noise.

Sound Generation. Melodic structures are derived from the positions and movement of the balls. In the *time domain* (rhythm), inter-onset intervals are inversely related to the speed of a ball. Pitch selections are made by projecting the continuous motion of the balls into a subdivision of discrete segments in the music *frequency domain*. An object collision (Fig. 2) initiates alterations to the global structure of the sonification, as high-level properties are changed based on (1) properties of the music at that point in time and (2) a set of predefined events. BilliARt's generative music algorithm moves between 3 primary behaviors.

State 1: melodies are derived dynamically from ball motion in real-time
State 2: melodic and harmonic material are locked into static structures with rhythmic material containing invariant elements
State 3: sonic material resulting from the above is recorded and reorganized by concatenative synthesis

By following important events in the session, the music highlights the structure of the interaction experience.

Inter System Communication. The authors of [1] do not discuss inter-(sub)system communication. BilliARt uses Open Sound Control(OSC) [12] as communication protocol between subsystems, e.g. to stream motion capture data as input for sonification and to remotely configure and calibrate the application.

4   User Evaluation

A structured questionnaire was administered by interview to visitors of a 10-day annual innovation exhibition [2]. 241 persons aged between 11 and 86 evaluated the installation (M=43,53; STD=21,18). The age distribution is bimodal with two data peaks around 25 and 65 years. 78,3% participants were male, 74,4% were experienced billiard players, and 17,7 % were familiar with interactive arts.

The questionnaire measures: (1) user evaluation (9 dimensions, scale from 0 to 10), (2) user perception of sound qualities (12 bipolar adjectives), and (3) user appreciation of the multi-modality of the installation. Rated usability dimensions are: attractiveness, efficiency, clearness, controllability, stimulating, innovative, creativity, entertaining, and sound to image mapping. See Figs. 5, 6 and 7.

Statistics

		Attractiveness	Efficiency	Clearness	Controllability	Stimulating	Innovative	Creativity	Entertaining	MatchSound/Image
N	Valid	217	217	217	217	217	217	217	217	217
	Missing	0	0	0	0	0	0	0	0	0
Mean		8,016	7,747	8,249	7,023	7,735	8,740	8,433	8,514	7,417
Std. Error of Mean		,0767	,0992	,1072	,1274	,1323	,0923	,1033	,0867	,1201
Median		8,000	8,000	8,000	7,000	8,000	9,000	9,000	9,000	8,000
Mode		8,0	8,0	9,0	8,0	8,0	9,0	9,0	9,0	8,0
Std. Deviation		1,1298	1,4618	1,5798	1,8762	1,9490	1,3600	1,5219	1,2774	1,7691
Skewness		-,514	-1,450	-1,137	-,553	-1,304	-2,426	-2,516	-,857	-,874
Std. Error of Skewness		,165	,165	,165	,165	,165	,165	,165	,165	,165
Minimum		3,0	,0	1,0	2,0	,0	,0	,0	4,0	,0
Maximum		10,0	10,0	10,0	10,0	10,0	10,0	10,0	10,0	10,0

Fig. 5. evaluation of usability dimensions

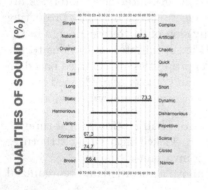

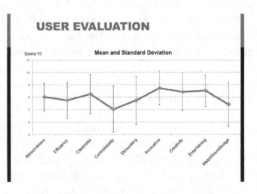

Fig. 6. perception of sound quality   **Fig. 7.** user evaluation overview

All usability dimensions received scores of 7 or higher by 85,7% of participants. *Innovative* (M=8,73; STD=1,36), *entertaining* (M=8,52; STD=1,28), *creativity* (M=8,44; STD=1,52), and *clearness* (M=8,25; STD=1,58) received the highest scores in Fig. 5. Although still rather high, the lowest scores were given to *controllability* (M=7,02; STD=1,87), and *sound to image mapping* (M=7,41; STD=1,77). The sound qualities observed most were *open* (74,7%), *dynamic* (73,3%), *compact* (67,3%) and *artificial* (67,3%), see Fig. 6. In 13,7% of the cases, participants were undecided about the bipolar adjectives *high/low* and *short/long*. Multi-modality was appreciated as follows: 46% found the total concept most important, 24% appreciated the game aspect most, 16% preferred the visuals and 14% chose the sound. Age or gender effects were not found.

5   Conclusion

BilliARt is an AR framework that enables the implementation of an AR Carom Billiard table. By combining auditive and visual texture synthesis, BilliARt can be used as a real-time collaborative art installation enabling creative and artistic human expression without imposing predefined interaction rules or restrictions.

Acknowledgements. This research is funded by Ghent University, iMinds, the Institute for the Promotion of Innovation by Science and Technology in Flanders (IWT), the Fund for Scientific Research-Flanders (FWO-Flanders), and the EU. The authors like to thank IPEM (Ghent University) for their infrastructure and support.

References

1. MacWilliams, A., Reicher, T., Klinker, G., Bruegge, B.: Design patterns for augmented reality systems. In: MIXER (2004)
2. Gent, J.: http://www.jaarbeursgent.be/
3. Smith, K.: Reversible-jump markov chain monte carlo multi-object tracking tutorial. IDIAP Research Institute, Communication IDIAP-COM-06-07 (2006)
4. Jacobs, M.C., Livingston, M.A., et al.: Managing latency in complex augmented reality systems. In: Proceedings of the 1997 Symposium on Interactive 3D Graphics, p. 49. ACM (1997)
5. Valente, L., Conci, A., Feijó, B.: Real time game loop models for single-player computer games. In: Proceedings of the IV Brazilian Symposium on Computer Games and Digital Entertainment, vol. (89), p. 99 (2005)
6. Naturalpoint: OptiTrack, http://www.naturalpoint.com/optitrack/
7. Hai-Xia, X., Yao-Nan, W., Wei, Z., Jiang, Z., Xiao-Fang, Y.: Multi-object visual tracking based on reversible jump markov chain monte carlo. IET Computer Vision 5(5), 282–290 (2011)
8. Reeves, W.T.: Particle systems a technique for modeling a class of fuzzy objects. In: ACM SIGGRAPH Computer Graphics, vol. 17, pp. 359–375. ACM (1983)
9. Akenine-Möller, T., Haines, E., Hoffman, N.: Real-time rendering. CRC Press (2011)
10. JackAudio, http://www.jackaudio.org
11. Letz, S., Orlarey, Y., Fober, D.: Jack audio server for multi-processor machines. In: Proceedings of the International Computer Music Conference, pp. 1–4 (2005)
12. UC Berkeley Center for New Music and Audio Technology: Open Sound Control, http://www.opensoundcontrol.org

Geometric Transformations and Duality
for Virtual Reality and Haptic Systems

Vaclav Skala

Department of Computer Science and Engineering, Faculty of Applied Sciences
University of West Bohemia, CZ 306 14 Plzen, Czech Republic
skala@kiv.zcu.cz

Abstract. Virtual reality and haptic systems use geometric transformations with points represented in homogeneous coordinates extensively. In many cases interpolation and barycentric coordinates are used. However, developers do not fully use properties of projective representation to make algorithms stable, robust and faster. This paper describes geometric transformations and principle of duality which enables to solve some problems effectively.

Keywords: projective space, homogeneous coordinates, principle of duality, barycentric coordinates, linear system of equations, outer product, cross product GPU computation.

1   Introduction

Geometric transformations with rigid objects are used in computer graphics, virtual reality and haptic systems. Homogeneous coordinates are mostly introduced with regard to geometric transformations only. However, if projective extension of the Euclidean space, which uses homogeneous coordinates natively, is used for reformulation of algorithms, not necessarily geometrical only, simple, faster and more robust algorithms are obtained. Also if principle of duality is used, users can obtain novel algorithms with better properties.

In this paper some principles are described and demonstrated on simple geometrical problems. Significant advantage of projective algorithms reformulation is that naturally supports vector-vector architectures like SSE and GPU.

2   Projective Representation and Principle of Duality

In geometry the Euclidean coordinates are used in general, as the Euclidean space has a "metric", i.e. a distance of two points in E^2 is computed as:

$$d = \sqrt{(\Delta X)^2 + (\Delta Y)^2} \tag{1}$$

A point X in E^2 is represented as $X = (X, Y) \in E^2$. However in geometry lines and planes are used as well and they can be described in an implicit form:

C. Stephanidis (Ed.): HCII 2014 Posters, Part I, CCIS 434, pp. 642–647, 2014.
© Springer International Publishing Switzerland 2014

$$F(X) = 0 \qquad (2)$$

This equation can be multiplied by any constant $q \neq 0$ and the given geometric primitive does not change. It means that a one parametric formulation is given.

Projective Extension of the Euclidean Space. The projective extension on the Euclidean space is simple and it is defined by:

$$X = {}^x\!/_w \qquad\qquad Y = {}^y\!/_w \qquad\qquad w \neq 0 \qquad (3)$$

Coordinates in projective representation are given by homogeneous coordinates [1], [10]. The point $X = (X, Y) \in E^2$ is represented by a vector $x = [x, y : w]^T \in P^2$. In many cases, especially in mathematically oriented texts, notification $[a_0 : a_1, ..., a_n,]$ is used, where homogeneous coordinate $w \equiv a_0$. This is more convenient notation especially for n-dimensional applications. Homogeneous coordinates are mostly used for a point representation. However in geometric algorithms lines and planes are also important primitives.

A line in E^2 is defined as:

$$aX + bY + d = 0 \qquad (4)$$

If multiplied by $w \neq 0$, then:

$$awX + bwY + dw = 0 \qquad (5)$$

and therefore a line can be defined, if homogeneous coordinates are used, as:

$$ax + by + dw = a \cdot x = a^T x = 0 \qquad (6)$$

where: $a = [a, b : d]^T$ and $x = [x, y : w]^T$. It can be seen that the formula is more "compact".

In the case of E^3 a point is given as $X = (X, Y, Z) \in E^3$ in the Euclidean space or as $x = [x, y, z : w]^T \in P^3$ in the projective space. A plane is given as:

$$ax + by + cz + dw = a \cdot x = a^T x = 0 \qquad (7)$$

where: $a = [a, b, c : d]^T$ and $x = [x, y, z : w]^T$.

It can be seen that homogeneous representation can be used also for a fraction a/b representation in order to postpone a division operation and obtain higher precision of computation as two float representations in the fraction are used and division operation is postponed.

Principle of Duality. Principle of duality is one of the most important principles used in geometry. From the line or plane equation $a^T x = 0$ can be seen that the meaning of symbols a and x is not fixed, as a can be a point representation and x can be line/plane coefficients. It means that those geometric primitives are *dual* [2].

The principle of duality in E^2 states that any theorem remains true when we interchange the words "point" and "line", "lie on" and "pass through", "join" and "intersection" and so on. Once the theorem has been established, the dual theorem is obtained as described above, see [3].

In other words, the principle of duality in E^2 says that in all theorems it is possible to substitute the term "point" by the term "line" and the term "line" by the term "point" and the given theorem stays valid. This helps a lot in solving some geometrical cases. In the case of E^3 point is a dual to a plane and vice versa etc..

Let us consider two simple problems in E^2:

- a line is given as a join of two points – this leads to a system of linear equations $Ax = 0$
- a point given as the intersection of two lines – this leads to a system of linear equations $Ax = b$

If solved in the Euclidean space two significantly different problems are obtained. However the principle of duality leads to a natural question:

Why two different problems are obtained if the given problems are dual?

Similarly in E^3 a plane is given as a join of three points and a point is given as an intersection of three planes.

An elegant, robust and fast solution is presented in the chapter 4.

3   Linear and Spherical Interpolation in Projective Space

Interpolation is very often used in geometrical problems; mostly linear interpolation in the Euclidean space is used.

Linear Interpolation with Linear Parameterization. Linear interpolation in the Euclidean d-dimensional space is defined as:

$$X(t) = X_1 + (X_2 - X_1)\, t \tag{8}$$

and has *linear parameterization*. If barycentric interpolation is used on a d-simplex:

$$X(\lambda) = \sum_{i=1}^{d} \lambda_i X_i \qquad \sum_{i=1}^{d} \lambda_i = 1 \tag{9}$$

where: $\lambda = (\lambda_1, \dots, \lambda_d)$, i.e. in E^2:

$$X(\lambda_1, \lambda_2) = \lambda_1 X_1 + \lambda_2 X_2 \qquad \lambda_1 + \lambda_2 = 1 \tag{10}$$

and in E^3:

$$X(\lambda_1, \lambda_2, \lambda_3) = \lambda_1 X_1 + \lambda_2 X_2 + \lambda_3 X_3 \qquad \lambda_1 + \lambda_2 + \lambda_3 = 1 \tag{11}$$

The question is what happens, if points X_i are given in the homogeneous coordinates.

Linear Interpolation with Monotonically Parameterized. If points are given in homogeneous coordinates, linear interpolation can be made directly in the projective space, i.e. $x = [x, y: w]^T$. In this case:

$$x(t) = x_1 + (x_2 - x_1)\, t \tag{12}$$

i.e.

$$
\begin{aligned}
x(t) &= x_1 + (x_2 - x_1)\, t & y(t) &= y_1 + (y_2 - y_1)\, t \\
z(t) &= z_1 + (z_2 - z_1)\, t & w(t) &= w_1 + (w_2 - w_1)\, t
\end{aligned}
\tag{13}
$$

It is again a linear interpolation. However, the coordinates X changes with the value of t *non-linearly, but monotonically* [6], [7]. This property can be used for efficient algorithms deciding which point is closer to an observer etc. Computation of the barycentric coordinates in with homogeneous coordinates is similar [6].

4   Computation in Projective Space

Let us consider following simple examples demonstrating the proposed approaches.

Intersection Operation. Let us consider a simple example when a point is given as an intersection of two lines p_1 and p_2. This leads to a system of linear equations $Ax = b$ with a usual solution:

$$\begin{bmatrix} a_1 & b_1 \\ a_2 & b_2 \end{bmatrix} \begin{bmatrix} X \\ Y \end{bmatrix} = \begin{bmatrix} -d_1 \\ -d_2 \end{bmatrix} \qquad X = \frac{Det_x}{Det} \qquad Y = \frac{Det_y}{Det} \qquad (14)$$

But there is question what happens, if the value of Det is small, i.e. when $|Det| < \varepsilon$. It does not generally mean that the given lines are parallel or close to parallel!

It can be proved that the intersection point x of two lines $p_1 = [a_1, b_1 : d_1]^T$ and $p_2 = [a_2, b_2 : d_2]^T$ can be easily computed using the cross product as:

$$x = p_1 \times p_2 = det \begin{bmatrix} i & j & k \\ a_1 & b_1 & d_1 \\ a_2 & b_2 & d_2 \end{bmatrix} = [x, y : w]^T \qquad (15)$$

In the case of E^3 the intersection point x of three planes ρ_1, ρ_2 and ρ_3 is given as:

$$x = \rho_1 \times \rho_2 \times \rho_3 = \begin{vmatrix} i & j & k & l \\ a_1 & b_1 & c_1 & d_1 \\ a_2 & b_2 & c_2 & d_2 \\ a_3 & b_3 & c_3 & d_3 \end{vmatrix} = [x, y, z : w]^T \qquad (16)$$

where: $\rho_1 = [a_1, b_1, c_1 : d_1]^T$, $\rho_2 = [a_2, b_2, c_2 : d_2]^T$, $\rho_3 = [a_3, b_3, c_3 : d_3]^T$.

Join Operation. Let us consider a simple example of a line p given by two points X_1 and X_2. This leads to a system of linear equations $Ax = 0$, i.e.:

$$\begin{bmatrix} X_1 & Y_1 & 1 \\ X_2 & Y_2 & 1 \end{bmatrix} \begin{bmatrix} a \\ b \\ c \end{bmatrix} = \begin{bmatrix} 0 \\ 0 \end{bmatrix} \qquad (17)$$

It means that one parametric set of solution is obtained. *How to solve it?* The answer is simple due to the principle of duality, as a point and a line are dual in E^2. Therefore the line p given by two points is determined as:

$$p = x_1 \times x_2 = det \begin{bmatrix} i & j & k \\ x_1 & y_1 & w_1 \\ x_2 & y_2 & w_2 \end{bmatrix} = [a, b : d]^T \qquad (18)$$

In the case of E^3 a plane given by three points is given as:

$$\rho = x_1 \times x_2 \times x_3 = \begin{vmatrix} i & j & k & l \\ x_1 & y_1 & z_1 & w_1 \\ x_2 & y_2 & z_2 & w_2 \\ x_3 & y_3 & z_3 & w_3 \end{vmatrix} = [a, b, c : d]^T \qquad (19)$$

It can be seen that the principle of duality applied with projective representation can lead to new, more stable and robust formula especially convenient for vector-vector architectures [5].

It means that *no division operation is needed* in the both cases.

5   Geometric Transformations

Geometric transformations are used in virtual reality and haptic systems and their efficiency and robustness must be considered. However it is necessary to note that *geometric transformations of points in homogeneous coordinates differ from transformation of implicitly defined objects*, i.e. lines, planes, and normal vectors, etc.

Geometric Transformations of Points. Geometric transformations of points are based matrix-vector multiplication, i.e. $\boldsymbol{x}' = \boldsymbol{T}\boldsymbol{x}$, where: $\boldsymbol{x} = [x, y, z : w]^T$ and matrix $\boldsymbol{T}$ is (4×4) size [4].

Geometric Transformations of Implicitly Defined Objects. In graphical applications positions of points are changed by an interaction etc.:

$$\boldsymbol{x}' = \boldsymbol{T}\boldsymbol{x} \tag{20}$$

The question is how coefficients of a line $\boldsymbol{p}$, resp. of a plane $\boldsymbol{\rho}$ are changed if points are transformed without a need of computation lines or planes from their definition.

It can be proved that:

$$\boldsymbol{p}' = (\boldsymbol{T}\boldsymbol{x}_1) \times (\boldsymbol{T}\boldsymbol{x}_2) = det(\boldsymbol{T})(\boldsymbol{T}^{-1})^T\boldsymbol{p} \triangleq (\boldsymbol{T}^{-1})^T\boldsymbol{p} = [a', b' : d']^T \tag{21}$$

or

$$\boldsymbol{\rho}' = (\boldsymbol{T}\boldsymbol{x}_1) \times (\boldsymbol{T}\boldsymbol{x}_2) \times (\boldsymbol{T}\boldsymbol{x}_3) = det(\boldsymbol{T})(\boldsymbol{T}^{-1})^T\boldsymbol{\rho} \triangleq (\boldsymbol{T}^{-1})^T\boldsymbol{\rho}$$
$$= [a', b', c' : d']^T \tag{22}$$

where: $\triangleq$ means protectively equivalent.

It means that *transformation matrix of a normal vector is generally different from the matrix for transformation of points*.

6   Solution of Selected Problems

There are nice examples how the projective representation can simplify a solution of geometrical problems [8].

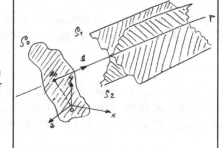

Fig. 1. Intersection of two planes

Line in E^3 as Two Plane Intersection
Let us consider a "standard" formula first. Planes $\boldsymbol{\rho}_1$ and $\boldsymbol{\rho}_2$ are defined as:

$$\boldsymbol{\rho}_1 = [a_1, b_1, c_1 : d_1]^T = [\boldsymbol{n}_1^T : d_1]^T \quad \boldsymbol{\rho}_2 = [a_2, b_2, c_2 : d_2]^T = [\boldsymbol{n}_2^T : d_2]^T \tag{23}$$

In the Euclidean space a line given as an intersection of two planes is given as:

$$\boldsymbol{s} = \boldsymbol{n}_1 \times \boldsymbol{n}_2 \equiv [a_3, b_3, c_3]^T \qquad \boldsymbol{x}(t) = \boldsymbol{x}_0 + \boldsymbol{s}t \tag{24}$$

and

$$DET = \begin{vmatrix} a_1 & b_1 & c_1 \\ a_2 & b_2 & c_2 \\ a_3 & b_3 & c_3 \end{vmatrix} \qquad x_0 = \frac{d_2 \begin{vmatrix} b_1 & c_1 \\ b_3 & c_3 \end{vmatrix} - d_1 \begin{vmatrix} b_2 & c_2 \\ b_3 & c_3 \end{vmatrix}}{DET}$$

$$y_0 = \frac{d_2 \begin{vmatrix} a_3 & c_3 \\ a_1 & c_1 \end{vmatrix} - d_1 \begin{vmatrix} a_3 & c_3 \\ a_2 & c_2 \end{vmatrix}}{DET} \qquad z_0 = \frac{d_2 \begin{vmatrix} a_1 & b_1 \\ a_3 & b_3 \end{vmatrix} - d_1 \begin{vmatrix} a_2 & b_2 \\ a_3 & b_3 \end{vmatrix}}{DET} \tag{25}$$

Line in E3 as Two Plane Intersection – Projective Solution. Directional s vector of a line given by two planes is $s = n_1 \times n_2$. Let us consider a plane ρ_0 passing the origin with the normal s vector, i.e. $\rho_0 = [a_0, b_0, c_0 : 0]^T$. Then the "starting" point x_0 can be determined as:

$$x_0 = \rho_1 \times \rho_2 \times \rho_0 \qquad (26)$$

How simple the formula is!

7 Conclusion

This paper describes new approaches to solutions of geometrical problems related to applications, especially applicable in virtual reality and haptic systems based on projective space representation. Shortly introduced principle of duality enables solving dual problems by one sequence resulting to more robust code. As the projective representation supports vector-vector operations naturally, application of GPU architecture or usage of SSE instructions is natural and significant speed up can be expected as well. If homogeneous representation is used, division operation is postponed in principle and a higher precision of computation can be expected as well.

Acknowledgment. The author thanks to colleagues at the University of West Bohemia for their critical comments, suggestions, to anonymous reviewers for their critical view and comments that improved the manuscript significantly. Supported by the MSMT CR projects No.LH12181, LG13047.

References

1. Bloomenthal, J., Rokne, J.: Homogeneous Coordinates. The Visual Computer 11(1), 15–26 (1994)
2. Coxeter, H.S.M.: Introduction to Geometry. John Wiley (1969)
3. Johnson, M.: Proof by Duality, Mathematics Today (December 1996)
4. Miller, J.R.: The Mathematics of Graphical Transformations: Vector Geometric and Coordinate-Based Approaches, DesignLab (1997)
5. Skala, V.: A New Approach to Line and Line Segment Clipping in Homogeneous Coordinates. The Visual Computer 21(11), 905–914 (2005)
6. Skala, V.: Barycentric Coordinates Computation in Homogeneous Coordinates. Computers & Graphics 32(1), 120–127 (2008) ISSN 0097-8493
7. Skala, V.: Intersection Computation in Projective Space using Homogeneous Coordinates. Int. Journal of Image and Graphics 7(4), 615–628 (2008) ISSN 0219-4678
8. Skala, V.: Projective Geometry and Duality for Graphics, Games and Visualization - Course SIGGRAPH Asia 2012, Singapore (2012) ISBN 978-1-4503-1757-3
9. Stolfi, J.: Oriented Projective Geometry. Academic Press (2001)
10. Yamaguchi, F.: Computer-Aided Geometric Design – A Totally Four Dimensional Approach. Springer (1996)

Data Fusion for Difficulty Adjustment in an Adaptive Virtual Reality Game System for Autism Intervention

Lian Zhang[1], Joshua W. Wade[1], Dayi Bian[1], Amy Swanson[3], Zachary Warren[2,3], and Nilanjan Sarkar[1,4]

[1] Electrical Engineering and Computer Science Department
[2] Treatment and Research in Autism Spectrum Disorder (TRIAD)
[3] Pediatrics and Psychiatry Department
[4] Mechanical Engineering Department
Vanderbilt University, Nashville, TN 37212
{lian.zhang,joshua.w.wade,dayi.bian,amy.r.swanson,
zachary.e.warren,nilanjan.sarkar}@vanderbilt.edu

Abstract. A virtual reality driving simulator is designed as a tool for improving driving skills of individuals with autism spectrum disorders (ASD). Training at an appropriate driving difficulty level can maximize long term performance. Affective state information has been used for difficulty level adjustment in our previous work. This paper integrates performance with affective state information to predict the optimal difficulty level. The participant's performance data, physiology signals, and eye gaze data are captured. The performance features and affective state features are extracted. Two classification methods, Support Vector Machine (SVM) and Artificial Neural Network (ANN), are implemented to predict difficulty level. The results demonstrate that performance together with affective state information outperform the separated features in difficulty level prediction. A highest accuracy of 83.09% is achieved with the integrated features.

Keywords: autism, pattern recognition, virtual reality, data fusion, cognitive load, difficulty adjustment.

1 Introduction

Researchers are increasingly utilizing virtual reality (VR) technologies as intervention platforms for individuals with autism spectrum disorder (ASD) [1, 2]. The capability for real-time adaptation makes VR games particularly appealing as a potential vehicle for teaching complex skills to individuals with ASD. In adaptive systems, a computer can utilize complex data streams in order to predict a human's cognitive and affective state, and then employ previous and current performance along with current context to modify the game's difficulty level. Such an adaptation to optimize difficulty levels has the potential to maximize the learner's long-term performance within and beyond the system.

C. Stephanidis (Ed.): HCII 2014 Posters, Part I, CCIS 434, pp. 648–652, 2014.
© Springer International Publishing Switzerland 2014

Typically, cognitive load is inferred using model-based data fusion methods [3]. Markov models have been used for an intelligent tutoring system and virtual reality applications [4]. Dynamic Bayesian network model as a data fusion method has the advantage of dealing with temporal information [5]. Artificial Neural Network (ANN) has been used to detect mental workload in real time [6]. The accuracy of these model-based methods, however, is limited by the accuracy of the models.

Additionally, classification methods have been used to recognize cognitive workload. In [7], linear discriminant analysis is applied to determine a game's difficulty level. Fuzzy logic is a simple method for cognitive workload classification [8]. Support Vector Machines (SVM) has a good accuracy in cognitive load recognition [9].

In our previous work, we implemented and evaluated SVM, Bayesian network, k-nearest neighbor and Regression Trees for difficulty level adjustment with affective state in an adaptive system [10]. In this paper, both affective state and performance are integrated using SVM and ANN for difficulty adjustment in a VR based driving task for ASD interventions. The rest of the paper is organized as follows. In Section 2, the VR-based driving task is described. Section 3 discusses the two difficulty adjustment methods used in this work. We present the results in Section 4.

2   VR-Based Driving Task

A VR-based driving simulator was developed to improve the driving skill of individuals with ASD. A set of driving tasks with different difficulty levels was designed to investigate the response of a participant under different cognitive loads. A total of seven ASD teenagers between the ages of 13 and 17 years participated in the driving experiment. Eye gaze data, physiological data, and performance of the participants were captured during the experiment.

The failure, achievement, and driving behavior were recorded as the performance. Biopac MP 150 [11] was used to acquire participant's physiological signals with a sample rate of 1000 Hz in our experiment. The Tobii X120 remote eye-tracker recorded eye gaze behavior [12]. The accuracy of the eye tracker is 0.5°. Considering the variation of both the gaze data and physiological data from person to person, we recorded physiological and eye gaze baseline data for each participant before the experiment.

During the experiment, a therapist observed and reported the participants' affective state every two minutes using a 1-5 Likert scale. The optimal difficulty levels for the driving task were also suggested by the therapist according to her understanding of the participants' affective states and performance. This was done to train and test the fusion methods.

3   Difficulty Level Prediction

We extracted performance features and affective features from the initial data mentioned above offline. Every two minutes of signal was processed in Matlab for the features extraction.

The mean of the driving speed, indicating driving performance, and the number of failures, reflecting the action error, were two essential performance features used in this work. The achievements during driving were reflected by the obtained score, which were the other performance feature.

The mean of the pupil diameter and the blink rate were chosen to be eye gaze features. Unfortunately, we lost some physiological data due to data collection error, so the physiological features were not used in this paper. Instead, the therapist's reports about the participants' affective state were utilized for the difficulty assessment. The consistency between the physiological signal and the therapist report has been studied in our previous work [13-15]. So the reported affective state was a reasonable choice for difficulty level prediction. We chose four affective states in this work: engagement,   enjoyment,   anxiety,   and   boredom.   Support   Vector Machine(SVM) and Artificial Neural Network(ANN) were presented in this paper for the purposes of estimating difficulty level. The Matlab functions of these two methods were used for classification-based fusion.

3.1   Support Vector Machine

Support vector machine is a supervised learning classifier which forms a hyperplane with labeled training data [16]. The defined hyperplane can be used for classification. Given a set of training data $= \{x_i, y_i\}_{i=1}^n$, the hyperplane satisfies the equation:

$$wx-b=1 \tag{1}$$

The hyperplane can be found by maximizing (in the Lagrange multipliers α) the function

$$L(\alpha) = \sum_{i=1}^n \alpha_i - \frac{1}{2}\sum_{i,j} \alpha_i \alpha_j y_i y_j k(x_i, x_j) \tag{2}$$

Subject to $0 < \alpha_i < C$ (for $i = 1, 2, ..., n$) . $k(x_i, x_j)$ is the kernel function, which can be replaced by different nonlinear kernel functions. The penalty parameter C is the weight for the misclassification.

3.2   Artificial Neural Network

Neural network model includes an input layer, one or more hidden layers, and an output layer. Each layer is composed of neurons. Neurons in different layers are connected by weighted connections. A two-layer feed-forward network with a sigmoid transfer function in both the hidden layer and output layer was used in this paper[17]. Every neuron receives inputs coming from the previous layers and calculates the sigmoid function of weighted inputs.

$$z_k = \sigma(w_k^T x) \tag{3}$$

$w_k \in \mathbb{R}^m$ is the weight vector pointing to the neuron z_k . $x \in \mathbb{R}^m$ is the input vector of the neuron z_k . The Backpropagation method updates the weights until the error is smaller than a threshold or the iteration number reaches the iteration threshold.

4   Results

ANOVA was used to select the most discriminative features for difficulty level assessment. The result showed that the number of failures from the performance features and the enjoyment level from the affective state features had strong relationship with the difficulty level (p<0.005 for each). These two features were selected for data fusion.

The five-scale difficulty levels were clustered into three classes: easier level (level 1 and 2), medium level (level 3), and harder level (level 4 and 5). The accuracies of multiple-class classification were 58.66% for SVM and 52.75% for ANN with selected features. After removing the medium level (level 3), we analyzed the binary classification methods with easier level (level 1 and 2) and harder level (level 4 and 5).

Table 1 shows the binary classification results of SVM and ANN with different features. These accuracies were generated by averaging over 100 computations. Affective state features coming from therapist proved to be most powerful features in difficulty level prediction. Eye gaze features had lower accuracy than other features. The highest accuracy was from the SVM method with the selected features.

Table 1. difficulty level estimation accuracy

	Eye	Performance	Affective	All features	Selected features
SVM	62.36%	65.36%	81.73%	74.82%	**83.09%**
NN	68.50%	68.13%	77.25%	75.38%	78.25%

5   Conclusions

Our previous studies [14, 15] have shown that affective state can be used for difficulty level estimation. This paper improved the game difficulty level assessment by combining multiple signals. Integrating all the features without feature selection did not increase the accuracy; however the selected affective features and selected performance features together lead to the highest classification accuracy.

In the future, we will use this ability to choose an optimal game difficulty level for each individual with ASD to provide a more challenging yet fruitful skill development opportunity.

Acknowledgment. This work was supported in part by the National Institute of Health Grant 1R01MH091102-01A1, National Science Foundation Grant 0967170 and the Hobbs Society Grant from the Vanderbilt Kennedy Center.

References

1. Lahiri, U., Bekele, E., Dohrmann, E., Warren, Z., Sarkar, N.: Design of a Virtual Reality based Adaptive Response Technology for Children with Autism. IEEE Transactions on Neural Systems and Rehabilitation Engineering 21(1), 55–64 (2013)
2. Lahiri, U., Warren, Z., Sarkar, N.: Design of a Gaze-sensitive Virtual Social Interactive System for Children with Autism. IEEE Transactions on Neural Systems and Rehabilitation Engineering 19(4), 443–452 (2011)
3. Novak, D., Mihelj, M., Munih, M.: A survey of methods for data fusion and system adaptation using autonomic nervous system responses in physiological computing. Interacting with Computers 24(3), 154–172 (2012)
4. Woolf, B., et al.: Affect-aware tutors: recognizing and responding to student affect. International Journal of Learning Technology 4(3), 129–164 (2009)
5. Rowe, J.P., Lester, J.C.: Modeling User Knowledge with Dynamic Bayesian Networks in Interactive Narrative Environments. In: AIIDE (2010)
6. Wilson, G.F., Russell, C.A.: Performance enhancement in an uninhabited air vehicle task using psychophysiologically determined adaptive aiding. Human Factors: The Journal of the Human Factors and Ergonomics Society 49(6), 1005–1018 (2007)
7. Novak, D., et al.: Psychophysiological measurements in a biocooperative feedback loop for upper extremity rehabilitation. IEEE Transactions on Neural Systems and Rehabilitation Engineering 19(4), 400–410 (2011)
8. Bergasa, L.M., Nuevo, J., Sotelo, M.A., Barea, R., Lopez, M.E.: Real-time system for monitoring driver vigilance. IEEE Transactions on Intelligent Transportation Systems 7(1), 63–77 (2006)
9. Kapoor, A., Picard, R.W.: Multimodal affect recognition in learning environments. In: Proceedings of the 13th Annual ACM International Conference on Multimedia. ACM (2005)
10. Liu, C., Rani, P., Sarkar, N.: An Empirical Study of Machine Learning Techniques for Affect Recognition in Human-Robot Interaction. In: 2005 IEEE/RSJ International Conference on Intelligent Robots and Systems (IROS 2005), August 02-06, pp. 2451–2456 (2005)
11. Biopac system, http://www.biopac.com/
12. Eye tracker X120, http://www.tobii.com/
13. Liu, C., Conn, K., Sarkar, N., Stone, W.: Physiology-based affect recognition for computer-assisted intervention of children with Autism Spectrum Disorder. International Journal of Human-Computer Studies 66(9), 662–677 (2008)
14. Rani, P., Sarkar, N., Smith, C., Adams, J.: Affective Communication For Implicit Human-Machine Interaction. In: IEEE International Conference on System, Man and Cybernetics, Washington D. C., pp. 4896–4903 (October 2003)
15. Liu, C., Rani, P., Sarkar, N.: Human-Robot Interaction Using Affective Cues. In: The 15th IEEE International Symposium on Robot and Human Interactive Communication - ROMAN 2006, United Kingdom, pp. 285–290 (September 2006)
16. Boswell, D.: Introduction to support vector machines (2002)
17. Beale, M., Hagan, M.T., Demuth, H.B.: Neural network toolbox. Neural Network Toolbox, The Math Works, 5-25 (1992)

Author Index